大学翻译学研究型系列教材

总主编　张柏然

文学翻译研究导引

An Introduction to Contemporary Literary Translation Studies

主　编　葛校琴　严晓江
副主编　郑　贞　杨淑华　万晓燕

南京大学出版社

图书在版编目(CIP)数据

文学翻译研究导引 / 葛校琴，严晓江主编. — 南京
:南京大学出版社，2013.6
(大学翻译学翻译型系列教材 / 张柏然总主编)
ISBN 978-7-305-11340-6

Ⅰ.①文… Ⅱ.①葛… ②严… Ⅲ.①文化翻译—高等学校—教学参考资料 Ⅳ.①I046

中国版本图书馆 CIP 数据核字(2013)第 072481 号

出版发行 南京大学出版社
社 址 南京市汉口路 22 号 邮 编 210093
网 址 http://www.NjupCo.com
出 版 人 左 健

丛 书 名 大学翻译学翻译型系列教材
总 主 编 张柏然
书 名 文学翻译研究导引
主 编 葛校琴 严晓江
责任编辑 金 晶 裴维维 编辑热线 025-83592123

照 排 南京南琳图文制作有限公司
印 刷 宜兴市盛世文化印刷有限公司
开 本 787×1092 1/16 印张 21.5 字数 536 千
版 次 2013 年 6 月第 1 版 2013 年 6 月第 1 次印刷
ISBN 978-7-305-11340-6
定 价 44.00 元

发行热线 025-83594756 83686452
电子邮箱 Press@NjupCo.com
Sales@NjupCo.com(市场部)

大学本科翻译研究型系列读本
大学翻译学研究型系列教材

总　序

张柏然

到了该为翻译学研究型系列教材写几句话的时候了。两年前的炎炎夏日，南京大学出版社委托笔者总揽主编分别针对高等院校翻译学本科生和研究生学习与研究需求的研究型系列读本和导引。俗话说，独木难撑大厦。于是，笔者便千里相邀"招旧部"，网罗昔日在南大攻读翻译学博士学位的"十八罗汉"各主其事。寒来暑往，光阴荏苒，转眼两年过去了。期间，大家意气奋发，不辞辛劳，借助网络"上天"，躲进书馆"入地"，上下求索，查阅浩瀚的文献经典，进而调动自己的学术积累，披沙拣金，辨正证伪，博采众长，字斟句酌，终于成就了这一本本呈现在读者面前的教材。

众所周知，教材乃教学之本和知识之源，亦即体现课程教学理念、教学内容、教学要求，甚至教学模式的知识载体，在教学过程中起着引导教学方向、保证教学质量的作用。改革开放以来，我国各类高校组编、出版的翻译教材逐年递增。我们在中国国家图书馆网站上检索主题名含有"翻译"字段的图书，检索结果显示，1980 至 2009 年间，我国引进、出版相关著作约 1 800 余种，其中，翻译教材占有很大的比重。近些年来，翻译教材更是突飞猛进。根据有关学者的不完全统计，目前，我国正式出版的翻译教材共有 1 000 多种。① 这一变化结束了我国相当长一段时间内翻译教材"一枝独秀"的境地，迎来了"百花齐放"的局面，由此也反映了我国高校翻译教学改革的深化。

但是，毋庸讳言，虽然教材的品种繁多，但是真正合手称便的、富有特色的教材仍属凤毛麟角。教材数量增多并不足以表明教学理念的深刻转变。其中大多都具有包打翻译学天下的纯体系冲动，并没有打破我国既往翻译教材编写从某一理论预设出发的本质主义思维模式和几大板块的框架结构。从教材建设看，我国翻译理论教材在概念陈设、模式架构、内容安排上存在着比较严重的雷同化现象。这表明，教材建设需要从根本上加以改进，而如何改进则取决于我们有什么样的教学理念。

有鉴于此，我们组编了"大学翻译学研究型系列教材"和"大学本科翻译研究型系列读本"这两套系列教材。前者系研究生用书，它包括《中国翻译理论研究导引》、《西方翻译理论研究导引》、《当代西方文论与翻译研究导引》、《翻译学方法论研究导引》、《语言学与翻译研究导引》、《文学翻译研究导引》、《汉语典籍英译研究导引》、《英汉口译理论研究导引》、《语料库与翻译研究导引》和《术语翻译研究导引》等 10 册；后者则以本科生为主要读者对象，它包括《翻译概论读本》、《文化翻译读本》、《文学翻译读本》、《商务英语翻译读本》、《法律英语翻译读本》、《传媒英语翻译读本》、《科技英语翻译读本》、《英汉口译读本》、《英汉比较与翻译读本》和《翻译资源与工具读本》等 10 册。这两套教材力图综合中西译论、相关学科（如哲学、美学、文学、语

① 转引自曾剑平、林敏华. 论翻译教材的问题及编写体系[J]. 中国科技翻译，2011，11.

言学、社会学、文化学、心理学、语料库翻译学等)的吸融性研究以及方法论的多层次研究,结合目前高校翻译教学和研究实践的现状进行创造性整合,编写突出问题型结构和理路的读本和导引,以满足翻译学科本科生和研究生教学与研究的需求。这是深化中国翻译学研究型教材编写与研究的一个重要课题,至今尚未引起翻译理论研究界和教材编写界的足够重视。摆在我们面前的这一课题,基本上还是一片多少有些生荒的地带。因此,我们对这一课题的研究,也就多少带有拓荒性质。这样,不仅大量纷繁的文献经典需要我们去发掘、辨别与整理,中西翻译美学思想发展演变的特点与规律需要我们去探讨,而且研究的对象、范畴和方法等等问题,都需要我们进行独立的思考与确定。研究这一课题的困难也就可以想见了。然而,这一课题本身的价值和意义却又变为克服困难的巨大动力,策励着我们不揣浅陋,迎难而上,试图在翻译学研究型教材编写这块土地上,作一些力所能及的垦殖。

这两套研究型系列教材的编纂目的和编纂特色主要体现为:不以知识传授为主要目的,而是培养学生发问、好奇、探索、兴趣,即学习的主动性,逐步实现思维方式和学习方式的转变,引导学生及早进入科学研究阶段;不追求知识的完整性、系统性,突破讲授通史、通论知识的教学模式,引入探究学术问题的教学模式;引进国外教材编写理念,填补国内大学翻译学研究型教材的欠缺;所选论著具有权威性、文献性、可读性与引导性。具体而言,和传统的通史通论教材不同,这两套系列教材是以问题结构章节,这个"问题"既可以是这门课(专业方向)的主要问题,也可以是这门课某个章节的主要问题。在每个章节的安排上,则是先由"导论"说明本章的核心问题,指明获得相关知识的途径;接着,通过选文的导言,直接指向"选文"——涉及的知识面很广的范文,这样对学生的论文写作更有示范性;"选文"之后安排"延伸阅读",以拓展和深化知识;最后,通过"研究实践"或"问题与思考",提供实践方案,进行专业训练,希冀用"问题"牵引学生主动学习。这样的结构方式,突出了教材本身的问题型结构和理路,旨在建构以探索和研究为基础的教与学的人才培养模式,让年轻学子有机会接触最新成就、前沿学术和科学方法;强调通识教育、人文教育与科学教育交融,知识传授与能力培养并重,注重培养学生掌握方法,未来能够应对千变万化的翻译教学与研究的发展和需要。

笔者虽说长期从事翻译教学与研究,但对编写教材尤其是研究型教材还是个新手。这两套翻译学研究型教材之所以能够顺利出版,全有赖各册主编的精诚合作和鼎力相助,全有仗一群尽责敬业的编写和校核人员。特别值得一提的是,在这两套系列教材的最后编辑工作中,南京大学出版社外语室主任董颖和责任编辑裴维维两位女士全力以赴,认真校核,一丝不苟,对保证教材的质量起了尤为重要的作用。在此谨向他(她)们致以衷心的感谢!

总而言之,编写大学翻译学研究型教材还是一项尝试性的研究工程。诚如上面所述,我们在进行这项"多少带有拓荒性质"的尝试时,犹如蹒跚学步的孩童,在这过程中留下些许尴尬,亦属在所难免。作为教材的编撰者,我们衷心希望能听到来自各方的意见和建议,以便日后再版修订,进而发展出更好更多翻译学研究型教材来。

是之为序。

二〇一二年三月二十七日

撰于沪上滴水湖畔临港别屋

前　言

文学翻译的历史非常悠久。在中国，从东汉佛经翻译开始，至今已有1700多年的历史；在西方，如果从公元前200年希腊、罗马时期的戏剧翻译算起，文学翻译也已历经了2000多年的历史。

大量文学作品的翻译和有关文学翻译的理论阐述，使得文学翻译及其研究成为翻译研究中的经典话题。人们谈论翻译，在不作说明的情况下，预设的往往就是文学翻译；谈论翻译理论，其讨论对象也是文学翻译。文学翻译通常被视为所有翻译形式中的"最高形式"(the highest form of translation)。

20世纪70年代，对翻译研究者来说，最具有历史意义的大事就是宣告"翻译研究"(Translation Studies)作为一门独立学科的建立。作为一门学科，翻译研究的对象不仅仅是语言问题，还涉及翻译家、原作、译作、译语读者、历史语境等一切与翻译相关的因素，其研究方法更注重描述，其研究视阈从文本内部拓展到文本之外。翻译研究作为一门学科，其系统性日渐显现。

20世纪90年代，翻译研究出现了文化转向，同时，也开始从原语取向研究向译语取向研究转化。译语文本在目标语中的接受以及相关的一系列问题得到更多关注。文化研究的勃兴，又助推了这股翻译研究的热潮，文学翻译研究开始进入文化研究视野。翻译研究视阈拓展，翻译理论新思涌现，在国际范围内进一步形成了翻译研究的热潮。国内的一些研究者对文学翻译研究中的新思想、新发展也日渐关注，研究成果不断推陈出新。在当今全球化的文化语境下以及"中国文化走出去"的战略思想指导下，非常有必要梳理中外文学翻译研究的现状，以期对翻译学学科的建设和不断完善有所裨益。

《文学翻译研究导引》是"大学翻译学研究型系列教材"的分册之一。编者结合目前国内高校翻译研究和教学实践的实际情况进行合理整合，以满足翻译学学科研究生教学与研究的需求。该教材共选文35篇，其中英文文章16篇，中文文章19篇，按论题分为9章，每章由"导论"、"选文"、"延伸阅读"以及"问题与思考"四部分组成，按照内在逻辑编排，主要内容包括：(1) 文学、文学翻译与文学翻译研究；(2) 文学翻译研究的语言学探索；(3) 文学翻译研究的文化转向；(4) 文学翻译研究的美学之维；(5) 文学翻译研究的社会学因素；(6) 文学翻译研究的阐释学钩沉；(7) 文学翻译研究的哲学考察；(8) 文学翻译研究的女性主义启示；(9) 文学翻译研究的后殖民主义视阈。

文学翻译包括从原本的产出、翻译文本的选择、译者的理解和表达，直至译本的产出等一系列环节，其中关涉历史语境、社会意识形态、主体作为、性别和文化的平等、译本的接受、文化的传承等诸多话题。文学翻译研究的方法众多，理论视角不同，本教材不可能面面俱到，尽收其中。就选文的研究类别问题，该教材依据欧洲传统文学分类法并结合现代文学分类法，确定戏剧、诗歌、小说为文学翻译的主要研究对象。选文对这三大类别的翻译研究都有不同程度的兼顾。同时，编者注重选取与中国文学翻译研究的相关文章，旨在引起译界学者对中国文学翻译研究发展状况的思考。

本教材由葛校琴和严晓江担任主编，郑贞、杨淑华、万晓燕担任副主编。葛校琴和严晓江负责确定选文、撰写提纲、导论和部分导言以及统稿与定稿；郑贞、杨淑华、万晓燕负责撰写部分导言、核对选文以及编排主要参考文献等；在读硕士研究生沈文涛、田福建也参与选文的输入。该套教材总主编——南京大学外国语学院博士生导师张柏然教授审核了全稿并提出了许多宝贵的改进意见，在此深表谢忱。南京大学出版社的领导和编辑们在该教材的出版过程中付出了辛勤劳动。此外，还要衷心感谢各位选文作者的大力支持。

由于编者水平有限，教材中的疏漏与不当之处，敬请专家、同行与读者批评指正。

主　编
葛校琴　严晓江

目　录

第一章　文学、文学翻译与文学翻译研究

导　论

研究文学翻译，还得从文学谈起。

“文学性”是文学作品的特性，也是文学翻译所要传达的核心内容。早在20世纪初，文学批评界和理论界就试图对“文学性”作出定义。罗曼·雅各布森在1921年指出：“文学科学的对象不是文学，而是‘文学性’，也就是使一部作品成为文学作品的东西。”（方珊，2002：102）这说明，文学具有其他学科所不具有的特性，即文学区别于其他学科之“文学性”。“文学性”是一切具有审美效果的文艺作品所必然具有的性质，是诗之所以为诗、小说之所以为小说的存在理由。

对于雅各布森和他同时代的俄国形式主义批评家来说，“文学性”主要存在于作品的语言层面。这里，“语言层面”主要包括作品的技巧、程序、形式、词汇、布局、情节分布等，而“文学性”正是作品的这些构成要素与构成方式的独特之处。“文学性”主要是指：雅各布森所说的“形式化言语”（formed speech），强调对日常语言进行变形、强化，甚至歪曲，什克洛夫斯基所倡导的对日常语言的“陌生化”（defamiliarisation）处理，布拉格学派的创始人穆卡罗夫斯基所提出的“突现”的诗的语言，以及托马舍夫斯基所注重的“节奏的韵律”（rhythmic impulse）的语言，等等。换言之，“文学性”即创新性，与墨守成规水火不容。

韦勒克和沃伦所论的“文学的本质”可以说是对文学最经典的定义。“‘文学’一词，如果指文学艺术，即想象性文学，似乎是最恰当的。”“‘虚构性’、‘创造性’或‘想象性’是文学的突出特征。”文学作为语言的艺术，被认为是有别于日常语言的具有创造性特征的独特结构。俄国形式主义批评家们和韦勒克、沃伦等人都是从文本的语言文体层面所体现的文学特质和美学效果来讨论“文学性”和定义文学，并努力描绘出文学文本相对确定的元素和艺术特质。这种对文学本体的定位，有助于研究者辨析文学文本与其他类型文本的差异，从而为文学翻译研究打好基础。

那么，何为文学翻译？文学翻译，顾名思义就是对具有文学特质的文本进行的跨语言转换。卡萨格兰德（J. B. Casagrande）曾将文学翻译定义为“审美—诗意的翻译”（aesthetic-poetic translation）：

> ... aesthetic-poetic translation thus refers to the translation of poetic texts, where it is necessary to retain the expressive and stylistic features of the author's work to as large an extent as possible. ... while the content is clearly important, "express consideration is given to the literary or aesthetic form of the message in

both languages." (Shuttleworth & Cowie, 1997: 7)

克拉塞(Olive Classe)在《英译文学翻译百科全书》(*Encyclopedia of Literary Translation into English*,2000)中指出:"文学"含有"美学目的,具有持久性和有意为之的文体效果的存在"(aesthetic purpose, together with a degree of durability and the presence of intended stylistic effects)。"文学翻译"因文本对象的"文学性"而使得对它的翻译也具有了独特性。

国内很多学者持有相同的观点。林语堂(1933)认为,翻译除了忠实和通顺的标准之外,还有美的标准;译者既有对原著者、读者的责任,也有"对艺术的责任"(罗新璋、陈应年,2009: 492-493)。傅雷的翻译原则是重神似而不重形似。他(1951)说:"以效果而论,翻译应当像临画一样,所求的不再形似而在神似","以甲国文字传达乙国文字所包含的那些特点,必须像伯乐相马,要'得其精而忘其粗,在其内而忘其外'"。(同上:623-624)钱锺书在《林纾的翻译》(1964)一文中提出:"文学翻译的最高标准是'化'。把作品从一国文字转变成另一国文字,既能不因语文习惯的差异而露出生硬牵强的痕迹,又能完全保存原有的风味,那就算得入于'化境'。"(同上:774)林语堂视翻译为艺术,译者得一艺术品,即要还它一艺术品。傅雷则把翻译从字句的推敲提升到了艺术的锤炼。钱锺书所言翻译的"化境",即是"艺术上臻于精妙超凡之境"。(罗新璋语)文学翻译作如此艺术的追求自然要求译者对原文的语言形式如音韵、修辞、篇章结构等等进行全方位的美学审视,并将自己的审美感受凝于笔端,再现于译文的语言形式之中,使译语读者产生与译者相同的审美感受。

当然,"文学性"在翻译中的传达并非易事。卡萨格兰德指出:诗意或审美的表达,如韵、格律、隐喻等,"恰恰是最不容翻译的,而它们又恰是个体语言的独特之处"("precisely those aspects of language which are most resistant to translation" as they "partake of the unique qualities of the individual language")。林语堂也承认意大利哲学家克罗齐(Benedetto Croce, 1866-1952)的话:"凡真正的艺术作品都是不能译的。"(同上:504)傅雷说:"即使最优秀的译文,其韵味较之原文仍不免过或不及。翻译时只能尽量缩短这个距离,过则求其勿太过,不及则求其勿过于不及。"(同上:624)可见,正是文学语言的独特性使文学翻译不同于其他类型的翻译,但同时也增加了翻译转换的难度。

其实,"文学性"也好、文学的本质也好,都是人们在长期认识过程中逐渐形成的比较笼统、广泛、可体会但又难以言传的概念。赫曼斯(Theo Hermans)指出:对于当今文学研究者来说,他们早已放弃那种单一地从语言形式和本体上对文学进行定义的努力,而是侧重从文学的功能和偶然性来作出定义。伊格尔顿(Terry Eagleton)指出:文学是一种带有价值判断的写作,价值观和价值的判断则受制于社会和意识形态。乔纳森·卡勒(Jonathan Culler)则说:文学,是体制或机构的一种标签,它意指一种言语行为或是一个文本事件,意在引出多样的关注;文学属于历史和意识形态范畴,具有社会功能和政治功能。

伊格尔顿和卡勒对文学别样的阐释拓展了传统文学认识的疆界,对文学翻译的界定和研究也带来了深刻的影响。赫曼斯认为,虽然文学作为具有独特性的文本而普遍得到认可,但对文学翻译的分类标准则模糊不清,几部大型词典对文学翻译也没有太清楚的陈述。在他看来,马克·沙特尔沃思(Mark Shuttleworth)和莫伊拉·考伊(Moira Cowie)的《翻译研究词典》(*Dictionary of Translation Studies*, 1997)中没有提供"文学翻译"词条,所列的卡萨格兰德"审美—诗意的翻译"也是含糊随意,约瑟·朗伯(Josè Lambert)在《文学翻译之研究》(*Literary Translation: Research Issues*)中对文学翻译也没有明确的定论,彼得·布什(Peter

Bush)在《文学翻译之实践》(*Literary Translation*：*Practices*)中则转而去写译者的技巧和作用，避主题而言他。凯瑟林娜·赖斯(Katharina Reiss)虽然对翻译的文本类型作了分类，但在表达性文本(expressive texts)类型中，她只是把叙事作品、戏剧和诗歌与电影、喜剧小品和圣经并列，并没有对“文学翻译”作专门的阐述，而一些专业的文学翻译词典则直言是沿用传统上人们对文学翻译的认识，不作概念的厘清，回避了矛盾。所以，文学翻译至今没有明确的定义。

本章围绕文学、文学翻译和文学翻译研究来选材。首选韦勒克和沃伦所著《文学理论》(*Theories of Literature*，1956)第一章《文学的本质》。该章节中对文学的阐述已成为文学研究中对文学本体认识的经典话语，也是研究文学翻译的学者必读的内容。赫曼斯的《文学翻译》(*Literary Translation*)一文则对不同历史时期的文学翻译进行了广泛的考察，尤其是对翻译研究文化转向后的翻译研究进行了回顾，如后结构主义对文本意义的阐述，读者接受反应理论的出现和解释学的勃兴，翻译的意义、对等、功能的重新认识，译者主体和主体性的重新拷问等等，为我们展示了上个世纪以来文学翻译研究的整体面貌。彼得·布什在《文学翻译之实践》中揭示了文学翻译的主体——译者所作的从文本的选择、推荐、翻译、出版、阅读等等方面，对传统文学经典的挑战和对“忠实翻译”的偏离。同时，也揭示了非译者主体所能左右的原因：编辑的修改、社会和各种文化因素的影响等。但译者是关键的“行动者”、能动的主体，译本主要是译者无数次决断的产物。谢天振的《文学翻译的创造性和叛逆性》不但揭示了创造性的生成原因以及和叛逆性的关系，而且阐明了创造性叛逆的必要性和重要意义。可见，没有创造性叛逆，也就没有文学的传播和接受。约瑟·朗伯(José Lambert)在讨论文学翻译时则对文学翻译的研究现状直接提出批评。他认为，以往的文学翻译研究都是在同一性和非历史性的前提下对翻译的不易、忠实的困难进行考察，对几百年来进行的翻译实践鲜有发人深省的真知灼见，也没有提供可资借鉴的文学翻译的综述，因此，也就很难对文学翻译作历史的回顾和深入的思考。

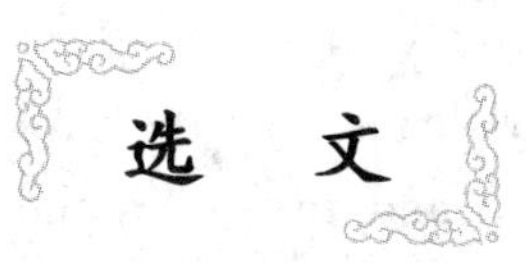

选　文

选文一　The Nature of Literature

Rene Wellek　Austin Warren

导　言

本文《文学的本质》选自文学批评经典之作——《文学理论》(*Theories of Literature*，1956)，作者是勒内·韦勒克(Rene Wellek，1903-1995)和奥斯汀·沃伦(Austin Warren，

1899-1986)。韦勒克是美国比较文学教授、20世纪西方杰出的文学理论家和文学批评史家，著有八卷本《现代文学批评史》；沃伦是美国文学评论家、作家，讲授英语。

"文学的本质"在区分了科学语言、日常语言和文学语言的基础上，揭示了文学语言的特殊性：充满内涵、语义含混、多同音异义字和语法上的不合理等等。文学语言不仅具有指示性，更具有表达性，在传达说话人语调和态度的同时，试图影响和改变听者的态度。文学语言深植于语言的历史结构中，强调符号本身，并具备表达和语用功能，它对语言的开发和利用更加系统和有目的。文章认为，虚构性、想象性和创造性是文学的本质特征，文学作品是一个交织着多种关系和意义的复杂组合体。因此，在研究文学作品时，必定要关注其存在方式及其层级系统。本文对文学本质的揭示，有助于更好地理解文学翻译研究对象的本质特征，并在文学翻译的实践中更加关注文学作品的文学性。

The first problem to confront us is, obviously, the subject matter of literature scholarship. What is the literature? What is not literature? What is the nature of literature? Simple as such questions sound, they are rarely answered clearly.

One way is to define "literature" as everything in print. We then shall be able to study the "medical profession in the fourteen century" or "planetary motion in the early Middle Ages" or "witchcraft in Old and New England." As Edwin Greenlaw has argued, "Nothing related to the history of civilization is beyond our province;" we are "not limited to *belles letters* or even to printed or manuscript records in our effort to understand a period or civilization," and we "must see our work in the light of its possible contribution to the history of culture." According to Greenlaw's theory, and the practice of many scholars, literary study has thus become not merely closely related to the history of civilization but indeed identical with it. Such study is literary only in the sense that it is occupied with printed or written matter, necessarily the primary source of most history. It can be, of course, argued in defense of such a view that historians neglect these problems, that they are too much preoccupied with diplomatic, military and economic history, and that thus the literary scholar is justified in invading and taking over a neighboring terrain. Doubtless nobody should be forbidden to enter any area he likes, and doubtless there is much to be said in favor of cultivating the history of civilization in the broadest terms. But still the study ceases to be literary. The objection that this is only a quibble about terminology is not convincing. The study of everything connected with the history of civilization does, as a matter of fact, crowd out strictly literary studies. All distinctions fall; extraneous criteria are introduced into literature; and, by consequence, literature will be judged valuable only so far as it yields results for this or that adjacent discipline. The identification of literature with the history of civilization is a denial of the specific field and the specific methods of literary study.

Another way of defining literature is to limit it to "great books," books which, whatever their subject, are "notable for literary form or expression." Here the criterion is either aesthetic worth alone or aesthetic worth in combination with general intellectual distinction. Within lyric poetry, drama and fiction, the greatest works are selected on aesthetic grounds; other books are picked for their reputation or intellectual eminence together with aesthetic value of a rather narrow kind: style, composition, general force of presentation are the usual characteristics singled out. This is a common way of distinguishing or speaking of literature. By saying that "this is not literature," we express such a value judgment; we make the same kind of judgment when we speak of a book on history, philosophy, or science as belonging to "literature."

Most literary histories do include treatment of philosophers, historians, theologians, moralists, politicians, and even some scientists. It would, for example, be difficult to imagine a literary history of eighteenth-century England without an extended treatment of Berkeley and Hume, Bishop Bulter and Gibbon, Burke and even Adam Smith. The treatment of these authors, though usually much briefer than that of poets, playwrights, and novelists, is rarely limited to their strictly aesthetic merits. In practice, we get perfunctory and inexpert accounts of these authors in terms of their specialty. Quite rightly, Hume cannot be judged except as a philosopher, Gibbon expect as a historian, Bishop Bulter as a Christian apologist and moralist, and Adam Smith as a moralist and economist. But in most literary historians these thinkers are discussed in a fragmentary fashion without the proper context—the history of their subject of discourse—without a real grasp, that is, of the history of philosophy, of ethical theory, of historiography, of economic theory. The literary historian is not automatically transformed into a proper historian of these disciplines. He becomes simply a compiler, a self-conscious intruder.

The study of isolated "great books" may be highly commendable for pedagogical purposes. We all must approve the idea that students—and even beginning students—should read great or at least good books rather than complications or historical curiosities. We may, however, doubt that the principle is worth preserving in its purity for the sciences, history, or any other accumulative and progressing subject. Within the history of imaginative literature, limitation to the great books makes incomprehensible the continuity of literary tradition, the development of literary genres, and indeed the very nature of the literary process, besides obscuring the background of social, linguistic, ideological, and other conditioning circumstances. In history, philosophy, and similar subjects, it actually introduces an excessively "aesthetic" point of view. There is obviously no other reason than stress on expository "style" and organization for singling out Thomas Huxley from all English scientists as the one worth reading. This criterion must, with very few exceptions, favor popularizers over the great originators: It will, and must, prefer Huxley to Darwin, Bergson to Kant.

The term "literature" seems best if we limit it to the art of literature, that is, to imaginative literature. There are certain difficulties with so employing the term; but, in English, the possible alternatives, such as "fiction" or "poetry," are either already pre-empted by narrow meanings or, like "imaginative literature" or *belles letters*, are clumsy and misleading. One of the objections to "literature" is its suggestion (in its etymology from *litera*) of limitation to written or printed literature; for, clearly, any coherent conception must include "oral literature." In this respect, the German term *Wortkunst* and the Russian *slovesnost* have the advantage over their English equivalent.

The simple way of solving the question is by distinguishing the particular use made of language in literature. Language is the material of literature as stone or bronze is of sculpture, paints of pictures, or sounds of music. But one should realize that language is not mere inert matter like stone but is itself a creation of man and is thus charged with the culture heritage of a linguistic group.

The main distinctions to be drawn are between the literary, the everyday, and the scientific users of language. A recent discussion of this point by Thomas Clark Pollock, *The Nature of Literature*, though true as far as it goes, seems not entirely satisfactory, especially in defining the problem is crucial and by no means simple in practice, since literature, in distinction from the other arts has no medium of its own and since many mixed forms and subtle transitions undoubtedly exist. It is fairly easy to distinguish between the language of science and the language of literature. The mere contrast between "thought" and "emotion" or "feeling" is, however, not sufficient. Literature does contain thought, while emotional language is by no means confined to literature: witness a lovers' conversation or an ordinary argument. Still, the ideal scientific language is purely "denotative." It aims at a one-to-one correspondence between sign and referent. The sign is completely arbitrary, hence can be replaced by equivalent signs. The sign is also transparent; that is, without drawing attention to itself, it directs us unequivocally to its referent.

Thus scientific language tends toward such a system of signs as mathematics or symbolic logic. Its ideal is such a universal language as the *charateristica universalis* which Leibniz had begun to plan as early as the late seventeenth century. Compared to scientific language, literary language will appear in some ways deficient. It abounds in ambiguities; it is, like every other historical language, full of homonyms, arbitrary or irrational categories such as grammatical gender; it is permeated with historical accidents, memories and associations. In a word, it is highly "connotative." Moreover, literary language is far from merely referential. It has its expressive side; it conveys the tone and attitude of the speaker or writer. And it does not merely state and express what it says; it also wants to influence the attitude of the reader, persuade him, and ultimately change him. There is a further important distinction between literary and scientific language: In the former, the sign itself, the sound symbolism of the word, is stressed. All kinds of techniques have been invented to draw attention to it, such as meter, alliteration and patterns of sound.

These distinctions from scientific language may be made in different degrees by various works of literary art: For example, the sound pattern will be less important in a novel than in certain lyrical poems, impossible of adequate translation. The expressive element will be far less in an "objective novel," which may disguise and almost conceal the attitude of the writer, than in a "personal" lyric. The pragmatic element, slight in "pure" poetry, may be large in a novel with a purpose or a satirical or didactic poem. Furthermore, the degree to which the language is intellectualized may vary considerably: There are philosophical and didactic poems and problem novels which approximate, at least occasionally, the scientific use of language. Still, whatever the mixed modes apparent upon an examination of concrete literary works of art, the distinctions between the literary use and the scientific use seem clear: literary language is far more deeply involved in the historical structure of the language; it stresses the awareness of the sign itself; it has its expressive and pragmatic side which scientific language will always want so far as possible to minimize.

More difficult to establish is the distinction between everyday and literary language. Everyday language is not a uniform concept: it includes such wide variants as colloquial language, the language of commerce, official language, the language of religion, the slang of students. But obviously much that has been said about literary language holds also for the other use of language excepting the scientific. Everyday language also has its expressive function, though this varies from a colorless official announcement to the passionate plea roused by a moment of emotional crisis. Everyday language is full of the irrationalities and contextual changes of historical language, though there are moments when it aims at almost the precision of scientific description. Only occasionally is there awareness of the signs themselves in everyday speech. Yet such awareness does appear—in the sound symbolism of names and actions. No doubt, everyday language wants most frequently to achieve results, to influence actions and attitudes. But it would be false to limit it merely to communication. A child's talking for hours without a listener and an adult's almost meaningless social chatter show that there are many uses of language which are not strictly, or at least primarily, communicative.

It is thus quantitatively that literary language is first of all to be differentiated from the varied uses of every day. The resources of language are exploited much more deliberately and systematically. In the work of a subjective poet, we have manifest a "personality" far more coherent and all-pervasive than persons as we see them in everyday situations. Certain types of poetry will use paradox, ambiguity, the contextual change of meaning, even the irrational association of grammatical categories such as gender or tense, quite deliberately. Poetic language organizes, tightens, the resources of everyday language, and sometimes does even violence to them, in an effort to force us into awareness and attention. Many of these resources a writer will find formed, and preformed, by the silent and anonymous workings of many generations. In certain highly developed literatures, and especially in certain epochs, the poet merely uses an established convention: the language, so to speak, poeticizes for him. Still, every work of art imposes an order, an organization, a unity on its materials. This unity sometimes seems very loose, as in many sketches or adventure stories; but it increases to the complex, close-knit organization of certain poems, in which it may be almost impossible to change a word or the position of a word without impairing its total effect.

The pragmatic distinction between literary language and everyday language is much clearer. We reject as poetry or label as mere rhetoric everything which persuades us to a definite outward action. Genuine poetry affects us more subtly. Art imposes some kind of framework which takes the statement of the work out of the world of reality. Into our semantic analysis we thus can reintroduce some of the common conceptions of aesthetics: "disinterested contemplation," "aesthetic distance," "framing." Again, however, we must realize that the distinction between art and non-art, between literature and the non-literary linguistic utterance, is fluid. The aesthetic function may extend to linguistic pronouncements of the most various sort. It would be a narrow conception of literature to exclude all propaganda art or didactic and satirical poetry. We have to recognize transitional forms like the essay, biography, and much rhetorical literature. In different periods of history the realm of the aesthetic function seems to expand or to contract: The personal letter, at times, was an art form, as was the sermon, while today, in agreement with the contemporary tendency against the confusion of genres, there appears a narrowing of the aesthetic function, a marked stress on purity of art, a reaction against pan-aestheticism and its claims as voiced by the aesthetics of the late nineteenth century. It seems, however, best to consider as literature only works in which the aesthetic function is dominant, while we can recognize that there are aesthetic elements, such as style and composition, in works which have a completely different, non-aesthetic purpose, such as scientific treatises, philosophical dissertations, political pamphlets, sermons.

But the nature of literature emerges most clearly under the referential aspect. The center of literary art is obviously to be found in the traditional genres of the lyric, the epic, the drama. In all of them, the reference is to a world of fiction, of imagination. The statements in a novel, in a poem, or in a drama are not literally true; they are not logical propositions. There is a central and important difference between a statement, even in a historical novel or a novel by Balzac which seems to convey "information" about actual happenings, and the same information appearing in a book of history or sociology. Even in the subjective lyric, the "I" of the poet is a fictional, dramatic "I." A character in a novel differs from a historical figure or a figure in real life. He is made only of the sentences describing him or put into his mouth by the author. He has no past, no future, and sometimes no continuity of life. This elementary reflection disposes of much criticism devoted to Hamlet in Wittenberg, the influence of Hamlet's father on his son, the slim and young Falstaff, "the girlhood of Shakespeare's heroines," the question of "how many children had Lady Macbeth." Time and space in a novel are not those of real life. Even an apparently most realistic novel, the very "slice of life" of the naturalist, is constructed according to certain artistic conventions. Especially from a later historical perspective we see how similar are naturalistic novels in choice of theme, type of characterization, events selected or admitted, ways of conducting dialogue. We discern, likewise, the extreme conventionality of even the most naturalistic drama not only in its assumption of a scenic

frame but in the way space and time are handled, the way even the supposedly realistic dialogue is selected and conducted, and the way characters enter and leave the stage. Whatever the distinctions between *The Tempest* and *A Doll's House*, they share in this dramatic conventionality.

If we recognize "fictionality," "invention," or "imagination" as the distinguishing trait of literature, we think thus of literature in terms of Homer, Dante, Shakespeare, Balzac, Keats rather than of Cicero or Montaigne, Bossuet or Emerson. Admittedly, there will be "boundary" cases, works like Plato's *Republic* to which it would be difficult to deny, at least in the great myths, passages of "invention" and "fictionality," while they are at the same time primarily works of philosophy. This conception of literature is descriptive, not evaluative. No wrong is done to a great and influential work by relegating it to rhetoric, to philosophy, to political pamphleteering, all of which may pose problems of aesthetic analysis, of stylistics and composition, similar or identical to those presented by literature, but where the central quality of fictionality will be absent. This conception will thus include in it all kinds of fiction, even the worst novel, the worst poem, the worst drama. Classification as art should be distinguished from evaluation.

One common misunderstanding must be removed. "Imaginative" literature need not use images. Poetic language is permeated with imagery, beginning with the simplest figures and culminating in the total all-inclusive mythological systems of a Blake or Yeats. But imagery is not essential to fictional statement and hence to much literature. There are good completely imageless poems; there is even a "poetry of statement." Imagery, besides, should not be confused with actual, sensuous, visual image-making. Under the influence of Hegel, nineteenth-century aestheticians such as Vischer and Eduard von Hartmann argued that all art is the "sensuous shining forth of the idea," while another school (Fiedler, Hildebrand, Riehl) spoke of all art as "pure visibility." But much great literature does not evoke sensuous images, or, if it does, it does so only incidentally, occasionally, and intermittently. In the depiction even of a fictional character the writer may not suggest visual images at all. We scarcely can visualize any of Dostoevsky's or Henry James's characters, while we learn to know their states of mind, their motivations, evaluations, attitudes and desires very completely.

At the most, a writer suggests some schematized outline or one single physical trait—the frequent practice of Tolstoy or Thomas Mann. The fact that we object to many illustrations, though by good artists and, in some cases (e. g., Thackeray's), even by the author himself, shows that the writer presents us only with such a schematized outline as is not meant to be filled out in detail.

If we had to visualize every metaphor in poetry we would become completely bewildered and confused. While there are readers given to visualizing and there are passages in literature where such imaginings seem required by the text, the psychological question should not be confused with analysis of the poet's symbolic devices. These devices are largely the organization of mental processes which occur also outside of literature. Thus metaphor is latent in much of our everyday language and overt in slang and popular proverbs. The most abstract terms, by metaphorical transfer, derive from ultimately physical relationships (*comprehend*, *define*, *eliminate*, *substance*, *subject*, *hypothesis*). Poetry revives and makes us conscious of this metaphorical character of language, just as it uses the symbols and myths of our civilization: Classical, Teutonic, Celtic and Christian.

All these distinctions between literature and non-literature which we have discussed—organization, personal expression, realization and exploitation of the medium, lack of practical purpose, and, of course, fictionality—are restatements, within a framework of semantic analysis, of age-old aesthetic terms such as "unity in variety," "disinterested contemplation," "aesthetic distance," "framing," and "invention," "imagination," "creation." Each of them describes one aspect of the literary work, one characteristic feature of its semantic directions. None is itself satisfactory. At least one result should emerge: A literary work of art is not a simple object but rather a highly complex organization of a stratified character with multiple meanings and relationships. The usual terminology, which speaks of an "organism," is somewhat misleading, since it stresses only one aspect, that of "unity in variety," and leads to biological parallels not always relevant. Furthermore, the "identity of content and form" in literature, though the phrase draws attention to the close interrelationships within the work of art, is misleading in being overfacile. It encourages the illusion that the analysis of any element of an artifact, whether of content or of technique, must be equally useful, and thus absolves us from the obligation to see the work in its totality. "Content" and "form" are terms used in too widely different senses for them to be, merely juxtaposed, helpful; indeed, even after careful definition, they too simply dichotomize the work of art. A modern analysis of the work of art has to begin with more complex questions: its mode of existence, its system of strata.

选文二 Literary Translation

Theo Hermans

导 言

本文《文学翻译》选自 Piotr Kuhiwczak 和 Karin Littau 编著的 *A Companion to Translation Studies*, 2007)。作者赫曼斯(Theo Hermans)是伦敦大学学院(University College, London, UCL)荷兰语和比较文学教授,翻译理论和翻译史研究专家。著有 *Translation*

in Systems (1999), *The Manipulation of Literature: Studies in Literary Translation* (1985), *Crosscultural Transgressions: Research Models in Translation Studies II* (2002)和 *Translating Others* (2006)等，其著述在译界影响很大。

选文描划了文学翻译作为翻译研究的重要分支其发生、发展及其研究领域不断拓展、研究主体不断深化的进程。作者在阐述文学翻译的研究内容、地位的确立、研究的理论化过程的同时，也阐明了什么是文学、文学与文学批评，文学与文学理论的关系，以及比较文学研究中人们如何看待翻译文学的问题等。文章跨越漫长的历史维度，揭示了文学研究从形式主义文论方法到解构主义和后殖民主义研究发展的进程中，文学翻译研究方法如何不断地被改进并予以修正。文章揭示了文学翻译理论发展所经历的从微观层面如译者的语言选择到宏观层面的如译者的意识形态、伦理立场等等各个方面的论争。在结论中，赫曼斯对文学翻译和翻译研究的前景充满乐观。他认为，翻译能够包容各类异质以抵制同质的统辖。

Rat Poison to Ted Hughes

What, if anything, is distinctive about literary translation? Few would doubt their intuitive sense that there is a difference between Ted Hughes' rendering of a play by Aeschylus and the English-language label on the packet of white powder in a Greek supermarket identifying the stuff in it, for the tourist's sake and good health, as sugar, salt, detergent or rat poison. But how are they different? Interestingly, Emma Wagner, a translation manager with the European Commission who mentions the Ted Hughes versus rat poison example in a discussion with a translation theorist, refers to the two kinds of translation as the top and bottom ends of the range, respectively (Chesterman & Wagner, 2002: 5). Not only is there felt to be a difference between literary and other forms of translation, but value enters the picture as well.

The standard view is that literary translation represents a distinctive kind of translating because it is concerned with a distinctive kind of text. The theory of text types, which seeks to classify texts according to their functions and features, duly places literary texts in a class of their own. The fact however that text typologies do not agree on what to contrast literary texts with—technical, pragmatic, ordinary? —suggests that what distinguishes literary from other texts may not be entirely obvious. And if there is no agreement on what makes literature distinctive, it may be equally hard to decide on what grounds literary translation should be awarded its own niche. In her *Translation Criticism*, first published in German in 1971 and now also in English, Katharina Reiss reviews various attempts to distinguish different kinds of translation. A. V. Fedorov, Otto Kade, J. B. Casagrande and Georges Mounin, among others, all include literary translation as a separate kind, but their criteria for doing so remain unclear or seem haphazard.

In recent years a number of general reference works on translation have appeared. Can they shed light on what makes literary translation special?

The *Dictionary of Translation Studies* (Shuttleworth & Cowie, 1997) has entries for "literal translation," "free translation" and the like but not "literary translation." Its entry on "aesthetic-poetic translation" turns out, with linguistic, ethnographic and pragmatic translation, to form part of J. B. Casagrande's fourfold and somewhat random list of translation types. The more encyclopedic reference works give out equally mixed signals. Writing on "Literary Translation: Research Issues" in the *Routledge Encyclopedia of Translation Studies* (Baker, 1998), Josè Lambert considers the definition of "literary" and the collocation "literary translation" but does not reach conclusions. Its companion piece "Literary Translation: Practices" by Peter Bush side-steps the issue by declaring: "Literary translation is the work of literary translators" and stressing the skill and worth of the latter. The German Handbuch Translation distinguishes only very broad text types: informative, appellative and expressive, the typology devised by Karl Bühler in the 1930s (Bühler, 1934). Under "primarily expressive" texts, narrative, drama and poetry make an appearance along with film, comic strips and the Bible, but "literary translation" as such is not featured (Snell-Hornby et al. , 1998).

There are now also a couple of reference works devoted specifically to literary translation into English. They must distinguish literary from "other" translation; but how? In the preface to her two-volume *Encyclopedia of Literary Translation into English*, editor Olive Classe (2000) merely notes that she has followed general usage. Just as translation commonly refers to interlingual translation, and "literature" and "literary" tend to imply "aesthetic purpose, together with a degree of durability and the presence of intended stylistic effects," so "literary translation" is read as conventionally distinguished from "technical translation." Peter France's *Oxford Guide to Literature in English Translation* makes a more determined effort. It speaks of literary translations as translations "designed to be read as literature" and cites with approval Gideon Toury's distinction between "literary translation" and the "translation of literary texts," the latter, nonliterary form of translation being described as "informational." Toury's distinction rests on his view, derived from Yury Lotman and, beyond him, Roman Jakobson and the Russian Formalists, that literature is characterised by the presence of a secondary, literary code superimposed on a stratum of unmarked language (Toury, 1980: 36-37). A formal definition of this kind no longer has currency in literary studies and anyway sits uncomfortably with the intentional aspect of accepting as literary any translation designed to be read as literature.

The search for a definition of literary translation leads nowhere. To students of literature this will not come as a surprise. They gave up trying to define literature some time ago. Today definitions of literature tend to be functional and contingent rather than formal or ontological. Let me use two introductory but influential textbooks to illustrate the point. Terry Eagleton's (1983) *Literary Theory* opens with a chapter "Introduction: What is Literature?" which argues that literature is best defined as "a highly valued kind of writing" and goes on to stress the social and ideological conditioning of values and value judgments. Jonathan Culler's (1997) *Literary Theory*: *A Very Short Introduction* adopts a two-pronged approach. The designation "literature" serves as "an institutional label," now denoting "a speech act or textual event that elicits certain kinds of attention". However, for historical reasons attention of the literary kind has been focused on texts displaying certain features, notably such things as the foregrounding of language, the interdependence of different levels of linguistic organisation, the separation from the practical context of utterance, and the perception of texts as both aesthetic objects and intertextual or self-reflexive constructs. The label and the features tend to correlate, so that the recognition of formal traits will trigger the institutionally appropriate kind of attention and vice versa. A conceptually sustainable way of modelling literary translation may then be based on prototype theory. In this view the prototypical literary translation is one perceived, and perhaps also intended, as a literary text, and hence as possessing literary features and qualities; around prototypical texts a host of other texts of more or less questionable membership will cluster, allowing the system to evolve in time.

For all that, Culler also notes that not much attention has been paid to the issue of the definition of literature in the last 25 years; what has attracted interest, he argues, is literature as a historical and ideological category, and its social and political functioning. Broadly speaking, this has also been the development with respect to the study of translation, and of literary translation in particular. Questions of definition and demarcation have given way to functional approaches that have been increasingly preoccupied with the roles assigned to and the uses made of translation by a variety of actors in varying contexts. In the case of the study of literary translation, however, another institutional issue had to be settled first. It concerned the acceptance, by the literary studies community, of translations as legitimate objects of study in the first place. Indeed comparative literature, the branch of literary study one might have expected to champion translation as an instrument of cultural transmission and negotiation, was decidedly slow to wake up to its relevance.

The changing attitude may be gauged from the three successive "Reports on Professional Standards" issued in 1965, 1975 and 1993 by the American Comparative Literature Association or ACLA. The first report stressed the need for "some access to all the original languages involved" and drew a stern line between teaching "foreign literature in translation" and comparative literature proper. Students of the latter were urged to read original works wherever possible and to rely on translation only as a last resort and for "remote languages." The 1975 report still called on teachers to work with original texts, not only for the benefit of those with a command of the relevant languages, but in order to "make the remaining students aware of the incompleteness of their own reading experience." The 1993 report strikes a different note. Not only is there the conciliatory statement that "the old hostilities toward translation should be mitigated," but translation is now held up as "a paradigm for larger problems of understanding and interpretation across different discursive traditions."

Coincidentally, Susan Bassnett's (1993) *Comparative Literature: A Critical Introduction* came out in the same year as the final ACLA report. Bassnett argued that traditional comparative literature was now well and truly dead and the new impulses were coming from cultural studies, gender and postcolonial studies, and translation studies. Rather than suggesting that the old hostilities towards translation be mitigated, she proposed translation studies as "the principal discipline from now on, with comparative literature as a valued but subsidiary subject area" (Bassnett, 1993: 161). The provocation did not go down well in comparative literature circles. Nevertheless, introductions to comparative literature today pay attention to translation.

Several things brought about the change in attitude signalled in the ACLA reports. Globalisation was one. As knowledge of Latin and Greek waned, comparative literary studies in the West found themselves in a postcolonial world full of potentially valuable texts in what the 1965 ACLA report could still refer to as "remote languages". Hermeneutics may well have been another. As early as the 1960s Hans-Georg Gadamer (1977: 98) observed that "[h]ermeneutics operates wherever what is said is not immediately intelligible." The operation takes place in the first instance within the same tradition, when the accidents of time and change have erected obstacles to the transmission of linguistic meaning, but applies *a fortiori* across languages and cultures. Negotiating these barriers requires translation. Hence, as Gadamer (1977: 19) put it, "[f]rom the structure of translation was indicated the general problem of making what is alien our own." How this process works in practice within one and the same linguistic and cultural tradition was illustrated in the opening chapter of George Steiner's (1975/1998) After Babel. Demonstrating the kind of deciphering needed to make sense, in contemporary English, of the language of English writers from Shakespeare to Noel Coward, the chapter was suitably entitled "Understanding as Translation." In his *What is Comparative Literature?* Steiner went on to insist on what he called "the primacy of the matter of translation" for all cross-cultural study. From a purely institutional point of view the fact that Andre Lefevere's *Translating Literature: Practice and Theory in a Comparative Literature Context* was published under the aegis of the Modern Language Association of America was no less significant.

There are similarities between the emergence of translation studies as an academic discipline and the recognition accorded to literary translation by comparatists. The study of translation generally had to emancipate itself from its ancillary status with respect to translation criticism and translator training so as to be able to approach translation as a phenomenon worthy of attention in its own right. In a parallel movement the study of literary translation had to legitimise itself in the context of comparative literature by pointing to the significance of translations, not just as vicarious objects standing in for originals as best they can, but as significant counters in the symbolic economy and carriers of ideas, attitudes and values.

Comprehending Translating

In the Anglo-Saxon world the traditional academic approach to literary translation went via the practical workshop, often supported by exercises in close reading as popularised by the New Critics of the 1930s and 1940s. The mutually beneficial combination of practical translation and criticism is summarised in Marilyn Gaddis Rose's Translation and Literary Criticism: "What translating does is to help us get inside literature." For D. S. Came-Ross, who became the editor of one of the first English-language journals devoted to literary translation, translation was "essentially an instrument of criticism." Came-Ross added that "true translation is much more a commentary on the original than a substitute for it." The statement highlights the alliance between translation and criticism while firmly assigning translation its place in relation to original writing.

Apart from serving as a workout and/or skills acquisition course for translators, the workshop employs translation as a means of probing the meaning of complex texts. Translating and understanding are two sides of the same coin. One of the leading New Critics, I. A. Richards, not only took a close interest in semantics but argued in the essay "Toward a theory of translating," later renamed "Toward a theory of comprehending," that in principle it is possible, though exasperatingly difficult, to reach an adequate understanding of a unique text through a careful mapping of all its denotative and connotative dimensions.

Hands-on experience of translating is the workshop's main strength. In addition, the concept invites reflection on the process of translating, on the aims and contexts of the exercise, and on other people's achievements. Broadly speaking, two lines emanate from the workshop concept. One consists of testimonies by practising translators, the other of translation criticism and, eventually, history.

The former line can boast some grand names of translator-writers, among them, in the 20th century, Ezra Pound and Vladimir Nabokov. Book-length testimonies in English include Ben Belitt (1978), Burton Raffel (1971, 1988), John Felstiner (1981), Suzanne Jill Levine (1991), Susanne de Lotbiniere-Harwood (1991), Douglas Hofstadter (1997), Robert Wechsler (1998), Clive Scott (2000) and Jin Di (2003). Collections like those compiled by Biguenet & Schulte (1989), Warren (1989), Weissbort (1989) and Boase-Beier & Holman (1999) feature shorter statements. The expositions fit old patterns. Much of the historical discourse on translation shows translators rationalising their own practice, more often than not in self defence. Some testimonies are more combative than others and slide from legitimising a particular mode of translating to legislating for all translation; Nabokov's vitriolic attacks on all styles of translating except his own are a case in point. Mostly, however, the shoptalk is concerned with concrete particulars; it is detailed, retrospective, introspective and experiential. As diagrams of the communication model hold theoreticians in their thrall, Clive Scott, for example, questions the received academic wisdom that translation is driven by communicative intent. Instead, he insists that reading and translating are intensely personal acts of self discovery and self-expression. Robert Bly's (1983) eight stages of translation, as exemplified by poetry, adopt the form of a masterclass. Having (1) scribbled a literal version, the translator (2) establishes the poem's overall meaning, (3) rewrites the crib in an acceptable linguistic form and adjusts the text to (4) a particular idiom and to (5) the poem's mood and (6) it's sound pattern, before (7) checking the draft with native speakers and (8) preparing the final version. Typically, however, Bly's account makes no mention of working conditions or of the social functioning of literary texts. Indeed many translators who would be part of literature's symbolic economy also buy into its public agenda of privileging artistic integrity over either economic or ideological considerations. The exceptions tend to be those who have followed academe's growing interest in the social conditioning and effects of literature; this applies to gender-conscious and postcolonial translators and to their fellow travellers (Venuti, 1995).

The historical prominence of translators' discourses about their art and craft lives on in the tendency, evident in several branches of translation studies, to approach translation from the translator's point of view. Jiff Levy's influential article (1967) on translating as constant decision-making, for example, depicts the process from the translator's angle, as does Gideon Toury's account of the operation of translation norms, which builds directly on Levy (Toury, 1995: 53-69). In the hermeneutic camp, George Steiner's so-called fourfold motion of initiative trust, invasive aggression, tentative incorporation and eventual restitution (Steiner, 1975/1998: 312ff.) seeks to portray the successive mental stages of the translator at work. In the same way Antoine Berman's call (1992) for an ethics of centrifugal rather than ethnocentric translation is primarily an appeal to translators to allow the foreignness of the foreign text to remain visible.

The other line emanating from the translation workshop found one of its earliest and finest illustrations in Reuben Brower's essay "Seven Agamemnon:"

> When a writer sets out to translate—say, the Agamemnon—what happens? Much, naturally, that we can never hope to analyze. But what we can see quite clearly is that he makes the poetry of the past into poetry of his particular present. Translations are the most obvious examples of works which, in Valery's words, are "as it were created by their public." (Brower, 1959)

The detailed comparison of texts, the workshop's strongest suit, here extends from aligning original and translation to inspecting serial translations. With this move from the pair to the series, the goal of the exercise also shifted from judgmental criticism to the historical embedding of texts. Brower's essay broke new ground in exploring seven English versions of Aeschylus' *Agamemnon* produced over several hundred years and reading each in relation to the dominant poetics of its time. The study of translation, for Brower, yielded insight into changing concepts of literature. The chronologically plotted renderings of a single original "show in the baldest form the assumptions about poetry shared by readers and poets"(Brower, 1959).

Brower's essay accords translations symptomatic value: because they conspicuously reflect a period style, they supply the researcher with a handy key to the larger picture. Rewarding as this view of translation was at a time when serious attention to literary translations needed justification in academic circles, it reinforced the perception of translation as merely reflecting prevailing conventions. Why translation should be so passive, Brower did not explain. More recent researchers have attempted explanations, and they have involved much broader categories. Andre Lefevere downplayed the importance of linguistic aspects of translation and highlighted instead the role of poetics and of ideological factors and institutional control. Recognising that translation means importing texts (containing potentially subversive elements) from outside a particular sphere, Lefevere stressed the desire of those in power to regulate translation. Because they mostly succeed, most translation offers "an unfailing barometer of literary fashions" (Lefevere, 1991: 129). Arguing from a gender position, Lori Chamberlain has claimed that translation is over-regulated because "it threatens to erase the difference between production and reproduction which is essential to the establishment of power." By analogy with Michel Foucault's (1986) "author function," Myriam Diaz-Diocaretz (1985) and Karin Littau (1997) have brought up the notion of a "translator function" to identify the ideological figure that restricts the dispersal of meaning and locks translation in both a legal system and a hierarchical symbolic order that privileges original work over secondary work.

Whether these explanations of the place and role of translation seem persuasive or not, they show that the debate has moved on. In the same way, the issue of the role of translation as merely conforming to prevailing period tastes or as an active shaping force has been redefined. As early as 1920 T. S. Eliot recognised translation's potential "vitalising effect," as he put it in "Euripides and Professor Murray"—in The Sacred Wood. Itamar Even-Zohar's polysystem theory would provide a theoretical framework for this potential. Revitalising Russian Formalist ideas, the model envisaged literature as permanent tug of war between conservative and innovatory forces, with translation joining now one and now the other side, either consolidating or undermining established modes of discourse. In this way translation was written into the broader scheme of things, along with other hitherto-neglected forms such as popular fiction or children's literature. The scheme of things grew even broader in the 1990s when translation came to be seen as helping to shape cultural identities. The selection of texts for translation and the way in which individual translations construct representations of foreign cultural products (and, metonymically, of foreign cultures as such) would now be read as offering a window on cultural self-definition. This is because domestic values inform both the process of inclusion and exclusion and the choice of a particular mode of representation (Hermans, 1999: 58ff.).

The workshop approach to literary translation held practice and observation in a precarious balance. However, as the above paragraphs indicate, ideas about translation have developed rapidly as translation studies gained momentum roughly from the 1980s onwards. As a result, new perspectives, approaches and concerns have come to the fore, more or less in step with the evolution of literary theory. In what follows I will discuss the main developments in the study of literary translation, grouping them for convenience under three headings: linguistics, functionalism and interventionism.

Linguistic Signatures

If Reuben Brower reckoned in 1959 there was much in translation "that we can never hope to analyse" (Brower, 1959), linguistic approaches have sought to supply tools to scrutinise the textual make-up of both literary and non-literary translations. The application of linguistic models to the analysis of literary texts had its heyday in the 1960s and 1970s, under the impulse of structuralism and transformational grammar. The momentum was not subsequently maintained, except in research on style. Linguistic approaches to translation seemed destined for a similar fate, but in recent years have bounced back with renewed vigour.

Early linguistically-inspired studies of literary translation concentrated on the semanticisation of form and on literary form as deviant usage. Richard de Beaugrande (1978) suggested ways in which translators might achieve "equivalence" by seeking to match in the translation the original's ratio of deviation versus standard usage. The approach slotted comfortably into the theory of text types deriving from Karl Bühler, as mentioned above. Bühler (1934) recognised three main functions of language (to represent, to express and to appeal) and distinguished three text types according to the dominance of one of these functions. Although text-type theory largely bypassed literature, Katharina Rein classified literature as "form-focused text." In the same way, text linguistics and pragmatics, which reacted against the decontextualised treatment of language characteristic of structuralism and transformational grammar, turned their attention mostly to non-literary texts.

More recently, however, two lines of linguistic enquiry, corpus studies and critical linguistics, have been making significant inroads into the study of literary translation. Corpus studies interrogate computer-readable texts in a variety of ways, with the intention of tracing patterns and common features across large amounts of data. For the machine to be able to respond, the questions fired at the corpus need to be formal and exact, and therefore linguistic in nature. One tendency of corpus-based translation studies has been to search for universals. For the time being, this exercise is compromised by the fact that the available translation corpora cover only a limited number of languages, lack a historical dimension and have no way of identifying whether the features encountered are exclusive to translation. Another line of enquiry, closer to traditional literary interests, has turned to stylistic investigation (Baker, 2000). Just as statistical data on individual usage enabled researchers to identify the author (Joe Klein) behind Primary Colors, the anonymously published insider novel about Bill Clinton's path from Arkansas to the US presidency, so corpus-based translation studies can pinpoint translators' personal voices across a range of apparently very different translations. The question of the coexistence of different subject positions in translated texts had been around in literary translation studies for some time. While a Bakhtinian emphasis on dialogism and heteroglossia might provide a suitable frame for their discussion, corpus-based studies were able to ask—and answer—much more precise questions, to extend their searches and come up with interesting correlations. For example, Mona Baker (2000) found that, for all their much-vaunted ability to wrap themselves around the style of their authors, translators leave their individual linguistic signature on texts belonging to very different genres and originally written in different languages. Today corpus-based translation studies are in full expansion across a broad spectrum of texts and languages. They work best when a sufficient volume of words can be scanned in and tagged; prose rather than poetry would seem to be their natural habitat.

Critical linguistics builds on pragmatics and discourse analysis, both of which made themselves felt in the study of translation in the 1980s. Indeed as early as 1986 Mary Snell-Hornby announced a "pragmatic turn" in translation studies, prefiguring the spate of "cultural" and other turns that would be declared later. In contrast to both structural and transformational models of language, M. A. K. Halliday's functional grammar views language as a social semiotic and has become an effective tool to delve into the way in which ideology is inscribed in the language we produce. Roger Fowler's (1981) *Literature as Social Discourse* demonstrated the relevance of this branch of linguistics for literary criticism. Among the earliest applications of Hallidayan concepts in literary translation studies was Kitty van Leuven-Zwart's model (1989-1990) for the analysis of shifts in translated narrative fiction. Van Leuven-Zwart sought to map semantic shifts logged at the microlevel of original and translated texts onto the macrolevel of narrative structure. To make this transition, she projected the various micro-shifts resulting from her analyses on Halliday's three so-called metafunctions: the ideational (i. e., roughly the way of presenting information), the interpersonal (which establishes the speaker-hearer relation) and the textual (the thematic organisation of a text). From this she came up with discursive profiles that could show differences in point of view, agency, modality and such like across entire texts.

In recent years Jeremy Munday (2002) has proposed combining the Hallidayan model with the potential unleashed by corpus studies to explore linguistic differences between originals and translations and relate them to social and ideological contexts. The three metafunctions are again the essential tools. The precision of linguistic concepts, together with the blanket coverage afforded by computerised searches, allows a type of investigation that is new, detailed and replicable, without seeking to sideline judicious interpretation.

Functioning Contexts

Functionalist ways of tackling the study of translation began to be mooted in the 1970s and 1980s out of dissatisfaction with the predominantly prescriptive and decontextualised approaches holding sway at the time. Two particular schools of thought emerged, skopos theory and descriptivism. Skopos theory ("skopos" is Greek for "aim" or "goal"), which flourished in Germany, is explicitly functionalist in that it views translating as goal-directed action. It makes much of the intended functions and likely effects of translations in comparison with the functions and effects of their originals, stressing that as a rule the two communication situations are not parallel. Different translations may be needed to suit different kinds of readers, as indeed Theodore Savory had pointed out 20 years earlier. The translator is meant to assess similarities and differences and act accordingly, bearing in mind the interests and expectations of all concerned. To the extent that institutional constraints and audience expectations figure prominently in the model, skopos theory falls in with literary reception studies. If it has had only limited impact on the study of literary translation, this is chiefly because audience expectations are notoriously hard to define in literature.

Descriptive work has focused less on the actual behaviour of translators than on the outcomes of their actions and decisions, less on process than on product. The textual orientation chimes with literary pedigree of most descriptivists. As with other functionalist approaches, the aim is not so much description as understanding and explanation, even though (especially in the early days) descriptivism flaunted its empirical streak in order to distance itself from the prescriptivism of the applied approaches and of translation criticism. The leading descriptivist questions are historical: Who translates what, when, how, for whom, in what context, with what effect, and why? The last question requires delving into the motivation behind the choices made by translators and other actors. How to interpret translators' actions? The answer was found in the concept of a "translation norm." If we know the prevailing norm of translation, we can assess whether individual translators' behaviour accords with it, and speculate about their reasons for compliance or defiance. More likely than not, these reasons will bear some meaningful relation to the individual's position in a social environment, as an agent in a network of material and symbolic power relations. With this, translation has lost its philological innocence.

The set of norms relevant to translation at a certain time amounts to a translation poetics. It determines what will be deemed acceptable as translation in a given culture. Ways of processing texts that fail to meet the criteria regarded as pertinent to translation in a given community may result in the product being called paraphrase, imitation or pastiche, but not translation. In this sense norms police the boundaries of what a culture regards as "legitimate" translation. Moreover, norms embody social and ideological values. The implication is that translation is not an immanent but a relative concept, culturally constructed and therefore historically contingent. By following lines of thought of this kind, descriptivism reached some fairly radical conclusions. At the same time, it dovetailed with literary research on conventions, historical poetics and interpretive communities. And just as literary studies grew sceptical about grand historical narratives and discovered the micro-stories of New Historicism, descriptivists have relished the detail of individual case studies.

While descriptivism helped to legitimise translation as a serious object of literary study, much of the historical work on literary translation fits the descriptive paradigm without being indebted to it. Nevertheless, descriptive researchers have invested much determined effort in literary translation, from comparative methodology and wordplay to translation as a catalyst of cultural and political change (Tymoczko, 1999). In the process, a substantial range of aspects, modes and functions of translation in different contexts was documented, mostly with respect to canonical Western literature. The history of Western thought about translation received attention from Andre Lefevere (1977), Lieven D'hulst (1990) and others, and bespeaks an ongoing interest, as testified by several international anthologies. The roll-call of canonical historical thinkers featured in each one of these readers, incidentally, consists of Cicero, St. Jerome, Luther, Vives, Du Bellay, Dryden, Goethe, Schleiermacher, Wilhelm von Humboldt, Mme de Stael and Matthew Arnold. The literary presence is strong.

Descriptivism built on Formalist and Structuralist principles. From an early preoccupation with a taxonomy of shifts between originals and translations it graduated to polysystem theory and to Gideon Toury's emphasis on empiricism and strict methodology (1995). The attempt to account for translators' choices led first to concepts such as norms and patronage (Lefevere, 1992a) and then, as awareness of the need to bring context into view increased, to a "cultural turn". A large amount of detailed historical-descriptive research on literary translation was carried out in the 1980s and 1990s in Gottingen. This was mostly on translations into German but also on such topics as genre, narrative technique and translation anthologies. By the 1990s, as descriptivism was being urged into a more self-critical direction, other, ideologically more committed approaches were making their mark.

Problematic Others

If the collection *The Manipulation of Literature* (1985) introduced the descriptive paradigm to Anglophone researchers, it is sobering to reflect that Jacques Derrida's altogether more daring "Des tours de Babel" appeared in the same year. While descriptivism was cultivating its structuralist lineage, post-structuralism passed it by.

Perhaps post-structuralism is best seen in this context as a persistent questioning of taken-for-granted assumptions about translation. It raises doubts about the very possibility of translation by calling attention to such things as the instability of meaning, the materiality of language and the performance enacted by multilingual texts. By highlighting the double bind of translation as simultaneously necessary and impossible it also shows up the illusory nature of the attempt to dominate translation by theorising it from outside. Just as post-structuralism remains wary of the distinction between original writing and criticism, it distrusts the division between object-level and meta-level. Derrida's "Des tours de Babel" presents itself as a translation—sympathetic, perverse and oblique—of Walter Benjamin's *The Task of the Translator* of 1923 (published in English in 1970). At once literary and philosophical, post-structuralist writing about translation partakes creatively of translating.

The post-structuralist levelling of the groundwork proved productive. Its critique of representation was taken up with a particular emphasis by the two main critical currents of the 1990s, gender and post-colonial theory. Both, in literary as well as in translation studies, have been concerned with the archive, with identity, with commitment and with ethics.

The history of translation has been viewed as an arena of conflict by gender-oriented and post-colonial researchers. They focus on what is excluded as well as on what is included in and for translation, on the hidden as well the declared agendas, the larger power structures underpinning particular events and acts. Following the example of gender studies in literature, translation scholars have dissected the social and educational systems that allowed some women to translate but not to write original work, or at least not in their own names, and to translate certain books and not others. Postcolonial researchers have reconsidered the West's image of other parts of the globe in the light of Edward Said's *Orientalism* (1978) and analysed translation as an instrument of domination and of information control: The metaphors speak of complicity and resistance rather than enrichment, of appropriation rather than transmission or transfer. If for the descriptivists the loss of philological innocence was a staging post, here it is the starting point.

Neither gender studies nor post-colonial studies distinguish absolutely between literary and other forms of discourse. All discourses are seen as contributing to the construction of identities and communities. This brings into play the researcher's own person, and the place of his or her discourse. Gender as well as post-colonial researchers emphatically speak from minority positions. The first group speaks as part of a non-masculine community under constant pressure from a predominantly masculine world; the other speaks as part of communities living under the historical aftermath of colonialism, the everyday reality of neocolonialism, or the exercise of other power differentials. The specifically literary forms they have been most involved with are ecriture feminine and hybrid writing. Both forms challenge translation in that they evoke particular kinds of experience and self-consciously turn the standard medium of expression against itself. Ecriture feminine invents its own body language outside the reach of male-dominated discourse. In the culturally-hybrid writing of post-colonial authors, the memory of other tongues is always inscribed, whether as the multilingual legacy of colonialism or through the migrant's lost speech. As profoundly displaced forms of writing, they establish not single but complex, polymorphous, uprooted identities.

If the translation of such ideologically committed texts pushes the translator's own allegiance to the fore, so does their analysis. The metalanguage of translation cannot shake itself free of translation. As a result, ethical considerations have come to be applied both to translating and to its academic study. One illustration of this is provided by the work of Antoine Berman and Lawrence Venuti. Berman sought to counter what he termed the ethnocentric deformation of "naturalising" translation by a dogged attachment to the letter, to the detriment of the restitution of surface meaning. Such refractory translating, he argued, refashioned the receptor language and made it more receptive to "the Foreign as Foreign," an ethically desirable goal (Berman in Venuti, 2000: 285-286). Lawrence Venuti is currently the main advocate of this approach in English. While he concedes that all understanding is necessarily positioned and therefore "domesticating," he remains keen to practise "minoritising" forms of translation, forms that privilege substandard, marginalised, unorthodox, volatile and sedimented registers, everything, in short, that makes language teeming and heterogeneous. Venuti regards such translating as politically beneficial as well as ethically responsible, despite some paradoxes. It assists global English in appropriating the world's cultural goods even as it works to diversify its expressive stock. It commends a wayward mode of translation in polished academic newspeak. It exhorts economically vulnerable translators from within secure university walls. It is a very literary, almost quixotic undertaking. Even so, it raises fundamental concerns not just about translation but also about discourses about translation.

The interventionist strategies of gender and postcolonial approaches oblige those studying translation to reflect on their own positions, presuppositions, agendas and methodologies. That does not mean the different schools of thought in translation studies are moving closer together. No doubt the interventionist tendencies could learn from critical linguistics how to pinpoint value and ideology in texts with greater accuracy. The descriptivist search for renewal matches the self-reflexive moment in both critical linguistics and the interventionist camp. But the global context of current academic research, like that of contemporary literature, fosters diversity as well as uniformity. For the moment at least, both literary translation and translation studies appear to possess enough pockets of fractious heterogeneity to resist what Derrida, in a different context, called the hegemony of the homogeneous. It is a comforting prospect.

选文三 Literary Translation, Practices

Peter Bush

导 言

本文《文学翻译之实践》选自蒙娜·贝克(Mona Baker)主编的 *Routledge Encyclopedia of Translation Studies*(上海外语教育出版社,2004)。作者彼得·布什(Peter Bush)曾是东英吉利亚大学的文学翻译教授和文学翻译不列颠中心主任,现居巴塞罗纳,是自由职业翻译家,翻译了许多西班牙语文学作品。2009 年,因出色地翻译了 Miguel Sousa Tavares 的《赤道》(*Equator*),获古班基恩奖(Calouste Gubenkian Prize)。他与苏珊·巴斯内特合编了《身为作者的译者》(*Translator as Writer*),编辑了古巴文集《海龟的声音》(*The Voice of the Turtle*)。

选文围绕译者展开。文学翻译是文学译者(literary translators)的工作,是处在复杂的社会文化网络中的一种原创性的、主体的活动。这样的观点颠覆了人们对"文学翻译"和文学译者的传统认识。文章论及译者的不同情况、译者对原著的研究、译者采取的不同翻译策略和过程、译者与作者的合作等,旨在说明:译者不完全受"对等"的规约,更多的是一种介入(intervention),译本都是多元阅读、多次书写的结果。为符合主流文化和接受者的需要,译者和出版方都会做出一定的修改。出版的译本是译者创造性努力的成果。译者是该项主体行为和社会实践的关键人物,译本是由译者的多次决断带来的原语文本在译语文化中的"再生"。文学家打破了原语的常规和文化观念,译者则打破译语的标准和文化观念。从中我们看到,文学译者所体现的不同于其他译者的创造性。

Literary translation is the work of literary translators. That is a truism which has to serve as a starting point for a description of literary translation, an original subjective activity at the centre of a complex network of social and cultural practices. The imaginative, intellectual and intuitive writing of the translator must not be lost to the disembodied abstraction which is often described as "translation."

Literary translators have to connive or contend with the well-established hierarchies in the definitions of what constitutes literature: poetry, drama and prose—usually in that order, of "high" culture as opposed to "lower" categories such as science fiction, children's fiction and "pulp" fiction. These hierarchies are reflected in general assumptions about both the relative worth and difficulty of translating the constituent sections of literary production. Such categorizations have been attacked by cultural theorists, post-modernists and some translation scholars who have pointed out how the construction of canons has been informed historically by value-judgements refracted through prejudices of class, gender, nation and race. These attacks have also undermined confidence in the author's interpretation of what s/he has written in favour of the multiplicity of readings by readers: the kingly or queenly author has been dethroned and replaced by a fragmented realm of individual readers (Venuti, 1992). The work of literary translators implicitly and sometimes explicitly challenges the authority of the canon, the nationalism of culture and the "death" of the author. A literary translator is bilingual and bicultural and thus inhabits a landscape which is not mapped by conventional geographies; s/he is at home in the flux that is the reality of contemporary culture, where migration is constant across artificial political boundaries. In self-styled monolingual dominant cultures, as in the Anglo-Saxon varieties, that flux is often portrayed as a threatening, if not a pathological state of being. Literary translators are involved at a keen point of cultural convergence because they translate those works which, for whatever reason, are selected for translation and which now exist where otherwise there would be silence. They often play a key role by suggesting works for translation or regularly writing readers' reports for publishers on books sent by foreign authors or their agents. The eventual selection implies the work is representative—even if it is anticanonical—of a particular quintessential use of language and feeling in the source culture. It also implies that the publishers believe there is a market for that literary translation. By definition, nevertheless, any literary translation breaks the nationalist canon because, however assimilated by the translation and publishing process, it introduces into the reading space of non-readers of the source language a work that would otherwise remain an array of meaningless letters or symbols. As the creator of the new work in the target culture, the literary translator operates at the frontiers of language and culture, where identity is flux, irreducible to every day nationalist tags of "Arab," "English" or "French," or to foreign talk seen as irritating jabber.

Literary translators also belong to a cash nexus of relationships and a tradition of social practices within the publishing industry. A contract has to be signed, payment agreed, and decisions about copyright and deadlines for delivery of manuscript have to be reached, usually in the course of the translator's lone negotiations with a publisher. Payment may be in the form of an advance on royalties. Usually, the originating author accepts a royalty of eight per cent that in principle leaves two per cent for the translator. For a publisher who sees the translator as an added expense, a small payment may be made as an advance on royalties or a flat fee worked out on the basis of a rate per thousand words. Many literary translators argue for an advance based on the actual amount of time they estimate the translation may take rather than such piece-work rates. Grants from sponsoring Ministries of Culture or bodies such as the Arts Council in Britain or the National Endowment for the Humanities in the United States are sometimes awarded to publishers to defray the cost of translation. Contracts usually include some line about "providing a language that is faithful to the original" and commit the translator to the correction of proofs.

These arrangements may differ from country to country. In countries with a buoyant demand for translations, a publisher may have an in-house team of translations and translators, and the whole chain of production is run by literary translators who are part of the professional administrative framework of the publishers. In Britain and the United States, it is more likely that publishers will work with freelance translators they know or will contract them on the basis of word-of-mouth recommendation (the "friend of a friend"), proof of previous work or by reference to directories of literary translators.

Literary translators often do not have an agent, because agents are not interested in the slender earnings to be gleaned from representing literary translators. There are translators' associations which will advise on contracts and legal help in disputes, but characteristically they do not become involved in the actual negotiations over individual contracts. Literary translators, like all writers, are a heterogeneous social grouping. Some can live on their inheritances or the windfall of a royalty from a best-seller, some may combine literary translation with full—or part-time academic posts or other work, but freelance literary translators throughout the world depend on the amounts they receive for their translations to pay for the electricity that powers the word-processor.

What then of literary translation and the "rebirth" of the author? The process of translation differs slightly from translator to translator and is influenced by the particular work translated. However, whether there is to be collaboration with a living author, or study of previous translations in the case of a "classic" work, there are common stages and problems in the work of literary translators. It used to be the case that translators did not write about these issues, but there are now a number of case-studies written by translators about their mode of operation. First, the literary translator confronts words set on the page—in a certain context and with particular resonances—by an author who may be dead physically or metaphorically and now lives in the variegated readings by a host of readers of the source language. There is at least a minimum commonality to those readings created by the original. The literary translator creates a new pattern in a different language, based on personal readings, research and creativity. This new creation in turn becomes the basis for multiple readings and interpretations which will go beyond any intentions of either original author or translator. Nevertheless, it is the fruit of thousands of decisions, large and small, and of creative activity on the part of the translator.

An essential preparation for the translation will be careful reading and re-reading and accompanying research of source text and other work by the author. This can include travel to the writer's country and historical and literary research. It often helps to read works that play a similar though different role in the target culture. For Felstiner (1980), this meant reading poetry by High Church T. S. Eliot in order to gauge the right voice for Pablo Neruda, the Chilean Communist. In the case of living author a range of collaborative possibilities offer themselves. Some authors enjoy participation in the translation to the extent that the final fruit of the collaboration is a new work in which they extend and add

new sections. Others may add marginal comments to a draft. Sometimes, a translator may decide on very limited collaboration with an author in order to further a strategy of translation that is not tied too closely to equivalence, and this can give more scope for intervention on the part of the translator. There are translators who opt not to research the scholarly background of the work they are translating, presumably in pursuit of a more "writerly," intuitive mode. Whatever the strategy adopted by the translator, any translation is ultimately the product of multiple readings and drafts which precede and determine the shape of the final draft delivered to the publishers. Context is crucial. The process may be truncated or altered by external forces: the publication of a book may have to coincide with the release of a film, a dramatic script may have to be handed to production so staging can be started and the translation by changed in that process, or in a tradition upheld by London theatre companies a "literal" translation may be given to well-known writer who then produces a literary version. Different strategies may be necessary to approach a short lyric poem or a long work of prose fiction. A translator of fiction has to engage with the different rhythms, the images and symbols an author will use in the course of hundreds of page. Repeated reading and research enable the translator to identify such patterns, though some will be translated subconsciously as part of the process of imaginative rewriting. In dense texts resonate with ambiguities and alternative meanings by a James Joyce a translator works at disrupting the target culture in the way the original work disrupted the standard language and received notions of the source culture. Literary translation is then a very social, culturally-bound process where the translator plays a key role in a complex series of interactions.

When a manuscript is submitted to a publishing house, the editing process involves the application of a new set of criteria to the translation. There may be house-style that an editor uses across the board, and this may be applied, appropriately or otherwise, to a literary text in translation. In the English, Spanish and Portuguese-speaking worlds, for example, there will be issues of different dialects and editors who will only accept their variety of standard. This often leads to partial and usually inconsistent adaptations of translations into, say, American English or British English. Some leading translators have argued against this practice, explain that "editors can play havoc as they try to anglicize the text," and some have called for the retention of the language of the translator. The editor's reading, however, need not simply be a threatening and standardizing project. A fresh reading brings new insights and can eliminate mistakes that would otherwise mar the final version.

Conscious decisions which involve changing the translation are made at every stage, by editors and translators, in order to cater for the perceived needs of the receiving, dominant culture; Kuhiwczak (1990), for example, discusses the case of cuts made to Milan Kundera's novel *The Joke*. It is also worth pointing out that any publishing houses do not employ editors with a knowledge of the source language and there is no tradition of sub-contracting freelance editors with such knowledge.

A published translation is the fruit of a substantial creative effort by the translator, who is the key agent in the subjective activity and social practice of translation. Whatever the restraints of the network of social and cultural factors, it is ultimately the literary translator who makes the thousands of decisions that give a literary work its "afterlife": an existence in other languages.

选文四　文学翻译的创造性和叛逆性

谢天振

导　言

本文选自谢天振的著作《译介学》第三章第一节。作者谢天振是上海外国语大学教授、博士生导师。主要成果有:《译介学》(上海外语教育出版社,1999)、《当代国外翻译理论导读》(南开大学出版社,2008)、《中西翻译简史》(外语教学与研究出版社,2009)、《比较文学与翻译研究》(复旦大学出版社,2011)等等。

译介学不同于传统的翻译研究,"出发语和目的语之间如何进行转换的实际问题不再是它的兴趣所在,关于不同的翻译方法、不同的译文,它无意作出高低优劣的价值判断;它关注的是两种不同文化背景的语言在转换过程中文化信息的失落、变形、扩张、增生等等;以及文学翻译在人类跨文化交流的桥梁作用,它所具有的特殊的价值和意义"(见《译介学》序二)"创造性叛逆"是"译介学"引入的一个命题,也是译介学的核心论题。作者认为文学翻译中的"创造性与叛逆性其实是根本无法分隔开来的,它们是一个和谐的有机体。"这个命题的意义是巨大的,它不仅指明了文学翻译的性质特征,也高度凝练地总结出了文学传播与接受的一个基本规律。这一命题的确立对翻译文学的地位问题以及译者的主体性问题都具有重要的意义。

任何翻译,不管是一般的日常翻译、科技翻译,还是文学翻译,其本质其实都是把一种语言中业已表达出来的信息传达到另一种语言中去。但是文学翻译与其他翻译有一个根本的区别——它所使用的语言不是一般的语言,也就是说,不是一般意义上的仅仅为了达到交际和沟通信息目的而使用的语言。文学翻译使用的是一种特殊的语言,正如茅盾在一次报告中所说的,"文学的翻译是用另一种语言",它"把原作的艺术意境传达出来,使读者在读译文的时候能够像读原作时一样得到启发、感动和美的感受。"[1]显然,这是一种艺术语言,一种具有美学功能的艺术语言。这种语言要能够重现原作家通过他的形象思维所创造出来的艺术世界、所塑造成功的艺术形象。

然而,翻译的实践表明,人们赋予文学翻译的目标与文学翻译实际达到的结果之间始终是

存在差距的。这其中的原因，有艺术上的，也有语言本身的。意大利著名美学家克罗齐分析说："如果翻译冒充可以改造某一表现品为另一表现品，如移瓶注酒那样，那就是不可能的。在已用审美的办法创作成的东西上面，我们如果再加工，就只能用逻辑的办法；我们不能把已具审美形式的东西化成另一个仍是审美的形式。"[2]这是从审美原理角度分析文学翻译的困难（在克罗齐看来，文学翻译简直就是不可能的），话虽偏激了一些，但不无道理。

另一方面，则是文学本身的特点所决定的。众所周知，文学与其他艺术相比，如音乐、绘画、雕塑、甚至电影等，它是唯一局限于语言框架之内的艺术。而语言之所以能产生艺术所要求的形象性、生动性，这是与语言本身的历史文化积淀、与该语言环境中的语言使用者本人的生活经验，有着密切的关系。特定语言环境内的历史的文化积淀和语言使用者的生活经验，使该语言的使用者在使用某一特定语汇时产生丰富的联想，从而赋予该语言以特定的形象性和生动性。譬如，"天高云淡"一语，寥寥四字，貌若平常，但在汉语这一特定的语言环境中，却能使人产生"海阔天空、壮志满怀"、或"秋高气爽"、或"秋风肃杀"等等的诗的意境，产生许多丰富的联想。但是当译者把这四个字照搬到另一种语言中去，如译成英语 The sky is high, the clouds are thin，英语读者恐怕就无法产生相似的联想。因此，当在一种语言环境中产生的文学作品被"移植"到另一种语言中去时，为了使接受者能产生与原作同样的艺术效果，译者就必须在译语环境里找到能调动和激发接受者产生相同或相似联想的语言手段。这实际上也就是要求译作成为与原作同样的艺术品。在这种情况下，文学翻译与文学创作已经取得了相同的意义，文学翻译也已显而易见不再是简单的语言文字转换，而是一种创造性的工作。仍然是茅盾的话："这样的翻译，自然不是单纯技术性的语言外形的变易，而是要求译者通过原作的语言外形，深刻地体会了原作者的艺术创造的过程，把握住原作的精神，在自己的思想、感情、生活体验中找到最适合的印证，然后运用适合于原作的文学语言，把原作的内容与形式正确无疑地再现出来。这样的翻译的过程，是把译者和原作者合而为一，好像原作者用另外一国文字写自己的作品。这样的翻译既需要译者发挥工作上的创造性，而又要完全忠实于原作的意图，……这是一种很困难的工作。但是文学翻译的主要任务，既然在于把原作的精神、面貌忠实地复制出来，那么，这种艺术创造性的翻译就完全是必要的。"[3]加拿大翻译研究家芭芭拉·格达德说："面对新的读者群，译者不仅要把一种语言用另一种语言传达出来，而且要对一个完全崭新的文化及美学体系进行诠释。因此，翻译决不是一维性的创作，而是两种体系的相互渗透。译者是传情达意的积极参与者，是作者的合作者。"[4]

这里也许可举王佐良先生翻译的培根的《谈读书》为例。译文不长，抄录如下：

> 读书足以怡情，足以傅彩，足以长才。其怡情也，最见于独处幽居之时；其傅彩也，最见于高谈阔论之中；其长才也，最见于处事判事之际。练达之士虽能分别处理细事或一一辨别枝节，然纵观统筹、全局策划，则舍好学深思者莫属。读书费时过多易惰，文采藻饰太盛则矫，全凭条文断事乃学究故态。读书补天然之不足，经验又补读书之不足，盖天生才干犹如自然花草，读书然后知如何修剪移接；而书中所示，如不以经验范之，则又大而无当。有一技之长者鄙读书，无知者羡读书，唯明智之士用读书，然书并不以用处告人，用书之智不在书中，而在书外，全凭观察得之。读书时不可存心劫难作者，不可尽信书上所言，亦不可只为寻章摘句，而应推敲细思。书有可浅尝者，有可吞食者，少数则须咀嚼消化。换言之，有只须读其部分者，有只须大体涉猎者，少数则须全读，读时须全神贯注，孜孜不倦。书亦可请人代读，取其所作摘要，但

只限题材较次或价值不高者，否则书经提炼犹如水经蒸馏，淡而无味矣。

读书使人充实，讨论使人机智，笔记使人准确。因此不常作笔记者须记忆特强，不常讨论者须天生聪颖，不常读书者须欺世有术，始能无知而显有知。读史使人明智，读诗使人灵秀，数学使人周密，科学使人深刻，伦理学使人庄重，逻辑修辞之学使人善辩：凡有所学，皆成性格。人之才智但有滞碍，无不可读适当之书使之顺畅，一如身体百病，皆可借相宜之运动除之。滚球利睾肾，射箭利胸肺，漫步利肠胃，骑术利头脑，诸如此类。如智力不集中，可令读数学，盖演题须全神贯注，稍有分散即须重演；如不能辨异，可令读经院哲学，盖是辈皆吹毛求疵之人；如不善求同，不善以一物阐证另一物，可令读律师之卷案。如此头脑中凡有缺陷，皆有特药可医。

如果不说明这是一篇译文的话，有谁能看出这是一篇翻译作品呢？略带古奥的、浅近的汉语文言文体，高度凝练而又极其准确的用词，流畅简约的行文遣句，通篇浑然一体的风格，令人不仅得到思想的教益，而且得到美的享受。

事实上，这篇译文除了思想是来自原作者英国著名哲学家、英语语言大师培根(Francis Bacon)之外，其余已经都是译者的贡献了。用这样的语言去表达原作的思想，谁说不是一种创造呢？难怪我国的文学大师郭沫若要说："翻译是一种创造性的工作，好的翻译等于创作，甚至还可能超过了创作。这不是一件平庸的工作，有时候翻译比创作还要困难。"[5]事实确是如此，因为译者在创造时并不是随心所欲，他要受到原作的许多因素的限制。如这篇《谈读书》，译者之所以用这样的语言去表达原作，是因为原作本身就是一篇古色古香、用词精炼、含义深刻的典雅散文。[6]所以有人把翻译喻为"戴着镣铐跳舞"，可谓极其形象地道出了翻译的艰难本质。

文学翻译的创造性性质是显而易见的，它使一件作品在一个新的语言、民族、社会、历史环境里获得了新的生命。但是，与原作的创造性质相比，翻译的创造性性质还是有所不同，它属于二度创造，即再创造。但是创造与再创造这两者之间的界限却是很难划分，这是因为文学翻译有许多种不同的类型。逐字逐句的、比较忠实的翻译，其性质自然属于再创造性质，但是那些"编译"、"译述"、"达旨"以及偏离原文较远的"意译"，其性质就很难界定了。实际上，这个问题与翻译的概念有关。有人说，翻译的概念随着时代的发展在不断变化，此话有理。现在如果再回过头去看看中国早期的译作，像林纾、苏曼殊等人的翻译，按照现在的翻译标准，是否还能算作是翻译呢？他们"译作"中的创造性成分实在是太大了。这种情况也不光是发生在中国，世界其他国家也都有。毕竟，人们对翻译的认识有一个过程。

深入探究一下的话，作为人类的一个文化现象，文学翻译实在是一种颇为微妙的矛盾现象。因为，作为文学，它理应把一件非本族语的文学作品变成一件地道的本民族语言写成的作品，像上面所引的王佐良的译文那样，否则它就不成其为文学作品了。但是，作为翻译，它又应该把一件外族的文学作品传达过来，使人感觉到它是一件外族文学的作品，否则又如何能算是"翻译"？各国的文学翻译工作者似乎一直就在这相互矛盾、甚至相互排斥的两点之间犹豫、徘徊，殚精竭虑，努力在这两点之间找到一个合适的切入点。

从创作心理学的角度看，文学翻译(其他翻译也一样)大致可分为两个阶段，即分析阶段和综合阶段。这两个阶段的区别当然不一定很明显，也不一定有明确的时间上的界限，它们更多的是存在于思考之中或潜意识之中，并存于同一个创作活动之中。两者之中，分析是文学翻译创作的前提。通常译者拿到文本后，首先总是要仔细研读原文——这里的研读也就是分析，接

着他要考虑如何用译语表达的问题——这时他就进入了综合的阶段。无论在分析阶段还是综合阶段，译者所使用的语言就是他的母语。而如果说，在分析阶段译者担任的还仅仅是读者的角色的话，那么，在进入综合阶段后，译者就已经担任起创作者的角色了，这时他所思考的问题几乎与原作者所考虑的问题一模一样：他要考虑如何使所述的事件生动有趣，如何使塑造的形象富有魅力，如何使人物的语言具有个性，如何使作品体现一定的风格等等。由此可见，文学翻译家所考虑的问题已经超出了原作文本的语言问题的框框，他所思考的很多问题许多已经进入了作家的创作领域。当然，作为翻译的文学创作与作为原作的文学创作是存在重大区别的，其中最根本的区别在于：原作的创作直接来源于生活，来源于作家的现实，译作的创作来源于原作，来源于原作家所表现的现实。但尽管如此，译者还是需要有能体会到原作人物感情、思想、行为的能力，需要有把这一切重新表现出来的能力，而这无论如何也是一种创造——人们通常称之为再创造。

然而，迄今为止，人们对文学翻译的再创造性质的认识还是不够的，人们往往以为，再创造比起原作的创造来总要低一等。其实，原作的创造与译作的再创造各有其特点，也各有其不可替代的独立价值。优秀的翻译家固然未必就能成为出色的大作家，但杰出的大作家也未必一定就能够成为优秀的翻译家，这种例子古今中外，可说比比皆是。因此，创造与再创造不能简单地归结为孰高孰低的问题，而应认清其各自的功用与特点。

如果把创造与再创造孰高孰低的问题推向极端的话，就引出了另一个翻译界一直有争议的话题，即译作能不能胜过原作的问题。从翻译的本义来看，这个问题应该是不成立的，因为翻译应该忠实于原作，不及原作的翻译固然不足取，但超过了原作的翻译同样也是与翻译的宗旨不符的。英国翻译研究家乔治·斯坦纳说："理想的翻译是既不要不及原文，也不要超过原文。"然而我们大家都知道，这仅仅是"理想的翻译"，而这样理想的翻译实际上是永远不可能完全实现的。

但是文学翻译的实践表明，译作胜过原作的现象不仅外国有，中国也有。外国的例子，如波德莱尔用法语翻译的爱伦·坡的诗，人们觉得波德莱尔的译作比爱伦·坡的原诗更为出色（幽默的美国人说，在"坡"的名字下有两个人，一个是平庸的美国作家，一个是天才的法国诗人）；奈瓦尔用法语翻译的《浮士德》，哥德读后的印象是其文字比原作的文字还要清晰；弗赖利格拉斯(F. Freiligraph)用德语翻译的《草叶集》，连惠特曼也不否认可能胜过他的英文原诗……在中国，精通英文的钱锺书"宁可读林纾的译文，不乐意读哈葛德的原文，理由很简单，林纾的中文文笔比哈葛德的英文文笔高明得多"。[7]著名语言学家吕叔湘在仔细对照了多首英译唐诗之后也说，其中的有些译诗"竟不妨说比原诗好"。[8]因此，有好几位学者都指出，"有些译诗经过译者的再创造，还可以胜过原作"，"有时译文的干净妥帖甚至胜过原作"[9]等等。

与译作胜过原作的现象相仿的另一种现象是译作对原作的"提高"，具体说来也即是对原作的"雅化"。譬如有的《圣经》译本"刻意雕琢，显得十分华丽"；有的莎士比亚译本，由于译者所处的社会环境可能比莎士比亚所处的环境更为高雅，所以译者把原作里的许多蠢话、粗话和可笑的对话都作了"提高"，译文因此比莎士比亚的原作"更为庄重，更为文雅"。[10]

在文学翻译里，无论是译作胜过原作，还是译作不如原作，这些现象都是文学翻译的创造性与叛逆性所决定了的。如果说，文学翻译中的创造性表明了译者以自己的艺术创造才能去接近和再现原作的一种主观努力，那么文学翻译中的叛逆性，就是反映了在翻译过程中译者为了达到某一主观愿望而造成的一种译作对原作的客观背离。但是，这仅仅是从理论上而言，在实际的文学翻译中，创造性与叛逆性其实是根本无法分隔开来的，它们是一个和谐的有机体。因此，法国文学社会学家埃斯卡皮(Robert Escarpit)提出了一个术语——“创造性叛逆”(creative treason)，并说：“翻译总是一种创造性的叛逆。”[11]

文学翻译的创造性叛逆在诗歌翻译中表现得最为突出，因为在诗歌这一独特的体裁中，高度精炼的文学形式与无限丰富的内容紧密结合在一起，使得译者几乎无所适从——保存了内容，却破坏了形式，照顾了形式，却又损伤了内容。试看一例：

杨巨源有诗名《城东早春》，诗曰“诗家清景在新春，绿柳才黄半未匀。若待上林花似锦，出门俱是看花人”。英国汉学家翟理斯(Herbert A. Giles)把它译为：

The landscape which the poet loves is that of early May,
When budding greeness half concealed enwraps each willow spray.
That beautiful embroidery the days of summer yield,
Appeals to every bumpkin who may take his walks afield.

有人指出，译者以 early May 译原诗中的“新春”一词不确，“因为在中国，五月初已经将近暮春了。译者没有研究中国的时序景物，就拿欧洲的时序景物来比附，结果违反了同一律”。[12]这一批评当然不错，因为中国与欧洲的时序确实不同，early May 不同于中国的“新春”，用 early May 译“新春”，这是对原诗的叛逆。但假若我们细细推究一下译诗的话，我们当能发现，这种叛逆似乎并非出自译者的本意，因为从整首译诗可以见出，译者对中文原诗的把握还是很准的，也是很严谨的，基本上传达出了原诗的诗意和意境。至于用 early May 译“新春”，显然是出于押韵的需要(与第二句中的 willlow spray 押韵)，不得已而为之。况且，对于英美读者来说，early May 也已经包含着“新春”的信息了，因此对这一译法似乎也情有可原。当然，与此同时这种译法也确实传达了一个错误的信息，使英美读者误以为中国的早春在五月之初，但这恐怕是诗歌翻译中普遍存在的一个难题，无法强求在一首诗歌中就给予解决，这个难题也许可以借助同一首诗的不同译本来加以完成。

例如，另一位汉诗的英译家宾纳(Bynner)所译的韦应物的诗句“春潮带雨晚来急，野渡无人舟自横”，也招致一点物议。宾纳的译诗为：

On the spring flood of last night's rain
The ferryboat moves as though someone were pulling.

有人指其以“似有人”译“无人”，两者反映的画面一动一静，“违反同一律”。[13]

同是这两句，王守义与约翰·诺弗尔合作，把它译为：

spring sends rain to the river
it rushes in a flood in the evening

the little boat tugs at its line
by the ferry landing
here in the wilderness
it responds to the current
there is no one on board

王译比较忠实地传达了原诗那种静态的画面，而且也没有了宾纳译本中那个"多余的人"，但是王译同样也没有了宾纳译本中那种与原诗相应的简洁与韵味。王译实际上是一首散文诗——这是对原诗韵律的一种叛逆，之所以如此，是因为在译者看来，在中国古典诗词中起很大作用的诗的外在美——诗的形式和诗的语言形式，主要是在音韵方面，而"这种音韵美在英译中是无法表达的"，因此，他们的译诗，如他们自己所宣称的，"看来是散文化的释义，而实际上是一首不错的英语无韵诗。如果它译出了原诗的意境、神韵、美感，它就是一首好的译诗。而且它会被英语读者接受，加以欣赏，甚至参与欣赏再创造，完成对诗美的享受和感应。"[14]

这两个例子可以让我们窥见创造性叛逆一些基本特点。由于文学翻译，一部作品被引入一个新的语言环境，于是也就产生了一系列的变形：翟理斯为了传达原作的韵味，结果把"新春"变成了"五月初"；宾纳为了追求原作诗的画面，结果却丢失了原作的诗歌形式和韵律……

文学翻译的创造性叛逆的特点当然不止于"变形"，它最根本的特点是：它把原作引入了一个原作者原先所没有预料到的接受环境，并且改变了原作者原先赋予作品的形式。文学翻译的创造性叛逆的意义是巨大的。正如埃斯卡皮所说："说翻译是叛逆，那是因为它赋予作品一个崭新的面貌，使之能与广泛的读者进行一次崭新的文学交流；还因为它不仅延长了作品的生命，而且又赋予它第二次生命。"[15]确实，在古今中外的文学史上，正是文学翻译的创造性叛逆，才使得一部又一部的文学杰作得到了跨越地理、超越时空的传播和接受。

创造性叛逆并不为文学翻译所特有，它实际上是文学传播与接受的一个基本规律。我们甚至可以说，没有创造性叛逆，也就没有文学的传播与接受。在人类的口头文学时期，许许多多的口头文学作品在一代又一代的口头文学家们的口口相传的过程中，不断接受他们的创造性叛逆，从而变得越来越丰富，越来越充实，越来越完满。进入书面文学时期，文学家们的创造性叛逆就变得有迹可循了——某些文学文本(版本)的变迁正是后代创作家对前人作品的创造性叛逆的证明。但这还仅仅是文学的创造性叛逆的一个方面，创造性叛逆的更重要的方面还在于它对文学作品的接受与传播所起的作用。一部作品，即使不超越它的语言文化环境，它也不可能把它的作者意图完整无误地传达给它的读者，因为每个接受者都是从自身的经验出发，去理解、接受作品的。一部《西游记》，政治家从中发现了"片听片信的主观主义干部"，"明辨是非敢于斗争的勇士"，文学人类学家从中发现了人类成年礼的原型模式，而普通百姓却只是看到了一部充满鬼怪打斗的有趣的神魔小说，其原因就在这里。

而一旦一部作品进入了跨越时代、跨越地理、跨越民族、跨越语言的传播时，其中的创造性叛逆就更是不言而喻了，不同的文化背景、不同的审美标准、不同的生活习俗，无不在这部作品上打上各自的印记。这时的创造性叛逆已经超出了单纯的文学接受的范畴，它反映的是文学翻译中的不同文化的交流和碰撞，不同文化的误解和误释。创造性叛逆的这一性质，使得文学翻译的创造性叛逆在比较文学研究中具有了特别的意义。正如《中西比较文学手册》中"翻译"条目所言："翻译是一种'创造性叛逆'这种'叛逆'表现在形式上就是翻译中的删减、添加和意译。……然而，不管翻译效果怎样，它无疑是不同语种间的文学交流中最重要、最富有特征的媒介，是比较文学的首要研究对象。比较文学家认为作家通过外国作品的翻译，领略到某些本国文学中没有的新的因素，并将其在自己的作品中表现出来，在这一过程中，翻译起到了媒介作用。一个国家翻译外国文学的作品本身意味着这个国家对外国文学的接受，也是外国文学对该国文学产生影响的表现。在我国现代文学的形成、发展中受到外国文学的很大影响，其中，翻译的文学媒介、实现影响方面所起的作用是极其明显的。……另外，'创造性叛逆'所带来的翻译的个性、翻译的理论,译者对原作的'选择性共鸣'及其译本的变迁等或表示了外国文学影响的踪迹,或反映了一国文学的情势,这些都是翻译研究的重要内容。"[16]

注释:

1. 矛盾《为发展文学翻译事业和提高翻译质量而奋斗》,载《翻译研究论文集》(1949-1983),第 10 页。
2. 克罗齐《美学原理》,外国文学出版社,1987 年,第 78 页。
3. 同注释 1。
4. Babara Godard, Language and Sexual Difference: The Case of Translation, in *Atkinson Review of Canadian Studies*, Vol. 2, No. 1, Fall-Winter, 1984, p. 13.
5. 郭沫若《论文学翻译工作》,同注释 1,第 22 页。
6. 王佐良的译文及培根的原文见王佐良《翻译、思考与试笔》,外语教学与研究出版社,1989 年。
7. 钱锺书《林纾的翻译》。
8. 参见吕叔湘编注《英译唐人绝句百首》。
9. 王佐良 Two Early Translators Reconsidered,载《外语教学与研究》1981 年第 1 期。
10. 乔治・斯坦纳《通天塔》,第 120 页。
11. 埃斯卡皮《文学社会学》,王美华、丁沛译,安徽文艺出版社,1987 年,第 137 页。
12. 张今《文学翻译原理》,第 59 页。
13. 同注释 12,第 55 页。
14. 王守义、约翰・诺弗尔《唐宋诗词英译》,黑龙江人民出版社,1989 年,第 167 页。
15. 同注释 11。
16.《中国比较文学手册》,四川人民出版社,1978 年,第 103-104 页。

选文五 Literary Translation, Research Issues

José Lambert

导 言

本文《文学翻译之研究》选自蒙娜・贝克(Mona Baker)主编的 *Routledge Encyclopedia of Translation Studies*(上海外语教育出版社,2004)。作者约瑟・朗伯(José Lambert)是比利时鲁汶大学教授、翻译和文化研究中心主任,*Target* 杂志主编之一。他是翻译研究文化转向的主要倡导者、描述性翻译研究学派的代表人物之一,从事文学翻译研究 30 多年,注重收集个案,运用系统的方法研究译语规范对翻译过程的制约。已发表论文 100 多篇,与人合编了 *Literature and Translation: New Perspectives in Literary Studies*(1978), *Translation in the Development of Literatures*(1993), *Translation and Modernization*(1995), *Translation Studies in Hungary*(1996), *Crosscultural and Linguistic Perspectives on*

European Open and Distance Learning (1998), *The Future of Cultural Studies* (2000)等。

选文涉及当下文学翻译研究的三个大问题:(1) 文学翻译的定义问题。作者从18世纪文学的确立谈起,论及文学概念和翻译概念的不定、文学和翻译合并为一专门术语的问题、文学翻译的原创伪装、文学翻译输入对译语文学传统的影响等;(2) 文学翻译的研究模式。这里主要谈及从事文学翻译这种跨文化现象研究的理论模式和方法论模式,如佐哈尔详述的多元系统论和图里的文学翻译规范论等,并描述了译者和翻译在译语文化中的地位,论及对等的多样性、文学翻译动力学等话题;(3) 文学翻译的描写研究。这部分论及描写研究对于了解文学翻译在译入文化中的中心或边缘地位,采取了创新的还是保守的翻译策略,以及验证翻译研究假设,阐述翻译标准和原则,颠覆翻译的传统理解等带来的重要作用。该研究方法也是未来翻译研究的主导方法。

Many of the books written on translation through the ages deal largely with literary translation, and in particular with the difficulty of "translating well" and of being "faithful." Such discussions are based on an assumption of universality and on ahistorical claims; they rarely offer any scholarly insight into the way actual translations have been produced and used through the ages. Scholarly work does exist, but it is rather heterogeneous, making it difficult to provide a reliable overview of either the history or current thinking about literary translation.

Literary Translation: A Problem of Definition

The very use and combination of literary and translation is symptomatic of the casual way in which the concepts of literature and of translation have so far been taken for granted. Neither concept is simple or well defined in most cultures. A historical exploration of the way in which the object of study has been conceptualized, with the aid of such things as dictionaries, encyclopedias and other key instruments of cultural knowledge, is therefore very much needed. The same applies of course to translation practices and their exact relationships with the more or less explicit theories elaborated at different points in history. The use of the term literature and its equivalents in various languages to refer to specific patterns of creativity in style, genre and so on seems to be a rather modern development, dating back only to the eighteenth century. Scholarship has not established clearly the extent to which literature and a literature are necessarily linked to one particular language and, even less, the extent to which particular literary traditions may be linked to a given territory, nation or state. It is generally assumed that such links exist *a priori*, but this assumption is untenable for a variety of reasons. A tenuous relationship between literature and other entities such as language, territory and nation would suggest that translated literature will not necessarily manifest signs of interaction between different literary traditions. The concept of translation itself is similarly far from being universal, and where it does exist, the borderlines between it and related concepts such as ADAPTATION and rewriting are not necessarily clear or uniformly drawn, whether historically or at a given moment in time, not even within the same linguistic tradition. The ubiquity of the type of event that is casually referred to in translation studies as literary translation makes it incumbent on scholars to define the conditions under which this type of event takes places, as well as to investigate the conditions under which it does not occur. This is no easy task, given the ambiguous status of translated literature, particularly in view of the problem of visibility/invisibility of the act of translation. A translation may be presented explicitly as a translation, in which case it is visible, or it may be disguised as an original, which explains why the majority of readers remain unaware of the foreign origins of some literary texts. The latter is particularly true of fairy tales and children's literature. What complicates the issue even further is that original texts are also sometimes presented as translations. But it is far more common for a translation to be disguised as an original than it is for an original text to be presented as a translation, particularly in the world of mass literature and in the business world. Both pseudo-translations and invisible translations provide interesting indicators of the value position of imported literature in a given culture and therefore deserve to be studied systematically as central issues in the development of literatures.

Another reason why translation is often invisible and ambiguous is that not only entire texts but also text fragments and discursive patterns may be imported into the target literature. In this sense, the difficulty of drawing a clear line between what is original and what is translated in a given literary tradition reflects the wider difficulty of identifying what is indigenous and what is foreign in any language: all languages contain many elements and patterns which are ultimately foreign in origin.

To the extent that literatures (as literary traditions or systems) are tied to particular languages, they have all developed, at least in part, with the aid of literary exchange via translations (Even-Zohar, 1978). It is not at all clear, however, where and how this exchange takes place nor what the exact impact of translation on a given literary tradition may be. Notwithstanding the long history of scholarship which asserts the innovative nature of the interaction between literature and translation, we can no longer justifiably assume that such exchanges are necessarily innovative (Even-Zohar, 1978). It is fair to say, however, that there are many instances where a literary tradition has been greatly influenced by imported and translated models on the level of stylistic devices, metaphors, narrative structures or entire genres (such as the modern novel) and entire genre systems (for example, the Aristotelian genre tradition in the West). What seems to play a decisive role in determining the extent of such influence, as well as the very definition of translation within a given literary tradition, is the position of literary translation as such and the extent to which it has become canonized (Even-Zohar, 1978). Indeed, in most western societies literary translation seems to have become so prestigious that the very concept of translation tends to be reduced to literary translation, as can be seen in the definitions offered by most dictionaries and encyclopedias. Most cultures will cite instances of literary translation, in the narrow sense, as examples of good or well-known translations, rather than say BIBLE translations, even though the latter have been imported more systematically and with far-reaching consequences into most cultures. The canonization of literary translation is a consequence of the prevalence of a NORMATIVE concept of translation and is restricted to literary translation *vis-à-vis* other types of translation and other texts in the target culture. It is rarely the case that a literary translator and his/her own text have acquired more prestige than the canonized source text and source author: translations of Virgil and Shakespeare belong to the core of canonized literary writing and their translators have benefited from this situation, but they hardly vie with the original authors in terms of prestige. Exceptions do occur as, arguably, in the case of Baudelaire as translator of Edgar Allan Poe, but only very rarely.

Literary Translation: Research Models

Given that translation is a culture-bound phenomenon, it is essential that we study the way in which it varies through time and across cultures, as well as the reasons for this variation. Clearly, there is a need here for theoretical and methodological models which can provide a research-oriented set of hypotheses for studies of this type. One such model has been proposed by Toury (1980, 1995) for both literary translation and for translation in general, based on the concept of norms which is borrowed from sociolinguistics and the social sciences. This model is an extension of polysystem theory, as elaborated by Even-Zohar (1978). Polysystem theory, and by extension Toury's model, assumes that translations never function as totally independent texts and that translators always belong in one way or another to a literary and/or cultural environment, even if this environment is geographically remote from their place of residence. The relationship between translations and their environment may vary, and may at times be negative, but it is always there, shaping translation behavior and influencing the position of translated literature. Identifying and describing the position of translators and translations *vis-à-vis* a given readership is no easy matter. Clear parameters need to be elaborated for locating translators and translations first and foremost with respect to the target literature, but sometimes also with respect to the source literature, and even with respect to an intermediary tradition on which a translation may be based (Toury, 1980: 53, 56); the latter, i. e., intermediate/indirect translation, is particularly common in a (post-)colonial context. By and large, translators and translations function as translators/translations rather than as writers/literature, as in the case of contemporary translations of the Greek classics, and this may be due either to their own strategies or to their position from the point of view of the dominant literary groups.

Translation is a type of communication which points, often explicitly, to a previous communication in another language, or to parts of it. This relationship with a previous communication assumes some form of equivalence (Toury, 1980: 54) which is nevertheless thought to be unattainable in practice. The concretization of the elusive notion of equivalence is essential for a description of the position of translated literature because it can explain how and even why value and power relationships between the traditions involved determine the very concept of translation. Numerous types of equivalence may be postulated in a given culture, and even within the same text, but the NORMS of equivalence are to certain extent predictable: For example, proper names in novels are often adapted to fit into the target tradition in France but hardly ever in the Netherlands. The norms, models and strategies employed in a given translation cannot be understood in isolation from the dominant and or peripheral literary and cultural environment in which the translation has to function. This environment is complex and is generally defined in terms of the target culture rather than the source culture. And yet, contemporary mass culture has gradually redefined, even partly erased, the borderlines between source and target worlds while placing (literary) translation within a multilateral rather than a bilateral frame of reference. Nevertheless, given that literary translation and literary imports in general are goal-oriented activities designed to fulfill a need in the target literary tradition, an analysis of these needs and the strategies employed to address them may help us explain the dynamics of literary relationships and traditions, and hence of literary translation.

Within this functional research paradigm, then it is assumed that all translation activity (whether it involves producing, using or commenting on translations) is guided and shaped by such things as the norms, value scales and models which are prevalent in a given society at a given moment in time. The study of literary translation therefore consists of the study of translation norms, models and traditions. Any translation activity, and any utterance about translation, is part of the data that can be used to elaborate a profile of a given translation environment and to establish the position that literary translation occupies on the cultural maps of the world, and indeed whether it plays a significant role in shaping the dynamics of such maps. In this respect, statements by translators and their critics or readers are interesting not so much in themselves but as objects of research. Most cultures have only a limited tradition of translation criticism and theory, but there is generally an obvious systematicity in their implicit discourse on translation. The entire network of relationships between translated texts, translators, their critics and readers becomes more intelligible when considered as a complex tradition or system.

Descriptive Studies of Literary Translation

According to Even-Zohar, it is possible to predict the conditions under which translations might occupy a central or peripheral position and might be innovative or conservative in the strategies they employ.

Descriptive studies are required to test the validity of this hypothesis and to provide a basis for elaborating general principles that can help us predict such conditions, if they are indeed possible to predict. Some descriptive studies have been undertaken in recent years, and the tradition of translation has been studied more or less systematically in certain cultures, in particular the European ones. The European Renaissance period and its contribution to the birth of the very concept of literary translation, French classicism with its strong and enduring tradition of *les belles infidels*, and the remarkably rich German translation culture have been covered by such studies. Some research has also been done on the reception (rather than the translation) of Greek and Roman classics and of SHAKESPEARE in Europe (Delabastita & D'hulst, 1993), where indirect translation has played a significant role.

There is still a need to investigate the beginnings of various European literary traditions, focusing on literary translation as one type of literary and cultural import. Most national literatures seem to have based their canons on the Greek and Latin models, often with the mediation of the French canon, and to have kept these canons alive with the help of translation as the supreme rhetorical exercise. The differentiation of literary traditions during the Romantic Age illustrates a double movement in the position of translated literature: On the one hand, the Shakespearean and other new models helped the various national traditions to establish their new rhetorics and genre systems, gradually substituting theatre and the epic with prose works; on the other hand, the classical tradition has been pushed further and further into the periphery of literary life and now survives mainly in didactic traditions rather than in literature, though it is fair to say that attempts have occasionally been made to reintroduce the classics into modern literature. In terms of theoretical models of translation, the German tradition has been by far the most influential. Lessing, Voss, Herder, Goethe, SCHLEIERMACHER and the German Romanticists, among other, have all used translation explicitly as a key instrument in developing German culture on the basis of a systematic interaction between the (more or less French) classical tradition and the new world.

Extending the range of descriptive research beyond this essentially restricted European frame of reference will most likely prompt us to revise our understanding of literary translation considerably, especially if we include oral literature and the history of colonization within our purview (Bassnett, 1993). The literatures of North America and Latin America seem to have developed almost entirely on the basis of translation, in much the same way as the Roman tradition was based on the Greek one. We may well discover that all colonial culture, writing systems and literacy have developed on the basis of translated literature. In Africa, and also in Korea, this process occurred with the aid of the Bible and John Bunyan. In Japan and in South East Asia, the novel use of colloquial language in translations has shaped contemporary written usage. DUBBING and SUBTITLING, two new genres used in the audiovisual representation of fiction and hence arguably belonging to the category of literary translation, have played and continue to play a similar role. Given that translated literature has been so influential in shaping the dynamics of discourse, communication and culture, its traditional treatment as an art that is best described by reference to individual, anecdotal experience no longer seems justifiable, and the need for serious, descriptive research in this area cannot be overestimated.

【延伸阅读】

[1] Lander, C. E. *Literary Translation: A Practical Guide*. Clevedon · Buffalo · Toronto · Sydney, NY: Multilingual Matters Ltd., 2001.

[2] Gentzler, E. *Contemporary Translation Theories* (Revised 2nd Edition). Clevedon · Buffalo · Toronto · Sydney, NY: Multilingual Matters Ltd., 2001.

[3] Toury, G. *Descriptive Translation Studies and Beyond*. Amsterdam: J. Benjamins Pub., 1995.

[4] Fowler, R. *Literature as Social Discourse: The Practice of Linguistic Criticism*[M]. London: Batsford Academic and Educational Ltd., 1981.

[5] Kuhiwczak, P. & Littau, K. (eds). *A Companion to Translation Studies*. Clevedon · Buffalo · Toronto, NY: Multilingual Matters Ltd., 2007.

[6] Wellek, R. & Warren, A. *Theory of Literature*. New York: Harcourt, Brace & World Inc., 1956.

[7] Hermans, T. *Translation in Systems: Descriptive and Systemic Approaches Explained*. Manchester: St. Jerome Pub., 1999.

[8] 吕俊.论翻译研究的本体回归.外国语,2004(4).

[9] 许钧.翻译论.武汉:湖北教育出版社,2003.

[10] 许钧.翻译研究之用及其可能的出路.中国翻译,2012(1).

[11] 孙艺风.翻译学的何去何从.中国翻译,2010(2).

[12] 张今,张宁.文学翻译原理(修订版).清华大学出版社,2005.

【问题与思考】

1. 文学的本质特征是什么?
2. 如何在文学翻译实践中更好地再现原文的"文学性"?
3. 谈谈当下文学翻译研究的模式和方法。
4. 谈谈你对文学翻译的微观研究和宏观研究的理解。
5. 如何理解文学翻译的创造性和叛逆性?

第二章　文学翻译研究的语言学探索

导　论

随着现代语言学的形成与日臻完善，20 世纪中叶以来，建立在语言学——普通语言学或结构主义语言学基础上的翻译研究获得了长足的发展，翻译研究在很大程度上摆脱了“经验陈述”的模式而更具有科学的特性。语言学范式强调意义的构成特征和语言结构，努力制定对等转换的规则，以语言分析代替直觉感受，克服了语文学派的主观主义，使翻译活动具有一定的科学性和客观性。因此，根茨勒把翻译的语言学派也称之为翻译的“科学派”。布龙菲尔德的结构语言学、乔姆斯基的转换生成语法、韩礼德的系统功能语法等为翻译语言学派提供了理论基础。

纵观语言学派研究文献，我们可以将它们分为两类：一类是结构主义语言学家关于翻译的论述；另一类是以现代语言学理论为基础专门从事翻译问题研究的学者的论述。前者立足于结构主义语言学自身的研究，仅将翻译问题作为语言结构分析的个例或个别途径，其有关翻译的论述与其说是翻译研究，不如说是借助翻译来探索语言研究的方法论；而后者在前者范式的指导下，对翻译过程、翻译方法等范畴进行描述，以期得出具有普适性的翻译模式——语言学模式。翻译研究的语言学派认为翻译只能是一门语言学学科，翻译活动就其实质来说是语言学的任务。如果说语言学翻译研究的第一类文献是基于语言学自身研究的需要，即功利性目的而对翻译现象进行分析，其结论给翻译研究带来极大的局限，从而从根本上否定了翻译理论作为学科的地位；那么，语言学翻译研究的第二类文献则是基于又一功利性：为实现译文“等值”或“等效”的实用性目标，同样得出具有理论偏向的模式。

随着语言学的发展，人们对语言的研究也由语言本身扩大到语言与社会、语言与心理、语言与生理等方面，后期的语言学翻译思想把原作、原作者、原文读者等因素都考虑了进去，所以也就更科学、更完整地描述了翻译过程，突破了微观语言学的文本模式，开始关注两种文化之间的交流。封闭的、静止的和自足的语言学翻译研究范式被 20 世纪 90 年代中期兴起的翻译理论研究的文化转向所打破。

法国著名翻译理论家乔治·穆南在《翻译的理论问题》这部被西方译界奉为译论经典的“划时代的著作”中，从语言学的角度，对翻译的理论问题进行了多角度的探索和审视，其中有的观点对我们客观地认识翻译活动、翻译研究与语言学的关系不乏启迪意义。乔治·穆南认为，翻译的许多问题，诸如翻译活动的正当性、可行性等基本问题，都可以从语言科学的研究成果中得到启示。他通过研究现代语言学的意义理论，指出人们对意义的传统认识并不科学，而索绪尔、布龙菲尔德、哈里斯、叶姆斯列夫等语言学家从某种程度上摧毁了人们的传统意义观，从而对翻译活动的正当性和可行性间接地提出了异议。除了传统的意义观，乔治·穆南还看到人们对语言结构的认识也同样受到了质疑。大多数人都认为人的思维，无论何时何地，都遵循普遍的逻辑或心理范畴对宇宙的经验进行切分。各种语言之间应该互通，其原因在于所有语言都无一例外地总是指称同一人类体验的同一宇宙，而这一宇宙又是遵照所有人都一致的认识范畴加以分析的。然而，事实并非如此简单。我们必须接受翻译的可行性的事实，只有在这一基础上，翻译的理论问题才有可能被理解，甚或得到解决。

认知语言学是一门研究语言的普遍原则和人的认知规律之间关系的语言学流派。20 世纪 80 年代，认知语言学作为语言研究的一种研究范式和独立学派得以确立。不同民族的相同认知心理基础和认知能力、与客观世界相互作用中所获得的共同体验，即不同民族相似的认知构成了语际翻译可译性的基础。认知语言学不仅是语言学研究的新视角，而且为翻译研究及文化翻译提供了新思路。认知语言学的翻译模式包含六个观点：翻译具有体验性，翻译具有多重互动性，翻译具有一定的创造性，翻译的语篇性，翻译的和谐性以及翻译的两个世界（即现实世界和认知世界）。

20 世纪 80 年代以来，在后殖民主义文化研究大潮的冲击下，翻译理论研究出现了“文化抗衡”。后殖民研究视角给予翻译研究的启示在于，它将翻译看作殖民文化的产物，是帝国主义强权政治及帝国主义文化思想观念对外进行霸权扩张的工具，是强势文化和弱势文化在权力差异语境中不平等对话的产物。一般来讲，翻译是在强势文化与弱势文化之间进行的，并且一般由强势文化向弱势文化输入。翻译的认知语言学视角关注译者在翻译活动中所经历的体验、认知和再现的过程。由于认知差异及文化上的不平等，译者在翻译策略的选择上带有不同的特征。作为强势文化地位国家的译者往往在翻译中操纵改写处于弱势地位国家的作品。大到文化心理意识形态，小到字、词、句的改写，以此来迎合强势文化的需求。

韩礼德所创立的系统功能语言学是当今世界上最具影响力的语言学流派之一。它研究语言的功能，重视语境对语言理解的影响和作用，强调形式是意义的实现手段，意义由形式来体现。系统功能语言学强调语言的三大纯理功能：概念功能、人际功能和语篇功能，重视语境对语言理解的影响和作用，认为语篇总是出现在一定的语境当中，情景语境是语篇直接产生的语境，位于外围的是文化语境，涉及特定言语社团的历史、文化、风俗习惯、思维模式、道德观念、价值观念、伦理范式等，具有民族性。特定的语境要求特定的语篇内容，语境与语篇相互影响。因此，译文与原文在纯理功能上的对等，实质上是译文与原文在相同语境中的功能对等。系统功能语言学中的纯理功能思想以及语境理论为《论语》等典籍英译研究提供了可操作性途径，也是系统功能语言学理论用于典籍研究的一种尝试。

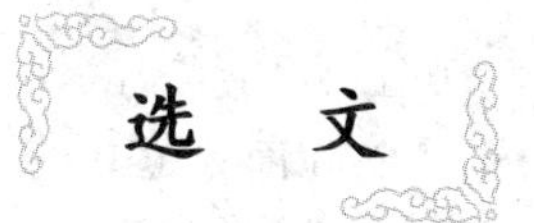

选 文

选文一 试析翻译的语言学研究

张柏然

导 言

本文选自《外语与外语教学》2008 年第 6 期。作者张柏然是南京大学外国语学院教授、博士生导师。

选文在肯定现代语言学对翻译理论研究的发展作出贡献的前提下，通过对西方翻译语言学派的几个代表人物的理论进行剖析，侧重研究这一学派的翻译研究存在的理论偏向。以雅可布逊、奈达、卡特福德、威尔斯、纽马克、斯坦纳、弗斯、弗米尔、费道罗夫和巴尔胡达罗夫等为代表的翻译语言学派为现代翻译研究奠定了学科和学理基础。然而，翻译研究的语言学派认为翻译只能是一门语言学学科，他们或以翻译研究作为结构主义语言学理论研究自身的途径和手段，或在结构主义语言学观照下对翻译过程作语言学的静态分析，最终偏离了翻译研究而归于对比语言学范畴。语言学范式的翻译研究太拘泥于原文的信息层，不甚注意作品的美学功能，忽视文艺作品的艺术再现，忽视文本主题结构以及文本的话语和语篇结构，忽视更大范围的文化与这些因素对译文的生成和接受所产生的影响；没有考虑语用维度、语用意义和文本的社会与文化语境，对这些方面的理论描述比较薄弱。

翻译思想史表明，随着现代语言学的形成与日臻完善，20 世纪中叶以来，建立在语言学——普通语言学或结构主义语言学基础上的翻译研究获得了长足的发展，产生了许多积极的理论成果，在翻译研究领域逐步形成了独具“范式”的语言学派。由于语言学派的努力，翻译研究在学科化进程中迈出了坚实的一步，从而也使得翻译研究在很大程度上摆脱了“经验陈述”的模式而更具有科学的特性。多年来，国内外学者就翻译的语言学研究取得的成就所作的介绍或论述，虽说不是汗牛充栋，却也是林林总总，举不胜举，在此就不赘述了。

然而，在对语言学派的研究文献作详尽的观察之后，我们就会发现，这一学派的翻译研究还存在着理论偏向。虽然交际理论、社会符号学等的引入使得这一理论偏向在一定程度上得到修正，比如，纽马克(Newmark)运用语义学理论分析了思维、言语与翻译的关系，阐述了语义翻译与交际翻译的特点，在其成名作《翻译研究途径》中所提出的“语义翻译”与“交际翻译”在理论上与实践上至今仍为人们所引用，但是，翻译的语言学研究的偏向始终存在着。

纵观语言学派研究文献，我们可以将它们分为两类：一类是结构主义语言学家关于翻译的论述；另一类是以现代语言学理论为基础专门从事翻译问题研究的学者的论述。前者立足于结构主义语言学自身的研究，仅将翻译问题作为语言结构分析的个例或个别途径，其有关翻译的论述与其说是翻译研究，不如说是借助翻译来探索语言研究的方法论；而后者在前者范式的指导下，对翻译过程、翻译方法等范畴进行描述，以期得出具有普适性的翻译模式——语言学模式。

布拉格学派的创始人雅可布逊(Jakobson，1959)较早注意到翻译问题与普通语言学理论的关系。他认为，语言符号的意义在于将一种符号翻译为另一种的符号，翻译实际上就是语符和信息的诠释，因此翻译是语言学方法不可分割的组成部分。雅可布逊在其著名论文《翻译的语言观》中列举了诠释语符的三种方式：语内翻译、语际翻译和符际翻译。其中，语际翻译涉及到一般意义上的翻译概念。在此雅可布逊意在强调在诠释语言现象时语言学对翻译行为的依赖性。

同样，英国语言学家弗斯(J. R. Firth)在《语言分析和翻译》一文中详尽地阐述了结合翻译进行语言分析的观点。弗斯肯定了翻译理论本身在语言学中的地位。他认为，把翻译作为语言分析的一种形式，用来阐明语义具有一定的可行性。弗斯指出，在英国语言学史上马林诺夫斯基首次系统地把翻译用于阐明某些民族话语的意义，并把这种方法称之为“语言分析”。弗斯提出了“全面翻译”的概念，既要全面运用一切可能的手段传达意义，在语法、词汇、词的搭配和语境等四个层次上进行语言分析。弗斯将翻译的意义归纳为：其存在这一事实的本身就是对语言理论和语言哲学的挑战；语言分析与翻译结合可以为语言学家和社会学家提供广阔的研究空间。

在语言学派翻译研究的第一类文献中，韩礼德(M. A. Halliday，1985)的观点较为著名。他指出句子是翻译的基本单位，翻译过程包括三个阶段：寻找等值物、检验等值物以及调整译语结构。然而，韩礼德对翻译的论述，其出发点是外语教学。他认为利用母语进行语言对比可以使学生注意到两种语言的异同，因为他认为翻译是一种特殊的语言对比形式，它包括两个方面：语际等值和语法结构的全面对比。因此，他得出结论：翻译理论是普通语言学的重要组成部分。

通过上述研究我们可以发现，语言学家在讨论翻译问题时，首先将翻译研究纳入语言学理论研究的框架，以结构主义语言学的理论与方法来描述翻译现象。他们研究翻译的根本目的在于将翻译研究作为语言研究的重要途径。因此，将翻译研究作为个例以补证语言学理论、突出翻译研究的工具性功能是第一类翻译研究的共同特征。

这类翻译研究由于其语言研究功利的前设性，直接导致其研究的理论偏向——研究的工具性目的，因而影响了其分析结论的普适性，给翻译研究带来了一定的局限。海德格尔认为，前设和前有、前见一样，是任何解释的基础，它们一起构成了理解的前结构，事物的作为结构出自理解的前结构。前设即运用一个观念来弄清作为结构。当我们面对研究对象时，总是对它预先做出假设，然后才能把它解释成“作为”某物。前设就是研究翻译前我们预先已有的假设。任何解释都包含了某种假设，问题在于这种前设的客观性。上述语言学家从普通语言学出发，以结构主义范式观照翻译问题，其理论视角本身无可厚非。然而，这种研究具有明确的功利性：将翻译研究视为对结构主义语言学结论的补证，将翻译理论视为语言学研究的途径或手段。这种以工具性为目的的翻译研究必然导致研究结论的理论偏向，从而从根本上否定了翻译理论作为学科的建构。或许法国语言学翻译理论的代表人物穆南(Mounin)从另一侧面揭示出语言学翻译研究第一类文献的特性：他主张研究翻译问题的语言学家至少在最初阶段不

要将翻译作为弄清某些普通语言学问题的手段，而应该运用语言学，特别是现代语言学的理论和方法，为译者解决翻译问题提出可能性。

如果说语言学翻译研究的第一类文献是基于语言学自身研究的需要，即功利性目的而对翻译现象进行分析，其结论给翻译研究带来极大的局限，从而从根本上否定了翻译理论作为学科的地位；那么，语言学翻译研究的第二类文献则是基于又一功利性：为实现译文"等值"或"等效"的实用性目标的观照下，同样得出具有理论偏向的模式。

语言学翻译理论的第二类文献，其理论基础是普通语言学理论或结构主义语言学理论。该理论基础的选定是根据这样一个常识：翻译是特定形式的言语行为，而语言学则是研究语言的科学，它能够提供关于语言研究的基本概念、理论模式和方法，因此翻译理论无法回避语言学。对翻译性质、过程和方法的分析和描述必然要用语言学的基本概念、范畴和方法。

从广义上看，索绪尔是结构主义语言学的创始人。他认为，语言是一个体系（或系统），即一种结构。语言的特点并非由语音和意义本身所构成，而是由语音和意义之间的关系构成的一个网络，即成为一个体系，也就是语言的结构。这种语言体系被视为一个符号体系。索绪尔认为，一切符号都可以分为能指和所指，语言的研究可分为共时性研究和历时性研究。共时性研究是对特定时期语言横断面的研究。索绪尔十分重视语言的共时性研究。他还指出，由词结合成一个结构有两种关系：组合关系和聚合关系。总之，索绪尔的语言学模式是以共时性研究为基础的、将语言与言语加以区别的语言体系，这个体系由组合关系和聚合关系构成语言中的差别体系。

继索绪尔之后，美国语言学家乔姆斯基（Chomsky，1957）则强调语言学研究对象为语言能力而非语言现象。他将语言分为深层结构和表层结构。乔姆斯基提出的短句结构规则和推导模式说明了他的结构与转换的方法。短语结构规则是形成句子的一整套规则。这个规则先有一整套短语结构改写规则。

在实践上，语言学翻译研究的第二类文献均以结构主义语言学理论的某种语言模式作为其理论基础，如奈达（Nida，1982）就以乔姆斯基转换生成语法为基础，提出由原语结构转换成译语结构的核心句模式，而卡特福德（Catford，1965/1991）则以韩礼德的系统语法理论为其翻译研究基础。

奈达（1964）认为，一般意义上翻译过程包括以下几个阶段：分析、转移和重组。即首先分析原作语言的信息。将其剖析成结构上最简单明了的形式，在此基础上转移，然后再重新组织成正常的译作语言。分析阶段包括三个方面，即各成分之间的语法关系，语义单位的外延意义以及语法结构和语义单位的内涵值。转移阶段：将事件名词从一种语言转移成另一种语言时，一般先将它转换成动词形式。同理，通常先将抽象名词转换成形容词和副词。奈达（1982）认为，在将表层结构的各种表达形式转换成核心结构时，产生了四种基本的结构单位，即事物单位（thing）、事件单位（event）、抽象单位（abstract）和表示关系的单位（relation）。另外，奈达提出了限制和确立词汇单位在特定上下文含义的方法，即通过句法结构限定词义，以及通过语义结构辨别含义。词义相近的关系有三种，即邻近关系、内涵关系和重叠关系。

奈达强调，对原语语言进行分析时，不能局限于研究语言单位间的句法关系和这些语言单位的外延意义，文体风格在传达信息中具有更为重要的意义，在转移阶段，奈达就语言的意义非对应现象——喻体差异、喻体缺省、语义缺省等现象提出了翻译对策。翻译时应注意内涵结构和外延结构，为此奈达提出了转移外延内容的三种方法：全新组合、分解组合和综合组合。

奈达认为,重组过程涉及到两个主要范畴:形式范畴和功能范畴。前者要求根据文体风格和文学体裁进行重组,后者则要求译者关注读者的接受效果。由此可见,奈达所谓的翻译时对原、译语两种语言的语法结构、语义单位、文体风格进行分析,在传达风格、功能的基础上为处理语义非对应现象设定语义层面上的对策,其核心在于语言对比分析和寻找语义对应。

卡特福德关于翻译理论的论述同样遵循与奈达相同的研究模式。他在其《翻译的语言学理论》(1965/1991)一书中开宗明义地指出:"翻译是用语言进行操作的工作:即把一种语言文本转换成另一种语言的文本。因此,任何翻译理论都必然利用语言理论普通语言学理论。"他还认为,翻译的中心问题是在译语中寻找等值物,而翻译理论的中心任务则是描述翻译等值的本质以及达到翻译等值的条件。卡特福德的理论核心在于它提出实现等值关系的途径:等值关系可以由"层面"(语法形式和词汇形式、语音实体和字形实体、语境)到"等级"(句子、子句、词组、单词、词素)在任何一个交叉点上建立。如果在较低的某一等级上不能确立等值关系,可以在较高等级上求得。与奈达相同,卡特福德翻译研究的中心仍然立足于语言分析,即界定等值成分的本质和条件。

语言学翻译研究的第二类文献表明,这种研究一般始于语言(双语)的结构分析,诸如语言各层次的划分、话语实用关系类别以及话语功能类别的确定,经由翻译单位的选定,最终规定翻译具体操作方法。这种方法在语言学翻译研究中通常表述为模式、方法和步骤等。

然而,我们应当指出,首先,翻译作为特定形式的文化活动,是以双语(原语和译语)的互动性转换为其表征的,但这并不意味着翻译仅仅局限于某种语言操作或语言活动。这种以语言为中介的双语互动或文化互动现象,以及由此导致的语音、语词、语法、文体等变异现象,决非语言学理论所能涵盖的。所以,现代语言学理论必然为翻译研究带来空白,从而造成语言学翻译研究的理论偏向。翻译研究的基点应为语言的差异性,亦即双语的非等值性。结构主义语言学对翻译中原语和译语之间并合现象(不同语言的共同之处)的认同表明,该研究偏离了翻译研究的本质问题;同时,它对原、译语这一现象及其对策的解释和选定则又使该理论由于强烈的功利性而成为教学研究或应用研究。对一个学科而言,舍弃基础理论研究而进行应用研究,其结论的偏向性是不言而喻的。

包括语言学翻译研究在内,世界范围内多数学派对翻译研究的核心是如何实现等值或等效。这表明,翻译研究始终停留在对翻译方法(翻译模式)的探索和选定上。语言学翻译研究以其对翻译过程的描述而获得了科学性或客观性,因为"过程"与"现象"总是联系在一起的。应当指出,这种对"过程"的考虑,其实质是对方法以及模式的操作程序的设定,和所有规范选择一样,它的研究结论带有浓重的经验色彩。

其次,语言学翻译研究的第二类文献认为,在具体翻译过程中,翻译家对原语文本接受的结果——深层结构的表述最初是由核心结构(核心句)来实现的。而所谓核心结构则指对特定深层结构最基本、最具代表性的表述形式。这类研究忽略了一个基本事实,即核心结构在其完形的初始,已经导致意义的缺省。事实上,在具体的翻译过程中,翻译家对深层结构的把握是通过"统觉"来实现的。然后,翻译家直接在译语中找寻与这种"非语言"或"超语言"的结构相对应的译语表层结构。再后,根据原文的深层结构对译语表层结构进行语义修正,以完成译语文本的建构。所谓的语体风格在此应列为语义构成。而"非语言"或"超语言"的结构通常表现为意义指向(在应用性文本中)和心理意象(在艺术性文本中)。总之,翻译家的基本任务是通过译语语言对意义指向和心理意象进行表述和修正。因此,对于奈达所谓的深层结构和表层

结构之说，尽管他在分析阶段和转移阶段表现出结构特性——层级性或步骤性，然而，这并未使翻译过程得到客观的、经验性的描述，同时也使得这种翻译模式即使作为教学型模式也失去了可操作性。同样，卡特福德的理论也缺乏得以实现翻译等值的可操作性。他的翻译模式的核心在于界定等值成分的本质和条件，认为等值关系可以在由“层面”到“等级”的任何交叉点上建立。这表明：他的论述与其说是对翻译模式的设定，不如说是在比较语言学范式中探求原、译语双语对应的可能性，只是卡特福德在此将双语对应表述为等值而已。换句话说，卡特福德虽然在主观上力求以结构主义语言学为基础对翻译问题进行详尽的探讨，但是，实际上在探讨翻译的过程中，他不自觉地偏离了翻译研究，而展开了原、译语双语的静态分析与比较。所以，卡特福德的翻译模式又可以界定为以翻译的语言学研究的第二类文献为表征的第一类文献。

翻译的语言学研究的第一类文献以及建立在这种范式基础上的第二类文献，他们或以翻译研究作为结构主义语言学理论研究自身的途径和手段，或在结构主义语言学观照下对翻译过程作语言学的静态分析。特别是由后者设定的翻译模式，他们或由于其层级性或步骤性使得自身失去了应用价值（可操作性），或以对双语言静态比较分析为转移，最终偏离了翻译研究而归于对比语言学范畴。

综上所述，17 世纪以来，随着当时社会的文化转型，在逻辑实证主义和唯理论的刺激和推动之下，新兴的语言理论受到青睐，西方译学的语言学范式亦随之渐露雏形。语言学家、翻译理论家们开始对语言分析、语篇分析产生浓厚兴趣，对从前一些零散的争论也开始了系统的整体性思考，既关注文本的结构层次，又重视形式本身，从而破除了语文学式的“得意忘言”的陈规。语言学范式强调意义的构成特征和语言结构，努力制定对等转换的规则，以语言分析代替直觉感受，克服了语文学派的主观主义，使翻译活动具有一定的科学性和客观性。因此，根茨勒把翻译的语言学派也称之为翻译的“科学派”。布龙菲尔德的结构语言学、乔姆斯基的转换生成语法、韩礼德的系统功能语法等为翻译语言学派提供了理论基础。以雅可布逊、奈达、卡特福德、威尔斯、纽马克、斯坦纳、弗斯、弗米尔、费道罗夫和巴尔胡达罗夫等为代表的翻译语言学派筚路蓝缕，为现代翻译研究奠定了学科和学理基础，翻译理论也开始走上了系统化、科学化、客观化的研究道路。然而，翻译研究的语言学派认为翻译只能是一门语言学学科，翻译活动就其实质来说是语言学的任务，重要的是对比原作和译作语言单位意义上的相同，以达到内容上的等值；认为语言是透明的，翻译是一种纯语言的转换过程，所涉及的只是两种不同语符中的两个对等信息；把翻译视为一门精确的科学，集中研究语言系统的差异和语言形式的转换，注意寻找语言转换规律以及语义的对等模式，迷信语言的共性；译者的任务只是按照语言规律去解码与编码。这样一来，整个翻译过程被简单化、机械化、程式化了，而起作用的只是语言的工具理性及其规律性。翻译理论由于长期受语言学的影响，形成了一种思维定势，认为语言是一个规范的、同一的和稳定的符号系统，是人们认识世界和把握世界的工具，因此，语言被类比为数学符号系统，成了理性和规律性的象征。翻译的语言学研究范式给人们带来了理性思维，破除了原来文学研究范式的神秘性和主观直觉的研究方式，从主观性走向客观性使翻译研究取得了很大进展。但由于语言学范式使译者过多依赖于语言的规律性，忽视主体的主观能动性，排除言语活动的社会制约性和规定性，从而突出了原文文本的中心性，追求同一性和一致性，最终堕入语言逻各斯中心。

由此可见，语言学范式的翻译研究太拘泥于原文的信息层，不甚注意作品的美学功能，忽视文艺作品的艺术再现，忽视文本主题结构以及文本的话语和语篇结构，忽视更大范围的文化与这些因素对译文的生成和接受所产生的影响；没有考虑语用维度、语用意义和文本的社会与文化语境，对这些方面的理论描述比较薄弱。其范式是封闭、静止的和自足的。随着语言学的发展，人们对语言的研究也由语言本身扩大到语言与社会、语言与心理、语言与生理等方面，后期的语言学翻译思想把原作、原作者、原文读者等因素都考虑了进去，所以也就更科学、更完整地描述了翻译过程，突破了微观语言学的文本模式，开始关注两种文化之间的交流。上述封闭的、静止的和自足的翻译研究范式被 20 世纪 90 年代中期兴起的翻译理论研究的文化转向所打破。

选文二 语言学与翻译

——乔治·穆南论翻译的理论问题

许 钧

导 言

本文选自《外语研究》1998 年第 1 期与第 2 期。作者许钧是南京大学外国语学院教授、博士生导师。

选文结合翻译研究中的一些基本问题，对法国著名翻译理论家乔治·穆南的《翻译的理论问题》中的基本观点进行评述。在乔治·穆南看来，任何翻译活动的基础部分包含着一系列隶属于语言学的分析和活动内容，而实用语言学能够比任何技巧性的经验之谈都更准确、更可靠地给予启示。翻译是一种建立于一门科学基础之上的艺术；他明确指出：布龙菲尔德、哈里斯、叶姆斯列夫的理论动摇了人们探索意义这一概念时所具有的传统的安全感。意义的捕捉不再出于文学和文体学的原因，而是出于语言学本身的、甚至符号学的原因；当我们在探讨翻译的时候，决不应该回避新洪堡学派在对语言思想与现实、语言与“世界映象”之间关系的思考时提出的观点，这些观点对我们打破以往过于简单化的认识，进一步认识到不同语言的传情达义规律的深刻差异，从而更全面地认识与发现翻译中的本质障碍，提高翻译活动的自觉性，无疑是有利的。

近段时间，译界不少同行对翻译研究的途径问题进行了思考，对翻译的语言学派提出了质疑，作为一种学术探索，这是再正常不过的。但遗憾的是，有的学者似乎走向极端，完全否定语言学对翻译活动和翻译研究的指导价值。最近，抽时间重读了法国著名翻译理论家乔治·穆南的《翻译的理论问题》。乔治·穆南在这部被西方译界奉为译论经典的“划时代的著作”中，从语言学的角度，对翻译的理论问题进行了多角度的探索和审视，其中有的观点对我们客观地认识翻译活动、翻译研究与语言学的关系，或许不乏启迪意义。本文试结合翻译研究中的一些基本问题，就书中的主要观点作一评述，供同行们参考。

1. 打开语言学的大门

在西方翻译理论界，最早且较为系统地提出翻译理论研究应属于语言学研究范围的，是前苏联的费道罗夫。他在1953年发表的《翻译理论概要》中明确指出翻译的过程是使用语言的过程，因此在翻译中，语言问题应放在头等重要的位置上。认为翻译研究，首先应当从语言学的角度加以研究，并宣称只有采用语言学的研究手段，才能科学地揭示出翻译的规律和本质。在他之后，移居加拿大的法国人让-保尔·达尔贝勒纳于1958年推出了以"翻译方法"为副标题的《法英比较修辞》，他们积极支持费道罗夫的观点，认为必须把翻译"列入语言学的范围"，并提出"翻译是一个真正的学科，具有自身特殊的技巧和问题"，值得在"目前倍受重视的语言学的分析手段"(Vinay et Dalbelnet，1958：23)的启示下进行系统研究。

在目前的中国翻译理论界，对语言学与翻译的关系问题讨论颇多。首先有一种误解，认为现代语言学雄心勃勃，不安于自己的领地，要把翻译纳入自己的范围。其次是认为翻译不仅仅是一种语言交换活动，因此，语言学不可能解决翻译的全部理论问题，把翻译纳入语言学的范围只能是把翻译研究引入一条狭窄的死胡同。实际上早在本世纪60年代初，乔治·穆南对这些问题就有过思考。关于语言学与翻译研究的关系，乔治·穆南经过多方面的考察，指出了这样一个事实：翻译作为一种特殊的语言活动，一个具有其独特客体的研究领域，在本世纪50年代之前，却一直被语言学研究所忽视。他指出，"关于翻译活动的科学研究，更为令人奇怪的是：任何一部完整的哲学论著都得将语言理论包括在内，但是语言理论却从不把翻译作为语言活动加以研究、列入自己的范围。翻译是一种特殊的，但也是普遍的语言活动，也许对语言和思维的研究都有一定启示。最近问世的有关语言学综合研究的重要著作对这一点也只字不提。翻译作为语言现象和独特的语言问题至今无人过问。在费尔迪南·德·索绪尔、叶斯柏森、萨丕尔、布龙菲尔德的论著中，难以寻找到四五处提及翻译的只言片语。被提及时，翻译事实也往往只起了旁注的作用，用于论证与翻译毫不相关的某个观点，几乎从未就翻译而论及翻译"。(Mounin，1963：11)他还发现，这种对翻译一无所知的必然结果就是在大百科全书中见不到"翻译"的条目：无论是法国的、英国的、还是意大利的或德国的百科全书，没有一行论及翻译及其历史与问题的文字，"只有狄德罗编纂的百科全书是个例外"。(Mounin，1963：11)在他看来，现代语言学对翻译这一特殊的语言现象继续熟视无睹，将翻译排斥在其大门之外，是"语言科学的耻辱"。因此，当费道罗夫，维纳和达尔贝勒纳等为翻译大声疾呼，要求获得科学研究独立客体或独立领域的地位时乔治·穆南认为这是翻译研究一个新的开端。

然而，乔治·穆南看到争取使翻译在普通语言学论著中获得一席之地，让翻译象双语现象，语言接触现象，语言地理学或词源学一样，受到语言科学的重视，并非一件易事。除了语言学界的排斥之外，这一为翻译争取科学研究领地的努力还受到了众多翻译家的异议，他们认为翻译是一门艺术，反对"把翻译说成是一种严格地隶属于科学认识范畴，特别是隶属于语言分析范围的活动"。(Mounin，1963：13)如法国的爱德蒙·加里，他是一位著名的翻译家，既有文学翻译，特别是诗歌翻译的丰富经验，又有在国际重要会议担任同声传译的经历。他认为费道罗夫和维纳等的论点"经不起事实的考验"。(Edmond Cary，1958：4)在他看来，翻译是一项极为复杂的活动，涉及多方面的因素，无法复归于语言学完全合理的科学定义的统一性。他指出,“文学翻译不是一种语言活动,而是一项文学活动”(Edmond Cary, 1958: 8),并认为诗歌翻译是一种诗歌活动,要译诗,译者必须善于表现出诗才,剧作翻译若要达到演出的要求,就不可能是语言活动的结果,而是戏剧活动的成果,不然,语言是译过来了,但因为不注意戏剧艺术,却不能供演出。至于电影译制,更是一种超越了语言学范围的特殊的电影艺术活动,因为对应词句的选择必须尊重演员的口形、语流、动作影片的音乐、画面和视象规定的情景,甚至还要考虑到群体观众的社会反应等。乔治·穆南充分意识到了加里提出的这些观点的合理性。但他认为,对于翻译研究而言,“这些观点与其说否定了费道罗夫和维纳的论点,毋宁说是对他们的论点的限定与补充。这些观点批评费道罗夫的观点提出的是一种‘文学的倾向’”。乔治·穆南指出,“这是两个极端,双方都仅仅看到一项至少包括两个方面的活动的一个方面。加里和苏联的同行主要说的是翻译(文学、诗歌、戏剧、电影等等)不仅仅是一项凭词汇、形态、句法问题的科学分析便可以解决其一切问题的语言活动。而费道罗夫则强调了另一方面:翻译首先是也始终是一项语言活动;语言学是所有翻译活动的共同点和基础。”(Mounin, 1963: 15)乔治·穆南反对加里的极端观点,认为加里之所以否认语言学对翻译理论的任何辅助作用,是因为他把语言学的定义限制到了形式描写语言学的定义:“他作为一个翻译家而非语言学家,把普通语言学和描写语言学混为一谈,不知除了内部语言学之外,还存在着一种外部语言学(语言心理学或心理语言学和语言社会学或社会语言学)和一种文体学,而文体学研究的问题正是他作为翻译家所关心的问题。

在乔治·穆南看来,翻译,尤其在戏剧、电影、口译方面,确实具有非语言和超语言的方面。但是,任何翻译活动的基础部分包含着一系列隶属于语言学的分析和活动内容,而实用语言学能够比任何技巧性的经验之谈都更准确、更可靠地给予启示。他说,翻译和医术一样,可以说是一种艺术,但是一种建立于一门科学基础之上的艺术。翻译的许多问题,诸如翻译活动的正当性、可行性等基本问题,都可以从语言科学的研究成果中得到启示。

2. “意义”与翻译

翻译中,意义的传达是最基本的问题之一。翻译,不应该只是译词,还要译意;不但要译意,还要译味。从一种语言到另一种语言,意义能否转换,如何转换是翻译理论界长期以来探索的主要问题。维纳和达尔贝勒奈就明确指出,译者往往从意义出发,在语义范围内进行所有的转换活动。在索绪尔之前,不少语言研究者认为“语言,归结到它的基本原则,不外是一种分类命名集,即一份跟同样多的事物相当的名词术语表,”“这种观念[…]假定有现成的,先于词而存在的概念。”(索绪尔,1982:100)法国语言学家马丁纳在他的《语言学概论》一书中也谈到了这一相当普遍的看法:“根据一种极为幼稚但也相当普遍的看法,一门语言不外是一份词汇表,即一份声音(或书写)产品的目录,每一件产品都与某一个事物相对应;如某一种动物,马,以法语命名而著称的特殊目录便相应地制造出一种特定的声音产品,以 cheval 这一书定形式加以表示;各种语言之间的差异最终只归结到命名的差异;如法语为 cheval,英语则说 horse,德语则为 pferd;再学习一门语言不过在于记住在各个方面都与原来的分类命名集相平行的新的分类命名集。”(Martinet, 1960:14)若按照这种普遍的观点,翻译中的语言转换自然不成问题,正如乔治·穆南所指出的:“既然世界被视作一个物质的或精神的,区别明确的事物大仓库,那么每种语言便以一种独有的标签,一种独特的编号给事物编目造册;这样一来既然原则

上每个事物大致只有一个标签，且每个编号只代表预先交给所有编目者的同一仓库中的一种物品，那么人们就可以毫无差错地从一种目录过渡到另一种目录。”(Mounin，1963：22)

然而，乔治·穆南认为，从一种语言到另一种语言的转换是非常复杂的，涉及多方面的问题。他深入地分析了索绪尔，布龙菲尔德、哈里斯、叶姆斯列夫等语言学家有关语言意义的论述，指出意义问题并非人们想象的那么简单。但也不像上述语言学家认为的那样不可捕捉。

索绪尔指出，“语言符号连结的不是事物和名称，而是概念和音响形象。后者不是物质的声音，纯粹物理的东西，而是这声音的心理印迹。我们的感觉给我们证明的声音表象。它是属于感觉的，我们有时把它叫做‘物质的’，那只有在这个意义上说，而且是跟联想的另一个要素，一般更抽象的概念相对立而言的。”(索绪尔，1982：101)他进而指出，语言符号是一种两面的心理实体，一面为所指，另一面为能指。能指和所指的联系是任意的，是约定俗成的。这就否定了被表达的概念和表达概念的语言链之间存在着内在的必然联系。那么意义与词，所指与能指到底是通过什么方式进行连结的？在索绪尔看来，“在词里，重要的不是声音本身，而是使这个词区别于其他一切词的声音上差别，因为带有意义的正是这些差别。”(索绪尔，1982：164)一个词的意义严格地取决于所有其他触及或可能触及该词所指的现实的词存在与否。根据索绪尔，“一个词可以跟某种不同的东西即概念交换，也可以跟某些同性质的东西即另一个词相比”。因此，我们只看到词能与某个概念“交换”，即看到它具有某种意义，还不能确定它的价值；我们还必须把它跟类似的价值，跟其他可能与它相对立的词比较。我们要借助于在它之外的东西才能真正确定它的内容。对于翻译来说，如何确定词的意义只是第一步，而从一种语言向另外一种语言转换，就有个转换是否等值的问题。然而，索绪尔认为，由于词是系统的一部分，在同一种语言内部，所有表达相邻近的观念的词都是互相限制的，而词的内容不是预先规定了的观念，而是由系统发出的价值。他指出，“如果词的任务是在表现预先规定的概念，那么，不管在哪种语言里，每个词都会有完全相对等的意义；可是情况并不是这样。”(索绪尔，1982：162)作为翻译理论研究者，乔治·穆南十分清楚地看到了索绪尔的命名观(把命名当作“系统”)和词的价值说与把语言当作分类命名表或编目的传统观念之间的根本差别。他说这一传统观念可以追溯到《圣经》，圣经把事物的命名描写为一种专有名称的分配，如《创世纪》第一段第5、8、10行中就写道：上帝称光明为昼，称黑夜为夜，称空间为天，称硬的部分为地，称积水的地方为海。乔治·穆南认为柏拉图在他的《对话录》中阐明的普通名词理论，即对一般事物的命名的理论，也同样表现出了“语言为分类命名集”的观点。这一古老的观念，把名称与事物的结合，亦即意义与词的连接，看作了一种命名，一种清点。然而，索绪尔的观点深刻地动摇了人们这种从古以来的简单认识，同时，从某种意义上揭示了翻译的基础障碍：词的意义不是一种简单的分配，翻译活动面对的不是词的意义的简单转换，而涉及到整个系统。不过乔治·穆南指出，索绪尔对词与意义连接这一概念的分析并没有损害翻译活动的正当性，因为这种分析是建立在古典的心理学之上，丝毫没有真正地对反映普遍的人类经验的概念的普遍性质——不管对价值的划分如何——提出异议。这一分析就其本身而言是难能可贵的，借助索绪尔对“意义”的传统观念的分析，我们可以对“词对词的翻译之所以不能进行”作出科学的解释。

布龙菲尔德的“意义”理论表现了与传统观念的彻底决裂，乔治·穆南认为，布龙菲尔德力戒对“意义”这一概念作出任何主观精神的定义，他所采取的行为主义的定义；一个语言陈述的意义就是“讲话者发出这一陈述的环境以及这一陈述从听话者身上引起的行为——反应”。

(转引自 Mounin, 1963: 27)布龙菲尔德明确指出,促使人们发出语言陈述的环境包括他们所处的世界的所有事物和所有情况。为了赋予一门语言的每一个陈述的意义以科学准确的定义,那我们必须对讲话者的世界中的任何事物都有一种科学的准确的了解。然而,问题是,我们对自己生活在其间的这个世界的了解是多么不完全,致使我们很少能对一个陈述的意义作出准确的阐述。因此,"……在语言研究中对'意义'的说明是一个薄弱的环节,这种情况一直要持续到人类的知识远远超过目前的状况为止。"(转引自 Mounin, 1963: 29)乔治·穆南看到布龙菲尔德的这一行为主义的"意义"理论实际上意味着对任何翻译活动在理论上的正当性或实践上的可行性的一种否定;既然一个陈述的意义永远难以(至少目前还不能)认识,那么人们就决不可能把一门语言的意义传达到另一种语言中去。不过乔治·穆南对布龙菲尔德的观点的有效性提出了质疑。他认为,即使在布龙菲尔德本人看来,对意义的这种定性表达了一种理想的程序,一种绝对性,它定能通过人类在无数个漫长的世纪中不断获得更多的知识而一步一步地得以接近。只是在目前阶段,由于方法上和暂时的原因,对意义的捕捉就科学性而言是不可能的。因此在目前阶段,翻译在科学意义上来说是不可能的。但是,布龙菲尔德是自相矛盾的,因为他提出了一个假设:"正因为我们没有办法确定大部分意义,也没有办法展示意义的恒定,因此,我们应该把每一个语言形式的特殊性和恒定性作为任何研究的一个假设,完完全全像我们与其他人的日常关系中假设的那样。我们可以提出这一假说,作为语言学的基本假设,此假说可以这样提出:在某些共同体(语言共同体),有一些语言陈述,就其形式与意义而言,是同一的。"换言之,这就意味着"每一个语言形式都有着一种特殊的、恒定的意义"(Mounin, 1963: 30)。乔治·穆南指出,应该说布龙菲尔德的观点对我们更好地了解意义概念的科学限度是有益的,但他的意义理论并不能真正从本质上否认翻译的可行性,因为他最终还是承认了社会实践以各种方式保证每一个语言形式所特有的,也是相对的恒定性和特殊性,并且承认这种手段的合法性,无论是事物指称,还是词语定义,甚或翻译。据此,乔治·穆南认为,布龙菲尔德的假设恰恰证明了翻译在实践上是可行的,尽管是有条件和限度的。

继布龙菲尔德之后,分布语言学派继续就意义问题进行大胆的探索,他们抛弃了布龙菲尔德的假说,试图通过意义的抽象化建立其语言分析方法。乔治·穆南指出,该学派力戒使用"意义"一词,其目的是为了赋予构成语言的结构的描写以更严格的科学性。面对一种语言素材,该学派的分布分析主动置身于环境之中;而这势必是一种破译者面对密码的环境:不再由意义给文本分析提供出发点,而由文本的形式分析最终导向意义。但分布语言学派在实际的研究中并不能彻底地实践他们的理论,比如哈里斯在后期的研究中就重新给意义以一定的位置,加以重视,将之作为分析的辅助标准。乔治·穆南还就叶姆斯列夫排斥意义研究的语言学观形成的原因和后果进行了探索和分析。他指出,叶姆斯类夫的研究理论与方法并没有摧毁语言学中的意义概念。叶姆斯列夫与索绪尔、布龙菲尔德、哈里斯等语言学家一样,试图把对意义的认识置于语言描写的终点,而不是置于起点。他们的目的在于为最终接近意义提供更为科学的方法。但在等到更为科学的方法得以建立、被接受与通过,并等到这些方法能更科学地分析内容实现之前,叶姆斯列夫基本上是将自己的观点建立在布龙菲尔德的那一假说之上;每个独立的语言陈述都具有一种比较特殊,比较恒定的意义,但也有一定的限度,而这些限度正渐渐地被认识,这一假说无疑在以人类的某些经验为基础,暂时支撑着任何语言研究的正当性。在乔治·穆南看来,现代语言学的诸派理论在一定意义上深化了对语言陈述形式及其意义之间准确的关系的分析。上述的种种理论出于方法上的原因,试图排斥意义,不借助意义这

一概念，达到确定构成语言的关系系统。但是，这一反对借助于意义的企图，哪怕在形式主义的描写语言学范围内，也是有争议的。他明确指出，布龙菲尔德、哈里斯、叶姆斯列夫的理论，具有正当的理由，将动摇人们探索意义这一概念时所具有的传统的安全感。它们表明了意义的捕捉——不再出于文学和文体学的原因，而是出于语言学本身的、甚至符号学的原因——是，或者也许是十分困难的，不够确切的，偶然的。它们虽然根据不同的情况和环境强烈地指出了一些迄今为止未被人们认识到的限度，但既未损害翻译活动理论上的正当性，也未损害翻译活动实践上的可行性。

3. 翻译与“世界映象”理论

在上文中，我们看到，乔治·穆南通过研究现代语言学的意义理论，指出人们对意义的传统认识并不科学，而索绪尔、布龙菲尔德、哈里斯、叶姆斯列夫等语言学家从某种程度上摧毁了人们的传统意义观，从而对翻译活动的正当性和可行性间接地提出了异议。除了传统的意义观，乔治·穆南还看到人们对语言结构的认识也同样受到了质疑。

乔治·穆南指出，长期以来，人们一直认为语言的结构或多或少都直接地源于宇宙的结构和人类思维的普遍结构，语言中有名词和代词，这是因为宇宙间有存在物，语言中有动词、形容词、副词，这是因为宇宙间有过程，有存在物的品质、有过程的品质与品质本身的性质。语言中有介词和连词，这是因为语言里，存在物之间，过程之间、存在物与过程之间存在着相关、赋与、时间、地点、状况、并列、从属等逻辑关系。按照这样的观点，翻译自然是可以进行的，因为：

① 一门语言将全等的符号置于某些词(a, b, c, d,…)和某些存在物，过程、品质或关系(A , B, C, D…)之间：a′, b′, c′, d′… =A, B, C, D

② 另一门语言将全等的符号置于某些别的词(a′b′c′d′…)和同一的存在物，过程、品质和关系之间：a′, b′, c′, d′… =A, B, C, D

③ 翻译的任务就在于复写出：

a, b, c, d … =A, B, C, D

a′, b′, c′, d′… =A, B, C, D

因此：a, b, c, d … =A, B, C, D

“翻译，是把一桶用升计算的液体用加仑来计算但液体始终不变，无论以升或加仑出售。人们普遍认为，以两种不同计量单位出售的是完全同一的现实事物，是同一数量的现实事物。”(Mounin, 1963：41-42)在乔治·穆南看来，人们对翻译的这种简单化的认识是十分普遍的。确实，无论在外国，还是在中国，人们对翻译活动缺乏深刻的认识。至今在中国，翻译在大多数人的眼里，只不过是一种语言的简单交换，一种纯模仿的技术性工作，不需任何创造性。这种观点，直接源自于人们对世界思维和语言之间的关系的简单化认识。虽然不同语言是以不同的方式切分语言内容实体和语言范畴，但大多数人都认为人的思维，无论何时何地，都遵循普遍的逻辑或心理范畴对宇宙的经验进行切分。各种语言之间应该互通，其原因在于所有语言都无一例外地总是指称同一人类体验的同一宇宙，而这一宇宙又是遵照所有人都一致的认识范畴加以分析的。然而，事实果真如此简单吗？乔治·穆南看到，新洪堡学派提出的有关语言哲学的观点，对宇宙与语言之间关系的传统看法提出了质疑。如新洪堡学派的加西尔就认为语言不是一种被动的表达工具，而是一种积极的因素，给人的思维规定了差异与价值的整体。

任何语言系统对外部世界都有着独特的分析,有别于其他语言或同一语言其他各阶段的分析。语言系统沉积了过去一代代人所积累的经验,向未来的一代提供一种看待与解释宇宙的方式;传给他们一面棱镜,而他们将用这面棱镜去观察非语言世界。他在《象征意识病理学》一文中明确指出:"世界并非仅仅由人们通过语言去理解与想象;人们对世界的观念以及在这一观念中生活的方式已经被语言所界定。"加西尔的这一观点得到了人们的关注。如特里尔就指出:"每一门语言都是一个通过并依赖客观现实进行选择的系统,实际上,每一门语言都创造了一幅完整,自足的现实图景。每一门语言也都以其独特的方式构建现实,因此而建立了这一特定语言所特有的现实要素。一门特定语言中的语言现实要素决不会以完全一样的形式在另一种语言中出现,也决不是现实的直接描摹。"(Mounin, 1963:43)叶姆斯列夫对特里尔的这一观点进行了精辟的阐述,认为人们并不能通过对所指事物的自然描述,就可有效地显示出某一共同体中所采用的语义习惯,群体评价与社会舆论的特征。因此,对内容实体的描写首先必须把语言与社会其他机构联系起来,构成语言学与社会人类学其他分支的接触点。正因为这样,同一的自然事物可以根据不同的文明对象,得到完全不同的语义描写,对类似于"好"与"坏"这样的直接评价的词语,对"房屋"、"座椅"、"国王"这类文明所直接创造的事物的语义描写如此,对自然界事物的语义描写如此。叶姆斯列夫还举例说:如"马"、"狗"、"山"、"冷杉"等等事物,在一个熟悉它们,(并认出它们)是本地事物的社会里,与在一个它们纯粹为陌生事物的社会里,人们对它们下的定义自然不同——但这并不妨碍语言拥有某个词指称这些事物。比如狗,在爱斯基摩人眼中,这首先是一种牵引动物;对琐罗亚斯教徒来说,它一是种神圣的动物;在印度社会里,狗象贱民一样遭受歧视,而在西方社会里,狗尤其是一种通过驯服,用以狩猎,警卫的动物,在这四种不同的社会里,"狗"的语义描写自然是不同的。叶姆斯列夫的观点是十分明确的,不同的社会的人对同一事物的经验是有别的,因此对同一事物的语义描写也自然有别。这就给翻译的可行性提出了疑问,既然不同社会对同一事物的语义描写可能不同,那么要把一门语言指称或指写中的事物用另一种语言传达出来,自然障碍重重。语言学家沃尔夫的观点更进一步,他认为"所有观察者并不必定从同一明显的自然事物中得出同一的宇宙图景,除非他们思想中的语言背景是相似的,或通过这种或那种方式可以达到同质。"而"每一门语言都是一个宏大的结构系统,与别的系统有着区别,在这一系统中,个人不仅仅借以交流,而且还借以分析自然,发现或忽视这一或那一类型的现象或关系的形式与范畴进行文化上的排列,个人在这些形式与范畴中注入了他思维的方式,并通过它们构建他的世界知识大厦。"总之,"我们是根据我们的母语预先规定的界限切分自然。"(Mounin, 1963: 46-47)乔治·穆南对这些观点进行了梳理和分析,从中看到了这样一个事实:每一门语言在现实中切分着不同的一面(忽视另一门语言所揭示的东西,发现另一门语言所疏忽的东西等),而且对同一现实的切分单位也有差别(你划分我合并,我合并你划分,你兼含我排斥,我排斥你兼含等),这几乎成了法国哲学界和语言学界的共识。他认为,这些观点对于翻译而言,是致命性的,"意味着在严格的意义上否认翻译活动的任何可能性。"他说,一旦意义没有普遍性的保证,便无法捕捉,因而也就无法翻译。若按照新洪堡学派的观点,不同语言对现实有着不同的切分,那么,不同语言所指涉的存在物、过程、品质和关系就不一致,因此,也就无法逻辑地证明 a、b、c、d…… 与 a′、b′、c′、d′……之间"传统"的等值性。但是,乔治·穆南对这些观点的理论依据提出了质疑:"难道我们真的只是在一个我们的语言已经定下模式的宇宙里思维吗?难道我们真的仅仅通过一门特殊语言的变形镜去看待世界,以至于我们从每一门特殊语言中得到的(同一现实)不同的图景永

远无法准确地重叠吗？难道真的当我们用两种不同的语言表述世界时，我们所表述的永远都不是一个完全同一的世界，致使不仅仅从一门语言到另一门语言的翻译不合理，而且科学意义上的任何翻译在实际上都是不可能的吗？他认为新洪堡学派的观点失之偏颇，但是，这些观点却可以给翻译以诸多的启迪。他指出我们必须承认宇宙的结构远远没有机械地，即逻辑地在语言的普遍结构中得到反映。确实，不同的语言往往是以不同的语言结构表述同一的自然现实，比如拉丁语与法语的语言结构就不同，虽然同样表达"皮埃尔打保尔"这一现实，但词序结构就相异。同时，不同的语言也往往以不同的结构来切分人类的客观经验。他举例说，假设宇宙中存在着方式结构（回答以"怎样"引出的、就行为提出的问题），那么法语中"il traversa la rivière la nage"（他游过了河）一句似乎完全反应了客观经验的结构。但是，对于这一包含着同一客观经验的同样结构的同一情景，英语却作如下的描述：He swam across the river. 可以看到，英语和法语对经验的切分完全不同。如此一来，如何确定这两种语言结构哪一种更准确地反映了客观经验的结构？而对于翻译来说，这两种结构是否能够完全对译？乔治·穆南认为，当我们在探讨翻译的时候，决不应该回避新洪堡学派在对语言思想与现实、语言与"世界映象"之间关系的思考时提出的观点，这些观点虽然有些极端，但是对我们打破以往过于简单化的认识，进一步认识到不同语言的传情达义规律的深刻差异，从而更全面地认识与发现翻译中的本质障碍，提高翻译活动的自觉性，无疑是有利的。他指出："我们必须接受——而不是回避、否认，甚至视而不见——这些看似摧毁了翻译的可行性的事实，只有在这一基础上，翻译的理论问题才有可能被理解，甚或得到解决。"（Mounin，1963：58）在《翻译的理论问题》一书中，乔治·穆南还就翻译、语言与人际交流，翻译的可行性和翻译的限度进行了深入的研究，并从文化人类学、文献学等途径探讨了翻译与文化的问题，从句法结构、词汇等层面，讨论了翻译的具体转换问题等，笔者将另文作有关评介。

选文三　从认知语言学角度看强势文化对翻译的影响

师　琳

导　言

本文选自《外语教学》2011年第6期。作者师琳是博士生、西安建筑科技大学文学院副教授，研究方向为认知语言学、英美文化、英语教学。

选文从认知语言学的角度，分析了处于弱势文化地位的《红楼梦》以及《骆驼祥子》翻译到处于强势文化地位的英语时，译者往往采用归化策略，对作品认知上的差异之处做出改动，以迎合满足强势文化的认知需求。认知语言学的翻译观强调体验和认知的制约作用，重视作者、作品和读者之间的互动关系，追求实现解释的合理性和翻译的和谐性。认知语言学建立在体验哲学的基础上，用认知语言学的视角去审视翻译，相比传统的以文本为中心的翻译观和传统语言学的翻译观，它突出了主体认知活动在翻译中的表现。作为强势文化地位国家的译者往往在翻译中操纵改写处于弱势地位国家的作品，大到文化心理意识形态，小到字、词、句的改写。

1. 引言

语言是文化的载体，文化是语言的土壤，语言和文化密不可分。语言是文化的重要有机组成部分，它记录着人类文化发展的历史，反映着社会文明进步的成果；但语言不能脱离文化而存在，总是生长在一定的文化背景中。语言作为文化的载体，它浸透了民族的文化；文化包含着语言又影响语言。翻译的实质体现为：在两种语言交流的同时进行文化交流。它不是简单的从一种语言转换成另一种语言，而是从一种文化中的语言表现形式转换成另一种文化中的语言表现形式。

随着各国文化交流的日益频繁和翻译研究方法多元化的发展，文化研究开始成为全球性研究，翻译学家们逐渐认识到翻译可以更加深入地剖析文本内及文本之间的关系从而达到跨文化目的。20 世纪 80 年代，翻译研究进入了一个崭新的阶段：翻译的文化论。此学派将翻译上升到跨文化交际过程的角度，脱离以往单层对文化的讨论，代之以多元文化研究。

文化翻译论强调与多门学科的结合以实现多元化翻译研究。社会学、符号学、语法学、阐释学及语言哲学等学科的引入为认识翻译这一文化现象提供了多方面视角，而恰恰是这些学科推动翻译研究走出语言学的局限，上升到文化层面。

认知语言学是一门研究语言的普遍原则和人的认知规律之间关系的语言学流派。20 世纪 80 年代，认知语言学作为语言研究的一种研究范式和独立学派得以确立。认知语言学认为，语言是人们通过认知与客观世界相互作用的结果，语言是与概念结构一致的象征符号系统。基于对客观世界相同的认知体现在不同民族语言中的共性不在语言形式上，而在于人的认知心理。不同民族的相同认知心理基础和认知能力、与客观世界相互作用中所获得的共同体验，即不同民族相似的认知构成了语际翻译可译性的基础。由此可见，认知语言学不仅是语言学研究的新视角，而且为翻译研究及文化翻译提供了新思路，输入了新鲜血液。本文从认知语言学角度研究翻译，分析强势文化对翻译的影响。

2. 认知语言学和翻译的关系

认知语言学在中国的发展始于 20 世纪 80 年代末，经过 30 年的引进、吸收与发展，中国认知语言学在语法研究、翻译、文学、诗学、外语教学等领域都得到了广泛的应用和发展。按照认知语言学的观点，“从理论上讲，不管是什么语言形式，我们都可以寻求理据并加以解释。因为任何一种语言现象，包括非常规的语言现象，其背后总是存在着人们的认知规律。”（汪立荣，2004：272）不同民族由于社会环境、历史传统、宗教信仰等方面的差异，通过源于人与人的互相作用获得的经验自然会有很多差异。这种社会文化的差异也同样会体现在语言表达形式中。语言学研究的结果也表明，语言与认知之间有密切的关系，而认知与文化背景有关。

30年来，认知语言学与翻译研究集中于三个方面：(1) 认知语言学视野下的翻译理论研究；(2) 认知语言学观照下的翻译实践；(3) 认知语言学对于翻译教学的指导作用。据初步统计，1980-2010年间中国期刊网论及认知语言学论文共计1 200余篇，其中核心期刊刊载计27篇。27篇核心论文中涉及认知语言学与理论研究15篇，翻译实践11篇，翻译教学1篇。王寅将体验哲学和认知语言学的基本原理扩展应用于翻译理论和实践的研究，提出了认知语言学的翻译观。认知语言学的翻译观认为，翻译是以现实体验为背景的认知主体所参与的多重互动作用为认知基础的，读者兼译者在透彻理解源语语篇所表达的各类意义的基础上，尽量将其在目标语言中表达出来，在译文中应着力勾画出作者所欲描写的现实世界和认知世界。认知语言学的翻译观强调体验和认知的制约作用，重视作者、作品和读者之间的互动关系，追求实现解释的合理性和翻译的和谐性。认知语言学建立在体验哲学的基础上，用认知语言学的视角去审视翻译，相比传统的以文本为中心的翻译观和传统语言学的翻译观，它突出了主体认知活动在翻译中的表现。

翻译活动的主体是译者，翻译的认知语言学视角关注译者在翻译活动中所经历的体验、认知和再现的过程。王寅提出认知语言学的翻译模式包含六个观点：翻译具有体验性；翻译具有多重互动性；翻译具有一定的创造性；翻译的语篇性；翻译的和谐性以及翻译的两个世界(即现实世界和认知世界)。

3. 强势文化对翻译的影响

“文化翻译”的概念最早是由社会人类学家提出的，埃德蒙·里奇在《我们自己与他者》一文中对这一概念给出了较为明确的界定。所谓文化翻译，指的是在文化研究的大语境下来考察翻译，即对各民族间的文化以及语言的“表层”与“深层”结构的共性和个性进行研究，探讨文化与翻译的内在联系和客观规律。换言之，文化翻译观从文化研究的角度研究翻译。20世纪80年代后期开始，随着文化批评和文化研究在西方学术理论界的兴起并逐步上升到主导地位，一大批学者开始从不同的文化研究角度切入翻译问题。Holz-Manttari(1984：7)用“跨文化合作”(intercultural cooperation)来指翻译；Lefevere(1992：4)则把翻译看作是“文化交融”(acculturation)；Snell-Hornby明确指出，翻译是一种“跨文化的活动”，并建议从事翻译理论研究的学者们抛弃他们的“唯科学主义”的态度，把文化而不是文本作为翻译单位，把文化纳入翻译理论研究中来。

“文化翻译观”的主要内容是：“翻译不仅仅是双语交际，它更是一种跨文化交流；翻译的目的是突破语言障碍，实现并促进文化交流；翻译的实质是跨文化信息传递，是译者用译语重现原作的文化活动；翻译的主旨是文化移植、文化交融，但文化移植是一个过程；语言不是翻译的操作形式，文化信息才是翻译操作的对象。”(杨仕章，2004)

20世纪80年代末以来，在后殖民主义文化研究大潮的冲击下，翻译理论研究出现了“文化抗衡”。后殖民批评消解霸权，弘扬弱势文化，承认文化的差异，主张不同文化的平等。后殖民研究视角给予翻译研究的启示在于，它将翻译看作殖民文化的产物，是帝国主义强权政治及帝国主义文化思想观念对外进行霸权扩张的工具，是强势文化和弱势文化在权力差异语境中不平等对话的产物。随着殖民体系的瓦解，殖民地人民在获得了民族解放和国家独立之后，更增强了解除、摆脱宗主国的精神控制的要求，这当然是一个比体制变革更艰难的文化政治工程。不少后殖民主义学者认识到要重塑民族身份，抵抗霸权文化的侵略。

一般来讲，翻译主要不是在势均力敌的文化而是在强势文化与弱势文化之间进行的，并且一般由强势文化向弱势文化输入。在此，以英美文化与中国文化的交流为例，从认知语言学角度，简述强势文化对弱势文化的影响及其在翻译上的体现。翻译的认知语言学视角关注译者在翻译活动中所经历的体验、认知和再现的过程。由于认知差异及文化上的不平等，译者在翻译策略的选择上带有不同的特征。

让我们从《红楼梦》的英译看一看中英文化间的不平等是如何影响这部文学名著翻译的。到目前为止，《红楼梦》的英译全本有两种，而且都是20世纪70年代完成的。一种是英国汉学家霍克斯的 *The Story of the Stone*，另一种是我国学者杨宪益的 *A Dream of Red Mansions*。关于这两个译本我国翻译界有不少讨论，其中崔永禄教授的评论代表了绝大多数人的意见。他认为："霍克斯的《红楼梦》译本，在传达主题信息和艺术信息方面应该说是取得了突出成就，尤其是艺术的再创造，远远超过了其他译本，但在文化信息的传达方面却有一种十分值得注意的倾向。说它是倾向，一是在霍的译文中，我们看到的一些问题不是个别现象，而是较普遍的、有一定思想指导的；二是不仅是霍克斯一个人的做法，其他西方人翻译中国作品或处于弱势文化地位国家的作品时也有类似倾向，这就值得我们非常注意。"(2007)在霍克斯的译本中"红"字的处理就是一个十分明显的例子。从人类的生理基础来看，红色由于波长、色度和饱和度三方面的物理特征，对眼睛的刺激最为强烈，因而最容易被感知。社会文化方面，在各原始民族生活中，红色的自然事物占有举足轻重的地位，崇拜太阳、火和血是原始社会及早期文化的一种普遍现象。中国人的认知和文化结构表现出明显的红色情结，这首先体现在中国人自古就把红色与喜庆事物联系起来。中国人对红色的特殊喜好源于古代对太阳的崇拜和祈望，祖先以祭祀巫舞的形式表达这种本能的依恋和崇拜，由此红色的喜庆之意应运而生。红色的吉祥之意逐渐延伸到逢凶化吉、美好、幸福、繁荣昌盛等褒义范畴。运用的政治领域，红色象征着革命和社会主义，这在中国人的认知结构中也属于褒义的范畴。与汉语的红色相反，英语中的 red 的文化意义则贬义多于褒义。英语文化的认知结构中常将 red 和鲜血联系起来，西方人则认为血液是奔腾在人体内的生命之液，一旦鲜血流淌，生命将面临危险，所以 red 在西方表达政治上的残暴和流血、经济上的亏损负债等。因此，如何处理"红色"就成了霍克斯棘手的问题。在小说的名称上，他用了 *The Story of the Stone*，除有原文版本等因素的考虑外也避免了"红"在汉英两种语言中因联想意义不同而引发的麻烦。然而在小说的正文中"红色"是无论如何也必须直面的。虽然霍克斯在英译本的前言中对包括"红色"在内的文化现象从汉英两种语言的角度进行了对比，但他还是通篇将"怡红院"译成了 Court of Green Delight，"怡红公子"译成了 Green Boy。同样是翻译《红楼梦》，杨宪益在处理中国特色文化现象时却采取了另一种策略。不仅书名《红楼梦》中的"红色"依旧，就是"怡红院"、"怡红公子"也分别被译成 Happy Red Court 和 Happy Red Prince，保持中国文化"不变色"。另外，《红楼梦》第七回中"周瑞家的"感叹语"阿弥陀佛"，霍克斯译为 God bless my soul，从而使"周瑞家的"改信了基督教，而杨宪益译为 Gracious Buddha，让"周瑞家的"仍然笃信佛教。第二十四回中有"巧媳妇做不出无米的粥来。"杨宪益译为 Even the cleverest housewife can't cook a meal without rice；霍克斯译为 Even the cleverest housewife can't make bread without flour！两个译文中 meal 和 bread、rice 和 flour 的差别其实就不仅仅是食品及其原料的差别了。

正如崔永禄教授所说的那样，霍克斯在《红楼梦》翻译中所采取的策略不仅是他个人的做

法，其他西方人翻译中国作品也有同样的倾向。作为强势文化国家的译者发挥主体性，能动性，操纵并改写翻译作品尤其是处于弱势文化地为国家的作品。小到具体的字、词、句的改译，大到作品文化心态不同引起的意识形态的改写。老舍先生的《骆驼祥子》英译本结局部分就是一个明证。原文以主人公未能团圆的悲剧结束，揭示了旧社会劳动人民不会有自救的可能。文中祥子战胜了刘四，燃起了重新生活的希望。他想找到曹先生和小福子，可情人小福子在妓院中不堪忍受自杀了，祥子的希望破灭了，从此消沉堕落下去。小说的结尾写道：

> 体面的、要强的、好梦想的、利己的、个人的、健壮的、伟大的祥子，不知陪着人家送了多少回殡，不知何时何地会埋起他自己来，埋起这堕落的、自私的、不幸的、社会病态里的产儿，个人主义的末路鬼！

但是在1964年的英译本中，译者Evan King(伊万・金)却带给人们一个充满诗意与浪漫的美国式大团圆结局：祥子去了曹宅，在曹先生的安排下，把小福子从下等妓院中拯救了出来。译文是这样的：

> In the mildness of summer evening the burden in his arms stirred slightly, nestling closer to his body as he ran. She was alive. He was alive. They were free. (King, 1964: 315)

为了使这一结局“顺理成章”，译者还加入了“女学生”和“Pock Li”两个角色。女学生的言行唤醒了祥子的灵魂，也点燃了他寻求新生的希望；而“Pock Li”的堕落更能衬托出祥子未来的光明。尽管这一改译引起了中国文艺界的批评，译文却在美国大获成功。原因在于当时美国人民的文化心态和意识形态。当时是在第二次世界大战后，经历过战争的惨痛，亲人们阴阳相隔，家庭悲欢离合，让无数的美国人渴望生而不希望死，期待战后的团聚而不是磨难后的毁灭。这种社会心理潮流迫使译者有意掩盖了现实的矛盾与痛苦，从而使读者在所谓的圆满中得到心理上的认可和满足。

由于认知的差异，翻译——两种不同文化地位的交流，势必遭受一定程度上的失真，才能更好地为强势文化服务。在这改写的过程中，译者发挥主观能动性，常采用归化这一翻译策略。

4. 结语

翻译活动的主体是译者，翻译的认知语言学视角关注译者在翻译活动中所经历的体验、认知和再现的过程。本文从译者主体性发挥入手，分析了处于强势文化地位的英美作品和处于弱势地位的中国作品之间的翻译。以《红楼梦》和《骆驼祥子》的英译为例，分析了认知差异在翻译上的体现。这些分析表明作为强势文化地位国家的译者往往在翻译中，操纵改写处于弱势地位国家的作品。大到文化心理意识形态，小到字、词、句的改写，以此来迎合强势文化的需求。

选文四 《论语》三个英译本翻译研究的功能语言学探索

陈 旸

导 言

本文选自《外语与外语教学》2009年第2期。作者陈旸是博士生、佛山科技学院文学院副教授，研究方向为功能语篇分析、翻译实践、应用语言学。

语境和纯理功能是系统功能语言学的重要概念。选文将这两个概念运用于《论语》英译研究之中。作者首先探讨系统功能语言学的语境理论和纯理功能思想用于《论语》英译研究的可行性和适用性，然后对取自阿瑟·威利、潘富恩和温少霞、赖波和夏玉和的三个《论语》英译本中的个别翻译范例进行功能语篇分析，旨在通过对比原文与译文的功能参数对译文的效果给予客观的评价。分析表明：系统功能语言学中的理论可为我们客观评估译本提供一定的依据。

《论语》是儒家的经典著作之一，也是了解中国传统文化最权威的文献典籍。据东汉班固《汉书·艺文志》载，"《论语》者，孔子应答弟子、时人，及弟子相与言而接闻于夫子之语也。当时弟子各有所记，夫子既卒，门人相与辑而论纂，故谓之《论语》。"《论语》一书言简意赅，内容博大精深。早在宋代，就有"半部《论语》治天下"之说；自16世纪末以来，《论语》开始被译为西方语言。《论语》的英文翻译，最早见于英国传教士马希曼(Joshua Marshman)的节译本 *The Works of Confucius*(1809)。随后是另一位英国传教士顾利(David Collie)翻译的 *The Four Books*(1828)，该译本成了英国著名汉学家"理雅各翻译四书的直接先驱"(参见程钢，2002)；理雅各(James Legge)翻译的《论语》(*Confucian Analects*)收入1861年在香港出版的《中国经典》(*The Chinese Classics*)第一卷，该译本是第一个具有广泛影响的学术版译本。理雅各之后，西方译界不断有新译本出现，较有影响的包括：威利(Arthur Waley, 1938 /1998 /2005)、庞德(Ezra Pound, 1951)、柯立瑞(Thomas Cleary, 1992)、道森(Raymond Dawon, 1993)、莱斯(Simon Leys, 1997)、安乐哲和罗思文(Ames Roger & Henry Rosemont, 1998)、斯林格伦德(Edward Slingerland, 2003)等。在国内，晚清学者辜鸿铭于1898年推出第一个译本。此后国内学者大约有20余人翻译过《论语》。目前，较有影响的全译本包括：刘殿爵(1979)、程石泉(1986)、丘氏兄弟(1991)、李天辰(1991)、老安(1992)、梅仁毅(1992)、潘富恩与温少霞(1993/2004)、赖波与夏玉和(1994)、王福林(1997)、黄继忠(1997)、李祥甫(1999)。而林语堂(1938)、丁往道(1999)、马德五(2004)、王健(2004)、金沛霖和李亚斯(2005)以及赖波与夏玉和(2006)等皆为节译本(详细参见汪福祥，1996；王勇，2006)。据不完全统计，到目前为止，国内外译本总数不下于40种。而译本研究也成为国内近20年《论语》英译研究的一个焦点话题。

1. 关于《论语》英译本的研究状况

从我们收集到的相关38篇期刊论文和15篇硕士学位论文来看，译界主要集中研究理雅各(1861)、辜鸿铭(1898)、威利(1938/1998/2005)、庞德(1951)、柯立瑞(1992)、赖波与夏玉和(1994)、安乐哲和罗思文(1998)等人的译本。其研究方法,一是将原文与译文作对比分析,然后集中评价译文的特色与不足;二是将两个或多个译本放在一起进行对比分析,然后归纳总结各个译本的特点或优劣;而研究视角主要从翻译风格、翻译策略、译者动机、读者对象和译本质量等五个方面入手;其最有代表性的研究成果有:汪福祥(1996)、崔永禄(1999)、甄春亮(2001)、柳士军(2002)、付桂桂(2002)、王辉(2003,2004)、张小波(2000,2004)、车欢欢、罗天(2006)、刘永利、舒奇志(2006)、刘洪涛(2007)、丁建海(2007)。

译界对理雅各(下称理译)和辜鸿铭(下称辜译)的译本的看法,其意见褒远大于贬。例如:王辉(2003)认为理译将语义翻译和详尽注释结合起来,最大限度地保证了经义的传达,是汉学界和翻译史上纪念碑式的作品,然理氏译经过于依赖朱熹,对中国典籍必多曲解附会。甄春亮(2001)认为理氏译经的目的是让对中国历史文化一无所知的外国读者了解并掌握《论语》表述的事实。因此,理氏译本具有详尽的学术注释并采取直译方法传达原意,"是天才的翻译成果又是最详尽的研究成果"。王辉(2004)比较了理雅各和庞德译本(下称庞译)的翻译风格后认为,两者都是异化的成分多于归化的成分,理译是"近代汉学的开山之作和重要文献",庞译"古怪精灵、轻松俏皮"。刘永利、舒奇志(2006)在对比研究理雅各和安乐哲的译本(下称安译)后认为,理译是基于文化中心主义基础上的语言翻译代表作品;而安译是基于多元化理论的文化翻译典范。张小波(2004)认为辜译"别出心裁",成功地以"归化"的方式将中国文化作为强势文化推介于西方。车欢欢、罗天(2006)认为辜译是在翻译规范运作下译作顺利进入到目标语文化的一个典型例子。丁建海(2007)从翻译策略的视角探讨了辜译和安译。认为辜译的目的是传播儒家文化并希望得到西方的尊重,因而采用"归化"策略;而安译则是顺应文化平等尊重、相互融合的背景而采用"异化"策略。

而对于威利的译本(下称威译),译界意见"褒贬不一"。柳士军认为威译能充分再现原文信息,"具有翻译美"。崔永禄(1999)从译者的意图入手,对比分析了威译和柯立瑞的译本(下称柯译),认为威译注意细节的传译,尤其宜于学者进行研究使用;柯译通顺易懂,适合非学者型读者研读。刘洪涛(2007)从翻译动机、翻译策略等方面对比研究了理译和威译,认为两个译本都是不可多得的"善本"。

但对于赖波与夏玉和的合译本(下称赖译),译界基本上持否定意见。如,汪福祥(1996)认为赖译"译文质量粗劣"。付桂桂认为赖译"很难捕捉到《论语》古朴风雅的美感,更难寻找到原文文采飞扬的风范","语言平铺直叙,结构松散,缺乏新意,译本本身也尚有许多需待改进之处"。

显而易见,理译、辜译、威译和赖译(1994)是一直以来译界最为关注的译本,译界对理译和辜译的评价意见较为一致,即褒远大于贬;而对威译则争议纷纷,褒贬不一;对赖译则全盘否定。

鉴于上述原因,本文在研究中所选取的翻译评析范例分别出自以下译本:(1) 孔子著. Arthur Waley(阿瑟·威利)译. 外语教学与研究出版社出版(1998/2005)的《论语》(*The Analects*);(2) 杨伯峻、吴树平今译. 潘富恩、温少霞英译. 齐鲁书社出版(1993/2004)的《论语》今译 *The Analects of Confucius*(下称潘译);(3) 蔡希勤中文译注. 赖波、夏玉和英译. 华语教学出版社出版(2006)的《论语精华版》(*A Selected Collection of The Analects*)。

我们的研究目的是尝试通过选择具有代表性的《论语》英译本为语料,以系统功能语言学的语境理论和纯理功能思想作为理论基础，通过对比原文与译文的功能参数对译文的效果给予比较客观的评价，为《论语》英译研究和《论语》新译本的产生提供参考和借鉴。

2. 本研究的理论基础

Halliday所创立的系统功能语言学是当今世界上最具影响力的语言学流派之一。它是一个普通语言学理论，同时也是一个致力于理论指导实践的"适用语言学"(appliable linguistics)理论。它研究运用中的语言，也就是研究语言的功能；重视语境对语言理解的影响和作用；强调形式是意义的实现手段，意义由形式来体现。近年来，这方面的研究与实践也引起我国学者的关注。如徐珺(2002)、黄国文(2002，2004，2006)、张美芳(2005)、王东风(2006)、司显柱(1999,2004)，等等。

但从文献上看，用系统功能语言学理论指导《论语》研究或《论语》翻译研究的论著目前还不多见。方琰刊登在《功能语言学与适用语言学》(黄国文、常晨光、戴凡主编，中山大学出版社出版，2006)上的《建立和谐世界——对孔子〈论语〉的语言学研究》一文首开《论语》研究之先河。作者在系统功能语言学框架内探讨了产生《论语》的"社会、历史及意识形态环境"和该经典的语境特征、孔子主要思想的层次结构以及为实现他的思想所选择的词汇、语法的特点；文章最后讨论了儒家学说对现在中国和世界所具的现实意义。邹春媚的硕士毕业论文《〈论语〉语篇体裁的系统功能语言学分析》(华南师范大学，2007)以系统功能语言学为理论基础，研究《论语》的语篇体裁如何在语篇中得以实现。而韦汇余、张新(2006)刊登在《连云港师范高等专科学校学报》第2期上的《系统功能语言学视角下的〈论语〉翻译研究》一文，则是以系统功能语言学语境理论为基础，通过实例分析，探讨《论语》语内翻译的"语境方法"。

总的来说，应用系统功能语言学理论探讨《论语》英译研究的论著至今尚不多见。因此，本文试图在系统功能语言学理论的框架中探讨《论语》的英译问题，这也是把系统功能语言学理论用于典籍研究的尝试的一种表现。

3.《论语》三个英译本研究的可操作性探讨

系统功能语言学强调语言的三大纯理功能：概念功能(ideational function)、人际功能(interpersonal function)和语篇功能(textual function)；概念功能又分为经验功能(experiential function)和逻辑功能(logical function)(Halliday，1994/2000)。经验功能主要由及物性(Transitivity)系统来体现；及物性把人们对现实世界和内心世界的经验通过若干个过程(Process)表达出来，并指明过程所涉及的参与者和环境成分。因此，经验功能中小句及物性的分析主要涉及过程、参与者、和环境成分的选择；逻辑功能主要体现为小句复合体中小句与小句之间的逻辑(语义)关系。其中，小句之间的相互依赖关系包含并列和从属；而其逻辑语义关系则有扩展或投射。人际功能指人们用语言来和其他人交往，建立和保持人际关系，用语言来影响别人的行为，同时用语言来表达自己对现实世界和内心世界的看法甚至改变世界。人际功能主要由主语和限定成分所构成的语气(mood)系统来体现；语篇功能是人们使用语言，根据交际目的来组织概念功能中所承载的信息，反映各信息之间关系的语言功能。语篇功能主要由主位系统、信息结构和衔接系统三个语义系统来体现。概念功能、人际功能和语篇功能是语言意义的三个方面，构成了系统功能语学中的三大纯理功能。

系统功能语言学重视语境对语言理解的影响和作用，认为语篇总是出现在一定的语境当中，情景语境是语篇直接产生的语境；而位于外围的是文化语境，涉及特定言语社团的历史、文化、风俗习惯、思维模式、道德观念、价值观念、伦理范式等，具有民族性。特定的语境要求特定的语篇内容，不同的语篇体现不同的语境意义，语境与语篇相互影响。因此，译文与原文在纯理功能上的对等，实质上是译文与原文在相同语境中的功能对等。如 Halliday 等(1964)所言，翻译的过程在本质上是一种语言活动，对等在本质上是语境的对等。寻求意义的对等实际上是寻求两种语言的语篇在相同的语境中功能的对等。由此看来，系统功能语言学中的纯理功能思想以及语境理论为《论语》英译研究提供了科学的可操作性途径，我们可以通过对比原文与译文的功能参数对译文的效果给予比较客观的评价。

4. 语料分析与讨论

从《论语》可以看出，孔子希望通过自己的言传身教，传播"仁"的思想，旨在恢复西周的礼乐政治，建立和谐、正常的社会秩序。因此，"礼"在《论语》中是一个非常关键的概念，主要体现为对至高无上的祖先的祭礼以及君、臣、父、子各自间由"内自省"而发的自律。《论语·乡党第十》之"食不厌精，脍不厌细"和《论语·颜渊第十二》之"君君，臣臣，父父，子子"，集中体现了"礼"在上述两个层面上的意义。下面的分析重点就在这几句话。

4.1 "食不厌精，脍不厌细"之解读

"食不厌精，脍不厌细"出自《论语·乡党第十》："食不厌精，脍不厌细。食饐而餲，鱼馁而肉败，不食。色恶，不食。失饪，不食。不时，不食。割不正，不食。不得其酱，不食。肉虽多，不使胜食气。惟酒无量，不及乱。沽酒市脯不食。不撤姜食。不多食。"杨伯峻、吴树平(1993/2004，见上文)今译为：粮食不嫌舂得精，鱼和肉不嫌切得细。饭食霉烂发臭，鱼和肉腐烂，都不吃。食物颜色难看，不吃。气味难闻，不吃。烹调不当，不吃。不到该吃时候，不吃。不是按一定方法宰割的肉，不吃。没有调味的酱醋，不吃。席上肉虽然很多，吃肉不超过主食。只有酒不限量，却不至于喝醉。买来的酒和肉干不吃。吃完了，姜不撤除，但吃得不多。这一段话表达了孔子对祖先的敬意，对周代祭礼的敬重。祭祀从周代开始以祭祖为主，而祭礼中食礼是主要的内容。因此，孔子认为祭礼时用的食品，用料和加工都要特别洁净讲究，不能像寻常饮食那样。

4.2 "食不厌精，脍不厌细"的纯理功能分析

从经验功能及物性系统过程类型来看，这组小句都属于心理过程，其感觉者分别是形式上没有出现的"人"；而"精(舂得精)"和"细(切得细)"则分别为两个小句的现象(phenomenon)。按照系统功能语言学的观点，现象使感觉者产生某种思想、感觉和认知。从人际功能语气以及情态系统来看，这组陈述小句所给的信息，其说话者的态度是显性的，由情态化动词"厌"和语气附加语"不"体现出来；再从语篇功能的角度来看，两个小句的主位由"食"和"脍"体现；两个述位中的"精"和"细"体现了同义词和反义词的复现，是这一组表示并列延伸关系的小句的衔接手段。

4.3 “食不厌精，脍不厌细”英译的纯理功能分析

在这里，我们将对“食不厌精，脍不厌细”的英译本进行及物性分析。在上述三个英译本所提供的英译分别如下：

威译：But there is no objection to his rice being of the finest quality, nor to his meat being finely minced.

.潘译：He did not dislike to have his rice finely cleaned, nor to have his eat finely minced.

赖译：Rice (staple food) can never be refined too much; nor can meat be minced too much..

从过程类型看，威译和潘译分别采用了存在过程(is)和心理过程(dislike)来描述一种状态，而赖译则通过物质过程(be refined/be minced)来表示动态的事件；威译和潘译分别体现了存在物(no objection)和感觉者(He)及现象(to have his rice finely cleaned/to have his meat finely minced)之间的关系；赖译用 be refined/be minced 表示物质过程，其目标为 rice 和 meat，动作者没有在句法上表现出来，环境成分 too much 表示程度；三个译文均为陈述小句，赖译含有情态操作词 can，表示的是一种可能和将来事件，威译和潘译没有情态成分，表示的是不受时间限制的一般事实；威译的主位 But there，潘译的 He，赖译的 Rice，均为信息的起始点；威译采用多重主位(语篇主位＋主题主位)，目的是把这句话与前面的话语紧密联系起来。三个译文中的小句均是并列延伸关系，通过 no/not/never … nor 衔接起来。以上的分析表明，三个译本均句式工整、一气呵成，注重意义的传译。但威译和赖译在传译作为原文信息载体的经验功能方面明显逊色于潘译，因为存在过程和物质过程远不如心理过程更能表达原文的意义；相比之下，赖译更好地传译了原文的人际意义，因为它注重的是可能性，并不像其他两个译文那样确定；而威译通过名词词组 no object ion to … 比赖译 can never … too much 和潘译 did not dislike to … 所表达的“厌”更接近原文简洁、轻松、自然的文风。

4.4 “君君，臣臣，父父，子子”的解读

“君君，臣臣，父父，子子”出自《论语·颜渊第十二》：齐景公问政于孔子。孔子对曰：“君君，臣臣，父父，子子。”公曰：“善哉！信如君不君，臣不臣，父不父，子不子，虽有粟，吾得而食诸?”杨伯峻、吴树平(1993/2004)今译为：齐景公问孔子怎样治理国家。孔子回答说：“国君要像个国君，臣子要像个臣子，父亲要像个父亲，儿子要像个儿子。”齐景公说：“好呀！假如国君真不像个国君，臣子真不像个臣子，父亲真不像个父亲，儿子真不像个儿子，即便有粮食，我能够吃得着吗?”孔子的话大概是说：做君主就应该像君主的样子，做臣子就应该像臣子的样子，做父亲就应该像父亲的样子，做儿子就应该像儿子的样子。大家自律，齐国才有希望。

4.5 “君君，臣臣，父父，子子”纯理功能分析

从及物性系统过程类型来看，尽管这四个小句的动词是隐性的，但不难看出，这是四个含有认同型关系过程的小句。胡壮麟等指出，在任何一个认同型关系小句中，都有一个实体是“标记”，一个实体是“价值”。标记指的是外表、符号、形式和名称；价值指的是实质、意义、职能和身份。标记和价值总是与认同者和被认同者结合在一起。因此，这四个小句的认同者/标记分别为各小句句首的“君”、“臣”、“父”、“子”；认同动词(identifying verb)“像”，是隐性的；而被

认同者/价值分别为各小句句末的“君”、“臣”、“父”、“子”。从人际功能情态以及语气系统来看,这是一组不带情态或意态的陈述小句,体现说话者感情投入(affective involvement)低,只是以正式的口吻在向听话者提供信息,叙述真理;从语篇功能看,各小句的均为无标记主题主位(topical theme),由其经验成分中的认同者/标记充当,述位则由隐性认同动词和被认同者/价值充当;从衔接角度看,这四个小句主要通过小句间同义词的重复,构成一个词汇链,贯穿于小句之间;第一句与第二、第三和第四句分别构成了两个表示并列关系的小句复合体,表示延伸关系。

4.6 “君君,臣臣,父父,子子”英译的纯理功能分析

下面我们看看“君君,臣臣,父父,子子”在上述三个英译本中的英译情况:

威译:Let the prince be a prince, the minister a minister, the father a father and the son a son.

潘译:Let the ruler be ruler, the minister minister, the father father, and the son son.

赖译:Rulers, subjects, fathers, and so s should observe their respective rites.

从过程类型来看,威译和潘译都采用了认同型关系过程(Let ... be),威译中的认同者/标记(the prince/the minister/the father/the son)以及被认同者/价值(a prince/a minister/a father/a son)与潘译中的认同者/标记(the ruler/the minister/the father/the son)以及被认同者/价值(ruler/minister/father/son)略有不同,但两者皆较完美地再现原文信息;从语篇功能的角度上说,威译和潘译在结构上是比较接近原文的,威译在述位上通过“a ... ”体现被认同者的一种身份;而潘译在述位上的 ruler/minister/father/son 则把被认同者的身份抽象化;威译和潘译句式工整流畅;为了使译文语篇与原文语篇语境对等,两个译本把“君”分别译成 prince 和 ruler,这样一来,中西文化下的读者对原文具有同样的反应;与威译和潘译不同,赖译仅使用一个陈述小句,所以不存在小句之间的逻辑关系这一层;赖译用的是物质过程(observe),所以其过程类型、参与者(动作者/目标 rulers, subjects, fathers, and sons/their respective rites)等成分与原文不一致,因此在传译作为信息载体的概念功能方面可能有误。

4.7 小结

综观上面对《论语》三个英译本翻译范例的功能语言学解释,我们认为,潘译较准确、充分地传译原文的经验功能而再现了原文的信息。而这一方面,威译稍显逊色,而赖译则远不及前两者;三个译本中,潘译和威译在寻找译文语篇与原文语篇语境对等这一层面,做得较为巧妙;赖译诚如在其前言所言,“为了帮助古文程度不高的青年读者能够读懂这部书”,换言之,赖译的目标读者是中国语境下年青的一代,因此,赖译能较为准确的再现原文的语气和情态系统,但因其对原文的某些地方理解有偏差,故所用语言形式未能再现原文意义。和潘译一样,更适合中国语境下在课堂学得英语的中国读者;威译不能完全准确地传译原文的信息载体,但其简洁、轻松、自然、典雅的文风更接近原文。

5. 结语

本文首先回顾了《论语》的英译文在海内外的传播历史以及近 20 年《论语》英译本研究的

状况;接着探讨系统功能语言学中语境理论和纯理功能思想用于《论语》英译研究的必要性、可行性和可操作性;最后对所选三个《论语》英译本中的个别翻译范例进行功能语篇分析。我们的分析表明:系统功能语言学中的理论一方面能帮助我们全面、细致地分析、揭示和解释《论语》不同译本语言选择的原因,另一方面为我们评估译本提供一定的依据。

最后必须指出,由于我们的理论根据、研究的出发点以及所采用的分析的局限性,因此所作出的结论不一定能够得到翻译学界的普遍认同,这也是意料之中的。当然,把系统功能语言学中的有关理论运用于《论语》英译的研究,本文还只是一个初步的尝试。因为,除了纯理功能思想,系统功能语言学中的层次、例示、级阶、精密阶、轴等等概念都可以用来探讨翻译问题。今后我们还会尝试把这些相关的理论运用于翻译研究,以期更全面、细致地为《论语》英译研究和《论语》新译本的产生提供参考和借鉴。

【延伸阅读】

[1] Halliday, M. A. K. *An Introduction to Functional Grammar*. London: Edward Arnold, 1985.

[2] Newmark, P. *Approaches to Translation*. Oxford & London: Pergamon Press. Reprint in 1998. New York: Prentice Hall International, 1981.

[3] Nida, E. A. *Translating Meaning*. California: English Language Institute, 1982.

[4] 刘放桐等. 现代西方哲学(下)修订本. 北京:人民出版社,1990.

[5] 乔姆斯基. 句法结构. 荷兰:海牙摩顿出版公司,1957.

[6] 索绪尔. 普通语言学教程. 高名凯译. 北京:商务印书馆,1982.

[7] 谭载喜,编译. 新编奈达论翻译. 北京:中国对外翻译出版公司,2002.

[8] 许钧,袁筱一. 当代法国翻译理论. 武汉:湖北教育出版社,2001.

【问题与思考】

1. 为什么"文学的译者"不同于其他文本类型的译者? 差异何在?
2. 翻译的语言学研究存在那些理论偏向?
3. 乔治·穆南如何从语言学角度探讨翻译问题?
4. 翻译的认知语言学视角关注译者在翻译活动中的哪些问题?
5. 谈谈系统功能语言学的语境理论和纯理功能思想用于文学翻译研究的可行性和适用性。

第三章　文学翻译研究的文化转向

导　论

在文化的大语境下考察翻译活动使翻译研究视野更为开阔。翻译不仅是语言转换，更是传递文化信息的媒介，文化构建的一种方式，文学发展的重要工具。当然，翻译研究无论从文化着手还是从语言着手都只是切入点不同。从语言的转换切入并不排除文化因素，从影响翻译的外部因素切入也不应该忽视或排除语言的转换规律。

翻译研究自20世纪70年代以来出现了"文化转向"，其视点已从语言文本转向翻译与文化的关系，即文化对翻译的影响与制约作用，将翻译置于社会文化、人类历史的大语境下加以认识。翻译文学作为社会多元系统的一个组成部分，其形态或内在结构必然受社会文化的影响和作用。一个民族文学的强弱决定了翻译文学在其社会多元系统内的位置，从而决定了翻译策略。当民族文学"处于年轻期，或正在建构过程中"，"处于边缘或弱小"，"处于危机或转型期"时，翻译文学在整个文学系统中占主导地位。反之，就会处于次要地位。文学地位、文化地位对翻译文学的整体取向具有直接影响，但对翻译策略的影响往往是通过社会文化环境、历史背景所形成的社会及个体意识形态产生的。可见，文学翻译与文化的关系是多重的、复杂的。

在中国文化和文学的现代性乃至世界性的进程中，翻译文学成为中国现代文学的重要组成部分。一方面，中国文学所受到的外来影响是无可否认的。通过翻译家的译介和作家本人的创造性转化，这种影响已经成为中国文化的一部分，它在与中国古典文学精华的结合过程中，产生了一种既带有西方影响同时更带有本土特色的新的文学语言；另一方面，在与世界先进文化和文学进行对话与交流的过程中，中国文化和文学也对外国文化和文学产生了不可忽视的影响。在当今全球化语境之下，文化翻译和文学翻译中的重点将体现在把中国文化的精华介绍到世界，让全世界的文化人和文学爱好者共同分享中国文化的博大精深。

中国历史上曾有过三次译入高潮：东汉至唐宋的佛经翻译高潮、明末清初的科技翻译高潮以及鸦片战争后至"五四"前的西方政治思想与文学翻译高潮。在第三次翻译高潮中，以文学翻译，尤其是小说翻译最为繁荣，影响也最大。近代翻译小说是中国翻译发展史中的一个重要阶段。从1840年至1918年大致可分为三个时期：1840-1894年为萌芽期，1895-1904年为发展期，1905-1918年为鼎盛期。其翻译特征主要表现为：由意译逐渐向直译发展，由文言逐渐向白话发展，名著和短篇小说翻译增多，专业翻译家开始出现。中国近代小说在发展过程中既受传统小说的影响，更受外来小说的影响。在外来小说的影响下，中国作家的文学观念发生了变化，小说的题材有了扩展，表现手法、表现技巧有所创新，典型人物的塑造、人物心理描写等方面也都起了变化。由于当时资产阶级民主革命运动进入了新阶段，形势的发展使中国人民迫切要求输入西方文化，以反对封建专制主义，这就促进了翻译小说的繁荣。此外，外国小说的输入给中国近代小说创作以多方面的影响，当然，中国小说彻底的变革至“五四”以后才完成。

英文 agent 一词，意指代理人、代理商、中介人；媒介、中介等。可指个人，亦可指集体。在翻译过程中，即翻译活动的行动者。文学翻译中，译者作为主要的行动主体，表面上所做的是完成了一项语言的转换，实际上却是一种翻译和被译的过程。在这个过程中，译者对文本进行创造性转化；同时，译者也被塑造，也被指导如何进行翻译。作为个体的和集体的文学翻译“行动者”，他们为文学艺术的传承、文学系统的完善，以及推进一国文学之建立和发展等，都发挥了重要的作用。这是主体的能动作为，但也是社会的诉求。

萨格尔认为，集体或机构的“行动者”往往能发挥多种作用，因为这些机构人员毕生致力于外国文学、作家或文学流派的研究、翻译和传播，他们往往逆流而动，挑战常规和主流，他们甚至不畏风险，只求文化的创新和发展。

哲巴齐(Christine Zurbach)论述了葡萄牙 1975 年成立的公司——埃武拉文化中心(CCE)作为文化代理机构(agent)译介西方戏剧并建立葡萄牙自己戏剧库(repertoire)的过程。1974 年 4 月 25 日葡萄牙发生了“康乃馨革命”，终止了萨拉查的长期独裁统治。新政权对新闻审查予以解禁，允许接触各种外语，文学上的自由度大大增加，文学艺术与权力的关系得以改善。这种状况决定了 CCE 选择作者和作品进入译语剧目库的自由度增加，艺术性要求得到强调。在政府的资助和支持下，作为文化代理的埃武拉文化中心，实际上承担了制定葡萄牙文化创新政策的任务，如针对新政权下的新观众怎样进行戏剧艺术的生产和传播。这样的“行动”在于引进具有创新意义的外国戏剧，影响本国观众的鉴赏水平，最终对葡萄牙的戏剧发展加以引领并产生深刻的影响。

博尔赫斯介绍了《一千零一夜》流传史上的译者及其他们的译本：加朗和马德鲁斯的两个法文译本、莱恩和伯顿的两个英文译本、利特曼等人的四个德文译本。这些译本，有的添加大量内容(加朗译本)，有的对文本加以净化(莱恩和加朗译本)，有的注释繁多(伯顿译本)，有的表达生动(莱恩译本)，但有的却缺乏生气(利特曼译本)。博尔赫斯认为，“加朗的版本是所有版本里最差、最荒谬、最愚蠢的一种，不过却是阅读量最大的一种。”马德鲁斯的翻译是“创造性的不忠”，但正是“不忠”成就了马德鲁斯的译本。《一千零一夜》的译本流传启发了许多作家的灵感，其中“故事套故事”的典型结构，被博尔赫斯所采纳，成为他创作的许多短篇小说的叙事模式。

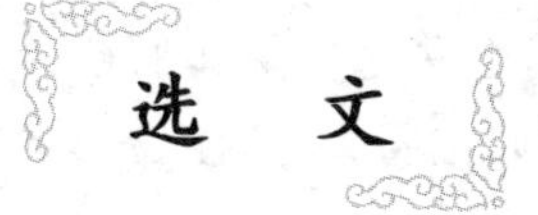

选　文

选文一　论社会文化对文学翻译的影响

姜秋霞　权晓辉　杨　芳

导　言

本文选自《外国文学研究》2003 年第 6 期。作者姜秋霞是西北师范大学外国语学院教授、翻译学博士，主要从事翻译教学与研究；权晓辉是西北师范大学外国语学院副教授；杨芳是江苏大学外国语学院讲师。

选文通过考察民族文学、社会文化地位及意识形态对翻译的影响，探讨翻译与社会文化之间的复杂关系。翻译文学作为社会多元系统的一个组成部分，其形态或内在结构必然受社会文化的影响和作用。一个民族文学的强弱决定了翻译文学在其社会多元系统内的位置，从而决定了翻译的策略；翻译会受到文化地位的影响，文化的强势与弱势会在很大程度上影响翻译的"归化"与"异化"取向。如果对翻译策略的选择出自不同的文化立场，便在一定程度上体现了文化的政治性；特定历史背景、社会文化环境所形成的意识形态对翻译文学的影响是多方面的。意识形态有社会群体意识形态与个体意识形态之分。译者的翻译个体文化意识对翻译策略的影响要远远大于民族文化地位的影响。

翻译与社会文化的关系既是一个古老的命题，又是一个新的课题。翻译是语言的转换，更重要的是语言所承载的文化信息的交流与转换，对民族文化的发展有着无可替代的意义。然而，翻译对于民族文化而言，并不是简单的文化输入或输出，还在某种程度上取决于与社会文化环境的相互作用，取决于译入语文化的接收方式等。换言之，社会文化对翻译也有着重要的影响和作用，对翻译的方式、翻译的取向有着各种制约和调节，两者之间是一种互为作用的关系。

翻译与社会文化之间(不是附着在语言符号上的狭义文化)的相互作用、相互影响的关系，特别是社会文化与历史背景对翻译的影响，是比较新的研究课题，是翻译研究自 20 世纪 70 年代出现"文化学转向"以来的焦点问题。在对翻译进行多元综合的考察和研究中，对翻译的认识不再限于语言或者文学文本的范畴，而是将其联系到更为广阔的社会文化语境。由以色列学者埃文·佐哈尔首先提出的"多元系统"理论将(文学)翻译纳入特定的社会文化系统，通过对社会文化系统中各种功能的解释研究翻译与目的语文化的互动关系。此后，比利时学者勒弗维尔等人又进一步提出了社会文化对翻译进行操纵的具体影响因素，如意识形态、赞助人、诗学对翻译的制约。随着翻译学文化研究的深入发展，翻译与社会的关系越来越带有政治的倾向，印度学者尼兰贾娜和斯皮瓦克运用后殖民主义理论对翻译的解读更深化了翻译的社会文化性质，他们对社会文化地位（强、弱势）对翻译的作用、翻译所反映的政治特性、所渗透的阶级张力等方面的研究充分揭示了翻译与社会文化的密切关系。

翻译研究的文化学转向不仅是对翻译认识的加深，是翻译学科的进一步发展，而且对语言与社会文化的关系、文学与社会文化的关系的认识都是极大的发展，对社会语言学、文学、文化学、人类学都有着很重要的启示。但翻译的文化学研究作为翻译学科的一个重要组成部分还远远没有成熟，还有待进一步的丰富和发展。本文将就这一领域已有的几个理论观点作进一步的讨论。

1. 民族文学对文学翻译的影响

根据埃文·佐哈尔的多元系统理论，翻译文学作为社会多元系统的一个组成部分，其形态或内在结构必然受社会文化的影响和作用。一个民族文学的强弱决定了翻译文学在其社会多元系统内的位置，从而决定了翻译的策略。他特别提出了译者的翻译行为或翻译策略是由翻译文学在目的语文化系统中的地位决定的，即翻译文学在整个文学系统中的“首位”和“次位”（强、弱）对翻译行为的选择具有重要的影响。根据他的观点，当民族文学“处于年轻期，或正在建构过程中”、“处于边缘的，或弱小的”、“处于危机或转型期”三种情况下，翻译文学在整个文学系统中占主导地位。反之就会处于次要地位。他指出，翻译文学占据中心地位时，译文会注重“充分性”（adequacy），即尽量忠于原文的结构、内容（“异化”策略）；反之，则译文为了迁就读者，尽量采用他们熟悉的语言、结构甚至内容（“归化”策略）。从理论上讲，民族文学处于弱势、翻译文学处于主导时，翻译策略倾向于异化，以便丰富和发展民族文学。应该说，这种观点具有一定的理论基础。我们知道，鲁迅主张“信而不顺”的翻译，为的是“……装进异样的句法去，故的，外省外府的，外国的，后来便可以据为己有”。（转引自陈福康）可见鲁迅异化倾向的翻译策略是出于引进和学习，以及对本土语言文学的丰富和发展。然而综观 20 世纪我国的翻译文学，无论是 20 世纪初，抑或 20 世纪末，各个时期都有着不同翻译策略的出现。20 世纪初，我国的民族文学处于新旧转型之时，亟待振兴，在文学的翻译上需要引进和吸收新的语言表现方式，即按照埃文·佐哈尔的观点在转换方式上忠于原文的结构、内容。然而对比那个时期的文学翻译文本，会发现同一时期，在同样的民族文学背景下，不同的译者采用了不同的方法。如 30 年代 *Jane Eyre* 的两个译本：伍光健翻译的《孤女飘零记》和李霁野翻译的《简爱》，虽然是同一时期，但在翻译方法上有很大的不同。李霁野几乎是逐字逐句的翻译，而伍光健的译本多有删节，其中有关西方文化典故的内容也被删削。茅盾评论说：“伍译是要避去欧化句法，即归化”。如果说不同历史时期、不同社会背景下民族文学地位的强弱对翻译策略有影响的话，那么这种影响是通过译者这一中介产生作用的，也就是说，如何看待本民族文学与他族文学、如何实现文学的交流与交融很大程度上取决于译者的文化意识和文化态度。译者是文学翻译与社会文化相互作用中一个重要的因素，是社会文化对文学翻译发生作用的中介。因此，翻译文学在社会多元系统中的位置及其对翻译的影响需要纳入译者主体的文化意识作为其中一个重要成分。

其次，民族文学对翻译的影响并不单纯体现在文学文本的转换策略上，更重要的是体现在译介的宏观结构上。考察不同历史时期的翻译主题，我们发现：民族文学地位对译介的内容有

较大的影响。20世纪初，我国民族文学处于转型期，文学精英们在批判旧的封建文化的同时，也在批判昔日的文学模式，不再提倡用旧有的格律体诗、章回体小说等，急于从外国文学中汲取新的血液，新的写作方法。这个时期的翻译文学内容广泛，在译介上引进了一些新的小说题材，如政治小说、教育小说、科幻小说和侦探小说。从这个意义上讲，当民族文学较弱，或处于"转型"之时，引进和吸收的需要会丰富翻译文学的内容，扩展翻译的范围，对翻译文学的整体结构产生很大影响。

另外，民族文学对翻译的影响不只局限于民族文学本身的地位，即民族文学在本社会系统内部的地位，还取决于民族文学相对它国文学的地位，有一个相对弱势概念。埃文·佐哈尔提出了三种翻译文学处于次要地位的情况，翻译文学在民族文学系统内部有主次或强弱地位之分，从而决定了翻译的导向、方式、策略等。但其主次或强弱地位还有与其他民族文学相对的强弱关系。从20世纪末我国大量翻译美国文学可以看出，虽然这个时期我国的民族文学形成了一定的范式，但相对迅速发展繁荣的美国文学而言，仍有许多值得借鉴和学习的地方，因而young，peripheral，weak不是绝对的，而是相对的。

2. 社会文化地位对翻译的影响

根据后殖民主义翻译理论，不同的民族，不同的文化，由于其政治经济地位的不同，在运用语言传递信息的过程中会在一定程度上表露出自己的社会身份和政治态度，在不同文化之间形成各种言说及对话方式，不同的政治意识与言说方式在翻译转换策略上会有所体现。从理论上讲，翻译应是双语转换与文化间的非政治性交流，是不同民族间的平等对话和相互接受。然而在此交流过程中，翻译会受到文化地位的影响，会因不同民族文化地位的差异在翻译的操作策略上出现不同的转换方式，具体而言，就是文化的强势与弱势会在很大程度上影响翻译的"归化"、"异化"取向。"归化"、"异化"这两个概念在技术层面分别被界定为"用译入语文化内容代替原语文化内容"和"保留、移植原语文化的形式和内容"。翻译中，译者会因其个体审美取向、价值判断以及文艺创作的主观特点对这两种不同的策略进行不同的选择，从而出现不同的翻译风格。但是，如果对此策略的选择出自不同的文化立场、渗透着文化地位的影响，"归化"或"异化"便在一定程度上体现文化的政治性，最为显著的便是强势文化的话语霸权与话语侵略。历史上，殖民者对殖民地的语言侵略早已有之，殖民者强制性的语言文化移植充分反映了权力话语的霸权与文化强势作用。随着殖民化的逐渐消解，语言文化的侵略越来越具有遮蔽性，强势文化往往以使者的身份通过翻译对"他者"文化进行普遍性渗透，在将文本转换成弱势文化语境过程中，用"异化"策略向目的语文化扩展其文化与政治意识。"异化"翻译策略可以是纯技术性的，只用于文化的交流，也可以承担政治性工具，为强势文化的侵略服务，使处于被言说地位的弱势文化在不知不觉中接受文化侵略；另一方面，强势文化在转换弱势文化语言文本过程中运用"归化"对弱势文化的文化特性进行歪曲甚至抹杀。民族文化地位对翻译转换策略的影响是社会文化在翻译中更大的渗透。

然而值得注意的是，文化地位对翻译的影响也包含着个体特性。正如民族文学对翻译策略的影响难以测量一样，文化地位在翻译转换中的体现也是比较模糊的。我们知道，《鲁拜集》的翻译，从波斯语言文本转换为英语时，译者采用了归化的方法，而当中国台湾译者将其转换为中文文本时也采用归化译法，这难道能够完全说明中国文化地位优于英国文化地位、英国文化地位优于波斯文化地位？再如《红楼梦》的翻译，在同一时期中西两位译者（杨译 1978，霍译 1973）笔下出现了明显的“归化”、“异化”两种不同翻译策略。因而文化地位对翻译的影响应该是间接的，要通过译者对特定文化的认同、接收或排斥产生作用。

目前，国内一些学者注意到，20 世纪末我国的翻译在策略上有异化的趋势，但这并不说明是民族文化地位的弱势趋向。从这个意义上讲，简单说文化地位影响翻译的策略，似乎难以解释社会文化影响翻译的复杂过程和方式。如果将译者主体的文化意识作为社会文化与翻译的中介环节也许更能说明问题。

3. 意识形态对翻译的影响

特定历史时期、特定社会背景下民族文学及文化地位对翻译文本转换策略的影响都有着一个共同的内容，即通过译者的主体文化意识发生作用。有关意识形态对翻译的影响，勒弗维尔有过比较详尽的论述，他认为，译者的行为受制于所处社会文化环境，在一定程度上体现其文化意识，翻译并不是在两种语言的真空中进行的，而是在两种文学传统的语境下进行的。译者对自己和自己文化的理解，是影响他们翻译方法的诸多因素之一。这一理论观点在很大程度上解释了社会文化各个层面对翻译的影响，即通过译者主体的文化认同、文化意识作用于翻译的转换策略。从不同时期文学翻译文本的对比发现，有些译者对原文中不符合当时社会思想意识的内容大量删减，如蟠西子翻译的《迦因小传》，将不符合当时封建礼教的诸如性爱描写的文字作了大量的删节，这样的翻译转换意味着文化意识在接受上的限制。然而对勒弗维尔的理论观点，也有进一步认识的空间。有两点值得我们注意：一是意识形态对翻译的影响是多方位的；二是社会意识形态与译者个体意识形态不是相等的同一概念。

第一，特定历史背景、社会文化环境所形成的意识形态对翻译文学的影响是多方面的，除对翻译的转换策略有影响，还对译介的内容起作用。不同时期的不同社会意识决定了读者的价值取向，从而决定了赞助人的翻译取向。20 世纪初至“五四”前后的 10 年间，我国仍是半封建半殖民地社会，一方面社会发展相对落后，急需进步的思想及先进的科学技术；另一方面时局动荡，没有固定统一的政治意识，需要借鉴新的政治思想。因而这个时期的翻译文学分两部分内容：“五四”前重在译介西方资本主义国家的先进科学技术及教育；“五四”后以译介俄国小说为主，从俄国革命中吸收新的政治思想和政治意识。20 世纪末则是我国改革开放的年代，经济发展意识影响到翻译时其文学主题有了转向，20 世纪初仅占翻译文学 0.22%（第 16 位）的经济类小说升至世纪末翻译小说的第 7 位。主题的选择在很大程度上说明了社会发展意识、文化形态作用于赞助人对翻译内容的取舍。

第二，意识形态有社会群体意识形态与个体意识形态之分。从各个时期文学翻译的方向、内容以及翻译方法看，都体现了社会文化语境下意识形态对翻译的影响，然而社会总体意识对译者个体的影响并不是完全一致的，还取决于个体与社会文化的关系。正如读者的阅读接受具有个体特性，译者的文化接受也有差异，对于各个时代、各种文化形态的理解在更大程度上决定了译者的翻译方法。林纾与蟠西子处于同一社会文化环境，但两人的翻译方法迥然不同，同一个民族的不同译者之间的策略选择充分体现了个体文化意识的差异，或者说个体文化意识中各种因素的作用。又如上面提到的《红楼梦》的翻译，同一时期两个译者所采用的不同翻译策略说明了不同译者的不同文化观念，或者说两种个体意识中的不同中西文化地位，体现了译者的翻译文化追求、翻译美学追求。从这个层面讲,译者的翻译个体文化意识对翻译策略的影响要远远大于民族文化地位的影响。

通过以上论述,我们得出三个方面的基本结论:

1. 社会文化对翻译文学有很大的影响作用,这些作用是多层面的,既有对翻译本体(如转换策略)的影响,也有对翻译文学整体结构、形态、内容取向等的作用,且更多地体现在对翻译作为社会文化系统的一部分在整体结构、价值取向上的影响作用。

2. 社会文化对翻译策略或翻译文本转换过程的影响和作用主要取决于译者主体,取决于译者的文化意识。无论是翻译文学主次地位、民族文化的强弱势地位在翻译转换中的作用都在很大程度上取决于译者的主体意识。社会文化环境、文化地位对翻译的影响不是直接的,而是通过对译者的意识的潜在影响和渗透间接影响翻译的策略。文学地位、文化地位对翻译文学的整体取向具有直接的影响,但对翻译策略的影响往往是通过社会文化环境、历史背景所形成的社会及个体意识形态产生的。这给我们一个很好的启发:对译者文化意识及其形态的研究将是翻译文化学的一个十分重要而有意义的内容。

3. 社会文化环境与翻译具有互动的作用。文化环境决定翻译的主题、内容及取舍程度,同时文学译介又反过来作用于文化环境的形态变化。翻译无论从宏观结构、价值取向上,还是在文本转换过程与方式上,都受社会文化环境的影响与制约;另一方面,社会文化对翻译的各种作用往往与主体的接收意识有关,社会意识形态、赞助人的作用均体现社会文化环境下主体意识的反应,因而文化接收、文化形态又受到翻译个体的作用。

文学翻译与社会文化的关系是多重、复杂的,本文只论及其中的一小部分,还有待于更深入的研究。

选文二　略论近代的翻译小说

王继权

导　言

本文选自王宏志编的《翻译与创作——中国近代翻译小说论》(北京大学出版社,2000)。作者王继权是复旦大学中文系教授,中国近代小说研究专家。曾与周榕芳编《台湾·香港·海外学者论中国近代小说》(百花洲文艺出版社,1991);与夏生元编《中国近代小说目录》(百花洲文艺出版社,1998),收近代小说(创作)6 400余种。

选文回顾了清末民初小说翻译的历史、方法及其深远影响。戊戌变法之前,虽有《四洲志》和《海国图志》的编译,但小说翻译却寥若晨星,不为知识分子重视。至戊戌变法之时,“且闻欧、美、东瀛,其开化之时,往往得小说之助”,让中国思想文化界视翻译小说为中国政治改良的必由之路,从政治小说开始,侦探小说、科学小说以及言情之说等都悉数翻译进来。至

"五四"之前,小说翻译进入鼎盛期,不仅译作数量剧增,且译介的档次和水平都有提高。早期翻译以意译为主,译者往往用中国章回小说的模式改造域外小说,删除"无关紧要"的闲文或"不合国情"的情节,或增补出原文没有的情节或议论。随着专业译者的出现及读者欣赏品味的提升,直译逐渐成为翻译小说的主要手段。翻译小说出现之初,因其目标读者是士大夫阶层,故采用文言文翻译,后来,随着白话报纸和杂志的创刊,读者群日渐平民化,翻译语言渐渐从文言文变为白话文。域外小说不仅输入有新的政治思想和观念,还有新的文学创作方法和技巧,促使了中国现代小说的诞生。

一

中国历史上曾有过三次翻译高潮。那就是东汉至唐宋的佛经翻译高潮、明末清初的科技翻译高潮和鸦片战争后至"五四"前的西方政治思想与文学翻译高潮。第三次翻译高潮中,以文学翻译,尤其是小说翻译最为繁荣,影响也最大。

从1840年至1918年,近80年,翻译小说大致可分为三个时期:

1. 1840-1894年为萌芽期

这一时期,翻译小说数量很少,有资料可查的,只发现七种翻译小说:(1) 最早的是《意拾喻言》(《伊索寓言》),系英文、中文、拼音的对照本,英国人罗伯特·汤姆译,共82则。最初发表于1840年《广东报》,后由广学会刊。(2)《谈瀛小说》(英国斯威夫特《格列佛游记》中的小人国部分)约5 000字,载《申报》1872年4月15日至18日。(3)《一睡70年》(美国华盛顿·欧文《瑞普·凡·温克尔》),约1 000余字,载《申报》1872年4月22日。(4)《昕夕闲谈》,蠡勺居士译,连载于1873年1月至1875年1月《瀛寰琐记》第3至28期,上卷31回,下卷24回,共55回。1904年,经译者删改重定,印成单行本,由文宝书局出版,署名改为吴县藜床卧读生。(5)《安乐家》,1882年画图新报馆译印。(6)《海国妙喻》(《伊索寓言》共70则),1888年天津时报馆印。(7)《百年一觉》(《回头看》)李提摩太译,1894年广学会出版。

这七种,有的是寓言(如《意拾喻言》),有的只有一个故事梗概(如《一睡70年》,只1 000余字),真正比较像样的是《昕夕闲谈》,有55回,可谓是近代第一部翻译小说。译者在《〈昕夕闲谈〉小序》中说:

> 今西国名士,撰成此书,务使富者不辱沽名,善者不必钓誉,真君子神采如生,伪君子神情毕露,此则所谓铸鼎象物者也,此则所谓照渚然犀者也。因逐节翻译之,成为华字小说,书名《昕夕闲谈》,陆续附刊,其所以广中土之见闻,所以记欧洲之风俗者,尤其浅焉者也。诸君子之阅是书者,尚勿等诸寻常之平话,无益之小说也可。

这一时期,不但翻译小说很少,还处在萌芽状态,整个翻译文学也很少。翻译较多的是公法和制造技术的书籍,如同文馆、制造局所译的书。当时流行的观点是西方的物质文明比我们强,但精神文明我们比他们优越得多,所以无须引进外来文化。统治阶级中比较开明的官僚,为了自强求富,兴办洋务事业,开始仿效西方资本主义的"船坚炮利",进行"练兵制器"活动,举

办近代军用工业以求强，创办近代民用企业以求富，所需要的是输入制造技术，不重视引进西方的学术文化。知识分子为传统思想所囿，也轻视西方文学，所以很少有人去翻译介绍外国小说，即使有几种，影响也不大。

2. 1895-1904 年为发展期

1894 年，中日甲午战争爆发，北洋水师全军覆没，中国战败。这一严酷的现实，极大地震动了全国人民，许多人开始认识到要使国家富强起来，只引进西方的技术是远远不够的，必须输入新学，必须变法。至此，整个思想界、学术界，开始进入了一个新的阶段。翻译方面也是如此。如严复，这时期先后翻译出版了赫胥黎的《天演论》(1898)、约翰·穆勒的《穆勒名学》(1899)、亚当·斯密的《原富》(1903)、斯宾塞的《群学肄言》(1903)、穆勒的《群己权界论》(1903)、孟德斯鸠的《法意》(1904)、甄克思的《社会通诠》等，系统地介绍西方的学说，影响极大。

文学翻泽，特别是小说翻译，也进入了一个新的时期。1899 年，林纾翻译的《巴黎茶花女遗事》出版，引起极大反响，译本"不胫而走"，大受读者欢迎，一时风行全国，被称为"外国《红楼梦》"，有洛阳纸贵之誉。严复有诗赞道："可怜一卷《茶花女》，断尽支那荡子肠。"接着，他又译了《英女士意色儿离鸾记》(1901)、《巴黎四义人录》(1901)、《黑奴吁天录》(1901)、《伊索寓言》(1903)、《布匿第二次战纪》(1903)、《利俾瑟战血余腥记》(1904)、《滑铁卢战血余腥记》(1904)、《英国诗人吟边燕语》(1904)、《埃司兰情侠传》(1904)。另外，曾广铨译英国哈葛德的《长生术》(1899，索隐书屋)，周桂笙译《1001 夜》(节译，1900)、杨紫驎、包天笑译哈葛德的《迦因小传》(1901，励学译编)、跛少年译英国笛福的《绝岛飘流记》(《鲁宾逊飘流记》，1902，开明书店)、戢翼翚译普希金的《俄国情史》(1903，大宣书局)、周桂笙译《新庵谐译初编》(1903，清华书局)、苏曼殊译雨果的《悲惨世界》(1904，镜今书局)、佚名译斯蒂文森《金银岛》(1904，商务印书馆)等等。

值得注意的是，这一时期的翻译小说，出现了一些新品种，如政治小说、科幻小说和侦探小说。这几种小说，在我国的传统小说是没有的，译者把它们介绍进来，给读者以耳目一新之感，很受大家欢迎。

首先是政治小说。梁启超 1898 年在《清议报》上发表《译印政治小说序》，大力鼓吹政治小说，他说：

> 在昔欧洲各国变革之始，其魁儒硕学，仁人志士，往往以其身之所经历，及胸中所怀，政治之议论，寄之于小说。于是彼中辍学之子，黉塾之暇，手之口之，下而兵丁，而市侩、而农氓、而工匠、而车夫马卒、而妇女、而童孺、靡不手之口之。往往每一书出，而全国之议论为之一变。彼美、英、德、法、奥、意、日本各国政界之日进，而政治小说，为功最高焉。

梁启超不但从理论上提倡，而且身体力行，亲自翻译日本柴四郎的《佳人奇遇》(1901，商务印书馆)。在他的带动下，许多译者也纷纷翻译政治小说，随后，陆续翻译过来的有矢野文雄的《经国美谈》(1902，商务印书馆)、末广铁肠的《香中梅》(1903，尊业书局)、《美国独立记演义》(1903，《大陆》本)、《游侠风云录》(1903，明权社)、《瑞西独立警史》(1903，译书汇编社)、《政海波澜》(1903，作新社)等等。翻译政治小说，是为了配合维新改良运动，是借"说部""发表政见，商榷国计”。这类作品，对于启发群众觉悟，增强民族意识，培养爱国主义精神是起到积极作用的。

其次是科幻小说。我国科学落后，在以往的小说中，没有这一类作品。这些作品的译入，扩大了中国读者的视野，增强了读者特别是青少年读者的阅读兴趣，所以颇受欢迎。这时期翻译的科幻小说有凡尔纳的《八十日环游记》（薛绍徽译，1900，经世文社）、《海底旅行》（卢藉东译，1902，《新小说》本）、《月界旅行》（鲁迅译，1903，东京进化社）、《环游月球》（1904，商务印书馆）、荷兰达爱斯克洛提斯的《梦游21世纪》（连载于《绣像小说》第1－4号；杨德森译，1903，商务印书馆）、押川春浪的《空中飞艇》（海天独啸子译，二册，1903，明权社）、《千年后的世界》（天笑译，1904，群学社）、井上园子的《星球游行记》（载赞译，1903，彪蒙译书局）等。

第三是侦探小说。1896、1897年间，《时务报》上连续发表了4篇英国柯南道尔的侦探小说：《英包探勘盗密约案》、《记伛者复仇事》、《继父诳女破案》、《呵尔唔斯缉案被戕》（1899，索隐书屋刊《新译包探案》收入此4篇）。1902年《新小说》杂志上设“侦探小说”专栏，登载侦探小说《离魂病》（披发生译述）、《毒药案》（无歆羡斋主译述）、《毒蛇圈》（法国鲍福著，上海知新主人译）。1903年《绣像小说》第4号起，连续刊载《华生包探案》：《哥利亚司考得船案》、《银光马案》、《孀妇匿女案》、《墨斯格力夫礼典案》、《书生被骗案》、《旅居病夫案》。其他出版的侦探小说还有：《泰西说部丛书之一》（柯南道尔著，黄鼎、张在新合译，1901）、《续译华生包探案》（1903，商务印书馆，此即《绣像小说》上刊载的6篇的结集）、《福尔摩斯再生案》（奚若译，1903年刊第1－3册，1900年刊第4册）、《唯一侦探谭四名案》（嵇长康，吴万邕合译，1903，文明书局）、《法国地利花奇案》（1903，江西尊业书馆译印）、《侦探谭》（冷血译，4册，1903-1904，时中书局）、《毒美人》（美乐林司郎治著，佚名译，1904，《东方杂志》本）、《侦探新语》（索公译，8篇，1904年，昌明公司）等等。

这一时期的翻译小说比上一时期有了很大发展，不但数量增加，而且品种增多，为以后翻译小说进一步发展，打下了基础。

3. 1905-1918年为鼎盛期

这一时期翻译小说有了很大的发展，据统计数字表明，约有1 000种，大大超过了前两个时期的总和。不但翻译小说的数量有了很大增加，而且翻译小说的品种更为完备。如短篇小说的大量涌现，虚无党小说、侦探小说热的出现，翻译质量明显提高，世界名著显著增多等等。到了“五四”前数年，翻译文体又鲜明地呈现出向新文学演变的趋势。

促使本时期翻译小说繁荣的原因是多方面的。(1) 这时，资产阶级民主革命运动进入了新阶段，形势的发展鼓舞了中国人民，使大家更迫切地要求输入西方文化，以反对封建专制主义，这就促进了翻译小说的繁荣。(2) 经过前两个阶段，翻译小说这一文学样式，已在中国的土地上生根，读者已习惯于这种读物，而译者也积累了经验，这就为大规模地译入翻译小说准备了条件。(3) 这一时期文艺报纸、文学刊物大量涌现，也是造成本时期翻译小说繁荣的又一原因。据统计，1872-1918年，有文学期刊132种，1905年以前创刊的只有《瀛寰琐记》（1872）、《新小说》（1902）、《绣像小说》（1903）、《新新小说》（1904）等10种，而1905年以后创刊的有122种。这些文学期刊，一般都刊载翻译小说，有的还以刊载翻译小说为主，这些杂志中，较为著名的有《小说世界》（1905）、《新世界小说社报》（1906）、《月月小说》（1906）、《小说林》（1907）、《竞立社小说月报》（1907）、《中外小说林》（1907）、《小说七日报》（1908）、《新小说丛》（1908）、

《扬子江小说报》(1909)、《小说时报》(1909)、《小说月报》(1910)、《自由杂志》(1913)、《游戏杂志》(1913)、《民权素》(1914)、《中华小说界》(1914)、《小说丛报》(1914)、《礼拜六》(1914)、《繁华杂志》(1914)、《小说海》(1915)、《小说新报》(1915)、《小说大观》(1915)、《青年杂志》(1915、第二年改名为《新青年》)、《小说画报》(1917)等等。其他有些综合性杂志及社会科学杂志、也有刊载翻译小说的。这许多阵地,为发表翻译小说创造了条件。(4) 留学生增多,使得翻译工作者队伍扩大。1905 年以后,出国留学的人数日渐增多,尤其是赴日留学的人数增加得更多,如 1905 至 1906 年之间,留日学生竟创下 8 000 人以上的纪录。留日学生之所这样多,一方面是由于当政者认为日本是君主立宪制,和他们的要求相符合。另一方面,客观上日本离中国近,费用省,如去日本的旅费,每人仅需 60－70 日元,而去美国则需 300－400 两;在日本的起居饮食,每年只需 250－300 日元,而在西洋,则岁需 1 500 两左右。这些留学生中的许多人,如苏曼殊、鲁迅、周作人、伍光建、戢翼翚等等,后来都成了翻译家,积极参加小说的翻译工作。(5) 广大读者群的形成,是翻译小说繁荣的又一重要条件。与过去不同,这时翻译小说的读者群大为扩大,这些读者,包括旧知识分子、新知识分子和市民。旧知识分子中的相当一部分人,除了旧学以外,也开始接触新学,阅读翻译小说。学堂的设立,造就了一大批新知识分子(包括在校学生),他们是翻译小说的忠实读者。而资本主义的发展、大中城市的繁荣,形成和扩大了市民阶层,市民中稍有文化者,也阅读书报杂志,阅读翻译小说。在商品经济的社会里,书籍杂志也是种商品,既然有这样广阔的市场。那么,它的繁荣是必然的。所以,广大读者群的形成、读者的需求,促成了翻译小说的进一步繁荣。

近代翻译小说,为"五四"以后翻译小说的新发展作了准备,是中国翻译发展史中的一个重要阶段。

二

近代翻译小说在发展过程中,具有下列特点:

1. 由意译(介绍故事梗概,有所删节,甚至有所增添)逐渐向直译(忠实于原著)发展

最初翻译外国小说,只介绍故事梗概,如《一睡 70 年》,只有 1 000 多字的梗概。许多人翻译长篇小说,主要是译介作品的主要情节,介绍作品完整的故事,把主要情节之外的副线或一些插入段落删去。这里明显可以看出是受了传统小说的影响,让读者听(看)一个有头有尾的完整故事,凡与这一故事无关的细节,尽行删除。至于删去景物描写和人物的心理描写,那更是普遍现象。所谓"译意不译词",颇为大家所信奉。又由于许多翻译家本身就是作家,在翻译作品时,不免有所"创造",常常添枝加叶,增加一些内容,如包天笑译《馨儿求学记》时,插进数节家事。苏曼殊译《悲惨世界》时,增添许多内容。吴研人把原译文仅 6 回的《电术奇谈》敷衍成 24 回,"改用俗语,冀免翻译痕迹",原有人名地名"经译者一律改过,凡人名皆改为中国习见之人名字眼,地名皆用中国地名",更"间有议论谐谑等,均为衍义者插入,为原译所无",实际上是半译半作。所谓"译述",是又译又述,成为一时的风气。随着小说地位的提高和译作的风行,翻译家对翻译工作也认真严肃起来,忠实于原著或基本上忠实于原著才成为风气,许多作品都能不失原著内容、风格,翻译的质量也明显提高。

2. 由文言逐渐向白话发展

当时翻译小说，大都用文言，不但林译小说是用古文翻译，其他许多作家也用文言翻译。这在当时是不足为奇的，有其历史原因。那时社会上通行的是文言(特别是在知识界)，而小说的读者大部分是知识分子，只有用文言翻译小说，才会被他们接受。但是，用文言翻译小说，在传播上必然受到一定限制，因为艰深的文字，很难在初通文字的读者中流传。为了在更大范围内传播，于是翻译家就用一些浅近的文体进行翻译。这种浅近的文体，介于文言和白话之间。后来，一些有识之士更大力提倡白话文。早在1887年黄遵宪就指出："盖语言与文字离则通文者少，语言与文字合则通文者多"；梁启超也注意文体的改革，他曾对人说："俗语文体之流行，实文学进步之最大关键也，各国皆尔，吾中国亦应有然。"1898年，裘廷梁发表著名论文《论白话为维新之本》，明确提出"崇白话废文言"的口号，系统地论述了推行白话的必要性，认为"有文字为智国，无文字为愚国；识字为智民，不识字为愚民：地球万国所同也。独吾国有文字而不得为智国，民识字而不得为智民"，其原因乃是"文言之为害"。他还详细论证了白话有"八益"。另一白话文运动的先驱者陈子褒也著文提倡白话文。在大家的倡导下，白话文运动迅速开展起来，白话报纸纷纷创刊，白话教科书、白话通俗读物大量印行。在翻译界，也用白话翻译小说。有的翻译家如周桂笙、周瘦鹃，既用文言，也用白话翻译小说，有的翻译家如吴梼、伍光建，基本上用白话翻译小说。后来，用白话翻译的人越来越多，白话译文的水平也日渐提高，到了"五四"前夕，一些翻译家的白话译文已相当流畅了，这为"五四"以后全面使用纯正的白话打下了基础。

3. 名著逐渐增多

早期的翻译，名家名作较少，二三流的作家作品较多。这是因为翻译家只注重作品的情节，为了向读者讲述故事，或者只着眼于改良群治，为了向读者进行宣传；也是因为翻译家对外国文学了解不多及受自身对作品的鉴赏能力的限制。所以，在选择翻译的底本时，标准不高，要求不严，著名作家的作品就很少翻泽。随着译者对外国文学了解的增多、艺术鉴赏能力的提高，许多名家名作才陆续介绍进来。陈平原曾作过一个统计，从1899年至1916年的翻译出版20部长篇小说中，1904年以前的只有3部，1905年至1916年的有17部，作者有司各特、笛福、斯威夫特、莱蒙托夫、大仲马、狄更斯、欧文、雨果、契诃夫、托尔斯泰、屠格涅夫等，作品如《鲁滨逊飘流记》、《格列佛游记》、《一千零一夜》、《当代英雄》、《三个火枪手》、《老古玩店》、《见闻杂记》、《大卫·科波菲尔》、《第六病室》、《海上劳工》、《93年》、《复活》、《春潮》等。以上说的是完整的长篇小说，还不包括节译本，也不包括短篇小说。如果连同节译本和短篇小说一并计算，那么，外家名作数字是很可观的。名家名作的增多，标识着翻译水平的提高，而且对读者了解世界文学、提高文学素养，是大有好处的。

4. 短篇小说翻译的增多

1905年以前，翻译小说以中长篇为主，短篇的很少，只有陈匪石译的《最后一课》(1903)、鲁迅译的《哀尘》(1903)、陈景韩译的《义勇军》(1904)等少数几种。1905年以后，短篇小说逐渐增多，不但翻译介绍了美国的马克·吐温、波兰的显克微支、英国的司各特的短篇小说，而且在翻译单篇短篇小说的基础上，还出版了短篇小说的作家专集和选集。专集如林纾和陈家麟

的托尔斯泰的两个短篇小说集:《罗刹因果录》(1915)和《社会声影录》(1917)、陈家麟和陈大镫译的契诃夫的短篇小说集《风俗闲评》上下册(1916),其中共收契诃夫的短篇小说23篇,可说是第一次较全面地介绍了契诃夫的作品。选集如周氏兄弟译的《域外小说集》一、二集,1909年出版,除收契诃夫、安特莱夫、王尔德、莫泊桑的作品外,特别注重收录东北欧的被压迫民族的作品(如波兰、芬兰、波希米亚作家的作品),有其特殊意义。鲁迅在序中说:"词致朴讷,不足方近世名人译本。特收录至审慎,译亦期弗失文情。异域文术,自此始入华土。"在选择的慎重、对原著的忠实上,这种严肃的态度确是独树一帜。此书虽只卖出21部,影响不大,但意义是深远的。另一种是周瘦鹃翻译的《欧美名家短篇小说丛刊》1－3集,1917年出版,收14国47家的作品,其中有一册专收英、美、法以外的,像荷兰、西班牙、瑞士、芬兰等国的作品。这一译本,曾得到教育部嘉奖,也颇受鲁迅称赞,誉之为"昏夜之微光,鸡群之鸣鹤"。

5. 专业翻译家的出现

近代翻译小说的译者,一般都有各自的职业,如作家、编辑、留学生等等,很少有专门以翻译为职业的。后来才出现以翻译为职业,或以翻译为主要职业的专业翻译家,如吴梼、伍光建等等。专业翻译家的出现,说明人们对翻译的作用认识有了提高,翻译家受到人们尊重。专业翻译家的出现,使译作的水平有所提高,他们专心致志从事翻译工作,翻译作品时,反复推敲,精益求精,为近代翻译事业作出了很大贡献。

三

中国近代小说在发展过程中,受到两方面的影响,一方面是受传统小说的影响,另一方面是受外来小说的影响。而后一种影响,是过去所没有的。下面简略地叙述一下在域外小说影响下,近代小说发生的变化。

1. 在域外小说影响下,文学观念起了变化

在中国的传统观念中,小说历来被视为小道,是不登大雅之堂的,处于文学的边缘地位,甚至被排斥在文学之外。到了近代,由于康有为、严复、夏曾佑,特别是梁启超的提倡和鼓吹,提出"小说界革命"的口号,重新估价小说的地位和作用,认为"仅识字之人,有不读'经',无有不读小说者。故'六经'不能教,当以小说教之;正史不能入,当以小说入之;语录不能喻,当以小说喻之;律例不能治,当以小说治之";"夫说部之兴,其入人之深,行世之远,几几出于经史之上,而天下之人心风俗,遂不免为说部之所持";"欲新一国之民,不可不先新一国之小说";"小说为文学之最上乘也";把小说提高到极重要的地位。更加上域外小说的大量输入,使人们的文学观念起了变化,不再把小说视为低下的文学样式,而和诗文同等看待,甚至看得比诗文还高。不但一般知识分子积极从事小说的翻译和创作,连那些饱学之士,也着手小说的翻译和创作。文学观念的转变,大大促进了小说创作的发展,出现了中国历史上少有的小说高潮。

2. 在域外小说的影响下,小说的题材有了扩展

中国传统小说多的是人情小说、神魔小说、侠义公案小说、历史小说、狭邪小说。随着域外小说的传入,政治小说、科幻小说、侦探小说相继介绍进来,即使是外国的言情小说,也比中国的人情小说更丰富多彩。这给中国作家以很大影响，使他们大开眼界。在外国小说的影响下，小说创作的题材有所扩展，作家们不仅学写政治小说、科幻小说和侦探小说，更重要的是，学习外国作家把视线转向下层社会，去描写普通人的日常生活，使小说的题材更加多样化，由此，出现了五彩缤纷的局面，这是中国历史上从来没有过的。

3. 在域外小说影响下，小说的表现手法、表现技巧有所创新

中国的长篇小说，由说书演变而来，在长期的发展过程中程式化了，形成了固定的模式，如章回体、回目诗、“话说”、“欲知后事如何，且听下回分解”，描写人物，形容美丑，也是千篇一律的词句，也很少景物描写，叙事方式则是全知叙事等等。最初，翻译外国小说时，也还是套用中国旧小说的模式，如分章分回、代拟回目、删去景物描写和心理描写，讲些套语套话；创作小说时，更是沿用中国旧小说的模式。到后来，翻译小说逐渐忠实于原著，不轻易删改，尽量体现原作的风格。而在创作上，则努力向外国小说学习，吸取外国小说的种种表现手法、表现技巧，出现了不分章分回、没有回目诗的中、长篇小说（如苏曼殊的小说），出现了倒叙的表现手法（如吴趼人的《九命奇冤》），也出现优美的景物描写（如刘鹗的《老残游记》），使中国的小说形式和世界的小说形式相接近。

4. 在域外小说影响下，典型人物的塑造、人物心理描写等方面，也都起了变化

由于中国古典小说表现手法的程式化，小说在塑造典型人物时，也不够多样化，更缺少人物的心理描写。域外小说艺术上的多样化，给中国作家以很大启示。在外国小说潜移默化的影响下，中国作家也学习外国小说塑造典型人物的方法（如曾朴的《孽海花》），学习外国小说心理描写的方法（如吴趼人的《恨海》），使中国的小说更丰富多彩。

5. 在域外小说的影响下，小说语言有了变化

小说语言，是小说创作的重要组成部分，语言的变革，是小说变革的重要方面。中国近代小说在外国小说的影响下，小说语言起了极大变化。一是由文言逐渐变为白话。起初是文言为主，白话较少，逐渐发展成为文白并存，后来白话逐渐增多，文言相对减少，为“五四”后全面提倡白话文作了准备。一是新名词的输入。这首先得益于翻译小说，先是在翻译小说中出现许多新名词，然后在创作小说中也有了新名词。一是句式的变化，如欧化语法（包括日本式的语法）、倒装句等等。一是标点符号的使用。中国原来只有句读，没有标点。标点符号刚输入时，还遭到一些人的反对和讥笑（如吴趼人），但随着翻译小说的大量流行，标点符号也为大家所接受，从而广泛地使用起来。

总之，外国小说给近代小说创作以多方面的影响，使近代小说引起变革。当然，中国小说彻底的变革，至“五四”以后才完成；但在从传统小说至现代小说的变化过程中，近代小说的变革，起着过渡的作用、桥梁的作用，是整个变革过程所不可缺少的。

选文三　The Theatre Translator as a Cultural Agent: A Case Study

Christine Zurbach

导　言

本文《戏剧译者作为文化代理：一个案例研究》选自 *Agents of Translation* (2009)一书。作者克里斯汀·哲巴齐(Christine Zurbach)是葡萄牙埃武拉大学(Universidade de évora, Portugal)教授、戏剧翻译博士(1997)，翻译和戏剧研究专家，著有《1975 至 1988 葡萄牙戏剧翻译与实践》(*Tradução e Prática do Teatro em Portugal de 1975 a 1988*, Lisboa, Colibri, 2002)。

选文描述了从 1975 年到 80 年代末由葡萄牙文化代理公司——埃武拉文化中心(CCE)——一群戏剧译者，在负责葡萄牙文化部 1975 年设立的戏剧翻译项目所发挥的重要作用。为了使这些翻译进来的剧目具有普适性，选译的都是经典作家的剧本。其中大部分是法国的剧作家，这充分显示了传统法国文化在葡萄牙的在场性。其他还有德国的作家，说明 1974 年后布莱希特戏剧在葡萄牙的影响。CCE 的介入类似于佐哈尔(Even-Zohar)所说的文化规划，是戏剧和文化模式的引进，这其中也显现了 CCE 作为文化代理的一种审美取向。1974 年 4 月 25 日革命后，葡萄牙新闻审查被解除，并寻求向其他语言和文化开放。在 CCE 所代理的这一翻译项目中，剧本的遴选等同于葡萄牙文化部在戏剧和艺术创新上的选择。这时期的剧本翻译大多与 1975 年后一些有重大影响力的剧院相关，尤其是一些新组建不久的剧院，在 CCE 的规划下，这些剧院不断地排练和演出这些翻译过来的剧本，从而在葡萄牙促成了一场去中心化的文化运动。

1. Introduction

The understanding of the role of translation and translators in societies and cultures has been the main aim of Translation Studies, which, confronted by the complexity of the phenomenon, continually reformulates its methodological and theoretical approaches (Delabastita, 2003). Nevertheless, the area of theatre translation has remained a poor cousin, despite the important studies on consecrated authors like Shakespeare (Delabastita & D'hulst, 1993), particular cases such as that of theatre in Québec (Brisset, 1990), or relations between text and mise en scène (Bassnett & Lefevere, 1998). More studies are needed in this area, especially on the position of the translator as participant in the artistic practice of the theatre and as theatrical specialist. Though Translation Studies has emphasized "the importance of placing the translator at the centre of thinking about translation" (Delisle, 1998: 1) or the historical role of translators (Baker, 1998: XIV) and contemporary training of translators (Gile, 2005), the role of the theatre translator has remained little known or even invisible (Venuti, 1995) despite the fact that the translator often plays a central role in the formation of company repertoires, not only as a translator but also as a cultural agent, as we shall see in this case study.

The study has been inspired by the approach developed by Anthony Pym, who has considered the role of the translator from the point of view of the concept of *frontier*, linked to those of negotiation and interculturality (2000). Pym, by considering in his first works (1998) the translators as agents who work in the space of the relations between languages and cultures, places his proposal in the area of those studies which are concerned with the cultural aspect of translations. In this way, translators will be a kind of intermediaries between cultures as their practice is that of mediation in the same way as are members of other professions. He here joins Even-Zohar, who insists on the specificity of their role in the importation and transfer of cultural repertoires: "(...) we should give much more attention to the *translators*, not only to their products, recognizing they may often produce much more than texts" (1998: 367).

Aware of the complexity of the phenomenon, our point of departure will be that of the researcher, who, wondering about the place of translation in (and through) the process of theatrical communication, does not merely examine the translated texts, but also examines the typology and limits of the tasks of the translators, the actions to which the translated texts are linked, and the institutional relations of the production and use of theatrical repertoires for cultural goals. Our empirical observation of the practice of theatre translation does in fact show us that it can contribute to the constitution or the transformation of what Even-Zohar calls the "cultural repertoire" (1997) of the target culture. Thus in the totality of the mode of production of the special repertoire which is the corpus to be studied, from its selection to its reception, it is possible to observe how, in a given socio-historical context, translation may correspond to an importation of institutionalized cultural practices, in the sense that Even-Zohar speaks of *transfer* (1997), thanks to a form of intervention which will engage the translator in various moments and levels of the process. In this case study, we will see how a concept of "public service theatre," as was experienced in France from the 1950s, was explicitly made to function, and how this project depended on a particular dramatic corpus that was translated and imported.

2. A Case Study: An Institutional and Cultural Project

Our case study will examine the professional production of plays by a cultural agent, the company of the évora Cultural Centre (CCE) in Portugal, from 1975 to 1988. The CCE, working in provincial Portugal, directed their work to a local and regional public in order to give them access to cultural goods they had not previously had access to, especially theatre. The particular sources which have been used in this study should be mentioned. The theatre historian will not be surprised to learn that, in this case, as in all theatre research, the indispensable archives for all research based on an empirical knowledge of the object in question are non-existent as such. Nevertheless, elements of the history of the institution can be found in the centre of documentation and the department in charge of organizing the diffusion of the repertoire to a specific public: young professional, amateur, university, trade union and professional association theatre groups. Thus, the work carried out by the group between 1975 and 1988, that of reproducing and making known the texts as part of a systematic task of teaching and supporting theatrical work carried out by other agents, is preserved in a large number of documents of an artistic and literary nature, especially translations. On the other hand, thanks to the continuing institutional relationship of those responsible for the company with their political interlocutors, the official administrative documents have also been preserved and may be consulted. In addition, on the twentieth and twenty-fifth anniversaries of the company (1995, 2000), they were partially reproduced and made public in issue no 15/16 of the *Adágio* (1995) revue, published by the Centre in order to describe and clarify its role during this period. In fact, the care given to the preservation of the documentary memory of the work undertaken may be considered a reflection of the cultural value which it has been given.

This case seems important as it provides a particular set of circumstances where the theatre translator performs his or her function as a contracted member of an institution which is carrying out a development strategy directed at a defined target public and whose innovatory work is formulated with the help of texts which make up a theatrical repertoire. Here, translation is a decisive element in the strategy of the importation of a foreign theatrical model. It is decisive in the choice of texts but also in terms of the dramatic and aesthetic treatment which orients communication with the target audience: as it was dominated to a great extent by the Brechtian model of critical thought on reality, it was linked to the rewriting of texts, supported by interpretative choices in translation, but also by aesthetic and pragmatic orientations which influenced production. Actually, the final aim was a play based on a translated text, and it was distributed and publicized as an artistic object.

In order to better understand the issue of such an institutional relationship, which closely links translation and theatrical practice to cultural aims, we can initially detail the organization and the aesthetic and theatrical choices of the institution to which the translator we describe here is attached, and which make clear his or her role as an agent of translation, then the way the translation is connected to the socio-historical context in which their collective and individual action takes place. We shall finish by making an analysis of the type of values/norms/ "performance instructions appropriate for and applicable to particular situations" (Toury, 1995: 55) which characterize the translations themselves in terms of their reception.

Initially we shall make a brief study of the corpus of the plays performed between 1975 and 1988, which are seen in Table 1 below. This shows a high number of plays translated by the CCE, both in quantitative terms, when one compares the number of Portuguese authors to those of non-Portuguese origin, who were imported and translated, and in qualitative terms, when one situates the translated works within a dramatic and discursive profile of the group, that of a universal theatrical heritage whose survival is ensured by systematic retranslation and contemporary productions.

Table 1 Chronology of the CCE Repertory between 1975 and 1988

Season	Origin	Author	Portuguese Title
1975	France	Richard Demarcy	A Noite do 28 de Setembro
1975	US	Luis Valdez	O Soktado raso
1975	US	Luis Valdez	As duas Caras do Patrâo
1975	Germany	Bertolt Brecht	Luz nas Trevas
1975	Cermany	Rertolt Brecht	O Senhor Puntila e o seu Criado Matti
1976	France	Marivaux	O Preconceito vencido
1976	Italy	A. Beolco	Historias de Ruzante
1977	Portugal	Almelda Garrett	O Conde de Novlon
1977	Britain	Shakespeare	Medida por Medida
1977	Portugal	José Réglo	Marlo ou eu proprlo-o Outro
1978	Germany	Peter Welss	A Noite dos Visitantes
1978	Germany	Bertolt Brecht	O que diz sim O que diznão
1978	Portugal	Gil Vicente	O Velho da Horta
1979	Germany	Welsenborn	Quinze Rolos de Moedasde Prata
1979	France	Molière	Jorge Dandin
1980	Germany	Kleist	A Biha quebrada
1980	Portugal	Camões	Auto de EI-Rei Seleuco
1981	Greece	Aristophanes	A Paz
1981	Russia	Gogol	O Inspector
1981	Portugal	Almeida Garrett	Falar a verdade a mentir
1981	Italy	Goldoni	O Amante militar
1982	Germany	Tankred Dorst	A grande Imprecaçâo
1982	Germany	Karl Valentin	Comoé que ele sechama?
1982	Germany	O. Horvath	A Fé a Esperança e a Caridade
1982	Portugal	Gil Vicente	Auto da India
1983	Portugal	sá de Miranda	Os Estrangeiros
1983	France	Prosper Mèrimée	O Céneo Inlerno
1983	France	Michel Vinaver	Dissidente、sō
1984	France	Anonymous	Amorosos
1984	Portugal	Passos/Barradas	Sem Alterações-As Alterações de Évora de1637
1984	Russia	Tchekhow	o canto do cisne/os maleficias do tabalo
1985	Britain	Ben Jonson	O Alquimista
1985	Portugal	Raul Brandão	O Doido e a Morte
1985	France	Corneille	Horàcio
1985	Portugal	Gil Vicente	Farsa de Inés Pereira
1985	Portugal	E. J. Viegas	O segundo Marinheiro
1986	Spain	Lope de Rueda	Cinco"Pasos"de Lope de Rueda

(Continued)

Season	Origin	Author	Portuguese Title
1986	France	Molière	A Escola das Mulheres
1987	France	Marivaux	O Legado
1987	Portugal	A. Prestes	Auto da Ciosa
1987	Portugal	Ernesto Leal	Afonso III
1987	Nor way	Henrik Ibsen	solness o Construtor
1988	Portugal	Gil Vicente	O Juiz da Beira
1988	France	Arthur Adamov	M. o Moderado

The reasons for such a repertoire by those responsible for the artistic side of the CCE is justified by the specific need to support the cultural and political policy of the CCE, both in terms of "a strategy aiming at the development of the Portuguese theatre, the surpassing of endemic backwardness, and the gestation of consummated facts which introduce the notion of *public service*(...)" (Repertórios, 1995), this last expression clearly pointing to a demand of the theatrical agents from the political system of the period. Greatest importance is given to a theatre of the text if one can judge by the statement according to which "the quality of the verb is the strongest instrument which this art has at its disposal" (Repertórios, 1995). It is not surprising then that the heritage of the "classics," associated with the literary canon, has a very important place. It is represented by famous authors like Shakespeare and Molière, through whom directors elaborate a discourse founded on their historical value, criticizing the essentialist and universalistic discourses which accompany them through a critical perception of their meaning for a contemporary usage. The choice of Portuguese authors shows the same dramatic coherence and privileges certain authors. Gil Vicente, from the beginning of the 16th century, is the most important point of reference in Portuguese drama, and his reception undergoes revision. Until 1974 his work had been ideologically manipulated by the Salazar regime. The work of Almeida Garrett represents romantic irony and the will to reform society. The discourse of contemporary texts also reflects a critical vision of history and of society that the production, inspired by Brecht's work, develops. These aesthetic choices affect the translation norms of the group. In Portugal in 1975, both as a company and a cultural agent, CCE was a new model whose creation was favoured by the novelty of the context of its creation. It was actually the only artistic project formally set up by a decree of the Secretary of State of Social Communication, to which it reported to and sent its accounts. It was basically made up of some 15 members, actors and directors, technicians and administrative workers. This structure, subsidized by the Ministry of Culture and organized according to the norms of a company or a professional organization, was directed by an artistic director, in this case a theatre director, who had both the functions of administrative and financial manager. However, the artistic director played a decisive role in the organization of the company, and the importance given to the choice of the repertoire determined the members of the team and the distribution of the tasks according to the specificity of requirements. In actual terms, the orientation of the project was that of supporting a policy of choosing a repertoire designed to promote the universal theatrical heritage and the "appropriation of a memory which is historical and which belongs to us" (Repertórios, 1995). In particular, the repertoire of the "classics," from Portugal or other cultural and linguistic traditions, presupposes the existence of a skilled artistic team which is aesthetically coherent, and which implies a multiplicity of agents, of whom a number, especially directors and actors, are also translators, as we shall see.

The project, established in the capital of a province in the centre-south of Portugal, is closely linked to the political transformations which came about as a result of the Revolution of the Carnations, which, in April 1974, put an end to the authoritarian regime which had been inherited from the Salazar period. An exhaustive study of the circumstances in which the work of translation took place, and, as a result, those of the links between the cultural-translation agent with history and the collectivity cannot be detailed here, but it is certain that an analysis limited to a corpus of texts, which ignores the historical origins of the institution that is responsible for their production and the relationships with the site of reception, will be incomplete. These political transformations brought about important structural modifications, such as the abolition of censorship, which had great repercussions in literary and theatrical life, especially in the relationships between the literary and the artistic on one hand, and power on the other. The identification of these interferences in the theatrical field will allow us to account for the fabric of the conditions of production of the repertoire, whether they are political, institutional, economic, cultural or social, as they played a role in literary and artistic communication in this period. In terms of a systemic relationship, the artistic work of this company which was subsidized by the State is that of a situation of economic and political dependence, which is not without its own consequences for its independence. The norms adopted for its translations are, in this initial period, marked by an opening emphasizing innovation and favour foreign influences and therefore the importation of texts and their translations, but they also show very precise ideological choices. Actually, the general effort to change cultural direction after 25 April 1974, supported by the new powers, and the abolition of political censorship, thereby allowing free access to new languages, are decisive for the orientations which were adopted in the choice of authors and texts which were introduced into the repertoire and their artistic treatment (see Section 4 below). It is in these circumstances that the company is seen as a cultural agent as it was responsible for a decentralized theatrical project, and, benefiting from institutional support, had the task of developing an innovative cultural policy, which consisted of pursuing the artistic production and diffusion, outside Lisbon and the cultural centre of Portugal, of plays which are addressed to a new public in the periphery.

Finally, we should mention that the project includes a programme of theatrical and cultural training in the drama school which was attached to the company from its establishment in 1975. This theatrical training unit was in charge of the preparation of future decentralized projects of the same type, which repeated the aesthetic choices of the CCE, especially the textual corpus used in the courses and interpretation exercises which included numerous translations, chosen to correspond to the educational and cultural vision which valued the literary and theatrical heritage.

3. A Cultural Agent of the Theatre and a Translator

According to the categories proposed by Toury (1995), it is initially at the level of preliminary norms, the choice of texts, the translation policy of what was to be translated from the universal theatrical heritage, that the CCE translator made an intervention. We shall see that in the majority of cases this function was mixed with that of the artistic director who was responsible for the programme for each season as it had been established by the directors of the CCE. Thus the translator played a central role in the composition of the repertoire for each season and influenced the importation of texts coming from foreign literatures, this being the result of his or her accumulation of functions within the project itself. The texts to be translated, which were part of the artistic choices of the CCE programme, resulted in the selection, production and diffusion of the plays to be presented to the public,

Table 2　Translators of the CCE Repertoire

Author	Text (Source/Target)	Translator	Eunction in the Play
Demarcy	La Nuit du 28 septembre (A Noite do 28 de Setembro)	Teresa Mota/ CCE collective	Actors
L. Valdez	Acto (O Soldado raso)	M. Barradas	Director
L. Valdez	Acto (As duas Caras do Patrão)	L. Varela	Director
B. Brecht	Lux in Tenebris (Luz nas trevas)	M. Barradas	-----------
B. Brecht	Herr Puntila und sein Knecht Matti (O Senhor Puntila e o seu Criado Matti)	M. Barradas (1)	Director
Marivaux	Le Préjugé vaincu (O Preconceito vencido)	M. Barradas/ actors	Director/ Actors
A. Beolco	*Due diatoght di Ruzante in üngua rus-tica*, *sententiosi*, *argutie rediculosissimi*; *Pariamento de Ruzante che iera vegmáde campo*; *Bitorn* (Histórias de Ruzzante)	I. Peixoto	Director
K Yacine	La Poudre d' Intelligence (O Pó da Inteligência)	L. Varela (1)	Director
Shakespeare	Measure Ior Measure (Medida por Medida)	M. Barradas	Director
Peter Weiss	Nacht mit Gasten (A Noite dos Visitantes)	M. Barradas	Director
Shakespeare	Measure for Measure (Medida por Medida)	M. Barradas	Director

(Continued)

Author	Text (Source/Target)	Translator	Eunction in the Play
Peter Weiss	Nacht mit Gasten (A Noite dos Visitantes)	M. Barrradas	Director
B. Brecht	Der Jasager/der Neinsager O que diz sim/O que diz não	L. Varela (1)	Director
G. Weisenborn	Fünfzehn Schnüre Geld (Quinze Rolos de Moedas de prata)	Clara Joona	Actor
Molière	George Dandin ou le mari confondu (Jorge Dandin)	E. Mora Ramos	Director
Kleist	Der zerbrochene Krug (A Bilha quebrada)	L. Varela (1)	Director
Aristophanes	Erench transl. La Paix (A Paz)	M. Barradas/L Varela	Directors
Cogol	Port. transl (O Inspector)	L. Varela (1)	Director
Goldoni	L'Amante militar (O Amante militar)	L. Silva Melo (2)	------------
T. Dorst	Grosse Schmahrede an der Stadtmauer (A grande Imprecação)	M. Barradas	Director
K. Valentin	Lachkabinelt (Comoé que ele se chama?)	"Cornucopia"(2)	Theatre Company of Lishon
Horvath	Glaube、Liebe、Hoffnung (A Fé, a Esperança e a Caridade)	L. Varela (1)	Director
Mèrimèe	Le Ciel et I'Enfer (O Céueo Inferno)	E. Mora Ramos	Director
Vinaver	Dissident, ilva sans dire (Dissidente, so)	L. Varela (1)	Director
Anonymous	Le Badin qui se loue. Un amoureux. Le Cuvier. (Amorosos)	V. Lemos (2)	Director (invited)
Tcheknov	Port. Transl. (O Canto do Cisne) Os Maleficios do Tabaco	(3)	------------
Ben Jonson	The Alchemist (O Alquimista)	L. Varela (1)	Director
Comeille	Horace (Horàcio)	M. Barradas	Director
Lope de Rueda	Pasos (Cinco"Pasos")	Gil Nave/ A. Passos	Director/ Actor
Molière	L'École des Femmes (A Escola das mulheres)	L. Varela (1)	Director
Marivaux	Le Legs (O Legado)	L Varela (1)	Director
Ibsen	Bygmester Solness (Solnesso Constructor)	L. Varela	Director
Adamov	M. le Modéré (M. o Moderado)	A. Maia Lobo (2)	------------

(1) Translation accompanied by the dramatic work of the author of this study, which implies the confrontation between the original of the translated text and an intermediary text.

(2) Does not belong to the CCE.

(3) Translation previously published by a commercial publishing company.

and all these tasks were coordinated and guided by the artistic direction team, which was made up by the director and his or her close collaborators, who were also the directors and authors of plays and who carried out the preliminary translation work, as we shall now see.

Among the tasks which support the work of artistic production and diffusion of the theatrical repertoire, the basis of the annual programme, the most decisive action in terms of the work of reproduction was that of the programming, the choice of works for the repertoire to be presented to the public. In addition to a number of original texts in Portuguese, the large number of translations reflected one of the essential characteristics of this procedure. Founded on a foreign model of theatre policy, which had been elaborated in France in the post-war period and which aimed at the promotion of decentralization of the theatre, established by political power as a programmed and structured strategy, this orientation was based on a repertoire of "popular" theatre, thus called as it is directed to large numbers of people and no longer to an elite, and should be addressed to a public whose loyalty should be guaranteed by various forms of organization of their relationship to the institution.

In addition, these text choices are associated with a reception aesthetics which was based on various procedures inspired by Brecht, in particular a reading of the theatrical fable according to a work of critical distancing based on the relationship between the actor and the mise en scène. This theatre policy, which was especially developed by the TNP of Jean Vilar in the 1960s, was familiar in Portugal in the professional theatrical milieu, which looked for ways of renewing theatrical practice. But it was only with the CCE that it became a cultural practice which was suitable for the Portuguese context, and its establishment coincided with a period of political and historical changes. The translation of the repertoire was thus carried out by the directors and actors as a coherent step in the development of the aesthetic and ideological orientation: that of the task of a dynamic cultural project developed by this group of professional actors, working with experimental theatre at a local level, part of a decentralization of the theatre.

Let us finally say that, in the case of translation as it is practiced in the CCE, the terminology turned out to be unsuitable, as when we speak of translators as agents who are exercising the profession of translator in the ordinary sense of the term, this term hardly corresponds to the socio-professional reality which the term here refers to. This form of translation is an action which is carried out by those who produce it as a function of an artistic programme. It is also transversally a part of the sequence of the actions which are necessary for the theatrical practice of the company. In reality, this position, which is relatively uncommon, shows the researcher how unstable the term translation may be and relativizes its use in function of the variety of observable practices. It should also be added that the target text, before being rehearsed and performed, is presented to those involved in the play, who are also able to contribute to the final version and introduce modifications. These usually come about as a result of the criteria of the acceptability of the text, its "theatricality" or speakability, and these alterations may also be made during rehearsals.

This will have an effect on the text of arrival, now submitted to a norm which privileges usage and the speaking of the text on the stage.

4. The Translated Texts and the Choice of the Translators

In this section, we shall examine the choice of the translators in the process of the production of the texts which were used, whether in the case of the directors or the actors. The following table shows a series of characteristics which are important for this study, attempting to combine elements of a linguistic and generic nature with the programmatic elements which have just been described here so we can see the extent of the importance of socio-cultural norms on the choice of works to be translated.

Table 3 Translations Performed by CCE between 1975 and 1988

Author	Translated Title	Source Text(s)
R. Demarcy	La Nuit du 28 septembre (A Noite do 28 de Setembro)	French original written for the inauguration of CCE, published in 1976
Luiz Valdez	Acto (O Soldado raso)	French tr. in *Travall Tnéâtral*, Ⅷ, 1972: "Simple soldat;" no translator's name; original "Actos b Luiz Valdezyel Teatro Campesino." Cucaracha Press, 1971, Fresno, California
Luiz Valdez	Acto (As duas Caras do Patrão)	French tr. ibid: "Les deux visages du patron"
B. Brecht	Lux in Tenebris (Luz nas Trevas)	French tr. in *Théâtre compiet*, Ⅺ, L'Arche, 1968: "Lux in Tenebris;" tr. Gilbert Badia
B. Brecht	Herr Puntila und sein Knecht Matti (O Senhor Puntilae o seu criado Matti)	French tr. in *Théâtre compiet*, Ⅳ, L'Arche, 1972: "Maitre Puntilaet son valet Matti;" rt. Michel cadot. German original: "Herr Puntila und sein Knecht Matti", in *Stücke*, Ⅸ, Suhrkamp Verlag, 1965
Marivaux	Le Prèjugé vaincu (O preconceito vencido)	Erench original: "Le Prèjugé vaincu", in *Théá tre complet*, Ⅱ, éd E. Deloffre, Garnier, 1968
A. Beolco	*Due dialoghi di Ruzante in ingua rustica*, *sententiosi*, *angutie rediculosissmi*; *Parlamento de Ruzante che iena vegnu de campa*: *Bilora* (Historias de Ruzzante)	French tr.; éd L'Arche
K. Yacine	La Poudre d'Intelligence (O poda Inteligéncia)	French original: "La Poudre d'intelligence," in *Le Cercle des Représailles*, Seuil, 1959
Shakespeare	Measure for Measure (Medida por Medida)	French tr.: "Mesure pour Mesure" by Erançois Victor Hugo, Garnier, 1964
Peter Weiss	Nacht mit Gasten (A Nolite dos Visitantes)	French tr. Armand Jacpb: "La Nuit des Visiteurs," éd. Seuil German original: "Nacht mit Gasten", Suhrkamp Verlag, 1963

(Continued)

Author	Translated Title	Source Text(s)
B. Brecht	Der lasager/der Neinsager (O que diz sim/O que diz nào)	German original: "Der lasager/der Neinsager," Suhrkamp Verlag, 1972
Weisenborn	Fünfzehn Schnüre Geld (Quinze Rolos de Moedas de prata)	French tr.: "Quinze Rouleaux dargenl", stage version by G. Jung, based on a French text by P. Grappin. Théâtre Populaire Romand. coll Répertoire, n⁰15, 1969
Molière	George Dandin ou le mari confondu (Jorge Dandin ou omarido enganado)	French original: "George Dandin oule mari confondu," in *Oeuvers complètes*. Ⅲ, Garnler-Flammarion, 1965
Kleist	Der zerbrochene Krug (A Bilha quebrada)	French/German bilingual edition; "La Cru-che cassée/Der zerbrochene Krug", Aubier, 1961, and Portuguese tr.: "A Bilha quebrada", unpublished by B. Silva for the Experimental Theatre Company of Porto, 1957
Aristophanes	French tr. La Paix (A Paz)	French tr.: "La Paix", by Marc-Jean Alfonsi. in *Théâtre complet*, I, Garnier-Flammarion, 1966
Gogol	Port Tr. (O Inspector)	Portuguese tr.: "O Inspector Geral", by Orlando Neves, Livr. Civiliz., 1968. Italian tr.: "L'Ispettore", by Renato Vecchione, Einaudi, 1978
Goldoni	*L'Amante militar* (O Amante militar)	Italian original, revised translation of Jorege Silva Melo (unpublished)
T. Dorst	Grosse Schmahrede an der Stadtmauer (A grande Imprecação diante das Muralhas da Cidade)	German original: "Crosse Schmahrede an der Stadtmauer;" Portuguese tr. by M. Barradas, published in *Teatro em Movimento*. n⁰5. now/dez. 1973
K. Valentin	Lachkabinett (Comoéque ele se chama?)	German original; translations by Teatro da Cornucópia
Horvath	Glaube、Liebe、Hoffnung (A Fè、a Esperança e a Caridade)	French tr. by Renée Saurel: "La Fol, I' Espérance et la Charité"ri Gallimard, 1967, German original, final version and variations: "Glaube、Liebe、Hoffnung," Suhrkamp Verlag, 1980
Mérimèe	Le Cielet I'Enfer (O Céueo Inferno)	French original: "Le Ciel et I'Enter", in *Theátre de Clara Galul*, Garnier-Flammarion, 1968
Vinaver	Dissident, il va sans dire (Dissident, só)	French original: "Dissident, ilva sans dire", in *Thèâtre de chambre*, L'Arche, 1978
French anonymous	Le badin qui seloue. Un amoureux. Le Cuvier (Amorosos)	French original: "Le Badin qui se loue;" "Un Amoureux;" "Le Cuvier," in *La Rarce en France de 1450a, 1550*, texts collected by A. Tissier, CDU-Sedes, 1976
Tchekhow	O Canto do Cisne Os Maleficios do tabaco	Portuguese tr.: "6 Peças em un acto," Portu-guese version, Porto, Minotauro, 1965

(Continued)

Author	Translated Title	Source Text(s)
Ben Jonson	The Akhemist (O Alquimista)	French tr.: "L'Alchimiste," adapt. by Marcel Moussy, in L'Arche, 1957 Spanish tr.: "ElAlquimista", by Marcelo Cohen, Bosch, 1983 English original.: "The Alchemist", *in Three Comedies*, Penguin Books, 1983
Corneille	Horace (Horacio)	French original: "Horace," in *Thèatre complet* 1. éd. Georges Couton, Garnier Frères, 1971
L. de Rueda	Pasos(Cinco "Pasos" de Lope de Rueda)	Spanish original
Mohère	L'Ecole des Femmes (A Escola das Mulheres)	French original: "L'Ecole des Femmes." in *Oewres complètes* Ⅱ, Garnier-Flammarion 1965 Portuguese tr.: "Escola de Mulheres", by M. Valentina Trigo de Sousa, Europa-América, 1974
Marivaux	Le Legs (O Legado)	French original: "Le Legs," in *Théátre complet* Ⅱ, éd. E. Deloffre. Garnier, 1968
Ibsen	Bygmester Solness (Solnesso Construt or)	French tr.: "Solnessle Constructeur," version by Gilbert Sigaux, Gallimard, coll. théátre du monde entier, 1973
Adamov	M. le Modéré (M. o. Moderado)	French original: "M. le Modéré," in *Théátre* Ⅳ, Gallimard, 1968

The first apparent characteristic, which can easily be checked by references to the source text, is that the dominant language is French, whether it is the case of French authors or of French translations of authors from other countries. This linguistic presence of the French language has a close link to the intercultural space in which these directors/translators have been educated, and which is conducive to the circulation of ideas, between two or more languages, cultures and theatrical traditions. This is the reason for the predominance of translations from French. As most of the translators had a university level education (especially in Law, Language and Literature, History and Philosophy), French was for them a means of direct contact with ideas coming from abroad. This is partially explained by the fact that French was an obligatory second language in Portuguese schools, but also due to the dominant position of French culture in the intellectual and artistic world of this generation, which was in opposition to the Portuguese regime in the pre-1974 period. In two cases, these directors/translators obtained a scholarship in theatre studies at the L'école Supérieure du Théatre National in Strasbourg in the 1970s. These courses and residence in France enabled them to consolidate the necessary skills needed to import the theatre model of the "public service theatre," which has already been discussed, and to establish a collection of works made up of the French editions of plays, which could be used for the CCE programme (here the role of L'Arche publishing house is central). This collection, centred

around the plays and the authors of the universal drama canon, is a coherent selection, which regroups original texts in French or foreign authors in French translations or often in adaptations, and which were used as intermediary texts. We can mention the case of the reception, through their French translations, of Brecht's plays, originally written in German, or the main European authors of modernity, such as Chekhov, Ibsen and Strindberg, whose languages were not known to the Portuguese translators.

Table 4　Generic Denomination and Translation

Genre (Source-texts)	Genre (Target-text)
La Nuitdu 28 septemore-fable theatrale surla révolution portugaise	Fabula teatral
Simpie Soldat-acto oumito	Acto
Lux in Tenebris-Einakter/piecoen un acte	Not specihed
Herr Puntlla [...]-Volksstick (B. B. 27. 08. 1940) ou pièce populaire. title original du manuscrit de Wuolijoki: A Finnish Bacchus. suivie d'une version en "Salonkomodie" de "Die Sagemehlprinzessin," surle modele du conte de fée d'Andersen	peçapopular
Lepréjugé valncu-comèdie en un acte et en prose	Comèdia
Due dialoghi di Ruzante in lingua rustica, sententiosi, argutie rediculosissimi; Parlamento de Ruzante che iera vegnú de campo; Bilora-dialoghi	"Histórias do Ruzante:" "Falatório do Ruzante de volta da guerra;" "Ruzante, o Bilora;" "Oração de boas vindas do Ruzante ao Cardeal Cornaro"
La Poudre de I'Intellgence-farce	Farsa
Measure for Measure-a play called *Measure for Measue*, dark comedy	Not specified; mentioned in the program as: "uma comèdia, uma tragèdia, uma 'moralidade'?"
Nacht mit Gasten-eine Moritat/une complainte	peça popular
Der Jasager und der Neinsager-Schulopern	Peça didactica
Fünfzehn Schnüre Geld/*Quince rouleaus d'argent*-adaptation d'un opera chinois en 8 tableaux, "un drame qui est aussi une comédie"	Not specified
George Dandin-comédie-ballet	Not specified
Der zerbrochene Krug La Canche cassée-comèdie en treize scènes	Comédia
La Paix-comédie antique	Comédia
Le Rèvizor-trad Arthur Adamoy: comédie en cinq actes	As in the Portuguese former translation by Orlando Neves: comédia em 5 actos; sàtira
L'Amante millitar-commedia; comédie	Comédia
Die grosse Schmanreàe	"imprecação" as genre (in the title)
Glaube, Liebe, Hoffmang 1 *La Fof, L'Espérance et la Charité*-Ein kleiner Totentanz/Petite danse de mort en cinq tableaux	Pequena dança de Morte em cinco quadros
Le Ciel et L'Enfer-comedia du"siècle d'or," comèdie, saynète	Comédia
Dissident [...]-pièce en 12 morceaux	Peça em doze fragmentos
farces (françaises du Moyen-âge)	*Amorosos, farsas medievais*
Pieces en un acte de Tchekhoy	*Serào Tchekhor*-teatro de câmara

(Continued)

Genre(Source-texts)	Genre (Target-text)
The Alchemist / L'Alchimiste-comédie en cinq actes et en vers	Comédia
Horace-tragedie en cinq acles et en vers	Tragédia
Cinco "Rasos" de Lope de Rueta-paso	Pasos
L'Ecote des Femmes-comédie en cinq actes et en vers	Comédia
Le Legs-comèdie en un acte et en prose	Comédia
Solness-trad. de Gilbert Sigaux. o. c. : piêce en trois actes	Peça em trés actos
M. le Modèrè-clownerie	Palhaçada

This table enables us to see a further dominant characteristic of this repertoire in terms of the question of genres and translation, that of the role of comedy and the comic theatre and its variants. This genre shows the critical aspect of the theatrical art and was central to the work of the CCE, together with the dramaturgy of the epic Brechtian theatre, which has transformed theatrical practice both at the level of textual and dramatic production and at the socio-political level on which cultural projects from the 1980s onwards have been based.

But what are the choices of the directors and translations in terms of translational norms? As these texts are not directed towards publication, they are defined from the beginning by a conception of the dramatic text which depends less on their literary value than on their "theatrical potential" (Pavis, in Angenot, 1989: 97). This initial choice implies a particular and specific conception of translation, which depends on intermediary texts in French, for reasons we have already shown. In addition, the documents which have been preserved clearly show, through the large number of variants of annotated manuscripts on the texts which were distributed in the rehearsals and introduced during the production of a play, the priority which was given to a textual version which was a result of the rehearsals of the texts. The modifications privilege the initial norm of acceptability (Toury, 1995) of the translations, valuing the stage action in detriment of the verbal and literary dimension of the texts. Lexical and syntactic elements were introduced that were determined by interferences of the socio-historical context, which are always translated into contemporary Portuguese. Actually, the operational norms in the CCE translations show us that, even in a strategy based on repertory theatre, thus of texts, the theatre translator is engaged to an even greater extent in an artistic, cultural and political rather than a literary project.

According to this description, the translations, their dramaturgy, interpretation, production, and the metatexts which accompany them form a whole whose coherence comes from the translation and which confirms the systematic orientation of the adopted norms towards the adaptation of the texts for the supporting structured project aimed at theatrical innovation. Differently to the theatre they had inherited, the translators produced new translations of Molière and Shakespeare, classics such as Aristophanes, canonized authors such as Ibsen and Strindberg, and translated unpublished plays such as those of Brecht and other German authors who broke with naturalism. It is clear that the texts represent a new

poetics or dramaturgy, for which it was necessary to rely on the French model, not only because of its prestige, but also because of the similarity with the post-1945 situation in France. Translating is an essentially pragmatic action, which seems to exclude all theoretical speculation if one judges it by the small number of commentaries on the translations in programmes which accompany the plays. More utilitarian than literary, it shows the main competence of these translators, that of their skill to produce texts which can fulfill theatrical goals, both in cultural and political terms. Their work is thus an example of the intersemiotic coherence which takes into consideration the theatrical issues behind their choices. In this imported cultural model that represents innovation and change, there is an attempt to replace tradition by means of questioning a certain elitist theatre of the past and also a concept of theatrical translation. These translations are less close to the conception of translation which has been called adequate than to processes of adaptation which are connected to the circumstances of production and the diffusion of texts through performed plays and a project, which is part of a period of the transformation of the Portuguese theatre, which, from 1975, was influenced by such projects coming from young companies in provincial capitals, who used and performed the same texts translated by the CCE to develop their repertoire and reflect on changing theatrical processes.

The final characteristic to be described is the fact that these translated texts are associated with a new production aesthetics, and it is this theatrical and textual model that is the object of transfer (see above), and this is particularly visible in the revision of the reception of the so-called "classic" authors. In this repertoire, the presentation of classic works, whether of foreign or Portuguese dramatists, contains a new "reading", which comes about in the procedures of rewriting and manipulation (Lefevere, 1992) of the text as an innovatory hermeneutic paradigm. This was the case of Molière, Marivaux and Shakespeare, and German dramatists such as Kleist and Büchner, but this procedure can be equally applied to the productions of Portuguese authors such as Gil Vicente, Sá de Miranda and Almeida Garrett, who received a dramatic treatment which stressed the historical and ideological aspect of their plays and was very different to their previous sacralization, with its definite "patriotic" connotations.

5. Coherence of the Programme and of the Intervention

Thus, the translation is no longer limited to textual or linguistic elements but is rather a model of rewriting bringing about a new stage poetics, which is materialized in the reception model of older texts. When translating the literary complexity of these texts, with their linguistic, textual and cultural specificity, the translators follow certain theatrical norms. In this case, these norms privilege political engagement and intervention that will act on the target public in terms of transformation.

In order to better understand these concerns, we can refer to the well-known position of

Even-Zohar, who, following Eichenbaum, conceives of literature as a set of systemic activities, where we must not forget the historical context of the production of the translations. In our case, the translations we are examining can be seen in a similar way to original plays as part of a highly politicized period of change and rupture with the past and in an emerging theatrical discourse, which is very close to what is called a theatre of intervention. In addition, as has already been seen, though a French influence is maintained, this influence now introduces a new language to both the stage and to artistic practices, and also to the theatrical space theatre and the civic element of the theatre. Helped by an integrated or systemic approach of the translators and the contextual elements of their work, it is easy to detach and succinctly describe that which may help interpret the links between the translator, his or her work, and the wider context of the production and its reception, in other words, with the historical and cultural aspects of its practice. In actual terms, the composition of the corpus of the repertoire presented to the public in this period shows the stability of the hierarchy of the intersystemic relations between Portugal and France, which still seemed to be dominated by the cultural prestige and superiority which have been traditionally attributed to French literature as a source literature (Casanova, 1999). This fact can be seen, as we have shown, by the recourse to a large number of French works, though through the procedure of an indirect translation, using the concepts we have already described.

In this case study of the CCE, we can see translation as a linguistic practice and a rewriting, according to the terminology of André Lefevere (1992), which no longer has an apparent, or at least, an explicit, literary character. It is used for an action in society, at both regional and national levels, through diffusion in the theatre. In this form of communication, and in this particular case, the choice of the repertoire and the construction of the final theatrical object, translated, interpreted and put on stage, are *focused on* performance. Theatre translation is a complex textual and cultural practice, marked by an oscillation between two major types of functions: that of the stage and that of reading (page/stage). But the analysis of the practice of theatrical companies shows that priority is given to the essentially theatrical function of texts for the stage and performance, made up of verbal and non-verbal elements. In the case of the CCE, priority was not given to reproducing the published texts but rather to theatrical performance. For the researcher the consequences of this secondary position of the text as a literary object are somewhat negative: the documentation is unsatisfactory, and the play texts and the translations, paratextual elements, statistics, etc., are disorganized or difficult to use, as, not having been published, they are badly preserved and are found in the form of successive versions of the same text, which has been corrected and modified during the course of rehearsals. However, this fact confirms the theatrical and non-literary vocation of the texts, which, as they are printed for immediate use for rehearsals, and are out of date when they are reused by other agents. A large amount of information is omitted: clear references to the fact that they are translations, such as the name of the translator, and the fact that the translation has been made by the directors, are rarely included despite the importance of this fact for the totality of the process. It is thus necessary to examine the list of credits published in the programmes and distributed to the audience before the performances. These translations are simple photocopies, showing the lack of importance given to this document and written texts in general, which are important only for the work of the actors and rehearsals.

Nevertheless, apparently contradicting this lack of interest in the written text as cultural heritage, it is in the complementary texts that we find confirmation of this aspect of the act of translation as cultural and political intervention. From the beginning of its activities until the end of the 1980s, the CCE published a particular type of publication directed to other users. This was a further selection of plays, privileging shorter texts or those which are more accessible in technical or artistic terms. These texts are addressed to a specific target audience, theatre companies, usually directed by young people, which would potentially continue the theatrical strategy followed by CCE. Actors trained by the CCE theatre school or by members of the company who set up their own groups and adopted the existing model spread from the North to the South of Portugal (Faro, Leiria, Portalegre, Braga, Viana do Castelo ...). This process, which is based on the partial repetition of the CCE repertoire or certain of its characteristics, demonstrated the acceptance of this theatrical and cultural strategy, and it was also used by cultural agents attached to amateur theatre groups, who were looking for a new or unpublished repertoire and were sensitive to the prestige of CCE from whom they received support at different levels. The CCE texts also entered the national Portuguese circuit, thanks to their distribution by the network of amateur groups and their use by FAOJ, an official organ which promotes youth leisure activities and which replaced a similar structure from the previous regime.

6. Final Considerations

The methodological choice adopted here, concentrating on the cultural role played by the translation as it was carried out by particular translators, has led us to look for certain answers to the questions which have been raised by such a vision of translation which is beyond the classical approach, based on text comparison. Actually, as we have attempted to show, the answers which have an explicative value and clarify possible factors of casuality, are situated outside the texts themselves and are linked to the circumstances of production and the reception of the translated work. Our case study has attempted to understand the translation in function of the intended aims, the target audience and the circumstances of the work of the translator in terms of a collection of translated texts, which constitute a form of communication in a particular socio-political context aiming at an intervention in the social structure. It has attempted to account for a mode of reworking the literary text in society, in certain historical and political circumstances, and the importance of the role given to the translators, who are the cultural agents responsible for the production of texts but who are also responsible for the implantation of a conception of a living theatre, which Even-Zohar describes in the following way: "(...) I suggest that we integrate into the concept of 'goods' (and 'products') also the images projected into society by the *people* engaged in the making of repertoire, who are in the particular case of transfer agents of transfer. The labor of these agents may introduce into the network of cultural dispositions certain inclinations towards repertoires engaged by them. In other words, the new repertoire is not restricted in such cases to the items imported as goods—or not necessarily to them alone—but what plays a role in the culture is the persons, the agents themselves who are engaged in the business" (1997: 361). To conclude, we can mention the fact that, during the 1980s, the founding director of the CCE played an important role at the Ministry of Culture in preparing a new legislation for theatre on a national level, which was inspired by other countries in Europe and would help to overcome the cultural backwardness of Portugal. Though this last action was not followed up, this would justify the use here of the concept of *intercultural site*, where contact between languages and cultures takes place through translation(s). This will help us to account for the characteristics of the cultural meaning of the project of the CCE as a concrete open space where this contact has been experienced.

(Translated from the French by John Milton)

选文四　The Translators of the *Thousand and One Nights*

Jorge Luis Borges

导　言

本文《〈一千零一夜〉的译者》选自 Lawrence Venuti 所编 *The Translation Studies Reader*(2000)的第三篇。作者豪尔赫·路易斯·博尔赫斯(Jorges Luis Borges, 1899-1986)是阿根廷作家,作品涵盖多个文学范畴,包括短篇小说、短文、随笔、诗歌、文学评论和翻译文学。其中以拉丁文隽永的文字和深刻的哲理见长。他对世界文学影响巨大,被称为"作家中的作家"。

《一千零一夜》又称《天方夜谭》可谓是多作者的作品。据英文版译者伯顿和西班牙文版译者坎西诺斯·阿森斯所说,最初的系列故事在印度形成,后来传到波斯,在波斯进行了修改和丰富,并使其阿拉伯化,最后才传到了埃及。15 世纪末编撰了第一个集子。博尔赫斯认为《一千零一夜》在西方比在东方更受珍爱。柯勒律治、托马斯·德·昆西、司汤达、丁尼生、埃德加·爱伦·坡、纽曼都曾撰文盛赞它。故事套故事的结构是它的典型结构,启发了许多作家的灵感。博尔赫斯评述了《一千零一夜》的主要译本及其译者,介绍了两个法文版,两个英文版,四个德文版本。在对译者的评述中,博尔赫斯揭示了译者与译者之间的关系,论及了翻

译的忠实性问题，以及译者对原文"篡改"问题，并表达了自己的翻译思想。正如书名所示，《一千零一夜》是无穷尽的，每一个译者都会给它一个不同的版本。《一千零一夜》总是处于创造和成长之中，生生不息。

1. Captain Burton

AT TRIESTE, IN 1872, in a palace with damp statues and deficient hygienic facilities, a gentleman on whose face an African scar told its tale—Captain Richard Francis Burton, the English consul—embarked on a famous translation of the Quitab alif laila ua laila, which the roumis know by the title, *The Thousand and One Nights*. One of the secret aims of his work was the annihilation of another gentleman (also weatherbeaten, and with a dark Moorish beard) who was compiling a vast dictionary in England and who died long before he was annihilated by Burton. That gentleman was Edward Lane, the Orientalist, author of a highly scrupulous version of *The Thousand and One Nights* that had supplanted a version by Galland. Lane translated against Galland, Burton against Lane; to understand Burton we must understand this hostile dynasty.

I shall begin with the founder. As is known, Jean Antoine Galland was a French Arabist who came back from Istanbul with a diligent collection of coins, a monograph on the spread of coffee, a copy of the *Nights* in Arabic, and a supplementary Maronite whose memory was no less inspired than Scheherazade's. To this obscure consultant—whose name I do not wish to forget: It was Hanna, they say—we owe certain fundamental tales unknown to the original: the stories of Aladdin; the Forty Thieves; Prince Ahmad and the Fairy Peri-Banu; Abu al-Hasan, the Sleeper and Waker; the night adventure of Caliph Harun al-Rashid; the two sisters who envied their younger sister. The mere mention of these names amply demonstrates that Galland established the canon, incorporating stories that time would render indispensable and that the translators to come—his enemies—would not dare omit.

Another fact is also undeniable. The most famous and eloquent encomiums of *The Thousand and One Nights*—by Coleridge, Thomas De Quincey, Stendhal, Tennyson, Edgar Allan Poe, Newman—are from readers of Galland's translation. Two hundred years and ten better translations have passed, but the man in Europe or the Americas who thinks of *The Thousand and One Nights* thinks, invariably, of this first translation. The Spanish adjective milyunanochesco [thousand-and-one-nights-esque]—milyunanochero is too Argentine, milyunanocturno overly variant—has nothing to do with the erudite obscenities of Burton or Mardrus, and everything to do with Antoine Galland's bijoux and sorceries.

Word for word, Galland's version is the most poorly written of them all, the least faithful, and the weakest, but it was the most widely read. Those who grew intimate with it experienced happiness and astonishment. Its Orientalism, which seems frugal to us now, was bedazzling to men who took snuff and composed tragedies in five acts. Twelve exquisite volumes appeared from 1707 to 1717, twelve volumes that were innumerably read and that passed into various languages, including Hindi and Arabic. We, their mere anachronistic readers of the twentieth century, perceive only the cloying flavor of the eighteenth century in them and not the evaporated aroma of the Orient which two hundred years ago was their novelty and their glory. No one is to blame for this disjunction, Galland least of all. At times, shifts in the language work against him. In the preface to a German translation of *The Thousand and One Nights*, Doctor Weil recorded that the merchants of the inexcusable Galland equip themselves with a "valise full of dates" each time the tale obliges them to cross the desert. It could be argued that in 1710 the mention of dates alone sufficed to erase the image of a valise, but that is unnecessary: Valise, then, was a sub-species of saddlebag.

There have been other attacks. In a befuddled panegyric that survives in his 1921 Morceaux choisis, André Gide vituperates the licenses of Antoine Galland, all the better to erase (with a candor that entirely surpasses his reputation) the notion of the literalness of Mardrus, who is as fin de siècle as Galland is eighteenth-century, and much more unfaithful.

Galland's discretions are urbane, inspired by decorum, not morality. I copy down a few lines from the third page of his *Nights*: "Il alla droit *à* l'appartement de cette princesse, qui, ne s'attendant pas *à* le revoir, avait reçu dans son lit un des derniers officiers de sa maison." [He went directly to the chamber of that princess, who, not expecting to see him again, had received in her bed one of the lowliest servants of his household.] Burton concretizes this nebulous officier, "a black cook of loath-some aspect and foul with kitchen grease and grime." Each, in his way, distorts: the original is less ceremonious than Galland and less greasy than Burton. (Effects of decorum: in Galland's measured prose, "recevoir dans son lit" has a brutal ring.)

Ninety years after Antoine Galland's death, an alternate translator of the *Nights* is born: Edward Lane. His biographers never fail to repeat that he is the son of Dr. Theophilus Lane, a Hereford prebendary. This generative datum (and the terrible Form of holy cow that it evokes) may be all we need. The Arabized Lane lived five studious years in Cairo, "almost exclusively among Moslems, speaking and listening to their language, conforming to their customs with the greatest care, and received by all of them as an equal." Yet neither the high Egyptian nights nor the black and opulent coffee with cardamom seed nor frequent literary discussions with the Doctors of the Law nor the venerable muslin turban nor the meals eaten with his fingers made him forget his British reticence, the delicate central solitude of the masters of the earth. Consequently, his exceedingly erudite version of the *Nights* is (or seems to be) a mere encyclopedia of evasion. The original is not professionally obscene; Galland corrects occasional indelicacies because he believes them to be in bad taste. Lane seeks them out and persecutes them like an inquisitor. His probity makes no pact with silence: He prefers an alarmed chorus of notes in a cramped supplementary volume, which murmur things like: I shall overlook an episode of the most reprehensible sort; I suppress a repugnant explanation; Here, a line far too coarse for translation; I must of necessity suppress the other anecdote; Hereafter, a series of omissions; Here, the story of the slave Bujait, wholly inappropriate for translation. Mutilation does not exclude death: some tales are rejected in their entirety "because they cannot be purified without destruction." This responsible and total repudiation does not strike me as illogical: what I condemn is the Puritan subterfuge. Lane is a virtuoso of the subterfuge, an undoubted precursor of the still more bizarre reticences of Hollywood. My notes furnish me with a pair of examples. In night 391, a fisherman offers a fish to the king of kings, who wishes to know if it is male or female, and is told it is a hermaphrodite. Lane succeeds in taming this inadmissible colloquy by translating that the king asks what species the fish in question belongs to, and the astute fisherman replies that it is of a mixed species. The tale of night 217 speaks of a king with two wives, who lay one night with the first and the following night with the second, and so they all were happy. Lane accounts for the good fortune of this monarch by saying that he treated his wives "with impartiality ... " One reason for this was that he destined his work for "the parlor table," a center for placid reading and chaste conversation.

The most oblique and fleeting reference to carnal matters is enough to make Lane forget his honor in a profusion of convolutions and occultations. There is no other fault in him. When free of the peculiar contact of this temptation, Lane is of an admirable veracity. He has no objective, which is a positive advantage. He does not seek to bring out the barbaric color of the *Nights* like Captain Burton, or to forget it and attenuate it like Galland, who domesticated his Arabs so they would not be irreparably out of place in Paris. Lane is at great pains to be an authentic descendant of Hagar. Galland was completely ignorant of all literal precision; Lane justifies his interpretation of each problematic word. Galland invoked an invisible manuscript and a dead Maronite; Lane furnishes editions and page numbers. Galland did not bother about notes; Lane accumulates a chaos of clarifications which, in organized form, make up a separate volume. To be different: this is the rule the precursor imposes. Lane will follow the rule: he needs only to abstain from abridging the original.

The beautiful Newman—Arnold exchange (1861-1862)—more memorable than its two interlocutors—extensively argued the two general ways of translating. Newman championed the literal mode, the retention of all verbal singularities: Arnold, the severe elimination of details that distract or detain. The latter procedure may provide the charms of uniformity and seriousness; the former, continuous small surprises. Both are less important than the translator and his literary habits. To translate the spirit is so enormous and phantasmal an intent that it may well be innocuous; to translate the letter, a requirement so extravagant that there is no risk of its ever being attempted. More serious than these infinite aspirations is the retention or suppression of certain particularities; more serious than these preferences and oversights is the movement of the syntax. Lane's syntax is delightful, as befits the refined parlor table. His vocabulary is often excessively festooned with Latin words, unaided by any artifice of brevity. He is careless; on the opening page of his translation he places the adjective romantic in the bearded mouth of a twelfth-century Moslem, which is a kind of futurism. At times this lack of sensitivity serves him well, for it allows him to include very commonplace words in a noble paragraph, with involuntary good results. The most rewarding example of such a cooperation of heterogenous words must be: "And in this palace is the last information respecting lords collected in the dust." The following invocation may be another: "By the Living One who does not die or have to die, in the name of He to whom glory and permanence belong." In Burton—the occasional precursor of the always fantastical Mardrus—I would be suspicious of so satisfyingly Oriental a formula; in Lane, such passages are so scarce that I must suppose them to be involuntary, in other words, genuine.

The scandalous decorum of the versions by Galland and Lane has given rise to a whole genre of witticisms that are traditionally repeated. I myself have not failed to respect this tradition. It is common knowledge that the two translators did not fulfil their obligation to the unfortunate man who witnessed the Night of Power, to the imprecations of a thirteenth-century garbage collector cheated by a dervish, and to the customs of Sodom. It is common knowledge that they disinfected the *Nights*.

Their detractors argue that this process destroys or wounds the good-hearted naivete of the original. They are in error; *The Book of the Thousand Nights and a Night* is not (morally) ingenuous; it is an adaptation of ancient stories to the lowbrow or ribald tastes of the Cairo middle classes. Except in the exemplary tales of the Sindibad-namah, the indecencies of *The Thousand and One Nights* have nothing to do with the freedom of the paradisical state. They are speculations on the part of the editor: Their aim is a round of guffaws, their heroes are never more than porters, beggars, or eunuchs. The ancient love stories of the repertory, those which relate cases from the Desert or the cities of Arabia, are not obscene, and neither is any production of pre-Islamic literature. They are impassioned and sad, and one of their favorite themes is death for love, the death that an opinion rendered by the ulamas declared no less holy than that of a martyr who bears witness to the faith ... If we approve of this argument, we may see the timidities of Galland and Lane as the restoration of a primal text.

I know of another defense, a better one. An evasion of the original's erotic opportunities is not an unpardonable sin in the sight of the Lord when the primary aim is to emphasize the atmosphere of magic. To offer mankind a new Decameron is a commercial enterprise like so many others; to offer an "Ancient Mariner," now, or a "Bateau ivre" is a thing that warrants entry into a higher celestial sphere. Littmann observes that *The Thousand and One Nights* is, above all, a repertory of marvels. The universal imposition of this assumption on every Western mind is Galland's work; let there be no doubt on that score. Less fortunate than we, the Arabs claim to think little of the original; they are already well acquainted with the men, mores, talismans, deserts, and demons that the tales reveal to us.

In a passage somewhere in his work, Rafael Cansinos Asséns swears he can salute the stars in fourteen classical and modern languages. Burton dreamed in seventeen languages and claimed to have mastered thirty-five: Semitic, Dravidian, Indo-European, Ethiopie... This vast wealth does not complete his definition: it is merely a trait that tallies with the others, all equally excessive. No one was less vulnerable to the frequent gibes in Hudibras against learned men who are capable of saying absolutely nothing in several languages. Burton was a man who had a considerable amount to say, and the seventy-two volumes of his complete works say it still. I will note a few titles at random: Goa and the Blue Mountains (1851); A Complete System of Bayonet Exercise (1853); Personal Narrative of a Pilgrimage to El-Medinah and Meccah (1855); The Lake Regions of Central Equatorial Africa (1860); The City of the Saints (1861); The Highlands of the Brazil (1869); On an Hermaphrodite from the Cape de Verde Islands (1866); Letters from the Battlefields of Paraguay (1870); Ultima Thule (1875); To the Gold Coast for Gold (1883); The Book of the Sword (first volume, 1884); The Perfumed Garden of Cheikh Nefzaoui—a posthumous work consigned to the flames by Lady Burton, along with the Priapeia, or the Sporting Epigrams of Divers Poets on Priapus. The writer can be deduced from this catalogue: the English captain with his passion for geography and for the innumerable ways of being a man that are known to mankind. I will not defame his memory by comparing him to Morand, that sedentary, bilingual gentleman who infinitely ascends and descends in the elevators of identical international hotels, and who pays homage to the sight of a trunk... Burton, disguised as an Afghani, made the pilgrimage to the holy cities of Arabia; his voice begged the Lord to deny his bones and skin, his dolorous flesh and blood, to the Flames of Wrath and Justice; his mouth, dried out by the *samun*, left a kiss on the aerolith that is worshipped in the Kaaba. The adventure is famous: the slightest rumor that an uncircumcised man, a *nasráni*, was profaning the sanctuary would have meant certain death. Before that, in the guise of a dervish, he practiced medicine in Cairo—alternating it with prestidigitation and magic so as to gain the trust of the sick. In 1858, he commanded an expedition to the secret sources of the Nile, a mission that led him to discover Lake Tanganyika. During that undertaking he was attacked by a high fever; in 1855, the Somalis thrust a javelin through his jaws (Burton was coming from Harar, a city in the interior of Abyssinia that was forbidden to Europeans). Nine years later, he essayed the terrible hospitality of the ceremonious cannibals of Dahomey; on his return there was no scarcity of rumors (possibly spread and certainly encouraged by Burton himself) that, like Shakespeare's omniverous proconsul,[1] he had "eaten strange flesh." The Jews, democracy, the British Foreign Office, and Christianity were his preferred objects of loathing; Lord Byron and Islam, his venerations. Of the writer's solitary trade he made something valiant and plural: He plunged into his work at dawn, in a vast chamber multiplied by eleven tables, with the materials for a book on each one—and, on a few, a bright spray of jasmine in a vase of water. He inspired illustrious friendships and loves: among the former I will name only that of Swinburne, who dedicated the second series of *Poems and Ballads* to him—"in recognition of a friendship which I must always count among the highest honours of my life"—and who mourned his death in many stanzas. A man of words and deeds, Burton could well take up the boast of Almotanabi's *Divan*:

The horse, the desert, the night know me, Guest and sword, paper and pen.

It will be observed that, from his amateur cannibal to his dreaming polyglot, I have not rejected those of Richard Burton's personae that, without diminishment of fervor, we could call legendary. My reason is clear: The Burton of the Burton legend is the translator of the *Nights*. I have sometimes suspected that the radical distinction between poetry and prose lies in the very different expectations of readers: poetry presupposes an intensity that is not tolerated in prose. Something similar happens with Burton's work: It has a preordained prestige with which no other Arabist has ever been able to compete. The attractions of the forbidden are rightfully his. There was a single edition, limited to one thousand copies for the thousand subscribers of the Burton Club, with a legally binding commitment never to reprint. (The Leonard C. Smithers re-edition "omits given passages in dreadful taste, whose elimination will be mourned by no one;" Bennett Cerf's representative selection—which purports to be unabridged—proceeds from this purified text.) I will venture a hyperbole: to peruse *The Thousand and One Nights* in Sir Richard's translation is no less incredible than to read them in "a plain and literal translation with explanatory notes" by Sinbad the Sailor.

The problems Burton resolved are innumerable, but a convenient fiction can reduce them to three: to justify and expand his reputation as an Arabist; to differ from Lane as ostensibly as possible; and to interest nineteenth-century British gentlemen in the written version of thirteenth-century oral Moslem tales. The first of these aims was perhaps incompatible with the third; the second led him into a serious lapse, which I must now disclose. Hundreds of couplets and songs occur in the *Nights*; Lane (incapable of falsehood except with respect to the flesh) translated them precisely into a comfortable prose. Burton was a poet: In 1880 he had privately published The *Kasidah of Haji Abdu*, an evolutionist rhapsody that Lady Burton always deemed far superior to FitzGerald's *Rubáiyát*. His rival's "prosaic" solution did not fail to arouse Burton's indignation, and he opted for a rendering into English verse—a procedure that was unfortunate from the start since it contradicted his own rule of total literalness. His ear was as greatly offended against as his sense of logic, for it is not impossible that this quatrain is among the best he came up with:

A night whose stars refused to run their course,
A night of those which never seem outworn:
Like Resurrection-day, of lonesome length
To him that watched and waited for the morn.[2]

And it is entirely possible that this one is not the worst:

A sun on wand in knoll of sand she showed,
Clad in her cramoisy-hued chemisette:
Of her lips honey-dew she gave me drink,
And with her rosy cheeks quencht fire she set.

I have alluded to the fundamental difference between the original audience of the tales and Burton's club of subscribers. The former were roguish, prone to exaggeration, illiterate, infinitely suspicious of the present and credulous of remote marvels; the latter were the respectable men of the West End, well equipped for disdain and erudition but not for belly laughs or terror. The first audience appreciated the fact that the whale died when it heard the man's cry; the second, that there had ever been men who lent credence to any fatal capacity of such a cry. The text's marvels—undoubtedly adequate in Kordofan or Bûlâq, where they were offered up as true—ran the risk of seeming rather threadbare in England. (No one requires that the truth be plausible or instantly ingenious: few readers of the *Life and Correspondence of Karl Marx* will indignantly demand the symmetry of Toulet's *Contrerimes* or the severe precision of an acrostic.) To keep his subscribers with him, Burton abounded in explanatory notes on "the manners and customs of Moslem men," a territory previously occupied by Lane. Clothing, everyday customs, religious practices, architecture, references to history or to the Koran, games, arts, mythology—all had already been elucidated in the inconvenient precursor's three volumes. Predictably, what was missing was the erotic. Burton (whose first stylistic effort was a highly personal account of the brothels of Bengal) was rampantly capable of filling this gap. Among the delinquent delectations over which he lingered, a good example is a certain random note in the seventh volume which the index wittily entitles "*capotes mélancoliques*" [melancholy French letters]. The *Edinburgh Review* accused him of writing for the sewer; the *Encyclopedia Britannica* declared that an unabridged translation was unacceptable and that Edward Lane's version "remained unsurpassed for any truly serious use." Let us not wax too indignant over this obscure theory of the scientific and documentary superiority of expurgation: Burton was courting these animosities. Furthermore, the slightly varying variations of physical love did not entirely consume the attention of his commentary, which is encyclopedic and seditious and of an interest that increases in inverse proportion to its necessity. Thus Volume Six (which I have before me) includes some three hundred notes, among which are the following: a condemnation of jails and a defense of corporal punishment and fines; some examples of the Islamic respect for bread; a legend about the hairiness of Queen Belkis' legs; an enumeration of the four colors that are emblematic of death; a theory and practice of Oriental ingratitude; the information that angels prefer a piebald mount, while Djinns favor horses with a bright-bay coat; a synopsis of the mythology surrounding the secret Night of Power or Night of Nights; a denunciation of the superficiality of Andrew Lang; a diatribe against rule by democracy; a census of the names of Mohammed, on the Earth, in the Fire, and in the Garden; a mention of the Amalekite people, of long years and large stature; a note on the private parts of the Moslem, which for the man extend from the navel to his knees, and for the woman from the top of the head to the tips of her toes; a consideration of the asa'o [roasted beef] of the Argentine gaucho; a warning about the discomforts of "equitation" when the steed is human; an allusion to a grandiose plan for cross-breeding baboons with women and thus deriving a sub-race of good proletarians. At fifty, a man has accumulated affections, ironies, obscenities, and copious anecdotes; Burton unburdened himself of them in his notes.

The basic problem remains: how to entertain nineteenth-century gentlemen with the pulp fictions of the thirteenth century? The stylistic poverty of the *Nights* is well known. Burton speaks somewhere of the "dry and business-like tone" of the Arab prosifiers, in contrast to the rhetorical luxuriance of the Persians. Littmann, the ninth translator, accuses himself of having interpolated words such as *asked*, *begged*, *answered*, in five thousand pages that know of no other formula than an invariable said. Burton lovingly abounds in this type of substitution. His vocabulary is as unparalleled as his notes. Archaic words coexist with slang, the lingo of prisoners or sailors with technical terms. He does not shy away from the glorious hybridization of English: neither Morris's Scandinavian repertory nor Johnson's Latin has his blessing, but rather the contact and reverberation of the two. Neologisms and foreignisms are in plentiful supply: *castrato*, *inconséquence*, *hauteur*, *in gloria*, *bagnio*, *langue fourrée*, *pundonor*, *vendetta*, *Wazir*. Each of these is indubitably the *mot juste*, but their interspersion amounts to a kind of skewing of the original. A good skewing, since such verbal—and syntactical—pranks beguile the occasionally exhausting course of the *Nights*. Burton administers them carefully: first he translates gravely "Sulayman, Son of David (on the twain be peace!);" then—once this majesty is familiar to us—he reduces it to "Solomon Davidson." A king who, for the other translators, is "King of Samarcand in Persia," is, for Burton, "King of Samarcand in Barbarian-land;" a merchant who, for the others, is "ill-tempered," is "a man of wrath." That is not all: Burton rewrites in its entirety—with the addition of circumstantial details and physiological traits—the initial and final story. He thus, in 1885, inaugurates a procedure whose perfection (or whose *reductio ad absurdum*) we will now consider in Mardrus. An Englishman is always more timeless than a Frenchman: Burton's heterogeneous style is less antiquated than Mardrus's, which is noticeably dated.

2. Doctor Mardrus

Mardrus's destiny is a paradoxical one. To him has been ascribed the *moral* virtue of being the most truthful translator of *The Thousand and One Nights*, a book of admirable lascivity, whose purchasers were previously hoodwinked by Galland's good manners and Lane's Puritan qualms. His prodigious literalness, thoroughly demonstrated by the inarguable subtitle "Literal and complete translation of the Arabic text," is revered, along with the inspired idea of writing *The Book of the Thousand Nights and One Night*. The history of this title is instructive; we should review it before proceeding with our investigation of Mardrus.

Masudi's *Meadows of Gold and Mines of Precious Stones* describes an anthology titled

Hazar afsana, Persian words whose true meaning is "a thousand adventures," but which people renamed "a thousand nights." Another tenth-century document, the *Fihrist*, narrates the opening tale of the series, the king's heartbroken oath that every night he will wed a virgin whom he will have beheaded at dawn, and the resolution of Scheherazade, who diverts him with marvelous stories until a thousand nights have revolved over the two of them and she shows him his son. This invention—far superior to the future and analogous devices of Chaucer's pious cavalcade or Giovanni Boccaccio's epidemic—is said to be posterior to the title, and was devised in the aim of justifying it ... Be that as it may, the early figure of 1 000 quickly increased to 1 001. How did this additional and now indispensable night emerge, this prototype of Pico della Mirandola's *Book of All Things and Also Many Others*, so derided by Quevedo and later Voltaire. Littmann suggests a contamination of the Turkish phrase *bin bir*, literally "a thousand and one," but commonly used to mean "many." In early 1840, Lane advanced a more beautiful reason: the magical dread of even numbers. The title's adventures certainly did not end there. Antoine Galland, in 1704, eliminated the original's repetition and translated *The Thousand and One Nights*, a name now familiar in all the nations of Europe except England, which prefers *The Arabian Nights*. In 1839, the editor of the Calcutta edition, W. H. Macnaghten, had the singular scruple of translating *Quitab alif laila ua laila* as *Book of the Thousand Nights and One Night*. This renovation through spelling did not go unremarked. John Payne, in 1882, began publishing his *Book of the Thousand Nights and One Night*; Captain Burton, in 1885, his *Book of the Thousand Nights and a Night*; J. C. Mardrus, in 1899, his *Livre des mille nuits et une nuit*.

I turn to the passage that made me definitively doubt this last translator's veracity. It belongs to the doctrinal story of the City of Brass, which in all other versions extends from the end of night 566 through part of night 578, but which Doctor Mardrus has transposed (for what cause, his Guardian Angel alone knows) to nights 338-346. I shall not insist on this point; we must not waste our consternation on this inconceivable reform of an ideal calendar. Scheherazade—Mardrus relates:

> The water ran through four channels worked in the chamber's floor with charming meanderings, and each channel had a bed of a special color; the first channel had a bed of pink porphyry; the second of topaz, the third of emerald, and the fourth of turquoise; so that the water was tinted the color of the bed, and bathed by the attenuated light filtered in through the silks above, it projected onto the surrounding objects and the marble walls all the sweetness of a seascape.

As an attempt at visual prose in the manner of *The Portrait of Dorian Gray*, I accept (and even salute) this description; as a "literal and complete" version of a passage composed in the thirteenth century, I repeat that it alarms me unendingly. The reasons are multiple. A Scheherazade without Mardrus describes by enumerating parts, not by mutual reaction, does not attest to circumstantial details like that of water that takes on the color of its bed, does not define the quality of light filtered by silk, and does not allude to the Salon des Aquarellistes in the final image. Another small flaw: "Charming meanderings" is not Arabic, it is very distinctly French. I do not know if the foregoing reasons are sufficient; they were not enough for me, and I had the indolent pleasure of comparing the three German versions by Weil, Henning, and Littmann, and the two English versions by Lane and Sir Richard Burton. In them I confirmed that the original of Mardrus's ten lines was this: "The four drains ran into a fountain, which was of marble in various colors."

Mardrus's interpolations are not uniform. At times they are brazenly anachronistic—as if suddenly the Fashoda incident and Marchand's withdrawal were being discussed. For example:

> They were overlooking a dream city... As far as the gaze fixed on horizons drowned by the night could reach, the vale of bronze was terraced with the cupolas of palaces, the balconies of houses, and serene gardens; canals illuminated by the moon ran in a thousand clear circuits in the shadow of the peaks, while away in the distance, a sea of metal contained the sky's reflected fires in its cold bosom.

Or this passage, whose Gallicism is no less public:

> A magnificent carpet of glorious colors and dexterous wool opened its odorless flowers in a meadow without sap, and lived all the artificial life of its verdant groves full of birds and animals, surprised in their exact natural beauty and their precise lines.

(Here the Arabic editions state: "To the sides were carpets, with a variety of birds and beasts embroidered in red gold and white silver, but with eyes of pearls and rubies. Whoever saw them could not cease to wonder at them.")

Mardrus cannot cease to wonder at the poverty of the "Oriental Color" of *The Thousand and One Nights*. With a stamina worthy of Cecil B. de Mille, he heaps on the viziers, the kisses, the palm trees and the moons. He happens to read, in night 570:

> They arrived at a column of black stone, in which a man was buried up to his armpits. He had two enormous wings and four arms; two of which were like the arms of the sons of Adam, and two like a lion's forepaws, with iron claws. The hair on his head was like a horse's tail, and his eyes were like embers, and he had in his forehead a third eye which was like the eye of a lynx.

He translates luxuriantly:

> One evening the caravan came to a column of black stone, to which was chained a strange being, only half of whose body could be seen, for the other half was buried in the ground. The bust that emerged from the earth seemed to be some monstrous spawn riveted there by the force of the infernal powers. It was black and as large as the trunk of an old, rotting palm tree, stripped of its fronds. It had two

enormous black wings and four hands, of which two were like the clawed paws of a lion. A tuft of coarse bristles like a wild ass's tale whipped wildly over its frightful skull. Beneath its orbital arches flamed two red pupils, while its double-horned forehead was pierced by a single eye, which opened, immobile and fixed, shooting out green sparks like the gaze of a tiger or a panther.

Somewhat later he writes:

> The bronze of the walls, the fiery gemstones of the cupolas, the ivory terraces, the canals and all the sea, as well as the shadows projected towards the West, merged harmoniously beneath the nocturnal breeze and the magical moon.

"Magical," for a man of the thirteenth century, must have been a very precise classification, and not the gallant doctor's mere urbane adjective... I suspect that the Arabic language is incapable of a "literal and complete" version of Mardrus's paragraph, and neither is Latin or the Spanish of Miguel de Cervantes.

The Book of the *Thousand and One Nights* abounds in two procedures: one (purely formal), rhymed prose; the other, moral predications. The first, retained by Burton and by Littmann, coincides with the narrator's moments of animation: people of comely aspect, palaces, gardens, magical operations, mentions of the Divinity, sunsets, battles, dawns, the beginnings and endings of tales. Mardrus, perhaps mercifully, omits it. The second requires two faculties: that of majestically combining abstract words and that of offering up stock comments without embarrassment. Mardrus lacks both. From the line memorably translated by Lane as "And in this palace is the last information respecting lords collected in the dust," the good Doctor barely extracts: "They passed on, all of them! They had barely the time to repose in the shadow of my towers." The angel's confession—"I am imprisoned by Power, confined by Splendor, and punished for as long as the Eternal commands it, to whom Force and Glory belong"—is, for Mardrus's reader, "I am chained here by the Invisible Force until the extinction of the centuries."

Nor does sorcery have in Mardrus a co-conspirator of good will. He is incapable of mentioning the supernatural without smirking. He feigns to translate, for example:

> One day when Caliph Abdelmelik, hearing tell of certain vessels of antique copper whose contents were a strange black smoke-cloud of diabolical form, marveled greatly and seemed to place in doubt the reality of facts so commonly known, the traveller Talib ben-Sahl had to intervene.

In this paragraph (like the others I have cited, it belongs to the Story of the City of Brass, which, in Mardrus, is made of imposing Bronze), the deliberate candor of "so commonly known" and the rather implausible doubts of Caliph Abdelmelik are two personal contributions by the translator.

Mardrus continually strives to complete the work neglected by those languid, anonymous Arabs. He adds Art Nouveau passages, fine obscenities, brief comical interludes, circumstantial details, symmetries, vast quantities of visual Orientalism. An example among so many: In night 573, the Emir Musa bin Nusayr orders his blacksmiths and carpenters to construct a strong ladder of wood and iron. Mardrus (in his night 344) reforms this dull episode, adding that the men of the camp went in search of dry branches, peeled them with knives and scimitars, and bound them together with turbans, belts, camel ropes, leather cinches and tack, until they had built a tall ladder that they propped against the wall, supporting it with stones on both sides... In general, it can be said that Mardrus does not translate the book's words but its scenes: a freedom denied to translators, but tolerated in illustrators, who are allowed to add these kinds of details... I do not know if these smiling diversions are what infuse the work with such a happy air, the air of a far-fetched personal yarn rather than of a laborious hefting of dictionaries. But to me the Mardrus "translation" is the most readable of them all—after Burton's incomparable version, which is not truthful either. (In Burton, the falsification is of another order. It resides in the gigantic employ of a gaudy English, crammed with archaic and barbaric words.)

I would greatly deplore it (not for Mardrus, for myself) if any constabulary intent were read into the foregoing scrutiny. Mardrus is the only Arabist whose glory was promoted by men of letters, with such unbridled success that now even the Arabists know who he is. André Gide was among the first to praise him, in August 1889; I do not think Cancela and Capdevila will be the last. My aim is not to demolish this admiration, but to substantiate it. To celebrate Mardrus's fidelity is to leave out the soul of Mardrus, to ignore Mardrus entirely. It is his infidelity, his happy and creative infidelity, that must matter to us.

3. Enno Littmann

Fatherland to a famous Arabic edition of *The Thousand and One Nights*, Germany can take (vain) glory in four versions: by the "librarian though Israelite" Gustav Weil—the adversative is from the Catalan pages of a certain Encyclopedia; by Max Henning, translator of the Koran; by the man of letters Félix Paul Greve; and by Enno Littmann, decipherer of the Ethiopie inscriptions in the fortress of Axum. The first of these versions, in four volumes (1839-1842), is the most pleasurable, as its author—exiled from Africa and Asia by dysentery—strives to maintain or substitute for the Oriental style. His interpolations earn my deepest respect. He has some intruders at a gathering say, "We do not wish to be like the morning, which disperses all revelries." Of a generous king, he assures us, "The fire that burns for his guests brings to mind the Inferno and the dew of his benign hand is like the Deluge;" of another he tells us that his hands "were liberal as the sea." These fine apocrypha are not unworthy of Burton or Mardrus, and the translator assigned them to the parts in verse, where this graceful animation can be an *ersatz* or replacement for the original rhymes. Where the prose is concerned, I see that he translated it as is, with certain justified

omissions, equidistant from hypocrisy and immodesty. Burton praised his work—"as faithful as a translation of a popular nature can be." Not in vain was Doctor Weil Jewish "though librarian;" in his language I think I perceive something of the flavor of Scripture.

The second version (1895-1897) dispenses with the enchantments of accuracy, but also with those of style. I am speaking of the one provided by Henning, a Leipzig Arabist, to Philipp Reclam's *Universalbibliothek*. This is an expurgated version, though the publisher claims otherwise. The style is dogged and flat. Its most indisputable virtue must be its length. The editions of Bûlâq and Breslau are represented, along with the Zotenberg manuscripts and Burton's *Supplemental Nights*. Henning, translator of Sir Richard, is, word for word, superior to Henning, translator of Arabic, which is merely a confirmation of Sir Richard's primacy over the Arabs. In the book's preface and conclusion, praises of Burton abound—almost deprived of their authority by the information that Burton wielded "the language of Chaucer, equivalent to medieval Arabic." A mention of Chaucer as *one* of the sources of Burton's vocabulary would have been more reasonable. (Another is Sir Thomas Urquhart's Rabelais.)

The third version, Greve's, derives from Burton's English and repeats it, excluding only the encyclopedic notes. Insel-Verlag published it before the war.

The fourth (1923-1928) comes to supplant the previous one and, like it, runs to six volumes. It is signed by Enno Littmann, decipherer of the monuments of Axum, cataloguer of the 283 Ethiopie manuscripts found in Jerusalem, contributor to the *Zeitschrift für Assyriologie*. Though it does not engage in Burton's indulgent loitering, his translation is entirely frank. The most ineffable obscenities do not give him pause; he renders them into his placid German, only rarely into Latin. He omits not a single word, not even those that register—1 000 times—the passage from one night to the next. He neglects or refuses all local color: Express instructions from the publisher were necessary to make him retain the name of Allah and not substitute it with God. Like Burton and John Payne, he translates Arabic verse into Western verse. He notes ingenuously that if the ritual announcement "So-and-so pronounced these verses" were followed by a paragraph of German prose, his readers would be disconcerted. He provides whatever notes are necessary for a basic understanding of the text: twenty or so per volume, all of them laconic. He is always lucid, readable, mediocre. He follows (he tells us) the very breath of the Arabic. If the *Encyclopedia Britannica* contains no errors, his translation is the best of all those in circulation. I hear that the Arabists agree; it matters not at all that a mere man of letters—and he of the merely Argentine Republic—prefers to dissent.

My reason is this: the versions by Burton and Mardrus, and even by Galland, can only be conceived of *in the wake of a literature*. Whatever their blemishes or merits, these characteristic works presuppose a rich (prior) process. In some way, the almost inexhaustible process of English is adumbrated in Burton—John Donne's hard obscenity, the gigantic vocabularies of Shakespeare and Cyril Tourneur, Swinburne's affinity for the archaic, the crass erudition of the authors of seventeenth-century chapbooks, the energy and imprecision, the love of tempests and magic. In Mardrus's laughing paragraphs, *Salammbô* and La Fontaine, the *Mannequin d'osier* and the *ballets russes* all coexist. In Littmann, who, like Washington, cannot tell a lie, there is nothing but the probity of Germany. This is so little, so very little. The commerce between Germany and the *Nights* should have produced something more.

Whether in philosophy or in the novel, Germany possesses a literature of the fantastic—rather, it possesses *only* a literature of the fantastic. There are marvels in the *Nights* that I would like to see rethought in German. As I formulate this desire, I think of the repertory's deliberate wonders—the all-powerful slaves of a lamp or a ring, Queen Lab who transforms Moslems into birds, the copper boatman with talismans and formulae on his chest—and of those more general ones that proceed from its collective nature, from the need to complete one thousand and one episodes. Once they had run out of magic, the copyists had to fall back on historical or pious notices whose inclusion seems to attest to the good faith of the rest. The ruby that ascends into sky and the earliest description of Sumatra, details of the court of the Abbasids and silver angels whose food is the justification of the Lord all dwell together in a single volume. It is, finally, a poetic mixture; and I would say the same of certain repetitions. Is it not portentous that on night 602 King Schahriah hears his own story from the queen's lips? Like the general framework, a given tale often contains within itself other tales of equal length: stages within the stage as in the tragedy of Hamlet, raised to the power of a dream. A clear and difficult line from Tennyson seems to define them:

> Laborious orient ivory, sphere in sphere.

To heighten further the astonishment, these adventitious Hydra's heads can be more concrete than the body: Schahriah, the fantastical king "of the Islands of China and Hindustan" receives news of Tarik ibn Ziyad, governor of Tangier s and victor in the battle of Guadalete... The threshold is confused with the mirror, the mask lies beneath the face, no one knows any longer which is the true man and which are his idols. And none of it matters; the disorder is as acceptable and trivial as the inventions of a daydream.

Chance has played at symmetries, contrasts, digressions. What might a man—a Kafka—do if he organized and intensified this play, remade it in line with the Germanic distortion, the *Unheimlichkeit* of Germany?

Notes:

1. I allude to Mark Anthony, invoked by Caesar's apostrophe: "on the Alps/It is reported, thou didst eat strange flesh/Which some did die to look on ... " In these lines, I think I glimpse some inverted reflection of the zoological myth of the basilisk, a serpent whose gaze is fatal. Pliny (*Natural History*, Book Eight, Paragraph 33) tells us nothing of the posthumous aptitudes of this ophidian, but the conjunction of the two ideas of seeing (*mirar*) and dying (*morir*) *vedi Napoli e poi mori* [see Naples and die]—must have influenced Shakespeare.

The gaze of the basilisk was poisonous; the Divinity, however, can kill with pure splendor or pure radiation of manna. The direct sight of God is intolerable. Moses covers his face on Mount Horeb, "for he was afraid to look on God;" Hakim, the prophet of Khorasan, used a four-fold veil of white silk in order not to blind men's eyes. Cf. also Isaiah 6:5, and 1 Kings 19:13.

2. Also memorable is this variation on the themes of Abulmeca de Ronda and Jorge Manrique: "Where is the wight who peopled in the past/Hind-land and Sind; and there the tyrant played?"

【延伸阅读】

[1] Robinson, D. *Who Translates? Translator Subjectivities beyond Reason*. Acbang: State University of New York Press, 2001.

[2] Said, E. The Public Role of Writers and Intellectuals. In Sandra Bermann & Michael Wood (eds.), *Nation, Language, and the Ethics of Translation*. Princeton: Princeton University Press, 2005.

[3] Milton, J. & Bandia, P. F. (eds.). *Agents of Translation*. Armsterdam & Philadelphia: John Benjamins Publishing Company, 2009.

[4] Reiss, K. "Type, Kind and Individuality of Text: Decision Making in Translation" in *The Translation Studies Reader*. Lawrence Venuti (ed.). London: Routledge, 2000.

[5] Venuti, L. *The Translator's Invisibility: A History of Translation* (Second Edition). London: Routledge, 2008.

[6] Bassnett, S. The Meek or the Mighty: Reappraising the Role of the Translator. In Román Álvarez & M. Carmen África Vidal (eds.), *Translation, Power, Subversion*. Clevedon · Buffalo · Toronto, NY: Multilingual Matters Ltd., 1996.

[7] 董洪川. 文学影响与文化过滤. 四川外语学院学报,2001(5).

[8] 郭延礼. 中国近代翻译文学概论. 武汉:湖北教育出版社,1998.

[9] 孔慧怡. 翻译·文学·文化. 北京:北京大学出版社,1999.

[10] 吕俊. 论翻译研究的本体回归——对翻译研究"文化转向"的反思. 外国语,2004(4).

[11] 王宁. 比较文学与翻译研究的文化转向. 中国翻译,2009(5).

[12] 王宁. 文化翻译与经典阐释. 北京:中华书局,2006.

[13] 谢天振. 译介学. 上海:上海外语教育出版社,1999.

[14] 谢天振. 翻译研究新视野. 青岛:青岛出版社,2003.

[15] 朱义华. 文化建构下的文学翻译研究反思. 江南大学学报:人文社会科学版,2008(2).

【问题与思考】

1. 谈谈民族文学的地位与翻译文学的关系问题。

2. 社会文化地位和意识形态对翻译产生了怎样的影响?

3. 翻译对中国文化和文学的现代性产生了哪些作用?

4. 请谈谈《一千零一夜》中文译本的特点。

5. 受葡萄牙文化部资助和支持的埃乌拉文化中心作为文化代理在戏剧翻译中发挥了那些重要作用?

第四章　文学翻译研究的美学之维

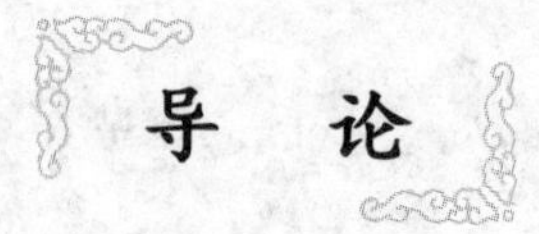

导　论

随着当代西方翻译理论研究视野的不断扩展，文学翻译研究的美学视角成为最近几年来比较热点的话题之一，翻译美学也因此成为翻译学研究的一个新领域。从美学视角探讨、阐释、实践文学翻译，在国内外都具有千年以上的历史。我国翻译思想的“十大学说”，诸如支谦的“文质说”、严复的“信达雅”、林语堂的“美学论”、朱光潜的“艺术论”、傅雷的“神似说”、许渊冲的“三美论”等译论，都蕴含着丰富的美学思想。同样，西方的译论之芽也是首先依附在哲学—美学之树上而枝叶渐丰的。

文学翻译意味着主体、客体的双向对话和交流，其实质是一种潜在审美心理的对话。翻译美学强调审美情感，其研究内容主要包括对翻译中的审美客体、审美主体和审美再现手段的研究。文学翻译的审美再现主要集中于三个问题：第一，就语言层面而言，原文中的各种形式美如何模仿？第二，就文化层面而言，原文中民族化的语言表达方式如何保留？第三，就艺术层面而言，原文中内容与形式的统一关系如何再造？翻译美学的研究价值主要体现在对文学翻译实践的指导功能。在如何传达原作之美的问题上，翻译美学所关注的问题为我们提供了方法论意义上的参考答案。现代文学翻译研究在理论上要有所突破，不但需要吸收哲学、文学、语言学、文化学等学科领域的研究成果，而且需要吸收美学尤其是接受美学领域的研究成果。接受美学强调文学的社会效果，重视读者的参与接受，主张从社会意识交往的角度去考察文学艺术的创作和接受现象。这一思潮反映了在结构主义思潮之后的人文主义思潮的新趋向。

大卫·康诺利(David Connolly)在《诗歌翻译》一文中指出：诗歌的形式具有一定的意义，诗的翻译只能是部分的，有缺失的，每一次翻译都不可能是最终的翻译。诗歌翻译模式和诗歌翻译理论不应忘记译者的倾情投入和创作灵感。译者只有对原作者的审美情感浓聚于其人、事、物、景中，才能传达原文之美。

在英语世界现有的中国古典文学英译文本中，诗歌是最瞩目的文类。古代诗人和他的目标读者之间那种关系是无法在中国古典诗歌传统以外再现的，这对翻译来说是一个相当大的障碍。在中国诗词传统里，《诗经》的地位是至高无上的。《诗经》第一代译者理雅各、戴维斯和翟理斯以及第二代译者韦理、高本汉的翻译意图和方法不同，但都对英美文化产生了一定影响。英美诗人对中国诗歌传统认识不全，他们往往按照自己的想象和理解阐释中国古诗，用以支持他们提出的新诗歌理论。自从20世纪60年代起，中国诗歌英译基本上成了西方大学中文系的领域。由于很多译作是为了满足大学课程某些需求而出版的，因此译者站在老师的位置，优先考虑比较实际的问题，而诗意反而就变得次要了。但是，如果我们着眼在“诗”，就要思索如何充分利用英美现代诗歌传统来表达中国古典诗词里常有的宁静致远的韵味和美学情致。

翻译美学对中国典籍英译和诗词英译尤其具有指导意义。如何让目的语读者感受美的意境是翻译工作者和研究者需要深入探讨的话题。刘华文教授通过分析叶威廉的诗歌模子论认为,中西诗歌都有塑造各自诗歌形态的"模子",诗歌的翻译者要有模子意识,对接受翻译的诗歌要进行模子分析和归类。这样,才能实现译诗和原诗之间模子上的对应。他认为,叶威廉的诗歌模子论涵盖了诗歌的阐释过程(传释学)、诗歌的表达过程(道家语言观)和诗歌的接受过程(主客关系)。叶威廉希望在中国古典诗歌的英译中能够将这些内容容纳进去,建立与原诗相似的模子,从而保证中国古典诗学的异质性在目的语中传达出来,而不至于被目的语所淹没。我国著名翻译家许渊冲先生在大量翻译实践和研究的基础上,总结出诗词翻译的本体论——"三美论",即译诗要尽可能传达原诗的意美、音美、形美。"三美"之间的关系是:意美是最重要的,音美是次要的,形美是更次要的。也就是说,要在传达原文意美的前提下,尽可能传达原文的音美,还要在传达原文意美和音美的前提下,尽可能传达原文的形美,努力做到三美齐备。如果三者不能得兼,那么,可以不要求形似和音似,但要尽可能传达原文的意美和音美。意、音、形三方面牺牲得最少的译文,才是最优秀的译文。如果译者能够发挥译文语言和文化的优势,运用深化、等化、浅化的方法,使读者知之、好之、乐之。那么文学翻译就有可能成为翻译文学。"楚辞"是中华传统文化的瑰宝,"楚辞"英译具有典籍翻译和诗词翻译的双重特征。从意美、音美、形美的角度分析许渊冲的《楚辞》英译文,可以管窥许渊冲的"三美论"对古诗词翻译和研究的理论和实践意义。

选 文

选文一 叶威廉的诗歌模子论与古典汉诗英译

刘华文

导 言

本文选自《译林》(学术版)2011 年 Z1 期。作者刘华文是南京大学外国语学院教授,翻译学博士。研究方向包括认知与翻译、诗歌翻译、语言哲学与翻译、译释学、双语词典学等。

选文阐述了叶威廉诗歌翻译的模子论思想。叶威廉的诗歌模子论涵盖了诗歌的阐释过程(传释学)、诗歌的表达过程(道家语言观)和诗歌的接受过程(主客关系)。他希望在中国古典诗歌的英译中同样能够将这些内容容纳进去,建立与原诗相似的模子。只有这样才能保证中国古典诗学的异质性在目的语中传达出来，而不至于被目的语所淹没。这种翻译观念是为了凸显原诗的模子，避免被译入语的诗歌模子所取代，是一种差异翻译诗学的理念。

中国古典诗歌作为英语世界介绍中国文学的主流体裁，其翻译体现了中国传统诗学和西方诗学的相遇与交汇。站在诗歌翻译文本的这个交汇点上，人们可以发现中西诗学对话的方式以及翻译为这种对话所提供的交流平台的特点。在中国诗歌英译的过程中，译者的翻译目的各有倾向：有强调中国诗学异质性的叶威廉，有用西方诗学观念比附中国诗歌的刘若愚，有借助翻译建构中国诗歌史的宇文所安，也有专门译介一位诗人的余宝琳，等等。这些中国古典诗歌的译者都有中西诗学的双重背景。在将中国诗歌译介到西方的同时，还用英语出版了关于中国诗学的专著。例如，叶威廉就著有 *Diffusion of Distances: Dialogues between Chinese and Western Poetics*，刘若愚著有 *The Art of Chinese Poetry*，*Chinese Theories of Literature*，宇文所安编著有 *Readings in Chinese Literary Thought*，余宝琳著有 *The Reading of Imagery in the Chinese Poetic Tradition*。这些学者所具备的双重诗学背景势必会影响到他们对中国古典诗歌的翻译。同时，他们对中国古典诗歌的英译也会反映出他们各自的双重诗学背景。这里将选择叶威廉的诗学理论及其中国古典诗歌的英译为考察对象，对他的差异翻译诗学的建构过程予以透视。

1. 叶威廉的中国古典诗歌的翻译：一种差异翻译诗学

叶威廉意识到汉诗译入英语之时会遭到扭曲或误表。他阅读了大量的诗歌翻译，而汉诗的英译对他的触动最大。他在其中发现了“各种背叛式的再现里面对中国本源美学思想可怕的扭曲”(Yip, 1993: 2)叶威廉所关心的是“本土的美学观念能否被允许如其所是地再现自身，而不会被西方的阐释习惯和诗学经济所框限”(ibid.: 1)。无怪乎叶威廉在英译中国古典诗歌的过程中，在强调中国美学观念有异于西方美学观念的同时，坚持将这种特异性在译诗中充分体现。他的这种翻译观念不仅仅是付诸实践的，同时也伴随着翔实的理论阐述。在《中国诗学》(2006)和《道家美学与西方文化》(2002)这两部著作中，他以道家美学为基础，建构了中国古典诗歌的模子论。这个理论为他的中国古典诗歌的英译提供了充分的支撑，这种理论准备在他的翻译实践中也获得了贯彻，使得译诗成为中西诗学之间差异性的载体，从而让他无意识地建构了一种差异翻译诗学体系。

2. 叶威廉的诗歌模子论

在叶威廉看来，每种文化都有自身塑造各自文化形态的“模子”(model)。“模子是一种构造活动，通过这一活动手头上的素材就被赋予了合适的形式。”(Yip, 1993: 8)叶威廉继而借助诗人的诗歌创作活动来说明模子的运作方式：“诗人在与存在经验协商时必须寻找表呈这些经验的形式，可能是商籁体或律诗；同时，还要寻找一套能够捕捉到这些经验的本质的美学策略或技巧，以便将一些抽象的概念具体化。最后从一种有序的启示中所具备的各种方面那里获

得一种澄明的视角。”(ibid.：9)“如果或者当所使用的模子无法兼容来自存在经验的素材时，那么诗人就会修改或转化这个模子，通过增加、删减甚至是颠倒原有形式的策略和观点的方式生成新的模子，借此实现既定的美学目的。”(ibid.)这种诗歌创作的模子论也同样适用于诗歌批评。“批评者在处理一件作品的时候，也要进入到这一结构活动的过程中去，必须首先了解所采用的模子，明白诗人在修改和转化模子时所采纳的选择和结合方式，这样才能彻底地掌控这首诗歌的原动力。”(ibid.)诗歌的翻译者同诗歌的批评者一样，对所翻译的诗歌对象要有模子意识，就是说要对接受翻译的诗歌进行模子分析和归类，这样才能实现译诗和原诗之间模子上的对应。中西诗歌有着不同的创作模子。诗歌的翻译者在进行翻译时需要意识到两者之间的差别。叶威廉在他的 *Chinese Poetry：An Anthology of Major Modes and Genres* 中同时为每一首诗歌给出了两个英语译文。实际上，这两个译文分别是两种模子的应用：第一个译文是中国诗歌创作模子的使用；第二个译文则是西方诗歌模子的应用。两个模子同时并用是为了避免单用西方模子所带来的对中国古典诗歌的诗性、诗意和诗质的遮蔽甚至是扭曲。

3. 模子论对叶威廉中国古典诗歌英译的影响

3.1　叶威廉翻译诗学中的传释学

在叶威廉看来，不同的语言有着不同的诗歌模子。在他建构自己的中西比较诗学的过程中，一再强调中国古典诗歌模子的特异性，这种特异性是不能够在翻译中被西方的诗歌模子所体现的。叶威廉对中国诗歌模子的建构一般是在中西诗歌对比的背景下展开的。在他的比较诗学的建构中确立了中国古典诗歌的模子。首先，中国古典诗歌的模子或形态包含有广阔的解读空间，而拒绝定位式的解读方式。意象在诗歌中的呈现会不受语法形式的囿限而表现出高度的灵活性。“这种灵活性让字与读者之间建立一种自由的关系，读者在字与字之间保持着一种‘若即若离’的解读活动，在‘指义’与‘不指义’的中间地带，而造成一种类似‘指义前’物象自现的状态。”(叶威廉，2006：16)中国诗歌翻译成英语时，翻译的成功与否从某种程度上讲就取决于这种所谓的“指义前”的状态能否被保留下来，以便让译入语的读者同样拥有原诗读者所具有的那种“若即若离”的解读效果。这种“指义前”的状态“使得读者与文字之间，保持一种灵活自由的关系，读者处于一种‘若即若离’的中间地带，而字，仿佛如实际生活中的事物一样，在未被预订关系和意义封闭的情况下，为我们提供一个可以自由活动、可以从不同角度进出的空间，让其中的物象以近乎电影般强烈的视觉性在我们目前演出”(ibid.：57)。叶威廉对这种解读效果的在译入语读者那里的获得是持否定态度的。他对文言文、英文和白话文这三种形态的语言进行了一下对比：“文言文常常可以保留未定位、未定关系的情况，英文不可以；白话文也可以，但倾向于定位与定关系的活动。”(ibid.：17)可见，他对在英译文中保持诗歌的这种中国古典诗歌“指义前”的物象之间的未定位和未定向关系是没有多少信心的。

叶威廉还强调诗歌解读的“事件性”特征。他试图剥离掉诗歌中事物的语言外壳，直接与“事物”接触。“我们和外物的接触是一个‘事件’，是具体事物从整体现象中的涌现，是活动的，不是静止的，是一种‘发生’，在‘发生’之‘际’，不是概念和意义可以包孕的。”(ibid.：22)中国古典诗歌模子的特征还包括诗歌文本对读者视觉、听觉、味觉、嗅觉等身体感官知觉的全面调动，而不只是诉诸理性思维。每一首诗歌的解读都是一次全方位的、立体的感知性事件。这种全面性的感知调动主要是由诗歌"指义前"的物象之间的原始性关系引发的。

叶威廉继而在他的中国古典诗歌的模子中强调视觉效果的重要性。中国诗歌是意象的铺排组合，这种铺排组合具现代性特点，符合电影的"蒙太奇"的叙事手法。实际上，中国诗歌的这一特点是为了贯彻中国诗学的言意观念。在中国诗歌里，言和意之间的关系是不对等的，相对于"言"，"意"总是会有盈余。在中国古典诗歌中，不难发现对这一言意关系的表述："此中有真意，欲辨已忘言"（陶潜）、"此情可待成追忆，只是当时已惘然"（李商隐）、"长恨言语浅，不如人意深"（刘禹锡）。在电影中，"蒙太奇"手法是电影这门视听觉语言生成意义的方式，那么中国诗歌中的"蒙太奇"手法也为诗歌生成"言外之意"创造了条件。如果在翻译中改变甚或缩小了这种蒙太奇的构意空间，那么就无法体现原诗歌中"意"大于"言"的言意关系，是对中国古典诗歌模子这一特点的破坏。

3.2 叶威廉翻译诗学的语言观

叶威廉认为，英语中"名"的符号性很强，也就是任意性很强。相比较而言，汉语的"名"则符号性较弱，也就是理据性很强。中国古典诗歌模子所负载的语言结构是从道家那里承接过来的，所以叶威廉在他的著述中对道家美学观念非常注重。他在《中国诗学》中就专辟一章论述道家的知识论。不过，与其说论述的是道家的知识论，还不如说论述的是道家的语言论，因为道家的知识获取主要是依靠语言实现的。在道家那里，要想获取关于事物的知识需要靠近事物，迫近事物。但是横亘在知识主体和知识对象之间的是语言中的"名"。"'名'的产生是在人与人之间，作为一种分辨，进而作为一种定位、定义，是一种分封行为。'名'之用，换言之，是产生于一种分辨的意欲，依着人的情况而进行。因为'名'是依附着人的情见、意欲，所以由各种'名'圈定出来的意义架构往往是含有某种权力意向。"（ibid.：45）可见，"名"的制定需要依靠人与人之间的权力关系，是一种"强之以名"。这种强制性的命名方式只顾及到命名主体这一端，而被命名的对象亦即被认识的对象则没有参与，于是"名"离开命名的对象就越来越远。那么，如何拉近"名"与被命名对象的距离，做到名实相符呢？道家认为只有"破名立象"才能做到"名即于物"的知识论目的。

道家破除"名"的强制性和任意性的方式就是加强"名"理据性也就是意象性这一面，力图让"名"具有可感性，尤其是可看性。所以，道家美学推崇一种用叶威廉的话来讲"'看而知'的原始语言"。那么，中国古典诗歌就是这种"'看而知'的原始语言"的终极体现者。这种"观看性"是叶威廉所构建的中国古典诗歌模子的最为关键的要件。在翻译中如果这一要件改变了，也就意味着对原诗模子的质的改变。所以，我们不难从叶威廉英译的中国古诗中清楚地发现这种对原诗意象及其排布的保留。

道家美学对"名言"表意的局限性认识还表现在启用反言、异言甚至无言上面。《庄子》里面充斥着诸如"正言若反"、"反者道之动"等等词类的反言性表述，同时还出现了扶摇之上的大鹏、物我难分的蝴蝶、游刃有余解牛的庖丁等等这些用异言表达的奇物奇人以及它们的"异事"。庄子抛弃"正言"，用反言、异言甚或是无言去表述"道"，这些言语形态也必然伴随着叶威廉所谓的"矛盾语法"，字词挣脱了语法、句法的束缚，做一种文字的"逍遥游"，直至达到噤声的"无言"境界："言无言，终身言，未尝言，终身不言，未尝不言。"（《庄子》）。叶威廉所建立的中国古典诗歌的模子也就自然地包含"空白美学"的观念，是一种弃有尚无的美学诉求。所以，他这样理解中国古典诗歌：

> 因为重视点兴、逗发万物自然的形现演化,“言无言”的另一个含义,可以说,还重视语言的空白(写下的是“实”,未写下的是“虚”)。空白(虚、无言)是具体(实、有言)不可或缺的合作者。语言全面的活动,应该像中国画中的虚实,必须使读者同时接受“言”(写下的字句)所指向的“无言”,使负面的空间(在画中是空白,在诗中是言外契合的物物关系)成为重要、积极、应作美感凝住的东西。(ibid.:57)

可见,从诗意的表达力上来讲,“无言”反而最强,而异言、反言次之,正言最弱。这样,中国古典诗歌在英译过程中其无言、异言、反言会遭受到“正言”规整,因为英语是具有“死板句法要求”的语言(Yip,1997:2)。叶威廉在英译中国古诗的时候力图抵制作为“正言”的英语对原诗模子的袭扰,尽量保留原初的反言、异言和无言的诗歌语言策略。

3.3 叶威廉翻译诗学的主客关系

叶威廉编译的*Chinese Poetry*:*An Anthology of Major Modes and Genres*选取的大部分是感物或体物诗歌,而格致物理的叙事诗相对来说占的比例较少。正如这本诗歌选集的标题所表明的那样,该选集是为了体现中国诗歌中的“主要模式和题材”。叶威廉在这本诗集所选译的中国古典诗歌透露了他对道家美学观念的推崇。

依循叶威廉所构建的中国古典诗歌模子,在将中国古诗翻译成英文的过程中,需要保持字词的“物象性”,反对将译文中的字词降解为经过逻辑思维加工过的纯粹概念。译诗的要求也要像原诗那样,“尽量要跳脱这些指义元素,欲托出‘指义前’属于原有、未经思侵、未经抽象逻辑概念化前的原真世界,究其基本原因,当然是由于道家所激发的观物感物的立场——为求不干预自然的衍化兴现——所必需带动的语法的调整。”(叶威廉,2002:9)在叶威廉对诗学的理解中至少有两个诗歌模子的存在:一种是“指义前”的模子,一种是“指义后”的模子。前一种模子保证诗人主体或读者主体与诗中物象的亲近,保证主体对诗中物象贴近的感知距离。而后一种模子则会让创作主体或欣赏主体落入到思维之中,启动逻辑性的概念及其互动对诗中的物象予以思虑,这样就拉远了主体同物象之间的距离。叶威廉在英译中国古典诗歌时表现得纠结在这两种诗歌模子之间。概念思维对物象的干预主要表现在把物象之间的关系明晰化,销蚀掉原诗物象之间诗人留白出来的模糊空间。这种明晰化的干预方式主要由动词来完成。叶威廉为了将这种干扰减少到最低程度,不惜词对字或词进行对译或者硬译,例如他对王维的《栾家濑》的英译:

飒飒秋雨中,浅浅石榴泻。
跳波自相溅,白鹭惊复下。

1. blast-blast—autumn rain/s middle
2. light-lightly—rock flow pour
3. jump wave/s self mutual splash each other
4. white egret startle again down (Yip, 1997: 227)

译文完全是对原诗物象直接呈现,没有进行理性的思维规整,最原始地呈现在读者面前,保持了“指义前”的原始状态。叶威廉随后又给出了另外一个译文:

1. Blasts of wind amidst autumn rains,
2. Patter-patter upon rocky clod.

3. Jumping beads splash against each other.
4. A white egret—startled—then down.（Yip，1997：227）

在这个译文中，叶氏只对第三行的译文做了句法的规整，将“跳波”之间的关系“定位”为相互地 splash，译者借机原诗的较为明确的物象关系对译文进行了明晰化。但是，就整个译文来将，译者仍然以尽量避免进行概念思维为上，所以该译文只比前一个译文的干预程度稍微多了一些，介乎一种“指义前”和“指义后”的中间状态，而没有像前一个译文那样是一种彻底的“指义前”的翻译，也没有像下面这个译文那样完全是一种对物象之间关系的彻底定位，呈现出一种完全“指义后”的概念思维状态：

The moaning of wind in autumn rain,
Swift water trickling over stones.
Leaping waves strike one another—
A white egret startles up，comes down again.（Owen，1981：39）

宇文所安的这个译文的第一句就给诗歌以情感定位，把风声比作是“哀怨（moaning）”的声音。这样就窄化了诗歌的解读空间，使得读者难以从不同方向、角度感知诗歌物象。宇文所安的译文从原诗纯感知的诉诸到译诗对情感的诉诸，再到后两行译诗动词对物象之间关系“思侵”式的定位，完成了诗歌模子的跨语转变。

叶威廉认为，道家美学崇尚“空白美学”，在绘画中表现为“留白”的手法，而在诗歌创作中则表现为营造一种空灵的代入感。“虚怀而物归，心无而入神，这个‘神’，就是我们的心进入了物象各具其性的内在机枢（‘道枢’）以后的状态。”（叶威廉，2006：58）这种“进入物象各具其性的内在机枢以后的状态”就是作品将欣赏主体代入进作品的解读空间，任由其进行物象的当下体认。如王维的《鹿柴》一诗：“空山不见人，但闻人语声；返景入深林，复照青苔上。”这首诗所描写的情景似乎就在读者的眼前，把读者的听觉和视觉调动了起来，因为诗歌没有呈现诗人的在场，这种主体的虚位让读者主体很快就感同身受地置身其中。这种强烈的情景代入感也体现在译诗中，叶威廉将主体“空白”出来，可以让译诗读者也同原诗读者那样毫无滞碍地将自身代入到诗歌所设置的情景之中。否则，充盈坐实的翻译将会填充原诗的“空白”，影响读者的自我代入。叶威廉的译诗是这样的：

1. Empty mountain：no man.
2. But voices of men are heard.
3. Sun's reflection reaches into the woods
4. And shines upon the green moss.（Yip，1997：225）

译诗也跟原诗一样，基本上做到了让主体虚位的状态，避免定位于一个人的视角。只要读者将自己身体的感官移入到译诗中，就会切身地感受到山、人声、返照的阳光、树林、青苔的自然呈现，并不需要理性的思维和判断，诗中情景的代入完全诉诸的是人的感官和感知。

叶威廉试图以道家美学观念建立中国古典诗歌的模子，同时又将这种模子作为中国古诗英译的参照。为了贯彻他的诗歌模子的跨语建立，他需要摆脱英语语言对建立这种模子的干扰。从主客关系的处理上，叶威廉一方面要确保译诗的物象性，方便译文读者诉诸自身的感知；再一方面，他为了拉近欣赏主体和诗中物象之间的距离，依然采取像原诗那样非定位的物

象处理模式，使物象之间构成的情景很容易就让读者把自己代入进去，使其身临其境、感同身受。上述两个措施的最终目的则是让译诗同原诗一样臻于物我两忘、天人合一的境界。叶威廉常常用中国画来说明中国古诗："中国的山水画，不用定点透视，而用散点透视，或回旋透视，仿佛各方面都可以看到，就是要突破'物眼'，就是距离的消解。"（叶威廉，2006：53）天人冥合的境界一方面体现在空间距离的消解上面，同时空间距离的消解也伴随着体认在时间上的即时性、当下性和并时性。"距离的消解、视限的消解所需要的不断换位的另一个含义即是并时性，即是观者同时从此看去，从彼看去。"（ibid.：53）主客之间的空间关系不是固定的，物我之间的时间关系不是恒久的。处于这种状态，主体在体认诗歌的时候就会实现"天地与我并生，万物与我齐一"（《庄子》）的诗意境界。

4. 结语

叶威廉的诗歌模子论涵盖了诗歌的阐释过程（传释学）、诗歌的表达过程（道家语言观）和诗歌的接受过程（主客关系）。他希望在中国古典诗歌的英译中同样能够将这些内容容纳进去，建立与原诗相似的模子。只有这样才能保证中国古典诗学的异质性在目的语中传达出来，而不至于被目的语所淹没。这种翻译观念是为了凸显原诗的模子，避免被译入语的诗歌模子所取代，是一种差异翻译诗学的理念。相比之下，华裔汉学家刘若愚翻译的李商隐诗歌集主要目的是为了彰显李商隐的人生轨迹，通过翻译他的诗歌建构他的生平传记。这种翻译理念是一种工具翻译诗学。翻译王维诗歌的华裔学者余宝琳的诗歌翻译理念也应忝入此列。美国汉学家宇文所安的中国古典诗歌的英译实践一方面体现在他所编译的中国文学选集中，另外他还用英文著述了《初唐诗》、《盛唐诗》和《晚唐诗》，这三部著述中都包含了唐诗的英译。他的诗歌英译主要是为了建构中国古代或者唐朝一代的诗歌史，所以不妨称之为建构翻译诗学。如果把叶威廉对中国古典诗歌的英译放置在整个汉学界对中国古典诗歌的翻译实践及其所持理念的背景之下，其差异翻译诗学的诉求就更能彰显出来。

选文二　从翻译美学看文学翻译审美再现的三个原则

党争胜

导　言

本文选自《外语教学》2010年第3期。作者党争胜是西安外国语大学欧美语言文学研究中心研究员、研究生部教授、博士，研究方向为文学翻译、翻译批评。

选文通过揭示翻译美学的渊源和发展以及翻译美学与文学翻译的关系，探讨当代翻译美学研究对文学翻译的启示意义以及对文学翻译原则的借鉴价值。翻译美学的任务，是运用美学和现代语言学的基本原理，研究和探讨语际转换中的美学问题，帮助读者了解翻译审美活动的一般规律，提高解决语际转换中碰到的具体问题的能力和对译文的审美鉴别能力。翻译美学的研究价值主要体现在对文学翻译实践的指导功能。翻译美学观照下的文学翻译审美再现三原则包括：象似原则——艺术模仿的原则；创作原则——艺术原创的原则；优化原则——艺术至美的原则。文学翻译研究需要吸收美学尤其是接受美学领域的最新成果，建构具有普遍适用性的翻译美学理论体系。文学翻译也只有与文艺学和美学联姻才能增强译作的审美效果。

1. 引言

文学翻译是翻译研究的重要组成部分，国内外浩如烟海的翻译研究著述中，有多一半成果是针对文学翻译而开展的。对于如何做好文学翻译，无论是翻译理论者，还是实践者，都从各自的研究角度，给出了许多答案和建言。在众多观点中，文学翻译的美学视角是最近几年来比较热点的话题之一，翻译美学也因此成为翻译学研究的一个非常崭新的领域。本文在总结梳理学界有关翻译美学研究成果的基础上，拟对该学科的历史渊源、研究对象和基本主张进行比较全面的论述。同时，结合典型例证，对翻译美学视域下的文学翻译实践原则进行探讨。

2. 翻译美学的历史渊源

一门独立学科的产生，通常是以这门学科的理论专著的问世并冠以该学科的名称为标志的。此外，它还应该具有两个显著标志：高校课程的设置和国际会议的召开。按照这个标准衡量，翻译美学作为一门独立的学科，其学科生命还很年轻。从现有的资料判断，较早以“翻译美学”命名并从理论上对这一学科进行系统描述和研究的著作在国外是 Shirley Chew 和 Alistair Stead 编著的 *Translating Life: Studies in Translational Aesthetics*(1999)，在国内则首推傅仲选的《实用翻译美学》(1991)。该书是我国首部以独立形态出现的翻译美学专著，标志着我国翻译美学研究在理论上的觉醒。此后，有关翻译美学的课程在我国的一些研究生教育机构也相继开设，如上海外国语大学研究生院、同济大学外国语学院，西北师范大学外国语学院，湖南大学外国语学院、湖南师范大学外国语学院、国立台湾师范大学文学院翻译研究所等。甚至有高校(如中国少数民族语言大学)在本科阶段就开设了这一课程。从理论专著的问世到高校课程的设置，翻译美学研究在我国的历史可以说只有短短 20 年的时间。

但是，从美学视角探讨、阐释、实践文学翻译，在国内外都具有千年以上的历史。在我国翻译思想“十大学说”(王秉钦)中，几乎所有的学说都有其美学渊源。例如，支谦的“文质说”、严复的“信达雅”、林语堂的“美学论”、朱光潜的“艺术论”、傅雷的“神似说”、许渊冲的“三美论”等译论，都蕴含着丰富的美学思想，具有显著的贵美倾向。而据译史研究，西方的译论之芽也是首先依附在哲学—美学之树上而枝叶渐丰的。从古罗马时期著名哲学家西塞罗针对文学翻译而主张的“辞章之美”，到后世翻译家杰罗姆的“自然之美”、翻译理论家泰特勒的“忠实之美”、以至加切奇拉泽的“艺术之美”，各家主张中，我们都可发现美学思想映照下的熠熠光辉。如果我们把20世纪90年代以前的美学视角下的文学翻译研究看作是翻译美学的孕育期的话，此后的20年间则可以被看作翻译美学的分娩期。这期间，在国外出版了 Shirley Chew 和 Alistair Stead 合著的 *Translating Life*：*Studies in Translational Aesthetics*（1999）；在国内则出现了傅仲选的《实用翻译美学》（1993）、刘宓庆的《翻译美学导论》（1995）、奚永吉的《文学翻译比较美学》（2004）、毛荣贵的《翻译美学》（2005）等研究著作。从国内四部著作在翻译美学理论建树过程中所起的推动作用来看，《实用翻译美学》和《翻译美学导论》最为值得学界关注和思考。前者对翻译中的审美客体、审美主体、审美活动、审美标准和审美再现手段等翻译美学的研究对象进行了分章详论，并在该书的概论部分对翻译美学的任务进行了简要论述。书中所探讨的内容与体系框架，正是当今翻译美学研究所应具备的指导原则、研究对象与范围。后者则"用现代美学的基本原理透视了翻译的运作机制，构建了现代翻译美学的基本框架，讨论了翻译的科学性、艺术性、审美客体、审美主体以及审美意识诸问题，提出了翻译不同文体的审美标准和对策"（毛荣贵，《翻译美学》，2005：16）。除了上面提到的四部学术专著，这一时期国内围绕翻译美学发表的科研论文也比较多。依据中国期刊全文数据库的统计，1994年到2010年之间，从翻译美学视角研究翻译的论文多达1226篇。其中，刘士聪的"散文的'情韵'与翻译"（2002），张柏然的"当代翻译美学的反思"（2001），赵秀明的"中国翻译美学初探"（1998）等文章在翻译研究界均引起热烈反响，争鸣继起。这些论著的出版，为翻译美学在中国作为一门独立学科而出现完成了理论上的准备。

3. 翻译美学的研究对象

与所有学科一样，翻译美学的研究对象与其研究任务有着密切的联系。有学者指出，"翻译美学的任务，是运用美学和现代语言学的基本原理，研究和探讨语际转换中的美学问题，帮助读者了解翻译审美活动的一般规律，提高解决语际转换中碰到的具体问题的能力和对译文的审美鉴别能力。"（傅仲选，1993：2）从理解的角度看，这段描述略显概括和笼统，对于我们了解这门新兴学科的研究任务帮助有限。结合刘宓庆（1995）、奚永吉（2004）、毛荣贵（2005）、方梦之（2004）等的观点，我们认为，翻译美学的任务，就是运用美学的基本原理，探讨美学对译学的特殊意义，分析、阐释和解决语际转换中的美学问题。在充分认识翻译审美客体和审美主体基本属性的基础上，剖析客体的审美构成和主体审美、复现美的能动性，明确审美主体与审美客体之间的关系，研究翻译中审美再现的类型和手段，以指导翻译实践。由此可见，翻译美学研究主要包括对翻译中的审美客体、审美主体和审美再现手段的研究。

目前，学界对翻译的审美客体的理解尚未统一。一种观点认为翻译涉及两种语言，因此翻译中的审美客体应该包括原文和译文。（傅仲选）另一种观点则认为，翻译的审美客体就是译者所要翻译加工的原文，这个原文必须具有审美价值，能够满足人的某种审美需要。（刘宓庆）从前面探讨过的翻译美学的历史渊源看，翻译美学所涵盖的审美客体不应将译文排除在外。否则，无论是支谦的"文质说"，还是严复的"信达雅"说，亦或是傅雷的"神似说"，都将失去审美比较所需的文本要件，成为无的之矢。这种审美客体也就成了文学意义上的审美客体，而非翻译学意义上的审美客体。由此我们可得出一个较为中肯的结论：翻译研究中的审美客体必然包括原文和译文。

值得注意的是，尽管傅仲选和刘宓庆在翻译审美客体所指对象的理解上不尽一致，但是他们在翻译审美客体的构成要素上却持有相同的观点。两位研究者所用的术语虽然不同,但所探讨的审美要素都与内容与形式这一对文学文本的二元系统密不可分。综合国内外目前的研究成果,可以看出,翻译审美客体的构成要素在文本的形式系统中主要包括语音层审美信息、字形(词形)层审美信息、句子层审美信息和篇章层审美信息;在文本的内容系统中则主要包括情志审美信息和意象审美信息。内容系统的隐含性导致情志审美信息和意象审美信息的模糊性和开放性,从而为接受美学理论关照下的文学翻译创造性叛逆主张带来可以阐释的理论空间。

学者们对翻译的审美客体的歧见同样反映在他们对翻译的审美主体的解释之中。刘宓庆认为翻译的审美主体就是翻译者。(刘宓庆,1995:168)而傅仲选则将译者、译文编辑和译文读者并列为翻译的审美主体,并指出这三个审美主体之间存在不同的分工:译者是原文的审美主体,读者是译文的审美主体,编辑既是原文又是译文的审美主体。(傅仲选)笔者认为,翻译美学在理论渊源上是基于国内外著名翻译家审美自觉基础上的翻译思想。总结和提出这些思想,目的是要为其他译者提供翻译的方法和经验,以便他们能够理解和鉴赏原文中的审美信息并在译文中将这些信息再现或创造。因此,将译文编辑和译文读者并列为翻译的审美主体对于译文的鉴赏而言是可以接受的,但是从译文文本的存在、译文质量的保障、译文对原文审美要素的再现这几个方面看,译者才是真正意义上的审美主体。

在翻译过程中,审美主体如果要将审美客体转换为另一种语介的文本,使其中的美学要素得以最大限度的保留,就必须娴熟地运用各种审美再现手段,确保译文与原文高度神似。审美再现手段因此成为翻译美学研究中最重要的研究对象。截至目前,学界对于翻译审美再现手段的分类研究并没有形成共识。有学者从具体技巧的角度出发,提出了增词法、减词法、引申法、替代法、反面着笔法、合译法和分译法等审美再现手段(傅仲选);也有学者从指导原则的角度出发,提出了模仿、重建、虚实转换、隐显转换和收放转换等再现手段。(刘宓庆)笔者认为,对于审美再现手段的合理分类应该建立在对"审美再现"这一翻译美学概念的正确理解之上。在文学翻译中,审美再现所要再现的,是原文的内容情志美、语言形式美、修辞模式美、音韵声律美和篇章结构美。由此可见,一切翻译的审美再现都集中于三个问题:第一,就语言层面而言,原文中的各种形式美如何模仿?第二,就文化层面而言,原文中民族化的语言表达方式如何保留?第三,就艺术层面而言,原文中内容与形式的统一关系如何再造?这三个问题决定了翻译审美再现手段所针对的重点对象,不是原文中的微小翻译单位(词汇和句子),而是较大翻译单位(段落和篇章)。因此,在审美再现手段的分类问题上,刘宓庆的分法更合理,也更适用。这个论断可以在刘著《翻译美学导论》中得到印证。篇幅所限,恕笔者在此不再例证。

4. 翻译美学的基本主张

著名翻译家泰韦特(Thomas Tyrwhitt)说过:"翻译贵在发幽掘微,穷其毫末。在造词与琢句方面,要译出其文;在性格与风格方面,要译出其人;在褒贬与爱憎方面,要译出其情;在神调与语感方面,要译出其声。"[转引自杨衍松:"果戈里——俄国散文之父"(译序)]泰韦特对翻译的要求言简意赅地包容了中外翻译美学研究的思想精髓。通过对已有翻译美学研究成果的梳理和解读,我们可以将泰韦特等翻译家和刘宓庆等翻译美学理论研究者的基本主张归纳为以下三点:第一,翻译既是科学,又是艺术。因此翻译艺术存在于一切翻译活动之中。不论译者面对的是什么文体的原语材料,翻译的过程自始至终存在着艺术选择和加工以及艺术优化

的任务。翻译艺术的普遍性和全程性促使翻译实践成为名副其实的审美活动。第二，在文学翻译中，对原文的艺术模仿和对译文的艺术创造同等重要，缺一不可。一部文学译著能否成为译入语国家翻译文学的一部分，能否得到该国文学评论家和史论家的肯定，既取决于原著作本身的艺术价值，也取决于译作的艺术价值。文学翻译的“二次创作”属性决定了在实践过程中对原文的艺术模仿和对译文的艺术创造的必要性。第三，语言形式在文学语篇的美学构建中具有不可或缺的意义。因此，文学翻译既要求内容之真，又要求形式之美。这就要求译者在不违背译入语语言使用规范的基础上，对蕴含在原文表达方式、篇章结构和交际意图之中的审美要素尽量予以保留。在此过程中，译语的准确性、生动性、表现力以及和谐美是保证译文语言审美效果的关键因素。

5. 翻译美学观照下的文学翻译审美再现三原则

作为翻译学学科下的一个子学科，翻译美学的研究价值主要体现在对文学翻译实践的指导功能。在如何传达原作之美的问题上，翻译美学所关注的问题为我们提供了方法论意义上参考答案。那么，如何从美学的视角来介入文学翻译呢？在回答这个问题之前，让我们先借用一下美学大师朱光潜先生关于审美的一段议论：

假如你是一位木商，我是一位植物学家，另外一位是画家，三人同时来看这颗古松。我们三人可以说同时都“知觉”到这一棵树，可是三人所“知觉”的却是三种不同的东西。你脱离不了你的木商的心习，你所知觉到的只是一棵做某事用、值几多钱的木料。我也脱离不了我的植物学家的心习，我所知觉到的只是一棵叶为针状、果为球状、四季常青的显花植物。我们的朋友——画家——什么事都不管，只管审美，他所知觉到的是一棵苍翠劲拔的古树。……他只在聚精会神地观赏它的苍翠的颜色，它的盘曲如龙蛇的线纹以及它的昂然高举、不受屈挠的气概。(朱光潜)

朱光潜议论中的三种人，对同一棵古树，怀抱不同的态度。木商从有用和有利的角度看古松，持的是功利的态度；植物学家从自然和研究的角度看古松，持的是科学的态度；画家从艺术和欣赏的角度看古松，持的是美学的态度。

如果我们把翻译比作这里的古松，作为译者，又该怀抱何种态度呢？是功利的，科学的，还是美学的？从翻译的职业诉求和翻译美学的基本主张看，译者应该同时怀抱上述三种态度，完成其翻译的过程。翻译的功利性是不言而喻的。不论是为了学习和就业的翻译专业的学生，还是为了文化传通和谋生的职业翻译家，他们都与朱光潜先生议论中的木商一样，在翻译活动开始的第一个阶段，对翻译任务本身持明显的功利态度。与此同时，翻译的标准、原理、规律、方法等又要求译者在具体的翻译过程中对原文信息进行客观、准确、忠实的反映，使得译文和原文在文本功能上“动态对等”。可见，译者还应该像植物学家一样，对翻译任务持科学的态度。而至于画家的态度，更是译者必须秉持的。文学翻译若止步于表面的准确和数学意义上的对等，就会像植物学家只见“针状的叶子、球状的果实”一样，失却画家眼中的“苍翠之艳、劲拔之美”。为表述方便而言，我们可以把文学作品的译者的工作分为三个阶段：第一阶段，为功利。追求译作的完成；第二阶段。为科学。追求译作的准确；第三阶段，为艺术，追求译作的优美。结合前述翻译美学三条基本主张，笔者认为，在文学翻译实践中，译者可以依循下面三条基本原则，提高其译文的审美效果。

5.1 象似原则——艺术模仿的原则

语言象似理论提出之后，翻译研究者很快发现，从象似性的视角切入翻译，将有助于解决原文形式的复现问题，实现以形示意的翻译效果，在最大程度上实现"形神皆似"的理想的翻译标准。根据王寅关于语言象似性分类的研究，我们可以把文学翻译实践的象似原则分解为数量象似性、时间象似性、空间象似性，心理象似性和意象象似性。译文对原文在这五个方面的属性进行自觉影像，符合美学中艺术模仿的原则。依循这个原则，有利于对原作形式审美效果的再现。比如在下面的例子中，译文2影像了朱自清语言的简洁之美，所以比较起来在数量象似性上要优于译文1：

我北来后，他写了一封信给我，信中说道，"我身体平安，惟膀子疼痛厉害，举箸提笔，诸多不便，大约大去之期不远矣。"(朱自清《背影》)

译文1　After I arrived in Beijing, he wrote me a letter, in which he says, "I'm all right except for a severe pain in my arm. I even have trouble using chopsticks or writing brushes. Perhaps it won't be long now before I depart this life. (张培基译，45字)

译文2　After I came north he wrote to me: "My health is all right only my arm aches so badly I find it hard to hold the pen. Probably the end is not far away. (杨宪益译，34字)

5.2 创作原则——艺术原创的原则

艺术之美，贵在原创。文学翻译是一门艺术，所以创作原则无疑适用于文学翻译。对于译文与原文的关系，古今中外多有精辟之见。意大利美学家克罗齐在《美学原理》中谈到翻译时指出："上好的译文除与原文有几分相似外，必须有它独创的艺术价值，本身即可成为一部独立的艺术作品。"(转引自方梦之《译者就是译者》)著名学者许钧教授也认为，"好的文学翻译不是原作的翻版，而是原作的再生。它赋予原作以新的面貌，新的活力，新的生命，使其以新的形式与姿态，面对新的文化与读者"。(许钧，2003)依循创作原则，有利于弥补文学翻译过程中因语际转换而造成的原文审美信息的损耗。例如在下面的译例中，译者尝试用"以创补失"的策略，再现了原文作者想要表现的"婆媳之间关系紧张"的交际意图：

姚氏：(念)亲生女儿真灵便，
取来个媳妇太讨厌。
人人都说我不公，
亲生的女儿谁不疼。
家家都说我媳妇好，
我看她是眼中钉。
靳氏：(唱)与婆婆捧来了一碗面，
未进门先觉得胆战心寒。
每顿饭不嫌早来就骂晚，
不嫌淡来就骂咸。

在娘家做姑娘样样都好办，
到婆家当媳妇事事为难。(悲伤)

——晏甬《小姑贤》

译文：

Mis. Yao：(monologue) My daughter is the apple of my eye，And my daughter-in-law the fly in my pie. All neighbors heap their praises upon my daughter-in-law，But I find her nothing but the sore in my eyeball.

Mis. Jin：(sing) I bring in a bowl of noodles to my mother-in-law，But my body trembles like a leaf before I step into her door. With me she never stops finding fault，Saying the meals cook with too little or too much salt. To what my mother would say good and okay，My mother-in-law tends to say shit and nay. (sadly)

——笔者试译

5.3　优化原则——艺术至美的原则

至善至美是艺术创作的最高理想，也是指导各种艺术实践的重要原则。就文学翻译而言，译者在遵循忠实通顺原则的同时，还应该遵循优化的原则，“尽力择优而从”(刘宓庆，2005)，以使译文接近“善译”(马建忠，《拟设翻译书院议》)的标准。从所指对象区分，文学翻译的优化原则可以分为语言优化和语序优化。语言优化指“发挥译文的语言优势，选用最合适的译语表达方式”(许渊冲，2006)；语序优化指在不变更原文内容的前提下，根据译语表达习惯和认知过程，对译文的句序进行优化重组。请看例示：

例1：语言优化

原文：

When my husband，Bill，and I were courting，just a phone call could send us quivering with excitement. We went on impromptu picnics，called each other Sweet Patoo tie and left mash notes in strange places. Cheeks flushed，hearts raced，palms sweated.

And then we got married.

Mortgage payment rolled in. A son，housekeeping，jobs and just plain old familiarity forced romance out. Faced with the choice of watching TV or sharing a passionate moment，I am embarrassed at how often we cast our vote for Jerry Seinfeld.

原译：

我们之间接到对方的电话就会激动不已。脸变红了，心在跳，手掌也在出汗。一个儿子、家务、工作，还有老一套平淡而又熟悉的东西让我们失却了浪漫。面对着是看电视还是大家高兴一会儿的选择的时候，我感到很窘迫，经常我们把选票投给Jerry Seinfeld。(注：Jerry Seinfeld是当代美国一肥皂剧的著名笑星。)

毛荣贵在《翻译美学》中评论这段译文时说，“如此译文，犹如一杯扑鼻的上等咖啡，换成了

一杯白开水。没了激情,没了文采,没了美感。”(毛荣贵,2005)两相比较,他的评论是比较中肯的。且看他改进之后的译文:

一个对方的电话,就能让自己因激动而心跳。双颊红通通,心头跳蹦蹦,手心汗津津。儿子出生、家务繁重、工作压力,再加上那亲热不起来的亲热,浪漫就这样被扫地出门了。夜幕降临,是看电视?还是两人亲热一会儿?我们每每选择前者,这使我内心真不是滋味。

和原来的译文比较,毛译在保留原文的修辞美、语言美和内容美方面,的确上升了一个层次。但是,毛译依然有改进的空间。首先,原译文和毛译都存在一定的漏译,把原文要表达的内容减少了;其次,毛译中的“一个对方的电话”的用语不符合汉语表达规范,改为“对方的一个电话”较好;再次,“儿子出生、家务繁重、工作压力”三个短语尽管在形式上做到了一致。但是经不起仔细推敲,因为“出生”、“繁重”、“压力”分类于动词、形容词和名词,并置起来存在词性不一致的问题。鉴于上述三点。我们认为,此文作如下翻译似乎更好:

对方的一个电话,就能让彼此激动不已。不经意的一个提议,双方都会欣然同意。他会柔情地叫我“小甜心”,我也会亲昵的叫他“乖宝贝”。我们所到之处,都会留下爱情的写意。总之,只要两人在一起,都会有那种甜蜜的感觉:脸颊发烫,心跳加速,掌心冒汗。

然而结婚之后呢?

房贷的压力,育儿的辛苦,家务的劳累,工作的重负,再加上彼此之间的审美疲劳,使得婚前那种浪漫的感觉早已不复存在。夜幕降临,是面对电视对一个自己并没见过的当红明星无谓投票,还是和那熟悉的不能再熟悉的爱人卿卿我我共度良宵?我们每每会选择前者,这使我内心真不是滋味。

例 2:语序优化

原文:

敕勒川,阴山下。
天似穹庐,笼盖四野。
天苍苍,野茫茫,
风吹草低见牛羊。

——北朝民歌:《敕勒川》

原译:

By the side of the rill,
At the foot of the hill,
The grass land stretches' neath the firmament tranquil.
The boundless grassland lies
Beneath the boundless skies.
When the winds blow
And grass bends low,
My sheep and cattle will emerge before your eyes.

(引自《汉魏六朝诗一百五十首》,许渊冲译,1996 年版)

改译：

At the foot of the hill,
By the side of the rill,
The grass land stretches' neath the firmament tranquil.
The boundless grassland lies
Beneath the boundless skies.
When the winds blow
And grass bends low,
My sheep and cattle will emerge before your eyes.

（引自《汉英对照新编千家诗》，许渊冲译，2000年版）

两个译文均为许渊冲先生的杰作。前后译文惟一的不同，是译诗第一、二两行句序的调整。虽然英语在表达习惯上有"从小到大，从微观到宏观"的定则，前译诗不改也可。但是在这首具有画面美感的民歌中，作为审美主体的读者的视野，则"正如电影镜头一样，从 hill 到 rill，渐退为背景，一望无际的 grassland 进入镜头，随着视野的扩大，出现悠然的 firmament，以及远景中的 sheep and cattle。前后顺序，层次井然"（张智中，2006：157）。可见，许渊冲调整的不是句序，而是读者审美视野的自然顺序。

6. 结语

综上所述，我们认为，现代文学翻译研究在理论上要有所突破，不但需要吸收哲学、文学、语言学、文化学等学科领域的研究成果，而且需要吸收美学尤其是接受美学领域的最新成果，在继承中外传统翻译美学研究成果的基础上，建构具有普遍适用性的翻译美学理论体系。在实践方面，文学翻译也只有与文艺学和美学联姻，通过这种联姻增强译作的审美效果，为译作在目标语国家的接受创造条件，才能破解近几十年来我国文学翻译领域缺乏翻译文学名著的困局，让更多的外国文学名著走进中国，同时也让更多的中国文学名著走向世界。

选文三　Poetry Translation

David Connolly

导　言

本文《诗歌翻译》选自贝克（Mona Baker）主编的 *Routledge Encyclopedia of Translation Studies*（上海外语教育出版社，2004）。作者大卫·康诺利（David Connolly）是爱尔兰裔英国人，1998年加入希腊籍，曾在希腊的雅典大学、亚里士多德大学教授翻译，拥有伯明翰大学、普林斯顿大学和牛津大学的荣誉学位(Honorary degree),翻译了希腊20世纪主要诗人和作家的25部作品。

选文探讨了诗是否可译,诗的风格、形式和情感等在翻译中的传达问题,以及诗歌创作与诗歌翻译的关系,还解释了诗歌翻译中的翻译、改写和拟作,以及"是诗人译诗还是译者译诗"、诗歌的译评等诸多方面的话题。作者从自己的诗歌翻译实践出发,提出了许多有见地的思想,如诗歌的形式具有的意义;诗的翻译只能是部分的,有缺失的,每一次翻译都不可能是最终的翻译;以译者的翻译目的为衡量标准,诗歌翻译模式和诗歌翻译理论不应忘记译者的倾情投入和创作灵感;诗歌翻译需要建立自己系统理论等等。这些诗歌翻译思想是对传统诗歌翻译理论的概括和总结。

The translation of poetry is generally held to be the most difficult, demanding, and possibly rewarding form of translation. It has been the subject of a great deal of discussion, particularly within the field of LITERARY TRANSLATION. Much of the discussion consists of a theoretical questioning of the very possibility of poetry translation, even though its practice is universally accepted and has been for at least 2000 years, during which translated poetry has influenced and often become part of the canon of the TL poetic tradition; Fitzgerald's *Rubaiyat of Omar Khayyam* (1859) and Pound's *Cantos* (1925-1970) are obviously examples. The views on the subject are many and varied, often anecdotal and, perhaps unavoidably, subjective. Robert Frost's definition of poetry as 'that which is lost in translation' is often quoted in the literature to highlight the difficulty of the task, yet discussions of the actual process of translating and attempts to define the particular problems involved and the strategies for dealing with these are relatively few.

(Im)Possibility of the Task

It is widely maintained that poetry translation is a special case within literary translation and involves far greater difficulties than the translation of prose. The language of poetry will always be further removed from ordinary language than the most elaborate prose, and the poetic use of language deviates in a number of ways from ordinary use. Poetry represents writing in its most compact, condensed and heightened form, in which the language is predominantly connotational rather than denotational and in which content and form are inseparably linked. Poetry is also informed by a "musical mode" or inner rhythm, regardless of whether there is any formal metre or rhyming pattern, which is one of the most elusive yet essential characteristics of the work that the translator is called upon to translate. And in addition to the difficulties involved in accounting for content and form, sounds and associations, the translator of poetry is also often expected to produce a text that will function as a poem in the TL. So, although it is crucial that the original be recognizable in the translation (if we are to talk of translation and not imitation or ADAPTATION), a further criterion for a successful translation is that of the intrinsic poetic value of the translated text. In short, "what an English-only reader wants is a good poem in English." Similarly, it is often suggested that, unlike other forms of literary translation, the translation of poetry must stand on its own as a poetic text, to a large extent. However, Nabokov, a firm believer in the impossibility of poetry translation, would disagree: "I want translations with copious footnotes, footnotes reaching up like skyscrapers to the top of this or that page so as to leave only the gleam of one textual line between commentary and eternity."

The often insurmountable difficulties involved have led many, like Nabokov, to the conclusion that poetry can only be rendered literally. A similar view is attributed to Robert Browning, namely that poetry translation "ought to be absolutely literal, with [the] exact rendering of [the] words, and the words placed in the order of the original. Only a rendering of this sort gives any real in sight into the original." Roman Jacobson's resolute belief that poetry is by definition untranslatable led to the somewhat different methodological approach that only "creative transposition," rather than translation, is possible where poetic art is concerned. Shelley, too, believed essentially in the impossibility of poetical translation, and yet he produced several verse translations from Greek, Latin, Spanish and Italian poetry and is a good representative of early writer on the subject, who tended to emphasize the futility of the undertaking whilst undertaking it none the less! A contemporary translator, William Trask, perhaps sumsup this attitude succinctly when he says, "impossible, of course, that's why I do it."

The view that it is impossible to translate poetry recognizes that it is impossible to account for all the factors involved and to convey all the features of the original in a language and form acceptable to the target language culture and tradition. However, from this sobering acceptance of the difficulty involved and of the enormity of the task comes a search for strategies whereby as much as possible of the original poetry may be saved in the translation.

Approaches: Pragmatic and Theoretical

Approaches to the problems involved in translating poetry fall into two basic categories: the pragmatic and the theoretical. The pragmatic approach is favoured by most practising translators, while the theoretical models of the process are mainly the work of linguists.

A typical example of the pragmatic approach is the view expressed by W. S. Merwin (in Weissbort, 1989: 139): "I continue in the belief, you know, that I don't know how to translate, and that nobody does. It is an impossible but necessary process, there is no perfect way to do it, and much of it must be found for each particular poem as we go."

There is, in fact, a noticeable reticence on the part of practising translators towards attempts by linguists to provide a formal basis for what has traditionally been considered a highly subjective and *ad hoc* activity. For example, Peter Jay (in Weissbort, 1989: 74) writes: "I've not yet come across any theoretical precept that's helped me make a line of any translation ring true." Practising translators tend to write of the specific problems they encounter in translating a particular poet and of the solutions they found—often in the form of an apology for the translation—or reflect on the various stages they pass through in the process.

Translators, however, rarely keep notes about the process of translating or any record of the choices made in the process. Even if translators could provide descriptions of solutions and strategies they have employed in dealing with specific translation problems, the question remains whether an examination of a skilled translator's personal experience can provide formal strategies and hence be of practical value to other translators. What is stressed continually by practising translators, over and above any particular approach or methodology, is the need for constant reworking and reassessment of the translated text in an attempt to make it correspond to the original poetic text on all levels, or rather on as many levels as possible.

However, although skilled translators' reflections on the process of translation may be unreliable, it is precisely insights into this process that are missing from most theoretical models and approaches to the translation of poetry. Nida (1964: 146) presents a diagram of how a message in the SL is decoded by the receptor and re-encoded into a message in the TL. The centre of the diagram is the process he labels **transfer mechanism**, and it is this stage of the process that is the most difficult to analyse. Most models of poetry translation focus on either the decoding of the ST or the product of the re-encoding in the TL. An approach often adopted is to compare one or more translations of a poem with some notional ideal translation, with the ensuing unavoidable and subjective value judgements. A somewhat more useful approach is to compare several translations of the same poem, not in order to make value judgements, but to examine the different strategies employed. Lefevere (1975) examines different translations of a poem by Catullus and distinguishes seven strategies, though it is rare in practice to find any of the strategies he discusses used exclusively. De Beaugrande (1978) formulates a model of poetic translation based not on a comparison of texts but on text linguistics and strategies of textual equivalence, focusing primarily on the analysis and comprehension of the ST and on reader-oriented theories of literature. Here again, however, the actual process of translating is lost somewhere in the maze of the complex diagrams of his model. A more empirical model of the processes involved in translating poetry is provided by Jones (1989), who suggests three main stages: the understanding stage, which involves close analysis of the source text; the interpretation stage, where the translator works item by item, though with continual reference to source and target texts; and the creation stage, where the target text is fashioned as an artefact that can be valid in target-culture terms. It is interesting to note how this model of the process

coincides with much of the existing reflections by skilled translators on their work.

The relationship between theory and practice in poetry translation has always been problematic. Few theories can account for the complexities involved in actual practice or indeed for the resourcefulness needed by the translator; and although it may be unrealistic to expect that a theoretical model of poetry translation should solve all the problems a translator encounters, such a model should arguably provide a description of the set of strategies available for approaching these problems and procedures for dealing with the various factors involved. Most scholars would probably agree with de Beaugrande that "certainly the very uneven quality of much translated poetry suggests the pressing need for more definite and regular procedures."

The Nature of the Task

Any translation of a poem will require attention to each of the various levels on which a poem functions. On the semantic level, a poem carries some message or statement about the real world or the author's reaction to it, and this is often considered the core which any translation must reproduce. However, the message of a poem is often implicit and connotative rather than explicit and denotative, giving rise to different readings and multiple interpretations. It has been pointed out repeatedly that translation is first of all an act of reading, and just as there is no single way of reading a poem, there is no one interpretation and translation of it. The translator, in fact, translates his or her own interpretation, though this should preferably be informed one. Alternatively, some scholars suggest that the translator believes the author would have expressed him/herself had he or she been writing in the target language (Lefevere, 1975: 103). However, the author's intension is rarely obvious or inferable with any great degree of certainty, and there is no reason to suppose that the translator has privileged access to it. One might suppose that semantic problems of interpretation could be dealt with by simply consulting the poet if he or she is still alive, but, as Socrates relates in *The Apology*, readers are often more informed than authors, and the meaning of a poem lies not with the author but within the text itself and the reader's interpretation of it.

A thorough stylistic analysis of the text is a prerequisite in poetry translation. Style is one of the features that distinguishes literary translation—and in particular poetic translation—from other forms of translation, and since readers expect to find in a translation those particular characteristics that mark the text as belonging to a particular poet, a poetic translation successful only if style has been conveyed together with content, and a stylistic analysis is often carried out unconsciously or intuitively by experienced translators and sensitive readers. Lefevere (1975: 99) suggests that the reason why most translations, versions and imitations are unsatisfactory is that they tend to concentrate exclusively on one aspect of the source text, rather than on the text as a whole, presumably because of an inadequate stylistic analysis on which to base methodological criteria.

Related to the question of style is another question prevalent in the discussions on poetry translation, namely whether verse should be translated into verse or prose. As might be expected, believers in the impossibility of poetic translation tend to assert that if poetry is to be translated at all, prose is the only medium for that purpose. One advocate of the translation of verse into prose is Stanley Burnshaw, who, in *The Poem Itself* (1960), gives the poem in the original language, discusses it and then gives a literal prose rendering. He advances the view that the only way to experience the poetry of an alien language is to hear the sounds of the original while reading literal renditions. In his Preface, he claims that since poetry cannot be poetically translated, the most satisfactory procedure is to provide the reader with a lexical and contextual commentary and an *ad verbum*, nonliterary translation alongside the original, thereby enabling the reader to experience the source text for him/herself.

Prior to the twentieth century, the translation of verse into prose was rarely defended; the prevailing view was that "to attempt... a translation of a lyric poem into prose, is the most absurd of all undertakings, for those very characters of the original which are essential to it, and which constitute its highest beauties, if transferred to a prose translation, become unpardonable blemishes." Similar views concerning the necessity of preserving a poem's formal rhymes and metre are still held by many in the twentieth century. Joseph Brodsky, for example, maintained that "metres in verse are kinds of spiritual magnitudes for which nothing can be substituted... They cannot be replaced by each other and *especially not by free verse*."

It is not only the individual words of a poem but also its form which acts as a signifier with a signified that changes from culture to culture and from age to age. In other words, the meaning of a poetic form changes with the passage of time and the transformation of social values, and may not be effective in another age and culture. For example, the sonnet form does not signify for the contemporary North American reader what it did for Petrarch's contemporaries in fourteenth-century Italy. Using the same form for a translation in a different age and a different culture may therefore carry quite a different meaning and produce the opposite of a faithful rendering. One solution is to look for a cultural equivalent (such as the English iambic pentameter for French Alexandrines) or a temporal equivalent (modern free verse for classical verse forms of the past). The form of a poem has to be translated, like all its other aspects, and, without going as far as Bonnefoy to say that it *must* be translated into free verse, translators of verse should at least be aware of the possibilities open to them and the strategies they have at their disposal. Holmes (1988: 25) identifies four such strategies, traditionally employed for the translation of verse forms.

(a) **mimetic**, where the original form is retained;

(b) **analogical**, where a culturally corresponding form is used;

(c) **organic**, where the semantic material is allowed to "take on its own unique poetic

shape as the translation develops;"

(d) **deviant** or **extraneous**, where the form adopted is in no way implicit in either the form or the content of the original.

The choice of strategy, of course, is itself a reflection of target language NORMS and the preferences of a particular cultural community at a particular point in time.

Poetry does not only function in terms of semantic content and aesthetic form; often, it is intended to arouse sentiment and to produce emotional effect. This pragmatic dimension of a poem is perhaps the most difficult to account for in translation. If there is disagreement as to what constitutes semantic and formal equivalence in poetry translation, it is even harder to define pragmatic (dynamic) equivalence. Yet the general belief is that the translator should try to achieve an "equivalent effect" and that "that translation is best which comes nearest to creating in its audience the same impression as was made by the original on its contemporaries" (Rieu, quoted in Lefevere, 1975: 103).

A fundamental problem, however, is the lack of a theoretical basis for standards of EQUIVALENCE in poetry translation, partly because there is no overall agreement as to what in a poetic text constitutes the basic UNIT OF TRANSLATION. Although equivalence remains an important factor in discussions about translation, there is disagreement as to what types of equivalence are most crucial, given that it tends to be different to achieve on every level. For example, in order to maintain equivalence of sound patterns, it will usually be necessary to sacrifice equivalence on a syntactic or semantic level. De Beaugrande and Lefevere (1975: 96) favour equivalence on a communicative level. No translation of a poem, though, can ever be "the same as" the poem itself, and what the translator should strive for, according to Holmes (1988: 54), are "counterparts" or "matchings," by which Holmes means words and other elements which fulfil functions in the language of the translation and the culture of its readers that are similar, "though never truly equivalent," to those fulfilled by the words and structures of the source poem in the language and culture of its own readers.

The ongoing dilemma of the translator of poetry is how to account as accurately as possible for the characteristic features of the original and at the same time create a poetic text in the TL that will have a similar pragmatic effect on the reader. The simultaneous achievement of equivalence on all the levels on which a poem functions is in practice impossible, so the translator is continually faced with choices and compromises. Poetry translation has been called the art of compromise and its success will always be a question of degree. The translation will always incur loss in relation to the original, irrespective of whether there may be gain in the translation, in the sense that the translation may be considered a better poem. If the goal of equivalence on all levels of a poem is impossible, it follows that no one translation is wholly adequate—a point which could perhaps be made of all translation, though it is clearly more obvious in poetry translation. It also follows that several translations of the same poem will be able to achieve what no one translation can do, that is highlight different aspects of the sane poem, and there is a good case to be made for multiple translations of the same poem (Holmes, 1988: 51).

Poet-translators and Translator-poets

There has always been a close connection between writing original poetry and translating it, and major poets are often themselves translators and concerned with the theoretical issues involved. Many writers have claimed that one must be a poet to translate poetry, though it could also be said that even if the translator is not a poet in his or her own right, he or she becomes one in the process. If artistic ability is needed to produce an original poem, then a very similar artistic gift is required in translating it, and the names of original poets and their translators are therefore frequently linked in the literature. Despite the traditional view of the translator of poetry as a secondary or failed poet feeding off the achievements of others, it is widely recognized that poetry translators are highly gifted, for they "must perform some (but not all) of the functions of a critic, some (but not all) of the functions of a poet, and some functions not normally required of critic or poet" (Holmes, 1988: 11). Perhaps it is these other functions required of a translator-poet that explain why many poet-translators may be great poets but not necessarily great translators. Many well-known poet-translators tend to impose their own style so thoroughly on the translated poems that these resemble their own poems rather than reflecting the particular characteristics of the author. For example, Ezra Pound's "translation" are Pound and are read for that reason, and Lowell admitted to producing not "translations" but "imitations." It is interesting to note that some poet-translators, like Lowell, use translation as a kind of workshop for practising their craft when their own work has reached an impasse.

Similarly, it is possible for a poet who is ignorant of the source language to produce a poetic text both aesthetically pleasing and intuitively accurate, as in the case of Pound's translations from Chinese. This is usually accomplished through the use of an intermediary or informant, someone with knowledge of the SL who prepares a primary or draft translation, sometimes known as **crib translation**.

There has been much discussion on the demarcation lines between translation, adaptation and imitation, and the difference seems to lie in the degree of interpretation. According to Lefevere (1975: 76), "The translator proper is content to render the original author's interpretation of a theme accessible to a different audience. The writer of versions basically keeps the substance of the source text, but changes its form. The writer of imitations produces, to all intents and purposes, a poem of his own, which has only title and point of departure, if those, in common with the source text." It is true that a lot of literature on poetry translation is about value judgments based on the critical method of comparison with the original, with the result that imitations and adaptations fare badly. Evaluation must, however, also be based on the translator's aims. A translation has to be

judged in terms of its consistency with these aims and not on something it was never meant to be. It cannot simply be assumed that the translator's aim is always to represent the original as completely as possible. All aims are valid provided they are clearly stated and motivated. What is not acceptable is inconsistency with these aims, mistakes in decoding and encoding, or loss that is due to incompetence on the part of the translator (see Lefevere, 1975: 101-3, for a five-point inventory for assessing the competence of a literary translator).

Translators often stress the need for a sense of affinity with the poet they are translating, and love for the poet's work together with some degree of inspiration are important factors usually missing from models and theories of poetry translation. As Octavio Paz suggests, "neither are sufficient, but both are indispensable." Perhaps it is this profound emotional involvement in translating poetry that motivates translators almost to the point of addiction to engage in what some have termed "the art of the impossible."

选文四 中国古典诗歌英译概述

孔慧怡

导 言

本文选自孔慧怡的《翻译・文学・文化》(1999)。作者孔慧怡是香港大学一级荣誉文学士,伦敦大学博士。学术论著有:《重写翻译史》(2005)、《翻译与文化变迁》(2005)、《亚洲翻译传统与现代动向》(2000)、《翻译・文学・文化》(1999)等;文学英译有《海上花列传》(*The Sing-Song Girls of Shanghai*)(2005)、《小城之恋》(*Love in a Small Town*)(1988)、《荒山之恋》(*Love on a Barren Mountain*)(1991)等。

选文较全面地勾勒出中国古典诗歌英译的历史。在回顾《诗经》第一代译者理雅各的 *The She King*,戴维斯的 *The Poetry of the Chinese* 和翟理斯的 *Gems of the Chinese Literature: Verse* 以及第二代译者韦理及其译作 *The Book of Songs*,高本汉的 *The Book of Odes* 之后,文章阐明了意图不同、译法不同的状况并介绍了中国诗歌英译对英美文化产生的影响。作者以庞德的 *Cathay* 为例,说明如果主体文化内部先产生变革的力量,那么外来的事物则是催化剂。另外,现在的译诗大多缺乏诗意,译者的翻译功力无法与前人相比,中诗英译的最好方法是通过中外译者合译。

在英语世界现有的中国古典文学英译文本中,诗歌是最瞩目的文类。这个现象本身就可以说明,中国文化传统与英语文化传统对文学的目标和看法,有着基本的分歧。事实上,从文学作品的分类来说，一般人把中国的散文类别与英语文学里的 prose 对等，本身就是个大问题，因为 prose 这个文种与 poetry 相对，凡是不属于诗歌类别的，一概算是 prose，所以连小说也是 prose 作品，一般英语 prose 选集都收录不少摘自小说的篇章。现在一般人做翻译时，惯于把中国的"文"与 prose 对等，"诗"与 poetry 对等，其实是一种以中国文学规范为依归的权宜做法，假如不加以解释，实在很容易误导英语读者。

在中国古典文学传统里，"文"的地位一直比诗高。大家都知道所谓的"诗缘情"，"文载道"。[1]这两句话清楚而又简洁地说明为什么"文"在中国古典文学传统里占有崇高的地位：作为道的载体，"文"在社会和道德范畴肩负起重要的使命，因此相对于诗，在中国传统文化体系里所占的位置就更显得重要了。当然，这并不是说诗歌没有广泛的影响力；正相反，诗也有它的政治功能，而写诗填词是中国传统文人都喜爱的一种活动，因为诗歌作为一种文体，得到传统认许，可以让文人言个人之志。我们还得注意一个事实，就是直到 20 世纪 20 年代，所有受过良好教育的中国人不但深谙写诗填词之道，而且不论为了交际或自娱，都写过一定数量的旧诗。这个事实告诉我们，中国古典诗歌原有的读者是很特别的一群人：他们既是读者，同时也是诗人（虽然不一定是第一流的诗人），对古典诗歌的规律有深刻的认识。中国古典诗词可以说是写给专家看的。

所有作者对自己的目标读者都有一定的假设和期盼，而作品往往建基于这些假设上。面对中国传统每个文人都会写诗这种现象，我们必须承认，古代诗人和他的目标读者之间那种关系，是无法在中国古典诗歌传统以外再现的。这在翻译来说，是一个相当大的障碍。但尽管如此，也尽管在中国古典传统里"文"的地位比"诗"高，从现代一般西方人对中国古典文学的概念来看，诗歌的地位远比任何其他文类突出。虽然西方人在介绍中国古典文学的初期，沿用中国文化传统的规范。但当翻译文学作品的人数开始多起来，而这些作品又和译入语文化的某些潮流达到一种契合，非汉学家的兴趣重心就明显地转移到诗歌了。到了 1947 年，Rrobert Payne（1911-?）就说诗歌是中国文化"最美丽的花朵"。[2]

《诗经》英译之始

18 世纪时在华的耶稣会士虽然也曾把《诗经》个别篇章译成欧洲语言，但他们的着眼点并非文学。时至今日仍被广泛引用的早年在中国古诗英译集，首推理雅各（James Legge，1814-1897）的 *The She King*。这本《诗经》英译 1871 年在香港出版，诗集名称的拼音正好反映中国南方口音的影响。《诗经》是中国文化传统里历史最悠久的经籍之一，而且也可说是笺注最多的经籍；在中国诗词传统里，《诗经》的地位是至高无上的。《诗经》古代笺注一个很大的特色，就是把收录的诗歌视为有浓厚政治寓意的作品，而整部《诗经》更被认为是想出仕辅政者必读的经籍。理雅各的翻译基本上跟随着这个传统，因此除了译诗之外，对于笺注也有详尽的解释，同时也就个别诗歌的政治背景作出说明。实际上，理雅各着手翻译《诗经》的时候，中国本土已有不少学者对《诗经》提出一些新的看法，但理雅各的翻译方向，基本上仍然跟随朱熹的论点；这很明确地显示出比较保守的态度；[3]另一位《诗经》译者高本汉（Bernhard Karlgren，1889-1978）后来就称此为"不幸的"保守。[4]

现在大家常看到的理雅各《诗经》译本是 1871 年出版的分行散文式译本；其实在 1876 年理雅各曾经推出另一个诗体英译本与 1871 年的译本有显著分别。我们可以推想，理雅各推出

第二个译本的原因，是希望把这些中国古诗放在英美诗歌的规范内，让他们以“诗”的面目和英语读者见面。[5]这种一诗两译的做法，让理雅各在中国古典诗歌英译史上占有一个很独特的位置：为了平衡源语学术知识与译入语诗歌规范的矛盾要求找寻实际的答案，他是个先驱者。他结果决定另外推出一个诗体版本，足以证明他认为译作的重点不可能同时兼顾学术与诗歌规范两方面的要求。毕竟理雅各对翻译工作的兴趣基础是文化方面而非文学方面的，《诗经》英译其实只是他翻译儒家传统经籍计划中的一部分，而他这个计划最大的目的，是为希望到中国传教的人介绍中国本土的知识和信仰传统，以期达到知己知彼的效果。理雅各这种文化取向，正好让我们理解为什么他翻译的1876年诗体《诗经》版本到了现在会鲜为人知——在理雅各翻译中国经典的计划里面，这些诗歌在中国儒家传统文化中的地位和评价，远比他们作为诗或民歌重要。18世纪在中国的耶稣会士也曾翻译过一些《诗经》中的作品和个别民歌，其目的亦并非为西方读者介绍中国文学传统，而是利用这些诗歌作为表达中国民族各方面特色的一种工具。[6]理雅各翻译中国经典的目的与18世纪耶稣会士所做的中国典籍欧译工作，在很大程度上可以说是一脉相承的。

诗歌作为文学作品的译介

首先推出中国古典诗歌英译选集的两名英国人，和理雅各可说是同时代的人。其中一人是曾任香港总督的戴维斯(John Francis Davis，1795-1890)，他的译诗集名为*Poeseos Sinensis Commentarii：The Poetry of the Chinese*；另一人是翟理斯(Herbert A. Giles，1845-1935)，译诗集名为*Gems of Chinese Literature：Verse*。这两本诗集和理雅各的《诗经》英译最不同的地方是译者的目标：两位译者都希望把诗歌作为文学作品介绍到英语世界，因此他们翻译的时候，就有了和理氏不同的考虑。

曾任香港第二届总督的戴维斯说明他出版这本诗集的目的，是希望改变中国文学在西方所受到的冷遇，而他认为要达到这个目标，最好的方法是“细心选择最佳的题材，同时处理手法应该尽量吸引有品位、有文化的读者，数量愈多愈好”。[7]戴维斯所说的“处理手法”，明显地指翻译的策略与方针。事实上，他的译本最大的特征是形式上富有弹性：视乎个别诗歌的需要，他运用不同的形式来表达，包括分行散文式、固定格律式、甚至是改编重写式。撇开翻译的实际效果不谈(因为这与个人的语言及文学能力有直接关系)，戴维斯这种不拘一格的做法，实在很适用于诗歌选集，因为这样更易于表达不同作家和不同诗种之间的分别。

不过，戴维斯这个选集最特别的地方，并不是他所做的翻译决策，而在于选材。戴维斯录取的作品，大多数是我们心目中的“歌体”(即verse)，而不是诗(即poetry)。他在译序中承认自己对采茶歌很有偏爱，因此全书有很大篇幅用于采茶歌；同时他也在传统小说及戏曲中抽取个别诗歌，独立翻译，收录在这本诗集中。另外他也收录了晚清学人王韬所写的有关伦敦风景习俗的10首旧诗，但并没有说明作者是谁。我们可以推想，选自小说和戏曲的个别诗歌也显示戴维斯个人的喜好，它们和采茶歌有一个相似的地方，就是通俗浅白，说不上是文学性强的诗作。描述伦敦景物的旧诗，对英语读者来说，当然也有一点与本土有关的趣味，可以作为一个吸引读者注意的焦点，所以戴维斯选用这些题材，是不难理解的。让人感到有点奇怪的是，这本诗集极少收录中国诗歌传统中著名诗人的作品，亦极少中国人心目中的佳作；全书收录的作品亦完全没有提及诗人的名字。从这一点我们可以看出，戴维斯心目中的“最佳主题”虽说是希望代表"中国诗歌",但事实上从他的选材建构起来的形象,却与中国诗歌传统本身并没有甚相似的地方。我们现在没有资料显示戴维斯对中国诗歌传统是否有深入理解,但从选材角度来看,他偏爱浅白和通俗的作品,似乎对中国诗歌传统的经典之作认识不深,而入选的作品很可能是他在学习中文的过程中碰上的材料。加入我们换一个角度,甚至可以说,正因为戴维斯对中国古典诗词的传统认识不深,意味着他不必背负这个传统的包袱,可以按照自己的兴趣和偏爱来建构这个诗歌选集。因为在他心目中,"有品位、有教养的读者"正是和他本人兴趣相近的人,所以他有信心凭自己建构的有"代表性"中国诗吸引读者。戴维斯这本诗选,固然可以看做在文化交流的早期,因为对原语文学传统缺乏深入了解而出现的产物,但更值得我们注意的是,戴维斯在译序中表明他的翻译目的,和他这本诗集的选材相对比,让我们清楚地看到译入语非专家读者的品位和兴趣,与原作文化的固有传统经典规范可以有多大的分别。这一种客观的理解对我们评价任何时代的翻译作品和他们背后的价值观,都有很大的帮助。

翟理斯在 *Gems of Chinese Literature*:*Verse* 的译序中说明,因为要顾及一般读者的需要,所以他在译诗中删除了英语读者难以理解的深奥典故,同时也省略了转换成英语后很难念出来的人名。这两类省略,其实都和翟理斯选定了什么样的人作为目标读者有很大关系。要解释中国古典诗词中所用的典故,不论是用脚注或者是在作品前面先详加说明,都是一种很明显的文化负重。这既不是翟理斯的主要翻译目的,也绝不是他心目中的一般英语读者会感兴趣的东西。至于省略音译的人名,则主要是就诗歌节奏和语感的考虑了。19 世纪的英语读者面对英译的中国人名,连如何发音也无所适从,[8]更别说理解这个人名背后有什么意义了。音译人名在节奏方面同样是突兀的外来成分,因此很容易打断译诗的节奏感,假如译者的目的是减轻译作所负担的文化包袱,希望可以用直接的方式打动英语读者,就非特别注重语感不可了。

翟理斯的译作立足于英国文化与文学规范,他为译诗选择的形式和节奏,都是他的目标读者非常熟悉的类别,而译诗中偶然用上希腊、拉丁和意大利语的典故,在当时的英语世界,也是被认为可以加强文学性和感染力的做法。一般来说,这种把译作植根于译入语本土文化的翻译方针,在文学作品翻译的早期是很常见的现象;中国人翻译外国文学作品的初期,就有极多相应的例子。这种做法有它的长处,就是很容易与目标读者沟通;但它自然也有短处。假如我们只希望译作读者体会到,另一个文化对人性和文学的表达也有美和善的追求,从而减轻一般读者对另一个文化的疏离感,这是很有效的做法;但如果我们的目标是让读者体会到两种文化之间的差异,希望他们可以领略另一种生活方式和世界观,这种做法就有相当大的缺陷了。缺陷在什么地方呢?我们且看一个简单的例子:

> With trembling heart and cautious steps
> Walk daily in fear of God ...

上面两句诗的文化背景显然是西方基督教式的传统,表达的绝不是中国古代诗人的思想。一般讨论翻译时说到的"同化"和"异化"问题,愈是靠近基础的文化层面就愈见尖锐,这里引的译诗句子就是最佳例证。这样的译例可以让我们理解到为什么后世评论翟理斯的翻译,往往认为他不论用语、节奏及翻译的文化方针都太古老了。但我们也不要忘记,大多数译者所赖以运作的文化框架,都建立于他们的教育和个人经验之上,也就是说,他们自觉或不自觉地把它们那个时代的价值观投射到翻译作品上,而译作之所以能吸引与他们同时代的读者群,原因也正在这里。翟理斯就是一个好例子。至于说他的遣词造句比较古老,其中一个原因应该是他

常年生活在中国，所以文学品味反而较他同时期的英国人为保守。但正因为他翻译的作品是中国古代文学，与他同时代的读者并不会因为他用比较保守的文风而感到格格不入；他们可以把这种风格理解为一种独特的表达手法。

《诗经》英译的"第二代"

上文提到，戴维斯和翟理斯的选材及翻译方法，除了反映出他们的个人背景外，也显示了译入语文化的当时规范。以下我们会举出理雅各以后最重要的译本，以说明英语的诗歌及翻译规范在数十年间经历了多大的转变。

到目前为止，20世纪最受瞩目的《诗经》英译本，分别是韦理（Arthur Waley）的 *The Book of Songs* 及高本汉的 *The Book of Odes*。韦理很清楚中国传统对《诗经》的看法，是把它视作政治讽喻，又或是道德教化的材料，但他却决定把英译《诗经》以民歌的面貌呈现给一般英语读者看，所以译本只有少量注释，而学术性的深入注解则另成一册。更重要的是他把《诗经》原来的分章结构打破，而以诗歌主题为译作分类的基础。韦理这个看来新颖而大胆的翻译决定，其实是有它很深厚的文化背景的：20世纪头20年，欧洲对民间文学——特别是民歌——兴起了广泛的研究兴趣，这个潮流甚至对当时中国学界和文坛也有过相当影响，而韦理决定把诗歌以民歌方式介绍给西方读者，并且打破原来以"国"为基础的分类，而就内容和主题重新编排，反映的正是当时让民间文学抬头的欧洲文化潮流。

从译诗的形式和风格来看，韦理也迈出了新的一步。他放弃了传统的英诗格律和押韵方式，转为依赖英语的自然节奏（sprung rhythm），同时他运用的词汇和语言层次幅度也极为广阔，以日常口语入诗的例子相当多。以上所说的种种，当然就是自20世纪初开始，英语现代诗发展出来的新方向。到目前为止，韦理的中、日文学英译本是少数真正吸引到广大英语读者群的译作，这一点固然显示了他的文学才华有独到之处，另一方面亦说明，他的翻译方法和目标，在译入语文化中正好引起共鸣。

上文说到的另一译者高本汉，在翻译方面的取向刚好和韦理相反。他的翻译方针是以学术需要凌驾一切。高本汉从1942到1946完成了可以称为逐字对译的《诗经》全译本。这种决定牺牲诗意（甚至不考虑诗意问题）的译诗方法，注定高本汉的译本不会在汉学界以外产生什么影响，更不会吸引大量英语读者。但作为"学术翻译"，他却可以说是一个重要的里程碑，因为这是学者译诗，而以学问完全压倒诗意的重要作品。随着汉学研究的发展，这种偏重知识而轻视诗歌特性的翻译方法，就愈来愈明显了。

中国诗歌在英美文化引起的反响及余波

虽然中国诗歌译成英语的只占极少部分，但我们都知道中国古典诗歌对20世纪英美现代诗歌传统的诞生和成长起过"推波叻澜"的作用。庞德（Ezra Pound，1885-1972）通过研究日本学者 Fenellosa 的笔记，翻译了一系列的中国古诗，收集在 *Cathay* 这本集子里，作为反英美诗歌传统规格和性质的一面旗帜，推动印象诗派的成长和发展，这对我们来说已经是耳熟能详的故事了。庞德英译中国古典诗歌的尝试，在意象派中后继有人，其中很著名的例子就是美国女诗人 Amy Lowell（1874-1975）。但对我们来说，这整个发展最有趣的地方，就是这场跨文化的孕育诗歌新芽运动,其实是一种源于误解的成果。中国古典诗歌格律严谨,但因为庞德及其他意象派诗人不懂中文,无法理解中国古诗在声韵和形式结构方面受到多大的约束;他们惟一能看到的,就是诗中的意象,因此对英美意象派诗人来说,中国古典诗歌是纯粹以意象为基础的。他们有了这种理解,就引中国古诗为范本,认为英美诗歌如果要摆脱传统的种种束缚,必须效法中国古诗;他们绝对没有想到的,是中国诗歌在中国的文学与文化传统中,事实上受到种种规条的约束和限制。正因为英美诗人对中国诗歌传统没有认识,他们才可以按照自己的想像和理解,把中国古诗引上适应他们本身需要的道路,用以支持他们提出的新诗歌理论。这个例子正好说明,变革的力量其实总是来自主体文化,外来的因素只是起了催化的作用,产生的实际影响远较表面看来的为轻。从这个角度来看,学术界经常讨论庞德翻译是否准确或忠实(通常是指责他不准确及不忠实),对我们尝试理解文化交流的实际运作方式,意义就实在不大了。

上述英美意象诗人向中国古诗借鉴的例子,还有一个更有趣的发展,因为它回过头来,又对中国白话文学运动的形成起过一定作用。胡适(1891-1962)在倡议中国文学革命的时候,明显是受到英美意象派诗人就诗歌所发表的宣言影响,因此他心目中的中国新诗就是以英美意象派诗为楷模的。但胡适却没有料到,中国古典诗歌在英美意象派诗歌运动中曾经扮演过什么角色;他要推翻的中国古典诗歌传统,却正是他要学习的英美意象诗派的曾引为创作目标的。上文所说有关主体文化内部先产生变革的力量,然后借助外来事物作催化剂,在此又一次得到证明。

译诗如何运作:寒山的启示

假如译入语文化会按照本身的发展需要,对中国古典诗歌传统的某一些层面加以强调,另一些层面加以弱化或忽视,那么同样的情况出现在对个别中国诗人的介绍,就不稀奇了。一般人都强调诗歌翻译的困难,但也有诗人通过翻译之后,在译入语文化取得一股新的生命力,因此达到比在原文化更高的地位;寒山就是一个好例子。这个唐代的出家人在中国诗歌传统里并非主流人物,但他的诗作却悉数译成英语,而且不只一种译本;这一点连中国诗歌传统中最著名的大诗人也没有几个可以与之相比。到底寒山为什么会如此受英语读者看重呢?虽然第一个把他介绍给英语一般文学读者的是韦理(1954 年韦理译了 27 首寒山的诗作,在有名的 *Encounter* 杂志刊登),但寒山能够在英语世界享有盛名,主要归功于美国 *Beat Generation* 的主将 Gary Snyder。五六十年代起,美国的文化环境出现重大变化,一群年轻人反思物质文明带来的束缚,希望寻找精神上的进步和灵性的解脱,因此把目光伸展到东方哲学及宗教,希望可以在此得到启发。Snyder 就是这一代人的旗手。他以简单直接而又充满美国式年轻活力的语言翻译寒山的诗,而更重要的是,他这个做法同时也把寒山传奇化和美国化,配合了当时美国年轻人的文化诉求,因此在中国诗歌传统中本来没有什么突出地位的寒山,就成了 60 年代美国前卫文化的偶像式人物。英美新一代诗歌读者通过 Snyder 的视野来看寒山的作品,会觉得这些译诗既有英美现代诗歌派的特色,又充满了东方宗教和哲学意味,与这一代英语读者所追求的配合得丝丝入扣。寒山的主要英语者——包括 Snyder、华兹生(Burton Watson)和赤松子(Red Pine,一名住在台湾的美国人)——全部都对佛教禅宗有很大兴趣,因此译者与其目标读者之间在文化诉求方面有很强的默契。

另外值得注意的一点,是韦理和 Snyder 在翻译寒山的过程中,都有一条非常明显的日本路线，而华兹生则是长期旅居日本的美国学者，这实在很有探讨价值。既然寒山诗作的英译在目前为止是惟一深入英美文化的中国诗歌，而它们的传播又以日本为桥梁，除了因为诗歌的宗教哲学味道在日本远比在中国受欢迎，而禅宗进入西方也是主要通过日本这条渠道之外，是否也显示了英美作为主体文化，在文学取向方面更倾向于某一种日本风格和传统呢？

寒山在英语世界的特殊地位可能只是机遇，也可能指向主体文化的某些偏向和特征，但无论如何，这个翻译的个案让我们清楚地看到，译作如果能在主体文化吸引大量读者，造成一定的文化反响，那么它在主体文化的规范里必定是已经建立起另一种生命，与它在原来文化中怎样运作并没有一定关系。

这里我们必须指出，像寒山诗英译这种情况是很独特的。除了他之外，没有任何中国诗人得到这种偶像式的待遇。此外，能够通过翻译而冲破在原有文化中划定的地位，除寒山外也没有别的显著例子了。一般来说，中国古典诗歌英译时，译者对个别诗人的评价还是与中国传统评价相辅相成的。假如我们看诗歌英译的频次，就会发现如李白、杜甫、王维、白居易和苏东坡等著名诗人，也是英语译者最乐于选用的。在翻译选材方面，译者亦会参考中国有名的诗歌集，例如《唐诗三百首》就有不止一个译本。[9]虽然到现在大家对别的诗歌种类如词和曲已经没有当年那种偏见，但以量而言，唐诗在翻译方面始终还是个重点。

一本相当特别的译诗选

译者和编者在处理中国古典文学传统和现代文学传统的时候，总是采取泾渭分明的做法，不会把分属两个传统的作品放在同一个选集里。但英译中国诗却有一个例外，就是 Robert Payne 所编的 *The White Pony*。这本英译诗集以朝代分章，全书大部分篇幅收录古典诗歌，时间直至清末，但最后一小部分却收入 1911 年后出版的白话诗。当时中国在文化和社会方面的急剧变化，让身处其中的 Payne 感到应该介绍新文化传统中的新作品，这是很可以理解的。但我们站在翻译的角度看，这种溶新旧诗于一炉的集子，明显地带出一个问题：译者如何表达新旧两个传统在语言和诗歌形式方面的天渊之别呢？这本诗集并没有为我们提供答案，因为光看翻译，我们实在无法看得出选集中的诗来自两个不同的文学传统。尽管如此，这本选集作出的尝试因为很罕见，所以始终有其参考价值，而时至今日，还没有同类的选集出现。也许所有译者和编者都考虑到如何表达古今传统分别的问题，也想不出上佳的解决办法。

The White Pony 的另一个特点，就是翻译方法也有别于一般一人独译或两人合作的方式。这是一本群体合作的翻译集，而很多译诗都没有列明译者名字，原因是一首诗随时会经过好几个人（全部都是以中文为母语的人）之手，因此译作的最后面貌，真的只有让编者负责了。

近 40 年的发展

自从 60 年代起，中国诗歌英译基本上成了西方大学中文系的领域。因为很多译作都是为了满足大学课程某些需求而出版的，因此译者站在作为老师的位置，优先考虑比较实际的问题，如词句与典故的意义，及诗人在中国文化传统的地位等，而诗意反而就变得次要了。1976 年出版的 *Sunflower Splendour* 正好显示这种由学者联手合作的做法，有何长处和弱点。这本诗集从中国古典诗歌传统最早期一直延伸到 50 年代，揭开了中国古典诗歌传统很重要而又为人忽视的一点，就是新文学运动之后，古诗并没有完全消失。以包罗性和资料性而言，这本诗集无疑是开创了新天地；但如果我们着眼在“诗”，这里所收的译作水准却非常参差，而且有很多往往让人大失所望。这一带的译者所受的教育与他们的前辈大不相同，普遍来说，西方古典语言、文学的底子相对地薄弱，而且也有部分人并非从小就接触英语的。他们在大学里任职，亦会带来很多间接影响翻译的因素，因此他们的翻译环境亦与前一辈的译者有所分别。凡此种种客观环境的变化，对文学翻译必定会产生影响。总的来说，今日置身学界的译者，在西方古典文学（classics）方面的功底远逊前人，而在大学教书又不一定要有写作才华，所以像上文提到高本汉式的翻译就愈来愈普遍了。假如译者缺乏理雅各那样的古典训练，也没有翟理斯对语言节奏的控制能力，又缺乏韦理那种文学天才和敏锐的直觉，那么标榜学问而忽视诗意，其实就是没有选择的选择了。

“学界译者”中的佼佼者

以上所说的，是近数十年的普遍发展。但幸运的是，在这种总趋势下，也有明显的例外；在二战后才投身学术界的人之中，也有出类拔萃的译者。霍克斯（David Hawkes）从50年代至80年代的译作都和诗歌脱离不了关系，而其中重要作品如楚辞（*Ch'u Tzu*，*The Song of the South*，1959）、杜诗（*A Little Primer of Tu Fu*，1965），特别是《红楼梦》（*The Story of the Stone*，1973-1980）中的诗词，显示了这一辈精英学者融合学术专长和上乘的文学触觉与语感，达到了怎样高的成就；上述几种译作风格和翻译方法都完全不一样，一方面显示霍克斯作为译者，数十年来不断探索和钻研不同的翻译手法，另一方面也显示出他个人的功力。翻译同类型、同风格的作品，远较翻译种类繁多而风格迥异的作品容易得多；从霍克斯数十年来的译作来看，他所掌握的文学翻译幅度，可以说是相当罕有的。

另一位值得一提的中诗英译者是华兹生，他和霍克斯的文风迥然相异。华兹生的文笔平淡自然，读来舒缓有致，正好配合他特别喜爱的带有退隐味道的中国古诗。以下所引华译苏东坡《鹧鸪天》一首，读者从译文自然节奏的起落，应该可以体会到华兹生如何充分利用英美现代诗歌传统，来表达中国古典诗词里常有的宁静致远的韵味：

Mountains shine through forest breaks, bamboo hides the wall;
Withered grass by small ponds jumbled cicada cries.
White birds again and again cut across the sky;
faint scent of lotus shining pink on the water.

Beyond the village,
by the old town walls,
with goosefoot cane I stroll where late sunlight turns.
Thanks to rain that fell at the third watch last night
I get another cool day in this floating life.

谈论诗歌翻译，到头来还是要把眼光放在个别作品上。译作的文学素质如何，并不是靠摇旗呐喊或编造口号就可以决定的；即使提出一套以文化传播为目标的理论，传播是否成功，还是得看译入语读者对译作有何反应。标出旗帜、长于理论是学界的特征，但这些是否可以演化为文学天分,从而让个别诗歌译作得到在英语文化里的新生命,则仍然只能看个别译者的语言和文学才能了。总的来说,二次大战后的教育体制和大学制度的种种架构,对于诗歌的发展可说是弊多于利;这种情况并不限于翻译的诗作,原创诗作亦明显地受影响。也许霍克斯和华兹生两人在事业上作出的选择,可以为我们提供某一种启示:他们两人为求专心从事翻译,都自动缩短了"正常的"学术生涯。同时我们也不能忽视另一点:他们这一辈学者现在都已过了退休年龄了。

如何寻求突破

目前的教育潮流仍然偏重实际知识而轻视文学触觉和感性,在这样的环境里,中国诗歌的英译本愈来愈难脱离由大学出版社构思成为教科书的框架,发展下去,大概其作为教学工具的分量愈重,则作为文学作品的分量就愈轻。这个问题当然并不限于翻译的诗作,但译诗和其他文种相比,所受的打击更大,因为本来诗歌读者就相对地少。翻译过来的诗如果文学性弱,而原因是译者把诗意成分的重要性减低——不论是故意如此,还是因为力有不逮——造成的后果,就是让译诗在英语文化里变得极度边缘化。诗歌翻译在对译者语感和语言运用方面的要求,远较其他文类的翻译为高,这也正是为什么一般在大学教书的人尝试翻译古典诗词,会遇上那么大的困难:他们有的是专业知识,学者身份更可以是一种权威的象征,但如果中国文学英译变成有"学"而无"文",那么译作的性质和功能,就和诗歌原来的文学功能脱节了。上文提到韦理和高本汉风格迥异的两种《诗经》译本,正好代表"文"和"学"两条道路;但要走哪一条路,其实并不是个人的选择,因为语言技巧和文学才华并不是去念研究院或拿个博士学位就可以换来的。

要为翻译成英语的诗歌注入生命力,合译是一个很好的办法。以往由学者和英美诗人合作带来良好成果的例子,也有不少。20 年代 Witter Bynner 和江亢夫合作翻译的 *The Jade Mountain*(《唐诗三百首英译》)与 Amy Lowell 和 Florence Ayscough 合作译出的 *Fir-flower Tablets*,都是美国诗人及懂得中国语言、文化的学者合作的成果。七八十年代类似的组合有 Kenneth Rexroth 和钟玲,以及 Vincent McHugh 和 C. H. Kwock。从译诗如何可以在译入语文化立足这个角度来看,这种合作形式实在是可以带来一定的突破。很可惜,到目前为止,这样的合作总是例外,而不是常见的事。

虽然从事翻译的人经常强调跨文化沟通的重要性,并强调通过文学翻译可以达到深层的文化交流,但从翻译文学在译入语文化如何运作的角度来看,主体文化的文学规范、文化需要和预期,几乎完全控制了读者如何接受从外语译入的诗歌。[10] 中国文学——特别是古典诗词——的英译,为我们提供一个很好的个案研究,证明无论是选材、翻译风格,甚至译作是否在英语世界被接受和产生影响,其实都完全不能脱离主体文化的规范和内在动力。正是因为这个原因,本文的讨论没有涉及在中国本土策动的古典诗词英译作品。撇开译者的英语能力和对英语文学与文化的各种规范的掌握是否足够不谈,[11] 这种在译入语文化以外策动的翻译活动,并非应主体文化的需要或期望而产生,因此他们能进入主体文化的机会就非常低了。以 20 世纪情况而言,英美文化是强势文化,即使要借助外来的文化力量时,亦只是按本身要求做出选择和调配[12](本文提到意象诗派和寒山的例子,正好做证明)。有了这样的背景,假如再加上中国译者在语言能力和文化理解方面都有问题,除非主体文化突然产生某方面的欠缺感,而又认为可以借助外来译者的力量，否则在英美文化范畴外策动的文学译作就根本不可能在主体文化的范畴内运作。到目前为止，提高英语语言、文化能力和在英语文化中找寻立足点，正是中国内地译者尝试在本国进行古典诗词英译所面对的两大问题。

注释：

1. 朱自清：《诗言志辩》，《朱自清文集》第4卷1129页，香港：文学研究社，1952.
2. Robert Payne, *The White Pony*, New York: The John Day Company, 1947, p. vii.
3. 假如我们考虑到理雅各翻译中国经籍的目的是以介绍儒家传统为重心，我们甚至应该承认他的做法是达到这个翻译目标的必然选择，而不一定涉及保守与否的问题。
4. Bernhard Karlgren, *Glosses on the Kuo Feng Odes*, *Bulletin of the Museum of Far Eastern Antiquities*, No. 14(1942), p. 75.
5. 详见 Lauren Pfister, "James Legge's Metrical *Book of Songs*," *Bulletin of the School of Oriental & African Studies*, Vol. 60, Part 1, pp. 64-85.
6. 这些诗全部译成拉丁文，见于耶稣会士 Jean-Baptiste Du Halde 所编的 *Description Gëographique, historique, chronologique, politique et physique de l'Empire de la Chine et de la Tartarie chinaise* 和 *Mëmoires concernant l'histoire, les sciences, les arts, les moeurs, les usages, etc. des Chinois*。前者于1735年出版；后者长达15册，于1776-1814年出版。
7. John Francis Davis, *Poseos Sinicae Commentari*: *The Poetry of the Chinese*, c. 1870, edition used New York: Paragon Book Reprint Corp., 1969, p. 33.
8. 这个现象维持到现在。汉语拼音系统中"c"、"q"、"z"、"x"等声母，没有学过这种拼音方法的人根本不会念。
9. 第一译是 Witter Bynner 和 Kiang Kang-hu 在1929年出版的 *The Jade Mountain*，这本诗集的翻译工作于1917年开始。
10. 某些国家在文学翻译方面的传统与英语文化的传统有异，倾向于认同异化；日本和德语文化都是好例子。这种情况之下，在译作中表现出来的异化(包括思想方式、词汇和语法各方面)，其实仍然是遵从本土文化对翻译定下来的规范，服从本土文化的参照系而运作，只不过此参照系的既成规范对翻译作品异化的要求远较英语文化参照系为高而已。
11. 假如当代以英语为母语的学界译者也因为教育制度和诗歌在某文化参照系中所占比重的改变，而显示出掌握诗歌语言方面的欠缺，那么以英语为外语或第二语言的译者面对何等障碍，自是不言而喻了。
12. 回顾中国近2000年的翻译传统，凡是对本土文化发展产生长远影响的"文化输入"活动，亦无不按照这种模式运作。

选文五　许渊冲《楚辞》英译的"三美论"

严晓江

导　言

本文选自《南通大学学报》(社会科学版)2012年第2期。作者严晓江是南通大学外国语学院副教授、硕士研究生导师、南京大学文学博士，研究方向为翻译学、比较文学。

选文从意美、音美、形美的角度以及微观层面分析许渊冲的《楚辞》英译文，旨在探讨许渊冲翻译观的精髓——"三美论"对古诗词翻译和研究的理论和实践意义。许渊冲以展现《楚辞》的艺术价值以及传播优秀的中华传统文化为翻译目的，更加注重英语世界读者的接受问题以及由此产生的社会影响。他采用以归化为主的翻译策略，将直译与意译相结合，在灵活变通中尽量发挥译语优势，使译诗既能传达原诗的精神风貌又符合英语的行文规范。许译《楚辞》传情达意，音韵和谐，形式工整，简洁流畅，使人感心、感耳、感目，其中渗透的"三美论"体现了西方文化的求真精神以及中国文化的求美传统，在很大程度上可以看作是具有中国特色的文学翻译理论。

楚辞是中华传统文化的瑰宝。在漫长的传播过程中逐渐形成三种涵义："第一，诗体。指出现在战国时代、楚国地区的一种新的诗体。第二，作品。指战国时代一些楚国人以及后来一些汉人用上述诗体创作的一批作品。第三，书名。指汉人对楚国人、汉人所写诗歌辑选而成的一部书。"这是我国著名楚辞研究专家周建忠教授对"楚辞"一词的界定。自19世纪以来，不少中外译者曾翻译过《楚辞》这部浪漫主义诗歌总集的若干篇目，尤其是以翻译屈原的诗篇为主。诸如霍克斯（David Hawkes）、翟理思（H. A. Giles）、理雅各（James Legge）、韦利（Arthur Waley）等西方汉学家以及杨宪益、卓振英、孙大雨、许渊冲等中国翻译家都进行了积极尝试。在这些各具特色的译文中，许渊冲的《楚辞》（*Elegies of the South*）英译文因其对"三美论"的实践而独树一帜。

翻译家许渊冲先生1921年出生于江西南昌，1943年从西南联大毕业后进入清华大学研究院，1948年赴法国巴黎大学留学，1983年起任北京大学教授，已出版中、英、法文译著60余本，是至今为止将中国历代诗词译成英、法韵文的唯一专家。在大量翻译实践和研究的基础上，许渊冲总结出诗词翻译的本体论——"三美论"，即译诗要尽可能传达原诗的意美、音美、形美。该理论是受鲁迅先生关于"习字"与"著文"论点的先期启发，他曾借用鲁迅的话说："诵习一字，当识形音义三：口诵耳闻其音，目察其形，心通其义，三识并用，一字之功乃全。其在文章，……遂具三美：意美以感心，一也；音美以感耳，二也；形美以感目，三也。"在论及这三者之间的关系时许渊冲认为："'意美'，是最重要的，'音美'，是次要的，'形美'，是更次要的。也就是说，要在传达原文'意美'的前提下，尽可能传达原文的'音美'；还要在传达原文'意美'和'音美'的前提下，尽可能传达原文的'形美'；努力做到三美齐备。""三美论"是许渊冲翻译观的精髓，国内学者对其研究主要集中在三方面：一是运用该理论分析许渊冲本人的翻译作品，比如《毛泽东诗词》的英译以及唐诗宋词的英译；二是运用该理论分析其他译者的翻译作品并总结译文的美学特征；三是对该理论提出某些质疑，比如刘英凯认为许渊冲的"形美说"与"音美说"往往拘泥于形似而有损神似等等。目前，学者对许渊冲的《楚辞》英译与"三美论"之间关系的研究甚少。相比较其他古诗词和典籍英译而言，《楚辞》因为主题深奥、文字晦涩而更加难译。因此，管窥"三美论"与许译《楚辞》的相互印证，对古诗词翻译具有以点带面的指导意义。

1. 感心:传译诗眼,再现意象

许渊冲所谓的“意美”就是保存原诗的情韵并传达其深层意义。“意”是作者的思想感情与客观景物相融合的产物,是诗的灵魂所在。“王国维说过一句名言:一切景语都是情语。这就是说,诗词中即使是写景,也是借景写情。而西方文字,一般说来,写景是写景,抒情是抒情,很难理解景中有情的中文,要用英文来表达就更难了。而文学翻译需要传情达意,达意是低标准,传情是高标准。”诗人往往借“诗眼”来传情达意,译者要善于巧抓诗眼、正确解读诗眼、恰当表达诗眼,才能充分展现诗的意美。《楚辞》经过历代文人的注疏释义之后,导致了阐释者对某些字句的弹性解读,译者也总是从不同角度去理解。例如,《离骚》中的“长太息以掩涕兮,哀民生之多艰”诗句中,“民生”一词就是该句的诗眼,也可以说是全诗的诗眼。“民生”究竟是指“人民的生活”呢,还是指“人生”呢?译者可以结合历史背景以及上下文语境进行分析,全诗用“朕、吾、余”等第一人称来抒写屈原的生命历程和精神之旅,表明了他虽深受迫害却依然怀有安邦之志的伟大胸怀。可以想象:这样一位坚贞之士此时此刻主要是在哀叹自己的命运多舛,它当然也包含了感叹普遍意义上的人生多艰。许渊冲将其译成:I sigh and wipe away my tears, oh! /I'm grieved at a life full of woes. 意思是说:“我长长叹息不禁泪流满面啊,可怜人生多么艰难!”译文中的叹词 oh 直抒胸臆,给读者留下深刻印象。a life full of woes 语意恰切,传达了屈原怀才不遇的愤懑与沉郁之情。翻译的本质是译意,意美要以意似为基础,也就是“从心所欲不逾矩”。由于“意美有时是历史的原因或联想的缘故造成的。译成另外一种语言,没有相同的历史原因,就引不起相同的联想,也就不容易传达原诗的意美。”鉴于此,译者要尽可能把语意隐晦的汉语原文译成具体明白的英文,以帮助西方读者从时代背景方面体物缘情。《楚辞》英译牵涉到古今阐释和汉英转换的过程,译者只有真正领悟作者的思想境界,才能以文寻情和以情入文,从而再现原诗的意美。

传情达意是以再现原诗艺术意境为依据的,“立象尽意”概括出中国诗词意境的创造离不开“意象”这一载体。意象传译犹如画龙点睛,需要译者重新创造出与原诗意境相似的审美意象。《楚辞》往往通过丰富隽永的意象刻画诗人的细腻情感,激发读者的想象力。例如,屈原在《九歌・云中君》中就勾勒了“云神”灵动生辉、行踪不定的形象:“灵皇皇兮既降,猋远举兮云中。览冀州兮有余,横四海兮焉穷。”意思是说:“伟大的云神已经降临啊,忽然又如旋风般远飞入云中。你的光芒岂止照临神州啊!泽披四海永不穷尽。”许渊冲将其译成:In silver drops, oh! you come with rain;/On wings of wind, oh! you rise again. /Upon the land, oh! you come with ease;/You float over, oh! and beyond four seas. “灵皇皇”一词指代“云神”,译者使用意译将其形象转换成 silver drops 一词,展现了“云神”晶莹剔透的色彩与飘忽不定的形态,同时又衬托了“云神”高洁美丽、惠泽人间的美好品格,将自然界中云的特征与诗人赋予其“英雄形象”的寓意融为一体。可见,译者可以适度转换原诗的意象以营造情景交融的意境。当然,译者也可以根据具体情况保留原诗意象。虽说《楚辞》中的某些意象是中华文化所独有的,但是由于人类有着共同的认知心理,就有可能产生某种心理契合。将原诗中的意象进行迁移,有助于保留异域文化的原汁原味。不论是意象的转换还是保留,译者的审美经验都要和作者的审美经验最大限度地统一起来,传达原诗的艺术意境。

2. 感耳:韵式灵活、叠词变通

许渊冲所谓的"音美",就是要保持原诗的神韵,使译文有"节调、押韵、顺口、好听"。《楚辞》的魅力之一在于音美,它的首要特征便是押韵。汉语往往比较容易押韵,同一个韵脚有多个汉字可供选择,而英语中对于同一个韵脚可供选择的单词数量则相对有限。关于汉诗英译的押韵问题,许渊冲认为:"即使百分之百地传达了原诗的意美,如果没有押韵,也不可能保存原诗的风格和情趣。"许译《楚辞》讲究押韵,但是韵式与原诗相比却有变化。例如,《湘夫人》中有一段描写湘君幻想为爱人修建居室的诗句:"荪壁兮紫坛,播芳椒兮成堂。桂栋兮兰橑,辛夷楣兮药房。"意思是说:"用荪草装饰墙壁啊紫贝砌满庭院,中堂里布满香椒的气息。用桂树作栋梁木兰作椽,辛夷作门楣啊白芷铺满房间。"许渊冲将其译成:In purple court, oh! thyme decks the wall;/With fragrant pepper, oh! is spread the hall. /Pillars of cassia, oh! stand upright,/And rooms smell sweet, oh! with clover white. 原诗采用的是 abcb 的韵式,也就是第二句的"堂"和第四句的"房"押韵。译诗采用的是 aabb 的变通韵式,也就是第一句的 wall 和第二句的 hall 押韵,第三句的 upright 和第四句的 white 押韵,读起来同样琅琅上口。此外,译诗中动词 deck,spread,stand 以及 smell 的使用构成了"无灵主语+有灵动词"的模式,赋予了香草佳木以灵性,增添了湘君和湘夫人栖息之处的梦幻色彩。屈原善以植物喻人,像荪草、辛夷、白芷这些古代的楚地植物在现在并不多见,fragrant 一词则是化深为浅的翻译,概括了这些稀有植物的总体特征,反映了男女主人公的高洁品行和浪漫情怀,表现了人们对美好爱情和幸福生活的无限憧憬。可见,由于英诗与汉诗都有各自的音律规则,译者应善于利用英语的语音特点,采用变通韵式的方法,让读者在体味意美的同时感受到音美。当然,如果译诗实在无法押韵,也不应强求,不能因韵害义而本末倒置。

叠词是传达诗词音美的又一常见的修辞手段,具有独特的美学价值。汉语叠词的功能在于"突出思想、强调感情、加强节奏感、增添音韵美。"英语叠词用得没有汉语那样普遍,叠词英译是《楚辞》英译的难点之一。《楚辞》蕴含着向往光明、追求真理、不屈不挠的求索情神,音韵婉转、节奏铿锵的叠词具有浓烈的抒情效果。例如《九辩》结尾的 10 句诗就连用了 10 个叠词:"乘精气之抟抟兮,骛诸神之湛湛。骖白霓之习习兮,历群灵之丰丰。左朱雀之茇茇兮,右苍龙之躣躣。属雷师之阗阗兮,通飞廉之衙衙。前轻輬之锵锵兮,后辎乘之从从。"这些叠词拟物状声,动静相宜,绝不是单纯的声韵重复,而是承载着情感的倾注。这段诗是说:"乘着天地的一团团精气啊,追随众多神灵在那苍穹。白虹作骖马驾车飞行啊,游历群神的一个个神宫。南方朱雀在左面翩跹飞舞啊,北方苍龙在右面奔行跃动。雷师跟着咚咚敲鼓跟随在后啊,风伯走在前面把路开辟。前面有轻车铃声清脆啊,后面有大车紧紧随从。"诗人展开浪漫主义的想象,描绘了不得志之人幻想穿过日月虹气,成为天上神灵的主宰。许渊冲采用重复英语单词的方法将其译成:I'd ride the ether round on round, oh! /And race with gods sky-bound, sky-bound. /I'd drive the rainbow white, so white, oh! /And pass through the stars bright, so bright. /And left the Red Bird beats its wing on wing, oh! /At right the dragons green swing and swing. /The Lord of Thunder rumbles past, past, oh! /The Master of Wind flies ahead, fast, fast. /In front, light coaches ring bell on bell, oh! /Behind, the heavy wagons utter yell on yell. 译诗中单词的重复营造出一种回环往复的气势,传达了朱雀、苍龙、雷师、风伯都听凭调遣的神气情形,这种虚幻的欢乐反衬了悲秋哀怨的主题。有的单词之间还用了介词 on,连词 and 以及副词 so,使衔接更加紧凑。当然,在有些情况下,译者只能采用意译来处理原文的叠词形式。例如,《九歌·湘夫人》中有两句描写秋风落叶的诗:"嫋嫋兮秋风,洞庭波兮木叶下。"意思是说:"绵绵的秋风吹过,洞庭湖泛起波澜落叶飘旋。"秋风冠以"嫋嫋",映衬了湘君凄凉孤独、悱恻深沉之情。许渊冲将其译成:The autumn breeze, oh! ceaselessly grieves/The Dongting waves, oh! with fallen leaves. 译者并没有用重复单词的方法翻译"嫋嫋"一词,而是以简练的用词以及完美的押韵进行意象叠加,autumn breeze 和 fallen leaves 给读者以丰富的遐想,传达了诗人复杂的思想感情以及一唱三叹的音美。可见,在诗词英译过程中有时需要舍弃原文的叠词形式,挖掘英语具有近似效果的艺术手段,呈现诗人内在情感与诗歌外在音美的契合,通过音美来加强意美。

3. 感目:长短交错,对仗工整

许渊冲所谓的"形美",就是译诗在句子长短和对仗工整方面尽量做到与原诗形似。也就是说,如果译诗与原诗行数相同并且分节相当,每行的长度也大致相等,那么译诗就基本体现了原诗的形美。形美本身的审美价值是诗词艺术魅力的重要因素之一,虽然不如意美与音美那样重要,但是在翻译中却不能忽视它对二者的影响。《楚辞》的文字排列错落有致,常规中有一定变异,某些诗句在整齐的对偶句中还穿插了一些长短不一的句式,以展示诗中人物内心情感的起伏变化。例如《九歌·湘君》中有一段描写湘夫人未见到心上人时而产生幽怨心理的诗句:"石濑兮浅浅,飞龙兮翩翩。交不忠兮怨长,期不信兮告予以不闲。"意思是说:"石上的清泉,湍急地流淌;飞龙船啊!翩翩掠过水面如飞鸟。交友不忠便长相怨恨,有约不守反而骗我说不得空闲。"诗中前两句是严整的五字对偶短句,第三句和第四句却分别转换成字数不一的两个长句,节奏也由轻快跳跃变得舒缓凝重,传神地刻画了湘夫人对湘君不能如约而至的失望与伤心之情。许渊冲将其译成:As on a shallow stream, oh! a dragon boat,/Though its wings beat fast, oh! can't keep afloat. /Faithless as you're, oh! you deceive me;/Breaking our tryst, oh! you say you're not free. 译文的前两行均为九个单词,第三行和第四行的单词数与前两行不一致。为了兼顾 boat 与 afloat 两个单词的韵脚,译者将"飞龙兮翩翩"进行了断行翻译,分别放在译诗的第一句和第二句,各诗行之间上下勾联,在变化之中求整齐,在整齐之中求变化。虽然英诗和汉诗都讲究分行和押韵,但形式上却各有特点。汉诗言简意赅,以意统形,寥寥数词便意境全出;英诗以形见长,介词、连词、冠词通常不可缺少,这就使得译诗的字数与原诗保持形似十分困难。许渊冲以诗译诗,并且加入了 as, though, on, you 等连词、介词和代词等等,在连贯性和衔接性方面符合英语的语法特征。所加的词都是原诗内容所有而形式所无的,其简洁顺畅的译诗达到了与原诗意境相似的效果。同样,译者也可以根据具体情况适当删减,增删都要以传情达意为原则。

在展现形美方面,许渊冲的《楚辞》英译文不但注意到诗句的长短起伏,而且还尽量使用押韵的对仗句。对仗句的平衡性反映了中国传统美学注重情感表达的中和之美。由于英语平行结构与汉语中的对仗句有相似之处,所以许渊冲常使用平行结构来保留原诗的视觉美感。例如,《湘君》中有这样几句诗:"朝骋骛兮江皋,夕弭节兮北渚。鸟次兮屋上,水周兮堂下。"意思是说:"早上起来就往水边高地走,到了黄昏还停留在北滩上。暮归的鸟儿栖息在屋檐之上,流水在华堂之前来回萦绕。”许渊冲使用跨行平行结构将其译成：At dawn I drive my cab，oh! by riverside;/At dusk on northern isle，oh! I stop my ride. /Under the eaves，oh! the birds reposed;/Around the house，oh! the river flows. 原诗中主语对主语，谓语对谓语，状语对状语，译诗中名词对名词，动词对动词，介词对介词，诗行之间的平行结构铺排整齐。另外，在译诗的第二句中，译者将状语 on northern isle 提到了句子的前半部分，这不仅为整首译诗 aabb 的韵式提供了方便，而且也起到强调的作用。《楚辞》具有独特的形式特征，译诗要再现原诗的风格就必须体现语言形式的文学性。好的译诗应该是内容与形式的完美结合，但是当二者产生矛盾的时候，译者要以诗人的感悟传达原诗的艺术效果。

4. 中学西传，求真求美

任何一种翻译活动都有一定的翻译目的和翻译策略。许渊冲翻译《楚辞》是以弘扬优秀的中华传统文化为己任，并且希望能将文学翻译发展成为目的语中的翻译文学。他说：“文学翻译的最高目标是成为翻译文学，……真正的翻译文学应该是既真又美的。”“如果译者能够发挥译文语言和文化的优势，运用‘深化、等化、浅化’的方法，使读者‘知之、好之、乐之’，如果译诗还要尽可能再现原诗的‘意美、音美、形美’，那么文学翻译就有可能成为翻译文学。”虽然译诗不能完全传达原诗的意美、音美、形美，但意、音、形三方面牺牲得最少的译文，才是最优秀的译文。为了达到翻译目的，译者就要对原文本进行适当改写。根茨勒(Gentzler)认为：“生活在任何一种文化里的人都会在该文化的熏陶下形成其特有的概念构架(conceptual grid)和文本构架(textual grid)。如果说概念构架使译者用自己文化的世界观和价值观来阐释原文的话，那么文本构架则决定了在特定社会中可以被接受的文学形式和文本类型，使读者对文本形式有一种期待，并以作品是否符合这一期待来评判译文的优劣。”也就是说，特定社会的文本构架形成了该社会的主流诗学，主流诗学会引导译者将原文改写为符合译入语社会审美取向或诗学特征的译文。许渊冲更加关注的是《楚辞》的“中学西传”，而西方的普通读者则是关系到文化传播的一股重要力量，因此他采取了以归化为主的翻译策略。异化策略与归化策略实际上是译者的一种思维趋向和价值取向，即趋向于原作者的思维还是读者的思维。许渊冲将直译与意译相结合，通俗流畅的译文更加有助于英语世界读者的理解与接受。有学者这样写道：“源远流长汇欧美，冲霄直上搅西东，诗骚词赋凭谁问，文化大使唯许翁。”

许渊冲以深厚的中英文功底和诗性感悟使《楚辞》的文化思想和艺术价值在异域土壤中得以再生。许译《楚辞》是对“三美论”孜孜以求的实践，体现了西方文化的求真精神以及中国文化的求美传统。虽然“三美论”还有一些可商榷之处，比如如何做到“三美”并举问题，如何最大限度地传达异域风味与发挥译文优势相统一的问题等等。但从总体上来讲，“三美论”不仅吸收了西方现代翻译理论的因素，更重要的是突显了中国传统文论的特质，对古诗词英译实践和研究具有重要的参考价值。作为许渊冲翻译观的核心组成部分，其中的深意赋予研究者许多有待探索的空间。

【延伸阅读】

[1] Chan，E. Translation Principle and the Translator's Agenda：A Systemic Approach to Yan Fu. In Theo Herman (ed.)，*Cross-cultural Transgressions*：*Research Models in*

Translation Studies Ⅱ: *Historical and Ideological Issues*. Manchester: St. Jerome Publishing, 2002.

[2] Hung, E. (ed.). *Translation and Cultural Change*: *Studies in History*, *Norms and Image-projection*. Amsterdam/Philadelphia: John Benjamins Publishing Company, 2005.

[3] 贺微. 翻译:文本与译者的对话. 外国语,1999(1).

[4] 胡安江. 文本的意义空白与不确定性——兼论文学翻译的审美效果. 四川外语学院学报,2004(3).

[5] 刘世聪. 文贵简. 中国翻译,2000(2).

[6] 刘世聪. 散文的"情韵"与翻译. 中国翻译,2002(2).

[7] 邵炜. 从傅雷《艺术哲学》的翻译看翻译的接受美学. 四川外语学院学报,2008(6).

[8] 王宏志. 重释"信达雅":20 世纪中国翻译研究. 东方出版社,1999.

[9] 许渊冲. 再谈"意美、音美、形美". 外语学刊,1983(4).

[10] 许渊冲. 翻译的艺术. 北京:中国对外翻译出版公司,1984.

[11] 傅仲选. 实用翻译美学. 上海:上海外语教育出版社,1993.

[12] 朱纯深. 从文体学和话语分析看《荷塘月色》的美学意义. 名作欣赏,1994(4).

[13] 宗白华. 美学与意境. 北京:人民出版社,1987.

【问题与思考】

1. 如何理解译者的审美体验有着显著的主动性和创造性?
2. 翻译美学有哪些历史渊源? 翻译美学的基本主张是什么?
3. 谈谈学界对翻译审美客体和审美主体的不同理解。
4. 许渊冲的"三美论"对古诗词翻译具有哪些指导意义?
5. 如何理解诗歌翻译中的审美移情?

第五章　文学翻译研究的社会学因素

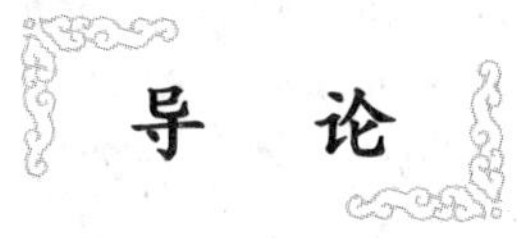

导　论

20 世纪 70 年代，佐哈尔(Itammar Even-Zohar)和图里(Gideon Toury)提出了与翻译原语中心论思想完全不同的观点：翻译属于译语系统，任何译本的认可，都要依赖目的语规范；"对等"不是翻译研究的中心概念，所谓"对等"都是一定历史阶段目的语"规范"的要求。这样，翻译的接受环境被带入翻译研究所关注的中心中来，从而开启了全新的译语取向的译学研究。在佐哈尔和图里那里，文学被视为一个多元系统，系统内外的各种"规范"侵入翻译活动的各个环节，制约着译者在翻译过程中的决策和策略；"规范"之间的互动使得多元系统内部的系统彼此形成张力，旧张力打破，创新的文学系统又会形成新的张力，从而使不同时期不同地区的文学多元系统呈现出不同的形态。图里的《翻译规范的性质和作用》一文详细地阐述了"翻译规范"的意义、类别、性质和作用。图里认为，主流的翻译规范、过时的翻译规范和新生的翻译规范有时会同场竞争，新的战胜过时的，边缘的战胜主流的，从而实现新旧规范的交替。译者的作用是完成一项社会赋予的任务，对译者来说，习得并适应翻译活动中的社会规范非常重要且也是必然。图里的翻译规范理论也带来了翻译研究方法上的突破，翻译研究开始从印象式的规定性言说转向重视翻译事实分析的、重视多文本比较研究的描述性研究上来，为翻译研究开辟了一条面向译语系统的、功能主义和系统性的描述性研究途径。此后，西方译学研究从理论阐述向文本描写转移。

1998 年，西米奥尼(Daniel Simeoni)在 *Target* 杂志上发文指出，图里着力于阐明规范的高度控制性，及其对译者行为的统治，但从社会学角度看，译者本身也是维护规范或创新规范的能动者(agent)，译者受"惯习支配"(habitus-governed)。"惯习"(habitus，又译"生存心态")是法国社会学家布尔迪厄提出的一个社会学概念。西米奥尼的重要文章《译者惯习的重要地位》将 habitus 引入翻译研究，带来了一系列社会学视角翻译问题探讨，翻译研究由此出现了社会学转向。

布尔迪厄在揭示社会结构及其运作逻辑时，提出了场域(fields)的概念。他认为，社会世界由各个场域构成；场域，即现实社会层面上所呈现出来的社会各行动者的力的关系网。"惯习"(habitus)是人在成长、教育、工作、交际等社会化过程中逐渐学会、内化并强化了的一套"性情系统"(system of dispositions)。在各种场域中活动着的人，具有各种秉性、情感、气质、习性和思想，它们不可避免的贯彻于他们的行为之中，但在反复的行为中，它们又不断地被改造和被更新。在一定时段的历史活动中，它们形成了相对稳定的体系化的"惯习"。场域和惯习是实践的产物，同时又是人的实践的社会制约性条件。一方面，各种社会性因素通过场域形塑和改变具体个体的“惯习”,另一方面,“惯习”通过“认知建构”甚至改变场域的结构来作用于社会。

默克尔(Denise Merkle)分析了身兼剧作家和译者双重角色的马耶,在选择翻译语言和翻译方法时的“惯习”。作为享有声誉、经济独立的作家,马耶有条件选择只翻译自己崇拜作家和喜欢的作品,并按自己意愿作翻译决定。但她希望取悦观众,因此她遵从现行的文学和翻译潮流,创造满足观众“期待视野”的翻译作品。

霍恩比(Mary Snell-Hornby)指出:20 世纪 70 年代,戏剧翻译讨论的焦点问题是:是提供忠实精准的学术翻译文本还是提供可供戏剧舞台表演的剧本。1971 年,德国翻译研究学者凯瑟林娜·赖斯(Katharina Reiss)在区分文本类型时指出:戏剧是一种多媒体文本,其目的不是提供阅读,而是提供给演员来说或唱,再通过音响和视频传达给观众,而其中的语言内容则是整个多媒体文本中的一小部分内容。到了 80 年代,戏剧文本区别于其他文学文本的特点得到认可:戏剧的独特之处是由“舞台说明”(stage directions)和“口语对话”(the spoken dialogue)组成。“人物对话”决定了戏剧翻译是“舞台翻译”(stage translation)。

勒菲弗尔(André Lefevere)的《翻译和经典形成:美国戏剧 90 年》阐明了文学选集的编撰是经典形成的主要方式。在译编过程中,场域中的规范和译者的惯习对经典的确立产生了重要影响。利益的追逐、编撰权力的行使、大学课时设置、译本版面的限制、意识形态和诗学上的规约等等,都导致译者去改写原文。选集编撰过程中仅录入欧洲及其附属国的作品,体现了当时相对稳定的惯习系统中的欧洲中心主义思想。

“范式”(paradigm)概念源自美国历史学家和科学哲学家托马斯·库恩的《科学革命的结构》,指常规科学所赖以动作的理论基础和实践规范,是从事某一科学的研究者群体共同遵从的世界观和行为方式。后来这个概念被社会学等学科所拓展,用来指某个历史时期大部分社会成员所认同的问题、方法、观点、过程和手段等等,即:理性的世界观。1825 年法国出版《英国杂志》,主要是刊登翻译的英国杂志文章。英国作为世界最发达的工业国和最大贸易国,其政治文化体系成为当时世界各国竞相效仿的对象。杂志作为一个即时消费的文化形式,不仅反映当时不断发展的城市化和工业化的社会现实,还融合知识普及和规范文化产品的作用。杂志是向读者传递文化、政治、经济和科学信息最有效的途径。莱米塞利(Maria Eulalia Ramicelli)的文章揭示了译者通过妙笔生花的编译法,来介绍和评论英国社会生活和政治文化,意在塑造一个新兴的巴西民族,给这个刚刚摆脱葡萄牙殖民统治的国家创造自己的文化体系、共同的价值观和民族感情,为国家的进步而奋斗。该杂志的翻译,对巴西社会及巴西叙事小说创作产生了全面的影响。

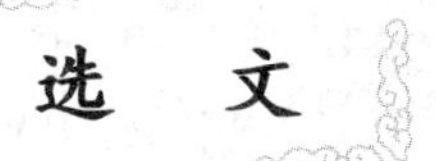

选　文

选文一　The Nature and Role of Norms in Translation

Gideon Toury

导　言

本文《翻译规范的性质和作用》选自劳伦斯·韦努蒂(Lawrence Venuti)所编 *The Translation Studies Reader*(2000)。作者吉迪恩·图里(Gideon Toury)是以色列特拉维夫大学的教授。他继承和发展了霍尔姆斯的译学构想，拓展了特拉维夫学派埃文-佐哈尔的多元系统理论。他的《翻译理论探索》(*In Search of a Theory of Translation*，1980)和《描述翻译研究及其他》(*Descriptive Translation Studies and Beyond*，1995)两部著作确立了描写译学的地位。

图里把社会学术语"规范"应用于希伯来文学翻译的研究。他指出翻译活动具有社会属性，译者必须完成社会赋予他的任务，翻译作为跨文化的交际活动，受到来自源语文化的和来自译语文化的两套"规范"体系的制约。译者如果遵循源语文化的规范制约，就实现"充分翻译"；遵从译语文化的规范制约就生产出"可接受的翻译"。该文详述了描写译学的核心概念"翻译规范"的定义、分类、性质和作用。翻译规范具有独特性、不稳定性和多样性的特点。图里提议，借用美国社会学家杰伊·杰克逊(Jay Jackson)的"U 形势能曲线"，通过图表来分析规范的强制程度、可容忍行为的幅度以及规范某个特定约束力相对于其他特定约束力的比率，寻找到区分各个规范之间的渐进差异。该文对文学翻译研究的社会学转向发挥了开拓性作用。

However highly one may think of Linguistics, Text-Linguistics, Contrastive Textology or Pragmatics and of their explanatory power with respect to translational phenomena, being a translator cannot be reduced to the mere generation of utterances which would be considered "translations" within any of these disciplines. Translation activities should rather be regarded as having cultural significance. Consequently, "translatorship" amounts first and foremost to being able *to play a social role*, i. e., to fulfil a function allotted by a community—to the activity, its practitioners and/or their products—in a way which is deemed appropriate in its own terms of reference. The acquisition of a set of norms for determining the suitability of that kind of behaviour, and for manoeuvring between all the factors which may constrain it, is therefore a prerequisite for becoming a translator within a cultural environment.

The process by which a bilingual speaker may be said to gain recognition in his/her capacity as a translator has hardly been studied so far. [...] In the present chapter the nature of the acquired norms themselves will be addressed, along with their role in directing translation activity in socio-culturally relevant settings. This presentation will be followed by a brief discussion of translational norms as a second-order object of Translation Studies, to be reconstructed and studied within the kind of framework which we are now in the process of sketching. As strictly translational norms can only be applied at the *receiving* end, establishing them is not merely *justified* by a target-oriented approach but should be seen as its very *epitome*.

1. Rules, Norms, Idiosyncrasies

In its socio-cultural dimension, translation can be described as subject to constraints of several types and varying degree. These extend far beyond the source text; the systemic differences between the languages and textual traditions involved in the act, or even the possibilities and limitations of the cognitive apparatus of the translator as a necessary mediator. In fact, cognition itself is influenced, probably even modified by socio-cultural factors. At any rate, translators performing under different conditions (e. g. , translating texts of different kinds, and/or for different audiences) often adopt different strategies, and ultimately come up with markedly different products. Something has obviously changed here, and I very much doubt it that it is the cognitive apparatus as such.

In terms of their potency, socio-cultural constraints have been described along a scale anchored between two extremes: general, relatively absolute *rules*, on the one hand and pure *idiosyncrasies* on the other. Between these two poles lies a vast middle-ground occupied by inter subjective factors commonly designated *norms*. The norms themselves form a graded continuum along the scale: some are stronger, and hence more rule-like, others are weaker, and hence almost idiosyncratic. The borderlines between the various types of constraints are thus diffuse. Each of the concepts, including the grading itself, is relative too. Thus what is just a favoured mode of behaviour within a heterogeneous group may well acquire much more binding force within a certain (more homogeneous) section thereof, in terms of either human agents (e. g. , translators among texters in general) or types of activity (e. g. , interpreting, or legal translation, within translation at large).

Along the temporal axis, each type of constraint may, and often does move into its neighbouring domain(s) through processes of rise and decline. Thus, mere, whims may catch on and become more and more normative, and norms can gain so much validity that, for all practical purposes, they become as binding as rules; or the other way around, of course. Shifts of validity and force often have to do with changes of *status* within a society. In fact, they can always be described in connection with the notion of norm, especially since, as the process goes on, they are likely to cross its realm, i. e. , actually become norms. The

other two types of constraints may even be redefined in terms of norms: rules as "[more] objective," idiosyncrasies as "[more] subjective [or: less inter subjective]" norms.

Sociologists and social psychologists have long regarded norms as the translation of general values or ideas shared by a community—as to what is right and wrong, adequate and inadequate—into performance instructions appropriate for and applicable to particular situations, specifying what is prescribed and forbidden as well as what is tolerated and permitted in a certain behavioural dimension (the famous "square of normativity," which has lately been elaborated on with regard to translation in De Geest, 1992: 38-40). Norms are acquired by the individual during his/her socialization and always imply *sanctions*—actual or potential, negative as well as positive. Within the community, norms also serve as criteria according to which actual instances of behaviour are *evaluated*. Obviously, there is a point in assuming the existence of norms only in situations which allow for different kinds of behaviour, on the additional condition that selection among them be nonrandom. ① Inasmuch as a norm is really active and effective, one can therefore distinguish regularity of behaviour in recurrent situations of the same type, which would render regularities a main source for any *study* of norms as well.

The centrality of the norms is not only metaphorical, then, in terms of their relative position along a postulated continuum of constraints; rather, it is essential: Norms are the key concept and focal point in any attempt to account for the social relevance of activities, because their existence, and the wide range of situations they apply to (with the conformity this implies), are the main factors ensuring the establishment and retention of social order. This holds for cultures too, or for any of the systems constituting them, which are, after all, social institutions ipso facto. Of course, behaviour which does *not* conform to prevailing norms is always possible too. Moreover, "non-compliance with a norm in particular instances does not invalidate the norm" (Hermans, 1991: 162). At the same time, there would normally be a price to pay for opting for any deviant kind of behaviour.

One thing to bear in mind, when setting out to study norm-governed behaviour, is that there is no necessary identity between the norms themselves and any formulation of them in language. Verbal formulations of course reflect *awareness* of the existence of norms as well as of their respective significance. However, they also imply other interests, particularly a desire to *control* behaviour, i. e., to dictate norms rather than merely account for them. Normative formulations tend to be slanted, then, and should always be taken with a grain of salt.

2. Translation as a Norm-governed Activity

Translation is a kind of activity which inevitably involves at least two languages and two

① "The existence of norms is a sine qua non in instances of labelling and regulating; without a norm, all deviations are meaningless and become cases of free variation" (Wexler, 1974: 4, n. 1).

cultural traditions, i. e. , at least two sets of norm-systems on each level. Thus, the "value" behind it may be described as consisting of two major elements:

a. being a text in a certain language, and hence occupying a position, or filling in a slot, in the appropriate culture, or in a certain section thereof;
b. constituting a representation in that language/culture of another, preexisting text in some other language, belonging to some other culture and occupying a definite position within it.

These two types of requirement derive from two sources which—even though the distance between them may vary greatly—are nevertheless always different and therefore often incompatible. Were it not for the regulative capacity of norms, the tensions between the two sources of constraints would have to be resolved on an entirely *individual* basis, and with no clear yardstick to go by. Extreme free variation may well have been the result, which it certainly is not. Rather, translation behaviour within a culture tends to manifest certain *regularities*, one consequence being that even if they are unable to account for deviations in any explicit way, the persons-in—the-culture can often tell when a translator has failed to adhere to sanctioned practices.

It has proven useful and enlightening to regard the basic choice which can be made between requirements of the two different sources as constituting an **initial norm**. Thus, a translator may subject him/herself either to the original text, with the norms it has realized, or to the norms active in the target culture, or, in that section of it which would host the end product. If the first stance is adopted, the translation will tend to subscribe to the norms of the source text, and through them also to the norms of the source language and culture. This tendency; which has often been characterized as the pursuit of adequate translation,① may well entail certain incompatibilities with target norms and practices, especially those lying beyond the mere linguistic ones. If, on the other hand, the second stance is adopted, norms systems of the target culture are triggered and set into motion. Shifts from the source text would be an almost inevitable price. Thus, whereas adherence to source norms determines a translation's adequacy as compared to the source text, subscription to norms originating in the target culture determines its acceptability.

Obviously, even the most adequacy-oriented translation involves shifts from the source text. In fact, the occurrence of shifts has long been acknowledged as a true universal of translation. However, since the need itself to deviate from source-text patterns can always be realized in more than one way, the actual *realization* of so-called obligatory shifts, to the extent that it is non-random, and hence not idiosyncratic, is already truly norm-governed. So is everything that has to do with non-obligatory shifts, which are of course more than just

---

① "An adequate translation is a translation which realizes in the target language the textual relationships of a source text with no breach of its own [basic] linguistic system" (Even-Zohar, 1975: 43; my translation).

possible in real-life translation: they occur everywhere and tend to constitute the majority of shifting in any single act of human translation, rendering the latter a contributing factor to, as well as the epitome of regularity.

The term "initial norm" should not be overinterpreted, however. Its initiality derives from its superordinance over particular norms which pertain to lower, and therefore more specific levels. The kind of priority postulated here is basically logical, and need not coincide with any "real," i. e., *chronological* order of application. The notion is thus designed to serve first and foremost as an *explanatory tool*. Even if no clear macro-level tendency can be shown, any micro-level decision can still be accounted for in terms of adequacy vs. acceptability. On the other hand, in cases where an overall choice has been made, it is not necessary that every single lower-level decision be made in full accord with it. We are still talking regularities, then, but not necessarily of any absolute type. It is unrealistic to expect absolute regularities anyway, in any behavioural domain.

Actual translation decisions (the results of which the researcher would confront) will necessarily involve some ad hoc combination of, or compromise between the two extremes implied by the initial norm. Still, for theoretical and methodological reasons, it seems wiser to retain the opposition and treat the two poles as distinct in principle: If they are not regarded as having distinct *theoretical* statuses, how would compromises differing in type or in extent be distinguished and accounted for?

Finally, the claim that it is basically a norm-governed type of behaviour applies to translation of all kinds, not only literary, philosophical or biblical translation, which is where most norm-oriented studies have been conducted so far. As has recently been claimed and demonstrated in an all too sketchy exchange of views in *Target*, similar things can even be said of *conference interpreting*. Needless to say, this does not mean that the exact same conditions apply to all kinds of translation. In fact, their application in different cultural sectors is precisely one of the aspects that should be submitted to study. In principle, the claim is also valid for every society and historical period, thus offering a framework for historically oriented studies which would also allow for comparison.

3. Translation Norms: An Overview

Norms can be expected to operate not only in translation of all kinds, but also at every stage in the translating event, and hence to be reflected on every level of its product. It has proven convenient to first distinguish two larger groups of norms applicable to translation: preliminary vs. operational.

Preliminary norms have to do with two main sets of considerations which are often interconnected: those regarding the existence and actual nature of a definite translation policy, and those related to the directness of translation.

Translation policy refers to those factors that govern the choice of text types; or even of individual texts, to be imported through translation into a particular culture/language at a particular point in time. Such a policy will be said to exist inasmuch as the choice is found to be non-random. Different policies may of course apply to different subgroups, in terms of either text-types (e. g., literary vs. non-literary) or human agents and groups thereof (e. g., different publishing houses), and the interface between the two often offers very fertile grounds for policy hunting.

Considerations concerning *directness of translation* involve the threshold of tolerance for translating from languages other than the ultimate source language: is indirect translation permitted at all? In translating from what source languages/text-types/periods (etc.) is it permitted/prohibited/tolerated/preferred? What are the permitted/prohibited/tolerated/preferred mediating languages? Is there a tendency/obligation to mark a translated work as having been mediated or is this fact ignored/camouflaged/denied? If it is mentioned, is the identity of the mediating language supplied as well? And so on.

Operational norms, in turn, may be conceived of as directing the decisions made during the act of translation itself. They affect the matrix of the text—i. e., the modes of distributing linguistic material in it—as well as the textual make up and verbal formulation as such. They thus govern—directly or indirectly—the relationships as well that would obtain between the target and source texts, i. e., what is more likely to remain invariant under transformation and what will change.

So-called *matricial norms* may govern the very existence of target-language material intended as a substitute for the corresponding source-language material (and hence the degree of *fullness* of translation), its location in the text (or the form of actual *distribution*), as well as the textual *segmentation*.① The extent to which omissions, additions, changes of location and manipulations of segmentation are referred to in the translated texts (or around them) may also be determined by norms, even though the one can very well occur without the other.

Obviously, the borderlines between the various matricial phenomena are not clear-cut. For instance, large-scale omissions often entail changes of segmentation as well, especially if the omitted portions have no clear boundaries, or textual-linguistic standing, i. e., if they are not integral sentences, paragraphs or chapters. By the same token, a change of location may often be accounted for as an omission (in one place) compensated by an addition (elsewhere). The decision as to what may have "really" taken place is thus description-bound: What one is after is (more or less cogent) *explanatory hypotheses*, not necessarily

① The claim that principles of segmentation follow *universal* patterns is just a figment of the imagination of some discourse and text theoreticians intent on uncovering as many universal principles as possible. In actual fact, there have been various traditions (or "models") of segmentation, and the differences between them always have implications for translation, whether they are taken to bear on the formulation of the target text or ignored. Even the segmentation of sacred texts such as the Old Testament itself has often been tampered with by its translators, normally in order to bring it closer to *target* cultural habits, and by so doing enhance the translation's acceptability.

"true-to-life" accounts, which one can never be sure of anyway.

Textual-linguistic norms, in turn, govern the selection of material to formulate the target text in, or replace the original textual and linguistic material with. Textual-linguistic norms may either be *general*, and hence apply to translation qua translation, or *particular*, in which case they would pertain to a particular text-type and/or mode of translation only. Some of them may be identical to the norms governing non-translational text-production, but such an identity should never be taken for granted. This is the methodological reason why no study of translation can, or should proceed from the assumption that the later is representative of the target language, or of any overall textual tradition thereof. (And see our discussion of "translation-specific lexical items.")

It is clear that preliminary norms have both logical and chronological precedence over the operational ones. This is not to say that between the two major groups there are no relationships whatsoever, including mutual influences or even two-way conditioning. However, these relations are by no means fixed and given, and their establishment forms an inseparable part of any study of translation as a norm-governed activity. Nevertheless, we can safely assume at least that the relations which do exist have to do with the initial norm. They might even be found to *intersect* it—another important reason to retain the opposition between "adequacy" and "acceptability" as a basic coordinate system for the formulation of explanatory hypotheses. ①

Operational norms as such may be described as serving as a model, in accordance with which translations come into being, whether involving the norms realized by the source text (i. e., adequate translation) plus certain modifications or purely target norms, or a particular compromise between the two. Every model supplying performance instructions may be said to act as a *restricting* factor: It opens up certain options while closing others. Consequently, when the first position is fully adopted, the translation can hardly be said to have been made into the target language as a whole. Rather, it is made into a model language, which is at best some part of the former and at worst an artificial, and as such nonexistent variety. ② In this last case, the translation is not really *introduced* into the target culture either, but is

---

① Thus, for instance, in sectors where the pursuit of adequate translation is marginal, it is highly probable that indirect translation would also become common, on occasion even preferred over direct translation. By contrast, a norm which prohibits mediated translation is likely to be connected with a growing proximity to the initial norm of adequacy. Under such circumstances, if indirect translation is still performed, the fact will at least be concealed, if not outright denied.

② And see, in this connection, Izre'el's "Rationale for Translating Ancient Texts into a Modern Language" (1994). In an attempt to come up with a method for translating an Akkadian myth which would be presented to modern Israeli audiences in an oral performance, he purports to combine a "feeling-of-antiquity" with a "feeling-of modernity" in a text which would be altogether simple and easily comprehensible by using a host of lexical items of *biblical* Hebrew in *Israeli* Hebrew grammatical and syntactic structures. Whereas "the lexicon ... would serve to give an ancient flavour to the text, the grammar would serve to enable modern perception." It might be added that this is a perfect mirror image of the way Hebrew translators started simulating spoken Hebrew in their texts: Spoken lexical items were inserted in grammatical and syntactic structures which were marked for belonging to the written varieties (Ben-Shahar, 1983), which also meant "new" into "old."

imposed on it, so to speak. Sure, it may eventually carve a niche for itself in the latter, but there is no initial attempt to accommodate it to any existing "slot." On the other hand, when the second position is adopted, what a translator is introducing into the target culture (which is indeed what s/he can be described as doing now) is a *version* of the original work, cut to the measure of a preexisting model. (And see our discussion of the opposition between the "translation of literary texts" and "literary translation" as well as the detailed presentation of the Hebrew translation of a German *Schlaraffenland* text.)

The apparent contradiction between any traditional concept of equivalence and the limited model into which a translation has just been claimed to be moulded can only be resolved by postulating that **it is norms that determine the (type and extent of) equivalence manifested by actual translations.** The study of norms thus constitutes a vital step towards establishing just how the functional-relational postulate of equivalence has been realized—whether in one translated text, in the work of a single translator or "school" of translators, in a given historical period, or in any other justifiable selection. ① What this approach entails is a clear wish to retain the notion of equivalence, which various contemporary approaches have tried to do without, while introducing one essential change into it: from an ahistorical, largely prescriptive concept to a historical one. Rather than being a single relationship, denoting a recurring type of invariant, it comes to refer to any relation which is found to have characterized translation under a specified set of circumstances.

At the end of a full-fledged study it will probably be found that translational norms, hence the realization of the equivalence postulate, are all, to a large extent, dependent on the position held by translation—the activity as well as its products—in the target culture. An interesting field for study is therefore comparative: the nature of translational norms as compared to those governing non-translational kinds of text-production. In fact, this kind of study is absolutely vital, if translating and translations are to be appropriately contextualized.

4. The Multiplicity of Translational Norms

The difficulties involved in any attempt to account for translational norms should not be underestimated. These, however, lie first and foremost in two features inherent in the very notion of norm, and are therefore not unique to Translation Studies at all: the socio-cultural specificity of norms and their basic instability.

Thus, whatever its exact content, there is absolutely no need for a norm to apply—to the same extent, or at all—to all sectors within a society. Even less necessary, or indeed likely, is it for a norm to apply across cultures. In fact, "sameness" here is a mere coincidence—or else the result of continuous contacts between subsystems within a culture,

① See also my discussion of "Equivalence and Non-Equivalence as a Function of Norms" (Toury, 1980: 63-70).

or between entire cultural systems, and hence a manifestation of interference. (For some general rules of systemic interference see Even-Zohar, 1990: 53-72.) Even then, it is often more a matter of apparent than of a genuine identity. After all, significance is only attributed to a norm by the *system* in which it is embedded, and the systems remain different even if instances of external behaviour appear the same.

In addition to their inherent specificity, norms are also unstable, changing entities; not because of any intrinsic flaw but by their very nature as norms. At times, norms change rather quickly; at other times, they are more enduring, and the process may take longer. Either way, substantial changes, in translational norms too, quite often occur within one's life-time.

Of course it is not as if all translators are *passive* in face of these changes. Rather, many of them, through their very activity, help in shaping the process, as do translation criticism, translation ideology (including the one emanating from contemporary academe, often in the guise of theory), and, of course, various norm-setting activities of institutes where, in many societies, translators are now being trained. Wittingly or unwittingly, they all try to interfere with the "natural" course of events and to divert it according to their own preferences. Yet the success of their endeavours is never fully foreseeable. In fact, the relative role of different agents in the overall dynamics of translational norms is still largely a matter of conjecture even for times past, and much more research is needed to clarify it.

Complying with social pressures to constantly adjust one's behaviour to norms that keep changing is of course far from simple, and most people—including translators, initiators of translation activities and the consumers of their products—do so only up to a point. Therefore, it is not all that rare to find side by side in a society three types of competing norms, each having its own followers and a position of its own in the culture at large: the ones that dominate the centre of the system, and hence direct translational behaviour of the so-called *mainstream*, alongside the remnants of *previous* sets of norms and the rudiments of *new* ones, hovering in the periphery. This is why it is possible to speak—and not derogatorily—of being "trendy," "old-fashioned" or "progressive" in translation (or in any single section thereof) as it is in any other behavioural domain.

One's status as a translator may of course be temporary, especially if one fails to adjust to the changing requirements, or does so to an extent which is deemed insufficient. Thus, as changes of norms occur, formerly "progressive" translators may soon find themselves just "trendy," or on occasion as even downright "*passé.*" At the same time, regarding this process as involving a mere alternation of generations can be misleading, especially if generations are directly equated with age groups. While there often are correlations between one's position along the "dated"—"mainstream"—"avant-garde" axis and one's age, these cannot, and should not be taken as inevitable, much less as a starting point and framework for the study of norms in action. Most notably, young people who are in the early phases of their initiation as translators often behave in an extremely epigonic way: They tend to perform according to dated, but still existing norms, the more so if they receive reinforcement from agents holding to dated norms, be they language teachers, editors, or even teachers of translation.

Multiplicity and variation should not be taken to imply that there is no such thing as norms active in translation. They only mean that real-life situations tend to be complex; and this complexity had better be noted rather than ignored, if one is to draw any justifiable conclusions. As already argued, the only viable way out seems to be to contextualize every phenomenon, every item, every text, every act, on the way to allotting the different norms themselves their appropriate position and valence. This is why it is simply unthinkable, from the point of view of the study of translation as a norm-governed activity, for all items to be treated on a par, as if they were of the same systemic position, the same significance, the same level of representativeness of the target culture and its constraints. Unfortunately, such an indiscriminate approach has been all too common, and has often led to a complete blurring of the normative picture, sometimes even to the absurd claim that no norms could be detected at all. The only way to keep that picture in focus is to go beyond the establishment of mere "check-lists" of factors which may occur in a corpus and have the lists *ordered*, for instance with respect to the status of those factors as characterizing "mainstream," "dated" and "avant-garde" activities, respectively.

This immediately suggests a further axis of contextualization, whose necessity has so far only been implied; namely, the *historical* one. After all, a norm can only be marked as "dated" if it was active in a *previous* period, and if, at that time, it had a different, "non-dated" position. By the same token, norm-governed behaviour can prove to have been "avant-garde" only in view of *subsequent* attitudes towards it: An idiosyncrasy which never evolved into something more general can only be described as a norm by extension, so to speak (see Section 1 above). Finally, there is nothing inherently "mainstream" about mainstream behaviour, except when it happens to function as such, which means that it too is time-bound. What I am claiming here, in fact, is that historical contextualization is a must not only for a *diachronic* study, which nobody would contest, but also for *synchronic* studies, which still seems a lot less obvious unless one has accepted the principles of so-called "Dynamic Functionalism" (for which, see the Introduction to Even-Zohar, 1990,① and Sheffy, 1992: passim).

① "There is a clear difference between an attempt to account for some major principles which govern a system outside the realm of time, and one which intends to account for how a system operates both 'in principle' and 'in time.' Once the historical aspect is admitted into the functional approach, several implications must be drawn. First, it must be admitted that both synchrony and diachrony are historical, but the exclusive identification of the latter with history is untenable. As a result, synchrony cannot and should not be equated with statics, since at any given moment, more than one diachronic set is operating on the synchronic axis. Therefore, on the one hand a system consists of both synchrony and diachrony; on the other, each of these separately is obviously also a system. Secondly, if the idea of structuredness and systemicity need no longer be identified with homogeneity, a semiotic system can be conceived of as a heterogeneous, open structure. It is therefore, very rarely a uni-system but is, necessarily, a polysystem" (Even-Zohar, 1990: 11).

Finally, in translation too, *non-normative* behaviour is always a possibility. The price for selecting this option may be as low as a (culturally determined) need to submit the end product to revision. However, it may also be far more severe to the point of taking away one's earned recognition as a translator; which is precisely why non-normative behaviour tends to be the exception, in actual practice. On the other hand, in retrospect, deviant instances of behaviour may be found to have effected *changes* in the very system. This is why they constitute an important field of study, as long as they are regarded as what they have really been and are not put indiscriminately into one basket with all the rest. Implied are intriguing questions such as who is "allowed" by a culture to introduce changes and under what circumstances such changes may be expected to occur and/or be accepted.

5. Studying Translational Norms

So far we have discussed norms mainly in terms of their activity during a translation event and their effectiveness in the act of translation itself. To be sure, this is precisely where and when translational norms are active. However, what is actually available for observation is not so much the norms themselves, but rather norm-governed instances of behaviour. To be even more precise, more often than not, it is the products of such behaviour. Thus, even when translating is claimed to be studied directly, as is the case with the use of "Thinking-aloud Protocols," it is only *products* which are available, although products of a different kind and order. Norms are not directly observable, then, which is all the more reason why something should also be said about them in the context of an attempt to *account* for translational behaviour.

There are two major sources for a reconstruction of translational norms, textual and extratextual:[①]

a. **textual**: the translated texts themselves, for all kinds of norms, as well as analytical inventories of translations (i. e., "virtual" texts), for various preliminary norms;
b. **extratextual**: semi-theoretical or critical formulations, such as prescriptive "theories" of translation, statements made by translators, editors, publishers, and other persons involved in or connected with the activity, critical appraisals of individual translations, or the activity of a translator or "school" of translators, and so forth.

There is a fundamental difference between these two types of source: Texts are *primary* products of norm-regulated behaviour, and can therefore be taken as immediate

① Cf. e. g., Vodička (1964: 74), on the possible sources for the study of literary norms, and Wexler (1974: 7-9), on the sources for the study of prescriptive intervention ("purism") in language.

representations thereof. Normative pronouncements, by contrast, are merely *by*-products of the existence and activity of norms. Like any attempt to formulate a norm, they are partial and biased, and should therefore be treated with every possible circumspection; all the more so since—emanating as they do from interested parties—they are likely to lean toward propaganda and persuasion. There may therefore be gaps, even contradictions, between explicit arguments and demands, on the one hand, and actual behaviour and its results, on the other, due either to subjectivity or naïveté, or even lack of sufficient knowledge on the part of those who produced the formulations. On occasion, a deliberate desire to mislead and deceive may also be involved. Even with respect to the translators themselves, intentions do not necessarily concur with any declaration of intent (which is often put down post factum anyway, when the act has already been completed); and the way those intentions are realized may well constitute a further, third category still.

Yet all these reservations—proper and serious though they may be—should not lead one to abandon semi-theoretical and critical formulations as legitimate sources for the study of norms. In spite of all its faults, this type of source still has its merits, both in itself and as a possible key to the analysis of actual behaviour. At the same time, if the pitfalls inherent in them are to be avoided, normative pronouncements should never be accepted at face value. They should rather be taken as *presystematic* and given an explication in such a way as to place them in a narrow and precise framework, lending the resulting explicate the coveted systematic status. While doing so, an attempt should be made to clarify the status of each formulation, however slanted and biased it may be, and uncover the sense in which it was not just accidental; in other words how, in the final analysis, it does reflect the cultural constellation within which, and for whose purposes it was produced. Apart from sheer speculation, such an explication should involve the comparison of various normative pronouncements to each other, as well as their repeated confrontation with the patterns revealed by [the results of] actual behaviour and the norms reconstructed from them—all this with full consideration for their contextualization. (See a representative case in Weissbrod 1989.)

It is natural, and very convenient, to commence one's research into translational behaviour by focussing on *isolated* norms pertaining to well-defined behavioural dimensions, be they—and the coupled pairs of replacing and replaced segments representing them—established from the source text's perspective (e. g., translational replacements of source metaphors) or from the target text's vantage point (e. g., binomials of near-synonyms as translational replacements). However, translation is intrinsically *multi*-dimensional: the manifold phenomena it presents are tightly interwoven and do not allow for easy isolation, not even for methodical purposes. Therefore, research should never get stuck in the blind alley of the "paradigmatic" phase which would at best yield lists of "normemes," or discrete norms. Rather, it should always proceed to a "syntagmatic" phase, involving the *integration* of normemes pertaining to various problem areas. Accordingly, the student's task can be

characterized as an attempt to establish what *relations* there are between norms pertaining to various domains by correlating his/her individual findings and weighing them against each other. Obviously, the thicker the network of relations thus established, the more justified one would be in speaking in terms of a normative *structure* (cf. Jackson, 1960: 149-160) or *model*.

This having been said, it should again be noted that a translator's behaviour cannot be expected to be fully systematic. Not only can his/her decision-making be differently motivated in different problem areas, but it can also be unevenly distributed throughout an assignment within a single problem area. Consistency in translational behaviour is thus a *graded* notion which is neither nil (i. e., total erraticness) nor 1 (i. e., absolute regularity); its extent should emerge at the end of a study as one of its conclusions, rather than being presupposed.

The American sociologist Jay Jackson suggested a "Return Potential Curve," showing the distribution of approval/disapproval among the members of a social group over a range of behaviour of a certain type as a model for the representation of norms. This model (reproduced as Figure 1) makes it possible to make a gradual distinction between norms in terms of *intensity* (indicated by the height of the curve, its distance from the horizontal axis), *the total range of tolerated behaviour* (that part of the behavioural dimension approved by the group), and the *ratio* of one of these properties of the norm to the others.

One convenient division that can be re-interpreted with the aid of this model is tripartite:[①]

a. **Basic (primary) norms**, more or less mandatory for *all* instances of a certain behaviour (and hence their minimal common denominator). Occupy the apex of the curve. Maximum intensity, minimum latitude of behaviour.

b. **Secondary norms, or tendencies**, determining favourable behaviour. May be predominant in certain *parts* of the group. Therefore common enough, but not mandatory, from the point of view of the group as a whole. Occupy that part of the curve nearest its apex and therefore less intensive than the basic norms but covering a greater range of behaviour.

c. **Tolerated (permitted) behaviour.** Occupies the rest of the "positive" part of the curve (i. e., that part which lies above the horizontal axis), and therefore of minimal intensity.

"A special group," detachable from (c), seems to be of considerable interest and importance, at least in some behavioural domains:

c′. **Symptomatic devices.** Though these devices may be infrequently used, their

① Cf. e. g., Hrushovski's similar division (in Ben-Porat & Hrushovski, 1974: 9-10) and its application to the description of the norms of Hebrew rhyme (in Hrushovski, 1971).

occurrence is typical for narrowing segments of the group under study. On the other hand, their absolute *non*-occurrence can be typical of other segments.

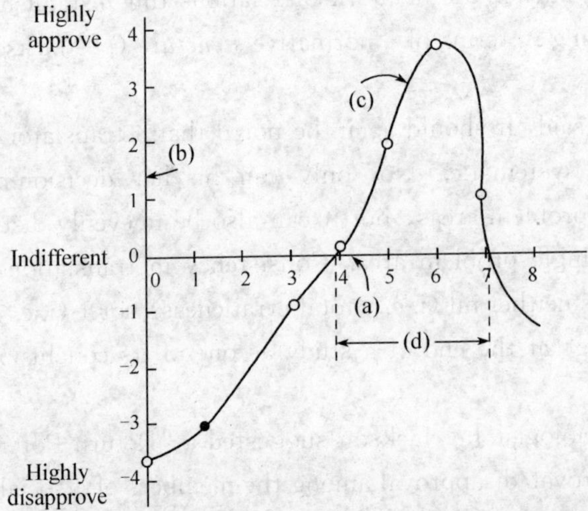

Figure 1 Schematic diagram showing the Return Potential Model for representing norms: (a) a behaviour dimension; (b) an evaluation dimension; (c) a return potential curve, showing the distribution of approval-disapproval among the members of a group over the whole range of behaviour; (d) the range of tolerable or approved behaviour.

Source: Jackson, 1960.

We may, then, safely assume a *distributional* basis for the study of norms: the more frequent a target-text phenomenon, a shift from a (hypothetical) adequate reconstruction of a source text, or a translational relation, the more likely it is to reflect (in this order) a more permitted (tolerated) activity, a stronger tendency, a more basic (obligatory) norm. A second aspect of norms, their *discriminatory capacity*, is thus reciprocal to the first, so that the less frequent a behaviour, the smaller the group it may serve to define. At the same time, the group it does define is not just any group; it is always a sub-group of the one constituted by higher-rank norms. To be sure, even idiosyncrasies (which, in their extreme, constitute groups-of-one) often manifest themselves as personal ways of realizing [more] general attitudes rather than deviations in a completely unexpected direction. ① Be that as it may, the retrospective establishment of norms is always relative to the section under study, and no automatic upward projection is possible. Any attempt to move in that direction and draw generalizations would require further study, which should be targeted towards that particular end.

Finally, the curve model also enables us to redefine one additional concept: the actual *degree of conformity* manifested by different members of a group to a norm that has already

① And see the example of the seemingly idiosyncratic use of Hebrew *ki-xen* as a translational replacement of English "well" in a period when the norm dictates the use of *lu-vexen*.

been extracted from a corpus, and hence found relevant to it. This aspect can be defined in terms of the distance from the point of maximum return (in other words, from the curve's apex).

Notwithstanding the points made in the last few paragraphs, the argument for the distributional aspect of the norms should not be pushed too far.

As is so well known, we are in no position to point to strict statistical methods for dealing with translational norms, or even to supply sampling rules for actual research (which, because of human limitations, will always be applied to samples only). At this stage we must be content with our intuitions, which, being based on knowledge and previous experience, are "learned" ones, and use them as keys for selecting corpuses and for hitting upon ideas. This is not to say that we should abandon all hope for methodological improvements. On the contrary: Much energy should still be directed toward the crystallization of systematic research methods, including statistical ones, especially if we wish to transcend the study of norms, which are always limited to one societal group at a time, and move on to the formulation of general laws of translational behaviour, which would inevitably be *probabilistic* in nature. To be sure, achievements of actual studies can themselves supply us with clues as to necessary and possible methodological improvements. Besides, if we hold up research until the most systematic methods have been found, we might never get any research done.

选文二　Translation Constraints and the "Sociological Turn" in Literary Translation Studies

Denise Merkle

导　言

本文《翻译的制约因素和文学翻译研究的"社会学转向"》选自 Anthony Pym, Miriam Shlesinger 和 Daniel Simeoni 编写的 *Beyond Descriptive Translation Studies: Investigations in homage to Gideon Toury* (John Benjamins Publishing Company, 2008) 的第十三章。作者丹妮丝·默克尔(Denise Merkle)是加拿大麦克墩大学(Université de Moncton, Canada)的教授，著有 *The Power of the Pen. Translation and Censorship in Nineteenth-century Europe*, *Francophone Dynamics in a Translated Canada: from the Margins to the Centre and Back* 等。她一直关注加拿大英法两种语言中法语在翻译中的地位。

选文以布尔迪厄的社会学观点切入，聚焦加拿大法语作家的文学翻译问题。文章指出，译者处在文学系统的中心地带，受翻译规范制约。安多瓦纳·马耶(Antonine Maillet)是法裔加拿大著名的作家和戏剧家，1979年曾获法国文学最高奖——龚顾尔文学奖。马耶出生在说阿卡迪亚方言的新不伦瑞克省一个小城，在说法语的蒙特利尔取得作家和戏剧家事业的辉煌。其写作语言是以阿卡迪亚方言为基础，浸淫着法国文学传统的一种自创语言——阿卡迪亚文学语言。作者分析了在翻译莎剧时译者在语言表达和方法选择上的"惯习"(habitus)及其译者希望取悦观众，从而遵从现行的文学和翻译规范，创造满足观众"期待视野"的翻译作品。作为翻译代理人的译者马耶是特定生活经历和社会文化语境的产物，熟悉并吸纳时代的翻译和文学规范让马耶成为加拿大法语社会文学的代言人。

> [W]hat is just a favoured mode of behaviour within a heterogeneous group may well acquire much more binding force within a certain (more homogeneous) section thereof, in terms of either human agents [...] or types of activity [...]. (Gideon Toury, 1995: 54)

Following the "cultural turn" in Translation Studies (Lefevere & Bassnett, 1990: 1) of the 1980s and 1990s, recent years have seen a "sociological turn" (or "social turn", as in Wolf, 2006: 9). This has been led, in Canada at least, by Daniel Simeoni (1998) and Jean-Marc Gouanvic (1999). The object increasingly being studied by translation scholars is the human agent, the translator, as a member of a sociocultural community called upon to interact with and within the community's structuring and structural dimensions, or Bourdieusian habitus, and as an agent of (inter-)cultural negotiation, rather than translations as cultural artefacts. This is, of course, not to say that translations are no longer being studied, rather that the emphasis has shifted. The result has been to provide literary studies, comparative studies and literary translation researchers with a broad range of methodologies and research techniques from which to choose, thereby greatly enriching the discipline or "interdiscipline" (see Snell-Hornby, 1988/1995: 133). This paper will attempt to consider the usefulness of Gideon Toury's emphasis on the target text, especially when considered in conjunction with the current interest in the (psycho-) sociology of translation and the translator. A close look at Toury's writings will show that he opened the door to this type of research, a fact that has been noted by Daniel Simeoni (1998), Reine Meylaerts (2004) and Michaela Wolf (2006), among others.

Over the years, Gideon Toury has been credited and criticized for shifting the focus of research in Translation Studies from the source text and culture to the target text and culture. When researchers take inspiration from Toury's publications, they invariably emphasize the target translation and how it functions in the target system, the link obviously being made between Itamar Even-Zohar's literary polysystem and Toury's work on how translations function within the target system, especially in relation to target system constraints.

Descriptive Translation Studies (DTS) was first introduced by James S Holmes (1972/2000) then further developed with an emphasis on "function" by Gideon Toury in *Descriptive Translation Studies and beyond* (1995). Certain scholars of literary translation have found the approach particularly productive, notwithstanding criticism of the over-emphasis on the text and target-orientedness (Hermans, 1995), especially when the corpus invites a longitudinal and historical approach. In the context of Spain's TRAducciones CEnsuradas (TRACE) project, Rosa Rabadán and Raquel Merino (2002) have succeeded in applying functional DTS to a "coherent corpus of translated text" (Baker, 1993: 240) and obtained revealing results. The researchers were careful not to limit their study to a product of censorship, i. e. , the censured text; rather they situated their analyses in the socio-institutional context (Robyns, 1992) of the receiving culture that controlled the reception (dissemination versus censorship) of translations. However, their work emphasizes the text, more so than the translator, perhaps, at least in part, because of the type of information that the researchers have been able to obtain from the Franco files in Madrid.

Through his work on DTS, Toury has thus provided a theoretical framework and research methodology for such large-scale projects as the TRACE project as well as his own projects. DTS theory is a logically self-consistent model for describing the behaviour of a related set of translation phenomena. It is supported by Toury's own experimental evidence and is testable. It is clear that this particular contribution to Translation Studies is far from negligible. However, the focus in this paper is more specifically the constraints hypothesis that is bound within DTS theory and its influence on translator behaviour. In fact, Toury's influence has reached beyond DTS methodology to participate constructively in research on textual manipulation and translation behaviour, an influence that was being felt in the 1980s and that is still being felt today (cf. Lefevere, 1983, 1992).

In the following pages, we would like to consider from the viewpoint of the sociological or social turn Toury's thoughts on various constraints on translator behaviour that range from idiosyncrasies to laws, first, by looking at his own writings in direct relation to some responses they have elicited from translation theorists, and then by presenting a brief study to demonstrate how certain hypotheses can be put to productive use. In keeping with Simeoni (1998) and Wolf (2006: 10-11), among others, I argue that by anchoring DTS in sociology and psychosociology, albeit behaviourist, Toury (1995: 54) laid the foundation for a sociological or social orientation in Translation Studies that by no means neglected cognitive and psychological factors. He essentially invited researchers to revisit his thinking in the light of advances in (psycho-)sociology research. Increasingly, emphasis is being placed on cognition and thought processes (Buzelin, 2005). Rather than concentrating on demonstrated behaviours as seen in cultural products, researchers are more interested in studying the agents who produce them, and how and why they do so, or in other words, researchers are opting for a "sociocognitive approach to cultural process and outcome" (Simeoni, 1998: 34). DTS subjected to the "sociological" turn, or "the study of habitus-mediated relations of norms" (Simeoni, 1998: 34) will be applied here to the case of the Acadian translating agent Antonine Maillet, a canonized writer in her own right. While we agree that it is important to put greater emphasis on the translator, agency, habitus and translation practices, we believe that the interaction of these and other elements, especially the prestige of a translated text as cultural artefact, the prestige of the translator within the target system and the target audience's horizon of expectation, must not be neglected.

Itamar Even-Zohar's polysystem theory transformed Translation Studies into an investigation of the position of translated texts taken as a whole (i. e., genre) in the historical and textual systems of the target culture. One of his students, Gideon Toury, took this transformation as his point of departure. Polysystem theory requires that a translated text, produced like the original text by a human agent, be studied as a part of an organic whole, although what the whole is remains unclear to many researchers and has thus sparked debate. For example, is the whole a sub-system of the literary polysystem grouping all genres of translated texts, the complete literary system, including foreign and indigenous texts, or the cultural system? We concur with Mary Snell-Hornby who affirms that the polysystem theory introduced by Even-Zohar has been "outstandingly influential" (Snell-Hornby, 1988/1995: 134); nevertheless, it must be acknowledged that Toury's work on target-oriented DTS, and more specifically his work on norms, has also been highly influential. The formal introduction of the notion of norms into the discipline is marked by Toury's 1976 doctoral dissertation *Normot shel tirgum veha-tirgum ha-sifruti le-ivrit ba-shanim* 1930-1945 [Norms of Literary Translation into Hebrew, 1930-1945], published a year later by the Porter Institute for Poetics and Semiotics, and his 1978 article "The Nature and Role of Norms in Literary Translation." In fact, Theo Hermans affirmed in the 1990s that by emphasizing the target rather than the source text, the concept of norms had effectively replaced equivalence as the operative term in translation studies (1995: 217; see also Baker, 2001).

Nevertheless, Theo Hermans (1999) and Daniel Simeoni (1998), among others, have recently argued that studies inspired by Toury's DTS relied too heavily on the target text, looking for trends in translation behaviour primarily in the translation product, thereby neglecting the translator, their thought processes, and the translation process. Yet Toury's thoughts on constraints take their inspiration from sociology and social psychology; his emphasis on positive and negative reinforcement and observable behaviour (the translated text being a "witness" to that behaviour) betray a Skinnerian influence. New socio-psychological theories have gained ground since the 1960s. Specifically, since the 1990s a Bourdieusian influence is being increasingly felt in Translation Studies, Jean-Marc Gouanvic being an early proponent well before the publication in 1999 of his *Sociologie de la traduction: la science fiction américaine dans l'espace culturel français des années* 1950. At

first, Bourdieu's influence was essentially limited to the concepts of habitus and field, but a broader understanding of his theory has added new elements to the discussion. Productive links have and can be made between Bourdieu's theory and DTS, as numerous translations scholars have demonstrated (Simeoni, 1998; Meylaerts, 2004; Wolf, 2006), given that Bourdieu's thoughts on habitus and control of discourse complement Toury's thoughts on translation behaviour and constraints.

Toury defines sociocultural constraints as a continuum with "diffuse" "borderlines", ranging from idiosyncrasies to rules (or laws) with norms falling between the "two extremes":

> Socio-cultural constraints have been described along a scale anchored between two extremes: general, relatively absolute rules on the one hand, and pure idiosyncrasies on the other. Between these two poles lies a vast middle-ground occupied by intersubjective factors commonly designated norms. [...] The borderlines between the various types of constraints are [...] diffuse. (1995: 54)

Under the "Norms" entry of the *Routledge Encyclopedia of Translation Studies*, Mona Baker explains that, in Toury's view, these "intersubjective factors" are the options that translators as members of a community living in a given socio-historical context select on a regular basis; translators are members of a community with shared values, norms and practices (2001: 164) who share a common understanding of what is correct and proper behaviour in a given situation. Baker goes on to explain the difference between norms and conventions, the latter covering preferences that are non-binding. In "Translation and the Consequences of Scepticism," Anne Mette Hjort (1990) refers to David Lewis's definition of conventions "in terms of common knowledge;" "[conventions] are based on common knowledge and on a preference to have one's behaviour conform to that of others" (43). The individual decides whether or not to be conventional, i. e., to be like their peers. On the contrary, directive norms that involve "regularity of behaviour in recurrent situations of the same type" (Toury, 1995: 55) appear to be binding since they are tied to "dictated" social expectations which exert pressure on members of a community to behave in certain ways under specific circumstances.

It would be useful at this point to make a link here with Hans Robert Jauss's reception aesthetics (1978) and how it can be applied to the reception of foreign literature within a given literary system. Jauss's concept of "horizon of expectation" considers the reader as a member of the target culture, and Translation Studies generally considers the translator to be a reader, par excellence. The potential overlap with Toury's thought is evident. The "horizon of expectation" also shares common ground with social expectations and can be used to compare a reader's reception of foreign products and indigenous products within the target system. Making the link between a translator/reader's horizon(s) of expectation, their natural inclination to conventional or conformist behaviour, social expectations imposed on the translator/reader and the (directive) norms that may influence translation behaviour can lead to fresh insights into the relationship between the foreign and the same in the sociocultural system under study. Of course, studying the relationship between the foreign and the same within the target system brings us face to face with what distinguishes the two, and this would necessarily be what sets apart the "general values or ideas shared by [the target] community" (Toury, 1995: 54) from the general values or ideas shared by the source community. Is there a clash between the translator's values and those expressed in the source text? Does the translator enjoy the freedom to be impartial (Hermans, 2006: 82)? From the point of view of an individual who functions within the system, these values or ideas may be referred to as the constraints that guide, even direct, behaviour so that it conforms to the combination of traits that distinguishes the individual's culture from another, much like one person's personality traits distinguish them from their neighbour. In other words, "[translators] simply operat[e] within different sociocultural settings and hence ha[ve] different norms as guidelines for their translational behaviour" (Toury, 1995: 277).

When there is no conflict between the values or ideas of the foreign and receiving cultures, the foreign cultural product will likely be welcomed. By contrast, when there is conflict, the target culture, and more specifically the translator, may "consent" to difference (Hermans, 2006: 82) or may resist what is perceived to be foreign "interference," taking it as an intrusion into the culture. In some cases, resistance to the linguistic or cultural alterity of the source text may take the form of "purification" of the target text.

Despite the very broad recognition of the usefulness of Toury's ideas, some weaknesses, above and beyond those already discussed, have nevertheless been pointed out. Toury's Descriptive Translation Studies and beyond has been repeatedly criticized for its mechanistic approach and under-emphasis of translators as members of a community (although I venture that the preceding discussion may lead the reader to wonder whether the latter criticism is justified). Toury appears to present a very top-down model that does not open the door to dialogue between translators or to dialogue between translators and those who might try to influence their behaviour. He seems to present professional translators as a discrete group working to some degree in isolation, despite their membership in a community. Norms seem to be imposed from above, and "sanctions" are attached to them. Toury states that "there would normally be a price to pay for opting for any deviant kind of behaviour" (1995: 55). Although he does discuss the reaction of translators to norms and acknowledges inspiration for his ideas on norms from sociology and social psychology, Toury does not explore the network of interactions between the translator as human agent with a personal history and a free will, and the various agents with whom translators must negotiate: other translators with whom they are competing or collaborating, the author, the client, the editor, the publisher, the reviser, the literary critic, etc. (Buzelin, 2005)

In response to this "gap," Simeoni explores "the possibility of nudging theory away from the properties of systemic constructs towards the main focus of translation norms, i. e., the translator" (1998: 1). He convincingly argues that "norms without a habitus to

initiate them make no more sense than a habitus without norms. Incorporating conflict in one single construct attached to the person of the translator should also help us better understand the tension behind the individual choices during the decision process" (1998: 33). Simeoni suggests emphasizing "practices of translating and authoring rather than texts and polysystems; translatorial habitus rather than translational norms" within a DTS framework (1998: 33). Here we shall explore this approach with respect to the case of a single translator, Antonine Maillet, who has developed a coherent corpus of translations for the theatre (four plays by Shakespeare).

Antonine Maillet and William Shakespeare: Setting the Stage

A decade or so after plays such as Robert Gurik's *Hamlet, Prince du Québec* (1968) and Michel Garneau's *Macbeth de William Shakespeare, traduit en québécois* (1978) dominated the Montréal theatre scene, the city experienced the Shakespearean spring of 1988. The former translations (and the term is used very loosely here) support Annie Brisset's argument (1990) that the cultural recycling of literary classics (from Molière to Shakespeare) reflected the tensions that Québec society was experiencing during the quiet revolution as well as during the two decades that followed it. By contrast, the plays produced in 1988, i. e., Michelle Allen's *Songe d'une nuit* [*A Midsummer's Night Dream*], Alice Ronfard's *La Tempête* [*The Tempest*] and François-Victor Hugo's *Cycle des rois* [*The Second History Cycle*], were respectively textual, simplified and nineteenth-century literal (cf. Mallet, 1993). The tensions felt by Québécois audiences that had provoked an ethnocentric reaction to alterity, especially to British and French colonial alterity, appear to have been assuaged as a result of acquiring greater cultural autonomy in the space of twenty years. In Sherry Simon's opinion (1988: 87), Québécois audiences were ready for translations that did more than simply enrich linguistic and cultural identity; their horizon of expectation had undergone a transformation. Instead of Gurik's parody translation or Garneau's perlocutionary translation (Brisset, 1990), a new approach to translating Shakespeare into French had been inaugurated. The following year, Antonine Maillet's *Richard III* was performed at the Théâtre du Rideau Vert. Maillet would consequently be a player in this Shakespeare revolution, for she would translate four of Shakespeare's plays between 1989 and 1999: *Richard III* (1989) [*Richard III*], La Nuit des rois (1993) [*Twelfth Night*], *La tempête* (1997) [*The Tempest*] and *Hamlet* (1999) [*Hamlet*]. The first three plays were published by Leméac; however, *Hamlet* remains unpublished.

Born and raised in Bouctouche, spending her early adulthood in Moncton, Maillet is the product of a small, rural and marginalized culture with a young literary tradition. Her rise to fame can be attributed to the phenomenal success of *La Sagouine* (1971); however, it was the recognition associated with winning the prestigious Prix Goncourt in 1979 for *Pélagie-la-Charrette* that catapulted her into the international limelight. Being the first "outsider" to win the coveted French prize has been linked by some to her literary French, which the French jury could read with greater ease than many literary products from Québec. Philip Stratford describes Maillet's French in the following manner:

> The crux of the matter is that Antonine Maillet doesn't write pure acadien at all. Acadien is just her base. To this she adds, instinctively, her own accent, images, rhythms, expressions. The product is an imaginative equivalent of acadien, heavily laced with Rabelais, Perrault, Molière, folk tales, the Catholic missal, Jean Giono and other sources that have influenced her. What she writes is an amalgam of all these parts, not academic acadien, but a new language. To give it its true name one should call it Antoninais or Mailletois, to give credit to the most important ingredient, her own originality. (Stratford, 1986: 326)

According to Stratford, Maillet's literary *acadien* is inspired by the writings of great canonical sixteenth- and seventeenth-century French writers, including Rabelais, Perrault and Molière. During an interview with Margaret Courchene, Maillet explained that she wished to "rehausser la langue populaire au niveau de l'art" (1992: 69). The Acadian woman of letters would in fact seize on the growing francophone interest in unadulterated Shakespeare at the end of the 1980s to maximize the use of all registers, including popular varieties of Canadian French, in her translations, registers that would be recognizable to a reader of Rabelais, Perrault or Molière—but also to a speaker of rural acadien whose French harks back to Rabelais's French, as Maillet's doctoral thesis proved. All of this to reject "un français restreint, contrôlé et châtré," Maillet thereby affirming "notre renaissance, c'est de découvrir que nous sommes un people et que ce peuple a une expression" (Courchene, 1992: 68), an affirmation that clearly echoes Québec sovereignist discourse.

Thanks to the 1979 Prix Goncourt, Antonine Maillet's status in French-Canadian letters was canonized. She was not on the outskirts of the literary system, rather she was formally recognized as a great French-Canadian writer who many considered a Quebecker. What may have contributed to the confusion regarding the author/dramatist's origins was her move to Montréal. Because Maillet is primarily a dramatist, who seeks large enough audiences to be able to mount plays on a regular basis, she moved to Montréal, the centre of Canadian francophone theatre and literary activity. In fact a number of Acadian expatriates have migrated there (e. g. , Claude LeBouthillier, Jacques Savoie), and this has led to resentment among some Acadians who have stayed *chez eux* in Acadie and paid the price of catering to a much smaller market, living in a primarily rural setting with rural values, and of being in constant contact with the immediate threat of English. It is in Montréal where Antonine Maillet not only wrote and staged her plays, she also started translating those penned by other playwrights, in particular William Shakespeare.

Antonine Maillet Re-translates Shakespeare: Confronting Translation Constraints

Gurik and Garneau had cut Shakespeare's plays from their source literary system to a certain extent through tradaptation, which was the "norm" in Québec until the late 1980s (Beddows, 2000: 11). Maillet, like those translators of the Shakespearean spring, would do the opposite. In terms of Toury's "initial norms," which involve the relationship between "at least two sets of norm-systems" (Toury, 1995: 56-57), Gurik and Garneau had opted for "acceptable translations" that minimized the foreignness of Shakespeare's plots, settings and language. However their respective, and very different, translation projects went beyond contesting the authority of Québec's traditional colonial masters by subverting their literary conventions and norms; these playwrights set out to create new literary and discursive norms for a culturally autonomous francophone Québec. For her part, Maillet opted for "adequate translation," deciding to put greater emphasis on the norms of the source literary tradition, or more precisely the norms that had been bequeathed to future generations by the canonized Elizabethan playwright whom she personally admires, in her words "l'un des plus grands auteurs de tous les temps" (Maillet, 1991: 7). However, as we have already seen, the stage was already set for this translation strategy; in fact, Maillet would appear to be conforming, at least to some extent, to the dominant literary and translation trends of the period.

In addition to the initial norms that we just looked at, operational norms enter into the equation. Different British and French literary conventions call upon norms that govern decisions taken by the translator during the translation process. In fact Maillet's translation of *Richard III* was criticized for having distributed certain linguistic elements in conformity with target norms instead of source norms. This criticism marks a stark contrast to the enthusiastic reception of Garneau's *Macbeth*, which cut scenes deemed unnecessary and which, more often than not, changed Scots cultural references to Québec ones. Theatre translation norms, at least when it comes to translating Shakespeare, would then appear to have evolved by the end of the 1980s. However, the questions to be considered here are (1) whether this evolution was a response to changes in the "general values or ideas shared by a community—as to what is right and wrong, adequate and inadequate" (Toury, 1995: 54); and (2) how Antonine Maillet reacted to these "values and ideas."

During the late 1980s there would appear to have been growing institutional support for unadulterated Shakespeare. First, Shakespeare's literary status in France, and, by extension, in Québec was undoubtedly bolstered thanks to the interest shown in the bard's dramatic literature by, among others, the Sorbonne's Centre de recherches en traduction et stylistique comparée de l'anglais et du français. The Centre published one issue of *Palimpsestes* in 1987 (translating dialogue) and two issues in 1990 (one on retranslating and one on translation/adaptation) that included at least one article on translating Shakespeare. Second, Charlotte Melançon's *translation Shakespeare et son théâtre* [*Northrop Frye on*

Shakespeare] was published by Montréal's Éditions du Boréal in 1988 and honoured the same year by the Association of Literary Translators of Canada with the John Glassco Prize for Literary Translation. It seems probable that a confluence of institutional support for the "real" Shakespeare contributed to the transformation of norms "into performance instructions appropriate for and applicable to particular situations, specifying what is prescribed and forbidden as well as what is tolerated and permitted in a certain behavioural dimension" (Toury, 1995: 54-55). Translators were put in the position where they could conform to or reject these new "performance instructions."

Antonine Maillet clearly admires Shakespeare. Furthermore, institutional support for source-oriented translation would have reassured a translator who apparently prefers to follow literary trends. These factors come into play when we consider Maillet's mental processes or her "habitus," that is, "the elaborate result of a personalized social and cultural history" (Simeoni, 1998: 32). The Acadian translator also greatly admires Rabelais, a bawdy pre-classicist French writer who was more or less a contemporary of the bawdy bard. A variation of Rabelais's French could conceivably be used to render Shakespeare's English. Maillet's preparatory work on Rabelais's French was done when she earned a doctorate at Université Laval; the topic of her dissertation was Rabelais and the lineage of Acadian language and culture. Her linguistic mastery and scholarly bent had prepared her well to meet the challenges of re-producing Shakespeare in French. Another factor to consider could be, specifically, the writer/translator's apparent inclination to conform to literary and translation trends, as her *Bourgeois gentleman* (1978) and *Évangeline deusse* (1975) appear to demonstrate when considered in their literary context.

Nevertheless, her 1989 translation of *Richard III* was considered inadequate by some critics, in particular Robert Lévesque, who published an incisive review "Du Shakespeare en réduction" the same year. While the Acadian writer had maximized foreignness (by contrast to Gurik's and Garneau's efforts), she had nevertheless not yet succumbed to the empire of the Shakespearean hexameter, choosing instead the conventional French alexandrine (Lévesque, 1989: 12-13), her *Richard III* betraying the traditional French tendency to make the translated text conform to French literary tastes and textual conventions. However, Maillet's approach evolved in direct response to the negative criticism penned by members of the target culture. Members of a cultural community are generally able to recognize linguistic practices as "belonging" to their culture and to spot "foreign" practices that may have been retained by a translator who has adopted the norms of the source culture (Toury, 1995: 56). In this case members of the target culture sought out foreign practices in the translation product and, in stark contrast to the preceding decade, expressed disappointment at not finding more examples. Maillet had initially resisted the interference of British literary conventions and received a "negative" sanction when her translation behaviour was evaluated (1995: 54-55). This "problem" was corrected in her 1993 translation of *Twelfth Night*, and the following review by Solange Lévesque is glowing:

> La dramaturge acadienne semble s'être retrouvée chez l'auteur britannique comme dans un univers familier; la multiplicité des tons, la raillerie, la roublardise, les équivoques, le plaisir du jeu (jeu des mots, jeu des rôles), la vivacité et le naturel des dialogues, tous ces traits brillamment entremêlés chez Shakespeare ont trouvé en français, grâce *à* la traductrice, des correspondances qui font de son texte une traduction d'une valeur indiscutable. (Lévesque 1993: 31)

Not all writers-cum-translators are as responsive to their critics as is Antonine Maillet. She is in the enviable position of being financially independent, in large part thanks to the success of *La Sagouine* and *Pélagie-la-Charrette*, and could have chosen to ignore them. In fact, she chooses to translate what interests her and what the Théâtre du Rideau Vert is interested in producing. Furthermore, it would appear that she wishes to please her audience by giving them the type of translation they are expecting.

It is interesting that the Acadian writer should have chosen a canonical Elizabethan writer to explore the limits of French (literary) language, especially considering the "irreconcilable philological differences" between the two language systems, "including the lack of elasticity of the arguably more regulated French language" (Beddows, 2000: 11). However, we have already seen that Maillet considers Shakespeare one of the greatest writers of all time, hence a model worthy of imitation. Maillet's international recognition had also transformed her into an "authorized spokesperson" (Bourdieu, 1982: 169) of not only the French-Canadian literary system, but also of the French language. And as Pierre Bourdieu has written, a culture's authorized spokespersons are called upon to reproduce officially sanctioned behaviour. Moreover, Antonine Maillet's "translations of Shakespeare demonstrate Québec's ability, in the 1990s, to tolerate the foreign on its stages" (Beddows, 2000: 102).

Conclusion

The preceding pages have made every effort not to "overlook the human agent, the translator" (Hermans, 1995: 222), by insisting on the study of "translatorial habitus." Clearly, Gideon Toury's thoughts on translator behaviour in response to norms have been useful in helping us arrive at the conclusion that Antonine Maillet is an agent of translation who is the product of her personal trajectory and sociocultural context. She is an accomplished writer in her own right; moreover, she has been attributed the socio-literary role on the national level of authorized spokesperson, apparently as a result of having acquired and internalized the dominant translation and literary norms of the period. Furthermore, the translator appears to have been seeking critical and social approval, and to obtain it bowed to critical expectations voiced in Québec and, to a lesser degree, in France. In this case, conforming to expectations has been positively received. In addition, Maillet's approach to translating Shakespeare has allowed "la fanatique de la défense et de l'illustration" of Acadian French (Maillet, 1999: 52) to give "*à* des mots qui sont parfois vieillis, parfois désuets, parfois inutilisés, parfois incompréhensibles, leur véritable noblesse" (Courchene, 1992: 69), an approach which could help explain her choice of the bawdy "barbare de génie" who allows her to exploit the full range of possibilities offered by the French language (cf. Merkle, 2000).

This comparative and systemic analysis represents but a tiny chapter in French-Canadian "translation historiography" (Meylaerts, 2004: 307, my translation) and has attempted to show that the relationship between the translator, her habitus-mediated relation to norms and translation agency must all be considered when examining translation process and function. Having brought into the discussion the thoughts of a number of translation theoreticians with a sociological bent does not diminish the fact that our point of departure was DTS and Toury's work on constraints. It is to be hoped that this case study might provide insights into the impact of convention and socio-cognitive constraints on the translation process.

选文三 Theatre and Opera Translation

Mary Snell-Hornby

导 言

本文《戏剧翻译》选自 Piotr Kuhiwczak 和 Karin Littau 编写的 *A Companion to Translation Studies*,2007)。作者玛丽·斯奈尔-霍恩比(Mary Snell-Hornby, 1940-)是维也纳大学教授,曾在慕尼黑、海德堡、苏黎世等城市的大学任教,也是英国沃里克大学(Warrick University)的翻译和比较文化研究中心名誉教授。主要从事翻译研究,也涉及词典编纂、语言学以及文学研究。著有 *Translation Studies: An Integrated Approach* (1988, 1995), *The Turns of Translation Studies: New Paradigms or Shifting Viewpoints*(2006)等。

选文介绍了戏剧文本翻译的各种方法,并详述了"恪守"忠实这一观念将大大影响了戏剧翻译文本搬上舞台的效果。文章认为,要获得舞台上的成功,话剧和歌剧文本的翻译需要采用一种合作式的"整体"翻译方法,即译者要与导演、演员等剧组人员合作,参与到剧本的制作和表演等整个过程中去。译者提供的翻译文本,要具有"可表演性"和"可理解性"。"可表演性"取决于它能否产生非语言的动作和效果,能否具有可说性(speakability)、个性化、简洁性和音律感。"可理解性"确保观众能够理解舞台上的演出。在涉及到语言、礼貌、道德标准、仪式、品味、意识形态、幽默感、迷信以及宗教信仰等社会文化因素时,译者必须做出适当的调整以避免误解的发生。

Introduction: Page or Stage?

Up until the 1980s the theatre was a neglected field in translation studies. In the world of academe the stage play was traditionally viewed as a work of literature, and in translating the dramatic text the same scholarly criteria (such as equivalence or faithfulness) were applied as to other types of literary translation. There were of course notable exceptions: in 1848 Ludwig Tieck, in his famous "Letter to the Translator of Elektra," wrote as follows:

> *Denn das scheint mir ein Hauptvorzug Ihrer Gbersetzung, dass die Sprache so ganz dramatisch, so ungeschwacht und ungezwungen ist, dass sie jedes Mal Leidenschaft richtig ausdriickt, ohne die oft etwas linkischen und erzwungenen Wendungen zu gebrauchen, in welche der Gelehrte, der Philologe oft verfällt, der sich nicht die wirkliche Rede, den natiirlichen wahren Dialog des Theaters deutlich machen kann.* (Tieck, 1848: 420f.)
>
> (For to me it seems to be one of the chief merits of your translation that the language is so entirely dramatic, so natural and undiluted that it is always a genuine vehicle of passion, without resorting to the often rather awkward and strained expressions frequently adopted by the scholar, the man of letters, who is unable to produce real spoken language, the true and natural dialogue of the theatre. *My translation.*)

Among literary scholars and the theatre world, the question of the faithful scholarly translation of dramatic dialogue on the one hand and the "actable," "performable" stage text on the other has been a common bone of contention. In the late 1950s there was a furore created among German academics—and fought out in the national weekly *Die Zeit*—by the Shakespeare translator Hans Rothe. His explicit aim was to produce, not a faithful reproduction of the printed English version with its wealth of imagery and meanwhile barely comprehensible allusions, but a text to be performed and understood on the mid-20th century German stage.

The Stage Play in Translation Studies

The 1970s: New Approaches and New Concepts

At this time translation studies had not yet established itself as a modern academic discipline, and the topic of translating for the stage was broached by only a few individual literary scholars and translators. Once again, the debate centred round the question of the "actable," "performable" stage text on the one hand and the faithful scholarly translation on the other. Theatre practitioners also objected that translated theatre texts often had to be changed during rehearsals to make them suitable for a stage performance (cf. Snell-Hornby, 1984). Early impulses from the emerging interdisciplinary perspectives of translation studies, though still within the framework of literary studies, came in the 1970s, in particular from the international colloquium "Literature and translation" held in Leuven in April 1976. In her contribution, "Translating spatial poetry: An examination of theatre texts in performance," Susan Bassnett described a play as "much more than a literary text, it is a combination of language and gesture brought together in a harmonious frame of timing" (Bassnett-McGuire, 1978: 161), and she presents "patterns of tempo-rhythm" and "basic undertextual rhythms" as new key concepts. In the French-speaking scientific community a semiotic approach was adopted: Anne Ubersfeld describes the theatre text as one that merges into a dense pattern of synchronic signs, and Patrice Pavis (1976) equates the staging of a written text, the *mis en scene*, with a *mis en signe*.

The 1980s and 1990s: Developing Independent Theoretical Approaches

The early contributions on stage translation unanimously point out that at the time this was an area previously ignored by translation theory, and it was during the course of the 1980s that the deficit was corrected. The first major step was to describe the specific characteristics of the dramatic text and what makes it so different from other kinds of literary text. One striking feature is that the stage text as such consists of two clearly separate components: the stage directions on the one hand and the spoken dialogue on the other. It is above all this latter component that is meant when the term "stage translation" is used. In her text typology of 1971 the German translation scholar Katharina Reiss had already identified "audiomedial" (later "multimedial") texts as those written, not to be read silently, but to be spoken or sung, and that are hence dependent on a non-verbal medium or on other non-verbal forms of expression, both acoustic and visual, to reach their intended audience. Unlike the case of the novel, short story or lyric poem, in multimedial texts the verbal text is only one part of a larger and complex whole—and this poses particular problems for translation. Examples of multimedial texts in this definition are film scripts, radio plays, opera libretti and drama texts. The latter two share the characteristic that they are written specifically for live performance on the stage, and they have been compared with a musical score which only realises its full potential in the theatrical performance (Snell-Hornby, 1984).

The semiotic approach

The theatrical sign as icon, index and symbol

In the early 1980s semiotics, as the study of signs, was systematically applied as a basis for the theoretical discussion of drama. The concept of the sign is indeed helpful in explaining the basic workings of theatre, particularly in the famous trichotomy established by Charles S. Peirce, according to which a sign can be an *icon*, an *index* or a *symbol*:

A sign can refer to an Object by virtue of an inherent similarity ("like-ness") between them (icon), by virtue of an existential contextual connection of spatiotemporal (physical) contiguity between sign and object (index), or by virtue of a general law or cultural convention that permits sign and object to be interpreted as connected (symbol).

The system of signs belonging to the world of the theatre presents a kaleidoscope of these three types, and the differentiation between them is essential for the spectator's interpretation of what s/he is seeing and hearing on stage. An iconic sign (such as a Tudor costume in a naturalistic production or a table set for dinner) can be taken as it stands, and it is fully interpretable as long as the spectator can situate it in context. An indexical sign is interpretable as long as the spectator can understand the point of connection (e. g., that smoke can stand for fire). A symbolic sign is only understandable if the spectator is familiar with its meaning in the culture concerned (e. g., that in Western cultures black is the colour of mourning). The theatrical experience varies with the spectator's previous experience and knowledge, and hence with his/her ability to arrange and interpret the abundance of sensory perceptions conveyed to him/her by the performance. The problem for stage translation is that the interpretation of the signs can also vary radically from one culture to another (particularly so with symbolic signs: the colour of mourning in Asiatic cultures for example is white), and much even depends on the acting styles and stage conventions of the country or cultural community concerned.

The above observations referred only to non-verbal signs. What is important for verbal language, and is therefore of special significance for translation, is the insight that the linguistic sign is essentially arbitrary and symbolic. In other words it is interpretable only if the recipient (or spectator) is familiar with its position or meaning within the language system and culture concerned. And this is where the stage text assumes its significance as dramatic potential.

Paralanguage, kinesics, proxemics and the stage text

As well as their potential for interpretation as signs, the naked words of the printed stage text provide a basis for action and co-ordination with the immediate environment of the dramatic world in which they are to be embedded. The means for such co-ordination are paralinguistic, kinesic and proxemic. The basic paralinguistic features concern vocal elements such as intonation, pitch, rhythm, tempo, resonance, loudness and voice timbre leading to expressions of emotion such as shouting, sighing or laughter. Kinesic features are related to body movements, postures and gestures and include smiling, winking, shrugging or waving. Proxemic features involve the relationship of a figure to the stage environment, and describe its movement within that environment and its varying distance or physical closeness to the other characters on stage.

The performability of a stage text as a dramatic "score" is closely connected with the possibilities it offers for generating such vocal elements, gestures and movements within the framework of its interpret-ability as a system of theatrical signs. An outstanding example of the performable stage text—not unsurprisingly taken from Shakespeare—with paralinguistic, kinesic and proxemic potential is Macbeth's famous monologue before the murder of Duncan, "Is this a dagger which I see before me?" What is generated by the text is a kind of optical illusion, described by Nicholas Brooke in his edition of *The Tragedy of Macbeth* as follows:

> Words play a great part here, but not words alone: The invisible dagger is necessarily created also by his body, gesture, and above all by his eyes, which focus on a point in space whose emptiness becomes, in a sense, visible to the audience. (Brooke, 1990: 4)

The focusing of the eyes on a point in space is the natural consequence of various verbal elements in the text—including the reiterated phrase "I see (thee)." I It is also a consequence of the personification of the object throughout the passage, whereby its presence is established in a quasi-dialogue as a kind of partner with whom the speaker naturally maintains eye contact. In this case the dramatic effect arises from the interaction of word, gesture and motion needed to create the ominous vision of the poised dagger. Usually, however, in dramatic discourse such interaction takes place within the framework of real dialogue involving two or more partners. Here, too, the same principle applies: The performability of the verbal text depends on its capacity for generating non-verbal action and effects within its scope of interpretation as a system of theatrical signs. Sometimes the methods used by the dramatist are amazingly simple: Misunderstandings arising from puns, for example, differing social conventions, irony or multiple associations have for centuries been the essence of stage dialogue.

The holistic approach

For the concert-goer the musical score is usually an abstract entity rationally analyzed only by the musicologist or critic: what counts is the global sensory effect of the music itself. A similar relationship exists between the stage text and the dramatic performance. But it is quite possible to analyse the dramatic score and identify the basic factors that make up its theatrical potential. The key words, much discussed over the last 20 years but still only vaguely defined, are performability/actability (jouabilite/Spielbarkeit) as discussed above, speakability (Sprechbarkeit), and in the case of the opera or musical singability (Sangbarkeit). What is considered performable, speakable or singable depends to a great extent on the theatrical tradition and on the acting styles of the language community involved. Back in 1985 Susan Bassnett aptly described the difference between British, German and Italian acting styles:

British classical acting requires the actor to physicalise the text, to reinforce possible textual obscurities with kinesic signs, to push forward through the language of the text, even at times against the text. The German tradition, which is more intensely intellectual, tends to the opposite extreme—the text acquires a weightiness that the spatial context reinforces and it is the text that carries the actor forward rather than the reverse. The Italian tradition of virtuosity on the part of the individual actor creates yet another type of performance style: the text of the play becomes the actor's instrument and the performance of that play is an orchestration of many different instruments playing together. (Bassnet-Maguire, 1985: 92)

Given such divergences, it seems inevitable that precise and at the same time generally accepted definitions will remain utopian. The term speakability (Sprechbarkeit) was discussed in detail in the 1960s by Jiri Levy (1969), for whom speakable language depends on the interplay of syntax and rhythm, vowels and consonants. More recently, in 1984, the term was complemented by the concept of Atembarkeit ("breathability"), which was introduced by the German stage director Ansgar Haag (1984) and means that stress patterns and sentence structures should fit in with the emotions expressed in the dialogue. All these features contribute towards making a text performable, a phenomenon that I investigated in the 1980s, partly on the basis of interviews with a stage producer and an actor from the Schauspielhaus in Zurich (Snell-Hornby, 1984). The conclusions I then reached, which contain various criteria of performability, can be summarised as follows (cf. Snell-Hornby, 1996):

(1) Theatre dialogue is essentially an artificial language, written to be spoken, but never identical with ordinary spoken language. If we compare a stage dialogue with a transcription of normal conversation, we find that the dialogue is characterised by special forms of textual cohesion, by semantic density, highly sophisticated forms of ellipsis, often rapid changes of theme, and special dynamics of deictic interaction offering large scope for interpretation. This is what since Stanislaysky has been known as the sub-text, which, as Harold Pinter put it, is "the language where, under what is said, another thing is being said."

(2) It is characterised by an interplay of multiple perspectives, resulting from the simultaneous interaction of different factors and their effect on the audience. Eminently effective on the stage are elements of paradox, irony, allusion, wordplay, anachronism, climax, sudden anticlimax and so on (as demonstrated in innumerable examples by Shakespeare or Stoppard).

(3) Theatre language can be seen as potential action in rhythmical progression; in this sense rhythm does not only refer to stress patterns within sentences, but also involves the inner rhythm of intensity as the plot or action progresses, the alternation of tension and rest, suspense and calm. This also applies to the structure of the dialogue, whereby rhythm is closely bound up with the tempo, which is faster in an exchange of short, sharp utterances and slows down in long sentences with complicated syntax.

(4) For the actor his/her lines combine to form a kind of individual idiolect, a "mask of language." For him or her, language is primarily a means of expressing emotion, through the voice, facial expression, gestures and movements. The dramatic discourse and the actor's performance should form a coherent and convincing whole, hence the demand for translations which are speakable, breathable and performable.

(5) For the spectator in the audience, language and the action on stage are perceived sensuously, as a more or less personal experience; s/he is not just a bystander, looking on curiously but uninvolved. As long as the stage events are convincing, the spectator should feel drawn into them and respond to them—either through empathy or alienation.

Theatre and audience: The sociocultural perspective

A "good" theatre text is invariably described by theatre practitioners as one that "works," and hence it must be interpretable by both actors and audience. To explain these mechanisms in terms of stage translation, Sirkku Aaltonen extended the semiotic approach to include a sociocultural perspective:

> In order to understand what is going on stage, the audience needs to be able to decode, if not all, at least a sufficient minimum of the signs and sign systems within the text. In consequence, adjustments may be made in the translation process in relation to the general cultural conventions covering the language, manners, moral standards, rituals, tastes, ideologies, sense of humour, superstitions, religious beliefs, etc. (Aaltonen, 1997: 93)

In other words, a translated text is closely bound up with the sociocultural circumstances of its conception:

> Although the text will always mean different things to different individuals and a multitude of meanings will always arise from the interaction between the content of the signs it emits and the spectator's competence to decode them, it all still happens in particular social and historical circumstances. When John Millington Synge wrote *The Playboy of the Western World*, it gave rise to riots in Dublin. It could never have the same impact again in another time or culture. The further the text recedes in time, the less relevant become the original meanings, and the more different the "message." The great advantage of stage drama lies in the fact that each translation and performance can take the particular cultural, social, historical and geographical situation of its audience into account and adapt the play to these changing circumstances. (Aaltonen, 1997: 94)

These apt observations focus on yet another special characteristic of stage translation as compared with the "faithfulness" required for "sacred originals" as in Bible translation or narrative prose. The need to adapt the play to changing circumstances applies particularly where, as with The Playboy of the Western World, specific historic circumstances or outdated ethical principles are involved. Similar scandals accompanied the first productions of Moliere's Tartuffe, Oscar Wilde's *Salome* and Arthur Schnitzler's *Reigen*, for example—for reasons that would be completely foreign to a modern audience.

The relationship between stage text and audience has been further investigated by Fabienne Hormanseder (2001) who, in her list of basic criteria for a successful stage text, has added to those discussed above the features Horbarkeit ("audibility"), Fasslichkeit ("comprehensibility") and Klarheit ("clarity").

It is, however, important to stress that no concrete, universally applicable rules can be drawn up for applying the terms discussed here. Actors are given intensive training in articulation and breathing techniques, and hence can master language that the layperson might consider "unspeakable," but which the dramatist used deliberately to create tension or special effects, and terms like "speakability" or "comprehensibility" must remain relative to the production and situation concerned.

Opera Translation

With texts written to be sung on stage—as in the case of opera or musicals—the problems only increase. The issue of opera translation has been investigated by Klaus Kaindl (1995), who advocates an approach that is interdisciplinary (combining insights from theatre studies, literary studies and musicology) and holistic—whereby the opera text becomes a synthesis of the libretto, music and performance (both vocal and scenic). The criteria of "performability" and "breathability" are here complemented by that of "singability" (Sangbarkeit). The call for singable opera texts is nothing new in the field—back in 1935 Edward Dent stated clearly: "It is essential to have words which can be easily sung and pronounced on the particular notes or musical phrases where they occur." One of the basic rules here is that open vowels like/a/are especially suitable for high notes and/o/and/u/for low notes, whereas consonant clusters are problematic. This applies especially with fast tempos that require rapid articulation from the singer.

This means that the translator of musical texts is faced with a challenging task. In her study of the translation of modern musicals, Claudia Lisa (1993) interviewed Herbert Kretzmer, the translator of the English text of *Les Misêrables* who correlated singability with characterisation. In describing his work, Kretzmer made the following remarks:

> I never finish a translation for Aznavour until I hear him sing a song. When I hear him sing the song there is (sic) always half a dozen ideas that come to me or certain words can be mistaken or misconstrued, or I can see that on that particular note of music the word I have given it does not sound right. It is to nasal or whatever and it needs a more open sound. (Lisa, 1993: 66)

Examples of the interplay of music, vocal performance and language are given by Kaindl (1995) in his discussion of Carmen and of various renderings through the centuries of the aria *"Fin ch'han dal vino" in Don Giovanni*, where it becomes clear that in opera, to an even more drastic extent than in spoken drama, the verbal text is only one of a whole complex of elements simultaneously at work. For the translator Edward Dent's words may still be valid:

> An opera libretto is not meant to be read as a poem, but to be heard on the stage as set to music; if the translator feels that his words may appear bald and

> commonplace he must remember that it is the musician's business to clothe them with beauty (Dent, 1935: 82).

Surtitling

In recent years opera houses have been adopting the practice of staging a work in its original language version and providing surtitles with the translated content of the verbal text similar to the subtitles of works on screen. Such translations are purely informative texts, of course, and criteria such as performability and singability do not apply. Surtitles are, however, growing increasingly sophisticated: apart from technical innovations such as installing small monitors in the seating so that the individual spectator can decide whether or in which language a text can be used, there have been attempts to integrate the translated text into the production on stage. Christina Hurt (1996) has compared French and English surtitles of Wagner's *Siegfried* based on the two different translation policies at the Royal Opera House Covent Garden and the Theatre du Chatelet in Paris. While at Covent Garden the surtitles are seen as part of the general service provided by the house, and standard versions are offered that are valid for all productions, at the Theatre du Chatelet surtitles are considered to be an integral part of the individual production and are created as part of an artistic whole. Hurt (1996) reaches the conclusion that the quality of the surtitles is superior if they form part of the production as in Paris, and if the translator is integrated into the production team—as an artist who uses technological media, but who can by no means be replaced by a machine.

The Stage Translator and the Production Team

Not only for surtitles has the need arisen for the translator to join the production team. In recent years this has been recommended by many scholars who have written on stage translation. Aaltonen describes two categories of translators:

> The first category of translators are those whose only connection with the stage is the translation work. They are fairly powerless and their relationship to the dramatic text is comparable to that of an actor. The text sets the parameters of the work, and both the translator and the actor must bow to the text. Their role is seen as that of mediators rather than of creators. The second category are translators who work within the theatre, such as dramaturges or directors. They exercise more power and retain this power when they work as translators. As translators they are closer to being creators than mediators. They can, if they so wish, make adjustments or interpret the text according to need. (Aaltonen, 1997: 92)

It is clearly this second category of translator who has the means and the influence to create and then produce the performable text. This does not only mean that stage directors can take over the translator's job, as has frequently been the case, but also that professional translators, as experts in text design, can cooperate with the production team. Working with Justa Holz-Manttari's (1984) concept of "*translatorisches Handeln*" (translatorial action), Klaus Kaindl has sketched modalities of interaction for opera translation, and Fabienne Hormanseder has made detailed and concrete suggestions for such cooperation in producing translated stage plays. Herbert Kretzmer, as indicated in the above quotation, has shown how such cooperation has already worked for the English production of *Les Miserables*. The German translator of the same musical, the rock-singer Heinz Rudolf Kunze—in an interview with Claudia Lisa (1993)—describes virtually ideal conditions for his work in the Vienna production. Kuntze approached his task holistically (as did Kretzmer for the English version): he first read Victor Hugo's novel, then saw the London and New York musical productions several times. He bought dictionaries of slang (including the 19th-century expressions) and listened to Claude Michel Schonberg's music, writing down his thoughts and ideas, which were later used in his text. As he was given 18 months to complete his task, he had time for contemplation and revision. During rehearsals and the preparation period, he was completely integrated into the production team, and like Kretzmer, he was able to change the text where necessary to make it more singable. He quotes one of the singers as saying: "*Ich kann das nicht singen. Ich muss dabei tanzen, und da stolpere ich über die Konsonanten. Mach das ein bisschen einfacher*" (Lisa, 1993: 77: "I can't sing that. I've got to dance at the same time and I stumble over the consonants. Make it a bit easier," my translation). Kuntze was only too willing to cooperate, and although he was not a dramaturge or director and so does not strictly speaking belong to Aaltonen's second category of translators, he was given the time and scope to work creatively and was given the necessary influence in the production. The result was a high-quality German text—and a resoundingly successful production.

Translation or Adaptation?

A question frequently raised is whether the creative, performable foreign language version of a theatre text is actually a translation at all. It is probably the low prestige and the lack of influence associated with the work of the translator that makes anyone who does more than merely transcode want to see the result as being a creative adaptation. Herbert Kretzmer was quite vehement in his refusal to see his work as a translation:

> The work that I did for *Les Miserables* can be described in any terms other than direct translation. It is a term that I absolutely reject. About a third of the piece might be described as translation of a kind, a rough translation following the line of the story, which was of course important to the project. Another third might be

> described as rough adaptation and the other third might be described as original material because there are at least six or seven songs now in the show that did not exist in the original French production at all. (Lisa, 1993: 62)

These remarks may be partially explained by the fact that Kretzmer—following common practice in stage translation—was provided with an interlinear translation of the French text along with English material from James Fenton, the first translator engaged for the project, and he did indeed add new material of his own. However, on being asked the reasons why he so vehemently rejected the term "translation" for his work, he replied:

> I resist and resent the word "translator" because it is an academic function and I bring more to the work than an academic function. It is very unacademic in fact. (...) I like to think that I brought something original to the project, that I was not a secretary to the project or a functionary, that I was as much a writer of *Les Miserables* than (sic!) Boublil and Schonberg and anyone else. So that is why I reject the term "translator." It is a soulless function. You do not have to bring intelligence, you do not have to bring passion to the job of translation, you only have to bring a meticulous understanding of at least another language. You have to understand the language and you have to translate it into another language. You do not bring yourself, you just bring knowledge and skill. (Lisa, 1993: 62)

It is interesting that Heinz Rudolf Kuntze—as well as being a rock singer he is a graduate in German Literature—did not pretend to do anything other than translate. However, he sees this absolutely as a creative and poetic activity ("*Nach—und Neudichten*") that aims at evoking a "similar effect" in the target language, and not at merely reproducing individual linguistic items (Lisa, 1993: 76). Kunze expresses complete disdain for those producers in London and the USA who, in the early stages of the venture, gave him no scope for creativity, but "*sich nicht nur Zeile fair Zeile, sondern Silbe fiir Silbe alles haben iibersetzen lassen*" ("had everything translated, not only line for line, but even syllable for syllable") (Lisa, 1993: 75).

As indicated above, interlinear versions such as these are common in theatre practice, reducing the translator's contribution even more to hack-work which is then refined and improved by the "creative" expert who produces the final version. This is especially the case when the expert concerned is not familiar with the language of the source version. An outstanding example is Tom Stoppard, who has created English versions of a Polish play (*Tango by Slawomir Mrozek*), a Spanish play (*La casa de Bernarda Alba* by Garcia Lorca), German plays by Arthur Schnitzler (*Liebelei and Das weite Land*), *Nestroy's Einen Jux will er sich machen*, and *Pirandello's Henry IV*, without being proficient in any of the source languages involved. The ensuing translation process was described by Stoppard as follows (he is referring to his version of *Schnitzler's Das weite Land*):

> [...] the National Theatre provided me with a literal transcript which aspired

> to be *accurate and readable rather than actable*. I was also given the services of a German linguist, John Harrison. Together—he with the German text, I with the English—we went through the play line by line, during which process small corrections were made and large amounts of light were shed on the play I had before me. After several weeks of splitting hairs with Harrison over alternatives for innumerable words and phrases, the shadings of language began to reveal themselves: carving one's way by this method into the living rock is hardly likely to take one around the third dimension, but as the relief becomes bolder so does the translator, until there is nothing to do but begin. (Stoppard, 1986: ix, *emphasis added*)

Stoppard goes on to describe how during rehearsals further changes between source and target texts:

> [...] were often provoked by the sense that in its original time and place the text gave a sharper account of itself than it seemed to do on the page in faithful English in 1979. The temptation to add a flick here and there became irresistible. (Stoppard, 1986: ix)

It is interesting that Stoppard has no inhibitions about describing himself as "the translator"—though definitely of Aaltonen's second category—but he does have reservations about calling the resulting version—*Undiscovered Country*—a translation:

> So the text here published, though largely faithful to Schnitzler's play in word and, I trust, more so in spirit, departs from it sufficiently to make one cautious about offering it as a "translation:" it is a record of what was performed at the National Theatre. (Stoppard, 1986: x)

One might well ask if the same remarks could not be made about any foreign language theatre text, and one can only take up Susan Bassnett's words in discussing the issue back in 1985:

> Because of the multiplicity of factors involved in theatre translation, it has become a commonplace to suggest that it is an impossible task. Translators have frequently tried to fudge issues further, by declaring that they have produced a "version" or "adaptation" of a text, or even, as Charles Marovitz described his *Hedda Gabler*, a "collage." None of these terms goes any way towards dealing with the issues, since all imply some kind of ideal SL [source language] text towards which translators have the responsibility of being "faithful." The distinction between a "version" of an SL text and an "adaptation" of that text seems to me to be a complete red herring. It is time the misleading use of these terms were set aside. (Bassnett-McGuire, 1985: 93)

Conclusion: Future Prospects

After long years of heated debate, it is now accepted in translation studies that translation as it is understood today goes far beyond the mechanical and "soulless" activity described by Herbert Kretzmer, performed by a secretary or functionary and needing only knowledge or skill, but no creativity or passion—although unfortunately outside translation studies such prejudices are still widespread. The conception of translation as mere interlingual transcoding unfortunately still exists in the minds of many who work with language, and it is also still kept alive in theatre practice when a translator is asked to provide raw material that is then "recreated" by someone familiar with the needs of the stage. We have seen that the theatre text, and the task of translating for the theatre, is immensely complicated, and the result might seem most promising if the translator is given the scope of a creative artist working within the production team. From the 19th century "man of letters" and the 20th century "functionary" the theatre translator of the future might develop into an expert working with texts in the theatre, and translation studies should get the message across to a larger audience that the issues involved lie between disciplines and across boundaries.

选文四　Translation and Canon Formation: Nine Decades of Drama in the United States

André Lefevere

导　言

本文《翻译和经典形成:美国戏剧 90 年》选自《翻译、权力、颠覆》(*Translation, Power, Subversion*, 1996)。作者安德烈·勒菲弗尔(André Lefevere, 1944-1996)原籍比利时,是美国得克萨斯州奥斯汀分校的翻译和比较文学教授,当代西方比较文学和翻译研究领域知名学者。主要著作有:《文学翻译:比较文学语境中的实践与理论》(*Translating Literature—Practice and Theory in a Comparative Literature Context*, 1992),《翻译、改写以及对文学名声的制控》(*Translation, Rewriting, and the Manipulation of Literary Fame*, 1992),《翻译、历史与文化:原始资料集》(*Translation/History/Culture: A Source Book*, 1992)等,发表论文上百篇,极享盛名。

选文从翻译史的角度论证了文学选集编撰是经典形成的主要方式,编撰过程受到多种主、客观条件的影响。戏剧翻译是重写，译者由于受意识形态或诗学的制约，在一定程度上会改写原文。而对于不懂原语的读者而言，译文就成了原文。高中生和大学生及一些文学爱好者，通过阅读选集得以获取知识，译文成了经典，其影响力不可低估。作者选择布莱顿·马修斯于1916年出版的第一本戏剧选集《主要欧洲戏剧家》，探讨了影响选集选本的因素：出版商的市场收益，选集页数的限制，大学是否设置该戏剧课程，入选的作家有限等；选择标准的保守；是否符合当时的主流意识形态等等，这些仍然是入选文集的重要标准。从国别来看，西方戏剧尤其是欧洲及其附属国作品的选录，强化了当时美国戏剧经典中的欧洲中心主义。此外，对选集的编写无法忽略编撰者的个人偏好。作者呼吁翻译研究应关注重写过程中的变化及塑造的形象，揭示背后的各种影响因素。

The basic premise of this essay if that a translation of a literary work is one way of rewriting a literary text. Other types of rewriting literary texts are the compilation of anthologies, the production of literary criticism and literary history, and the ending of texts. These types are listed, and the rationale for listing them is explained more extensively in my *Translation, Rewriting, and the Manipulation of Literary Fame*.[1] Some of these rewritings merely refer to the texts they rewrite, as when titles and short plot summaries of literary works are mentioned in literary histories. Other rewritings reproduce the texts they rewrite to some extent, as when comic strip, or some movie versions of literary texts succeed in mainly reproducing the plot lines of their originals. Still other rewritings claim to represent the texts they are rewriting. Translation in the more traditional understanding of the word would be a prime example of this category. In fact, prospective readers who walk into most bookstores in the United States wanting to buy Brecht's *Mother Courage*, will only be able to buy the English translation/rewriting of that play, since the original is likely to be available only in a very select number of specialized bookstores. If they do not have German, and if they are not familiar with German literature, they will not mind this at all. They will, in fact, read the translation, the rewriting, as if it was the original text, and they will experience this state of affairs as normal, leaving professional readers of literature, such as critics and theoreticians, to agonize over it.

The way in which a translation is made therefore does matter enormously for readers who need translations because they cannot read original. This is all the more ironic because translations are usually judged and criticized by those who are able to compare them with their originals and therefore, by definition, do not need translations at all. The way in which translations are produced matters because translations represent their originals for readers who cannot read those originals. In other words: translations create the "image" of the original for readers who have no access to the "reality" of the original. Needless to say, that image may be rather different from the reality in question, not necessarily, or even primarily because translators maliciously set out to distort that reality, but because they produce their translations under certain constraints peculiar to the culture they are members of. These constraints may be ideological in nature, as when most translations of the classics of Greek and Roman antiquity produced in the nineteenth century either omitted passages then considered "obscene" altogether, or rendered passages of that type found in Greek originals into Latin in the translations, and passages of that type may also be poetological in nature, as when Homer and Virgil were translated into prose in the fifties of this century because the epic had been pronounced dead and it was widely believed that readers would only want to read novels from then on. The fact that Homer and Virgil are now routinely translated into verse again is as good an indication as any of the much more important fact that these constraints are by no means eternal and unchangeable; rather, they, too, are subject to changes in the socio-cultural environment in which translations and their originals are produced. Finally, these constraints may be of an obvious economic nature, as when a third of the songs were cut from the Broadway production of Brecht's *Mother Courage* because the play would otherwise have been classified as a musical by the Broadway unions, and the production costs would have increased accordingly.

If a translation provides its readers with an image of its original, another type of rewriting, often produced to meet more obviously didactic goals, namely the compilation of anthologies, tries to provide its readers/students with an image of a literature, a period in a literature, a type, such as drama in general, as opposed to narrative prose, for instance, or the lyric, and a genre, a subdivision of a type, such as Brechtian epic theatre, for instance, as part of the more encompassing concept of drama. If anthologies contain translations, they provide their readers with a double image. There is a macro-image the anthology as a whole tries to project, and the micro-images different translations collected in the anthologies project in their turn. We realize the importance of these images as soon as we wake up to the fact—and those of us who are professionally engaged with the study of literature are usually not too quick to do this—that these anthologies are the vehicle by means of which non-professional readers, not just the proverbial (wo)man in the street, but also students on the High School and University level who have no intention of becoming professional readers of literature, make literature's acquaintance in the first (and last) place.

Anthologies of drama of the type that will be discussed here are used in the US High Schools and Universities to introduce students to the evolution of the genre from the Greeks to the present. Students who do not go on to study literature will be left with these images for the rest of their lives. For them, the texts put together between the covers of these anthologies represent the canon of drama (or poetry, or the novel, or what have you). Or perhaps it would be closer to the truth to say that these anthologies try to pass themselves off as the canon to readers who read them either for educational purposes or to satisfy an interest or a curiosity. The power wielded by these anthologies is therefore not to be underestimated (and neither is the power wielded by individual translations). And yet these (and other) rewritings are hardly studied or analyzed at all. They are simply taken for granted, they seem to remain invisible, as if the "spirit" or what have you of the original passes through them to the readers by means of some undefined process of osmosis. These (and other) rewritings have to be taken for granted, they have to remain transparent, if the main premise of much of literary studies since Romanticism is to be kept alive, that is, if the writer, touched by genius, is to speak to his or her fellow (wo)men directly, out of the fullness of his or her emotions, even if he or she speaks another language altogether. By contrast, learned tomes have been written, and continue to be written about canons and canon formation, without touching once on what I propose to discuss in what follows: the hidden makers of what to many people does indeed become a living canon, and their agendas, hidden or otherwise.

I shall try to illustrate the points made above by a brief and (very) preliminary analysis of the corpus of drama anthologies published in the United States between 1900 and 1988. One of the earliest anthologists, Brandon Matthews, who will be introduced here as representative, in many ways, of those who were to follow in his footsteps, very definitely defines himself as a maker of canons in the introduction to his *The Chief European Dramatists*, published in 1916:

> Hitherto, however, no adequate attempt had been made to select, out of the drama of the remoter past and out of the drama of other tongues than English, a group of plays, tragic or comic, which might illustrate and illuminate the development of dramatic literature from the Greek of the fifth century BC to the Scandinavian at the end of the nineteenth century AD.[2]

Having described the task he set himself, Matthews goes on to list the difficulties he had to cope with in trying to carry out that task:

> It has been his duty to ascertain who, among the scores and the hundreds of playwrights that have flourished in the different countries of Europe during the past twenty-four centuries, were entitled to be recognized as acknowledged masters of the art of the drama or as indisputable representatives of their race and of their era.[3]

Some characteristic features of these two statements will be found in many, if not all subsequent introductions. The anthologist has to assume the burden of selection. Interestingly enough, the corollary to this is almost never discussed, namely: on what authority does the anthologist shoulder this burden? My contention is that this point is never discussed because the answer to the question would not quite match the lofty tone prevalent in the statement quoted above and in other, similar statements made later. That answer is likely to be that the authority in question is not conferred by any muse or other vaguely angelic and allegorical figure, but rather by publishers trying to tap into what they think is likely to be a lucrative market. Anthologies like the ones under discussion here were and are aimed at both the college market and the interested individual. Even in 1916 the college market must not have been negligible and it has, of course, grown more than exponentially by 1988 and beyond.

If we accept the premise that it is really the publisher who confers the mantle of authority, we must also accept that the framework within which makers of canons make their selection is delimited by factors other than just excellence and/or considerations of a pedagogical nature. That framework is also delimited by the number of pages the publisher is willing to invest in any given authority, and those numbers of pages are closely tied to the hours of course work required by institutions of (higher) learning. The basic framework may, therefore, well turn out to be that of the semester or year of study, in which a number of playwrights/plays need to be "done," and which does not allow for much, if any time over and beyond that number.

If this is true, it should become obvious that the semester framework also allows for relatively little in the field of radical change. It is not easy to suddenly bring an anthology on the market that doubles the number of selections, for instance. Rather, it would appear as if a (more than) relatively finite number of niches has been reserved for select playwrights and plays, a number that corresponds to the alloted class time per semester or year, so that for a new playwright or play to occupy a given niche its previous occupant will have to vacate it. The same holds true for genres, not just in the "fundamental" opposition between such basic types as comedy and tragedy, but also in the differentiation between historical drama, bourgeois drama, drawing room comedy, and other genres that have developed throughout the history of drama.

If most of the anthologies under discussion here are indeed aimed at the education market, the margin for competition among these anthologies will be relatively small, and room for innovation will be limited accordingly. As a result—and this is also the reason why so much attention is devoted here to an anthology published in 1916—the first anthology to enter the market is likely to set the tone for the many others to come. The first anthology, it could be said, delimits the parameters within which further anthologies can be put together, since different institutions of higher learning cannot be seen to be teaching wildly different selections under the same course heading likely to read "Introduction to Drama."

As a result, the anthologies under discussion here will—and do—display an inbuilt weighting toward the conservative. It is not easy to introduce new playwrights and/or plays, or even new translations: Archer's translations of Ibsen only definitely disappear from these anthologies as late as the 1950s. Add to this that it is not always easy to find translations of plays recognized as new and important within their own culture; this mere fact of literary life creates a time-lag that can delay the inclusion of new plays and their authors in anthologies by a number of years, or even a decade. That anthologies are weighted toward the conservative end of the scale is already obvious in the following statement also made by Matthews' introduction: "The principles of dramatic art are unchanging through the ages, the same today in Paris or in New York that they were in Athens twenty-four hundred years ago."[4]

These principles tend to be equated mainly with the concept of genre, as practiced by the "masters of the art" referred to by Matthews above. The problem for the anthologists then becomes which genres to include and which to leave out, or even whether to recognize new genres, such as Brecht's epic theatre, or the plays of Pirandello. In fact, many anthologists did not do so until the early sixties. Overall, anthologists appear to be more comfortable with the genres they consider "established," such as the classical and neo-classical tragedy, and the nineteenth century "well-made play," which developed out of the bourgeois drams of the eighteenth century. Not infrequently the uneasy coexistence between the established and he new give rise to formulations so cautious that they get perilously close to the grotesque, as in the introduction to Johnson, Bierman, and Hart's *The Play and the Reader*: "We have reserved the special problems of Pirandello's philosophical drama, or Brecht's 'epic' theatre, and of the Theatre of the Absurd, represented by Max Frisch, to the end of the volume."[5] It should be added, of course, that Frisch was, and is, not really associated with the Theatre of the Absurd, at least not within the framework of German language theatre, or the wider framework of European theatre as whole.

Finally, the anthologist has to also solve the problem of which playwrights to recognize as "indisputable representatives of their race and of their era." Matthews includes one play by Aeschylus, Sophocles and Euripides, thereby establishing a classical Greek trinity that will return in a fair number, though by no means in most of the anthologies put together by most of his successors. He also includes Aristophanes' *The Frogs*, in the translation made by John Hookham Frere about a hundred years before, but his successors did not follow him in this, for obvious ideological reasons: many of Aristophanes' plays were considered "obscene" and therefore either not included in most anthologies, or included only in an expurgated form. Matthews also includes one play by Flautus and one by Terence. Subsequent anthologists settle for one Roman comedy writer only, not two. Medieval theatre is conspicuously absent in Matthews' anthology, and the historical thread is taken up again with one play each by Lope de Vega and Calderon. In many subsequent anthologies, the theatre of the Spanish Baroque was to receive much less attention. Matthews further includes one play each by Corneille, Moliere and Racine, introducing another trinity, but one that is not likely to reappear in most subsequent anthologies, which tend to prefer Racine to Corneille, making Racine, in effect, the "token" French neo-classical dramatist. Many anthologies also tend to include Moliere more often than they exclude him. Moving along chronologically, French theatre is heavily represented with Beaumarchais, Hugo, Alexandre Dumas fils, and a play called *The Son-in-law of M. Poirier*, written by the now obscure team of playwrights Augier and Sandeau.

The appearance of this play raises the question of the possible incorporation of contemporary, or near-contemporary plays into canon, arguably the area in which the room for "mistakes" is the greatest. Many subsequent anthologists also include playwrights or plays that were popular at the time the anthologies were published, but vanished from subsequent anthologies, never to return.

Strangely enough, Matthews' anthology ends by including not only Goldoni, after Alexandre Dumas fils, thus interrupting, for no apparent reason, the chronological sequence observed until then, but also one play each by Lessing, Goethe, Schiller, Holberg, and Ibsen. Matthews' selection seems to suggest that the "true," or rather, the dominant tradition of the European theatre is the French one, at least since neo-classical times, which the Italians, Germans, and Scandinavians somehow tacked on. This, too, is a pattern that does not altogether disappear until the 1950s, and can be said to live on in an attenuated form even later. The reason for this may well be that French plays in translation were incorporated into the British repertoire at a much earlier date than other European plays. In his influential 1933 anthology, *World Drama*, about which more later, Barrett H. Clark, for instance, includes a 1973 translation of Moliere's *Le bourgeois gentilhomme*, entitled *The Cit Turned Gentleman*. The problem of the "universality" of the canon is thus raised time and again, but never resolved. Certain national traditions are definitely privileged above others. Some, predominantly non-Western, are hardly ever included, or even considered for inclusion, presumably between competing anthologies at any given time. This fact again reinforces the impression one has of the power, not only of institutions as such (of higher learning and others), but also, maybe even more predominantly so, of the inertia of those institutions as a significant factor constraining the anthologists' selections.

A chronological survey of the anthologies published between 1990 and 1988 illustrates the problems referred to above. The problem of the niches filled and/or vacated by authors is perhaps best illustrated by the fate of the Danish dramatist Holberg: he appears in 1916 an 1933, and never again thereafter. In terms of including or excluding, or even recognizing different genres, the historical play disappears after 1939. Schiller's *Wilhelm Tell* appears in 1961, 1933, and 1939; Goethe's *Goetz von Berlichingen* appears in 1916 only, and his *Egmont* in 1933 only. Victor Hugo's *Hernani* also appears only in 1916 and 1933. No other historical plays appear in any of the anthologies surveyed here. The bourgeois comedy suffers a similar fate: Lessing's *Mina von Barnhelm* appears in 1916 and 1933, as does Beaumarchais' *The Marriage of Figaro*. No other representatives of the genre appear in any anthology published during the time-frame adhered to in this essay.

In terms of the choice of authors considered representative for a certain "era," to use Matthews' words again, the Roman comedy writer Terence only appears in 1916, 1933, 1946, and 1957. All other anthologies prefer Plautus instead. Conversely, Sophocles is most often the token Greek Classical dramatist, being left out only in 1944, 1953 and 1961. Aeschylus and Euripides, on the other hand, are left out about twenty times each in the period surveyed here. In the same vein Racine is obviously the token French neo-classicist dramatist: he appears in virtually all anthologies published between 1900 and 1988, whereas Corneille only appears in 1916 and 1933. Also in terms of "eras" and "races," to speak with

Matthews one last time, all medieval plays, where they appear in the anthologies at all, are English, except for the French *Master Patelin* in 1933 and 1939, the French *Adam* in 1933, the Latin *Quem Quaeritis* in 1927, and the German *The Wandering Scholar* in 1933.

As mentioned above, inclusion of all "races" never seems to have been even a remote objective in the composition of drama anthologies, most of which silently identify "drama" with "western drama." In fact, non-Western plays are only included in three anthologies: five in 1933, one in 1957 and again one in 1964. It should be added that the 1933 anthology which included five non-Western plays, B. H. Clark's *World Drama*,[6] in two volumes, was published as the drama anthology to end all drama anthologies, not least because its publisher had obviously decided to allow for more choice by almost doubling the number of plays usually included. Clark's anthology did not supersede all others, but it was definitely considered to be in a class of its own, and its influence made itself felt well into the fifties, and some would argue, even beyond. It probably represents the most extensive attempt at creating a canon to be found in any of the anthologies analyzed here. It contains the four Greek dramatists—Menander had not yet been rediscovered in 1933—the three Latin ones (Clark is among the very few to include a play by Seneca), five medieval plays (*Adam*, *The Second Shepherd's Play*, *The Farce of Worthy Master Pierre Patelin*, *Everyman*, and even the German playwright Hans Sachs' *The Wandering Scholar from Paradise*). The Jacobeans are represented with three plays, as are the Restoration dramatists. The Italian eighteenth century is represented not only by Goldoni, but also by Beoleo, Scala, and Alfieri. Spain's Golden Age is represented by Cervantes, Lope de Vega, and Calderon. The French drama of the neo-classical era and beyond is represented by Corneille, Moliere, Racine, Beaumarchais, Hugo, Alexandre Dumas fils, but also the enigmatic Augier and Sandeau which, incidentally, also raises the problem of filiation: do certain anthologists include certain plays simply because they are to be found in other anthologies, and are therefore easily accessible in translation? This problem becomes even more acute, as has been touched on above, when "new" playwrights and plays are to be included. The plays usually exist in one translation only, which is then dutifully included in many subsequent anthologies, more often than not for lack of an alternative. German drama is represented with Lessing, Goethe, and Schiller; Holberg and Ibsen represent Scandinavia, and Russian drama is included by means of an Ostrovsky play. But most significant of all, Clark's anthology also includes *Sakoontala*, *The Chalk Circle*, an anonymous Japanese play called *Abstraction*, Seami's *Nakamitsu*, and Chikamatsu's *Four Ladies at a Game of Poem Cards*. The five non-Western plays, grouped together here to emphasize the point I am making, are fully integrated into the chronological unfolding of the development of what can here truly be called "World Drama." No other anthology under discussion here can stake the same claim, which is a further reminder, if one were needed, of the extent to which the canon of "drama" has remained Euro-centric, in the sense that it has been limited to the drama of Europe and its historical dependencies.

Obviously lacunas in Clark's anthology are Strindberg, who is not represented at all, and O'Neill. In the latter case it might conceivably be argued that O'Neill could still, in 1933, be regarded as not "fully established," or, at any rate, not established enough to merit a place among the classics of all time. It would be more difficult to make the same argument for Strindberg, however. The absence of both Strindberg and O'Neill must, therefore, in my opinion, be regarded as much more symptomatic of tenacious reluctance to include plays that do not conform to either the (neo-)classical or the well-made play muster. The canon, it seems, must be limited to the categories just mentioned, even though certain compromises with "the other side" are occasionally made, no doubt under the pressure of this side's popularity at any given time, which remains the barometer for inclusion or exclusion. The most striking observation, in this context, is that no dramatist who can be regarded as belonging to "the other side" has managed to permanently occupy a niche in the anthologies published since 1933, nor has any single non-well made play established itself to the extent of Moliere's *Tartuffe*, for instance, or Sophocles' *Oedipus the King*. Strindberg himself enters the anthologies with *Miss Julie* in 1939, which is again included in anthologies published in 1967, 1970 and 1988, but not between 1939 and 1967. Strindberg's *The Father* appears in anthologies in 1940 and 1957, and not before or since. *The Ghost Sonata* is included only once, in 1961, as is *The Dance of Death*, 1962. Finally, Strindberg's *The Stranger* makes two appearances, one in 1970 and in 1973, whereas *There Are Crimes and Crimes* appears once only, in 1957. It is no exaggeration to conclude, therefore, that neither Strindberg nor one of his plays managed to establish himself/itself as part of the canon of what is regarded as drama by those in the United States who saw it as their task to educate the theatre-going audience to appreciate excellence.

Similar fates have befallen three other writers often associated with the avant-garde in drama. Pirandello enters the anthologies in 1940, with *Six Characters in Search of an Author*, is dropped until 1946 for what must have been mainly ideological reasons at the time, and reappears, often with the same play, in 1957, 1964, 1968, 1970, 1971, 1972 and 1973. Yet, he disappears completely after 1973, whereas it could be argued convincingly, to my mind, that he should have established himself as a "modern classic" by the sixties, or definitely by the seventies. Not that his plays were performed all the time during those decades, but neither were those of Plautus or Racine, for instance, whereas the latter two are usually represented in anthologies published after 1973.

Brecht enters the anthologies in 1961, about twenty years later than Pirandello, presumably because the ideological resistance he had to overcome was much greater. Significantly, her is also most often represented with plays that can be interpreted as having "least" to do with Marxism. *The Private Life of the Master Race*, included in a 1957 anthology, can easily be read as primarily a satire on Nazi Germany. *Mother Courage*, included only in 1968 and 1970 can, by means of a judicious introduction and a few equally judicious "interventions" in the translation, easily be turned into a "tragic" figure in the

more or less classical mode, whereas *The Good Woman of Setzuan*, included in 1961, 1967 and 1972, can just as easily be transformed into a parable. This is exactly what happened to bother plays in Eric Bentley's translations, which are, not surprisingly, the translations used by the anthologies under discussion here. All the more surprising, therefore, that *The Caucasian Chalk Circle* should have been included four times, in 1967, 1970, 1971 and 1972, although even in this case it can be argued that the audience may well be counted on to remember the "actual" play much more than the introductory and concluding scenes framing it. because of their position in the original, these scenes can also easily be downplayed, or even dropped in translation.

Ionesco appears for the first time in 1961, with *The Lesson*. *Maid to Marry* follows in 1967, *The Leader* also in 1967, and *The Gap* in 1972. A greater surprise where non-well made plays are concerned is that Durrenmatt, Frisch and Adamov only appear once each, Durrenmatt in 1961, with *The Visit*, Frisch in 1971 with *The Firebugs*, and Adamov in 1972 with *Professor Taran*e. The greatest surprise of all in this context is undoubtedly that Beckett is only included three times, whit *Happy Days* in 1968, and again in 1988, and with *Act Without Words I* (admittedly no great sacrifice in terms of the investment to be made in terms of pages) in 1967. Although it can be argued that *Waiting for Godot* drastically changed the course of drama from the sixties onward, readers of these anthologies would have to gather this information from other sources.

The anthologies under discussion here are not only fundamentally conservative in terms of poetics, that is in terms of how they define (good) drama; they are equally conservative in terms of ideology. Not only does Marxism never really make it beyond the fringes, and if then, only in a much watered-down version, thoughtfully packaged by means of introductions and notes, but Ibsen's *Ghosts*, arguably not the least important of his plays, is never included at all, undoubtedly on account of its subject matter. No doubt Aristophanes' *Lysistrata* is only included twice in almost ninety years for the same reason. Significantly, the rise of feminism, also in the field of literary theory and criticism, seems to have been virtually powerless to influence selection in the Greek comedy writer's favour.

If the selections in most of the anthologies under discussion here are conservative in both ideology and poetics, they also tend to be conservative in that they favour two national traditions, the English, because that is the most obvious one for the readership aimed at, and the French, partially because, of the other national traditions, the French was the one that established itself first on the English stage, and partially because of the American fascination with things French and the peculiar identification of "high culture" with whatever is (or can be made to sound) French. The discrepancy between the treatment meted out to the French and the German traditions, no doubt also reinforced (twice) in the course of the century by ideological reasons, is striking: Geothe's *Faust*, not exactly an unimportant piece of dramatic art, nor an obscure one, is only included twice, first in 1900, and then not again until 1957, probably also because quite a few anthologies include a more "native," though fundamentally different treatment of the same theme, namely Marlowe's *Dr. Faustus*. Of the other German-language inclusions, over and beyond Brecht, Durrenmatt, and Frisch, Hauptmann's *The Assumption of Hannele* (1927), can be interpreted as something approaching a medieval allegorical play, and *The Weavers* (1940, 1957) is a well made play in structure, if not in diction. Hebbel's *Maria Magdalena* would also still fit the category of the well made play, which may be the reason why it appears three times, thereby surpassing Goethe, namely in 1940, 1946, 1953 and 1957. George Kaiser's *From Morn to Midnight* appears in 1962, and then again in 1967, at a time when interest in the dramatist and his works had already waned in Germany. Kaiser may have been included as an ideologically more palatable alternative to Brecht, even though a poetological terms his work is as far removed from the well made play muster as that of his one time rival. Bucher also makes two appearances, one with *Danton's Death* in 1957, and one with *Woyzeck* in 1972. Whether Buchner appear "in his own right," meaning as a playwright who wrote his novel plays in isolation, or as a "representative" of German Expressionism, and a more famous one than Kaiser at that, is hard to say. Finally, the long appearance of Wedekind's *The Tenor* in 1957 in a reminder of the very important fact that no discussion of anthologies like the present one can afford to ignore personal idiosyncrasies on the part of anthologists, who might either like a play so much that they want to include it at all costs, or who might include certain plays, no more than a sprinkling compared to the solidly conservative/traditional choices, as part of a very cautious attempt, always subject to abrupt termination at the publishers' displeasure, to extend the boundaries of the canon somewhat.

The fact that the great majority of these anthologies were designed to serve as textbooks for classroom teaching, goes a long way towards explaining the fundamental and tenacious conservatism underlying the selections, both in terms of ideology (no ethically objectionable or potentially subversive subject matter) and poetics (no, or definitely not too many, experimental plays whose presence might disturb the tax payers, who are, in their great majority, arguably not professional readers of literature, because they would not strike said tax payers as immediately intelligible). In the introduction to their 1927 anthology Hubbel and Beatty even take care to appease the tax payer on another score, when the state: "For the inclusion and discussion of foreign plays we have no apology,"[7] implying that the 1927 US audience, whose insularity was admittedly even greater then than it is now, might expect such an apology after all. Hubbel & Beatty's introduction is further remarkable for the fact that it is not overtly didactic. Their statement "the chief purpose of every writer of plays is to give pleasure to the spectators who come to his plays; and the spectators come primarily to be amused,"[8] stands in marked contrast to the statements made in other introductions. Yet they, too, produce a statement that could be found in other, more avowedly didactic introductions: "The permanent and the temporary conventions need to be clearly distinguished for they are easily confused."[9] About forty years later, Small and Sutton agree that:

> Though each culture, each reader, and even the same reader at different times,

> reads a literary work differently, knowledge of what can be factually known about it and its times is a protection against an anarchic subjectivity of interpretation that could eventually destroy its continuum of identity. [10]

The pedagogically motivated desire for clarity and order shines through most obviously in the introduction Hogan & Molin wrote in 1962: "The audiences that fill the theatres, however, are not especially informed one." The anthologists, therefore, see it as their task to overcome the "critical cleavage that reflects the absence of a theatrical heritage and experience"[11] admittedly by the most conservative of means: since "the ideas of genre today are confused and confusing," Hogan and Molin resort to "an Aristotelian notion of genres" to provide "a key to understanding and judgment."[12] In other words, Aristotle's poetics are still seen as the "true" yardstick against which all subsequent drama is to be measured, not least for pedagogical purposes. Aristotle becomes the venerable name, elevated above all suspicion, used to justify the undergoing conservative tenor of most selections in most anthologies, even if that tenor is occasionally masked by means of a "folksy" style in statements like "trying to hazard a definition is like trying to grab a bowl of jello."[13]

Yet the conservatism of the anthologies must still be packaged in such a way that it appeals to both students and the general reader. The most obvious way to do this is to topicalize the past. Perhaps the most extreme formulation of this strategy is to be found in Alice Venezky Griffin's introduction to Plautus' *Mostellaria* in her 1953 anthology *Living Theatre*. She rightly wants to point out Plautus's contribution to the development of drama, and does so by stating that "Plautus was the Rodger and Hammerstein of his day."[14] Millet & Bentley state essentially the same in their introduction to Plautus in their own 1933 anthology, *The Play's the Thing*: "Perhaps his most notable innovation (unobservable in the translation of his works) is the development of lyrical passages and of recitatives to be intoned or chanted to the accompaniment of the flute."[15] The ways in which the two statements are expressed could not be more different. Millet and Bentley admit that Plautus' main contribution is lost in translation anyway, whereas Alice Venezky Griffin appeals to readers' and students' imagination by putting Plautus' text squarely into a tradition they are thought to be familiar with: that of the musical. She goes on to say that "just as *Oklahoma* greatly influenced the pattern of American musical comedy, so the works of the Greek comedy playwright, Menander, became a model for the Roman dramatists."[16]

The topicalization strategy (as opposed to a strategy that would leave Plautus "untouched" in his own time, and translate his texts into a diction associated with that of the classics over the years: slightly archaic, slightly dull, and heavily footnoted) can also be found in the actual translations included in the anthologies under discussion. I shall round off this essay by briefly comparing two translations of Plautus' *Mostellaria*, one by Lynn Boal Mitchell in the Alice Venezky Griffin anthology mentioned, and one by A. S. Downer in his own anthology, *Great World Theater* published about thirty years later.[17]

Mitchell, as befits a translator translating for an anthology entitled *Living Theater*, is more radical in trying to turn Plautus into a writer of well made plays, and she wants to put him in the Shavian tradition. She therefore adds stage directions like the following at the beginning of Scene 3:

> In front of the house of Theopropides are disclosed a table provided with boxes for jewelry, cosmetics, perfumes, manicurist's buffer, etc. There are two couches near the table, on the one farthest from Philolaches sits Philematum. Scaphia stands behind her, arranging her hair.[18]

The stage direction, which is not there at all in the original, anchors the translation in the tradition of the drawing room comedy, and more specifically in its Shavian variant because of its length and the profusion of objects mentioned in it. The translation also tries to keep the punning of the original. Downer professes to do the same justifying his practice in a rather defensive footnote: "For those readers who (unlike the translator) detest puns, it should be pointed out that here, too, the English text attempts to be conscientious."[19] Maybe he felt he had to apologize for trying to be "clever," or maybe he wanted to counteract the audience's tendency not to associate puns with Romans. Neither translator is too successful, though, in trying to render the pun in "*detexit, tectus qua fui*" (line 163 in the Loeb Classical Library edition,[20] which translates *Mostellaria* as "*The Haunted House*"), likening the beloved to a storm that uncovered, but also tore off the roof where the lover was covered/roofed, to such an extent that he "*neque iam umquam optigere possum*" (Line 164), will never be able to re-cover/re-roof again. Mitchell writes: "That rainstorm which unroofed me ... Nor can I now repair the damages."[21] Downer tries: "Ripped off the roof of modesty ... too late to repair it."[22] Both are more successful in rendering Line 257: "*Nunc adsentatrix scelesta est, dudum adverstrix erat,*" something like: "Now the wicked woman is a 'consentress,' who was an adversary until now." Downer writes: "Is now a Yes-woman, a minute ago she was a No-woman."[23] Mitchell renders: "She was a 'No-No-er', now she is a 'Yes-Yes-er'."[24] When it comes to translating "*Te ille deseret aetate et satietate*" (Line 196), something like "He will desert you because of your age and his satiety," though, Downer tries "when you're dated and he is sated"[25] to render the Latin opposition "*aetate et satietate*," whereas Mitchell simply writes "when his love's grown cold,"[26] thereby missing a Shavian opportunity.

Throughout, Mitchell tries to make Plautus' text correspond to the image of Rome and things Roman she suspects her prospective readers to have. When the *order* "*capiundas crines*" (Line 226) is given, something like "fix up your hair," Downer translates: "put your hair up,"[27] but Mitchell makes the heroine "wear orange blossoms for him,"[28] no doubt because Roman girls are often portrayed in paintings and sculptures wearing blossoms in their hair. For the same reason Mitchell adds another stage direction at the end of this scene. In that stage direction she lets Philolaches, the heroine's master and lover, treat Sphaerio, another slave, as follows: "Sphaerio ... kneels. Philolaches washes his hands and dries them

on Sphaerio's hair."[29] In doing so, Mitchell evokes shades of Sienkiewicz, Bulwer Lytton, and other writers of popular historical novels dealing with ancient Rome, who offered their readers at least one such scene per book. Downer adds nothing here, preferring to leave his Plautus closer to the original, or trusting more in his readers' imaginative powers.

Mitchell is also closer to Shaw in diction; Plautus' "*lepida*" (Line 170) becomes "deucedly smart" in her translation,[30] whereas in Downer the heroine "merely" knows a bag of tricks.[31] Mitchell further tries to translate in such a way that the dialogue affects the audience more directly. When the master/lover has set his slave girl/beloved free, that slave girl's servant and former fellow slave makes the following observation: "*ille te nisi amavit ultro/id pro tuo capite quod dedit perdiderit tantum argenti*" (Lines 210-211). The Latin means something like: "unless he [your master/lover] will love you beyond this [or: go on loving you], he will have lost all that money that he gave for your head." Mitchell translates: "He is hanging around to be repaid for the money he invested in your freedom."[32] The audience obviously does not have to decipher here; Downer translates much more literally, and lets the audience do more of the thinking work. When Mitchell later translates the master/lover's statement: "*quae pro me causam diceret, patronum liberavi*" (Line 244), something like "I have freed a lawyer who will plead my cause," she adds "I have an Athena to defend me,"[33] obviously banking on the "name recognition" a name like "Athena" will bring. Downer does not do anything of the kind.

Topicalization may be taking Mitchell too far when she translates the Latin "*meretricium*" (Line 190), something like "mistress," by "Geisha."[34] The ensuring "cultural clash" may well be too great if one thinks of the most obvious, Japanese meaning of the word "geisha," without reducing it to its other, second accepted meaning of "courtesan." Attempts at "acculturating" the Latin sometimes lead both translators astray. When Plautus has one character tell another: "*accumbe*" (Line 308), something like "lie down," because the Romans did, after all, eat lying down, Mitchell uses the somewhat vague, and also, in the context, somewhat disconcerting: "take your place,"[35] whereas Downer simply translates "sit down,"[36] certainly de-romanizing Plautus while possibly making him more acceptable to the audience likely to read the translation.

Both translators feel the necessity to expand on Plautus' Line 289: "*pulchra mulier nuda erit quam purpurata pulchrior*," something like "a beautiful woman will be more beautiful naked than dressed in purple." Downer adds "ornament doesn't do much good if natural charm is lacking. Women who are unattractive only spoil beautiful clothing. And if they're beautiful they need no ornament."[37] Mitchell goes even further and adds: "For the lover of a Geisha buys favors with gold and purple ... Purple is fit for hiding old age, and gold is for an ugly woman (to take one's thoughts off her looks) ... Besides, she loves her pains in togging herself out, if she has a mean disposition."[38] It is rather doubtful whether the audience learns more from Downer's elaboration than from the original text, whereas Mitchell, not satisfied with making the woman old, proceeds to make her spiteful as well, a transformation for which there is no warrant in Plautus, though there is in much popular lore.

Yet there is no point in trying to construct the opposition between the two translations in stringent terms: both Downer and Mitchell are, after all, people of flesh and blood who translate not just according to a strategy, but also according to their own idiosyncrasies. Consider their translations of Line 304 and 305. The Latin reads: "*Bene igitur ratio accepti atque expensi inter nos convenit;/tu me amas, ergo te amo; merito id fieri uterque existimat.*" A translation might read: "The ratio of what is taken in and what is paid out fits well among us;/you love me, therefore I love you; we both think that is how it should be." Mitchell translates: "You love me (that is a receipt): I love you. (that is a disbursement. The two are identical in amount)," [39] capturing the mercantile metaphor. Downer gives the lines a Shakespearean ring, perhaps promoted by the fact that they are to be found close to the end of the scene, by translating: "our credit and debits thus balance precisely;/Your love and my love pair off very nicely," [40] the kind of translation one would have expected from Mitchell, whereas Mitchell's translation would seem better suited to Downer, and yet both translations are precisely where they are, presumably because Mitchell is Mitchell and Downer is Downer.

It is perhaps wise to end this essay with a caveat about its underlying methodology, which should definitely not be applied in a mechanistic way. Yet this caveat by no means detracts from the basic premise underlying what goes before: the great, yet hidden power wielded by those who rewrite literature, as opposed to those who write it, and the vital necessity to investigate what precisely happens in the process of rewriting, why, and what image of a text, a literature, a genre rewritings project, and why.

Notes:

1. Andre Lefevere, *Translation, Rewriting and the Manipulation of Literary Fame*. London and New York: Routledge, 1992.
2. B. Matthews (ed.), *The Chief European Dramatists*. Boston: Houghton Mifflin, 1916, p. ix.
3. Ibid.
4. Ibid., p. x.
5. Stanley Johnson, Judah Bierman and James Hart (eds.), *The Play and the Reader*. Englewood Cliffs: Prentice Hall, 1971, p. xi.
6. B. H. Clark (ed.), *World Drama*. New York: Dover Publications, 1993.
7. Jay B. Hubbel and John O. Beatty (eds.), *An Introduction to Drama*. New York: Macmillan, 1972, p. vii.
8. Ibid., 1.
9. Ibid., 16.
10. Norman M. Small and Maurice L. Sutton, *The Making of Drama. Idea and Performance*, Boston: Holbrook Press Inc., 1972, p. 4.
11. Robert Hogan and Sven Eric Molin (eds.), *Drama: The Major Genres*. New York and Toronto: Dodd, Mead, and Company, 1962, p. xiii.
12. Ibid., p. xiv.

13. Small and Sutton, *op. cit.*, p. x.
14. Alice Vnezky Griffin (ed.), *Living Theatre*. New York: Twayne, 1953, p. 85.
15. Fred B. Millet and Gerald Eades Bentley (eds.), *The Play's the Thing*. New York and London: D. Appleton-Century Company, 1933, p. 161a.
16. A. V. Griffin, *op. cit.*, p. 85.
17. Alan S. Downer (ed.), *Great World Theatre*. New York: Harper and Row, 1964.
18. *Living Theater*, p. 90a.
19. A. S. Downer, *op. cit.*, p. 88.
20. Paul Nixon (ed. and trans.), *Plautus*, vol. 3. London: Heinemann and New York: G. P. Putnam's, 1924. The Loeb Classical Library.
21. Mitchell *apud* Griffin, *op. cit.*, p. 90a.
22. Downer, *op. cit.*, p. 95.
23. Ibid., p. 97.
24. *Apud* Griffin, *op. cit.*, p. 92a.
25. Downer, *op. cit.*, p. 96.
26. *Apud* Griffin, *op. cit.*, p. 91a.
27. Downer, *op. cit.*, p. 97.
28. *Apud* Griffin, *op. cit.*, p. 91b.
29. Ibid., p. 93a.
30. Ibid., p. 90b.
31. Downer, *op. cit.*, p. 95.
32. *Apud* Griffin, *op. cit.*, p. 91a.
33. Ibid., p. 92a.
34. Ibid., p. 90b.
35. Ibid., p. 91b.
36. Downer, *op. cit.*, p. 99.
37. Ibid., p. 98.
38. Mitchell *apud* Griffin, *op. cit.*, pp. 92b/93a.
39. Ibid., p. 93a.
40. Downer, *op. cit.*, p. 99.

选文五　Translating Cultural Paradigms: The Role of the *Revue Britannique* for the First Brazilian Fiction Writers[1]

Maria Eulalia Ramicelli

导　言

本文《翻译文化范式：巴西第一小说家在不列颠时事讽刺剧中的角色》选自 *Agents of Translation* (2009)。作者玛丽亚·尤拉莉亚·莱米塞利(Maria Eulalia Ramicelli)在巴西南里奥格兰德圣玛丽亚联邦大学(Federal University of Santa Maria, Rio Grande do Sul, Brazil)讲授英美文学,研究领域为比较文学,关注英国小说及思想在19世纪巴西期刊中的传播状况。

19世纪的欧洲,杂志是向读者传递文化、政治、经济和科学信息最有效的途径。英国的杂志出版最为繁荣。作为世界最发达的工业国和最大贸易国,英国的政治文化体系成为当时世界各国竞相效仿的对象。法语《英国杂志》,主要刊登译自英国的杂志文章,通过介绍和评论英国社会生活方式和政治文化现实来反思或改变在政治、经济、文化等方面都陷入困境的法国社会。19世纪初的巴西,刚刚摆脱葡萄牙的殖民统治。当时的统治者既要维护国家领土完整,又要塑造一个新兴的巴西民族。翻译来自英国和法国(而不是葡萄牙)的文化可以帮助刚独立的巴西创立自己文化体系。1839年5月以《英国杂志》为模型《国内外评论》在巴西创刊,主要刊登译自英语和法语杂志中的大量文章,供巴西读者阅读。法语《英国杂志》所采取的"意译法"(为突出中心事件而删除一些细节、次要人物或次要事件;突出叙事者,让叙事者重复叙述或解释故事情节或故事中的异域情景,让读者通过叙事者的讲叙看故事)被巴西译者采纳并成为巴西小说的创作模式。可见,翻译不仅输入新的思想和文化,也输入新的书写形式和技巧。

1. Introduction: Periodicals in the Nineteenth Century

The French *Revue Britannique* was an important mediator, or agent of translation, of British ideas and cultural forms for Brazilian men of letters and their readers in the city of Rio de Janeiro, which was the capital and cultural centre of the Brazilian empire in the nineteenth century. This fact can be seen by the numerous fictional and non-fictional texts that were translated from the *Revue Britannique* for Brazilian newspapers and magazines from the first half of the nineteenth century, texts that had been originally published in British magazines or books and, therefore, reached Brazil via French translation. French mediation was not exclusive to Brazil as France had also been publicizing in Europe, since the eighteenth century, its particular view of British intellectual production and general achievements through translations which were free manipulations of the source-text in English.

Due to particular conditions of periodical production and circulation of texts, besides the particular historical context of Great Britain, France, and Brazil at the time, translation constituted a means of cultural contact of special complexity. This article thus discusses the Brazilian grounds for the selection of the *Revue Britannique* as an agent of translation of British fiction. Such a discussion implies considering the position of Brazil in relation to the larger context of European cultural production, led by the two most powerful nations at the time, namely Great Britain and France. Therefore, one must first consider the most important aspects of British and French periodical production before focusing on the role of the *Revue Britannique* in Brazilian literature.

In nineteenth-century Europe, periodicals were the most effective means by which cultural, critical, political, economic, and scientific production could be made available to a diversified and ever-growing readership. Britain, in particular, produced a variety of magazines that addressed the different social classes. In fact, if most British magazines such as the Scottish *Edinburgh Review* and *Blackwood's Magazine*, or the London *New Monthly Magazine* were produced by and addressed to the middle-classes, there were a number of magazines which were devoted to the instruction and amusement of the lower classes, such as *The Mirror of Literature, Amusement, and Instruction* or the *Servant's Magazine* for maids, also published in London.

The fact that more and more British readers looked for education and entertainment in the pages of periodicals was due to the specific British context of the time. From the Industrial Revolution onwards, British society experienced increasing industrial development, the multiplication of scientific discoveries and technical innovations, besides urban growth. Therefore, for a society in continuous change, moving towards industrialization and urbanization, information meant power. It is then not just a coincidence that access to formal education considerably increased in the first half of the nineteenth century and, consequently, led to the growth in a readership that wanted to be informed about bits and pieces of different areas of human production rather than devote itself to a more lengthy study of a particular subject, such as one finds in books. At the same time, the continuous development of printing techniques resulted in a much more efficient process of production and reproduction of printed material which kept up with the demands of the readership. In this context, there was a two-way relationship between magazines and readers: magazines had the task of spreading knowledge in a pleasant way exactly because readers wanted this kind of content. Moreover, as Henry Colburn (the polemical owner of the *New Monthly Magazine*) claimed, magazines constituted a literature that satisfied the readers' wishes for sheer entertainment in addition to social inclusion and affirmation through access to information. This situation had been developing since the late seventeenth century, when a number of more popular periodicals aimed at meeting the readers' demand for knowledge, by providing them with palatable information (Graham, 1930). One can thus see that the didactic purpose of the periodical press developed together with the gradual consolidation of the bourgeoisie in England, from the period of the English social revolution in the seventeenth century to the establishment of a bourgeois society in the nineteenth century. In their aspiration towards gentility, the middle classes regarded reading as a means of both cultural refinement and social consolidation in the new social structure. This situation was particularly noticeable in Great Britain, which became the most powerful nation in the Western world due to its leadership in industrial capitalism and worldwide trade. Its representative political system was often held up as a model for other countries to follow. In this sense, the nineteenth-century British periodical press managed to reflect the way of life of this ever-growing urban industrialized society by incorporating the fragmentation of knowledge and the standardization of cultural production as a consequence of the development of mass production and mass consumption of the written word.

The significance of magazines as a cultural form in nineteenth-century Britain is clearly stated by Mark Parker (2000: 27) at the beginning of his analysis of British literary magazines of the 1820s and 1830s:

> ... In a moment marked by expensive books, a collapsing market for books, and, despite the abundance of gift books and annuals, a perceived dearth of poetry, literary magazines largely become literature for the middle-class reading audience. Such magazines deliver literature, providing original essays and poems directly and relatively cheaply to their audience, and, through extensive quotation in reviews they disseminate it indirectly. They produce the official discourse on literature, through reviews and running commentary throughout their pages. And ultimately, literary magazines themselves aspire to be literature ... [2]

Parker also discusses the implications of the analysis of a text originally published in a periodical. As his argument goes, the periodical constitutes a specific type of publication aimed at immediate consumption; therefore, its meaning is intrinsically related to the moment of its production. The case studies presented by Parker help one realize how texts previously published in literary magazines had their meaning changed when they were republished in book form, being read and interpreted in a context other than the magazine itself. In other words, the meaning of a text published in a periodical also comes from this discursive unit (namely, the periodical itself and all the texts it contains in a certain issue) as the format of the periodical is determined by the context of its production. By context of production one should understand editorial and/or authorial interests besides specific contemporary circumstances.

The importance of the British periodical press in the nineteenth century can be seen in the numerous appropriations of British magazines in France. As a matter of fact, a number of French magazines took their British counterparts as models to follow and/or devoted themselves to Great Britain and its cultural production; among these magazines one can find *Revue Britannique*, *Revue Françise*, *Revue Encyclopédique*, *Revue des Deux Mondes*, *Journal des Débats*, and *The Athenaeum* (Devonshire, 1929: 13-27).

2. The *Revue Britannique*

The *Revue Britannique* was founded in 1825 by liberals Louis-Sébastien Saulnier, Jean-Michel Berton and Prosper Dondey-Dupré. It consisted mostly of translations of various kinds of texts which were lifted from British magazines. These translations usually did not follow the original text in full but were adapted versions that expressed the French translator's critical view of the British subject in question. In fact, Léon Galibert (the second editor of the *Revue Britannique*) stated the parameters that underlined the task of translating at a time when there was very little if any concern about the original author's own ideas and words:

> Il s'agissait non seulement de choisir, mais d'éliminer [des textes]; non seulement de communiquer au public les meilleurs articles, mais de les résumer et de les élucider quelquefois; non seulement de les transporter dans notre langue, mais de les approprier *à* notre civilisation; non seulement de prêter l'oreille aux cris de l'une des factions qui divisent l'Angleterre, de l'un des intérêts qui s'agitent dans son sein, mais de comparer les diverses opinions sans les confondre, et de faire jaillir la vérité de leur choc. Cette tache délicate, et qui exige une connaissance exacte des deux nationalités, a été remplie, avec un talent que l'estime publique a couronné, par les hommes auxquels M. Saulnier l'avait distribuée.[3]

Therefore, translation should be understood both as a cultural process and a cultural product; in other words, as a means of interpretation of a certain culture by the foreign context that receives it through written texts. This is exactly the idea that is conveyed by the concept of *cultural translation*, a concept that was devised by social anthropology to express the notion of culture as a text which is creatively and actively interpreted by the anthropologist who, just like the translator, aims at rendering the *text* (that is, culture) intelligible to another culture (Pallares-Burke, 1996: 12-13). Apart from the contribution of social anthropology, one also finds in Translation Studies a helpful theoretical basis exactly because it broadens the scope of analysis as it considers translation to be a significant type of *rewriting*. As a consequence, Translation Studies gives prominence to the *context* in which translation takes place and establishes a dialectical relationship between the literary system in which the text was produced (source-system) and the literary system which receives the translated text (target-system). According to André Lefevere and Susan Bassnett (1995: 11), "... translation, like all (re)writings is never innocent. There is always a context in which the translation takes place, always a history from which the text emerges and into which a text is transposed."

Returning to the founding of the *Revue Britannique*, it is important to consider that, given the French context of the time, this magazine reflected its founders' beliefs and ideas about Great Britain. On the one hand, the restoration of the Bourbons to the French throne, marked by Charles X's ultramonarchist reign from 1824 on, put the liberals on their guard and made them concerned about the maintenance of constitutional monarchy in France. In this context, the considerable political and economic stability of England, even after a long period of war, attracted the attention of the French defenders of the representative and constitutional regime, which had only recently been achieved but not definitely established by the French bourgeoisie. In fact, the editors of the *Revue Britannique* always acknowledged that Great Britain was a cultural and economic power with strong political institutions and a widely developed trade that reached all parts of the world. Nevertheless, such great interest in British achievements could not hide the strong feelings nurtured in France after the French defeat by England in 1815 and the resulting disintegration of the Napoleonic Empire, amidst the historical rivalry between these two nations for hegemony in the international arena. As Kathleen Jones (1939: 17) states, for Saulnier (the first editor of the *Revue Britannique*), "... la défaite de Napoléon avait été une rude leçon qui lui révéla la supériorité de la civilisation anglaise de l'époque." This resentment on the French side against English superiority found its way into the *Revue Britannique* by means of a sharp analytical treatment of British issues in fictional and non-fictional texts selected for translation.

All in all, the close and critical attention paid by the editorship of the *Revue Britannique* to all aspects of British life was part of a broader social-cultural French process that had been in vogue since the eighteenth century, called *anglomania*. Since the previous century and for reasons that varied according to the period, the French had been showing a strong interest in all issues related to England and its progressive economic and political system due to the unfavorable social, political and economic conditions in France. As a consequence, a number of British novels were translated and sold in bookshops in Paris, and the French intelligentsia knew about contemporary British publications in all fields of human knowledge (Jones, 1939: 1-11, 79-90; Pallares-Burke, 1995: 27-48). As Great Britain was considered to be a parameter in all areas of human knowledge and production, its achievements should be seen by other European countries as a starting point for their own development. This was the principle that guided the editorial policy of the *Revue Britannique*, which can be noticed in the frequent justifications of such recurrent attention to British periodicals from which all kinds of texts were taken: texts that conveyed criticism and reflection in social, political, economic and cultural areas; reports of scientific and industrial discoveries and development; fictional narratives; pieces of news about faraway regions sent by British travelers who had been attracted by the spirit of adventure and commercial enterprise. As Léon Galibert summed up, British magazines constituted "... un réservoir commun; foyer général des documents et des idées qui ont changé le monde ou qui le changeront. Que l'on ne s'étonne donc pas de leur influence, et de celle dont la REVUE BRITANNIQUE s'est entourée: *Savoir, c'est pouvoir.*"[4]

The articles to be translated and published in the *Revue Britannique* were chosen on a comparative basis: Apart from making general comments in prefaces, translators and/or editors usually attached footnotes to point out how the text as a whole or a certain passage in it would relate to the French context and be of interest to the French reader. Therefore, the real focus of the editors and translators of the *Revue Britannique* was on the French people themselves. Moreover, if one considers that the *Revue Britannique* also aimed at reaching European readers in general, it is possible to conclude that the editors of this magazine were, in fact, indirectly selling an image of their own country through their criticism of British affairs. Such an attitude can be seen in the selection of British fiction for the *Revue Britannique*, which was basically presented as a form of entertainment but was selected critically. On the one hand, British literature (especially fictional narratives) would amuse the reader and, therefore, counterbalance the general weighty content of the magazine. On the other hand, it would also bring some novelty to French literature as the French liked to read: "... [les] tableaux de moeurs où nos voisins excellent; car, comme l'a dit Mme de Staël, ils semblent avoir une fenêtre intérieure avec laquelle ils s'examinent eux-mêmes."[5]

In fact, the British fiction selected for the *Revue Britannique* could serve the utilitarian purpose of making British customs known to French readers. Hence, one can find footnotes attached to the narratives in order to present the translator's justification for the selection of the story, as happens in the following passage attached to "Mes campagnes parlementaires:"

> (1) NOTE DU TR. Cet article est un tableau fort piquant de la corruption sans pudeur qui s'était glissée dans la gestion des affaires publiques de la Grande-Bretagne, avant la réforme du Parlement. Les roués du régent et les courtesans de Louis XV montraient moins d'impudence que les prétendus élus du peuple qui siégeaient *à* la seconde Chambre. Félicitons nos voisins de ce qui le souvenir de tant de corruption et d'infamies n'ait pas entraîné le Parlement réformé dans des réactions violentes. Il a pu jeter l'ancre sur des pentes et s'y maintenir sans glisser.[6]

This note contains the translator's critical comment on the subject matter of this narrative in which the narrator reveals how he managed to get a seat in the British Parliament by taking advantage of the common but illegal procedures that ruled the negotiation of political positions. This narrative is also an example of how obscure the procedures of periodical production could be in the nineteenth century since the periodical indicated as its original source—*New London Journal*—did not exist in Britain at the time. As one can find other similar cases in the *Revue Britannique*, one can conclude that there must have been a mistake in the indication of *New London Journal* as the title of the periodical in question or even that this story may have been originally written in French rather than translated from the English, in which case a British title would have been cunningly provided to delude the readers about the true origin of the narrative. Therefore, "Mes Campagnes Parlementaires" would be a case of pseudotranslation.

Still in regard to the French taste for narratives which were informative about and critical of the British way of life, one can read in the *Revue Britannique* a narrative such as "Un logement *à* portée du tout," which tells the story of a typical rich London merchant (Mr. Rufus Wadd), who buys a country house at such a "convenient distance" from his working place that he could frequently go to London to run his business. This narrative was originally entitled "The Inconveniences of a Convenient Distance" and was written by John Poole (an obscure author nowadays) for publication in the *New Monthly Magazine*, in

1830.[7] Although the French translator usually made significant changes in the British fictional texts during the translating process, he seems to have approved of the original sarcastic tone of this story since he kept it in his translation. Therefore, the narrator of "Unlogement *à* portée du tout" is highly important in this narrative since he is strongly ironical in his description of Mr. Wadd's petit-bourgeois taste, which is expressed in the decoration of Mr. Wadd's country-house and his literary preferences.

The *Revue Britannique* frequently advertised the self-imposed mission of conveying information and reflection on a number of subjects to French and European readers alike. As a consequence of such a comprehensive and lofty purpose, the editors hoped that the magazine would be read as a book or encyclopedia rather than a periodical with a transitory value:

> Notre ambition était qu'un jour la collection de la REVUE BRITANNIQUE fût comme des espèces d'annales, comme une vaste histoire, non des faits dont la presse quotidienne alimente ses feuilles, mais de l'esprit humain, de ses travaux, de ses découvertes dans les diverses branches de l'arbre encyclopédique.[8]

The *Revue Britannique* was well received in France, where there were at least three editions of the 1825 issues in order to meet subscribers' demand. In addition, Kathleen Jones states that other French periodicals published texts borrowed from the *Revue Britannique*, and that this magazine was an important means of publicizing British authors, both those who were already known and those who were new to the French readership. But the *Revue Britannique* also achieved a large circulation abroad. It was illegally reproduced in Belgium, and the Belgian copies were widely sold around Europe.[9] Also, when praising the translations published in the *Revue Britannique*, the editors claimed that the translators had been able to *improve* the texts in such a way that the route of the borrowings could be reversed:

> ... plumes habiles qui plus d'une fois les [les textes] ont même améliorés, en les traduisant, comme semble l'indiquer la faveur que la REVUE BRITANNIQUE a obtenue en Angleterre et aux états-Unis, où cependant nous ne faisions le plus souvent que renvoyer, sous les formes d'une autre langue, les richesses que nous en avions tirées.[10]

3. The *Revue Britannique* in Brazil

As previously stated, the main aim here is to consider the presence of the *Revue Britannique* in nineteenth-century Brazil by highlighting the appropriation of fiction published in this French magazine by Brazilian men of letters, in a particular historical period. To start with, one has to consider the fact that after the censorship of printed material ceased in 1821, the periodical press continuously expanded in the city of Rio de Janeiro. It is then in periodicals from the Brazilian court, especially those published in the

1830s and 1840s, that one finds several fictional and non-fictional texts borrowed from the *Revue Britannique*. It is interesting to note, though, that only one periodical (namely, *O Cronista*) gives some hints about the immediate source of these texts. On the whole, one is led to think that the British articles and fictional narratives were directly taken from the British periodicals or books which are indicated as their original place of publication. In other words, the mediation played by the *Revue Britannique* was not revealed by the Brazilian men of letters, who were not only the translators of these texts but also the founders, editors, and most frequent contributors to the periodicals in which these foreign texts were published.

The *Revue Britannique* was also taken as a model for the *Revista Nacional e Estrangeira* whose opening article in the founding issue in May 1839, signed by the founders and editors (João Manuel Pereira da Silva,[11] Pedro d'Alcantara Bellegarde,[12] and Josino do Nascimento Silva[13]), states the following:

> Because we do not trust our restrictive lights and acknowledge our own insufficiency, we will turn to others' writing rather than to ours, by modelling this publication on the Revue Britannique. Most Brazilian men of letters know this collection of articles on science and art, and this knowledge sets us free from the task of praising it.
>
> As we subscribe to a large number of periodicals, both English and French alike, which are published under the title of *Magazine*, we are able to satisfy our readers' wish by translating and publishing the best of what we could find in them.[14]

The self-consciousness of the editors of the *Revista Nacional e Estrangeira* allows one to realize how precarious the cultural conditions and the means of production of printed material in nineteenth-century Brazil were, especially up to the 1850s. As a matter of fact, from 1821 onwards, a growing number of newspapers and magazines were published in Rio de Janeiro despite numerous difficulties to produce and keep a periodical running at the time: there was lack of appropriate printing machinery, a shortage of skilled workers at all levels of the printing process, and financial problems in running a periodical as the number of subscribers must have been very limited in a society which was basically illiterate. Thus, most Brazilian magazines had a very short life in the first half of the nineteenth century, usually of less than a year. Nonetheless, the fact that they existed implies that there was a demand, or rather, there were readers.

A comparative analysis of the first Brazilian fictional narratives and the British fiction that reached Brazilian periodicals via the French translation of the *Revue Britannique* shows that this French magazine was appropriated by Brazilian men of letters with a view to their project of founding Brazilian literature. Literature should convey a certain image of the country to its own people in order to help keep Brazil an independent and unified nation. In fact, the time was one of the most trying for the Brazilian ruling courtly classes as they experienced strong internal conflicts and had political and intellectual interests that went against those of the local elite and popular leaders of certain provinces.

In September 1822, Dom Pedro I proclaimed the independence of Brazil from Portugal and became the ruler of the new empire. However, as early as 1824, he managed to centralize political power in his own hands and consequently open the way to the dominance in government decisions of a small circle of bureaucrats and merchants, the majority of whom were Portuguese. Increasing dissatisfaction from Brazilian politicians, army generals, and the people in general led Dom Pedro I to abdicate from the throne in April 1831. As his son was too young to rule (Dom Pedro II was then only five), subsequent groups of three regents, and later a sole regent, were in charge of the central government. This period is known as the Regency and lasted until 1840 when 15-year-old Dom Pedro II was declared to be of age to become emperor.

The Regency was a very turbulent period. The frequent changes of regents went hand in hand with struggles among the ruling classes in the court and with bloody popular revolts that took place in a number of provinces to call for provincial independence and/or republicanism. As a matter of fact, the Brazilian provinces were not integrated either politically or economically as, after independence, the country's economy remained directed towards exportation, which meant that all attention was diverted from the development of an internal market. Besides, there were neither material conditions (due to the precariousness of the means of transport and communication) nor political or economic interest to promote thorough national integration. As a consequence, the Regency was also marked by frequent attempts from Portugal to recolonize Brazil by fomenting dissatisfactions in the provinces with the central government in Rio de Janeiro. On the other hand, the central government related political independence to the maintenance of the integrity of the Brazilian territory; the concept of nation in Brazil was, therefore, very limited as it was restricted to territorial integration.

Despite the political crises, the Regency was the first period when the Brazilian ruling classes had political power in their own hands, and, for them, it was not only important to ensure the conquest of political independence by means of territorial unity but also to organize the country as a new-born nation. As historian Jean Marcel Carvalho França (1999: 82) points out, this project, only apparently bureaucratic-administrative, had deep ideological implications:

> [this purpose] meant two things at least: on the one hand, to provide the country with its own cultural structure, that is, to provide it with a history, with a literature, with a geography; in short, with a community of values that would be able to create in the Brazilian the feeling for the nation. On the other hand, and complementarily, it meant educating the people, making them *enlightened*, *orderly and hardworking* enough so as to be able to cooperate more decisively in the

progress of the country.[15]

This is the context one must bear in mind when one reads the opening articles of Brazilian magazines published in Rio de Janeiro in the 1830s and 1840s, which claimed that Brazilian periodicals should both symbolize and lead the country to *civilization* by publishing Brazilian production and translations of a wealth of various articles borrowed from European periodicals, notably from French and British ones. In this context, translating meant the promotion of the development of the Brazilian civilization since the texts translated brought modern ideas and new cultural forms into a country which was just coming out of a long period of colonization marked by severe restrictions on intellectual production. The Brazilian periodical press also had another important task: to encourage the mostly illiterate Brazilian people to read and be instructed in order to cooperate with the desired move towards civilization. Therefore, the pleasure of reading, that is, of acquiring knowledge and entertainment, was widely advertised as the main aim of a number of magazines, such as *Gabinete de Leitura* and *Museo Universal*, or as the reason for the insertion of a new section in the newspaper *O Cronista*, on 5 October 1836, namely, the *feuilleton*, a French invention from the early nineteenth century, consisting of a detachable section at the bottom of the first pages of newspapers, and which brought entertainment in the form of fiction. So, after a didactic presentation of where to find and how to read this entertaining section in newspapers, the editors of *O Cronista* stated that, by bringing this French novelty to Brazil, they were encouraging Brazilians to read.

As can be seen, borrowings from French and British written culture attended to certain cultural and ideological interests on the part of the Brazilian men of letters who employed and/or adapted the foreign production according to their own needs, which basically consisted of the project of creating a cultural structure for the recently independent nation by distinguishing Brazilian identity from that of Portugal. In this sense, these men of letters were interested in and contributed to a number of fields: theatre, history, literary history and criticism, politics, economics, and literature. As my focus is on the role of the *Revue Britannique* as a cultural agent of translation of British fiction for Brazilians, it is worth remembering that, at the time, literature held the central position in the formation of national culture and identity. Besides, the period when there was more intense translation of foreign fiction in nineteenth-century Brazil corresponds to the initial stage of Brazilian fiction itself. Consequently, as fiction was an important means of nationalizing literature in Brazil, it is important to examine the reasons for the strong correspondence between the narrative pattern used by Brazilian men of letters in their own fiction and that emphasized and/or created by the French translator during the translating process of British narratives for the *Revue Britannique*.

4. The Translations of the *Revue Britannique*

A comparison of the French translation and the original version of these British narratives shows a recurrent set of translation procedures that led to the formation of a particular formal structure of the narratives in their French version. Among these British narratives, there is one which is paradigmatic of such a translating process since the deep reformulation of its formal structure not only provided the text with a more didactic tone but also impregnated it with the French translator's view of the British context portrayed there. The narrative in question was taken from *Pickwick Papers* and is the free translation of Chapter 13. In French, this extract is called "Les élections anglaises" (*Revue Britannique*, June 1837) and, consequently, in Portuguese, "Eleições inglesas" (*Museo Universal*, April 1840). In the *Revue Britannique*, the story is introduced by two long paragraphs that present Charles Dickens and his fiction to the French readers. This introduction was left out of the Brazilian translation; however, the rest of the French version was closely followed by the Brazilian translator.

Much of the fun and interest roused by *Pickwick Papers* comes from the way the narrative is structured: The narrator lets the reader notice the nuances between the narrator's and the central characters' point-of-view. As the narrator introduces himself as the *editor* of the notes taken by the members of the Pickwick Club, he follows the central characters' point-of-view, but, at the same time, reveals his own interpretative hypotheses of the facts, which do not agree with those of the characters. As a consequence, the clash in the disagreement between the narrator's and the characters' views creates an irony that permeates the whole novel and allows the reader to apprehend the narrator's sharper and more comprehensive understanding of the different situations. This type of point-of-view would serve Dickens' aim of impregnating his fiction with criticisms of various aspects of contemporary English society. Therefore, there is in *Pickwick Papers* an intentional interpretative gap between the various meanings conveyed in the text by the central characters and by the narrator, who has on his side a rather wise character, Samuel Weller, who is Mr. Pickwick's valet. The reader is then supposed to fill in this interpretative gap with his own interpretation of the ironical treatment given to the members of the Pickwick club by this *editor*.

However, the translation published in the *Revue Britannique*, and later in the Brazilian *Museo Universal*, presents a narrator who, by leaving aside this ironical subtlety in favour of a categorical interpretation of facts and characters, imposes his own opinion and personal judgment on the reader. The story itself starts differently: the first paragraph is completely new and comprises a summary of the idea of the book and a brief presentation of the central characters. The second paragraph corresponds to the opening of Chapter 13 in *Pickwick Papers*, but the beginning of the French translation follows a different tone: the narrator

himself introduces the members of the Pickwick club as ridiculous, whereas, in Dickens, these characters are free to act by themselves and, therefore, to get involved in various awkward situations which make them subject of derision to other characters and even to the reader. It is exactly this change in the narrative tone, which leads up to an important corresponding change in the role of the narrator, which is the most striking characteristic of the French translation (and, consequently, of the Brazilian one). The subtle irony is turned into overt irony; the *editor* of the papers, who sometimes shows uncertainty about some of Mr. Pickwick's interpretations, is turned into a narrator who forcefully presents his own view and whose discourse guides the reader's own understanding of the story. In other words, the French translator turned the narrator into an overt interpreter of the narrative. Therefore, the reader receives a text in which the narration develops in conjunction with its interpretation within a narrative format that can be easily *digested*. The French version reads as follows: in "Les élections anglaises" the Pickwickians stop at a town called Eatanswill in order to observe the election procedures to select a member of the House of Commons. Amid the confusing rivalry between the two opponents, the two main newspapers of Eatanswill fight each other, each supporting one of the two candidates. As Mr. Pickwick, in a moment of confusion, sides with the *bleues*, he is introduced to Mr. Polt, who is the editor of the *Gazette*, the organ of this party. Hence, when Mr. Polt speaks up about the universal importance of the press, the French translator created the following passage to allow the narrator to judge this character:

> Après avoir terminé ce discours empreint du lieu commun de la diffusion et de la niaiserie qui constituent le mérite du genre, M. Polt s'essuya le front avec un foulard, et notre héros [Mr. Pickwick] lui tendit la main en lui exprimant l'admiration profonde dont le pénétraient une éloquence aussi généreuse et des sentiments aussi magnanimes... [16]

In the sequence, when Samuel Weller firstly appears in "Les élections anglaises," the narrator praises him with these words:

> ... M. Pickwick était charmé; il venait d'achever sa toilette, l'oreille au guet, et regardant de temps en temps par la fenêtre, lorsque *son fidèle domestique*, Samuel Weller, entr'ouvrit doucement la porte, et fit apparaître *le profil malin et jovial d'une excellente figure de valet madré.* [17]

In the quotation above, the phrases in italics were created by the French translator and clearly illustrate how he made the text be more *didactic* as the narrator sums up in his own speech the perception that the reader himself would have of Sam Weller during the extensive reading of *Pickwick Papers*. In fact, these translating procedures recur in the translation of the other British narratives. They are: (1) emphasis on the central action at the expense of details, secondary characters, and secondary narrative actions; (2) greater prominence of the narrator who facilitates the reader's comprehension of the text by repeating and explaining in

detail information regarding both the narrative itself and the foreign context portrayed in the story; the narrator also guides the reader's own interpretation as he already interprets what he narrates. Therefore, the French reader (and, consequently, the Brazilian one too) reads a story whose meaning has already been deciphered by another previous reader—the translator—who voices through the narrator's speech his own critical view of the foreign cultural aspects in the narrative. By translating these British narratives from the *Revue Britannique*, Brazilian men of letters were acquainted with a certain narrative structure that would prove to be useful for their own production of fiction, as one can see below.

I have already stressed how clear it was for the leading political, economic and cultural groups in Rio de Janeiro that the nation and its literature were being founded during the Regency and, consequently, that it was crucial to ensure the sovereignty of Brazilian culture and territory. This process, nonetheless, implied a necessary exchange with Europe; no longer with Portugal, but rather with Great Britain and France. Here one can establish a plausible relationship between the first Brazilian fictional writings and the French mediation in the translation process of this British fiction, as this mediation altered the formal structure of the narratives by intensifying the role of the narrator as an interpreter. So it is more than a coincidence that the role of the narrator in the first pieces of Brazilian fiction corresponds closely to that found in the French translation of this British fiction, but with a different purpose: In the Brazilian fiction the narrator aims at explaining and guiding the reader's interpretation of the Brazilian context itself rather than of a foreign context.

"As Duas Órfãs" ["The Two Orphan Girls"], by Joaquim Norberto de Sousa e Silva, is paradigmatic of the kind of fiction that was written in the first half of the nineteenth century in Brazil.[18] It takes place in the colonial period, at the time of the battles against the Dutch invasion of the Northeast of Brazil, and is the story of two young women (cousins and orphans), called Mariana and Isabel, who fall in love with the same man, Dinis Gonçalves. This love triangle gets more complicated as Dinis loves and is engaged to Mariana but does not reject Isabel. The plot is divided into five short sections that can be organized into two blocks: the first block contains Sections I and II, which center on the historical content and introduce considerable information about the Dutch and the real Brazilian characters (including women) who fought to defend Brazilian territory; the second block is formed by Sections III to V, in which the content of historical chronicle is abandoned in favour of the conflicts resulting from the love triangle. The narrator dominates the development of the plot by giving information and making frequent comments about the unfolding of the facts and what the characters think, feel, and do. At two moments of the narrative the narrator freezes the action in order to insert long descriptions of local flora and fauna: a landscape that resembles a postcard for its static perfection. In another passage, the narration of the battle between Brazilians and the Dutch provides the narrator with a timely opportunity to praise the heroism of those who defended the integrity of the Brazilian territory. Among them, one finds black slaves and Indians who are said to have fought "voluntarily" for the rescue of this

region from the hands of the Dutch. Finally, the story has a gothic-like end: the three characters involved in the love triangle meet violent deaths, and Dinis turns into a ghost that haunts the banks of the River San Francisco where he drowned.

As Sousa e Silva emphasized the patriotic feeling by focusing on the urgent defence of the territorial integrity of Brazil, "As Duas Órfãs" would help delineate what should be understood as *the* identity of Brazil. Hence the insertion of long descriptions of a typically Brazilian natural setting as a means of nationalizing literature. However, the analysis of the narrative structure shows that these natural descriptions are rarely integrated into the development of the plot as their insertion invariably causes interruption of the action. As for the plot, it comes mainly from the European sentimental, domestic and occasionally gothic type of fiction. In other words, the story opens with a political issue, which allows the author to work on patriotism and national union, but is then diverted to a love story that leaves the historical-patriotic theme behind. In this narrative mélange, the narrator, by overtly controlling the development of the action, tries to hold together the narrative components which nonetheless keep a permanent friction: (1) the historical chronicle to reinforce the patriotic feeling; (2) the sentimental plot with a melodramatic dénouement as one could easily find in the bulk of European novels that reached Brazil; (3) the description of natural Brazilian settings to nationalize the narrative.

As in "As Duas Órfãs," the first pieces of Brazilian fiction have a centralizing narrator that made it possible for the Brazilian men of letters to write narratives of a rather simple structure without the need to coherently develop the other narrative elements (characters, setting, time) or to establish a proper connection between the different phases of narrative action as the narrator was given the task to keep a tight rein on the fictional discourse, at all its levels. This kind of narrative structure is very similar to that of British fiction, especially after the French translator's interference, which was published alongside Brazilian narratives in periodicals from Rio de Janeiro. At this point, one should consider the fact that these Brazilian and British fictional narratives were mostly written for periodicals. This type of fiction invariably has its structure centered on the narrator and serves a pedagogical function as the stories are usually developed in order to provide the reader with a comprehensive understanding of the narrative itself. One can also find the frequent overt expression in the narrator's speech of the author's own ideas and beliefs, which make it difficult to specify fictional discourse. In addition, it is important to recall that both in Europe and in Brazil translation and free appropriation of texts were still quite unrestrained by formal regulation in the first half of the nineteenth century. As a consequence, the French translation of this British fiction turned the narrator into a prominent character who worked as a spokesperson of the translator's own critical view of the British context portrayed in the narratives. In the *Revue Britannique*, this procedure served the editorial aim of critical scrutiny of the British achievements and cultural habits. In the Brazilian context, though, such a prominent narrator guided the reader's understanding of the text itself (which is perfectly understandable in a country where most people—rich and poor alike—were illiterate), but also took on the task of *presenting a certain view and certain aspects of the Brazilian culture and habits for the reader of his own country*. In this sense, the first Brazilian writers of fiction employed the narrator as a tool to convey to the reader information about cultural aspects that *should characterize an authentic Brazilian identity*, which was always proudly given a nationalistic and patriotic feeling.

To conclude, it is important to mention that these Brazilian men of letters also had access to other types of European fiction, including novels that reached Brazil in book form, fiction that they themselves translated into Portuguese to be published in various newspapers and magazines in Rio de Janeiro. In addition, literary critic Flora Süssekind (2000) also establishes a plausible connection between the early stage of Brazilian fiction and the writings of European travelers on Brazil in order to explain this position of the narrator. One should therefore consider this British fiction in its particular French version as *another interlocutor* of the first Brazilian fiction writers, who found in the *Revue Britannique* a fictional structure that was particularly suitable for their ideological and literary project in the Brazilian context of the time.

Notes:

1. This text is based on my doctoral thesis: Ramicelli, Maria Eulália. *Narrativas Itinerantes. Aspectos franco-britanicos da ficção brasileira, em periódicos do século XIX*. PhD thesis, University of São Paulo, 2004.
2. Gift books and annuals were popular small ornate books usually sold from October onwards to be given as Christmas presents. They were famous for their gorgeous engravings which provided themes for the writers who were engaged to produce fictional narratives or poems to go with the pictures.
3. Extract from an insert in the September 1835 issue, p. xii.
4. Extract from an insert in the September 1835 issue, p. viii. Italics in the text.
5. Extract from the preface in the January 1834 issue, p. 10.
6. *Revue Britannique*, October 1833, p. 254.
7. John Poole (1786[?]—5 February, 1872) was a successful dramatist whose farces and comedies were produced in London between 1813 and 1829. Popular actors such as Charles Kemble, John Liston, and William Farren appeared in his plays, the most famous of which was *Paul Pry* (1825). Although in his heyday Poole moved in fashionable society, his last twenty years were spent in obscurity. Through Charles Dickens's influence, Poole received a yearly pension of £100.
8. Extract from the preface in the January 1830 issue, p. 6.
9. For instance, the copy of the *Revue Britannique* that belongs to the collection of the British Library mentions on the front page that it was published in Brussels.
10. Extract from the preface in the January 1834 issue, p. 11.
11. Pereira da Silva was born on 30 August 1817 in Iguaçu (in a rural area in the province of Rio de Janeiro) and died on 16 June 1898 in the city of Rio de Janeiro. From 1834 to 1838, he lived in Paris, where he graduated in Law. In this period, he joined other Brazilian men of letters (namely, Domingos J. Gonçalves de Magalhães, Francisco de S. Torres Homem, and Manuel José de A. Porto Alegre) to found the

magazine Niterói (1836) which has been called the official launcher of Romanticism in Brazil. Back to Rio de Janeiro, Pereira da Silva was a very active man of letters who worked as a lawyer and held several political and bureaucratic offices, always as a conservative. He was the editor of certain periodicals from Rio de Janeiro, such as the important newspaper *Jornal do Comércio*, and founded, directed and/or contributed to a number of other magazines and newspapers. Pereira da Silva was a member of several important cultural institutions in Rio de Janeiro and was one of the founders of the Brazilian Academy of Letters. He wrote many historical works about Brazil and was the most prolific writer in the initial stage of Brazilian fiction. Being sympathetic to the regulation of the profession of literary writer, Pereira da Silva joined the group that founded the Men of Letters Association of Brazil in 1883.

12. Bellegarde was born on 3 December 1807 in Brazilian waters as his parents fled with the Portuguese royal family to Brazil to escape from Napoleon's army. He graduated in Mathematics and became a member of the Brazilian army under the protection of Dom Pedro I, who was the eldest son of King Dom João VI and the first emperor of Brazil. Bellegarde was also elected as a deputy to the General Assembly in 1863, but did not take office. He contributed to another magazine, the *Minerva Brasiliense*. Bellegarde died on 12 February 1864.
13. Nascimento Silva was born on 31 July, 1811, in Campos, a rural area of the province of Rio de Janeiro, and died on 6 June 1886. He studied Law in the College of Law of São Paulo and occupied several offices in this field. Nascimento Silva was the president of the provinces of Rio de Janeiro and São Paulo, a provincial and general deputy, and also a member of the emperor's counseling group. Just like Pereira da Silva, Josino do Nascimento Silva was a member of several important cultural institutions in Rio de Janeiro. He was the owner of the typography where the periodicals *O Cronista* and *Gabinete de Leitura* were printed and was the editor of two important newspapers: *Diário do Rio de Janeiro* and *Jornal do Comércio*.
14. "Por não confiarmos em nossas acanhadas luzes, reconhecedores da própria insuficiência, recorreremos antes aos escritos alheios do que aos nossos, modelando esta publicação pela Revista Britanica. A maior parte dos literatos brasileiros conhecem esta coleção de artigos sobre ciências e artes, e esse conhecimento forra-nos ao trabalho de elogiá-la. Assinantes de grande número de periódicos, tanto ingleses como franceses, publicados com o título de *Revista*, estamos ao alcance de satisfazer os desejos de nossos leitores, traduzindo e publicando o melhor que deles pudermos colher ... " Extract from the opening article of the *Revista Nacional e Estrangeira*, May 1839, p. vi. Italics in the text. My translation.
15. "[esse propósito] significava ao menos duas coisas: de um lado, dotar o país de uma estrutura cultural própria, isto é, dotá-lo de uma história, de uma literatura, de uma geografia, enfim, de uma comunidade de valores apta a gerar no brasileiro o sentimento de pátria; de outro lado, e complementarmente, significava formar o povo, torná-lo *esclarecido*, *ordeiro e trabalhador* osuficiente para que pudesse colaborar mais decisivamente para o progresso do país. " Italics in the text. My translation.
16. *Revue Britannique*, June 1837, p. 552.
17. Ibid., p. 553. My italics.
18. This narrative seems to have been originally published in a book entitled *Mosaico Poético* and in a brochure in 1841. Sousa e Silva was born in the city of Rio de Janeiro on 6 June 1820 and died in Niteroi (also in the province of Rio de Janeiro) on 14 May, 1891. As a student, Sousa e Silva was a constant visitor to the National Library, where he met priest Januário da Cunha Barbosa, who became his protector and employed him as his assistant in the library. From then on, Sousa e Silva remained in close contact with the imperial government and held several bureaucratic posts. He was a member of important cultural institutions in the

court. Sousa e Silva deserves special attention for having had an extensive literary production (poetry, fiction, and drama) and for having been a precursor of literary history in Brazil.

【延伸阅读】

[1] Sirkku, A. *Time Sharing on Stage: Drama Translation in Theatre and Society*. Clevedon · Buffalo · Toronto, NY: Multilingual Matters Ltd., 2000.

[2] Lefevere, A. *Translation, Rewriting and the Manipulation of Literary Fame*. London & New York: Routledge, 1992.

[3] Gentzler, E. *Translation and Identity in the Americas: New Directions in Translation Theory*. London: Routledge, 2008.

[4] Anderman, G. (ed.). *Voices in Translation: Bridging Cultural Divides*. Clevedon · Buffalo · Toronto, NY: Multilingual Matters Ltd., 2007.

[5] Corbett, J. *Written in the Language of the Scottish Nation: A History of Literary Translation intoScots*. Clevedon · Buffalo · Toronto, NY: Multilingual Matters Ltd., 1999.

[6] Faiq, S. (ed.). *Cultural Encounters in Translation from Arabic*. Clevedon · Buffalo · Toronto, NY: Multilingual Matters Ltd., 2004.

[7] Simon, S. Germanine de Stáel and Gayatri Spivak: Culture Brokers. In Maria Tymoczko & Edwin Gentzler (eds.), *Translation and Power*. Amherst, Mass.: University of Massachusetts Press, 2002.

[8] Bassnett, S. & Lefevere, A. *Constructing Cultures: Essays on Literary Translation*. Clevedon · Buffalo · Toronto, NY: Multilingual Matters Ltd., 1997.

[9] 冯文坤. 由实践哲学转向理论哲学的翻译研究. 四川师范大学学报,2007(2).

[10] 冯文坤. 论翻译与翻译的生存本体论意义. 四川外语学院学报,2008(2).

[11] 葛校琴. 后现代语境下的译者主体研究. 上海:译文出版社,2006.

[12] 倪梁康. 胡塞尔:现象学概念通释. 北京:三联书店,1999.

【问题与思考】

1. 请列举图里译语取向的翻译规范并作简要说明。
2. 说说文学翻译“社会学转向”的理论基础是什么?
3. 谈谈文学经典的形成与翻译的关系。
4. 如何理解美国戏剧经典中的欧洲中心主义?
5. 结合文学翻译实践谈谈行动者网络理论、活动理论和社会游戏理论之内涵。

第六章　文学翻译研究的阐释学钩沉

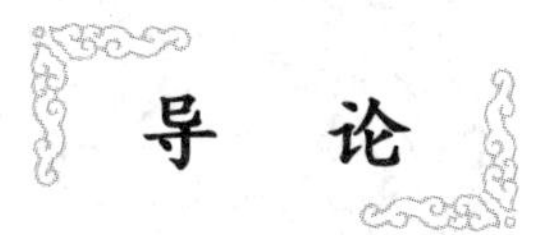

导　论

诠释学(Hermeneutics)是关于理解和解释的学科,亦称阐释学或解释学,已成为西方哲学人文主义思潮中的一个重要的哲学流派。现当代诠释学的代表人物主要有施莱尔马赫(Schleiermacher)、狄尔泰(Wilhelm Dilthey)、马丁·海德格尔(Martin Heidegger)、伽达默尔(Hans-Geog Gadamer)、哈贝马斯(Jürgen Habermas)、保罗·利科(Paul Ricoeur)。二十世纪六七十年代存在三种主要的诠释学理论模式:以施莱尔马赫、狄尔泰、贝蒂(Betty)为代表的浪漫主义传统诠释学,以布尔特曼和早期海德格尔为代表的存在主义诠释学以及伽达默尔的哲学诠释学,其中以伽达默尔为代表的哲学阐释学影响最大。

诠释学所关心的问题总是与翻译学所关心的联系十分紧密。从诠释学角度来看,翻译即解释,文学翻译更是如此。伽达默尔的代表作《真理与方法》被称为现代阐释学的经典之作,他在该书中提出的理解的历史性、视域融合以及效果历史三大哲学原则对文学翻译具有强大的解释力。首先,理解与阐释的文学文本作为历史性客体而存在,总会受到特定的历史背景、文化传统及社会习俗等因素的限制。文学翻译则会受到各种主客观特定历史条件的限制。其次,从视域融合的角度看,文学翻译是译者竭力将理解者视域和文本视域交融的过程。译者一方面需运用自己所掌握的知识结构和思维习惯对原文进行理解和诠释,另一方面还要充分考虑文本生成时的社会历史因素。再次,效果历史原则强调从艺术作品的效果历史中理解作品,这就把历史与现在密切相连,历史的有价值的文学文本重译对现在具有重要的意义。

艾柯诠释学的基本原则也同样能正确评价当代翻译研究的认识论精髓。艾柯认为,所有的翻译都是一种诠释,而这种诠释在作者意图、文本意图和读者意图之间复杂且又不稳定的关系中基本都表现为过度诠释。翻译也必须先梳理清这三者的关系和相互作用。"有限性"是艾柯诠释学的核心。过度诠释在大多数的文本翻译里其实是一种普遍现象,如何使译文忠实于原文取决于艾柯的"翻译的界限"。据此,翻译者需要严肃地考虑目标文本(译文)在哪些方面,又在多大程度上实现了或扭曲了原文本的结构或预期意义。翻译活动是一种高度的操纵行为,因为原文潜在意义被正确诠释的可能性是受到译者文化背景、知识、甚至目的影响的。艾柯诠释学里所坚持的把文本和历史背景结合起来的历史—哲学的调查方法是避免过度诠释的有效方法,译者要在意识到诠释局限性的前提下,尊重史实,考虑怎样翻译更接近标准作者意图和文本意图。

从总体上讲,文学翻译都反映出对源语文本的多样性理解和"阐释"特征,出现多样翻译文本结果。其中既有作品本身的语言文化环境和历史语境的客观影响,也有译者本身主观因素影响所致。译者要在把握源语文本“精髓”的前提下，在一定的限度内，尊重翻译过程的开放性，理解和“容忍”多样性存在，正确地看待不同目的语文本与源语文本的“距离”。

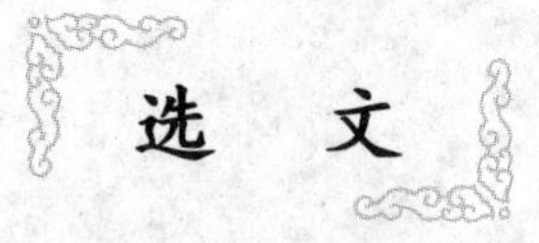

选　文

选文一　视域差与翻译解释的度

——从哲学诠释学视角看翻译的理想与现实

朱健平

导　言

本文选自《中国翻译》2009 年第 4 期。作者朱健平是湖南大学外国语学院教授、翻译学博士。

翻译标准要求译者在翻译中应把握理想的解释度，翻译现实则表明，翻译中实际的解释度常会偏离理想的解释度。理想的解释度和实际的解释度均与视域差有关：目的语文化与源语文本的视域差影响理想的解释度，译者与源语文本的视域差影响实际的解释度，译者与源语文本的视域差以及译者与目的语文化的视域差则是导致实际的解释度偏离理想解释度的根本原因。理想的解释度是一种动态的存在，它与目的语文化和源语文本的视域差成正比。

一、导　言

解释是翻译的普遍特征，但翻译是有限度的解释。作为翻译的解释，其限制主要来自两方面：一是文本的特征，二是译者的视域。文本在具有未定性和开放性的同时还有确定性，文本的确定性是导致翻译解释有限性的主要因素之一；译者除有独特视域外还有公共视域，公共视域要求翻译的解释限制在一定范围内。即是说，翻译的解释虽然不可能是唯一的，但也不可不着边际，而是要求译者在解释中把握一个理想的“度”。那么，翻译中理想的解释度应该是什么？可以确定一个确切的理想解释度吗？影响理想解释度的因素有哪些？既然有理想的解释度，肯定还有实际的解释度，那么实际的解释度是怎样的？它与理想的解释度是何关系？是什么造成了实际的解释度偏离理想的解释度？本文拟从哲学诠释学视角对这些问题进行探讨。

二、视域差

翻译即解释，解释即视域融合。在翻译中，解释之所以不可避免，是由视域差（horizon

gap)造成的。视域差是指与翻译密切相关的各因素的视域之间的差异。翻译涉及的因素很多，主要有译者、源语文本、目的语文化和目的语读者。这些因素均具有视域。

1. 译者视域。译者是翻译的执行者，他因具有历史性而不可避免地具有前见，前见构成了译者译前的初始视域，即译者在接触源语文本前所具备的知识、观点、认识和态度，包括译者在译前所储备的各种知识，对待源语文化、目的语文化、翻译标准和策略的态度，以及对目的语文本预期要达到的目的和预期的目的语读者对象的基本认识等。但译者的最终目的是形成目的语文本，译者从最初接触源语文本到目的语文本形成前，还会不断拓展视域，尽可能多地将源语文化和目的语文化纳入自己的视域，试图使目的语文本尽量达到目的语文化的要求，这样就形成了译者视域。因此，译者视域(the translator's horizon)是指译者在目的语文本最终成形前所具有的全部视域，或具备的一切知识、观点、认识和态度的总和，不仅包括译者在译前的全部前见，而且包括译者在译中获取的全部信息。

2. 源语文本视域。源语文本是译者的工作对象。按接受美学观点，在结构上，源语文本是一个由未定点、空白和确定点构成的图式化结构，因此既具未定性和开放性，又具一定程度的确定性；在内容上，源语文本反映了源语在语言、文化、思维、思想等方面的特征，这些构成了源语文本视域。因此，源语文本视域不仅体现了源语的语言特征、思想内容和思维特征，在更深层次上还体现了源语所在的文化特征。

3. 目的语文化视域。翻译，即译者视域与源语文本视域的融合，不是发生在真空中，而是完成于文化语境中。译者在重新固定视域融合后形成的新视域时所使用的目的语并非一尘不染，由于长期沐浴在目的语文化中，它不可避免地浸润着浓厚的目的语文化，而且目的语本身就是目的语文化的积淀物，目的语与目的语文化密不可分。目的语文化并不是静止的，而总是处于不断变化中，同样具有历史性，而且作为集体意识，同样具有前见，前见构成了目的语文化的视域，并对翻译产生影响。

4. 目的语读者视域。翻译的目的是为了促进文化交流，因此译者视域与源语文本视域的融合不是最终目的，也不是最后结果。新视域形成后，译者必须用目的语重新固定下来，形成新文本，即目的语文本。在目的语文本生成过程中，译者不可避免地要考虑目的语读者的接受能力，尽管目的语读者在译者的翻译过程中不可能是一个个具体的对象，而只是译者对目的语读者的虚拟，是一个抽象的读者群。译者这时所想象的目的语读者的接受能力和期待就是译者假想的目的语读者的视域。因此，目的语读者虽未直接参与翻译过程，但译者在翻译中所虚构的目的语读者群所拥有的公共视域同样会间接影响译者的翻译策略，进而影响目的语文本的生成。

可见，与翻译过程密切相关的四大因素都有视域，由于各自都有历史性，因此不可能完全叠合，而是存在差异。各个视域之间的这种差异，我们称之为视域差。以上因素至少构成6种视域差，即：译者与源语文本的视域差、目的语文化与源语文本的视域差、译者与目的语文化的视域差、译者与目的语读者的视域差、目的语读者与源语文本的视域差、目的语读者与目的语文化的视域差。

视域差是导致翻译具有解释性的根本原因，视域差的大小决定翻译解释度的大小。但这六种视域差对翻译解释行为造成的影响并不一样，而是有大有小，有轻有重，有直接有间接。如上所述，目的语读者视域对于译者而言只是一种虚拟的存在，虽然无论是作为个体的读者还是作为群体的读者，都会对译者的翻译行为作出一定的评价和反馈，并影响译者在目的语文本生成过程中采取的翻译策略，但无论如何，他们对译者解释行为产生的影响都只是间接的，因而与目的语读者相关的三种视域差对翻译解释度的影响相对要小些。

直接影响翻译的解释度的是前三种视域差，其中，目的语文化与源语文本的视域差直接影响着翻译中"理想的解释度"，译者与源语文本的视域差直接影响着翻译中"实际的解释度"，而"译者与源语文本的视域差"和"译者与目的语文化的视域差"之差则是导致实际解释度偏离理想解释度的根本原因。下面拟对这一观点作深入探讨。

三、视域差与理想的解释度——一种动态的翻译标准观

翻译中理想的解释度也即翻译标准。翻译标准一直是译界争论得最激烈的问题。语文学派和语言学派强调忠实或对等，目的论认为翻译标准应依翻译目的及目的语文本的功能而定，文化学派和解构主义则否定标准的必要性。

从哲学诠释学视角出发，翻译即解释，解释是翻译的根本特征，翻译的解释性从根本上否定了忠实和对等的可能。因此，所谓翻译标准，不应是对译者或目的语文本应在何种程度上忠实或对等于源语文本或原作者的规定，而应是对译者被允许在多大程度上超越源语文本、对源语文本进行何种程度的解释的规定。但它并不全盘否定翻译标准的必要性，它在强调文本的未定性和译者视域的历史性的同时，又承认文本的确定性和译者视域中公共视域的存在。相应地，它在承认翻译的解释性的同时，又强调限制翻译解释的度。即是说，承认翻译有标准，不等于认为标准只能是忠实或对等；否定忠实和对等，不等于否定为翻译制定标准的必要。承认翻译标准与承认忠实和对等并非一码事，否定忠实和对等与承认翻译有标准其实并不矛盾。

但对翻译的规定并不像传统上所认为的只是取决于原作者，因为作者在完成文本写作后，只能作为自身文本的一名解释者而存在，作者的解释并不具绝对的权威；同时也不像翻译研究学派所认为的只是取决于目的语文化的规范，规范只能是确定翻译标准的决定因素之一，而非全部。相反，对翻译作出规定，是源语文本与目的语文化的共同要求。一方面，源语文本除未定性外还有确定的一面，它客观上要求译者在翻泽过程中将解释限制在一定范围内；另一方面，目的语文化在长期演进过程中对代表源语文化的源语文本以及翻译标准和策略等各方面都形成了一定共识，要求译者在翻译过程中对源语文本的解释限定在一定范围内，译者的解释一旦超出目的语文化规定的限度，便会引起不满甚至惩罚。

但译者究竟应将解释限定在何种程度？目的语文化对该问题的看法往往只是一种主观的要求或期待，它与源语文本的客观视域之间往往存在一定的差异，即目的语文化与源语文本的视域差。所谓目的语文化与源语文本的视域差，指的是目的语文化作为集体意识对某源语文本所负载的源语语言、文化、思想等各方面的认识、观点和态度（即目的语文化对源语文本的视域）与源语文本自身所蕴含的源语语言、文化、思想等各方面内容（即源语文本视域）之间存在的差异。一方面，源语文本自身必定负载着它产生时所在的文化语境的各种特征，即源语文本视域；另一方面，目的语文化在面对该源语文本时也必定会对它负载的这些特征形成一个群体认识，即目的语文化视域。两个视域虽有相同之处，但由于目的语文化自身独特的历史性，其视域不可能涵盖源语文本视域的全部内容，从而使目的语文化作为一个群体意识对源语文本视域的观点和态度产生一定的偏差。目的语文化正是按照这种对源语文本含有偏差的群体认识来要求译者在翻译过程中应该如何对待源语文本，并期待或要求译者应该再创造一部什么

样的目的语文本的。即使这时目的语文化要求或期待目的语文本应忠实或对等于源语文本，但这种忠实或对等不可能是真正的忠实或对等，而是目的语文化视域下的忠实或对等，即这种要求或期待明显打上了目的语文化自身的烙印。正是这种视域差真正决定了目的语文化对某源语文本所要求的“理想的解释度”。

具体而言，“理想的解释度”与目的语文化和源语文本的视域差成正比，该视域差越大，目的语文化所允许的理想解释度就会越大；反之，目的语文化所要求或期待的理想解释度就应越小。就是说，“理想的解释度”不是依译者与源语文本的视域差而定，而是依目的语文化与源语文本的视域差而定。目的语文化与源语文本的视域差决定了“理想的解释度”的大小。但目的语文化与源语文本的视域差是一种动态的存在，它会因源语文本的类型、目的语文化所处的历史阶段、目的语文化内部的亚文化及其读者群、翻译涉及的两种语言以及翻译方向等不同而不同，因此，目的语文化会在不同的历史时期针对不同的文本类型提出不同的翻译要求和理想解释度。

（一）不同类型的源语文本需要不同的理想解释度

文本是一个图式化结构，不仅含有未定点和空白，而且含有确定点，是未定性和确定性的统一体。但不同类型的文本，无论是未定点和空白还是确定点，它们无论是在数量上还是质量上，都互不相同。文学文本与非文学文本自不用说，单就文学文本而言，在其他因素不变的情况下，诗歌的未定点和空白往往比小说多，未定性更强；(后)现代主义文学文本的未定点和空白比现实主义文学文本多，未定性更强。因此，目的语文化对诗歌的把握比对小说的把握更难，即是说，目的语文化与源语诗歌的视域差比与源语小说的视域差要大，因此，对源语诗歌的理想解释度相对小说而言可以而且必定更大。同样，目的语文化与(后)现代主义文本的视域差比与现实主义文本的视域差要大，因此，相对于现实主义文本而言，对(后)现代主义文本的理想解释度可以而且必定更大。

解释的极端形式是加注，译者通过加注从文本中跳到文本外，直接干扰读者视线。比如，萧乾夫妇译《尤利西斯》时共加注 6 000 余条，近 340 页，占正文的近 40%。之所以要加这么多注，是因为文本中空白和未定点太多，不加注不足以让汉语读者理解。正因为大部分空白和未定点在翻译中已被译者“具体化”，所以汉语读者阅读《尤利西斯》，若同时参考译注，就不太难了。这种极端的解释方式在译《尤利西斯》这样的“天书”时不仅为目的语文化所允许，而且深受读者欢迎，但在译《傲慢与偏见》等现实主义作品时却较为少见，译通俗小说时则更应杜绝。这表明，源语文本因类型不同而含有不同的未定点和空白，因而目的语文化会对不同类型文本的翻译提出不同要求和期待。

（二）不同的历史阶段需要不同的理想解释度

目的语文化与源语文本的视域差与目的语文化所处的历史阶段密切相关。目的语文化视域是一种历史的存在，它不可能永远处于静止而封闭的状态，而是会随时间的推移而不断变化。就某一部作品而言，源语文本视域虽然总是保持不变，但由于目的语文化视域发生了变化，二者的视域差也总是处于变化之中。即是说，在不同的历史阶段，同一目的语文化对同一源语文本的认识会不同，对同一源语文本中未定点、空白和确定点的数量和性质的认识也会不同。由于视域差的改变，目的语文化在不同历史阶段对同一源语文本的理想解释度的认识也会不同。这就是不同历史阶段会出现不同翻译标准和策略的根本原因，也是不同历史时期对同一源语义本需要不同目的语文本的根本原因。比如，林纾、苏曼殊的翻译对原文作了很大解释，虽在当时深受读者欢迎，得到了目的语文化的肯定，但若按现在的翻译标准，无疑是无法作为严格的翻译来接受的。正如谢天振指出，"现在如果再回过头去看看中国早期的译作，像林纾、苏曼殊等人的翻译，按照现在的翻译标准，是否还能算作翻译呢？他们'译作'中的创造性成分实在是太大了。"(谢天振，1999：134)这表明，人们对翻译解释度的期望和要求会随目的语文化的变迁而不断改变，而不会总是处于静止状态。

同样，目的语文化视域的不断改变还反映在它在不同历史阶段对翻译目的的认识的不断变化上，翻译目的的变化导致了目的语文化对翻译所允许或期待的理想解释度的变化。比如，在近代翻译文学发展期，"翻译的目的在于输入文明或借鉴其思想意义"，而不考虑文学价值，因此以意译和译述为主，译者常可"根据自己对作品的理解"对源语文本任意增删、改译，甚至将作品中的人名、地名、称谓乃至典故中国化。这时翻译的解释度可以说不受任何限制，译者可以天马行空，毫无约束。如苏曼殊译的《悲惨世界》"简直是近乎创作"，周桂笙译的《毒蛇圈》不仅增加了原文没有的描写，而且增加了很多自己的议沦。对于这种现象，当时的评论家不仅未加批评和制止，反而为之辩护甚至鼓励。比如，对于周桂笙那种想当然的随意增添，吴研人辩护说，"故虽杜撰，亦非蛇足"；有人甚至明确主张"译者宜参以己见，当笔则笔，当削则削"。(郭延礼，1999)

"五四"以后，我国文学界开始倡导白话文学，但由于当时白话文尚不成熟，受新文化运动影响，翻译的目的也随之发生转移，由原来重视思想的输入转移到重视语言形式的输入，希望通过翻译达到输入新的表达法的目的。因此，原来只注重输入思想而不注重输入新的表现形式的任意增删现象便自然要受到译界批评。比如，当时为误译辩护而主张"宁错而务顺"的赵景深以及和他持类似观点或在翻译中采取类似做法的译者都受到了主张直译的鲁迅和瞿秋白等人的严厉批评(瞿秋白，1931；罗新璋，1984)。尽管直译也是对源语文本的解释，但与任意增删情节和内容、增添译者观点的做法相比，其幅度显然小得多。

五六十年代，随着白话文日渐成熟，人们已不再满足通过直译得来的不太通顺的译文了，于是对目的语文本自身的文学性提出了更高要求。为达此目的，我国译界先后提出了神似和化境的翻译标准。这时对文学作品的认识已不仅仅局限于其语言性，也"不单单是事物的概念和情节的记叙"，而是"用语言创造的艺术"和"有能够吸引读者的艺术意境"。因此，这时对文学翻泽的要求是"把原作的艺术意境传达出来"，让读者"得到启发、感动和美的感受"(茅盾，1954；罗新璋，1984)。这种使译文达到神似、化境、传达原作"艺术意境"的要求必然要对源语文本的语言形式进行更大程度的解释，而语言形式的改变必然导致源语文本内容和神韵的改变，因此，尽管他们强调应充分体现原文"神韵"和"艺术意境"，但由于语言形式的改变，源语文本中的未定点和空白也在更大程度上发生了改变，从而使源语文本的内容和神韵随之得到了更大程度的解释。

(三) 目的语文化内部不同的亚文化会提出不同的理想解释度

每一种文化都会因地域、宗教、思维方式、生活方式的不同而具有不同特征，因而都区别于其他文化。一方面，每一种文化作为一个整体，其内部常会表现出许多共同特征，尤其是与其他文化相比显得更加突出。但另一方面，任何文化作为一个较大的群体，其内部会包括许多小

群体，它们会因地域、种族、宗教、职业、社会阶层、生活方式等不同而具有不同的价值观、道德观和行为规范，这些小群体常被称为亚文化。就翻译而言，目的语文化同样由许多亚文化组成。正因如此，翻译标准即使在目的语文化内部也不是统一的，因为各亚文化对源语文本往往会有不同的认识，并且常会根据自己的需要提出不同的翻译标准。因此，即使是在同一历史阶段，目的语文化也会对翻译的理想解释度提出不同的要求和期待。亚文化之间常会为了翻译标准和策略等问题展开论争，试图论证自己的标准是合理的。当两种(或多种)亚文化势力相当时，就可能会出现同一历史时期两种(或多种)翻译标准同时并存的现象。但这种局面往往无法维持长久，因为经过激烈论争，总有一方会败万阵来，而另一方就占据了该文化的主导地位，掌握了话语权，这种文化就自然成了主流文化。这时，虽会出现各种翻译标准，但主流文化的标准往往会成为某一历史阶段的主要标准，其他标准则会受到主流文化翻译标准的指责。因此，说某个历史阶段的翻译标准是什么，其实是说某个历史阶段主流文化的翻译标准是什么。比如 19 世纪末 20 世纪初，我国主流文化对翻译的要求是通过意译(改译、译述)输入西方思想，30 年代是通过直译输入西方语言的表达形式，五六十年代则是通过意译使目的语文本具有与源语文本相似的文学性，但这并不是说，在同一历史阶段不存在其他翻译标准。

(四) 不同的读者对象需要不同的理想解释度

目的语读者是目的语文化的具体代表，也是通过目的语文本传递过来的源语文化的直接接受者，源语文化只有通过目的语读者的阅读才能在目的语文化中真正发挥作用。但目的语读者在目的语文化中并非统一的整体，作为目的语文化的成员，他们虽有许多共识，但也有很大差异，这种差异体现在年龄、性别、性格、智力、学历、语言能力、认知能力、审美情趣. 社会地位等各个方面。这些因素会不同程度地影响他们对翻译的态度，并间接影响译者在翻译过程中要参照的翻译标准和要采取的翻译策略。但在实际翻译时，译者不可能将所有因素都考虑进去，他只能选取其中一项或几项，将读者归类(多半是无意识的)，概括其共同特点，有针对性地确定翻译策略。即是说，在实际翻译中，译者面对的不可能是所有目的语读者，而是目的语文化的某个具有某些共同特点的读者群，这种读者群其实就代表着上文所说的亚文化，他们的视域就是该亚文化的视域。因此译者在每次翻译中实际面对的是目的语文化的某种亚文化，所采取的翻译策略实际上是由源语文本与该亚文化的视域差决定的。由于不同的亚文化与同一源语文本的视域差不同(见图 1)，所以它们会对同一源语文本要求不同的理想解释度，因此译者需要针对不同的亚文化采取不同的翻译策略。

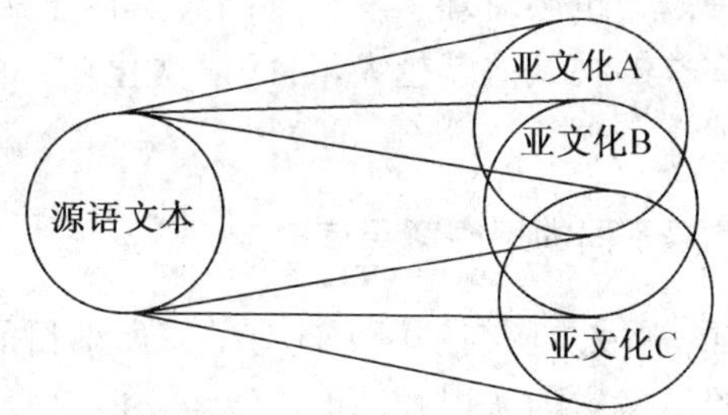

图 1　目的语文论各亚文化与源语文本的视域差

即是说，译者在确定翻译策略时已将假定的目的语读者视域纳入到自己的考虑中，而且正是按假定读者对翻译可能提出的要求或期待确定翻译的解释度的。这表明，目的语读者与源语文本的视域差同样会间接影响翻译中理想解释度的确定。若该视域差接近目的语文化与源语文本的视域差，翻译中理想的解释度就可与目的语文化作为一个整体所要求或期待的理想解释度基本保持一致，这时就可进行“正常”翻译，如将成人读物译成成人读物，儿童读物译成儿童读物，严肃作品译成严肃作品，通俗作品译成通俗作品等，即按目的语文化对该源语文本的整体态度来翻译。这时的翻译虽也有解释性，但其程度和目的语文化所要求的理想解释度会基本一致。

但若目的语读者与源语文本的视域差和目的语文化与源语文本的视域差相差较大，这类读者所期待的理想解释度就会偏离目的语文化作为一个整体所期待的理想解释度，这时译者就要对源语文本进行“不正常”翻译，即所谓改译。改译其实就是翻译加改写，是在“正常”翻译的基础上再进行改写。之所以要改写，是因为要满足某特殊读者群体的特殊需要和期待，如将成人读物改译成儿童读物，将严肃作品改译成通俗作品等。因此，安徒生的小说译成汉语时变成了童话故事，《西游记》译成英语时变成了猴王的故事，严复译《天演论》为吸引当时的士大夫而将译文“雅”化，使之透出“先秦子书的风味”（贺麟，1925；罗新璋，1984），傅东华译《飘》为了不“使读者厌倦”，“替读者省一点气力”，不惜将人名地名全都“中国化”，将“幽默的、尖刻的、下流的成语，都用我们自己的成语代替进去”，甚至将“冗长的描写和心理的分析”“老实不客气地整段删节”（傅东华，1940；罗新璋，1984）。不难想象，这种改译中的解释度常常是最大的。而且这种翻译常会因实际解释度过多偏离目的语文化期待的理想解释度而受到主流文化指责。但从译者锁定的读者对象考虑，这正好反映了某些特殊读者群对翻译的期待和要求，或者说，正是某些特殊读者群与源语文本视域差的具体反映。从这种意义上说，改译有其存在的合理性和必要性，它们体现的不是整个目的语文化所期待的理想解释度，而是目的语文化中某读者群所期待的理想解释度。

（五）不同语言之间的互译需要不同的理想解释度

目的语文化与源语文本的视域差还因翻译涉及的两种语言的差异不同而不同，从而导致不同语言的互译需要不同的理想解释度。比如英汉互译时，由于英语和汉语属于不同语系，存在很大差别，因此目的语文化似乎允许译者进行较大程度的解释；而日汉互译时，由于两种语言都有大量可资借用的汉字，很多汉字可直接移植而不会使目的语读者产生异样感，如“时间”、“天气”、“旅行”、“科学”、“社会”等词语在日语和汉语中除字形稍有区别外，意义上均可通用。这表明，翻译涉及的两种语言也会对理想解释度的规定产生影响：一般来说，两种语言相差越大，目的语文化与源语文本的视域差就越大，目的语文化允许的理想解释度也越大，反之亦然。

（六）不同的翻译方向需要不同的理想解释度

目的语文化与源语文本的视域差还与翻译方向有关。所谓目的语文化与源语文本的视域差，实质是指目的语文化对源语文本的认识和态度与源语文本自身蕴含的源语语言、思想和文化等方面的特征之间所存在的差异。不同的文化对另一文化的本质特征必定有不同的认识，比如，汉语文化对英语文化的认识和态度明显不同于英语文化对汉语文化的认识和态度，因此，同样涉及汉英两种文化，汉语文化与英语文化的视域差就不同于英语文化与汉语文化的视

域差。正因如此，英译汉时汉语文化期待的理想解释度会不同于汉译英时英语文化期待的理想解释度。英译汉时，汉语文化由于长期以来已对西方文化习以为常，对源语文本负载的西方文化往往较易认同和接受，因此二者的视域差会较小，汉语文化期待的理想解释度（相对于汉译英）往往也较小；汉译英则相反，由于英语及英语文化在相当长的时期内一直居于强势，而汉语及汉语文化相对居于弱势，因此汉语文化在西方的传播远不如西方文化在中国的传播那么广。相应地，汉译英时，英语文化对反映汉语文化的汉语文本的认识远不如汉语文化对反映英语文化的英语文本的认识那么容易产生认同感，即是说，英语文化与汉语文本的视域差比汉语文化与英源语文本的视域差要大，因而汉译英时英语文化允许的理想解释度往往比英译汉时汉语文化允许的理想解释度要大。

综上所述，与翻译密切相关的各因素都会影响目的语文化与源语文本的视域差，这些因素的改变都会导致目的语文化与源语文本视域差的改变，并最终导致人们对理想解释度的期待的差别。因此可以说，翻译中理想的解释度由目的语文化与源语文本的视域差决定，但由于视域差不是封闭而静态的概念。而是开放而动态的概念，因此，理想的解释度也不是封闭而静态的规定，而是开放而动态的规定。这就是哲学诠释学的动态翻译标准观。

四、视域差与实际的解释度

理想的解释度实际上不可能达到，译者给予源语文本的解释会或多或少地偏离理想的解释度。实际的解释度偏离理想的解释度，除了由于译者与源语文本的视域差外，更主要是由译者与目的语文化的视域差所致。

这里需要认识译者视域、公共视域和目的语文化视域的关系。目的语文化视域与公共视域是两个不同的概念。公共视域是指译者与某特定群体在某特定历史阶段对某特定事物共有的知识、观点、认识和态度，即公共视域是译者视域的一部分。若将“特定群体”上升为整个目的语文化，则公共视域是指进入译者视域的目的语文化视域，公共视域与目的语文化视域也是部分与整体的关系。三者关系如图 2 所示：

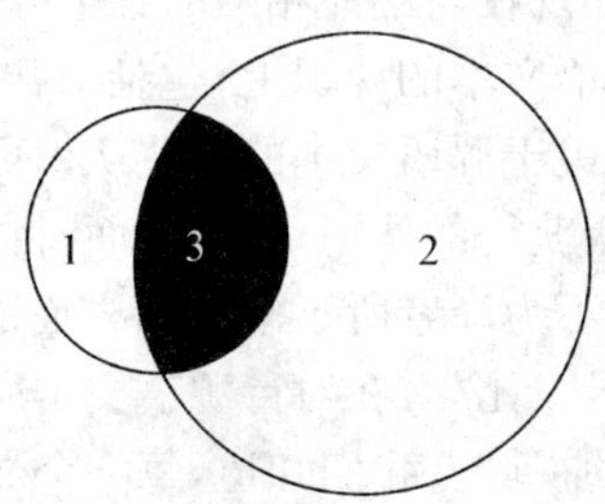

图 2　译者视域、公共视域与目的语文化视域的关系

（说明：1. 小圆为译者视域；2. 大圆为目的语文化视域；3. 阴影部分为公共视域）

可见，译者视域与目的语文化视域存在明显差别。首先，译者会因自己独特的个性和能力而从外界摄取独特的信息，形成独特的经验，这类信息和经验由于并不具有普遍性而暂时未获目的语文化认可，未能上升到目的语文化这一更高的层次，因而成了译者独有的部分，即译者的独特视域。其次，译者不可能将目的语文化视域的一切内容毫无遗漏地纳入自己的视域。

将外语译成母语的译者,虽然长期生活在目的语文化中,受其浸染熏陶,但由于受经历和能力的限制,无法将整个目的语文化纳入自己的视域,他所摄取的只是其中极小的一部分,而绝大部分是译者视域中所没有的;将母语译成外语的译者,生活在目的语文化的时间更短,从中摄取的内容可能更少,目的语文化中可能有更多的内容未能进人译者视域。由于这两方面的原因,译者视域与目的语文化视域不可避免地存在差异。

由于译者和目的语文化视域差的存在,加上译者与源语文本的视域差以及译者能力和翻译条件等因素的限制,而且有的译者还有很强的个性,总想努力表现自己的独特视域,甚至将自己的视域强加给读者或影响读者,因此,译者在翻译中的实际解释度常会偏离目的语文化期待的理想解释度。

但同时,译者有时也会努力使自己的实际解释度尽可能向着理想的解释度靠拢,因为实际的解释度一旦过于明显地偏离理想的解释度,便会在一定程度上受到目的语文化的惩罚,如出版社会要求译者对不合要求的目的语文本进行返工,甚至会另觅更理想的译者进行重译,译评家会对偏离行为提出批评等。因此,为了使实际的解释度尽量靠近理想的解释度,译者一方面会尽力抑制独特视域,另一方面则会努力扩大公共视域,将目的语文化视域纳入自己的视域中。译者正是通过这两种途径尽量缩小自己的视域与目的语文化视域的差距,从而相应地缩小实际解释度与理想解释度的差距,因为该差距越小,目的语文本就越符合目的语文化的要求和期待,因而越容易得到目的语文化的认同和接受。比如,严复译《天演论》"用汉以前字法、句法"使译文"雅"化是为了满足代表当时主流文化的士大夫的要求和期待(王佐良,1982),林纾译《巴黎茶花女遗事》因满足了目的语文化的期待而获得了"始料未及的"社会反响,从此一发不可休,"和翻译文学结下了不解之缘"(郭延礼,1999),刘重德时隔半个世纪重译《爱玛》,是为了使译文的语言满足当代汉语的语言规范,使当代"读者读了能懂而且读起来通顺"。(郑诗鼎,1998)

尽管如此,由于译者视域与目的语文化视域无法消除的视域差的存在,加之有些译者具有强烈的表现独特视域的欲望,因此,不同的译者翻译同一源语文本必定会得到不同的目的语文本。

译者与目的语文化的视域差体现在与翻译相关的各个因素上。

首先,这种视域差体现在对源语文本的认识上,包括对源语文本的语言、思想和文化等要素的认识。一方面,译者独特视域关于源语文本的某些认识可能得不到目的语文化的承认,或不符合目的语文化作为集体意识所获得的认识;另一方面,目的语文化视域对源语文本的某些认识可能未被纳入译者视域,因而不为译者所了解。两方面的原因都会导致译者与目的语文化在对源语文本的认识上出现差异。比如,在对待源语文本所反映的文化内涵上,译者很难将目的语文化所有的认识纳入自己的视域。我们知道,每一个文本都具有互文性,都是一种复杂的构成,它反映的远不只是字面含义,而是隐藏在背后的更为深刻的文化内涵。翻译时,每一个有责任心的译者当然应该尽可能地将这些内涵准确反映出来,但由于每一种文化在漫长的演进过程中变得十分复杂,因此源语文本中有些文化内涵在目的语文化中经过长期的集体积累已经认识到了,但作为个体的译者由于精力和能力有限而未能纳入自己的视域,这时译者的解释常会偏离目的语文化所期待的理想解释度。比如:

> What a piece of work is a man! ... and yet to me, what is this Quintessence of Dust? (Shakespeare, *Hamlet*)

对于 dust 一词，梁实秋译为“尘垢”，曹未风译为“烂泥”，孙大雨译为“尘土”，林同济译为“小粒黄土”，朱生豪和卞之琳都译为“泥土”。陈国华（1997）认为，只有“朱译、卞译才是确译”，其他译法都是误译，因为 dust 在此与 clay 有关，只能是“上帝用来造人的泥土”。这表明，将 dust 译为“泥土”尽管也是解释（因为中国文化既无上帝这个形象，更无上帝用“泥土”造人这个典故），但这种解释符合目的语文化所期待的理想解释度，而其他译文均偏离了理想的解释度。①

其次，译者与目的语文化的视域差体现在对翻译标准的把握上。传统译论强调忠实或对等，但在该忠实于谁、在哪方面忠实、在什么层次上忠实、忠实到何种程度等问题上却看法不一。即使译者对翻译标准的认识能与目的语文化达成一致，在具体操作中也会对同样的标准作出不同的理解和把握，并最终导致实际的解释度偏离理想的解释度。译者有时自认为“忠实”的译文却得不到目的语文化的承认，原因就在于此。

再次，译者与目的语文化的视域差有时还体现在译者的翻译能力和气质无法满足目的语文化的要求和期待。比如，我们常常要求译者应有很强的语言文化能力，甚至具备和作者同样的才情，在艺术个性和审美观等方面与作者旗鼓相当，认为只有这样才称得上合格的译者，但实际上，真正能全面满足这些要求的译者并不多。就译者的艺术个性和审美观而言，其实很少译者能与作者保持一致。这无疑会导致译者的实际解释度偏离目的语文化所要求的理想解释度。

综上所述，目的语文化与源语文本的视域差决定理想的解释度，但由于译者视域与目的语文化视域存在一定差异，因而译者的实际解释度常会偏离目的语文化期待或要求的理想解释度。

五、结　语

翻译研究中最突出的矛盾就是翻译的现实与理想之间的矛盾，翻译现实常常无法完全满足翻译理想。本文以哲学诠释学为理论背景，以笔者（2007）提出的“解释是翻译的普遍特征，但翻译是有限度的解释”的观点为基本前提，将翻译理想（或标准）假定为目的语文化所要求或期待的理想解释度，将翻译现实假定为通过译者的实际操作最终得到的目的语文本中所体现的实际解释度，探讨了翻译现实与理想之间的矛盾，试图找到一个更为动态、包容力更强的翻译标准，同时分析了翻译实践偏离翻译标准的根本原因。

① 为这并非陈国华个人的见解，而是得到了李赋宁、索天章、张中载、吴冰、王克非、傅浩、黄虹炜，周轩进、方平等学者的认可（见陈国华，1997），因此可认为是代表了目的语文化对 dust 的共同认识。而且，即使该观点暂时尚未得到专家认可，但若能言之成理，也应视为代表目的语文化对源语文化的共同认识，因为对源语文化的共同认识总是由少数人开始，再渐渐得到目的语文化认可的。

选文二　从艾柯诠释学看翻译的特性

张广奎

导　言

本文选自《外语教学》2007年第2期。作者张广奎是南开大学哲学系美学方向博士后、广东商学院外国语学院教授,研究方向为英语诗歌与诗歌理论、翻译理论、美学。

选文从艾柯诠释学的角度出发来探讨翻译现象和本质,以及在翻译过程中应当遵循的翻译原则。意大利哲学家安贝托·艾柯认为诠释涉及到关于文本的三种意图:文本意图、作者意图和读者意图;艾柯诠释学的中心思想是受原始文本限制的,许多时候表现为过度诠释。艾柯强调关联文本和历史情结的历史和哲学调查方法的重要性。翻译作为一种诠释也应当如此。翻译诠释受译者主、客观因素,甚至人类认知局限性的影响。科学的方法是用艾柯所倡导的历史和哲学的调查方法考察文本以及诠释、翻译文本。

近些年来,在翻译研究的热潮中,许多学派和学者在著书立说,打造着各自的理论框架,他们标新,他们也立异,从而使翻译研究进入了空前活跃的阶段。比如,从学派上有自从20世纪70年代以来在比利时和荷兰等西欧国家兴起的以探讨译文产生和作用为主的研究学派"翻译研究"(Translation Studies);从研究方法上,也开始从更大的领域对翻译进行跨学科研究;在大学里,国内已经有多所大学专门成立了翻译学院培养翻译实践和翻译理论研究的专门人才。但是,不管学者专家们多么沉迷于自己的(或经巧妙改造冠名以新的术语变成自己的)理论或观点,从翻译现象上讲都没有离开安贝托·艾柯(Umberto Eco)的诠释学范畴,作为意大利著名哲学家、文学理论家、美学家及符号学家的艾柯认为,所有的翻译都是一种诠释,而这种诠释在"作者意图"(intentio auctoris)、"文本意图"(intentio operis)和"读者意图"(intentio lectoris)(Umberto Eco, 1992: 25)(译者意图应包含在读者意图里)三者的复杂且又不稳定的关系中基本都表现为过度诠释。那么,在翻译实践中究竟如何才能尽量避免或降低这种诠释的过度性呢?本文将从艾柯诠释学的角度出发来探讨翻译现象和本质,以及在翻译过程中应当遵循的翻译原则。

1. 诠释的局限性

诠释学本来是指采用文法和历史的方法进行的圣经诠释与研究,后来经逐步发展与演变,它成了一种解释和理解文本的哲学方法。因此,哲学诠释学可以被看作是圣经诠释学的发展。它变成了人们诠释和理解文本的一种哲学方法,为各种各样的诠释活动提供了理论上的依据。

艾柯诠释学就属于此类,它的原则除了可用来诠释普通文本之外,也同样可用来诠释文本的翻译。艾柯诠释学认为，诠释关系到三种“意图”，即上文所说的“文本意图”、“作者意图”和“读者意图”。这三种意图在艾柯诠释学的框架中起着举足轻重的作用；诠释文本和翻译也必须先梳理清这三者的关系和相互作用。

那么什么是“文本意图”呢？以艾柯的小说《傅科摆》(Faulcault's Pendulum)为例，它的文本并不是所有普通读者都能读得懂的。要彻底理解文本的内涵，它既要求读者有一定的古典文学、欧洲中世纪历史和神话知识，又要求读者具有一定的现代知识，如计算机科学知识和很多诸如数学等跨学科的知识。文本对读者知识面的要求已经决定了一些读者肯定会中途失去阅读的兴趣而放弃阅读。所以，文本本身已经告诉了我们它所假定的或要求的读者类型。标准型的假定或要求就是文本之意图。进而，从作者和读者身上，艾柯又把他们进一步分为标准作者(Model Author)和标准读者(Model Reader)。标准作者事实上是真正持有文本意图者，他是文本的生产者，是从原主观作者升华出来的作者。而标准作者所期遇的读者就是标准读者。标准读者是想象中的，能够像作者原生产文本一样去诠释文本。他能成功地抓住标准作者赋予文本的意图。而确定文本的意图正是艾柯界定合理阅读范围的关键。然而，他也认为作者意图又是难以获得的，而读者意图又具有诸多可变的主观因素。于是，在艾柯的《诠释与过度诠释》(1992)一书中，作者这样论述到，“在不可获得的作者意图和可辩的读者意图之间有一种明晰的文本意图，这种意图被用来反驳站不住脚的诠释。”(Umberto Eco, 1979: 10)

虽然诠释并不是去发现一个文本当中的永恒意义，可是艾柯深信“被诠释的文本对它的诠释者们是存在着某种约束力的”，文本包含着某种结构的设计和符号的策略，这种结构上的设计或符号上的策略“鼓励并招引着某种阐释的选择”。即使一个开放的文本也服从这种普遍的规则，即文本已经假定了它的标准读者。这种开放的文本是一种信息沟通的或符号的策略。它表现出这样的一个事实，那就是，在它作为文本一旦生成的时候，它所指向的标准读者也随即生成定位。开放文本所表现的基本要素包括句法的、语义的和实用的。这些要素所指望的诠释只是诠释被生成过程的一部分。因此，一个开放的文本不管它是多么的开放，它都不应当被任意地诠释。

然而，当诠释者不尊重标准读者，也就是说，当诠释者不能尊重文本的符号策略时，他就超过了文本所设定的标准读者的预期指望。于是，他就自然地会进行一个异常的阅读。这种异常阅读是指有异于标准作者期望的阅读。这种异读其实就是“过度诠释”的一种形式，因为它因此产生了过度的符号指示，产生了意义的过剩，并从一定程度上没有尊重文本意图。从读者反映理论角度来看，这是读者参与了文本意义的重新构建——这也就是一个文学文本的内涵有时被译文“丰富”了的原因。

尽管文本意图的发现是艾柯诠释理论的一个中心组成部分，但是，他更热衷于保持这种意图三分法的某种关系。用艾柯的话说，通过尊重文本意图读者能把文本内部固有的这种不明确的结构加以具体化。如果读者不尊重文本，他/她就会产生对文本的异读。在艾柯的认识论里，文本意图和读者意图被认为是最有争议的。在某些情况下，艾柯是坚决否定经验作者的意图的。他认为这种经验作者意图是“不可获得的”，并坚持说“它从根本上是无用的。我们必须尊重文本，而不是作者或其他人。”(Umberto Eco, 1992: 78)然而，在其他情况下，艾柯也准许读者意图扮演次要的或从属的角色(因为读者即诠释者必然受到其种族文化背景的影响，下文将有所论述)。因此，在艾柯的诠释学里，他显然降低了经验读者的作用，经验读者在符号语言的舞台上只能绝望地扮演着从属演员(或二流演员)的角色。

那么,究竟什么是艾柯诠释的标准呢?艾柯认为,事实是开放的,具有潜在无限性,即它是一个"无限的符指过程"。但是,这样的一个事实"并不会导致诠释是没有标准的结论"。这种诠释标准是文本内部的或固有的,也是文本外部的或先验的。最难解决或有争议的还是文本内部标准。这些都取决于文本内部的第一个标准:一致性及其伴随的"同一原则"。据此,"一个文本是不可能支持相互矛盾的诠释的"。艾柯用文本内部一致性原则阐述到:"对于一个文本的任何诠释,如果它被同一文本内部的任一部分所印证,它都是可以被接受的。如果被同一文本内部的任一部分所挑战或质疑,对这个文本的任何诠释都应当拒绝接受。"(Umberto Eco, 1992: 66)他还认为,文本的一致性从根本上限定了诠释:在确立文本一致性方面,研究者应当搜寻那些有限的根据或一致性原则,而不是"那些数目不确定的相异的根据"或解释。重要的是诠释应当在这些限制(即这些有限的根据)的内部操作,而且应当避免这些矛盾与冲突。用原因所做的解释不应当是相异的而应当是一致的。第二个文本内标准是"经济"原则。假如一种诠释"不能更经济",这种诠释可能从诠释度上是可行的。这个标准是避免纯粹建立在过度或受限阅读基础上的猜测阅读的保证,因为它不允许信息的过度传递。

事实上,艾柯试图在文本内标准和文本外标准之间搭起一道桥梁。他认为,建立在文本"一致性"原则和"经济"原则基础上的诠释假设必须符合其他的证据,即他所指的历史证据。"经济"标准不适用于把文本孤立起来的情况。它必须着眼于文本产生的那个时期。这也就是说,文本内部标准强调的是文本诠释的历史特性,它必须依赖于诠释者对文本产生的历史背景的了解,通过历史的哲学的调查才能产生证据或文献。这种证据或文献才能使某种诠释性的推测比其他更合理。同时,研究者还必须把文本产生时词汇的语义,即把历史的语义考察进去。这样的语义才可能是与历史背景相关联的,包含这样语义的诠释才是可以被接受的,才是更接近文本意图的。

总之,文本的意图与施加其上的"文脉压力"潜在地限制了无限的符指过程与诠释过程。"有限性"是艾柯诠释学的核心。换句话说,艾柯诠释学的中心思想是受原始文本限制的。否则,无论如何都将是一种过度诠释。

而关于文本翻译,既然它也是一种诠释,那么在艾柯诠释学的框架下翻译的本质及特征又是怎样的呢?翻译又到底要遵循什么样的原则呢?

2. 作为诠释的翻译

事实上,艾柯诠释学的基本原则也同样能正确评价当代翻译研究的认识论精髓。就像他本人所说的那样,"翻译是一种现实化、明确化的诠释"。而这种"现实化、明确化"的翻译,要么是一种合理的诠释,要么就是一种过度诠释。特别要说明的是,过度诠释在大多数的文本翻译里其实是一种普遍现象,例子也垂手可得,比如复旦大学的陆扬先生在其著作《西方美学通史》的第二卷《中世纪文艺复兴美学》里提到了亚里士多德的《诗学》翻译的过度诠释问题:11世纪阿拉伯哲学家阿威罗伊的《亚里士多德〈诗学〉定解》后来证明大多是误解和曲解。(陆扬,1999: 460)

但是,如何使译文忠实于原文取决于艾柯的"翻译的界限",因为意义不是被译者(诠释者)任意创立或建构的。据此,翻译者的确需要严肃地考虑目标文本(译文)在哪些方面,又在多大程度上实现了或扭曲了原文本的结构或预期意义。为了达到如此的目的,译者应当能够区别什么是过度诠释,什么又是出自原文本潜在意义的合理诠释(翻译)。

在卡里(Henry Francis Cary，1772-1844，英国诗人和翻译家)的译著《神圣的喜剧》(也称《神曲》，*Divine Comedy*，但丁著)里，卡里主张翻译在本质上是一个文学上的，认识论的操纵过程。而所谓的“操纵”就是在译者意识的影响下的背离原文本意图的诠释；其实，也正是艾柯所说的“过度诠释”。而这种操纵又是很难避免的，因为读者(或译者、诠释者)的意图很难成为标准读者意图，诠释(或翻译)肯定会受到读者本土思想观念和意识形态的操纵。于是，操纵就成了译者意识形态对文本入侵的有意识或无意识的手段，译文也就成了译者操纵原文本的结果。这种诠释不管是故意的还是无意的，它都是一种曲解，是从很大程度上受译者信仰、理念、政治观点启发的对原文本的曲解。译者有意识扭曲原文的意思是为了推广或展示或施展自己的政治理念或意识形态(不排除有时候因为缺乏原文本背景知识无意识地误读)。在这种情况下，不管译文(或称诠释)读起来多么优雅，它都背离了原文，因为它终究是一种过度诠释。

在这个层面上，译者可以被说成是改写者。他们总是怀着某种个人的理念去诠释文本。这种理念不管是隐藏的还是表露的，不管是有意识的，还是无意识的，它在一定层面上是的确存在的。当然，我们不能排除如上文已经提及的译者误读(这里指无意误读)的可能性。于是，原文本和目标文本(译文)就有了不对称的符指，也从而导致了目标文本(译文)对原文本的背叛。因此，在翻译过程中曲解往往是固有的、内在的。艾柯的过度诠释是一种普遍现象，对原文本的不忠是每一个译者和读者不可回避的命运。翻译总是伴随“不对称关系。它从来就不是对等的简单的信息转换。因为它从根本上就是种族中心主义的”。所以我们常听说的“不可译性”是指在原文本和目标文本之间没有一种完全对称的符指系统。也就是说，只要民族是种族的，合理的诠释(或翻译)在很多情况下就不可能存在。

这重新把我们引向了艾柯认识论的核心——意义不是由诠释者任意建构的。由于各种主观与客观因素，诠释有它的局限性。翻译活动是一种高度的操纵行为，因为原文潜在意义被正确诠释的可能性是受到译者文化背景、知识、甚至目的影响的。也就是说，翻译不仅可能是，也不可避免地成为一种过度诠释的活动。换句话说，译者的意识形态的偏见造成了对原文的许多干涉，这种干涉体现在接近合理的解释上，也体现在毫不含糊的过度诠释上。而过度诠释的例子是随处可见的。

这里以英国诗人威廉·华兹华斯(William Wordsworth，1770-1850)的诗歌 *A Slumber Did My Spirit Seal* 为例，用艾柯诠释学来说明诠释和作为诠释的翻译过程和现象，以及翻译应当遵循的原则。诗歌原文如下：

A slumber did my spirit seal;
I had no human fears:
She seemed a thing that could not feel
The touch of earthly years.
No motion has she now, no force;
She neither hears nor sees;
Rolled round in earth's diurnal course,
With rocks, and stones, and trees.

一般来说，就此诗原文而言，读者阅读原诗不会产生太大的误读。因为，很显然，在文本的表面之下是关于死亡的主题。这种诠释也似乎更接近标准读者的诠释。作为经验读者，他/她不难发现诸如可指向死亡的 die，urn，corpse 和 tears 在文本里以某种方式被暗示体现。它们是 diurnal，course，fears，years，hears。但是，这些联想未必是华兹华斯的初衷，也就未必是标准读者的意图和文本的意图。或许，诗人使用这些词汇只是为了压韵，根本没有期望产生某种联想。所以，我们的诠释只是在原文本的基础上，由读者制造的一种假设。在这点上，我们似乎又可以回到艾柯的诠释理论上来——作者的意图是“不可获得的”，而读者的意图又是“有争议的”。这就是诠释的局限性，这一点在艾柯的《诠释的局限性》(*The Limits of Interpretation*)一书里有进一步的论述。

尽管诠释面临着这种尴尬，但诠释在人类文化的传播中又是必要的，也是不可避免的。语内诠释尚且如此，那么作为语际翻译的诠释又是怎样的呢？事实上，翻译作为一种诠释也是这样，也只能这样，或者说，由于语际符号的转换，翻译会是更加复杂的过程。还以以上同一首诗为例，从翻译的角度来看艾柯诠释学在翻译实践中的应用，以及我们应当遵循什么样的原则来从事这种无奈的诠释活动（这里的无奈是指不可回避的过度诠释和翻译在人类文化传播中的必要性）。那么，恰巧我们就从汉译本的《诠释与过度诠释》来摘录诗歌 *A Slumber Did My Spirit Seal* 的译文作为例证（译者在文中省略了该诗第一行的译文）：

（睡眠蒙蔽了我的心）
我没有丝毫人间的恐惧：
她已与万物同化
再也无法感受尘世的沧桑。
她一动不动，声息全无；
她已闭目塞听，
跟着大地在昼夜运行
连同那岩石，石块和树林。

在以上符号转换的过程中（即翻译的过程中），我们来看看译者的误读与过度诠释（此处并非刻意评论译者，只是把译文作为一个普通的诠释文本来论）。在原文的题目里，seal 的意思是 to close with or as if with a seal（以印，或好像以印封），或 close hermetically（密封）。但是，译者使用了“蒙蔽”一词来诠释它（这里指翻译）。其意义（虽然此处“蒙蔽”是比喻的用法）为“隐瞒真相，欺骗人”(hoodwink; hide the truth from; befool; befuddle; cheat; etc.)等等。显然，这是译者的误读，虽然可能是故意的，但也可能是无意的，也可能是不得不或无奈的选择。翻译后这两种符号是不对称的，其能指和所指自然也是不对称的。它通常不是标准译者或标准读者所期望的。同样，在原文中 touch 的意思是 the physiological or psychological sense by which external objects or forces are perceived through contact with the body or body's sense organs（通过与身体或身体的感官而感受到外部身体或力量的生理或心理感觉），这和被诠释后译文的“沧桑”（虽然更具有文采）同样具有信息不对称的关系。因为“沧桑”在汉语里的意思是“世事的变迁，人生的变化”(the changes of human life)。也就是说，译者背叛了原文和标准作者的意图。当然，如果站在他的立场上来说，翻译又“从来就不是一种对等的交流，因为它从根本上就具有种族文化特性”。因为在翻译过程中曲解是内在的、根深蒂固的，艾柯所阐释的“过度诠释”其实是一种普遍现象，而且在很大程度上可以说是不可避免的现象。对原文本的不忠是每一个译者和每一个读者不可避免的命运。“不对称关系”在诠释和翻译过

程中也是随处可见的。

3. 翻译诠释的原则

以上的例子说明了在翻译实践中诠释过程的复杂性。译者无论是有意识的，还是无意识的，甚至是潜意识的，都是在操纵文本，特别是当涉及到意识形态的问题时。那么，在翻译的过程中，是否应当遵循一定的原则呢？答案是肯定的。英国著名的翻译理论家波斯盖特(J. P. Postgate)把翻译的种类分为前瞻式(prospective)翻译和后顾式(retrospective)翻译。这里当我们强调诠释的科学性的时候，虽然无法从根本上避免“前瞻”的后果(这里用来指由于译者或诠释者方的主、客观因素所导致的过度诠释)，可是，我们可以把重点放在“后顾”上。译者(诠释者)所决定的译文的所指要尽可能遵循、忠于原文；否则就会造成能指和所指之间，以至于和读者方面文本的能指之间的更大的扩张。用艾柯的话来说，就是更大程度上的过度诠释。这种扩张和差异，或称过度诠释，(也)正如德里达(Jacques Derrida)所说的那样，是难以弥合的。不过，这种诠释的过度性至少是可以在一定程度上缩小的，这就要求译者尽量在彻底理解原文(及原文产生的历史背景)的基础上，尽可能地“后顾”——尊重原文。也就是说，为了确保诠释(译文)的准确性，“后顾”的原则是应当坚持的，因为原文本产生的历史背景在很大程度上决定着作者意图和文本意图(尽管我们不可能真正地获得)。于是，不管是从波斯盖特的“后顾”原则还是从德里达难以弥合的文本扩张，我们似乎都可以回到艾柯诠释学里所坚持的把文本和历史背景结合起来的历史—哲学的调查方法，这才是根本的哲学方法。

总之，由于艾柯所坚持的诠释方法和原则是从根本的哲学方法出发的，所以，他关于诠释学的思想在认识理论上是非常有效的，也是非常有力的。他关于文本权利的阐释在往诠释学的正确方向上前进了一大步(也正因为他的哲学回归)，读者和译者作为诠释者都不应当任意建构文本的涵义。他的诠释框架能比较接近完美地诠释原文本，并能有效地利用它来解释翻译现象和指导翻译实践。他的诠释学框架的优势在于，它是开放式的结构，它是根本的方法，具有能被进一步修订和发展的可能性，因为它是基于几条有价值的原则之上的：方法结构论(而不是存在结构论)防止了集权主义的诱惑；诠释的理性让人们意识到人类的局限性；把文本和历史背景结合起来的历史—哲学的调查方法意味着诠释者的任务从来就不是抽象的。尽管有它的局限性，艾柯还是给我们提供了有价值的诠释标准；没有这样的标准，文本描述和诠释将注定会是失败的，那将是一个完全主观的自我确定的话语。

然而，为了诠释文本或翻译，改善提高艾柯认识诠释学的功能也是有必要的，它值得进一步研究和思考。文本意图、作者意图和读者意图之间的关系是动态的、辨证的。虽然我们不能完全确定文本的意图，但是，关键要搞清什么影响着诠释的过程。正因为诠释是相对的，所以过度诠释就是绝对的。从某种程度上讲，翻译是操纵性的诠释，准确地说，就是过度诠释。因为诠释是有局限性的，也因为人类的认识也是具有局限性的，它应当是历史的。

当然，不能因为过度诠释的存在我们就不再翻译，问题是怎样翻译而不太过于过度诠释，或怎样翻译更接近标准作者意图和文本意图。那就是尽量考察文本产生的历史背景，也即上文所提及的多坚持“后顾”的原则。在意识到诠释有它的局限性的前提下，尊重史实，尊重作者意图和文本意图，从而使诠释或翻译更接近文本意图。

选文三　别样的语境　多样的阐释

——从解释学视角探究翻译理解中的多样性

杨晓斌

导　言

本文选自《外国语文》2011 年第 3 期，作者杨晓斌是四川美术学院教授，主要从事现代艺术、英美文学和翻译等研究。

选文着重从哲学解释学的角度展开对翻译理解的多样性问题的探讨，有助于我们更好地理解翻译的本质，从而有效地指导翻译实践。翻译就是从源语文本向目的语文本转化的过程和结果。这种不同语言间的转化过程也可理解为对源语文本的"解释"过程。翻译文本必然千差万别。影响翻译多样性的因素比较复杂，既有作品本身的语言文化环境和历史语境的客观影响，也有译者本身主观因素影响所致。译者影响翻译多样性集中体现在以下方面：作者与译者处在不同文化与历史语境中；译者身份不同会产生解释的多样性。在翻译原则和标准多样化的情况下，持不同标准的译者对同一文本就会有不同的翻译阐释，毫无疑问会产生阐释文本的多样性。

在人类历史的发展过程中，翻译一直扮演着十分重要的角色。操各种不同语言的人在交往的过程中必然会以口头或者书面形式实现语言的转换。当代解构主义哲学家和语言学家德里达认为，"翻译就是那在多种文化 多种民族之间，因此也是在边界处发生的东西"。其实质，翻译就是从源语文本向目的语文本转化的过程和结果。这种不同语言间的转化过程也可理解为对源语文本的"解释"过程。按照传统的翻译标准看，"阐释"要尽可能达到"信、达、雅"的理想境地。然而，译者在"解释"的过程中，因受历史时代、文化语境的客观限制和译者主观性等诸多因素影响，对源语文本的理解不会完全相同，必然会产生多样性，由此形成目的语文本的多样性结果。就理论上而言，通常，"一部作品译为另一种语言，必然存在以下三种情况：劣于原著，等值原著，优于原著"。这样，不同的译者对同一作品的翻译就会出现或劣或优或者等值的翻译。但事实上，从严格意义上讲，如世界著名的翻译理论家卡特福德和奈达等所谓"等值翻译"是不可能绝对实现的。等值于原著的译作几乎不可能，多少都会偏离原著，或优或劣。但无论翻译质量是优是劣，都反映出对源语文本的多样性理解和"阐释"特征，出现多样翻译文本结果。

鉴于等值论不是本文重点讨论范畴，姑且从略。为了更好地认识翻译过程中对源语文本解释的多样性，加强对翻译多样性本质的认识，本文着重从哲学解释学的角度展开对翻译理解的多样性问题的探讨。

1. 理想的阐释与多样的翻译文本

阐释是解释学(亦为阐释学)的核心。何为解释学？解释学(Hermeneutics)一词，源于古希腊神话中的信使之神赫尔墨斯(Hermes)，赫尔墨斯担当着向诸神和人间传达宙斯旨意的重任，并负责解释其意义，“对神谕加以解释而使其变得意义明晰”。因此解释学就与理解和解释密切关联起来。“理解”和“解释”便成为解释学的基本范畴。按照伽达默尔的说法，“解释学可以宽泛地定义为关于理解和解释文本意义的理论或哲学，是所有那些解释人们作品的人文学科的基础”。解释学的历史可以追溯到古希腊时期，在中世纪时期尤其应用在《圣经》的解释中。事实上，奈达也一直以《圣经》等翻译为基础和例证阐述翻译理论问题。在20世纪初，是哲学家海德格尔开启了现代解释学的大门，他使解释学发生了根本性的转向。解释学已不再是狄尔泰式的简单的关于心理学意义的理解，而是关于研究理解本身的本体论哲学。伽达默尔继承和发展了海德格尔的本体论阐释学，提出一系列构成阐释美学和接受美学理论基础的思想和观点，建立起一套对于文本意义的理解和解释的解释学体系，将文本置于阐释学的研究中心，构成阐释的基础。伽达默尔从现象学和解释学的角度对作品的本体论进行思考。他认为，开放性对作品的理解和诠释具有重要作用。开放性构成多样性，在开放性结构中，对一个文本或一部艺术作品里的真正意义的汲取是永无止境的，它实际上是一种无限的过程，也就是说对文本的理解和解释，是一个不断开放和不断生成阐释的过程。为便于更好地理解作品，他视作品为阐释学的核心，把作品放在与主体的欣赏关系中去阐释。因阅读和欣赏者的不同，对作品的语言理解也会显示出或多或少的差异。而我们的译者实际上首先就是源文本的阅读者和欣赏着，然后将源文本转换成目的文本，这构成了转换过程和翻译结果的多样性前提。

正如伽达默尔所说：“如果我们回想起解释学这个名字的起源，那么很清楚，我们所处理的是一种语言事件，是把一种语言翻译成另一种语言，因而也就是处理两种语言之间的关系。”在伽达默尔看来，从一种语言转换成另一种语言的翻译完全可以认为是一种阐释活动事实上，阐释是翻译的基本特征。译者翻译的过程亦为理解与阐释的过程。译者在翻译过程中冥思苦想，殚精竭虑，都希望对源语文本达到“理想的阐释”，但“理想的阐释”往往会因人而异，因为“理解并不是一种简单的复制过程，而是一种创造的过程……完全可以说，只要人在理解，那么总是会产生不同的理解”。正如有一千个观众，就有一千个哈姆雷特。因此，不难理解的是，翻译活动之后的目的语文本必然会五花八门、千差万别，不尽相同，意即译文不可能完全对等、丝毫不差地再现原文，必然会出现有距离的多样性文本，抑或优，为源语文本锦上添花，抑或劣，未能充分传达出源语文本的韵味 但也正是优劣共存的多样性理解和解释的多样翻译文本形成比较的前提条件，构成了丰富多彩的翻译世界。

2. 历史、文化语境差异和译者主观因素对翻译多样性的影响

总体上讲，影响翻译多样性的因素比较复杂，既有作品本身的语言文化环境和历史语境的客观影响，也有译者本身主观因素影响所致。由于翻译是不同语言之间的转换，转换过程中因不同译者的知识背景各异、理解能力所限、语言表达所需或误读所致等原因造成目的语文本的多样性。学贯中西，从事过大量翻译实践的钱锺书先生对此体会颇深。他认为“一国文字和另

一国文字之间必然有距离，译者的理解和文风跟原作品的内容和形式之间也不会没有距离，而译者的体会和他自己的表达能力之间还时常有距离。从一种文字出发，积寸累尺地度越那许多距离，安稳到达另一种文字里这是很艰辛的历程。一路上颠顿风尘，遭遇风险，不免有所遗失或受些损伤。因此，译文总有失真和走样的地方，在意义或口吻上违背或不尽贴合原文”。而译者影响翻译多样性集中体现在以下方面。

2.1 作者与译者处在不同文化与历史语境中

译者与作者通常不生活在同一文化环境中，或者同一历史语境里，译者和作者因文化与历史差异对作品的认知和感受不可能完全相同。尽管一些译者会千方百计，积极努力地查阅和研究作者生平、生活环境和写作习惯等有助于理解和“阐释作品的档案资料”，极力希望保持原作内容和风貌，然而遗憾的是，在翻译阐释中还是会发生译者在解读和阐释原语文本时同作者原意出现偏差的现象，不可能有一一对应的等效翻译，因为等效只是一个理想的效果，其实，原文和译文之间有着明显的文化鸿沟。例如，我们翻译莎士比亚，但我们不可能返回到莎士比亚时代；翻译希腊哲学，也不可能回复到古希腊时期。生活在不同时代的历史语境差异和生活在不同国家的文化语境差异显然会形成翻译的多样性，深深地打上不同文化背景和历史时代的烙印。

另外，鉴于源语文化对于目的语读者来说也可能是陌生的，或者说理解起来有困难，译者为了让目的语读者更好地理解作品，特意增添一些原文上没有出现的内容加以说明和解释，或者表明自己的观点。“比如，萧乾夫妇译《尤利西斯》时共加注释 6 000 余条，近 340 页，占正文的近 40%。之所以要加这么多注，是因为文本中空白和未定点太多，不加注不足以让汉语读者理解”。“凡在人们所说的东西不能直接被我们理解之处，解释学就开始起作用”。一方面是翻译时对原文的阐释，另一方面是阐释之外的解释。萧乾、文洁若夫妇在翻译时，采用“解码”的方式，对晦涩难懂的地方进行“解读”和“注释”。因此，译者要满足读者的需要，就要对源语文本进行阐释性处理或者改译。“之所以要改写，是因为要满足特殊读者群体的特殊需要和期待”。

2.2 译者身份不同会产生解释的多样性

众所周知，不同译者对同一源语文本会有不同的阐释，因此译者必然会在译作中留下“烙印”，形成自己独特的翻译文体与风格，导致翻译的多样性。

首先，译者身份不同是导致翻译多样性的重要因素。译者之间的身份差异包括内容较多，既有出生背景、生活背景、教育背景等不同、也有年龄、性格、个人偏爱、理解力、语言表达力等差异。以歌德的《少年维特之烦恼》为例。此作品自郭沫若翻译以来，“维特”热一直持续不断，并有多种版本问世。罗牧、钱天佑、黄鲁不、杨武能、侯俊吉、韩耀成、刘维成、胡其鼎等不同时代的译本构成了繁花似锦的《少年维特之烦恼》译文世界。由于译者的个性、爱好、气质、修养、经历等不同，以及各个译者中外文水平的高低有别，尽管他们殚精竭虑，都在努力地使自己的实际解释度达到他们理想的解释度，力争实现目的语文本对源语文本的完美再现，但实际情况是因他们对原著的个人理解和阐释显然不尽相同，译本的风格明显地呈现出很大的差异。

其次，翻译易于受译者主观情感因素影响。人们常说翻译是第二次创作。译者的主观情感在“第二次创作中发挥着巨大作用，译文常带有强烈的个人情感，使译文呈现出差异性。

例如：

The first elected Russian president, the man who declared what once was the world's largest nation, the Soviet Union, extinct, Boris Yeltsin resigned on December 31, 1999 after eight years in power.

作为俄罗斯第一位民选总统，作为宣布世界上最大国家——苏联——解体的一代巨人，叱咤俄罗斯政坛八年的叶利钦于20世纪的最后一天黯然辞职。

"对照原文和译文，我们可以看到，原文(英文版)用词客观、朴实；而译文(中文版)带有强烈的评价成分与浓烈的感情色彩。译者按照自己的经验与判断，增加了原文没有的评价意义，评价叶利钦为'叱咤俄罗斯政坛'的'一代巨人'，用带有伤感的词'黯然'来形容叶利钦的辞职"。这些带有强烈感情的词语实际表达出译者对叶利钦的称赞和惋惜之情。

此外，译者的个人偏爱和喜好也影响翻译理解的多样性。"在翻译的时候，如果译者选择与自己性情相近、阅历相似，风格相近的作品来翻译的话，译者就能和原作者产生共鸣，'性情相投'，'感同身受'，也就更能够调整其主观能动性"。译者在解释原作时能够更加自由地发挥，达到"传神"、"化境"之地步。如林纾在翻译时十分投入。翻译《巴黎茶花女遗事》时，主人公的爱情悲剧深深地感染着此时刚刚失去娇妻的他。他在鼻涕眼泪齐下的状态中译完了全书，成为风行海外的不朽之译作，其缠绵悱恻、哀感顽艳的恋爱故事打动和感染了大批的读者。郭沫若翻译歌德的《浮士德》，冰心翻译泰戈尔的《吉檀迦利》、傅雷翻译罗曼.罗兰的《约翰.克利斯朵夫》和巴尔扎克的《高老头》等神似甚于形似的优秀汉译本无不与译者对作品内容的偏爱和深切感受紧密联系在一起。他们以无法抑制的情感投入对原作进行了恰到好处的精彩阐释和合理演绎，使译文散发出强烈的艺术感染力。

对于莎士比亚的作品，从解放前到现在有多位译者都进行过翻译。比较著名的翻译版本也有多个。其中朱生豪、卞之琳、梁实秋和王佐良等人的莎翁译作都自有特色，各有秋千。由于译者的个人风格差异，这样就形成了与译者风格一致的不同翻译文本。但实质上是对同一原作的不同解释。

3. 翻译标准与阐释的多样性

翻译标准是翻译活动中的重要问题，不但影响翻译的质量，而且决定翻译的风格，与译者、读者和评价者都形成密切的关系。"翻译标准不仅是译者在翻译实践中遵循的原则和努力的方向，也是评价者用以鉴赏 阐释和评论译作的尺度。"在翻译原则和标准五花八门的情况下，不同的译者遵循的原则和持有的标准绝非相同，那么，持不同标准的译者对同一文本就会有不同的翻译阐释，毫无疑问会产生阐释文本的多样性。无论是严复追求完美、平衡相行的"信达雅"，鲁迅宁信而不顺，强调异化的"直译"，还是林纾、傅雷等追求神似、倡导晓畅明白译风的"意译"都在翻译实践中产生重要影响，为文本翻译构成多样阐释的前提。

在翻译过程中，就理论而言，持"信达雅"标准的译者力求在"信"、"达"和"雅"这三方面达到完美的平衡，唯恐失去偏颇。但在实践中，他们在阐释文本时，不可能完全能达到那样难以企及的理想标准的。再且，译者对"信、达、雅"的理解不同，在阐释中也会采用不同的方式和表达，造成译文本的多样性。同样，遵循"直译"或者"意译"的译者也是会对同一文本造成多样性阐释。以莎翁的戏剧翻译为例,目前公认的比较全面的莎士比亚戏剧译文有梁实秋和朱生豪的两大译本。比较梁氏和朱氏的译本不难看出他们对文本的阐释的不同。“梁实秋在翻译英语修辞格时用的基本上是直译,而朱生豪的译文则多为按汉语习惯的意译。”如此多样阐释的译本满足不同胃口的读者需求,领略和欣赏到多彩的译文世界。

巴比塔的倒塌,致使翻译成为人类相互交往中不可或缺的重要问题。翻译即解释,但并非任意的解释,而是有限度的解释。翻译的过程就是解释的过程。因受文化和历史语境的局限,受个人身份的影响和表达风格左右,虽然都希望达到“理想的解释”,尽可能保持源语文本风貌,但不同的译者对同一文本有着不同的解释,构成翻译文本的多样性。从解释学角度看,即或最神圣的《圣经》也因解释者的不同而存在多样的版本和不同的解释。因此,在翻译活动中,依据解释学观点,我们要在把握源语文本“精髓”的前提下,在一定的限度内,尊重翻译过程的开放性,理解和“容忍”多样性存在,正确地看待不同目的语文本与源语文本的“距离”,进入“百花齐放,百家争鸣”的翻译世界,达到缤纷多彩的繁荣目的,推动翻译事业蓬勃健康发展。

【延伸阅读】

[1] Eco, U. *Interpretation and Overinterpretation*. Cambridge: Cambridge University Press, 1992.

[2] Eco, U. *The Role of the Reader*. Bloomington & Indianapolis: Indiana University Press, 1979.

[3] Eco, U. *The Limits of Interpretation*. Bloomington & Indianapolis: Indiana University Press, 1990.

[4] 伽达默尔. 真理与方法. 洪汉鼎,译. 上海:上海译文出版社,2004.

[5] 伽达默尔. 哲学解释学. 夏镇平,宋建平,译. 上海:上海译文出版社,2004.

[6] 刘云虹. 解释的合理性:文学翻译批评的基础. 外语与外语教学,2002(5).

[7] 屠国元,李静. 距离合法性视角下译者当译之本的知情选择与情感同构. 中国翻译,2009(4).

[8] 王岳川. 现象学与解释学文论. 济南:山东教育出版社,1999.

[9] 谢天振. 作者本意和本文本意——解释学理论与翻译研究. 外国语,2000(3).

[10] 袁洪庚. 阐释学与翻译. 外国语,1991(5).

[11] 张隆溪. 道与逻各斯——东西方文学阐释学. 南京:江苏教育出版社,2006.

[12] 仲伟合,周静. 译者的极限与底线. 外语与外语教学,2006(7).

【问题与思考】

1. 诠释学中理解的历史性、视域融合和效果历史对文学翻译有何启示意义?
2. 艾柯诠释学的文本意图、作者意图和读者意图之间有什么相互关系?
3. 为什么说翻译是有限度的? 如何避免翻译中的过度诠释?
4. 如何理解“有一千个观众,就有一千个哈姆雷特”?
5. 译者影响翻译多样性集中体现在哪些方面?

第七章　文学翻译研究的哲学考察

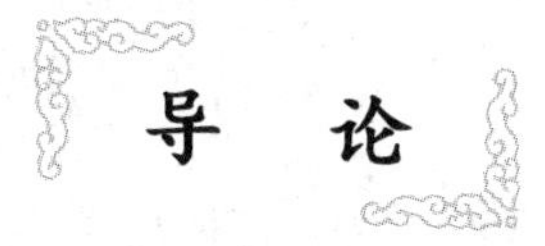

导　论

大致而言，翻译研究经历过三个时期或阶段：经验总结式翻译研究阶段、语言学派翻译研究阶段、后语言学派或语言学外翻译研究阶段。后一阶段不是对前一阶段的全部否定，而是超越。

各种翻译研究思潮或思想都有哲学基础。在某些阶段，翻译研究明显受超验主义、解构主义、怀疑主义和实用主义影响。超验主义翻译研究把原文意义看成是超越时空与超越语言的不变实体，并因此把翻译任务看成是认识这一实体、将它从原来语境中抽象出来、再“万分忠实”地用另一语言来传达出来。解构主义翻译研究认为原作身份是随着每次阅读或翻译发生改变的，文本意义由译文决定。没有翻译，原文就不复存在。怀疑主义置于翻译研究中，导致对翻译规律的质疑和否定以及对翻译主体的关注和重视。翻译理论的缺陷之一就是理论研究实用主义倾向强烈，实用性和可操作性成为研究者孜孜以求的目标。理论来源于实践并指导实践，但不能要求每一次理论研究，特别是基础理论或纯理论研究，都必须解决具体实践问题。理论应用，相对于理论主体来说，只不过是枝节；但是很多人却把它当成理论研究的全部。

20世纪初西方哲学发生的语言学转向使西方译界开始以理性的方式系统地分析翻译的语言学问题。钱锺书正是受西方哲学深刻影响的中国翻译家之一。他的翻译思想既吸收了中国传统哲学重“悟性”和整体观照的特点，又兼取了西方近现代哲学重理性和逻辑思辨之长。在西方各大哲学家中，休谟哲学对钱锺书启示颇深。休谟哲学体系中最重要的也是最具特色的部分是建立在怀疑论基础之上的因果关系问题。钱锺书在一定程度上接受了休谟哲学的因果观，他一方面提出“化境”为翻译的“最高境界”，另一方面又认为“化境”是“不可实现的”，这实际上与休谟承认外部事物的客观规律性的同时又认为这种客观规律性是超乎于人的理性认识之外有着同样的“怀疑”色彩。此外，西方阐释学也对钱锺书的翻译思想产生很大影响，他的“阐释循环”这一提法就是直接借自西方阐释学。钱锺书将“信达雅”中的“达”纳入“传达”渠道，契合了阐释学中所述的阐释的任务——“把诸神的旨意传达给凡人”；“把一种用陌生的或不可理解的表达的东西翻译成可理解的语言”。钱锺书对于翻译中“是”与“应该”之间存在不可否认的差距的感慨，在某种程度上而言也是以事实对理性中心主义者所描画的价值世界的颠覆。

运用翻译研究的哲学视角分析翻译现象有不少典型例子。例如，祖利军采用译者主体与“他者”的互动这一哲学框架对《红楼梦》中俗谚互文性的翻译进行了探讨。主体作为哲学范畴，与客体相对，指实践活动和认识活动的承担者。主体具有能动性、自主性、自为性等。能动性侧重于主体能力，表现为主体活动的自觉选择和创造；自主性侧重于主体权利，表现为对活动诸因素的占有和支配；自为性侧重于主体目的，表现为主体活动的内在尺度和根据。就《红楼梦》中的俗谚来说，它们基本典出中国古籍，其文化积淀博大精深，作为有中国特色的“他者”，在英译时也就很难找到对应的语言现象，其根本动因是译者主体与“他者”的互动关系。二者相互依存，既对立又统一。译者主体占上风时，互文性在译文中可以体现；“他者”占上风时，互文性在译文中难以体现。然而，译者主体与“他者”谁占上风与主体的知识水平有关。

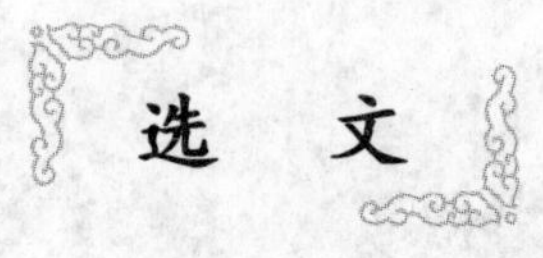

选　文

选文一　翻译研究的哲学层面考察

申连云　张少雄

导　言

本文选自《外语与外语教学》2005年第8期。作者申连云是长沙理工大学教授，研究方向为翻译学、比较文化；张少雄是中南大学外语学院教授，研究方向为教育思想史、翻译理论。

选文对各种翻译研究思潮或思想所蕴哲学基础进行概括描写。研究表明：在相当长的历史阶段，翻译研究明显受超验主义、解构主义、怀疑主义和实用主义等哲学思维的至深影响。翻译研究中的超验主义把原文意义看成一个超越时空、超越语言的不变实体；解构主义否定原作超验特性；怀疑主义质疑和否定翻译活动的客观性和规律性；实用主义要求每一次翻译理论研究都必须能指导翻译实践。反思翻译理论研究历程，有利于比较全面地认识翻译学，也有利于构建翻译学的层面。

1. 引言

科学研究不可能摆脱哲学的影响或制约，各种翻译研究思潮或思想都有哲学基础。翻译研究可以有形而下的考察，更应该有形而上的思辨。本文从哲学层面探讨翻译理论的拓展空间。

就哲学与翻译学的联系而言，以往的研究可分为三类：(1) 采用某种哲学研究模式或某种哲学理论解决翻译问题；(2) 从翻译视角探讨哲学问题；(3) 对翻译问题进行形而上思辨。(1)类是翻译研究常见模式。学科之间相互借鉴与引证有利于学科发展；但是，翻译研究在其他学科面前似乎不具备平等对话权，一旦与其他学科发生联系就处于臣服或受制地位。研究

者不是用翻译实际、即经验世界中的翻译现象，来验证及修正所举理论，而是用所举理论来评判翻译作品与规约翻译行为。这样，理论往往同实践背道而驰。(2)类研究跟(1)类方向相反，不是利用哲学理论来指导翻译实践，而是利用翻译现象来探讨哲学问题(如真值问题)。进行这种研究的主要是一些国外哲学学者，如 Davidson(1984)和 Quine(1996)等。在中国内地，这种研究尚属新领域，有钱冠连(2003)等少数人涉及。(3)类研究考察翻译本体论问题，主要议题有“翻译是什么”和“翻译是如何存在的”等；国内涉足者主要有张柏然、辜正坤和蔡新乐。张柏然(1998)认为上世纪译学研究由“(作)译者研究系列”、“(作)译品研究系列”和“读者研究系列”三大显流鼎足成势。蔡新乐(2002)注意到翻译哲学的形而上之维是翻译学研究的盲点，克服办法是从方法论向本体论转移。他还提出元翻译、反翻译、非翻译三个“新概念”，其中对元翻译论述最为卖力。“可以将元翻译视为一种事物变为另一种事物的那种潜在的可能性，语言的可能性或语言的吸收以及表达的可能性。”这种“转化或转变的可能性，即元翻译，普遍存在于人、文化以及语言中。所以，翻译的问题便不再是翻译学的问题或者不单单是一种技术性的、实用性的工具论问题，而是一种根本性的、与人本质相关的重大本体论问题。”辜正坤(2002)认为，在本质上讲翻译不但是语言转换，也是物质和精神交流(matter-spirit communication)；比如，所见东西转换成信号反映到头脑中，这就是翻译。因此，翻译是一切生物的存在方式，也是一切非生物的存在方式；因为在最高层次而言，翻译无非就是刺激与反应(stimulus-response)，即从刺激到反应的转换。翻译理论在最高层次上看就是关于存在的哲学。这种翻译学辜正坤称为玄翻译学(metatranslatology)。

在已有研究的激励下，本文对各种翻译研究思潮或思想所蕴哲学基础进行概括描写。研究发现，在某些阶段，翻译研究明显受超验主义、解构主义、怀疑主义和实用主义影响。

2. 翻译研究中的超验主义

创作凭空而出，而翻译却要对既在文本做转换处理。在人们观念里，译文忠实于原文是天经地义，“信”被认为翻译本质属性。再往前探究，不难发现这一观念背后隐藏着另一观念：原作意义一经诞生，就固定为“思想化石”，经历万古而不变——只要著作不失传；而这种观念的潜件(underlying wares)或潜行理论(underlying thesis)，是隐在的(implicit)或显在的(explicit)超验主义。

超验主义翻译研究，把原文意义看成是超越时空与超越语言的不变实体，并因此把翻译任务看成是认识这一实体、将它从原来语境中抽象出来、再“万分忠实”地用另一语言来传达出来；超验主义翻译批评，考察译作与原作的对应关系，具体表现为“枝枝叶叶的‘挑错儿’”。

我国传统翻译理论，从案本、求信，到神似、化境等，无一不在这个框架下演进与展开，无一不在寻找一种传达原作意义(或“精髓”或“精神”或“风姿”或“风采”)的超时空的理想翻译模式及理想译文。

我国大规模文字翻译活动发端于佛经翻译。宗教经典，自然被赋予永恒教义；译僧们“推经言旨，唯惧有失”，只好“案本而传”。道安的“五失本”与“三不易”，和玄奘的“五种不翻”等，不仅表现出译经僧人对经义的敬畏，更表现出译论家的价值取向。

翻译如此演进，无论是明清时期科技文献翻译，还是五四时期文学翻译，译家们都强调“如何去理解已存在的意义和发现其精神实质”(吕俊，2003)。道安提出“三不易”千多年后，严复发出相似感叹:"译事三难:信、达、雅。"严复三字诀一经提出,便被奉为"译事楷模"。虽然后来有人挑战严氏三字诀,而且"达、雅"受到很多人批判,但"信"受到一致肯定:"译文学作品只有一个条件,那便是要'信'"(陈西滢);"文学翻译的质量标准只有一个字——'信'"(常树枫);翻译标准是"准确性标准"(殿兴),等等(刘超先)。肯定"信",与"唯惧有失",构成跨时代呼应。

"五四"以降,译论家纷纷发凡"信"论,探讨如何"信"于原文、或"信"于原文什么等问题。诸家之中,"神似"说可谓一大显学。陈西滢、茅盾、郭沫若、闻一多、林语堂、朱生豪、傅雷等均有论述,而傅雷更以辉煌的翻译实践成为"神似"说代表。他认为凭借"艺术眼光",译者有能力认识先在意义,有能力把"隐藏在字里行间的微言大义""慢慢咂摸出来",有能力把"原文的意义、神韵全部抓住了"。林以亮(1984: 204-228)赞同 Savory 把同情心(sympathy)和直觉(intuition)等看成是良好译者应备条件。译者要具备对原文语言文字的理解力和对本国文字的操纵力以外,还必须具备感悟原作"气氛"的心灵,即同情心。只有这样,译者和原作者才能"超越了空间和时间上的限制,打破了种族上和文化上的藩篱",达到心灵契合。钱锺书"化境"说亦属显学,它要求译文"能完全保存原有的风味",译作是原作的"投胎转世"。在钱氏看来,认识和确定原作"风味"或"种子"不成问题,问题在于如何转换,如何保存。这也就是说,原作"风味"或"种子"是确定不变的;如果说有所变化,也是在转换阶段:"从一种文字出发,积寸累尺地度越那许多距离,安稳到达另一种文字里,这是很艰辛的历程。一路上颠顿风尘,遭遇风险,不免有所遗失和受些损伤。"

总之,认定不变原文及其先在意义,认定者自然会以译文"信"或忠实于原文为共同理想。理想达成与否,主要取决于能否用译入语"忠实"地传达先在意义。翻译艺术论认为决定于译者语文修养;翻译科学论则以为决定于译者是否穷尽相互转换的语言结构规律大概是传统翻译理论的视界与边线。

在很大程度上,西方翻译研究也没超越这一视界与边线。在西方翻译史上,直译与意译之争贯穿始终;不过,双方在忠实原文这点上却十分一致,异议只是哪种方法更能保存原文意义。西方超验主义翻译思想最典型、影响最大的代表是美国圣经翻译家 Nida。他从大量翻译实践中,发现民族文化和世界观差异,影响圣经教义传播;于是,他提出一个读者反应对等(equivalent reader's response)原则,目的是保证同一个教义在不同人群中有相同反应。对他来说,语言符号并不重要,只不过标签而已,重要的是符号在特定社会中的作用。他要建立教民和上帝之间的对话,而不是读者和语篇之间的对话。他认为原文意义不仅可以确定,而且可以翻译,可以让译文读者的感受和原文读者的感受"基本一致"。在他的翻译理论中,原文意义和原文意义给人的感受都成为从历史语境中抽象出来的、没有时间的永恒概念。译者有能力认识这个意义实体,并知道读者将如何接受。要传达这个确定意义,并确保所有读者反应一致,他有权增添、删减与简化。

在对待原作意义这点上,传统翻译理论都是超验性的;即便是具有现代翻译理论色彩的早期翻译研究学派(Translation Studies),也没有完全越出这一认识。虽然他们认识到翻译是一定历史时期的产物,必然受到该时期观念的制约;但是,他们仍然认为译者能够渡入原语文化中,通过对原语历史背景的研究,找到那个被命名(naming,即言说或语言——作者注)扭曲和模糊的作者意图,然后,采用陌生化策略(defamiliarizing device),选用当今社会译文读者感到陌生的语汇来实现对读者现有观念的解构,以此取得原文原有的效果和反应。(Gentzler, 1993: 157)其实,原作意义到底是不是不变实体,这很成问题。刘宓庆(2001: 74)指出翻译研

究中存在将客体简单化、直观化和凝滞化的弊端。凝滞化是指"将客体看作既没有共时变异也没有历时变异的对象，客体成为思想化石，忽视了客体本身可能存在的种种矛盾，也忽视了主体可能存在的矛盾"。翻译客体本身存在种种矛盾，翻译主体也存在"无限的可变性"，因此翻译应该不存在永恒的不变目标。

3. 翻译研究中的解构主义

超验主义赋予原文的种种属性，在存在主义思想大系中，基本上不被认可。存在主义试图提示人的本真存在，并以此来提示一切存在物的存在结构和意义。存在(existence)或在(being)，没有确定意义，也没有统一意义；存在或在的基本意义，是意识对象在意向活动中的显现。Heidegger 认为"在"的意义，与此在(Dasein)，即人自身密切相关，每个人领会的"在"总是他自身的在，因此，"在"是个别的，具有"我的"属性。作品，作为存在或在，确定意义与统一意义都是缺席的；所谓的意义，不是公共认知与普遍属性，而是私人意指。站在存在主义，特别是 Heidegger 立场上看翻译，原作不具备确定意义与不变意义，译文之"信"因此没有逻辑理据。

存在主义对超验主义原文观及原文意义观，应该说已经是巨大的解构和反动。然而，在解构主义创始人 Derrida 眼中，存在主义意义观仍然没有摆脱超验主义藩篱，Heidegger 的"在"只不过是超验主义的在，在的意义只不过是超验主义意指，因为《存在与时间》中关于在的问题是"在超验主义时间地平线的基础上提出的"。

在否定原作超验特性这点上，解构主义比存在主义更明确、更直接、更接近翻译理论。解构主义理论认为原作没有固定身份，原作身份是随着每次阅读或翻译发生改变的。文本意义不由原文而由译文决定。原文在历史长河中存在下来，不是由于自身具有固定品质，而是由于译文包含种种品质。没有翻译，原文就不复存在。

Derrida 认为翻译不是把确定意义渡过语言疆界，因为原文中不存在一个可以把握、认识和理解的固定意义或身份(identity)，谈不上固定意义复制或重现。原文身份非固定化、原文意义缺席和翻译非复制等观点，是 Derrida 解构主义翻译理论的基石。对他来说，译文同原文不是派生关系，而是共生关系，相互补充、相互限定。译文和原文分属两串不相关的表意活动。一切都是处于流变之中(at play)，无法界定、谈论和表现。传统翻译理论设定一个能够移植到另一表意系统的纯粹或固定意义，解构主义否认独立于语言之外的深层结构和意义，认为翻译时，译者看到或听到的只有语言。语言并不指向语言外部事物，而只指向语言本身，翻译转换中两种语言都处于两条相互影响、相互补充的语言链上。表意符号链无限倒退、延宕，犹如无边线棋盘(bottomless chessboard)。

解构原作也意味着解构原作者。不是原作造就译者，而是译者创造原作，这是解构主义观点之一。超验主义翻译理论赋予原作原生地位，肯定原作神圣地位；解构主义理论与此大相径庭。解构主义认为作品不是作者灵感的产物，而是社会的产物。创作行为是一种复杂行为，不能简化成作者个人行为。作者实际上不是独立个体，而是多种主观立场的复合体，是由多种社会因素决定的复合体。文本创作或生产(production)，不由个体意识进行，而由时代进行，是时代话语创造(create)作者，作者消解在自己参与产出的文本中。作者不是语言使用者，不独立语言之外；作者存在于语言之中，受到语言控制。作者的消解使话语成为自身主体

(subject)和权威(authority),并自我言说与自我演进。作品中,不是作为人的作者在说,而是语言在自述(speaking itself),并进行自指(self-reference),人只不过是在听。人不是什么都能听到,因为语言中有一些无声(mute, silent)的东西或意义,在言说发生时被掩盖。语言这种无声之面,Foucault 称为"他者"(the other),Derrida 称为"遗迹"(trace)。"他者"是意识思维的盲区(blind spot, dark region),伴随思维发生而发生,如影随形,不声不响。它是能指和所指间的空白,既在又不在,无法听见(inaudible),无法把握(grasp)。它永远无法像现象一样呈现出来,因为它总在运动、延异(defer and delay),一旦有人试图阻止它的运动,用言辞把它确定下来,它就扩散、蒸发,还没抓住它,它就已像回声一样消失。

在 Derrida 看来,考察语言被言说掩盖的遗迹,最好的领域就是翻译。译者在选用词汇时,发现语言间同义词也有细微差别,"正确"翻译和精确复制也会带有不同于原文的意义。这是语言的局限,一个两种语言都无法达到的灰色地带,一个既在又不在的无声意义或思想。一旦译者下笔,这种无声思想就会被选定的特定词汇延异和消除。

正因为语言具有这样无声特性,翻译不仅仅是去确定不变意义,去划定文本疆界,也要为遗迹运动(the play of traces)留下空间,为变异开辟道路。译者的任务是通过变形(transformation)给原作赋予生命,让它在原作者力不能及的时间和空间生存得更好、更长久。同时,通过延伸原作,译者赋予语言新生命。

解构主义者本意似乎不是提出翻译理论,只是想"利用"翻译来考察语言性质,"利用"翻译表明在文本翻译中人们最能接近和体会语言的变动特性,"利用"翻译使人们理解他们的核心概念"延异"。然而,这种对语言和翻译本质的思考对翻译理论非常重要,因为它打破超验主义一统天下,让翻译理论从"忠实"与"对等"等框框中解脱出来,从而获得深化和拓展。

有人将解构主义看成是一个翻译理论流派,更多的人不承认它是一种翻译理论。无论是自发的翻译思想,还是自觉的翻译学说,它已经实实在在为翻译理论增加了新维度和新发展空间。

4. 翻译研究中的怀疑主义

解构主义挑战和解构超验的不变意义,怀疑主义质疑和否定客观性和规律性。相当多的人认为自然界事物运动存在规律性;怀疑主义代表人物休谟却认为自然界并没有规律,认为所谓规律只是认知者的心理期待和联想。怀疑主义另一位代表康德也认为,普遍规律性不是外在世界自有的,而是认识主体给予自然的,即人为自然立法。

怀疑主义置于翻译研究中,导致对翻译规律性和客观性的质疑和否定。表现有两种:一种是对翻译规律的质疑和否定;另一种是对翻译主体的关注和重视。前者表现在翻译研究艺术论和科学论争论中。科学论认为翻译是科学,因为翻译活动中有一定规律可以遵循,比如英汉翻译中动词、冠词、定语从句等,翻译都有一定规律。只要对两种语言进行足够对比分析,某一方面规律就可以建立起来。把两种语言结构上的规律都建立起来后,翻译学也就因此建立起来,机器翻译也就变成事实。Nida 在 60 年代就是致力于建立起这样的翻译科学,这一意向从他著作标题 *Toward a Science of Translating* 可以看出。他(Nida, 1964)试图建立关于翻译转换活动(translating)的科学,一种探索从语言到语言的转换以及从表层结构到深层结构的逆转换的科学。然而,这种经验行为不可预测。Nida 的翻译科学理想给中国翻译研究策略和模式带来深远影响；Nida放弃科学论主张后，中国很多学者依然在执着地追求着翻译科学。据张经浩介绍，近年在中国一次全国性翻译理论研讨会议上，由于无法说服反对派，有位翻译界名人号召鼓掌通过“翻译是科学”的主张。

如果说翻译科学论有几分对流行语言学的攀附、有几分矫情的话，那么艺术论则要实在得多。杨宪益谈到自己一生翻译经验和体会时说：“我个人是从事文学翻译的，却觉得从搞文学翻译的角度来说，说翻译是一门科学，不如说它是一种艺术，或者说是一种技巧。”翻译科学论随着语言学发展而呼声日盛，一度独占翻译理论阵地。就在这种形势下，艺术论者表现出极大勇气。劳陇(1996)站出来，要“揭破翻译(科)学的迷梦”，号召人们“丢掉幻想，联系实际”。吕俊(1999)在世纪之交，对翻译研究的出路进行冷静思考：“这些纯语言学的操作追求的是一种分析哲学所谓的精确性、唯一性以及确定性。文学翻译离不开艺术，何况文学作品是一种虚构性质的东西，不是一种真理的追求，而恰恰是一种模糊性、多元解阐性以及不确定性。也就是说人们必须在文学研究中摆脱科学主义的束缚。”许渊冲(1999，2000)不仅坚持艺术论立场，还针锋相对提出“1＋1＝3”和“竞赛论”或曰“优化论”等理论主张，以否定翻译的规律性。艺术论者反对翻译是科学的主张，进而质疑和否定语言学派一切翻译理论。语言学派翻译理论以克服语言系统间结构对立为目的，忽略语言符号的语用意义和文本的社会与文化语境，研究所得翻译技巧和翻译规律在一定语境中适用，在另一语境中往往不适用。这导致翻译理论话语众说纷纭、莫衷一是。科学论者号召以通过议案或提案的方式来解决学术争议，也就成为一种必然。

翻译研究中怀疑主义另一种表现是对翻译主体、主观性的关注和重视。怀疑论实际上是一种人本主义副本；借着否认外部世界的客观确实性，怀疑论者希望把人的思想引回到人本身的存在上来。Baker(2003)指出，当前包括翻译研究在内的学术界的一个总体特征是关注主体或主观性(subjectivity)，承认研究者主观性对研究阶段进展和研究结果的影响。译者，作为跨文化交际主体，不是超然于两种文化的旁观者；翻译作品的形成自然受译者思想观念、知识水平甚至心理状态等因素影响。要想达成对翻译全面认识，译者主观因素必须纳入研究者考虑范围。

怀疑主义在翻译研究领域的两种表现都存在内在必然性，对客观规律性的否定和摧毁必然导致对主观性和主体的肯定和建构。前者表现为对翻译理论和翻译学的否定和鄙视，后者却是对理论(或纯理论)和翻译学的极大重视和推崇。前者反对翻译学，后者提倡翻译学；但是，两者不是成对立，而是一致，一致于否定翻译活动客观性和规律性的。前者是艺术论，后者并非翻译科学论。科学论倡导翻译是科学，坚持认定翻译活动是科学，其根据是翻译转换过程中有规律可循。怀疑论者认为翻译是科学，是指翻译是一门独立学科。在这里，“科学”的内涵悄悄地发生改变。艺术论和科学论合流，是翻译研究的飞跃，是学科走向成熟的信号。

5. 翻译研究中的实用主义

上文提到翻译科学论者提议举手表决通过“翻译是科学”的案例。这个案例反映出我国翻译界的窘迫状态：既没有权威，也没有确切知识，有的就是意见纷呈、答案对立的问题。最令人尴尬的是，在改革开放、翻译需求急剧增长的形译理论“无用”。不知情者对翻译理论或翻译学表现出冷淡和蔑视。翻译学者们则企图通过建立翻译学来提升学术地位；事与愿违，这种做法只从反面加强反对派信念。否定翻译理论的见解在 20 世纪 90 年代曾盛极一时，很多人宣布过翻译理论的命运：翻译研究进入死胡同，翻译学是幻想和迷梦。Nida 本人的转变更成为人们否定翻译学的有力证据。到如今，反对派依然振振有辞："到底应该根据理论来检验实践，还是根据实验来检验理论呢？换句话说，好的译文如果不符合理论提出的标准，应该修改的是理论还是译文？"（许渊冲，2003）面对此种质问，有人低头承认：应该修改理论。那么，翻译理论的缺陷到底在哪里呢？

翻译理论的缺陷之一就是理论研究实用主义倾向强烈。实用性和可操作性成为研究者孜孜以求的目标，可是事与愿违，理论往往跟实践背道而驰。比如"翻译单位"研究，巴尔胡达罗夫从现实的翻译行为或作品中发现翻译单位可以是语篇、句子、词组、词甚至词素和音位。中国学者先是将巴氏理论引进，接着是不满足于以翻译现象为研究对象的客观描写，纷纷从翻译以外的理论出发，论证对于某一层级翻译单位的偏好，"谈任何翻译活动中都必须使用何种层次的翻译单位。"（彭长江，2000）这里，研究的初衷是直接指导翻译实践，让人照着葫芦画瓢，有法可依。然而，研究不是以现实翻译现象的全面描写为基础，而是靠某一时髦理论模式和少数孤立例句来论证个人想法；因此，所得理论缺乏普适性：在一定语境中适用，在另一语境中不适用。对实用性的追求，恰恰沉沦为导致翻译理论跟翻译实践脱节、导致翻译研究话语相互矛盾与尖锐对立的重要原因之一。

理论来源于实践并指导实践，但不能要求每一次理论研究，特别是基础理论或纯理论研究，都必须解决具体实践问题。语言学不用来指导人们说话和写作，美学不用来指导人们穿着打扮，翻译学也着力于解决一时一地翻译转换问题。总体而言，理论用于指导实践，但是，理论研究与理论应用是两次行为。理论研究是一次完整的、自足的行为，以自身为目的；应用是它数年、数十年甚至数百年之后的另一次行为。Toury（2001：2）说："翻译学，作为一门经验科学，应用只不过是它向外部世界的延伸。"也就是说，理论应用，相对于理论主体来说，只不过是枝节；但是很多人却把它当成理论研究的全部。

与国内翻译界相反，国外翻译界是完全另一番景象，翻译研究深度和广度不断扩大，出现令人激动的繁荣局面。20 世纪 80 年代，也就是我们"翻译是科学还是艺术"争论正浓时，翻译成为语言学、文学、历史学、人类学、心理学、经济学等多种学科的研究对象，翻译研究成果广泛应用于诸多学科研究中，翻译学成为一门独立学科，获得和其他学科平等的地位。人们不仅用其他学科理论来观照翻译问题和翻译现象，而且从翻译出发、用翻译视角来审视和解决语言学、文学、心理学等领域问题。比如 Hatim（2001）就认为：只有仔细考察从一种语言转移到另一语言、从一种文化转移到另一种文化时，某语篇发生的变化，才能对该语篇有正确的和全面的认识。即便是在古代，在翻译框架内的语言研究也是卓有成效的。德国著名语言学家 Humbolt 认为一个语言民族的语言跟他们的精神是同一的，语言以及构成语言的词汇是一个语言民族对现实世界的独特反映；因此语言之间的区别不是声音和符号，而是世界观的根本不同。站在这种哲学立场上，他认为翻译是不可能的，"所有翻译都是企图完成一个无法完成的任务"。然而事实上，翻译却实实在在地进行着。为解决这种二律背反，Humbolt 对语言进行辨证分析，为后来建立语言二分观奠定基础（Wilss，2001：34-36）。可以说，是翻译事实或翻译现象让 Humbolt 初步认识到语言和言语的区别。Gentzler（1993：1）在指出翻译对文学的重要性时说："尽管学术界把翻译学视为一门边缘学科，但是在文学研究领域翻译理论却是处于中心地位；在一个各种文学理论纷呈的历史时期，越来越离不开翻译理论。"Bassnett（1993：

160-161)在论述比较文学和翻译学时说:"当比较文学还在争议它是否能看成一个学科时,翻译研究已经大胆地展示它是一个学科。应该重新审视比较文学和翻译研究之间的关系了,而且,应该有新的开端了。在比较文学与翻译研究的关系中,要改变力量平衡,把翻译研究看成合作伙伴,比较文学不再处于控制地位。在女性研究中,在后殖民理论中,在文化研究中,跨文化运作已经整体地改变文艺研究的面貌。从现在起,我们应该把翻译研究看成一个主要学科。"

在多学科的背景中和在多学科的关系中,审视翻译与进行翻译研究,的确是一种新的开端。这种新的开端,应该预示着实用主义翻译研究的终结。

大致而言,翻译研究已经历过三个时期或阶段:经验总结式翻译研究阶段、语言学派翻译研究阶段、后语言学派或语言学外翻译研究阶段。每一阶段都在一定历史语境中展开,或多或少受到当时学术气候影响。后一阶段不一定是对前一阶段的全部否定,而是超越。

Baker 指出当前包括翻译研究在内的学术界的另一个特征是普遍反思风气及元理论(metatheory)兴趣。元理论即理论的理论。本研究不是讨论某种翻译问题,而是宏观探讨各种翻译思潮及它们的哲学背景与哲学潜件;这样做,一方面是元理论兴趣所致,另一方面是想寻找翻译研究层面构架的拓展空间。

选文二　论钱锺书翻译思想的西方哲学基础

蓝红军　穆　雷

导　言

本文选自《外语与外语教学》2009 年第 12 期。作者蓝红军是广东外语艺术职业学院副教授、博士生,研究方向为翻译学研究;穆雷是广东外语外贸大学教授、博士、博士生导师,研究方向为翻译理论、翻译教学。

选文尝试性地探讨西方近现代哲学对钱锺书翻译思想的形成产生的影响,发现他的翻译思想中有着休谟哲学和哲学阐释学的基础,也体现了他对西方理性中心主义思想的反拨。钱锺书的翻译思想吸收了西方哲学的合理元素,又有着深厚的佛道渊源和辩证内涵。休谟哲学体系中最重要的也是最具特色的部分是建立在怀疑论基础之上的因果关系问题。钱锺书一方面提出"化境"为翻译的"最高境界",另一方面又认为"化境"是"不可实现的",这实际上与休谟承认外部事物的客观规律性的同时又认为这种客观规律性是超乎于人的理性认识之外有着同样的"怀疑"色彩;阐释学所关心的问题总是与翻译学所关心的联系十分紧密,"阐释循环"论是钱锺书重要的文论思想。钱锺书的"不隔"说的内涵与海德格尔思想的契合体现出了中华文化的传统思想融会、融化最新动向中的西方现代哲学的可能性。钱锺书对于翻译中"是"与"应该"之间存在不可否认的差距的感慨,在某种程度上也是以事实对理性中心主义者所描画的价值世界的颠覆。

1. 引言

钱锺书一生倾注于学术研究，撰写了一系列视野广阔、识见独到、议论精湛的极富思想原创性和学术开拓性的论著，使得"钱学"研究成为中国现代学术史研究中的一个重要课题。作为"钱学"的一个重要组成部分，钱锺书的翻译思想在我国译论史上也占据着重要的地位。他论述翻译的文章主要有：1963 年 3 月写的《林纾的翻译》(初载于 1964 年 6 月《文学研究集刊》第一册)，1981 年重写的《汉译第一首英语诗〈人生颂〉及有关二三事》(初载于 1982 年香港《抖擞》第 1 期)，1979 年《管锥篇》(中华书局)中《译事三难》、《翻译术开宗明义》、《译诗》、《译音字望文穿凿》等几则札记。钱锺书对翻译虽然没有鸿篇巨制的探讨，但他对于翻译的重大问题于《谈艺录》、《管锥编》、《七缀集》等著作中有着精辟的论述；郑延国(2003)发现钱锺书对翻译的灼见还出现在其诗和诗序之中。钱氏可谓全方位地论及翻译的性质、方法、规则，以至翻译中的文化与社会功用等问题，他最具代表性的译论是在译界如雷贯耳的"化境"说，人们将之和傅雷的"神似"论一起合称为中国传统翻译思想的"神话说"。

一代鸿儒的翻译思想自然引起了学界极大的关注，学者们多围绕"化境"开展研究：对"化境"进行文字发生学意义上的语义诠释；争论"化境"是"翻译标准"还是"翻译理想"；结合"化境"开展翻译批评；探讨"化境"的美学价值；批判"化境"的虚无神秘，等等。此外，还有少数学者对钱氏翻译思想的现代性意义进行了挖掘，如蔡新乐、黄汉平将钱氏翻译思想与西方解构主义联系起来考察，认为"钱锺书的翻译思想从根本上来说是反传统的，他比西方以德里达为代表的解构主义翻译学派更早地形成了一种中国式的'解构'翻译思想"。无疑，这些研究深化了我们对钱氏译论的认识。

钱锺书翻译思想之形成是在 20 世纪中国这一特定的历史时空中发生的，社会结构的剧烈变化，中西文化的冲突碰撞，传统学理与现代思潮的风云流变，不可能不对学问纵贯古今、会通中西文化的钱氏带来影响。他的译论看似集中在一个"化"字之上，实则蕴意深远、博大精深，译界对其"化"字的长期多样性解读便足以证明。他的翻译思想既吸收了中国传统哲学重"悟性"和整体观照的特点，又兼取了西方近现代哲学重理性和逻辑思辨之长。从这个角度而言，已有的研究还不够全面和系统，基本没有涉及其翻译思想之所以形成的哲学基础以及其所反映出来的文化意识。中西哲学思想和文化在钱锺书身上产生的影响以及他对之的接受、批判、继承与反思都值得深入地研究，据此，本文拟尝试性地探讨西方近现代哲学对他翻译思想的形成产生的影响，希望可以提供管窥钱氏翻译思想的另一个视角。

2. 休谟哲学对钱锺书翻译思想的影响

钱锺书青年时期曾留学欧洲，精通多国语言，熟读西方经典，并一直十分关心世界各国新事物新思想，他"在一定程度上凭借着西方思想资源，实现了对传统士大夫哲学、文学思想及其治学方式的超越。"(徐庆年)钱锺书对西方哲学有着浓厚的兴趣，西方哲学史上的家家户户他几乎都"上门做过客"，甚至"曾有过研究西洋哲学的念头"(党圣元)，他曾发表过《一种哲学的纲要》、《大卫·休谟》、《休谟的哲学》、《约德的自传》、《旁观》、《作者五人》等有关哲学方面的文章，分别讨论了英国哲学家休谟的思想，分析了英国新实在论者摩尔、新黑格尔主义者布拉德莱以及罗素和美国实用主义者詹姆斯、批判实在论者桑塔亚那等人的文章特色。他甚至在 30 年代当西班牙哲学家加赛德正在著述之时就论述过其思想，在 1947 年发表评论辨析了英文的"存在主义"一词，提到了雅斯贝尔斯 1938 年出版的《生存哲学》、萨特的《存在与虚无》、卡缪的《希齐夫对话》以及克尔凯郭尔、海德格尔等人的著作。甚至连我们现在所说的解构主义的"解构"(deconstruct)一词，最早还是钱锺书应人之请翻译的。

在西方各大哲学家中，钱锺书对休谟有过较深入的研究，休谟哲学对钱锺书也产生了很大的影响。在钱锺书撰写过的为数不多的书评中，有关休谟的就有两篇：评莱格的《大卫·休谟》和《评莱尔德的休谟的哲学》，分别刊载于 1932 年 10 月 15 日和 11 月 5 日的《大公报 世界思潮》。从书评看，"钱锺书对休谟哲学的渊源实质、特征以及学术个性都有深入的解和把握，并对休谟哲学研究史也相当熟悉"。

休谟哲学体系中最重要的也是最具特色的部分是建立在怀疑论基础之上的因果关系问题，即休谟问题，它在西方近现代哲学史上产生了极其深远的影响，"几乎重大哲学原理、哲学流派和哲学转折都发源于对休谟问题的研究和再认识"(张华夏，1998：6)，直到今天休谟问题仍然是西方科学哲学研究的重要课题。休谟贯彻经验论观点，对感觉之外的存在和外部世界的客观规律性持怀疑态度。他看到了经验知识的片面性和局限性，虽然承认"每一个有开始存在的东西也都有一个原因"，但认为"因果关系的发现不是凭借理性，而是凭借于经验"。(张志林，1998：78)人们日常生活使用的因果关系原则不能以理性证明其客观必然性，因果关系的必然性只存在于我们的思想之中，是人们经过长期的经验积累把近似关系和接续关系想当然地认为是因果关系，并把前者称为原因把后者称为结果。

钱锺书在一定程度上接受了休谟哲学的因果观，尽管他并不认同休谟关于因果必然性的主观主义观点，但是休谟对于"人类经验并不能告诉我们客观世界的必然联系"的观点，对于人类理性能力可以帮助人们认识客观世界中的因果关系的质疑，使钱氏走出了俗世因果决定论，并且抛弃"主观独断"走向"合理怀疑"。钱锺书对西方理性主义的否定和他在学术研究中对权威或固有观念的质疑都体现了"怀疑主义"在钱氏心中的影响。钱锺书一方面提出"化境"为翻译的"最高境界"，另一方面又认为"化境"是"不可实现的"，这实际上与休谟承认外部事物的客观规律性的同时又认为这种客观规律性是超乎于人的理性认识之外有着同样的"怀疑"色彩。在休谟看来，尽管物体存在不可知，但是人们对物体存在却又有着不可动摇的信念。钱氏也认为，尽管化境不可能实现，但人们对之的追求却始终不渝。

钱锺书根据这种因果关系的认识，批评了我国文论中曾经流行的"社会造因说"，并主张在历史研究中区分"史的事实"与"史家的事实"，还提出要善于从传统之中发现"现在性"，从现在的东西中寻找传统的"因子"，认为人们对传统的诠释与评价无不受影响于现实的认识条件，而传统资源无不可以被利用于当下的文化建设。钱锺书继承性地发展中国传统译论，"提出了'化境'翻译理论，把中国的传统翻译理论推向顶峰"，就表明他利用"传统资源"于"文化建设"的动因。

休谟在知识论中区分出"观念的关系"和"实际的事情"两种知识，在价值论中则区分开"是"与"应该"，认为前者可以用理性加以认知，而后者则是从情感(道德感)而来的，两者属于不同的领域。钱锺书也是严格区分"是"与"应该"或"事实"与"价值"的，他曾强调不能将"存在判断与价值判断合而为一"。他对翻译"化"与"讹"的解释："彻底和全部的'化'是不可实现的理想，某些方面、某种程度的'讹'是不能避免的毛病。"这实际上就是关于翻译应然理想与翻译实然价值关系的阐述，完全可以在休谟那里找到学理上的依据。

钱锺书在《汉译第一首英语诗〈人生颂〉及有关二三事》中最后有一番感慨："西洋的大诗人很多，第一个介绍到中国来的偏偏是朗费罗。朗费罗的好诗或较好的诗也不少，第一首译为中文的偏偏是《人生颂》。那可算是文学交流史对文学教授和评论家们的小小嘲讽或挑衅了！历史上很多——现在也就不少——这种不很合理的事例，更确切地说，很不合学者们的理想和理论的事例。这些都显示休谟所指出的'是这样'(is)和'应该这样'(ought)两者老合不拢。在历史的过程里，事物的发生和发展往往跟我们闹别扭，恶作剧，推翻了我们定下的铁案，涂抹了我们画出的蓝图，给我们的不透风、漏水的严密理论系统捅上大大小小的窟窿。"

现在看来，这篇文章就是用其所考证的翻译史实来注解休谟的思想，指示我们：翻译现实中的"是"往往与翻译理想中的"应该"是两码事。

3. 阐释学对钱锺书翻译思想的影响

钱锺书以博学强志闻名于世，其学术研究横跨中西，纵贯古今，会通文史哲大师对于西方近现代哲学的了解程度也许远远超出我们的想象，正是钱锺书对西方哲学的涉猎使得其学术思想中有着深厚的西方哲学底蕴。除了休谟哲学之外，对他翻译思想，乃至整个学术思想形成产生重大影响的还有西方阐释学。

阐释学是一门对于意义的理解和解释的哲学，它在西方有着悠久的历史。对阐释学的现代化发展作出巨大贡献的有施莱尔马赫、狄尔泰、海德格尔和伽达默尔等人。伽达默尔是哲学阐释学的创始人，他从海德格尔的阐释学出发，确立了阐释学以理解为核心的哲学与独立地位。理解的历史性、视阈融合和"效果历史"是伽达默尔哲学阐释学的三大原则。伽达默尔认为历史性是人类生存的基本事实，读者和文本都处于历史的发展演变之中，读者对文本的理解有其历史特殊性和历史局限性。历史性使得对象本和读者形成各自的"视阈"，而理解就是文本视阈与读者主体视阈的拉近。任何理解者都无法消除由于时空变化而引起的两种视阈存在的差距。伽达默尔主张文本和读者之视阈的融合，从而超越两者，达到全新的视阈。另外，伽达默尔还认为文本的意义是和理解者一起处于不断形成过程之中，理解者是在"效果历史"中理解作品。文本意义的开放性决定了文本是超越生成它的那个时代的，这也就为不同时代的人们对于文本产生多样性理解提供了可能。

阐释学所关心的问题总是与翻译学所关心的联系十分紧密。伽达默尔可以说是"翻译哲学"历史上最为重要的哲学家之一，其关于理解的历性原则解释了人们对文本的多元理解、误读、偏见、增删和改译等现象，因为译者(理解者)会受到各种主客观历史条件的限制，绝对"信"的译文是不可能存在的。而伽氏关于视阈融合的观点在一定程度上也确切地道出了翻译过程中不可避免的文化过度现象，因为译者总是不自觉地把自己的前有理解带进原文世界。

"阐释循环"论是钱锺书重要的文论思想，是钱氏由讨论汉语"不X不Y"句型引发而提出的，有学者甚至认为，钱锺书的"阐释循环"论是其整个学术思想的核心观念，不仅包括了总的纲领、具体途径、运行机制以及相应的具体方法等多个层面，而且有着坚实的学理依据。虽然学界对于钱氏"阐释循环"论的实质与西方阐释学的关系还存在争论，但可以肯定的是，"阐释循环"这一提法就是直接借自西方阐释学，钱锺书对于西方阐释学源流相当了解。由于阐释与翻译的密切联系，阐释学毫无疑问要处理翻译问题，凭此，我们便可推知，哲学阐释学对钱氏翻

译思想产生过重大影响。阐释学关于翻译就是阐释的思想在钱锺书的译论中都可找到反映。

钱锺书在《论"不隔"》中曾有这样的表述，"在翻译学里，不隔的正面就是'达'，严复《天演论》绪例所谓'信达雅'的'达'，翻译学里的'达'的标准推广到一切艺术便变成了美学上所谓的'传达'说（theory of communication）——作者把所感受的经验、所认识的价值、所运用的文字、或其他媒介物来传达给读者。"钱氏并没有将"信达雅"中的"达"的解释为通常人们所说的"通顺畅达"，而将之纳入"传达"渠道，这恰好契合了阐释学中所述的阐释的任务——"把诸神的旨意传达给凡人"；"把一种用陌生的或不可理解的表达的东西翻译成可理解的语言"。

阐释学认为理解的历史性和两种语言之间的差异决定了任何翻译都不可能是原文所有意义因素的完全再现，亦即是说，翻译中绝对的"信"是必然缺失的。但在理解和翻译中，译者绝不能将任何原文不存在的意义强加于文本，而是要找到最好的方式使在一种语言中表达的内容在另一种语言中得到表达。而钱锺书也认为，一国文字和另一国文字之间，译者的理解和文风跟原作品的内容和形式之间，而且译者的体会和他自己的表达能力之间必然存在距离，因而翻译过程不免有"讹"，也不可能实现彻底和全部的"化"。按他的"化境"说，理想的翻译应基于以下几个方面：第一，内容准确，尽量忠实于原文和原作者的意图；第二，易于理解，其实质是以读者为中心，注重译文读者的理解力，确保译文自然、易懂；第三，形式恰当，既要紧密依托原文，又应充分考虑译入语规范，避免生搬硬造。所以钱锺书对林纾增补删节的翻译风格并不否定，但对林纾翻译中的各种错讹现象，却予以了明确的批驳。

伽达默尔从现象学出发，重新审视了原文与译文的关系。他认为，"译文并不是原文的简单模仿，而是原文的表现与再现，是一种以原文为基础的再创造，是一种突出原文重点的解释。钱锺书在《林纾的翻译》中肯定了林纾翻译价值的存在，"许多都值得重读，尽管漏译误译随处都是"，说明在钱氏的翻译观中，译文并不附属于原文，而是作为原文所是的东西继续存在，是原文自身存在的扩充，而"坏翻译会发生一种消灭原作的效力"。

钱锺书曾多次提到伽达默尔，还将伽达默尔所说的"视阈融合"译为"读者与作者眼界溶化"。伽达默尔主张阐释者只与文本发生关系而并不与作者发生关系，文本在视阈融合中具有根本性的地位，在理解原作方面，原作者本人并不具有高于读者和译者的权威。因而伽氏注重的是阐释者与文本之间的"视阈融合"。钱锺书将"读者与文本之间的视阈融合"译为"读者与作者眼界溶化"似乎是一种错误，但钱氏的译才为世人所公认的"臻至化境"，而他的博学又不至于使之连阐释学的这一重要观点都不知道。鉴于钱氏曾认为伽达默尔和饶斯的学说"漏洞颇多"，笔者更倾向于认为钱锺书是在伽氏的"视阈融合"基础之上提出的自己的"眼界溶化"之说。

1934年钱锺书提出"不隔"说，讨论涉及翻译理论以及文学创作两个方面。钱锺书说："'不隔'不是一桩事物，而是一个境界，是一种状态（state），一种透明洞澈的状态——'纯洁的空明'，……'不隔'并不是把深沉的事物写到浅显易解；原来浅显易解的依然浅显；原来深沉的写到让读者看出它的深沉，甚至于原来糊涂的也能写得让读者看清楚它的糊涂……"应用到翻译中，亦即，翻译应该起到一种"解蔽"的作用，使得译文读者能与原文作者的视阈到达融合。这种"不隔"的状态是翻译的最终归宿与文学的最终指向，与海德格尔的"去蔽"以及"非对象性的思"趋向一致。钱锺书的"不隔"说的内涵与海德格尔思想的契合"体现出了中华文化的传统思想融会、融化最新动向中的西方现代哲学的可能性"，这在某种程度上也表明了西方阐释学的思想对钱锺书产生的影响。

4. 钱锺书对理性中心主义的反拨

自苏格拉底用“追问”的方式让人们知道了自己的无知，并佐以“知识即理性，无知即罪恶”信念的灌输，西方世界便走上了理性主义求知的道路。工业革命时期科学技术的发展带来的巨大成就日益强化了人们对理性知识的崇拜和对人类自身理性认知能力的迷信，在进化论思想的推波助澜之下一步步引发了理性中心主义的滥觞。理性中心主义把理性视为先验，将理性等同于上帝，坚持思维与存在的同一，认为整个世界具有一种可以用理智把握的结构，坚信人的理性能够认识整个世界，能够把握事物内在不变的本质和规律。理性中心主义关注和寻求事物的确定性、稳定性和规律性，因而片面张扬人的主体性，以人类理性抽象的普遍性来吞食个体的独特性。在理性主义的背景之中，人在实现对于知识追求的过程中，自身也逐渐沦为了工具。

这种推崇自然科学至上的工具理性渗透进了人文社会科学的各个领域，逻辑—数学的研究方法和思维方式在社科领域也变得十分盛行起来。在工具理性的观照下，翻译研究慢慢放弃了以往的直觉感悟的方法，转向了对翻译文本和语言的静态结构分析，强调语言的规律性、系统性和可转换性，翻译研究取得了长足的发展。但同时，工具理性“把语言视为理想的工具，翻译活动成了一种简单化与程式化的技术操作，译者主体也被物化，成为可以任意转换而结果不变的机器零件，因而失去了主观能动作用与创造性。”(吕俊，侯向群，2006：141)

钱锺书对这种理性中心主义关于人具有万能理性能力的“神话”却表现了深度的怀疑，他“不但不相信理性万能，反而在其学术作品和文学作品中，不断感叹人之渺小与无力，既无法达到对外部世界的穷尽认知，也无法真正认识自身，并且按理性设计的目标、愿望总是脱离理性力量的支配与控制，无法真正实现，因而人生充满不尽的无奈与遗憾。认为愿望总是脱离理性力量的支配与控制不断感叹人之渺小，既无法达到对外部世界的穷尽认知，也无法真正认识自身”(参见罗新河，2006：218)。钱氏这种对人之理性力量的怀疑主义也反映在他的译论思想中。

20世纪初西方哲学发生了的语言学转向，在此影响之下，西方译界将眼光从多个世纪以来对翻译的语文学意义的探讨中转移开来，开始以理性的方式系统地分析翻译的语言学问题。熟谙西方哲学、紧密关注西方学术发展的钱锺书对西方哲学这一重大动向不可能失察不闻，但在他对于翻译问题的论述中，他所采用的依然是中国传统的“神秘”、“虚幻”而“有失科学性”的话语。同时，他所坚持的一些观点，如：翻译的最高理想是不可实现的；译者的体会和表达存在差距等，实际上就是对于人的语言能力的质疑，也是对于理性中心主义对达到知识的确定性加以绝对化的一种否定。易言之，在翻译的问题上，人的能力是有限的。他对于翻译中“是”与“应该”之间存在不可否认的差距的感慨，在某种程度上而言也是以事实对理性中心主义者所描画的价值世界的颠覆。

理性中心主义强调知识的系统性，无疑，钱锺书对于翻译的诸多问题都有过严肃的思考，但他的翻译思想散落在他的几则札记之中，绝无巍然体系可言，我们只能从他信手拈来的杂谈似的评论中体会他的微言大义。然而，“‘体系’对于钱锺书而言，非不能也，而不为也”。钱氏正是以实际的方式来消解理性中心主义的“体系”观。工具理性放大作为普遍的人的主观能动性，而抹杀作为个体的人的独特性和个性发展要求，人自身也异化成了实现目的的工具。钱锺书在对林纾的翻译的评价中，对于林纾普遭人们病诟的增删创作的个性不无肯定，而对林纾后期沦为实现商业目的的工具时的翻译加以批驳，这也从一个侧面批判了工具理性所带来的消极后果。

钱锺书在其翻译思想中所体现的对西方理性中心主义的反拨是与其整个学术思想相一致的。这种对于盲目相信人类理性能力至上的怀疑与反思体现出他对世界和人类自身存在价值的深沉思索。

5. 结语

在如何对待中西思想和文化的问题上，有不少人陷入了非此即彼的二元对立的困境，而钱锺书则表现出一种清醒的头脑和一种深锐的洞察力，睿智而科学地借鉴、吸收和扬弃外来思想，"打通"与"融会"中西。他反对"重货利而轻义理"的"中体西用"，也鄙夷只知"排比欧故"以炫博识而实际上对西学义理全然不通的"鲁莽灭裂"(党圣元)。作为钱氏学术思想的一部分，他的翻译思想中既吸收了西方哲学的合理元素，又有着深厚的佛道渊源和辩证内涵，其中所寄寓的深意赋予了我们许多探究的空间。

本文尝试性地探讨了钱锺书翻译思想哲学基础的一个方面，限于篇幅，还未涉及其翻译思想中的中国传统哲学内涵，"通变"发展的文化意识，以及"破我"对话的伦理意蕴。笔者拟另著文加以探讨，也希望其他学者指正和加入讨论。

选文三 《红楼梦》中俗谚互文性翻译的哲学视角
——以"引用"为例

祖利军

导 言

本文选自《外语与外语教学》2010 年第 4 期。作者祖利军是北京华北电力大学外语系教授，研究方向为普通语言学和翻译研究。

选文采用译者主体与"他者"的互动这一哲学框架对《红楼梦》中俗谚互文性的翻译进行了探讨。互文性指能指符号的位置转移，与新的能指符号组成新的文本；能指符号在转移到新的语境之后能发挥新的功能。《红楼梦》原文中"引用"的互文性在英译中是否得到体现，其根本动因是译者主体与"他者"的互动关系。译者主体占上风时，互文性在译文中可以体现；"他者"占上风时，互文性在译文中难以体现。如果译者主体的知识能够驾驭"他者"，那么译者主体就会占上风，原文的互文性也能够得以传递。

1. 引言

作为中国文学史上最灿烂的阆苑仙葩之一,《红楼梦》自经问世以来,就一直以其博大精深的文化内涵与极富魅力的语言文字吸引着古今中外的各类读者。鲁迅说:"《红楼梦》是中国许多人所知道,至少,是知道这名目的书。谁是作者和续者姑且勿论,单是命意,就因读者的眼光而有种种:经学家看见《易》,道学家看见淫,才子看见缠绵,革命家看见排满,流言家看见宫闱秘事……"20 世纪 70 年代以来,随着《红楼梦》英文全译本(英国汉学家霍克思和闵福德的译本和中国翻译家杨宪益及其夫人戴乃迭的译本,以下简称为霍译本和杨译本)的出现,中国学者逐渐掀起了对《红楼梦》翻译研究的高潮,尤其是 21 世纪初,在中国引进了大量的西方翻译研究理论著作后,学者们纷纷从不同的翻译理论视角对《红楼梦》的英译进行了富有成效的研究,从而使《红楼梦》的英译研究成为了"《红楼梦》英译事业"。

俗谚是《红楼梦》中叙事的一个重要手段,它通俗易懂的表述和凝练睿智的哲理对人物的刻画和性格的揭示具有重要意义,因此有关俗谚的翻译也自然成为了学者们的研究焦点。张培基(1980)讨论了《红楼梦》的霍译本和杨译本对习语的处理,提出了自己的见解,并旁征博引有力地证明了自己的观点;刘泽权、朱虹(2008)对《红楼梦》三个英译本(包括乔里的前 56 回译本)中包括俗谚在内的习语进行了统计,探讨了译者们在处理这些习语时的规律性策略;袁翠(2001)从文化内涵的视角指出杨译本在成语翻译上存在的瑕疵;范敏(2007)以目的论为依据,分析了译者在《红楼梦》谚语翻译过程中选用翻译方法的目的性,探讨了翻译目的与谚语翻译策略的重要关系。

以上几篇文章是迄今为止笔者所能发现的有关《红楼梦》习语翻译研究的文章。我们不难发现,这几篇文章虽然研究视角各异,但都没有触及俗谚的互文现象及其翻译,也没有谈及译者主体以及"他者"在俗谚翻译中的影响作用。本文在这些研究的基础上,采用译者主体与"他者"的互动这一哲学框架对《红楼梦》中俗谚互文性的翻译做一探讨。

2. 何为"互文性"

互文性(intertexuality)的意义可以通过对该词英语词源的追溯而得到理解:inter 意思是"相互",text 来自拉丁文 texere,等同于英语的 weave(纺织),两部分合并起来意为"交织"。在现代英语中,text 作为"文本"的意义是以隐喻的方式获得的,即文本中的文字交织在一起。在理顺词源之后,我们可以清楚地看到,intertextuality 一词的内涵是"文本交织在一起"。

克里斯蒂娃(转自萨莫瓦约,2003: 5)认为,"互文性一词指的是一个(或多个)信号系统被移至另一系统中。但是由于此术语常常被通俗地理解为对某一文本的'考据',故此我们更倾向于取'易位'(transposition)之意,因为后者的好处在于它明确指出了一个能指体系(systme significant)向另一能指体系的过渡,出于切题的考虑,这种过渡要求重新组合文本——也就是对行文和外延的定位。"

另一位西方学者菲利普·索莱尔斯也对互文性进行了定义。他认为,"每一篇文本都联系着若干文本,并且对这些文本起着复读、强调、浓缩、转移和深化的作用。"

从以上两个定义来看,互文性首先指能指符号的位置转移,与新的能指符号组成新的文

本；其次，能指符号在转移到新的语境之后能发挥新的功能。

根据互文性的特点，《红楼梦》里具有互文性特点的俗谚可以划分为四类：引用、缩略、仿辞、用典。这四类的具体使用被称之为互文。引用指某俗语完整地借用了古代某一言辞；缩略指某俗语部分借用了古代某一言辞；仿辞是通过对古代某一词语的模仿而得到的新词；用典指某俗语里含有古代某一典故。限于篇幅，本文只对引用加以研究。我们预设的研究问题是：引用这一互文现象在翻译成英语后，其源语互文性信息是否得到了传递？如果没有得到传递，原因是什么？如果得到传递，传递的方式有哪些？要回答这些问题，我们先列举《红楼梦》中引用互文性的来源并分析其翻译策略。

3. 引用的互文来源及其翻译策略分析

引用指某俗谚完整地借用了古代某一言辞。所谓完整，指的是曹雪芹没有对借用对象做任何改动，一字不差地将古代的某一言辞引用到文中。这一定义使得《红楼梦》中能被称之为引用的俗谚的数量没有通常想像得那么多。笔者从上海市红楼梦学会、上海师范大学文学研究所编撰的《红楼梦鉴赏辞典》(1987)摘录了所有含有引用的句子和这些引用的互文来源，现整理如下：

1）后至蘅芜苑去看湘云病去，史湘云说他："你放心闹罢，先是'单丝不成线，独树不成林'……"(第56回)

单丝不成线，语出《水浒传》第49回："只是单丝不成线，孤掌岂能鸣。"独树不成林，语出古乐府《紫骝马》题解引《古今乐录》："梁曲曰：'独柯不成树，独树不成林'。"

2）贾蓉道："叔叔回家，一点声色也别露，……就是婶子，见生米做成熟饭，也只得罢了……"(第64回)

语出清代李光庭《乡言解颐》卷五"开门七事"条："'生米做成熟饭'，慎终于始也。"

3）平儿笑道："'得饶人处且饶人'，得省的将就些事也罢了。能去了几日，只听各处大小人儿都作起反来了，一处不了又一处，叫我不知管那一处的是。"(第59回)

语见宋代姚宽《西溪丛话》："蔡州有一道人，善棋，凡对局，辄饶人一先。有诗云：'自出洞来无敌手，得饶人处且饶人'。"

4）说着向鸳鸯道："这两日因老太太的千秋，……俗语说，'求人不如求己'……"(第72回)

语见宋代张端义《贵耳集》："宋孝宗幸灵隐，见观音像手持数珠。问曰：'何用？'僧净辉对曰：'念观世音菩萨。'问：'自念则甚？'对曰：'求人不如求己'。"

5）自古道："成人不自在，自在不成人。"你好生记着我的话。(第82回)

宋代罗大经《鹤林玉露》卷九引朱熹小简："谚云：'成人不自在，自在不成人'。此言虽浅，然实切至之论，千万勉之！"

6）岫烟笑道："他这脾气竟不能改，竟是生成这等放诞诡僻了。从来没见拜帖上下别号的，这可是俗语说的'僧不僧，俗不俗，女不女，男不男'，成个什么道理。"(第63回)

语见元代王实甫《西厢记》第二本"楔子"惠明唱词："[滚绣球]我经文也不会谈，逃禅也懒去参；戒刀头近新来钢蘸，铁棒上无半星儿土渍尘缄。别的都僧不僧，俗不俗，女不女，男不男，只会斋得饱也只想那僧房中胡渰，哪里怕焚烧了兜率伽蓝。则为那善文能武人千里，凭着这济困扶危书一缄,有勇无惭。"

7）宝钗因笑道:"妹妹知道,这就是俗语说的'物离乡贵?',其实可算什么呢。"(第 67 回)

语出明代孙鑛《〈书画跋〉跋》卷一《文太史三诗》:"谚云:'物离乡贵'。"

8）岫烟听了宝玉这话,且只顾用眼上下细细打量了半日,方笑道:"怪道俗语说的'闻名不如见面',又怪不得妙玉竟下这帖子给你,又怪不得上年竟给你那些梅花。既连他这样,少不得我告诉你原故。"(第 63 回)

语见《北史烈女传》:"房景伯为太守,有不孝者欲案之,入白其母。母曰:"吾闻闻名不如见面,小人未见礼教,但呼其母子来,令其见汝事吾,或应自改。"

我们看到,以上的俗谚皆引自古代某一文献且没有改动文献原文。每一俗谚都与其所引原文形成引用这一互文关系。那么这些俗谚的英译是否也体现了同样或类似的互文关系呢?

为了方便分析,我们先把以上俗谚的霍译和杨译依次按直译和意译两种策略列出。在列出前,有必要指出,直译和意译的定义一直处于百花齐放、百家争鸣的状态。翻译理论家们各执一词,莫衷一是。本文拟采用冯庆华(1997: 44)在《实用翻译教程》里提出的标准:"所谓直译,就是既保持原文内容、又保持原文形式的翻译方法或翻译文字。译文的语言与原文的语言常常拥有相同的表达形式来体现同样的内容,并能产生相同的效果。在这种情况下,我们就采用直译。所谓意译,就是只保持原文内容、不保持原文形式的翻译方法或翻译文字。译文的语言与原文的语言在许多情况下并不拥有同样的形式来体现相同的内容,更谈不上产生同样的效果。在这种情况下,一般采用意译为好。"

下面笔者把以上的俗谚依次按直译和意译两种策略列出。

3.1 霍直杨直

原文:单丝不成线,独树不成林。

霍译:The single strand makes not a thread nor the single tree a wood.

杨译:A single thread can't make a cord nor a single tree a forest.

原文:生米做成熟饭。

霍译:Don't say any thing about this when we arrive, said Jia Rong ... And as for Aunt Feng herself, when she sees that the rice is cooked and knows that it can't be uncooked, she'll have to put up with it.

杨译:When Aunt Xifeng sees that the rice is already cooked, she'll have to put up with it ...

3.2 霍意杨意

原文:得饶人处且饶人。

霍译:Where mercy is possible, mercy should be shown.

杨译:It's best to be easy on people—saves trouble.

原文:求人不如求己。

霍译:Self-help is the best help.

杨译:It's better to ask of one's own folk than of outsiders.

原文:成人不自在,自在不成人。

霍译：Perfection comes through ceaseless effort.

杨译：Men must choose between progress and comfort.

3. 3　霍直杨意

原文：僧不僧，俗不俗，女不女，男不男。

霍译：Xiu-yan ran her eye over it and laughed. "She'll never change. The same whimsical, preposterous A daman tina as always I Who but A daman tina would use her nom-de-plume in a birthday greeting? Talk about 'a monk no monk and a maid no maid!' What sort of etiquette is that?"

杨译："She hasn't changed in the least," observed Xiuyan with a smile. "She was born like this" headstrong and eccentric. "I've never seen other people use appellations like this in greeting cards. Why, this, as the saying goes, is neither fish, flesh nor fowl! It doesn't make sense."

原文：物离乡贵。

霍译：The farther from home, the more precious the object.

杨译：just some local products from far away, some novelties to amuse us.

3. 4　霍意杨直

原文：闻名不如见面。

霍译：The sight of it exceedeth the report thereof.

杨译：To know someone by repute is not as good as meeting face to face.

从以上不同俗谚对应的两个译本中我们不难看出，汉语原文中的互文关系在译文中大多没有得到体现。所谓互文性在译文中的体现，即互文性翻译，指两种情况：一、原文中的互文关系在译文中得到完整体现，也就是说，译文读者意识到了原文中存在着这种互文关系；二、译文读者读到这句俗谚时，能意识到这句译文与自己本族语的另一文本存在互文关系，就像中国读者读到"人生自古谁无死，留取丹心照汗青"时，知道或有可能知道，此句出自南宋爱国将领文天祥著名诗篇《过零丁洋》。

以"单丝不成线，独树不成林"为例，霍译是 The single strand makes not a thread nor the single tree a wood，杨译是 A single thread can't make a cord nor a single tree a forest. 读此译文之时，英语读者很难会想到此句分别出自《水浒传》和《紫骝马》，就是说体会不到互文性翻译的第一种情况，也体会不到第二种情况。对于以上几个例句来说，大多数是这种情况，即互文性翻译的两种情况读者都体会不到。

再以"得饶人处且饶人"为例，此句原本描写一个棋艺高超、天下无敌的道人，与他人下棋总是先让对方一步棋，最后仍能战胜对方。从译文来看，霍译是 Where mercy is possible, mercy should be shown，杨译是 It's best to be easy on people—saves trouble，读者丝毫看不出哪里有道人下棋的痕迹，也看不出英译与哪句英语成语有关联。可见，原文的互文性没有得到传递。

然而，也有两种情况其中一种被成功翻译的时候。以"僧不僧，俗不俗，女不女，男不男"为例，在《西厢记》中，这句唱词的意思是"我能力有限，才华并不出众"。再看译文，霍译是 a monk no monk and a maid no maid，读者看不出这个译文与才能有什么关系，也就是说读者体会不到互文性翻译的那两种情况。然而，杨译的 neither fish，flesh nor fowl 还是较好地反映了互文性翻译的第二种情况。该成语的原文是 neither fish，flesh nor good red herring 说的是 16 世纪英国社会等级的一种划分方式，即牧师吃鱼，平信徒吃禽肉，贫民吃熏鲱。英语读者读到此句时可能会联想到这一出处。

另外，霍译的 Self-help is the best help. 似乎模仿了 God helps those who help themselves. 这句谚语。也就是说，读者读到前者时，可能想到后者，既体现了互文性翻译的第二种情况。总之，二位译者虽然或直译或意译，原文的意义也得到了传达，但多数译文没能体现原文的互文性，尤其是互文性翻译的第一种情况根本得不到体现，第二种情况偶尔可得。那么造成这一尴尬的原因是什么呢？

4. 译者主体与"他者"的互动对引用互文性的诠释

笔者认为，《红楼梦》原文中的引用互文性在英译中没有得到体现的根本动因是译者主体与"他者"的互动关系。要了解这一互动关系，我们先来分别了解主体和"他者"的概念及特点。

主体作为哲学范畴，与客体相对，指实践活动和认识活动的承担者。主体具有能动性、自主性、自为性等。能动性侧重于主体能力，表现为主体活动的自觉选择和创造；自主性侧重于主体权利，表现为对活动诸因素的占有和支配；自为性侧重于主体目的，表现为主体活动的内在尺度和根据。这三个特点也是主体的本质属性。Regenia Gagnier 也认为，主体这一术语同时可以有很多意指：

> First, the subject is a subject to itself, an "I," how ever difficult or even impossible it may be for others to understand this "I" from its own view point, within its own experience. Simultaneously, the subject is a subject to, and of, others; in fact, it is often an "Other" to others, which also affects its sense of its own subjectivity ... Third, the subject is also a subject of know ledge, most familiarly perhaps of the discourse of social institutions that circumscribe its terms of being. Fourth, the subject is a body that is separate (except in the case o f pregnant women) from other human bodies; and the body, and therefore the subject, is closely dependent upon its physical environment. [首先，主体是自身的主体，即"我"，尽管他人很难或根本不可能从主体自身的角度、在主体自身的经验范围内理解这个"我"；同时，主体也是他人的主体、属于他人。实际上，主体对他人来说常常是"他者"，而"他者"影响着主体自身的主体感；第三，主体也是知识的主体，大家最熟悉的就是主体拥有限制它自身存在的社会机制的话语权；第四，主体是一个独立于其他躯体的躯体（孕妇除外），这个躯体，进而这个主体，紧密依赖于它所在的物理环境。]

根据以上的定义和解释，我们可以把主体的主要特点总结为：（1）主体具有能动性；（2）主体具有自主性；（3）主体具有自为性；（4）主体具有个体性；（5）主体具有"他者"性；（6）主体具有社会机制制约性；（7）主体具有物理环境依赖性。

译者作为翻译的主体，同时具有以上七个特点。

那么，“他者”指什么呢？“他者”是英文 the Other 或 Otherness 的汉译，在汉语中是一个地道的舶来品。黑格尔、费希特、胡塞尔、萨特、拉康、列维纳斯等哲学家对“他者”都做过详细的阐释，由于跟本文主题相关性不大，这里不予赘述。本文只选取“他者”在哲学上的外延意义，即“另类”、“差异”、“不和谐”、“格格不入”。有必要指出，主体本身也可以是“他者”，也就是上文主体特点的第五条。

在译事活动中，译者作为主体总是会努力发挥自己的能动性、自主性、自为性以及个性，比如，译者可以通过自己的母语和外语语言知识对句子结构进行调整、对措辞进行精心选择甚至微调语篇结构，等等。然而，译者主体的这些能动特点有时难以得到顺利发挥，“他者”作为“另类”因素常常会跳出来设置障碍，制造不和谐。这一点尤其表现在翻译异族文化的差异上。我们知道，中国文化博大精深，源远流长，其文化积淀也往往迥异于其他民族。俗语谚语可谓此种差异的典型代表之一。就《红楼梦》中的俗谚来说，它们基本典出古籍，而中国古籍是中国文化历史所特有的，很难在英语文化中找到对应的古籍，何谈对应的词语。有鉴于此，曹雪芹使用的引用互文现象，作为有中国特色的“他者”，在英译时也就很难找到对应的语言现象。上文的例句分析已经证明了这一点。

然而，“他者”不是孤立地存在，它与主体总是处于一种互动状态。在“他者”与主体的互动中，“他者”有时也被译者主体的能动性制服。上文提到，霍译的 Self-help is the best help.（求人不如求己）模仿了 God helps those who help themselves. 这句谚语，杨译的 neither fish, flesh nor fowl（僧不僧，俗不俗，女不女，男不男）模仿了 neither fish, flesh nor good red herring 这个典故。也就是说，原文具有互文关系，相应的译文也有互文关系。这里，“他者”之所以被制服是因为译者具有社会机制制约性和物理环境依赖性，也就是说，霍克思是英国本族人，他所处的社会和语言环境赋予了他对本族语言使用的纯熟性。杨宪益早年留学英国，并娶英国本族女子为妻，这对伉俪的英语语言水平之合力非同小可。

综上，译者主体与“他者”的关系很像中国古代“天人合一”的思想，即，“天”和“人”既是二元对立，也是一元统一，“天”即“ 他者”，“人”即译者。此二者相互依存，既对立又统一。译者主体占上风时，互文性在译文中可以体现；“他者”占上风时，互文性在译文中难以体现。然而，译者主体与“他者”谁占上风与主体的知识水平有关。如果译者主体的知识能够驾驭“他者”，那么译者主体就会占上风，原文的互文性也能够得以传递；如果译者主体的知识无法驾驭“他者”，那么“他者”就会反客为主，原文的互文性也就无法传递。

应该说，译者主体与“他者”的互动是翻译中的恒定参数。就互文性翻译来说，涉及中国历史文化的古典作品都比较难。这一点是可以理解的。即使我们这些以汉语为母语的本族人，对互文现象的意识也不同，有的人能意识到，有的人意识不到。这和我们受过的教育程度有关。相关领域的专家学者会有意识地注意互文现象，但在交际过程中大多数人只注重交际目的是否达到，基本不会对某词语的考据或互文性感兴趣。对于《红楼梦》这部差不多能当做中国文化百科全书的宏大作品来说，互文现象英译的难度更是可想而知。单就《红楼梦》中引用互文的英译而言，“他者”显然占了上风。也就是说，二位译者只将原文一小部分引用的互文性成功地再现给英语读者，而大部分引用的互文性没能再现。

王宏印（2008：144）认为，“在理论上，译文应当反映原文中所包含的一切互文关系，而且越充分越好。但实际上，由于翻译中的‘语义优先’原则的确定，以及由于文本所能容纳的复杂成分的有限性，即可容性，在不影响正常语义表达的前提下，究竟有多少互文可以体现在译文中呢？这是很成问题的。"

笔者同意王宏印的观点，所有的互文手段都是很难翻译的，因为在新的语境中这些俗谚获得了新生，即语境重置，读者很少或根本不会考虑它们在原文中的互文性，因此翻译者只需将它们在语境里的意义准确传达就足够了。

《红楼梦》的这两位译者是否意识到了俗谚中存在的互文性我们不得而知，但从二位的译文中我们可以看出，他们都尽可能地用俗谚或诗文来表达原文的意义。这种做法的好处是准确、生动地传达了原文的意义，对译文中那些互文关系的缺失也算一种弥补。

这里有必要指出，有人提出可以用异化并加注的方法保留中国特有的文化元素，这样既保留了互文关系，又彰显了中国文化。但笔者认为，异化并加注虽保留了互文性，但译文读者的阅读负担会增加，由于思路被打断，读者甚至有可能放弃阅读。译者主体的确进退维谷！

5. 小结

综上分析，引用互文的翻译在译者主体与"他者"的互动中处于一种尴尬的境地，也就是说，译者主体很难再现原文中的互文性。一方面，译者主体有极高的能动性、自主性和自为性，主观上想方设法传递原文的互文关系；另一方面，译者主体也受到"他者"的制约，这里的"他者"除了指中国特有的文化元素外，也指译者主体自身知识水平和目的语本身规则的限制，也就是说，译者成为了自身的"他者"。应该说，霍克思和杨宪益两位翻译家的主体性已充分发挥，因为他们基本把这些俗谚翻译成了谚语或诗文，对原文互文性的缺失也算是一种补偿。读者在阅读这一鸿篇巨著时，并不会因互文性没有得到翻译而认为二位翻译家的翻译是败笔。然而，互文性的翻译的确给我们提出了新的课题：到底怎样翻译互文性？可译度有多大？必要性有多大？有没有专门的互文性翻译策略？这些问题还有待于《红楼梦》译爱好者们做进一步研究。

【延伸阅读】

[1] 蔡新乐. 论翻译学的三个新概念：元翻译、反翻译与非翻译. 外国语，2002(1).
[2] 蔡新乐. 翻译学研究的一个盲点：翻译哲学的形而上之维. 中国翻译，2002(5).
[3] 辜正坤. Metatranslatology. 中国翻译，2002(4).
[4] 刘超先. 中国翻译理论的发展线索研究. 中国翻译，1994(4).
[5] 刘宓庆. 翻译与语言哲学. 北京：中国对外翻译出版公司，2001.
[6] 吕俊. 世纪之交的译学三思. 外语与外语教学，1999(1).
[7] 吕俊. 理论哲学向实践哲学的转向对翻译研究的指导意义. 外国语，2003(5).
[8] 钱冠连. 语言哲学翻译论. 中国翻译，2003(5).
[9] 张柏然. 翻译本体论的断想. 外语与外语教学，1998(4).
[10] 张经浩. 没有理论的实践是盲目的实践吗？上海科技翻译，2003(1).

【问题与思考】

1. 翻译研究中的超验主义、解构主义、怀疑主义、实用主义有何体现？

2. 为什么说钱锺书的翻译思想从根本上来说是反传统的？
3. 休谟哲学以及阐释学对钱锺书翻译思想产生了哪些影响？
4. 什么是“互文性”？《红楼梦》里具有互文性特点的俗谚有哪几类？
5. 举例说明译者如何弥补在再现《红楼梦》互文性中的缺失。

第八章　文学翻译研究的女性主义启示

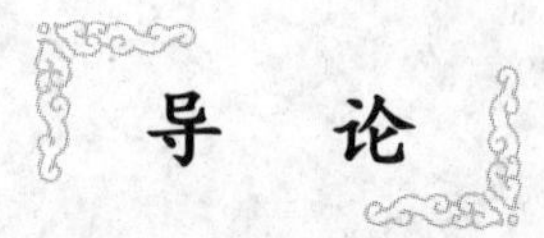

导　论

西方女性主义(feminism,也译为“女权主义”、“男女平权主义”、“女性主义”)一词缘于妇女解放运动。“性别”惯常视为人的生理属性。性别差异是社会文化建构起来的,是由文化和政治上的父权统治造成的。20世纪60年代末至70年代初的女性主义运动聚焦于女性差异的两个方面。首先它致力于以各种形式展现女性与男性的不平等差异,说明造成这些差异的原因是人为的性别行为模式;其次,相比女性之间的差异,它更强调的是女性的共同经历以及一致性和团结性。女性主义运动的重要影响之一是促成当代女性主义翻译研究的兴起。

女性主义翻译研究揭示了传统翻译研究将翻译女性化和将翻译边缘化的过程。翻译研究中隐藏着许多二元对立的概念,如创作与翻译、原文与译文、作者与译者等等。其中,前者常被视为权威性的、强壮的,后者则是地位低下的、附属的;前者应该主宰后者,后者则必须服从前者,忠实于前者。翻译的这种弱势地位是长期受父权语言压制的结果。自古以来,人类社会长期处在父权控制中。语言这一必不可少的交流工具也被纳入了父系社会的控制之中。长久以来女性在语言使用上处于被男性统治和歧视的地位。女性主义运动让西方女性认识到语言是操纵社会的工具,妇女希望通过改造语言而获得自身解放,翻译就是以女性主义的方式再改写。女性主义翻译研究致力于消除翻译中的性别歧视,批判将女性和翻译置于社会和文学最底层的观点,颠覆了传统的翻译观,从而,重新定位原作与译作、作者与译者、翻译与性别的关系,并主张对文本进行操纵和改写。弗洛图(Luise von Flotow)论述了女性主义翻译的三种实践方式:增补(supplementing)、劫持(hijacking)以及加写前言和脚注(prefacing and footnoting)。增补是为了弥补语言间的差异,要求译者进行干预。前言和脚注用来解释原文意旨,概括自己的翻译策略。“劫持”是指女性主义译者对并不一定具有女性主义意图的文本的剥夺和挪用。可见,翻译的过程不是简单的再现原文的意义,而是对原文意义的补充和延伸,译者不是机械地复制和再现原文,而是创造性地阐释原文。

女性主义翻译研究倡导的是一种差异哲学,将视线转到二元对立中的弱者,使文化中不为人知的边缘角色被展示出来。然而,它也有自身的内在缺陷,被诟病最多的是有重构二元对立之嫌,其过激的叛逆立场无法从根本上解决男女性别对立的问题。伍尔芙(Woolf)、西苏(Helene Cixous)、克里斯蒂娃(Kristeva)、伊瑞格瑞(Irigaray)等女性主义者提出了在坚持男女两性差别的基础上,以一种可以包容男女差异的同一境界的思想——“雌雄同体”来对抗和解构父权制的二元对立。女性主义翻译研究曾经取得了很大的成就,并仍在发展着,它为翻译研究的多元化提供了新视角。

选　文

选文一　Gender and Translation

Luise von Flotow

导　言

本文《性别与翻译》选自 Piotr Kuhiwczak 和 Karin Littau 所编的 *A Companion to Translation Studies*(2007)的第六章。作者路易斯・冯・弗洛图(Luise von Flotow)是渥太华大学翻译学教授,研究兴趣集中在翻译的性别和文化、视听翻译、翻译与文化外交以及文学翻译等。著《翻译与性别:女性主义时代的翻译》(*Translation and Gender: Translating in the "Era of Feminism,"* 1997),编有《翻译女人》(*Translating Women*, 2011)等。

选文分为三个部分。第一部分"从身份认同到多元"是对翻译研究中的性别问题所作的概括性总揽。第二部分和第三部分细述两种性别研究的范式。第一种范式认为,社会由男人和女人组成,但女人往往处于从属地位。性别的不平等是由社会造成的,社会让人认同自己的性别再依此认同进行作为;女人不是生成的而是父权制社会造成的。这一范式的认同来源于女性主义的理论和实践。第二种范式认为,性取向的差异造成了性别的不稳定性,酷尔、男同性恋、女同性恋等性别身份问题,通常与个人在这类事情上选择有关。性别被作为话语行为或附属行为的述行性得到研究。述行性的概念尤其在戏剧翻译的对话中体现出来。

From Identities to Pluralities

Transcultural and translingual developments in the women's movement and its various offshoots since the 1970s have implicated translation in every aspect of text production and reception, and have enormously expanded the thinking about and research on translation and gender. Diverse research initiatives have investigated the role played by translation in transmitting new socio-political ideas focused on gender and their literary expression across cultural boundaries; the roles played by women translators in the present and the past, their reception and influence have been studied; the importance of and the dangers involved in translating women's writing in an era of universalist notions about women, and the challenges involved in facing and recognising great differences between women have been discussed at length. Women's representation in language, through language, and across languages, and women's participation in this work of representation have underlain the entire period since the early 1970s. More recently, ideas about gender instability have added new dimensions to the discussions, and undermined the categories "man" and "woman" on which earlier debates were founded. Queer as well as gay and lesbian studies, concerned with other gender identities and in particular with individual choice in these matters, have taken debates into other, though not necessarily new, areas. In the Anglo-American realm especially, the focus on gender over the last part of the 20th century has powerfully affected translation, and been powerfully reflected by translation.

In this chapter I will re-trace the first gender paradigm, the paradigm that was shaped by the women's movement, feminist thinking, and feminist activism, and that strongly affected translation and translation studies. After briefly reviewing a number of early publications, I will explore the work that has been done in the field since those first articles and books' appeared. In the second part of the chapter, my focus will be on the destabilization of the term gender, on what I have called the second paradigm (von Flotow, 1999), which took hold in the early 1990s and is beginning to be reflected in translation studies, criticism and theory. Both paradigms reflect the interest in identity that became so important in post-1960s North America, and which, in Canada, was exacerbated by the French/English and American/Canadian divides. While these issues seem to have garnered enormous interest and exposure in the Anglo-American realm, they are widespread—European, Latin American, and increasingly, Arabic and Asian cultures are also taking an interest.

The first paradigm reflects the conventional assumption that there are groups of people in each society/culture that can be identified as women or men, and who, because of this identification and self-identification, are perceived and treated differently, with the group called women usually located in a subordinate position. To date most publications bringing together gender issues and translation have subscribed to this first paradigm—the notion of gender as a set of characteristics and behaviours imposed by society, as a construct that forms an individual and according to which that individual identifies. As Simone de Beauvoir's dictum "on ne nait pas femme, on le devient" ("one is not born a woman, one becomes one") so neatly implies, gender has been seen to imprint the dominant cultural expectations upon the male-sexed or female-sexed individual. Work in translation studies carried out under this first paradigm tends to subscribe to ideas derived from feminist theories and practices and thus focuses on women as a special minority group within "patriarchal" society that has been subject to usually biased treatment, including the area of translation as well.

The second paradigm derives from the relatively new idea that the diversity of sexual orientation and gender, class distinction, ethnicity, race and other socio-political factors is so great that it is impossible, or unwise, or meaningless to identify anyone as primarily male or female, since so many other factors come into play. Still in development, this paradigm has been spawning work that focuses on gender as a discursive and contingent act, and on its performative aspects. The idea that a translation, too, is a performance causes a certain tentative overlap between gender and translation in this second paradigm, where gender issues are often aligned with gay and lesbian identities and interests, and the translation analyses tend to deal with works in which traditional ideas about two genders are called into question. The notion of performativity seems to have led translation researchers to focus largely on the role played by theatricality and linguistic markers in dialogue that signify "gayness" (Harvey, 1998: 305). Just as in the theatre each performance is a passing phenomenon, so translation under this paradigm is viewed as a contingent, performative act. The first paradigm, in contrast, is based on more fixed notions about gender identity, which are limiting and restrictive, yet can be overcome or subverted, and the work is typically revisionist. It posits a powerfully assertive translator, exploring the (mis)representation of women authors in translation, the invisibility of women translators, and the patriarchal aspects of translation theories.

First Paradigm, with Follow-up and Backlash

Because of the powerful influence of language in applying and enforcing a society's notions about gender, gender expectations and gendered behaviour, and in producing, creating and manipulating texts in translation, the two areas of study developed a productive overlap from the late 1970s onward. Feminist critiques of the so-called mainstream "patriarchal" language that imposes gender restrictions through language, and feminist ideas about women's agency, activism, creativity and production soon countered traditional ideas about translation as a typically feminine activity of passive, yet often devious, repetition, re-production or mere procreation rather than creative production. Probably the most voluble and influential proponent behind the idea of feminist translation as production of meaning has been Barbara Godard, a translator of experimental feminist writing from Quebec and a professor of Canadian literature. Godard uses the term "womanhandling" to describe feminist approaches to translation and considers that feminist translators should "flaunt" their presence and agency in the text, making themselves and their work visible, and thereby reversing the age-old order of translators' and women's public and literary/scholarly invisibility (Godard, 1990).

While Godard's approach has been oriented toward creativity and visibility, thus revising the traditional quietist stance of the translator, various other forms of revisionism have also been highly visible in work on gender and translation. The title of Susanne de Lotbiniere-Harwood's (1991) *Rebelle et infidele* signals an attack on established notions that connect translation with a patriarchal view of women, as implied in the expression "*les belles infideles.*" The term was, and still is, used to describe translations done in the 17th and 18th century France that "improved" the foreign text in translation, making it more beautiful, until it corresponded to aesthetic notions of the time. *Re-belle et infidele* challenges the implicit misogyny of this saying, showing how such translation practices have occulted women's interests, ideas and presence in texts, and demonstrating how powerful a critically informed attitude on the part of the woman translator, and translation more generally, can be.

Sherry Simon's *Gender in Translation. Cultural Identity and the Politics of Transmission* (1996) also focuses on the interface between gender and translation, citing the famous dictum by John Florio (1603) that because they are necessarily "defective," all translations are "reputed females" as the opening. In a historical revision of translations, Simon then discusses influential, though largely ignored, women translators and their histories of working with male writers. She presents women's/feminists' versions of the Bible, and studies the difficulties involved in translating the polysemous neologisms of "French feminism" as well as the more general problems involved in translating women's writing across cultures. Espousing the current idea that translation produces knowledge and meaning and not just repetitions, and examining this idea in terms of women's struggle for political, social and scholarly influence, Simon's (1996) work problematises fidelity both in translation and human relations. Her work places this problem squarely within the climate of intellectual indeterminacy and relativism that developed in the last decades of the 20th century, due in part to women's/feminists' contentious struggle over language and meaning as well as women's roles.

Flotow's (1997) *Translation and Gender: Translating in the "Era of Feminism"* (1997) makes a further clear connection between feminist politics and translation. It shows how cultural politics deriving from the women's movement and feminism have affected writing and translation, how translations examined from a feminist perspective may be seen to require revision and re-translation, and how feminist theories and translation theory come together to counteract what one critic has called the "androcentric slide into gender as trope in the postmodern translation theory" (Chance, 1998: 183), i. e., the gendered tropes of translation, such as "les belles infideles," that continue to proliferate.

Much of this work has been supported by an important theoretical/historical text entitled "Gender and the metaphorics of translation" by Lori Chamberlain (1992). Chamberlain examines how theoretical and philosophical questions about language, mythologies, ancient "authoritative" texts and the symbolic intent and impact of gendered metaphors of translation are linked to and reflect the power relations within heterosexual unions that regulate marriage, reproduction and especially the control over offspring through the control of women's sexuality. Chamberlain's contention is that the ancient and ongoing derogatory link between women and translation, which has been expressed in countless metaphors used to describe translation over the centuries, has to do with a struggle for power and authority between the sexes that results directly from men's fears about women's sexual infidelity.

Chamberlain's work continues to incite theoretical approaches, among them an important recent piece, "Pandora's tongues" (2000) by Karin Littau, which reviews and

contrasts the two main myths in Western thinking upon which translation hinges: the mythic tale of the tower of Babel and that of Pandora. Littau sets out to re-appropriate Pandora's story for feminist translation theory, and locates the source of the traditional view of Pandora "releasing linguistic chaos" in "phallocentric anxieties about Woman, both as regards language—the mother tongue, and as regards her gender—female sexuality" (Littau, 2000). She then develops a complex argument around the psychoanalytic work of Luce Irigaray that posits women's sexual and psychological multiplicity to argue against the search for one "true" meaning in translation that has underlain translation theories based on Babel, traditional psychoanalytic sexual anxieties and the mythic, messianic notions about a "return" to one language. Multiplicity in meaning and in textual and visual representations of meaning, and especially in the "seriality of translation" is connected here to plenitude, to the cornucopia that Pandora is sometimes pictured with, and to a deconstructive revision of gender symbolics. Both Chamberlain and Littau provide theoretical approaches that go beyond the earlier revisionism and re-writing of translation history with regard to gender, and stimulate more speculative work on the myths and symbols that underlie Western culture and play into the work of representation and rewriting that is translation.

However, a very important body of work that addresses theory, mythology and symbolics began to appear a good ten years before Chamberlain's article: the earliest feminist revisionist translation interests were focused on Bible translation. Simon (1996: 111-33) makes clear that Bible translation has always been a political activity that produces text for a specific community or readership and, hence, adapts the text for that particular purpose. There is no absolute, original biblical truth, though there are many claims to truth. Feminist translation approaches have also sought to re-interpret and rewrite the Bible differently in order to reflect the new understanding of women's positions in society. They have sought to minimize the masculine bias in the language (Haugerud, 1977), proposed a more "inclusive" language not only for the biblical materials but also for the services and ceremonies of Christian churches (*The Inclusive Language Lectionary*, 1983), and provided new translations of key passages from the original Hebrew (Korsak, 1992). This work is always prefaced and accompanied by explanations and discussions of the intricacies of the language and the meaning that were being wrestled with. Moreover, the purpose is generally stated as making the biblical messages accessible and meaningful to women in the contemporary social and intellectual climate, as the title of Haugerud's (1997) translation of four books of the New Testament implies: *The Word for Us*. On the one hand, the idea of writing a contemporary text, for a reading public that is learning from and responding to the upheavals caused by the women's movement and feminist thinking, has been important throughout these Bible translations. On the other, contemporary feminist thought has opened translators' eyes to new ways of interpreting old, ingrained meaning; since translations are initiated and carried out in a certain context and for certain reasons, any political and cultural changes in this context will allow new ways of understanding. Von

Flotow's (2000) article on two differently "literal" English versions of the Creation myth, translated from Hebrew and published in 1876 by Julia Evelina Smith and in 1992 by Mary Phil Korsak, presents this problematic of perception and context and its impact on the final text.

A combination of gender interests, translation and historical research and revisionism has been the most productive of new knowledge. A large and growing body of work in several different languages has unearthed and assessed the work of women translators throughout history, and the most recent publication is a series of portraits of women translators, *Portraits de traductrices* (Delisle, 2002). The translation and presentation of a large number of thus-far untranslated women authors has been undertaken (Kadish & Massardier-Kenney, 1994; Schwartz & Flotow, 2006), and many individual articles have examined existing translations of important authors in light of new feminist research and approaches. This labour of reexamination and often subsequent re-translation has spread well beyond the Anglo-American sphere with a productive working group focused on German and located in Austria (Grbic & Wolf, 2002; Messner & Wolf, 2001), further research interests developing in Spain (Godayol Nogue, 2000) and in other parts of Europe.

Other research initiatives have been triggered by the problems encountered in translating contemporary, often experimental, feminist writing across cultures, or simply in translating between very different cultures, especially once the realisation set in that feminist ideas and politics are culturally (and even subculturally) specific, and their impact is contingent upon social class, education, mobility and many other factors. Critics Gayatri Spivak (1993), Christine Delphy (1995) and Beverley Allen (1999) have all written about thoughtlessly imperialist aspects of certain approaches in Anglo-American feminisms which are based on the undifferentiated notion that translation is a harmless, even benevolent, form of communication and that feminist ideas are transcultural. These critics show that translations can serve those who commission them by uncritically appropriating the texts of the other cultures (see Delphy, 1995, on the appropriation of "French feminist" texts), by translating away from the original culture and imposing certain hegemonic versions on the translated texts (see Spivak, 1993, on texts from developing countries in Western translation), or simply by disregarding the important cultural differences between closely related cultures (see Allen, on the translation of Italian feminist writings).

The revisionist work inspired by new perceptions of and positions on gender has proven enormously fruitful, both in terms of producing different knowledge and in shaking up conventional perceptions of translation that have for many years assumed that a translation produces a nearequivalent, though always weaker, version of the source text, and can usually be read and accepted in place of the foreign text. This attitude had not only rendered translators' work and intellectual achievements invisible, but also allowed them to dissemble their interventions in the text. The critical voices of feminist, and other, translation critics of the past decades have now led to the increasing visibility and responsibility of the

translator and the entire translation process—publishers, editors, translation patrons, reviewers and readers included.

In one predictably conservative and politically touchy area, this opening of the translation process is, however, suffering a backlash: in "genderneutral" or "inclusive" translations of the Bible. The "gender-neutral" translation recently produced for evangelicals (the most conservative, fundamentalist Christians)—the *NLV*, *New Living Translation*—set off an enormous storm of controversy (Marlowe, 2001). Prepared and published in two versions in England, one version had "gender-neutral" language and ostensibly used the translation technique of "dynamic equivalence," derived from Eugene Nida, also an evangelist Bible translator. It met with enormous resistance from evangelical organisations in the United States. Similarly, the Vatican has recently cracked down on "gender-neutral" liturgy. Having undermined and delayed developments in the English liturgy in this regard over the course of the 1990s, the Vatican is now trying to put an end to the attempts by the International Commission on English in the Liturgy (a group responsible for translations of biblical materials, the production of lectionaries and other Church instruments for Englishspeaking Catholics in 26 countries) to integrate gender-sensitive language into these texts. As a recent commentator has said:

> Jesus may once again invite Peter and other apostles to be "fishers of men" instead of "fishers of people," and the Nicene Creed may say "the Son of God was made man," instead of the Son of God "became truly human." (*Ottawa Citizen*, 2002: January 20)

The Vatican document condemning the "faulty translations" produced over the past 25 years in English-speaking countries is entitled *Liturgiam Authenticam*, and claims that there is nothing in the Church's sacred texts that would allow prejudice or discrimination on the basis of gender or race. Everything depends on the "right interpretation" which is the responsibility of the catechist or the homilist—not the translator, or the translating committee. What the Vatican calls for is very simple: "liturgical books marked by sound doctrine, which are exact in wording, free from all ideological influence." The Vatican's English press release on the document has a special section entitled Gender. I cite that passage here in full:

> Many languages have nouns and pronouns capable of referring to both the masculine and the feminine in a single term. The abandonment of these terms under pressure of criticism on ideological or other grounds is not always wise or necessary nor is it an inevitable part of linguistic development. Traditional collective terms should be retained in instances where their loss would compromise a clear notion of man as a unitary, inclusive and corporate yet truly personal figure, as expressed, for example, by the Hebrew term *adam*, the Greek *anthropos* or the Latin *homo*. Similarly, the expression of such inclusivity may not be achieved by a quasi-

mechanical change in grammatical number, or by the creation of pairs of masculine and feminine terms.[2]

The traditional grammatical gender of the persons of the Trinity should be maintained. Expressions such as *Filius hominis* (Son of Man) and *Patres* (fathers) are to be translated with exactitude wherever found in biblical or liturgical texts. The feminine pronoun must be retained in referring to the Church. Kinship terms and the grammatical gender of angels, demons and pagan deities should be translated, and their gender retained, in light of the usage of the original text and of the traditional usage of the modern language in question (N/ccdds/documents/rc_con_ccdds_doc_20010 507_ liturgiam-authenticam, May 2002).

These two paragraphs seem to order the reinstatement of many of the most conventional aspects of biblical language that were beginning to change under pressure from feminist thinkers and translators: the generic male term to refer to all humans; the "traditional grammatical gender" of the Trinity which masculinises every member of this group from God to the Holy Ghost; and traditionally-gendered terms for the Church, angels, demons, *et al*. The issue of "filius hominis" and "patres" are concrete examples of this masculinist language of the Church, which rewriters such as Haugerud (1971) and the committee responsible for *The Inclusive Language Lectionary* (1985) sought to diminish. In their view, the sex/gender of Jesus is inconsequential, God's gender cannot be known, and the power vested in the "Patres/Fathers" has historically filtered down to and been mistakenly appropriated by normal, everyday men of Christian societies—to the detriment of women. These concerns are evidently being swept aside in the name of "a clear notion of man as a unitary, inclusive and corporate yet truly personal figure."

While there may be a backlash from the Vatican, the scholarly sphere continues to burgeon with research and publications that derive from the first paradigm in gender and translation. An international conference at the Universite de Montreal on women translators of the Middle Ages and the Renaissance (September 2002), another conference at the Universidad de Valencia on "Gender and translation" (October 2002), two recent publications in German (Wood & Messner, 2000, 2001), as well as numerous MA and PhD theses—in English, French and other European languages—are concrete signs of such activity. Through its revisionist historical approaches and reconfiguration of translation as a creative, powerful, influential act in any context this is re-interpreting women's activities, visibility and influence in the field.

Other areas such as theatre and film translation and the translation of songs and libretti, all dealing with texts that arguably reach a much wider audience, are just beginning to be scrutinised in this vein. Klaus Kaindl's (1991) work on the romanticisation of women's roles in opera through the translation of opera libretti (in this case into German) is an early piece that examines the effect of 19th century German mores on the translation of Bizet's Carmen—her transformation from a sexually powerful street urchin to a coy and sentimental young lady. Similarly, recent work on the translations of musicals (cf. the unpublished manuscript on the German version of La Cage aux folles by Jurgen Weilert, Vienna, 2001, and on English translations of the 1920s Berlin cabaret texts by Ryan Fraser, Ottawa, 2001), as well as on particular aspects of dialogue in theatre texts (Harvey, 2000; Limbeck, 1999) examine the constant of conservative, censorious tendencies in translating for the stage, where colloquialisms and double-meanings with regard to sexuality abound, and are systematically toned down or erased.

Second Paradigm: Gender Instability and Translation

The contemporary focus on theatre/stage and media translation accompanies the equally contemporary trend to view gender as a theatrical representation, as a performance, or as a "performative" activity in which the individual discursively and often parodically struts his or her particular gender affiliation. Gender as performance, as an act that adults can choose to perform, counters the assumption of a seamless, stable identity imposed or acquired from childhood. Based on the much-discussed Gender Trouble (1990) by Judith Butler and other work in queer studies, the notion has highlighted one of the great weaknesses of early Anglo-American feminist theorising and current "UN-style feminist universalism" (Spivak, 1996: 253)—i. e. , that the term "woman" is stable—across history, cultures, ideologies, and can be used as a basis or a category from which to engage in abstractions or political theorising. Much has been written on this topic (see David Gauntlett on "Judith Butler," www. theory. org. uk) and translation studies has felt the impact.

One of the first to connect gender instability and translation was Carol Maier. Indeed, she and Francoise Massardier-Kenney claim that translation is wonderfully suited to reveal such instability:

> Recent work [...] subjects the terms "feminism" and "woman" themselves to what could be likened to exercises in translation, in which those terms are shown to be unstable points of departure for either theory or practice. Such questioning has made evident—and to a degree perhaps possible only through the practice of translation—the extent to which gender definitions are neither universal nor absolute manifestations of inherent differences but relatively local, constantly changing constructions contingent on multiple historical and cultural factors. (Maier & Massardier-Kenney, 1996: 230)

It has probably always been clear to translators that translation reveals such differences. By and large, however, translation has sought to minimize difference, and translation in the "era of feminism" has focused on differences between the two first paradigm genders, tending to occult those between women. Now, in the wake of queer theory, gender instabilities and post-colonial critiques by authors such as Spivak, Maier is advocating a:

> woman-interrogated approach to translation, which she explains as an endeavour to work less from confidently held definitions than from a will to

> participate in re-definitions, to counter the restrictions of a gender-based identity by questioning gender as the most effective or the most appropriate point of departure for a translator's practice. (Maier, 1998: 102)

This may seem paramount to striking the first paradigm from translation and translation studies—yet, as Maier explains, though gender may no longer be a clearly identifiable or even an important issue, this contingency need not lead to a feeling of impotence. Translation is always a representation, always a performance of another author's work, and hence, is invested with power. The point is that translators may choose to privilege women authors, say, or emphasise their own understanding of gender issues in a text, yet these are selective, performative aspects of the translation and do not represent intrinsic qualities of the text. An example of such "selected" performativity has been noted and criticised by Harveen Sachdeva Mann (1994) in her article on the massive two-volume collection entitled *Women Writing in India* (see Tharu & Lalita, 1991, 1993). Mann points out that the editors of the collection focused on first paradigm gender in compiling the materials, with the major criteria being that the work be written by women. Mann sees this as eliding issues of class differences and ethnicity, which she considers of far greater importance in the Indian context. Similarly, Maier's "woman-interrogated" translation practice leads her to produce a translation of Delirio y destino. *Los veinte afios en la vida de una espatiola* (Zambrano, 1999), a book on the philosophical writings of María Zambrano, that first-paradigm translation practitioners would doubtless find hard to understand. Maier translates the second part of the title as "Twenty Years in the Life of a Spaniard," deliberately eliding the fact that "una espatiola" refers to a Spanish woman.[3] Maier's explanation is that, since the book has appeared in a series on women writers, there is a danger of misrepresenting Zambrano, who did not see herself as a woman philosopher (Godayol Nogue, 2000).

Similar ideas about gender as a contingent and only subjectively meaningful aspect of texts and translations are evident in recent studies focusing on gay men's writing and translation (with the exception of brief passages in De Lotbiniere-Harwood [1991] there is very little material on lesbian textuality in translation). Echoing the realisation that there is no one definition of woman that would hold within one culture or across diverse cultures, Keith Harvey's recent work notes the "whole range of homosexual identities in French and English fiction" (Harvey, 1998: 295), which must be taken into account in the evaluation and translation of "camp" talk. There is no one homosexual identity either. Instead, diverse contexts produce diverse identities, and performances of these. Harvey argues that the camp style privileged by certain of these (Anglo-American) homosexual groups signifies "performance rather than existence" which leads to "a deliberately exaggerated reliance on questions of (self-)representation" (Harvey, 1998: 304). He also describes 1990s queer theory notions of identity as a "pure effect of performance" (Harvey, 1998: 305). Under this performance paradigm, then, certain types of writing and speech, in this case "camp," are "extrasexual performative gestures" (Harvey, citing Butler, 1998: 305) that both denote

and generate gay self-identificatory activity. In other words, "camp" talk is a code used by some gay individuals to signal their "gayness," identifying themselves to others in the public sphere, and generating a special exclusive language for a group of insiders.

Much like earlier feminist thinkers, Harvey is concerned with the translation of a coded, encrypted, neologistic language across cultural boundaries where different linguistic markers, and different socio-political contexts, influence linguistic performativity. The same question arises: how can linguistic phenomena that both derive from and generate a particular socio-cultural phenomenon be translated across cultural/language borders? Harvey notes the tendency on the part of the French translator of Gore Vidal's *The City and the Pillar*, for instance, to tone down the "camp" language, and surmises that this may be due to French homosexuals' reluctance to "self-identify according to the variable of sexuality" (Harvey, 1998: 311). It may indeed be an expression of a certain scepticism about the construction of a subcultural community that challenges and parodies heterosexual hegemony, while the "gayed" English translation of Tony Duvert's *Paysage de fantaisie* reflects the self-confident existence of such a community in the Anglo-American sphere.

In more recent work (2000), Harvey pays even closer attention to the presence of gay communities and their influence in allowing and encouraging certain types of textual, translational, transformances. This is also a topic explored by Eric Keenaghan (1998) in his work on the "gayed" American rewriting of Garcia Lorca's encrypted homosexual images. Though Lorca can hardly be seen as having produced discursively performative gay texts of the type Harvey describes, his American translator/adaptor, Jack Spicer, with the gay community as a backdrop, could turn Lorca's subtleties into a "vulgar (some might say obscene)and sexual register [...] importing a concrete sense of male sexuality and rendering the male body and sexual activity highly visible poetic objects" (Keenaghan, 1998: 274). Here, too, are echoes of the assertive "feminist translator" who takes charge of the text and rewrites it for her identity-reinforcing purposes. As Matthew Kayahara (2002) has argued, Alberto Mira (1999: 112) makes this question of gay identity and consciousness-raising through translation central to his argument that "bringing homosexuality in translation out of the closet has to be regarded, first and foremost, as a political gesture." Again, much like translators working under the first paradigm, Mira takes the position that translators must locate and recognise gay meaning in texts, and then activate it through translation for the sake of community building. Questions about where that meaning is located—in explicit sexual references, in "camp" dialogue or slang, in subtle evocations of homoeroticism, in intertextual appropriations from pop culture or in some other discursively performative gesture—are complicated, essentially located in the culture of the moment, and therefore contingent.

It is interesting to note the close parallels between the translation challenges that the two gender paradigms have triggered and the strong similarities between the strategies and solutions they call for. In terms of the activist positions taken by translators and by many researchers on gender in the past decades, both paradigms are based on identity-formation and group affiliations, and it is up to the translator to accept or refuse this identification. Moreover, both are constructivist (Nussbaum, 1999), viewing sexual identity as either being unwittingly constructed from childhood or deliberately constructed and acted out as an adult. Both paradigms are reflected in language and can be evoked, displayed, activated, enacted, suppressed or erased both in source texts, and in translated texts when this language is carried over into other cultures and contexts. In this transfer, political or ideological reasons play an important role. Under both paradigms, the producers—translators, publishers, editors—can choose to take assertive activist positions, rendering gender aspects and their own interventions deliberately visible, choosing to translate only those authors/texts that suit their politics, or deliberately intervening to make a text fit their particular mindset. Similarly, translation research in historical areas, such as Limbeck's (1999) work on the translations of Plautus that erase all intimations of homosexuality and DeJean's (1989) work on the many French versions of Sappho, can exploit the theoretical and epistemological categories devised in these gender paradigms to do revisionist analyses, and propose new readings of classical and more recent writers, and other key texts. Though deemed to be different, or theorised as differently constructed, the two gender paradigms have so far provoked stimulating versions of similar types of work. Even the warnings about erasing differences, engaging in imperialist processes, or stabilising an identification that is inherently unstable or diffident apply to both, and can be heeded.

Notes:

1. Interestingly, three books on gender and translation were written in Canada (De Lotbiniere-Harwood, 1991; Simon, 1996; von Flotow, 1997). Located within the Anglo-American "gender realm," Canada has also been strongly affected by translation owing to its politics of bilingualism.
2. The Vatican document was published in several languages, yet only the English has a subheading clearly entitled Gender; the German and French consist of numbered paragraphs and include a conciliatory justification of this ban on inclusive language. Reproduced here is the first part of the German text plus explanation (my italics mark the text missing from the English), which even recognises and employs the word "inclusive:"

   In vielen Sprachen gibt es Substantive and Pronomina, die fur das meinnliche und weibliche Genus dieselbe Form aufweisen. Darauf zu bestehen, dass dieser Sprachgebrauch geandert wird, darf nicht notwendigerweise als Wirkung oder Zeichen echten Fortschritts der jeweiligen Sprache gelten. Obwohl wit Hilfe der Katechese dafiir zu *sorgen ist, doss solche Wiirter weiterhin in diesem "inclusiven" Sinn verstanden werden, kann es in den Uberseztungen selbst dennoch nicht oft vorkommen, doss verschiedene Wiirter verwendet werden, ohne dass die im Text geforderte Genauigkeit, der Zusammenhang seiner Wiirter und Ausdriicke und seiner Stimmigkeit Schaden nehmen.*

   The special title and the lack of explanation in the English version make it much more pre-emptory.
3. The published version of this subheading reads "A Spaniard in her Twenties" (Zambrano, 1999), thus maintaining, or returning to pre-feminist notions of the feminine being included in or connoted by masculine/neutral forms. Maier had surmised that the final version might remain untranslated as una which

could have avoided the problem (Maier, 1998: 22ff.).

4. The "lesbian and gay translation project" located in Budapest at is a wonderful example of a publisher's initiative.

选文二　女性主义翻译之本质

葛校琴

导　言

本文选自《外语研究》2003 年第 6 期。作者葛校琴，博士、解放军国际关系学院教授、博士生导师。其研究兴趣集中在文化批评、文学翻译、传播学等领域。

选文从文化批评视角，阐述了女性主义翻译思想的起源，探讨了女性主义翻译的认识论、实践论和方法论以及女性主义翻译的解构主义理论来源，最后指出女性主义翻译的本质及对译学和文化批评的贡献。

一

译学研究的文化转向使人们必然关注翻译活动的政治、社会及历史等文化本质层面。随着文化身份(cultural identity)研究的日渐升温，作为身份研究重要内容的性别(gender)话题由此浮出水面。

性别惯常视为人的生理属性。男性和女性的差异是生理上的，生理上的差别带来男性和女性之社会差别。这似乎在告诫人们，男女间的不平等是必然的、无可奈何的，是女性必须接受的境状。但是，女性主义思想认为，用牛理差异来解释男女不平等的社会现状是差强人意。波伏娃指出，一个人之为女人，与其说是"天生"的，不如说是"形成"的。没有任何生理上、心理上或经济上的定命，能决断女人在这社会中的地位，而是人类文化之整体，产生出这居间于男性与无性中的所谓"女性"。唯独因为有旁人插入干涉，一个人才会被注定为"第二性"。换言之，女性的现状是社会造就的，是社会对她的期待造就的，是包围她的大文化、小文化、道德伦理、宗教信仰和教育造就的。因此，男女间的不平等，从来不是天生的、自然的，而是后天的、人为的存在。

性别差异是社会文化建构起来的，是由文化和政治上的父权统治造成的。在性别建构过程中，语言扮演了重要角色。语言是交流的工具，更是权力操纵的手段。自柏拉图和亚里士多德以来，语言的生成和发布都是由社会权力机构操纵，而社会权力机构的运作大多由男人掌控，男人们掌握着语言的生产和使用。这样的语言一直以来述说着男人的生活、描述着男人的世界并一直宣扬父权意识，由此形成了父权统治的权威话语——“父权语言”(patriarchal language)。在文本世界中，父权语言掌控着文本的创造、文本的阅读和文本的阐释，不知不觉地将女性逐渐塑造成他们要求的社会角色。男女相对的一系列概念因此而出现：理性与感性、坚强与软弱、主动与被动、独立与附属等等。这些概念不断地使用，逐渐地被强化，发展成为有形和无形的社会规约来生成女人的社会形象。而女人的内心世界、女人的社会经验和个人体验则没有人、没有她们自己的语言来描述。因此女性主义呼吁用女性主义话语来言说女性的特殊性、差异性，让这个话语构建的世界拥有女性自己的声音并努力使女性获得与男人精神上平等的地位。

女性主义思想家认为，女性与语言疏远太久，与她们的女性经验疏远太久，使她们不能将自己的经历符号化。传统的标准句法和确定的文类都代表父权制话语结构，因此女性主义试图找到新的语言和新的文学形式来对女性现实作出反映。她们批评并激烈地改变即存语言，大胆地进行创作实验；她们使用新词、新拼写、新语法结构、新意象和新隐喻以远离父权语言的权威结构，为女性寻求一片新的话语空间。正如法国女性主义者伊丽格瑞指出：如果我们继续讲这一语言，我们会重叙男人故事，重复男人话语。我们要向制定当今律法的话语挑战，因为这种话语为一切立法，包括性差异；如果依这种话语，另一性的存在，一个他者的存在，女人的存在，似乎仍然是无法想象的事情。女性主义的口号之一就是“妇女通过语言获得解放”。

二

女性主义对语言中性别问题的深刻揭示为翻译中性别问题的研究提供了独特的视角和方法论的指导，从而使传统的翻译认识论、翻译实践论和翻译方法论之基础都发生了根本性的动摇。

女性主义对翻译的认识是一种全球宏观关照，局部微观透视的文化翻译概念，它所涉及的不仅仅是本源语和译入语的问题，更是两种迥异文化相遇时使用谁的话语，为谁，为何种目的和如何阐释的问题。尤其当翻译跨越东方和西方、强势和弱势之时，翻译的问题更为复杂。因此，在女性主义看来，翻译是跨文化、跨语际的“违犯”(transgression)过程，是译者传达、重写并操纵一个文本使它适用于第二语言的公众的过程，此时，种种文化张力尽显其中。翻译，无论是作为过程还是作为结果，不但是现实之镜，同时也促成现实。译者可以利用翻译即翻译时使用的语言作为文化干预的手段，来抵制并改变父权话语的支配性结构。翻译因此成为一种创造性的写作实践，介入到文本意义的创造之中。

基于这样的翻译认识，女性主义翻译研究揭示了传统翻译研究将翻译女性化(feminized)和将翻译边缘化的过程。在以往的翻译阐述中长期存在的对女性的歧视性表述，如论及译本与原本的关系时，经常引用“漂亮的女人不忠实，忠实的女人不漂亮”之说法。这一譬喻使用社会中性别歧视的语言来喻说翻译的忠实问题，将性别歧视扩充到翻译研究领域，并暗示了翻译研究中隐藏的许多二元对立的概念，如创作与翻译、原文与译文、作者与译者等等。其中，前者常被视为权威性的、强壮的、生产性的，后者则是地位低下的，有缺陷的、附属的；前者应该主宰后者，后者则必须服从前者，忠实于前者；原创是完美的，翻译总是有欠缺的；原作是强壮而具有生产力的男性，译本则是低弱派生的女性。女性主义认为，翻译的这种弱势地位是长期受父权语言压制的结果；女性主义翻译研究就是要揭示和批判这种即将翻译又将女性逐入社会底

层和他(她)者处境的状况,以动摇维持这种状况的男性权威和父权话语。

女性主义翻译在实践上极力提倡一种译者干预性的(interventionist)翻译实践,要求对翻译文本进行女性主义的创造。弗洛图(Luise von Flotow)论述了女性主义翻译的三种实践方式:增补(supplementing)、劫持(hijacking)以及加写前言和脚注(prefacing and footnoting)。“增补”是为了弥补语言间的差异。她列举女性主义翻译家戈达德(Barbara Godard)翻译的女性主义作家 Nicole Brossard 的小说 *L'Amèr*。*L'* 为 *La*(*the*);*Amèr* 代表三个词:mère(*mother 母亲*),*mer*(*sea 海*),*amer*(*bitter 辛酸*)。原文标题即是文字游戏。戈达德的翻译将 the 放在左边,将 e, our, mothers 右边竖排,左右之间置大写 S 表示海,该标题成为

```
          e
the—S<—our
          mothers
```

组合成 These Our Mothers(这些我们的母亲)或 These Sour Smothers(这些辛酸的溺爱者),将以上三词的意思包含进去。在原女性主义表述的标题上再创新意。“劫持”是指女性主义译者对并不一定具有女性主义意图的文本的剥夺或挪用(appropriation)。如哈沃德(Hartwood)翻译丽芝·高文(Lise Gauvin)《她人的信》(*Lettres d'une autre*)。原作使用了许多阳性词,译者对此进行了“改正”(correct),如将 *Quebecois* 全改为 *Quebecois-e-s*,挪用原词创造阴性词。“加写前言和脚注”是女性主义翻译的常规。“前言”通常被女性主义译者用来解释原文意旨,概括自己的翻译策略,目的是让译本读者充分了解译者的翻译过程,并借此发挥女性主义翻译的教喻作用。哈沃德在译本《她人的信》的“前言”中解释说:“我的翻译实践是一项政治活动,目的是让语言为女性说话;我的署名意指我采取了所有翻译策略,让女性在语言中显现。”(Sherry Simon, 1996: 15)

女性主义翻译策略还有多种。如对原本的语法性别提出质疑。语法性别通常是语言结构性约法,是组成语言的结构成分,被认为跟意义毫无关系。但雅各布森(Roman Jacobson)指出,语法性别在某些情况下如诗歌和神话中也被赋予象征意义。女性主义从雅各布森的观点中受到启发,并认为这种诗学上的意义更具意识形态性。阳性通常是词的无标记(unmarked)形式,是词的简单形式,可以作一般性使用,具有相对中立的意义;阴性却是有标记形式,不能作为常规用法。英语名词虽无性别之分,但仍然隐含着性别意味。如“国会议员和*他们的*夫人”,女人总是成为男人的附属;mankind 是“男人类”的含义,用来指普遍的“人类”。这样的表述,表面上性别中立,但实际上是意指人类等同于人类中的男性。还有,署名问题也成为女性主义突现主体性的翻译策略。译者署名、突现译者、“把自己对操纵文本的标记昭示天下”,用以抵抗作者、原语文本的权威。女性主义专门创造了女译者(translatress)一词,突出女性译者的创造性地位。此外,她们还采用女性常用文本类型如翻译随笔或翻译日记,或撰写翻译理论文章,对父权文类的统治予以抵制。总之,女性主义译者使用一切可以使用的方法使翻译成为女性一种强有力的表达方式。

当然,女性主义这种重写的翻译实践通常需要文本、作者、译者三者的共谋和合作。文本通常是后现代实验小说或女性主义作品,作者本身也是女性主义作家,由女性主义译者进行翻译。所以女性主义翻译的忠实,不是对原文和原作者的忠实,而是忠实于她们的写作计划,一项女性主义的写作计划。

三

女性主义翻译理论和实践的出现并非无本之木无源之水，我们可以从法国心理分析家拉康、后结构主义思想家巴尔特和解构主义思想家德里达的相关思想中找到理论来源。

拉康是结构主义者，但他的理论启发了法国女性主义使之成为女性主义的直接来源。在拉康的理论中，想象界（the Imaginery）与象征界（the Symbolic）是两个与现实界（the Real）相异的两个术语。想象与前俄狄浦斯阶段一致，在此阶段，孩子认为自己是母亲的一部分，自己与世界之间没有分别，没有压抑、没有缺失，也就没有潜意识。到了象征界，父亲的出现离间了母子浑然一体的亲密关系，对孩子来说，失去了母亲的肉体，对母亲的占有欲望则受到了压抑，无意识由此展开。无意识是作为欲望压抑的结果而浮现的，从某种意义上说，无意识就是欲望。象征界的秩序就是现代社会中父权制的性别和社会文化的秩序，它由围绕男性的菲勒斯构成，受父亲法律（the Law of the Father）的支配。无论主体是否愿意进入象征界，由于它是社会文化和社会生活的主宰，主体必须进入象征界才不至于成为精神病患者。拉康思想中对女性依然有一种偏见，但他思想却启发了法国女权主义。回到前俄狄浦斯的想象界来抗拒象征秩序对女性的压抑，这是法国女性主义一种策略；在语言中建构主体则成为法国女性主义理论特色。

法国文论家巴尔特属于从结构主义到解构主义转变的人物，1970 年他发表的重要著作《S/Z》公开摒弃了结构主义的分析方法。在该书中，巴尔特对传统的文本意义、作者权威、阅读方式进行了后结构主义的阐述。这些阐述对女性主义翻译产生了极大的影响。巴尔特认为作品没有不变的内核，作品的意义是游移变动的，不为文本所凝固，没有终极意义；他提出文本的意义在于读者与文本接触时的体验。针对作者权威的看法，他认为作者不是作品意义的最高权威，作者一写下文字，意义的游移是他本人无法支配的。因此作者对于自己的“产品”不是主人，只是一个“客人”罢了。他把文学作品分为“可读的”和“可写的”两类。前者以写实主义小说为代表，后者以晦涩难读，不具可读性的先锋小说为代表。对于“可读性”小说，读者只是一个“消费者”，而对于“可写性”小说读者则是一个“生产者”。前者只需读者被动地消耗文本，后者则要求读者作出创造性贡献，读者一面阅读，一面思考并补充作者的未尽之言。“作者死了，读者诞生了”。女性主义翻译对传统翻译理论与方法的反动可以清晰看到巴尔特思想的影响。翻译成为“能指的游戏”，读者/译者在“可写性”文本上进行意义的创新或文本的再造。原作者的权威不再，原文的意义不定，翻译的对等同一无法企及。

现代西方社会的理性传统是在二元对立的思维模式的基础上建立起来的。如善与恶、好与坏、理性与感性、主体与客体等，彼此相对形成意义。语言也被认为是包含着能指与所指的对称性单位结构，能指反映所指，意义是确定一致的。但是，解构大师德里达却认为意义产生于一种能指与其他能指的横向开放性关系，不存在词与物一对一的纵向联系模式。人们对意义的确立不过是语言因其不同的排列而生出的效果。因此符号的意义并非自足，而是在与别的符号形成的对立、差异和对比中显现出来。语言是一张无限伸展的网，网上的成分不断交换和循环，没有一个成分受到绝对的限定。德里达创造的新词 différance（延异），就包含了两种意义：一是差别和区分；二是延搁和推迟。符号的意义处于不断的运动状态，是一种阐释替代另一种阐释的游戏。différance 由此成为解构西方传统二元对立思维方式的理论武器。德里

达在分析现代社会时认为，这种二元对立在社会中表现为菲勒斯中心和逻各斯中心的倾向，也就是父权中心和终极存在论思想。他将这两种倾向复合成一个词——菲逻各中心(phallogocentric)，即将父权和终极的追寻并列，将两者都视为支配自然和社会的合乎规律的真理。解构主义者就是要解构这一中心。德里达对确定意义和菲逻各中心主义的解构，成为女性主义和女性主义翻译的理论依据和实践目的。

四

综上所述，女性主义翻译理论倡导的是一种差异哲学。它使我们意识到翻译是文化、政治、历史、意义等各种差异剧烈碰撞和交锋的场所。翻译致力于消除差异，但翻译又造成差异。女性主义翻译理论强调女性身份，后殖民主义翻译理论标扬异化策略都是这一点最好的明证。女性主义翻译研究把视线转到差异上，转到二元对立中的弱者，转到众多的他(她)者，使文化中不为人知的边缘角色被展示出来，被人们注视，为差异的合法性辩护，为当今文化批评，为文化的健康发展，提供了丰富的思想资源。

女性主义翻译理论让我们看到合理使用翻译可以为建立健康的两性社会和良好的国际关系发挥作用。翻译促成全球文化的交流，更促成全球文化的生产；翻译是差异的碰撞，更是文化的争斗。贝尔·胡克斯(Bell Hooks)说，语言是斗争之场。跨语言、跨民族、跨文化的翻译何尝不是？后殖民翻译理论告诉我们，翻译既可以成为强势文化实施文化霸权的同谋，也可以成为抑制文化霸权的锐器。女性主义翻译也是。在历史上，它和任何话语方式一样，也曾是父权语言的捍卫者和维护者，但它同样可以成为女性的一种言说方式，为女性赢得男女平权作出贡献。性别歧视的改观不能等待男权的施舍，要女性自我的觉醒，要女性自己的参与。在强势和弱势文化的交汇中，同样需要弱势文化自身的努力。

女性主义翻译理论是在传统翻译研究基础上的进步。女性主义在更加宏观的文化翻译的概念下实施对具有普遍意义的"对等"、"忠实"、"同一"这些传统翻译概念的颠覆。"对等"诸概念视翻译为两种语言间的操作过程，确信意义同一，确信价值中立。女性主义视意义是性别的建构(the gendered construction of meaning)；"'意义'是一特定的个人，在其所处的特定的语境，为特定的目的而构建的特定时期的特写。"("'Meaning' is a feature of a specific time, constructed for a specific purpose, by a specific individual working within a specific context." Flotow, 1997: 96)翻译的问题应该是"谁，因为什么，在什么情况下，为哪些读者而重写?"("Who rewrites, why, under what circumstances, for which audience?" Lefevere, 1992: 7)可见，翻译并非是简单的语言转换问题，翻译是多层次展开的、各因素动态发展的、各种张力作用的语言操作过程。女性主义翻译理论深化了翻译研究的课题，拓展了翻译研究的思路，是对译学发展的重大贡献。

当然，女性主义所倡导的翻译给人一种矫枉过正的感觉。如对女性经验的过分张扬有落入色情文学之嫌；在理论的阐述中也使用一些过激性词汇，如剥夺、侵占、劫持等，有形成新的二元对立(女/男)的趋向；在翻译策略上和翻译的效果上也有矛盾的地方。这一切都有待于女性主义翻译理论和方法自身的不断发展和完善。女性主义翻译和其他任何学派一样，必将为文明的发展、社会的民主和公平作出贡献。

选文三　雌雄同体:女性主义译者的理想

何高大　陈水平

导　言

本文选自《四川外语学院学报》2006 年第 3 期。作者何高大是华南农业大学外国语学院教授,主要从事外语教学与教育技术、翻译理论与实践研究;陈水平是湖南科技大学外国学院硕士生,主要从事翻译理论与实践研究。

选文探询翻译之所以被性别化的历史根源和哲学根源,阐述女性主义者为了凸显女性主体的差异性所做的努力,论证了女性主义之所以运用这些过激的手法并不是要重新建构一个"母权制中心",而是为了建构一种可以包容男女性别差异的真正意义上的平等——"雌雄同体"来最终消除性别歧视。雌雄同体的理想的提出,不仅使女性主义理论不至于流于新的二元对立,而且为整个翻译研究提供了新的视角,有助于推动翻译研究的多元化发展。

1. 引言

男女两性分类,是一个多学科的分类系统。它既具有生物学意义,也具有心理学、社会学化人类学意义,同时还是一个可以进行多层面分析的现象。既可以从个体层面,也可以从人际层面、群体层面、社会类别层面、社会制度层面、文化类型层面等予以解释。解释的不同,其意义也有所不同。西方女性主义 feminism(今译为"女权主义"、"男女平权主义"、"女性主义",本文均采用"女性主义")一词缘于妇女解放运动,经历了许多演变和重新解释,甚至目前自称是女性主义者的人,对于它的确切含义也仍然莫衷一是。需要指出的是无论是"女权主义"还是"女性主义",在中国翻译语境中,似乎并不是一个受欢迎的词。人们更愿意使用内涵较为模糊的"女性翻译意识"。女性主义借用了德里达的解构主义理论,对传统的等级制度和性别角色提出了质疑,认为意义与价值不再是固定不变的,从而颠覆了传统的结构主义翻译范式和典律。70 年代以来,女性主义来势凶猛,其手法之激进令人咋舌,所以女性主义的翻译观点和实践遭到某些反对也是不足为奇。罗斯玛利阿罗约(Rosemary Arrojo)就认为,女性主义翻译的理想看起来完全就是男性主义种种形式建构的一个反面形象。她追问:为什么男性主义的阐释模式是偏离背叛而女性主义的阐释则意义丰富?既然她们总是想要代替或至少是增补其他的行为或其他的理论,女性主义译者的这些行动和欲望,自身难道不也是暴力性的吗?在此,女性主义有重新建构新的二元对立之嫌。同样,我国许多学者在承认女性主义翻译理论有一定启示的同时,也认为她的"某些观点对我国翻译界显得有些超前"(廖七一,2002),从某种角度来说甚至"会导致译者主体意识的过分张扬","会把翻译实践和翻译研究引向极端"(张景华,2004)。所以,正如洛丽钱伯伦指出的:女性主义译者应该接受的挑战之一就是超越作者和

译者的生理性别问题。在此，弗吉尼亚伍尔芙(Woolf)、埃莱娜西苏(Helene Cixous)、克里斯蒂娃(Kristeva)、露丝伊瑞格瑞(Luce Irigaray)等女性主义者提出了在坚持男女两性差别的基础上，以一种可以包容男女差异的同一境界的思想——“雌雄同体”来对抗和解构父权制的二元对立。

2. 翻译研究中性别歧视的历史和哲学根源

女性主义翻译理论的目标就是要识别、批判那些将女性又将翻译逐入社会和文学底层的概念。为此它必须探讨翻译被女性化的过程，并试图动摇那些维持这种联系的权威结构。(Simon, 1996)那么，翻译又是怎么被性别化的呢？从历史的角度看，翻译与女性有着不解之缘。首先，翻译是女性、尤其是欧洲中世纪的女性进入文学世界的途径。19至20世纪，法国、俄国、德国现代主义的伟大作品一半是由妇女翻译的。由于长久地被排斥在创作权力之外，妇女便把翻译作为写作的一种训练，利用这非常有限的着手点来达到自己的政治目的。另外，这种性别差异还体现在描述翻译的隐喻中。“女人”和“译者”同被归入话语的低等地位，译者被视为作者的侍女，女人低于男人。同样，在我国也有把翻译比做媒婆的歧视隐喻，而歌德甚至把翻译家比作是下流的职业媒婆。不但译者、原作和译作也与阳性和阴性的意象连在了一起，原作被视为强壮而有生产力的男性，而译本则是低级的派生的女性。而此中突出的是由法国翻译家梅纳日(Gilles Menage)杜撰的那个双关语“不忠的美人”，在男人心目中女人是“漂亮的不忠实，忠实的不漂亮”。从而将“漂亮”与“忠实”对立起来。无论是古典的翻译理论还是结构主义的翻译观都将“忠实”和“信”看作不可违抗的翻译伦理。翻译活动被比喻成一桩婚姻，忠贞(忠实)是后代(译文)惟一合法的保证。(廖七一,2002)这种将女性和翻译等同的观念，既表达了女性处于弱者的地位，也显示了翻译的从属状况。而女性主义认为，要求译文绝对忠实原文，就像要求女性绝对服从男性一样是不平等的，这样的婚姻实际上是建立在欺骗的婚姻合同基础之上的。首先，这些将“忠实”视为圭臬的译论都是建立在中心论和二元论的哲学基础上的。他们往往假定某种性别的二元对立，对立的其中一方处于决定性地位的中心，而另一方则是被决定的边缘，从而把译作与原作的关系就像男性和女性关系一样对立起来。作者被认为是权威，而译者和女性一样，是处于第二位的。男女间的生理差异是毋庸置疑的，但用生理差异来解释男女不平等的社会现状却难以差强人意，正如波伏娃认为的那样：“女人并非生来就是，而是后天变成的。”在文本世界里，父权掌控着文本的创造、文本的阅读和文本的阐释，不知不觉地将女性逐渐塑造成他们要求的社会角色。女性主义认为，导致男女不平等的根本原因是“差异”与平等的对立。在父权制社会中，这种男女的差异被夸大成为了不可调和的两极。事实上，男女同一的观念认为：从生理学角度来看，男女在性方面生理构造是一一对应的、同质的，只不过具体的表现形态有些不一样。这种差别应该是相对的，他们的关系应该是一个连续体，任何一个个体都是连续体上的一个点，既没有绝对的男性气质，也不会存在绝对的女性气质。同样，作者和译者、原文和译作之间也应该是一个连续体，在这个连续体中原文与译作相互映衬、相互补充，构成一种共生关系。其次，传统语言学派强调意义的普遍性，认为所有的语言都是异质同构的，意义的所指和能指存在着一一对应的关系。作品背后都隐藏着一个固定不变的意义等着译者去发现，然后亦步亦趋地把它加以传达。译者被看成一个仆人，一只看不见的手，机械地把一种语言转换成另一种语言，译作也被认为是一个摹本，而不是创造性的话语。这种结构主义的翻译理论过于强调语言的确定性，过分强调所谓一对一的转换规律，而忽视了语言文化间的差异和译者的主体因素，这种对主体因素的抹杀压制了译者的主观能动性，译者被看成是“隐形”的。女性主义者借用德里达的解构理论，认为意义产生于一种能指与其他能指的横向开放性关系，不存在词与物一对一的纵向联系模式。翻译是意义有差别的重复，全息图(hologram)成为这一自觉再现过程的独特象征。“连续曝光中多重影像的一种叠加，一种交叉叠盖，对于互文性，话语相互作用的一个比喻，一个展示着事实的转换的虚像。全息图并不固定不变地描绘其形象，它演示它。”(Simon，1996)意义是多重性的，允许有多重理解，因而翻译是有差异的，也就不存在惟一的标准。正如本雅明指出的那样，和原作完全相同的译作是不可能存在的。法国文论家巴尔特也认为作品没有不变的内核，作品的意义是游移变动的，不为文本所凝固，也没有终极意，文本的意义在于读者与文本接触时的体验；作者一旦写下文字，意义的游移是他本人无法支配的。这一思想一旦被女性主义利用，翻译就成为“能指的游戏”，原文的意义不再是有待发现的真值，而是有待创造的一系列话语。贝尔曼(Berman)指出：只译者把游戏摆上台面，她“他们就拥有了所有的权利”。(Simon，1996)

3. 突显女性主体的差异性

女性主义译者坚持维护她那根本性的差异，她那无穷尽地再阅读和改写的快乐，把自己对操纵文本的标记昭示天下。女性主义译者坦率宣称翻译就是重写，并用种种手段突显女性在文本中的地位，让女性在语言中“可见”，从而使女性在真实世界中被“听见”和被“看见”。女性主义认为，在旧的男性中心意识形态里，男性是作为整个人类代表的身份出场的，“一部人类历史实际上是一部男性中心主义的单一性别史”。为此，除了让许多“失落”的女性作品被发掘出来以外，女性主义译者还进行了大量大胆的翻译实践。首先，我们应该提到的是女性主义者的《圣经》翻译。女性主义者为了争取女性在基督教中应有的位置，从女性主义角度重新翻译了《圣经》。在她们的强烈呼吁下，1983年，《语言兼顾两性的圣经选文集》(*An Inclusive Language Lectionary*)的英译本终于正式出版。迄今，至少已出版了17种不同版本的“中性”或“语言兼顾两性的”《圣经》英译本。苏姗妮(Susanne)把这两种方法分别定义为“中性化”(neutralization)和“减性化”(desexiation)。然而，这些“中性”和“两性兼顾”的语言真能令人满意吗？苏姗妮指出这两种方法在使用范围和效果上实际上是不能令人满意的，往往会发生掩盖女性身影的现象。比方说，在翻译实践中，人们常常会用一些中性词来代替那些男性概括词，然而事实却是：普通读者的阅读思维过程多是习惯性地以男性为中心的，离开女权作品的语境，当人们看到或听到诸如person之类的中性词时，思维定势还是以男性为主。而且无论是在语言中还是现实中，从来都不存在中性这种东西。同样，“减性化”实际上也是有问题的。常见的例子为以s/he代替he。可是转而一想，我们就会发现一个问题，“减性化”似乎是一个很奇怪的概念。因为英语本身就是减性化了的男性语言。现实中，人们经常会希望能把he和man减性后当中性词使用，从而能把男女都包括在内。可是这些词没有一个被人们看成是中性词。所以，为了把女性的身影表现得更明确、更清楚，苏姗妮提出了“重新性化语言”(resex language)——为了女性的声音被听到，女性的身影被看到，而在语言方面所做的性化标志。在此，苏姗妮认为为了达到这样一种性化标志，翻译者可以尽情发挥自己的创造力，运用一切语言技巧使女性在文本中能够出现。那么女性主义者又是怎样利用自己的创造灵感在翻译中

体现女性主体的差异性呢？在戈达尔德、阿特伍德、卡萝梅尔、卡茜麦兹(Kathy Meizei)、弗洛图等人的努力下，词语的力量以新鲜、甚至是扎眼的面貌呈现出来。比如，弗洛图提出了三种实践方式：增补、加写前言和脚注以及“劫持”。增补是为了弥补语言间的差异，要求译者进行干预。她列举了女性主义翻译家戈达尔德(Bar-bara Godard)翻译的尼古拉·布罗萨尔(Nicole Bros-sard)的小说*L'Am. r*的例子。Am. r至少包含了三个词：mre(mother 母亲)、mer(sea 海)、amer(bitter 辛酸的)。戈达尔德利用图示把它组合成 These Our Mothers(这些我们的母亲)或“These Sour Smothers”(这些辛酸的溺爱者)，将以上三词的意义都包含进去了。其次，女性主义通常用前言和脚注来解释原文意旨，概括自己的翻译策略。戈达尔德显然是最好的例子，她在翻译布罗萨尔《图象理论》时，在日记和前言中记录了她在翻译这种在科学、哲学和后现代主义地带展开的文本所遇到的难处。而最具争议的是第三个技巧——“劫持”，也就是说，女性主义译者对并不一定具有女性主义意图的文本的剥夺和挪用。如阿特伍德翻译丽兹高文(Lise Gauvin)的《她人的信》(Letters d. une autre)；作者在文本里使用的全是阳性词的地方，译者给予了“纠正”，比方把原作中所有的 Qu becois(阳性复数)都替之以 Qu becoisesa(阴性复数)。除此之外，女性主义译者还在译本上署名，让译作带上译者自身的标记。女性主义者阿特伍德说：我在一个译本上署名意味着这一译本使用了所有的翻译策略。要使女性在语言中清晰可见。在此，译者被赋予了与原作者同等的权威，而译作是反映女性意识的“二次写作”。正如戈达尔德就此所论，阿特伍德的署名肯定不是一个解构行为，而是一次重建主导地位的尝试；阿特伍德对署名作为“固定一个单独、具体的女性主体”的行为的强调，的确意味着她期望建立“个人”的位置而非“话语”的位置。(Simon，1996)回想以前女性发表译文时只能采取匿名形式，否则译文就只能以手稿形式在家族中传阅。即使在女译者可以公开身份受到嘉奖之时，她们的态度也十分谦恭，把自己描述为扛着货物沉默地跟在主人脚步后的搬运工，是不同文化之间跑腿运送材料的船夫，称自己的工作是“暂时的”和“过渡的”而现在，女性主义译者提倡要在翻译中“粗暴的妇占”(womanhandling)文本，这就意味着她要取代那个谦虚而自惭形秽的译者。在此，作者对 womanhandling 一词的翻译“粗暴的妇占”是取自张南锋先生的翻译，正如徐来先生谈到的那样，“粗暴”二字虽不很悦耳，但女性主义者未必会反感，因为她们正是要以“矫枉过正”的方式来引起人们对译者主体性的足够兴趣。(徐来，2004)

4. 雌雄同体的理想

然而，对于法国女权主义文学批评家埃莱娜·西苏来说，女性文体或“女子气作品”这样的术语会使她厌恶，因为诸如“男性”和“女性”之类的术语本身就把我们限死在一个二元逻辑中，限死在“男女之间性对比的陈旧观念”之中。她坚信所有人类的天性中都蕴含着雌雄同体的因素，并且提出了她所谓的“另一雌雄同体”来区别“两性共体”的陈旧观念。陈旧的观念认为“双性的，因而是中性的”，是排除差别的；而对于女性主义者西苏来说，所谓的“另一雌雄同体”就是“每个人在自身中找到两性的存在，这种存在依据男女个人。其明显与坚决的程度是多种多样的。既不排除差别也不排除其中一性”。(西苏，1981)这种雌雄同体并不消灭差别，而是鼓动差别，追求差别。并增大其数量。而女性主义译者的最终目的就是要达到这样一种境界——在承认差异性基础上要求个人的心灵中保持男性和女性的平衡。正如克里斯蒂娃认为的那样，一个解放了的人是能够在“女性气质”和“男性气质”、混乱与秩序、革命与现状之间自由行动的人。英国女作家弗吉尼亚·伍尔芙也在《自己的房间》中写道：“心灵要有男女的通力协作才能完成艺术的创造，必须使一些相互对立的因素结成美满的婚姻，整个心房必须大敞四开，才能感觉到作家在美满地交流她的经验。”性别的认同可以是流动多变的。比如，中国诗词里就有一种以美女及爱情来托喻“政治情感”的悠久传统。古代诗人通常借恋歌来比喻他们的政治遭遇，把自己表述为诗中的女性角色，以达到自我掩饰的目的。孙宜康先生把这种通过女性声音所建立起来的托喻美学称做“性别面具”。“这种艺术手法也使男性文人无形中进入了性别越界的联想；通过性别置换与移情作用，他们不仅表现了自己的情感，也能投入女性角色的心境与立场。”(孙康宜，2002)例如曹植的《弃妇》，表面上是描写女主人公的哀怨之情，实际上是诗人暗示自己被兄长曹丕迫害与深埋内心的无能为力之感。而女性作家也可以利用这种“性别倒置”的手法，通过虚构的男性声音来说话。19 世纪的著名女词人兼剧作家吴藻就是最典型的例子。在其《饮酒读骚图》中，吴藻“女扮男装”，把自己比作屈原，却唱出比男人更加男性化的心曲。此剧在当时引起许多男性作家的热烈反应，他们都强调：最有效的寄托笔法乃是一种性别的跨越。屈原以美人自喻，吴藻却以屈原自喻。两性都企图在性别面具中寻求自我发抒的艺术途径。重要的是，要创造一个角色、一种表演、一种意象、一种与“异性”认同的价值。(孙康宜，2002)中国的“宫体诗”也是一个典型的例子，这些诗的大部分作者都是男性，却传神地描绘了宫里女子的悲惨心境。“个人化写作”被视为“女性写作”的主要形态。翻译就是“写作”，也要求译者内心达到男性和女性的平衡。所以，与“雌雄同体”相呼应，谢莉西蒙(Sherry Simon)也提出了跨写(cross-writing)或跨译(cross-translating)的概念。她认为女性译者可以成功翻译男性作者的作品，性别不匹配的译者也力可胜任。刘军平先生(2004)也认为，如果女性译家翻译男性作家的作品能够把握男性的刚强，如果男性译家翻译女性的作品能够传递其柔美，其译作一定是天作之合。有足够的事实证明，写作允许自我对其他身份的想像投射，而天生就属于一种文化身份并不能保证亲和关系。(Simon，1996)正是女性译者洛波特尔的翻译，才使男性作者托马斯·曼(Thomas Mann)的作品超越了狭隘的语言、地域和文化的限制而获得了“重生”；女性主义译者阿特伍德在翻译摇滚诗人和歌手卢西安弗朗哥(Lucien Franeoeur)的男子汉诗歌时，她意识到诗歌的立场、语言迫使她“以男性的方式话，”(Simon，1996)最终，阿特伍德沿用了弗朗哥的风格，继续了他的追求，再造了弗朗哥糅合了美国摇滚文化和法国僭越诗歌的语调和精神。同样，作者和译者的关系、原作和译作的关系也是不可分割的、平等的，既合作又独立的。“雌雄同体”中的双方相互依存、不可分割、合而不同，通过对话相互影响对方。形成一种共生的关系。事实上。许多女性主义译者都在翻译过程中充分表达了“雌雄同体”的思想。比如 17 世纪英国的诺斯考门伯爵(Earl of Roscommon)在他那首著名的诗中谈到了作者和译者的关系：译者应该仔细选择作者，这个作者应该是能与译者“情感相通”的，他们之间应该存在着“情感的纽带”。有了这种关系，再通过译者对原文的细读，一种共生的关系就产生了，作者和译者在一种神秘和极度的兴奋中融合在一起，从此，他们都不再作为个体而存在，而是合二为一，成为一个不可分割的整体。苏珊·巴斯奈特主张一种“高潮亢奋”的翻译理论，即翻译是一种“在愉悦、互敬的彼此相遇中把所有的成分融合进一个新的整体”的结果。斯皮瓦克认为译者首先必须完全帖服于原文，译者必须在文本中苦苦求索，付出努力赢取成为亲密读者的权利，否则便不能帖服于文本，不能对其特有的呼唤作出回应。“译者的任务是促进原文及其影子之间的爱，让散佚发生，免受译者的能动机制和她想像的或真实

的读者对她的要求的牵制。”(Spivak)在我国,许钧(2003)也用姻缘关系来描述译作和原作之间的关系:“翻译是一种相遇、相知与共存的过程,在这个过程中,有冲突,有矛盾。为相知,必尊重对方;为共存,必求两全之计,以妥协与变通,求得一桩美满的婚姻。”在此所体现的既不是作者高于译者,也不是译者高于作者,而是两者求同存异、和谐共存的完美境界。既不能抹杀译者在翻译中的主体性,让译者完全屈服于作者,也应该避免翻译主体的过分张扬而对文本的阐释所带来的不利因素,避免过多地对原文进行意识形态操控而对翻译理论和实践造成负面的影响,译者的诞生不需要译者的死亡作为代价译者与作者和谐共处才能更充分体现整个文本生命流变的历史过程,才能更深刻理解“源文”与译文之间不可分割的生命纽带。文本的互文性告诉我们世上不存在任何原创的文本,任何文本都与稍前出现的文本略有区别,都是“翻译的翻译的翻译”——首先是从非语言世界的翻译;其次,因为每一个符号,每一个短语都是另一个符号、另一个短语的翻译,因此没有什么文本是完全创新的。(Bassnett, 2002)而文化正是在不断“翻译”前人的作品而呈螺旋轨迹前进的,译文是原文生命的延续,是原作的“转世”。所以本雅明认为所有的译者的任务就是让原作超越时空的限制,让原作“转世”而获得“重生”。翻译不但没有诋毁原作的“纯洁”,而是为原作注入了新的血液,把原作带到一个新的语言世界,扩大了原作的影响。从此,译作和原作构成了一种共生的关系,原作对译作的依赖并不比译作依赖原作更多。用伽达默尔的阐释学观点来说,文本是作者的原初视阈与理解者的当下视阈的交融,即“视阈的融合”,融合后既不同于原文作者的视阈也有别于译者的视阈,它是两者视阈的丰富。

5. 结语

这是一个男女两性共生、雌雄同体的世界,一方的改变肯定会对另一方的在场有所影响。女性主义译者刻意追求翻译中的性别表现的差异,以凸显女性译者的文化身份,以颠覆男性在社会和文化中的统治地位。在女性主义眼中,差异变成一个积极的字眼,是人类认知过程和实践过程中的不可缺少的因素。因此,女性主义翻译理论倡导的是一种差异哲学,她把视线转到差异上,转到二元对立中的弱者,转到他(她)者,使文化中不为人知的边缘角色被展示出来。(葛校琴,2003)毫无疑问,雌雄同体的理想的提出,不仅为女性主义指明了发展的方向,使女性主义理论不至于流于新的二元对立,而且为整个翻译研究提供了新的视角,输入了新的血液,注入了新的活力,最终推动了翻译研究的多元化发展。女性主义翻译研究曾经取得了很大的成就,并仍在发展着,它非常有可能成为翻译理论史上又一座不朽的里程碑,但前提必须是它的理论拓展者能够认真审视其理论体系中的内在缺陷,并以求真务实的批判精神和理论勇气对此加以彻底修正。危机也可以是一种机遇,希望在学术界同仁的不懈努力下,女性主义翻译理论最终能够被纳入辩证和历史唯物主义的轨道,成长为健全、科学的理论体系。

【延伸阅读】

[1] Knellwolf, C. Women Translators, Gender and the Cultural Context of the Scientific Revolution. In Roger Ellis & Liz Oakley-Brown (eds.), *Translation and Nation: Towards a Cultural Politics of Englishness*. Clevedon · Buffalo · Toronto, NY: Multilingual Matters Ltd., 2001.

[2] Larkosh, C. Translating Woman: Victoria Ocampo and the Empires of Foreign Fascination. In Maria Tymoczko & Edwin Gentzler (eds.), *Translation and Power*. Amherst, Mass.: University of Massechussetts Press, 2002.
[3] Chamberlain, L. Gender and the Metaphorics of Translation. In Lawrence Venuti (ed.), *The Translation Studies Reader*. London: Routledge, 2000.
[4] Simon, S. *Gender in Translation: Cultural Identity and the Politics of Transmission*. London: Routledge, 1996.
[5] 蒋骁华. 女性主义对翻译理论的影响. 中国翻译,2004(7).
[6] 廖七一. 重写神话:女性主义与翻译研究. 四川外语学院学报,2002(3).
[7] 刘军平. 女性主义翻译理论研究的中西话语. 中国翻译,2004(7).
[8] 许宝强,袁伟. 语言与翻译的政治. 北京:中央编译出版社,2001.
[9] 徐来. 在女性名义下的"重写". 中国翻译,2004(7).
[10] 张景华. 女性主义对传统译论的颠覆及其局限性. 中国翻译,2004(7).

【问题与思考】

1. 女性主义翻译研究出现了哪两种范式? 两种范式的差别何在?
2. 什么是"坎普话语"(camp talk)? 翻译"坎普话语"有何意义?
3. 女性主义翻译理论给翻译研究拓展了哪些思路?
4. 为什么说女性主义翻译理论倡导的是一种差异哲学?
5. 在对女性主义翻译理论的阐述中有哪些过激性词汇? 如何理解"雌雄同体"?

第九章 文学翻译研究的后殖民主义视阈

导 论

后殖民主义(postcolonialism)是20世纪80年代末期在西方文化界和文学理论界异军突起,从边缘走向中心的最新理论思潮之一。西方翻译界开始重视殖民和后殖民语境里的翻译活动,着手分析研究翻译与帝国、翻译与文化身份、翻译与殖民主义霸权的历史共谋关系等问题,这促使我们重新审视传统译论里的一些基本问题。传统的翻译理论一直假定翻译是两种文化之间的平衡对话。但是,在后殖民语境下,文学翻译作为文化交流的一种形式,呈现出强势文化与弱势文化之间的不平等状态。弱势文化倾向于大规模地译介强势文化,而强势文化的情况则完全相反,文化的不平等关系使平衡的对话根本无法实现。鉴于此,人们将翻译的角色置于广阔的国际政治文化框架内进行重新审视,越来越意识到翻译与殖民关系、文化霸权等之间的密切关系,使后殖民翻译研究成为当前翻译研究的焦点之一。

美国翻译理论家劳伦斯·韦努蒂(Lawrence Venuti)在《译者的隐形:翻译历史》里揭示了两种翻译策略,分别是:"采取民族中心主义的态度,使外语文本符合译语文化的价值观,把原作者带进译语文化"的归化策略以及"对这些文化价值观的一种民族偏离主义的压力,接受外语文本的语言及文化差异,把读者带入外国情境"的异化策略。(Venuti, 1995)韦努蒂考察了从17世纪到当代的西方翻译,揭示了"通顺的翻译"策略一直在西方翻译史上占主导地位,其根本原因是要以西方的意识形态为标准,在英语中形成一种外国文学的规范。韦努蒂认为翻译的目的不是要消除语言和文化的差异而是要在翻译中表达这种语言和文化的差异。译本是读者了解异国文化的场所。翻译应把差异放在异国文化之中,追求文化的多样性,突出源语文本语言和文化上的差异。他指出,"反对英美传统的归化,主张异化的翻译,其目的是要发展一种抵御以目的与文化价值观占主导地位的翻译理论和实践,以表现外国文本在语言和文化上的差异。"

强势文化与弱势文化之间的权力差异也影响到翻译选材方面。以英美为代表的强势文化一般偏爱弱势文化里那些符合自己想像的模式化人物和意象的作品。塔维亚诺(Stefania Taviano)研究了多部现当代意大利戏剧在英国的译介。这些戏剧翻译实践反映出英国表演外国戏剧的策略。英国采用抵抗的方式表演外国戏剧颠覆了只关注外国戏剧"异域色彩"的传统,而更多强调其政治功能。

翻译理论话语同样深受强势文化与弱势文化之间的权力差异的影响。翻译理论研究从近代以来一直都是以西方话语为中心的,并直接影响着弱势文化的翻译理论和实践。弱势文化往往以译介和借用西方的翻译理论话语系统,面临失去自己的文化传统和文化身份的危险。其实,在中国长达两千年的翻译传统中,形成了如"信、达、雅","案本、求信、神似、化境"等等概念范畴，其中蕴含着丰富的中国哲学、美学、文学思想和观点。中国翻译学者应该对传统话语进行发掘和整理，在对西方翻译理论思想广取博收的基础上，建构和完善独特的中国译论话语体系。

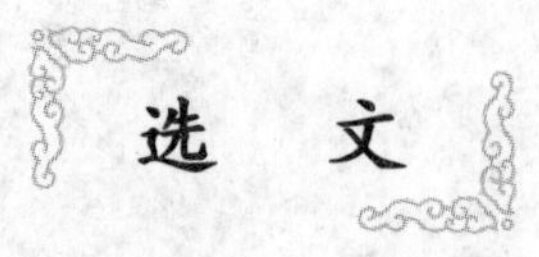

选文

选文一 Strategies of Translation

Lawrence Venuti

导 言

本文《翻译策略》选自蒙娜·贝克(Mona Baker)主编的 *Routledge Encyclopedia of Translation Studies*(上海外语教育出版社，2004)。作者劳伦斯·韦努蒂(Lawrence Venuti，1953-)是美国翻译理论家、翻译历史学家、坎普尔大学英文教授。从事意大利语、法语和加泰罗尼亚语(Catalan)的英译。1980 年获美国哥伦比亚大学(Columbia University)博士学位，因翻译 Barbara Alberti 的小说 *Delirium* 同年获 Renato Poggioli 翻译奖(Renato Poggioli Translation Award)。2007 年翻译 Giovanni Pascoli 的诗文(poetry and prose)获得人文学古根海姆研究基金。凡努蒂的研究领域非常广泛，被认为是现代翻译理论界最具深刻思想的人物。著有 *Our Halcyon Dayes: English Prerevolutionary Texts and Postmodern Culture* (1989)，*The Translator's Invisibility: A History of Translation* (2nd ed.，2008)，*The Scandals of Translation: Towards an Ethics of Difference* 等，主编 *Rethinking Translation: Discourse, Subjectivity, Ideology*(1992)，*The Translation Studies Reader* (2nd ed.，2004)等，大部分著作已成为翻译研究的经典之作。

选文探讨了翻译策略及决定翻译策略的因素。与形式主义的研究视角不同，凡努蒂从文化、经济和政治方面切入翻译策略，他通过丰富的例证，说明归化策略和异化策略的内涵、发展源流及其出现的原因，并对归化和异化的策略进行了比较。他得出结论，翻译策略是由译入语文化中特定时期的价值观决定的。该文对翻译策略的探讨不再停留在语言内部层面，而是将其放在更为广阔的文化和历史背景之下，扩展了译策研究的领域。

Strategies of translation involve the basis tasks of choosing the foreign text to be translated and developing a method to translate it. Both of these tasks are determined by various factors: cultural, economic, political. Yet the many different strategies that have

emerged since antiquity can perhaps be divided into two large categories. A translation project may conform to values currently dominating the target-language culture, taking a conservative and openly assimilationist approach to the foreign text, appropriating it to support domestic canons, publishing trends, political alignments. Alternatively, a translation project may resist and aim to revise the dominant by drawing on the marginal, restoring foreign texts excluded by domestic canons, recovering residual values such as archaic texts and translation methods, and cultivating emergent ones (for example, new cultural forms). Strategies in producing translations inevitably emerge in response to domestic cultural situations. But some are deliberately domesticating in their handling of the foreign text, while others can be described as foreignizing, motivated by an impulse to preserve linguistic and cultural differences by deviating from prevailing domestic values.

Domesticating Strategies

Domesticating strategies have been implemented at least since ancient Rome, when, as Nietzsche remarked, "translation was a form of conquest" and Latin poets like Horace and Propertius translated Greek texts "into the Roman present:""they had no time for all those very personal things and names and whatever might be considered the costume and mask of a city, a coast, or a century" (Nietzsche, 1974:137). As a result, Latin translators not only deleted culturally specific markers but also added allusions to Roman culture and replaced the name of the Greek poet with their own, passing the translation off as a text originally written in Latin.

Such strategies find their strongest and most influential advocates in the French and English translation traditions, particularly during the early modern period. Here it is evident that domestication involves an adherence to domestic literary canons both in choosing a foreign text and in developing a translation method. Nicolas Perrot D'ABLANCOURT, a prolific French translator of Greek and Latin, argued that the elliptical brevity of Tacitus's prose must be rendered freely, with the insertion of explanatory phrases and the deletion of digressions, so as "to avoid offending the delicacy of our language and the correctness of reason" (1640: preface; translated). The domestic values that such a strategy inscribed in the foreign text were affiliated with an aristocratic literary culture (D'Ablancourt's translation was dedicated to his court patron, Cardinal Richelieu) but they were also distinctly nationalsit. Under D'Ablancourt's influence, the English translator Sir John DENHAMF rendered Book 2 of the *Aeneid* in heroic couplets, asserting that "if Virgil must needs speak English, it were fit he should speak not only as a man of this Nation, but as a man of this age" (1656: A3r). In domesticating foreign texts D'Ablancourt and Denham did not simply modernize them; both translators were in fact maintaining the literary standards of the social elite while constructing cultural identities for their nations on the basis of archaic foreign cultures (Zuber, 1968; Venuti, 1993a).

Economic considerations sometimes underlie a domesticating strategy in translation, but they are always qualified by current cultural and political developments. The enormous success that greeted the English version of Italian writer Umberto Eco's novel *The Name of the Rose* (1983) drove American publishers to pursue the translation rights for similar foreign texts at the international book fairs. Yet what most contributed to the success of the translation was the sheer familiarity of Eco's narrative to American readers fond of such popular genres as historical romances and murder mysteries. By the same token, the Italian novelist Giovanni Guareschi was a best-seller in English translation during the 1950s and 1960s largely appealed to American readers absorbing the anti-Soviet propaganda of the Cold War era. The eponymous hero of Guareschi's first book in English, *The Little World of Don Camillo* (1950), is a priest who engages in amusing ideological skiermishes with a Communist mayor and always comes out the victor.

Domesticating translation has frequently been enlisted in the service of specific domestic agendas, imperialist, evangelical, professional. Sir William Jones, president of the Asiatic Society and an administor of the East India Company, translated the Institutes of Hindu Law (1799) into English to increase the effectiveness of British colonialism, constructing a racist image of the Hindus as unreliable interpreters of their native culture (Niranjana, 1992). For Eugene Nida, domestication assists the Christian missionary: as translation consultant to organizations dedicated to the dissemination of the Bible, he has supervised numerous translations that "relate the receptor to modes of behavior relevant within the context of his own culture" (1964). The multi-volume English version of Freud's texts known as the *Standard Edition* (1953-1974) assimilated his ideas to the positivism dominating the human sciences in Anglo-American culture and thus facilitated the acceptance of psychoanalysis in the medical profession and in academic psychology (Bettelheim, 1983; Venuti, 1993b).

Foreignizing Strategies

A foreignizing strategy in translation was first formulated in German culture during the classical and Romantic periods, perhaps most decisively by the philosopher and theologian Friedrich SCHLEIERMACHER. In an 1813 lecture "On the Different Methods of Translating," Schleiermacher argued that "there are only two. Either the translator leaves the author in peace, as much as possible, and moves the reader toward him. Or he leaves the reader in peace, as much as possible, and moves the author toward him" (quote in Lefevere, 1992b: 149). Scheleimacher acknowledged that most translation was domesticating, an ethnocentric reduction of the foreign text to target-language cultural values, bringing the author back home. But he much preferred a foreignizing strategy, an ethnodeviant pressure on thoes values to register the linguistic and cultural difference of the foreign text, sending the reader abroad.

The French theorist Antoine BERMAN viewed Schleiermacher's argument as an ethics of translation, concerned with making the translated text a site where a cultural other is not erased but manifested—even if this otherness can never be manifested in its own terms, only in those of the target language. For while foreignizing translation seeks to evoke a sense of the foreign, it necessarily answers to a domestic situation, where it may be designed to serve a cultural and political agenda.

Schleiermacher himself saw this translation strategy as an important practice in the Prussian nationalist movement during the Napoleonic Wars: he felt that it could enrich the German language by developing an elite literature free of the French influence that was then dominating German culture, which would thus be able to realize its historical destiny of global domination (Venuti, 1991).

Yet in so far as Schleiermacher theorized translation as the locus of cultural difference, not the homogeneity that his imperialist nationalism might imply, he was effectively recommending a translation practice that would undermine any language-based concept of a national culture, or indeed any domestic agenda. A foreignizing strategy can signify the difference of the foreign text only by assuming an oppositional stance toward the domestic, challenging literary canons, professional standards, and ethical norms in the target language. Hence, when foreignizing translation is revived by twentieth-century German theoriest like Rudolf Pannwitz and Walter Benjamin, it is seen as an instrument of cultural innovation. For Pannwitz, "translator makes a fundamental error when he maintains the state in which his own language happens to be instead of allowing his language to be strongly affected by foreign language" (1917: 242; translated).

From its origins in the German tradition, foreignizing translation has meant a close adherence to the foreign text, a literalism that resulted in the importation of foreign cultural forms and the development of heterogeneous dialects and discourses. Johann Heinrich Voss's hexameter versions of the *Odyssey* (1781) and the *Iliad* (1793) introduced this prosodic form into German poetry, eliciting Goethe's praise for putting "rhetorical, rhythmical, metrical advantages at the disposal of the talented and knowledgeable youngster" (Lefevere, 1992b: 77). Friedrich Holderlin's translations of Sophocles' *Antigone and Oedipus Rex* (1804) draw on archaic and nonstandard dialects (Old High German and Swabian) while incorporating diverse religious discourses, both dominant (Lutheran) and marginal (Pietistic) (George Steiner, 1975: 323-333; Berman, 1985: 93-107). Holderlin exemplifies the risk of incomprehension that is involved in any foreignizing strategy: in the effort to stage an alien reading experience, his translations so deviated from native literary canons as to seem obscure and even unreadable to his contemporaries.

Foreignizing entails choosing a foreign text and developing a translation method along lines which are excluded by dominant cultural values in the target language. During the eighteenth century, Dr. John Nott reformed the canon of foreign literatures in English by devising translation projects that focused on the love lyric instead of the epic or satire, the most widely translated genres in the period. He published versions of Johannes Secundus

Nicolaisus (1775), Petrarch (1777), Hafiz (1787), Bonefonius (1797), and the first book-length collections of Propertius (1782) and Catullus (1795). Nott rejected the "fastidious regard to delicacy" required him to delete the explicit sexual references in Catullus' poems, because he felt that "history should not be fixed". His translation provoked a moral panic among reviewers, who renewed the attack decades later when expressing their preference for George Lamb's bowdlerized Catullus (1821).

Domesticating vs. Foreignizing Strategies

Determining whether a translation project is domesticating or foreignizing clearly depends on a detailed reconstruction of the cultural formation in which the translation is produced and consumed; what is domestic or foreign can be defined only with reference to the changing hierarchy of values in the target language culture. For example, a foreignzing translation may constitute a historical interpretation of the foreign text that is opposed to prevailing critical opinion. In the victorian controversy that pitted Francis Newman's *Iliad* (1956) against Matthew Arnord's Oxford lectures *On Translating Homer* (1860), what was foreignizing about Newman's translation was not only that it used archaism to indicate the historical difference of the Greek text, but that it presented Homer as a popular rather than an elite, poet. Newman cast his translation in ballad meter and constructed an archaic lexicon from widely read genres like the historical novel; he thought that Sir Walter Scott would have been the ideal translator of Homer. Arnold argued, however, that Homer should be rendered in hexameters and modern English so as to bring the translation in line with the current academic reception of the Greek text. Whereas Newman wanted to address an audience that was non-specialist and non-academic, composed of different social groups, Arnold aimed to please classical scholars, who, he felt, were the only readers qualified to judge translations from classical languages. Newman's translation strategy was foreignizing because populist; the translation that Arnold preferred was domesticating because elitist, assimilating Homer to literary values housed in authoritative cultural institutions like the university. Translation strategies can often be determined by comparing contemporary versions of the same foreign text. Translation strategies can often be determined by comparing contemporary versions of the same foreign text. In the early 1960s, for instance, the American translators Norman Shapiro and Paul Blackburn were both translating Provencal troubadour poetry. Consider their versions of the first stanza from a poem by Gaucelm Faidit:

> A knight was with his lady fondly lying—The one he cherished most—and gently sighing as he kissed her, complained: My love, the day soon will arrive, chasing this night away. Alas! Already I can hear the watchman crying: Begone! Quickly, begone! You may not no longer stay. For it is dawn. (Shapiro, 1962: 72)
>
> A knight once lay beside and with the one he most desired, and in between

their kisses said, what shall I do, my sweet?

Day comes and the knight goes Ai! And I hear the watcher cry: "Up! On your way! I see day coming on, sprouting behind the dawn!"(Blackburn, 1978: 195)

Shapiro adopts a domesticating strategy. His lexicon, while intelligible to contemporary English-language readers, makes use of archaisms that are recognizably poetical, drawn from the tradition of nineteenth-century verse: alas, begone, cherished. Although his verse structure, both metrical and rhythming, is intended to approximated Faidit's musical stanza, Shapiro effectively assimilates the Provencal text to the traditional forms favoured by noted American poets, such as Robert Lowell and Rechard Wilbur, who had achieved national reputations by the 1960s (Perkins, 1987). Blackburn adopts a foreignizing strategy. His lexicon mixes the standard dialect of current English with archaism (to lie with, meaning "to engage in sexual inter-course"), colloquialism (in between, coming on), and foreign words (the Provencal ai). Although his verse structure, both rhythmical and intermittently rhyming, aims to approximate the musicality of Faidit's stanza, Blackburn actually assimilates the Provencal text to the open forms favoured by experimental poets, such as Robert Creeley and Charles Olson, who at the time were on the fringes of American literary culture (von Hallberg, 1985). Shapiro's dometicating version relies on canonical values, whose authority fosters the illusion that it is an exact equivalent or a transparent window on to Faidit's peom. Black-burn's foreignizing version relies on marginal values, whose strangeness invites the recognition that it is a translation produced in a different culture at a different period. The distinction between their strategies is particularly evident in their additions to the Provencal text: Shapiro makes his version conform to the familiar image of the yearning courtly lover by adding gently sighing and complained, Black-burn seeks estranging effects that work only in English by adding the pun on night in Day comes and the knight goes, as well as the surreal image of the sun sprouting.

As this example suggests, foreignizing strategies have been implemented in literary as opposed to technical translation. Technical translation is fundamentally domesticating: intended to support scientific research, geopolitical negotiation, and economic exchange, it is constrained by the exigencies of communication and therefore renders foreign texts in standard dialects and terminologies to ensure immediate intelligibility. LITERARY TRANSLATION, in contrast, focuses on linguistic effects that exceed simple communication (tone, connotation, polysemy, intertexuality) and are measured against domestic literary values, both canonical and marginal. A literary translator can thus experiment in the choice of foreign texts and in the development of translation methods, constrained primarily by the current situation in the target-language culture.

选文二　Staging Italian Theatre: A Resistant Approach

Stefania Taviano

导　言

本文《上演意大利戏剧:一种抵抗的方式》选自 *Voices in Translation*(2007)的第四章。作者塔维亚诺(Stefania Taviano)是英国沃里克大学(University of Warwick)翻译学博士、意大利墨西拿大学(University of Messina, Italy)讲师。著有 *Staging Dario Fo and Franca Rame: Anglo-American Approaches to Political Theatre* (2005)和有关意大利现代戏剧家和意大利的美国戏剧及表演艺术等相关文章,她也翻译意大利著名剧作家的作品。

选文研究了多部现当代意大利戏剧在英国的译介。这些戏剧翻译的实践反映出英国表演外国戏剧的策略。选择翻译和演出这些戏剧,有的出于政治上的考虑,有的则是因为该表演方式具有颠覆性(作者称之为抵抗式方法),即对英国戏剧传统构成挑战。2002 年演出的"奥德赛"采用了新的表演手段和表演舞台,让普通民众参与演出;彼得·泰尼斯伍德翻译的《那不勒斯百万富翁》采用了苏格兰方言,在英语中颠覆了外国戏剧中的人物形象。这种戏剧翻译和表演方式使本地观众和戏剧中的社会事件和人物共同产生共鸣,从而真正体会到故事的主题。文章认为,英国采用抵抗的方式表演外国戏剧颠覆了只关注外国戏剧"异域色彩"的传统,而更多强调其政治功能。

Introduction

An analysis of key British productions of modern Italian theatre testifies to the cultural and linguistic transformations affecting foreign plays when they are translated from one language into another; it also illustrates the peculiarities of theatre translation into English. While acculturation is an inherent aspect of the translation of theatre texts, there are specific ways in which foreign plays are appropriated by British theatre companies, due to cultural and theatrical constraints peculiar to this society.

This chapter looks at contemporary strategies adopted in staging foreign plays in the UK by taking into account the role of theatre audiences and the function of theatre in affecting and determining social practices. After briefly analysing a predominant British approach to foreign theatre, a number of recent productions of Italian plays, which seem to indicate a tendency towards an alternative strategy in stagings of foreign theatre in the UK, are examined. These include the 2002 joint production of *The Odyssey* by the Italian theatre group Stalker Teatro and the Glasgow-based Working Party, together with some key productions of plays by Luigi Pirandello, Edoardo De Filippo, Dario Fo and Franca Rame. These productions have been chosen for their political content, in some cases, but mainly for their provocative form and function in that they challenge common British stage traditions, such as the tendency to focus on the cultural identity of foreign plays, as well as dominant acting styles. The use of non-standard languages and the commitment of theatre collectives to physical acting will be shown to constitute central elements of a *resistant* approach that distinguishes itself for its challenging interpretations of foreign theatre.

Most British productions of Fo and Rame's plays, reveal, to different degrees, the main aspects of a predominant approach to political theatre which aims at appropriating foreign plays by focusing on their entertainment value and their cultural identity while undermining their political function. The success of the 2003 West End staging of *Accidental Death of an Anarchist* at the Donmar Warehouse Theatre, for example, was achieved thanks to a specific strategy, including the choice of the well-known Simon Nye, both as the author of the play's new translation and as the actor playing the part of the protagonist. Nye's excellent performance of farcical sketches and stereotypical figures, which were not included in the original text, made British audiences laugh but, at the same time, forget the political message of the play, aimed at revealing police brutality and corruption. This staging, together with many others, indicates the tendency to a comic reading of Italian theatre, which is the result of a compromise between the political function of the source text and its assimilation into the British theatrical system, aimed at ensuring the success of stage productions. In other words, Fo and Rame have been, and continue to be, the best known and most performed Italian playwrights in the UK thanks to the commercialisation of their plays, which makes them easy to stage and above all funny, hilarious Italian satire (see Taviano, 2005).

Nevertheless, it is important to acknowledge that a different approach to foreign theatre is now starting to emerge from a number of productions. I have defined such an approach resistant, according to a notion of postmodern performance, which, rather than transgressing the limits imposed by society, is *resistant* within the dominant culture. In otherwords, postmodernist artists and their art cannot be separated from the context in which they belong, but at the same time they can subvert predominant forms of representation. This definition of a resistant approach is based on Philip Auslander's (1992) view of transgressive and resistant politics applied to postmodern American performance. Similarly, a resistant approach to foreign playwrights subverts strategies centred on the "exotic" nature of foreign plays by focusing instead on their political role in stimulating and provoking theatre audiences. The opportunity for British audiences to (re)discover foreign theatre might reside precisely in *resistant* stagings, as in the case of the 2002 joint production of *The Odyssey*. This was a project funded by the Scottish Arts Council, and, despite the fact that the play was staged in a traditional theatre, challenged traditional notions of performance through an active involvement of the local community and the audience by extending its impact beyond the performance itself through workshops, as well as proposing innovative ways to use the Tramway theatre as a performative space.

The Odyssey was part of a month-long season of theatre and literary events in Glasgow between October and November 2002. The show was described in the programme as follows:

> Turin's Stalker Teatro fuses a 25-year history of site specific performance and visual arts to re-create this thrilling epic in Glasgow. In this UK premiere, co-produced by The Working Party, Stalker collaborates with installation artists and participants from communities throughout Glasgow to bring the poetry of *The Odyssey* alive in English and Italian.

Audiences were invited to "enter the World of the Hero," "to become the Hero" and "to embark on Homer's classic voyage of discovery." This was a truly interactive performance; as audience members when entering the theatre were metaphorically and literally taken through Odysseus's voyage. An actor with a blanket covering his/her shoulders would welcome us, give us a bag full of stones and show the way to our seats by taking us through a dark path with a torch and reciting lines from The Odyssey, with the sound of the sea in the background. The programme provided a journey guide with the breakdown of the eight scenes as follows:

> *Scene 1*, Telemachus; *Scene 2*, At the Court of Alcinous; *Scene 3*, Journey across the Seas; *Scene 4*, The Land of the Lotus Eaters; *Scene 5*, On the Enchanted Island of Circe; *Scene 6*, Hades; *Scene 7*, Homecoming and Slaughter; *Scene 8*, Banquet of Reconciliation.

Each scene took place in a different area of the theatre and represented a different stage in the voyage of Odysseus and the audience. The Lotus Eaters Scene, for example, consisted of a display of local artists's interpretation of Homer's voyage and of the Lotus Eaters chapter in James Joyce's *Ulysses*. The scene included: the artist Vrnda Daktor sitting in front of a mirror while drawing herself surrounded by discarded drawings to symbolise the artist in search of truth and inspiration; a cyclical action performed by Michella Dunne and Gillian Lees working with large blocks of lard and fruit, materials resonant of the Lotus Eaters' experience (in the artists' view) since, when they are exposed to time andhumancontact, their state is altered. The audience was invited to take an active role by deciding the order in which to observe each piece and the amount of time spent watching each of them. Spectators were also able to interact with the soundscape of the scene through two sound beams that were part of *The Dream of the Sea*, a multi-tracked musical piece. Throughout the performance two narrators, one speaking in English and the other in Italian, marked crucial points in the development of the story, contributing to the rhythm of the performance. The nature of the performance led to an interesting use of the Tramway Theatre, taking advantage of back stage spaces and corridors never used for performances, and above all it encouraged the audience to take an active role throughout the evening. In the concluding scene, that of the reconciliation banquet, audience members were asked to put on a large table the flat stones kept in the bags they were given at the entrance, thus creating an interesting mosaic. They were also given fruit and vegetables to put on top of each stone. As a result, a visually fascinating banquet table was laid, framed by hundreds of glasses of wine that were offered by the actors to the audience as the conclusion to the performance.

The Glasgow co-production of *The Odyssey* was a community theatre performance whose political efficacy was maintained in translation. The co-production, in fact, was the result of four weeks of collaboration between Stalker Teatro, The Working Party, local visual artists and members of the local community who had never performed before. Moreover, it ended with a one-day workshop where artists from the two cities exchanged ideas and experiences. *The Odyssey*, together with the workshop and other related events, aimed at strengthening the artistic collaboration between Turin and Glasgow. While *The Odyssey* would not be classified as political according to traditional notions of political theatre, its political meaning and efficacy were testified by the audience response and above all by the local artists and participants' response. The latter shared their enthusiasm for *The Odyssey* as an opportunity to discover their voice, their creativity and to challenge their role within society.

It is interesting to note that another performance with significant political implications took place in Glasgow 12 years earlier. This was *Glasgow All Lit Up!*, part of the community programmein Glasgow as European City of Culture. For 18 months Welfare actors trained local artists in lantern making using Japanese techniques, and the local artists worked with 250 community organisations from Strathclyde. As a result, on 6 October 1990 there was a parade of 10,000 people carrying about 8,000 lanterns across the city. The gathering ended with the Welfare State performance followed by a fireworks display. As Paul Kershaw argues, the semiotics of the lanterns, that is the politics of representation at work in the parade, expressed a plurality of voices signifying the cultural diversity of the city, as well as producing a sense of solidarity and collective belonging. The performance also dealt with state politics. While the police had decided to keep the city centre open to car traffic, in reality the procession dominated the city, and the traffic came to a standstill. Since as a non-violent political demonstration the lantern procession transgressed the decision of the local government, in Kershaw's (1996: 149) view, it "opened up, metaphorically and literally, a new space for politically democratic action."

Similarly, *The Odyssey*, as part of a one-month season, created a space for effective political action in its innovative use of the Tramway Theatre by offering an opportunity for a challenging theatrical and artistic exchange between Scottish and Italian cultures, and by encouraging the active involvement of local artists and common citizens in both the production and reception of the performance. Like *Glasgow All Lit Up!*, the plurality of visual artists contributing to the performance guaranteed the expression of Glasgow's cultural diversity. It also created a sense of solidarity between professional artists and common citizens with no previous artistic experience. Most importantly, all this was achieved through the co-production of an Italian community performance.

It is not by chance that such challenging productions took place in Glasgow. Scotland has a long history of staging foreign theatre that makes it a very fruitful and stimulating context for politically effective performances. The Glasgow Citizens Theatre is renowned for staging foreign playwrights such as Molière, Carlo Goldoni and Dario Fo, to name a few. Moreover, because of the role of its language, Scotland offers fascinating examples of the transposition of plays fromone regional context to another. Martin Bowman and Bill Findlay collaborated for a number of years on the translation of Michel Tremblay's works from Montreal French, Joual, into Scots. In Bowman's view, Quebec and Scotland are compatible in many cultural and social aspects, and Scots functions as a valid medium to translate the idiom of the Montreal working class, and vice versa—in 1998 Bowman and Findlay also adapted Irvine Welsh's *Trainspotting* into Joual (Bowman, 1998). In their approach to the source text, Bowman and Findlay tend, whenever possible, to avoid the introduction of target cultural material as a replacement for foreign cultural references. Their work, among other things, testifies to the current tendency to use Scots as the language in which to translate foreign plays, as opposed to English (see also Corbett, in this volume).

The Scottish approach to the translation of foreign plays indicates that the use of non-standard languages, such as regional varieties and dialects, might represent a vital element of productions that challenge British images of foreign theatre. Jatinder Verma's productions of Molière's *Tartuffe* for the Royal National Theatre in 1990 and *Le Bourgeois Gentilhomme* for Tara Arts in 1994, based on his own translations, represent a fascinating example. They are the product of what Verma defines as Binglish theatre, "a contemporary theatre praxis featuring Asian or black casts, produced by independent Asian or black theatre companies" that challenges dominant practices of the English stage (Verma, 1996: 194). Verma is the artistic director of Tara Arts, an independent company created in 1977, that searches for a distinctive theatrical form, based on classical Indian aesthetics and on "a rejection of the dominant convention of the modern English stage: the spoken word" (Verma, 1996: 199). Through Binglish productions British audiences are confronted with varieties of what Verma calls "langues"—intended as language and theatre praxis—such as Caribbean, Punjabi, Urdu, Nigerian and Somali. Verma uses varieties of English in his productions to contest the ownership of texts such as *King Lear*. The fact that Binglish productions draw upon non-European traditions of music, movement and imagery is precisely what distinguishes them. As Verma emphasises, Binglish productions are seen as provocative and stimulating by critics and audiences because they "negotiate a foreign-ness" (Verma, 1996: 200). His productions of Molière were "exercises in tradaptation," a term he borrows from Robert Lepage (Verma, 1994) referring to annexing old texts to new cultural contexts. By having Indian performers acting in his productions of Molière, Verma challenged British common notions of "authenticity" in stagings of French theatre.

Similarly, the adoption of English working-class regional idioms, such as Liverpudlian in the case of Peter Tinniswood's adaptation of Eduardo De Filippo's *Napoli Milionaria* in 1991, helped to convey the social status of De Filippo's characters. The play, set in war-time Naples, tells the story of a family kept together and fed by a mother who sells black-market goods. Her husband, Gennaro, who disapproves of his wife's illegal business, is captured by the Germans and by the time he comes back in 1944 his family is destroyed. His wife, who has continued to be a racketeer, has a relationship with another man and his son has turned into a thief (Billington, 2000).

The production received public acclaim, and the show was sold out for months. Michael Billington praised Tinniswood's choice of Liverpool and its language:

> The most radical aspect of Peter Tinniswood's new version is to employ Liverpool speech rhythms. The result gives the show a working-class authenticity and spares us the delight of listening to British actors sounding like a convention of ice-cream vendors. (Billington, 1991)

Billington pointed to two advantages of the Anglicisation of *Napoli Milionaria*. First of all, Liverpool speech rhythms help to convey the social status of De Filippo's characters. The use of an English working-class regional idiom recreates the connection between the language of the characters and their class identity present in the source text. Secondly, it avoids the use of fake Italian accents which, associated with Italian-style gesticulation, has caricaturing effects. In other words, Tinniswood's adaptation contributed to making the social and human issues dealt with in the play resonate with local audiences. In this way *Napoli Milionaria* became a coherent theatre text that spoke to target spectators on an emotional level, rather than being a spectacle of Italianness. This is confirmed by Billington's appraisal of "the broad-based humanity of a play that shows how ordinary people are all but destroyed by the economic imperatives of war" (Billington, 1991).

All the above productions reflect a translation practice that aims at toning down the cultural identity of foreign plays and at making their *mises en scène* relevant to target audiences for reasons other than their cultural connotations. This strategy, which became more common in British stagings of Pirandello and De Filippo in the 1990s, indicates a different phase and tendency in the process of integration of the otherness of foreign plays into the target system. Peter Hall's production of De Filippo's *Filumena*, translated by the dramatist TimberlakeWertenbaker, and Nicholas Wright's version of Pirandello's *Naked*, staged at the Almeida Theatre in 1998, constitute two further examples of British stagings of Italian plays that focused on evoking their validity as theatre texts within a coherent theatrical structure (De Filippo, 1998; Pirandello, 1998).

Wertenbaker chose to translate the Neapolitan dialect of the source text in plain English, without adopting any particular regional connotations, as she explained in an interview with *Corriere della Sera*, but to convey the dialect inflections of the Neapolitan dialect through the rhythm of the dialogue (De Carolis, 1998). The long speeches of the source text, often organised in a crescendo of repetitive statements, are replaced by concise dialogues and punchy phrases in the style of contemporary British stage prose. In John Gross's view, Wertenbaker's new translation of the play was one of the aspects that made Hall's staging successful (Gross, 1998). Critics were unanimous in praising Judy Dench and Michael Pennington's performance and spectators gave them standing ovations. The following remark by John Stokes's indicates that De Filippo was no longer perceived as an exotic Italian playwright, but one accessible to European audiences: "Children are children—it is this creed—banal, heartbreaking—that makes Filumena both as Neapolitan as a painted effigy and, at the same time, broadly European" (Stokes, 1998). This means that Hall's production of *Filumena* struck a cord with English audiences. The unique bond between parents and their children, instead of being perceived as a specifically Italian phenomenon, became relevant to local receivers of De Filippo's text.

Similarly, according to Charles Spencer, it was "the passion and the anguish" of Pirandello's theatre that the Almeida production of *Naked* "powerfully captured" (Spencer, 1998). Spencer also described the show as an "intense, atmospheric experience that will trouble the memory." The positive response that both the above productions received seems to suggest that British audiences and critics are becoming more receptive to challenging stagings of foreign plays.

I have been involved in a theatre project that aimed to make the human and social significance of Italian plays resonate with Anglophone audiences. This was the British première of Spiro Scimone's play, *Nunzio*, during the International Playwrighting Festival at the Croydon Theatre in London, in October 1999. The play is set in a one-bedroom flat, and the protagonists are two Sicilians who have emigrated to the North of Italy. Nunzio is seriously ill because of the fumes he breathes at work, Pino is a killer and travels all over the world. The flat is a claustrophobic environment where both characters hide from the surrounding world. The outside world is constantly threatening through phone calls, cars passing by the flat and mysterious envelopes pushed under the door. In this environment Nunzio and Pino develop a co-dependent relationship: they care for each other, but often get close to fighting, in the way that Estragon and Vladimir do in *Waiting for Godot*. In the isolation of the kitchen, they begin to discover each other: Pino realises how serious Nunzio's illness is and tries to protect him; Nunzio, in his naiveté, dreams about travelling to Brazil, like his friend. Both the claustrophobic setting and the repetitive nature of the dialogue remind us of Harold Pinter's theatre, particularly *The Dumb Waiter*.

Jennifer Varney and I, as translators of the play, decided to set *Nunzio* in Glasgow and to translate it into Scottish English to convey the cultural and linguistic distance between standard Italian and the Sicilian of the source text, which was written in the dialect spoken in Messina, my hometown (Scimone, 1999). The decision to translate into Scottish English automatically excluded the adoption of a stage Italian accent, or any other aspect of the stage

representation of Italians, such as excessive gesticulation. The nature of the relationship between the two characters, their inability to communicate with each other on a very basic human level as a result of their difficulty in expressing themselves through words, were aspects of the play that we tried to bring out in this production because they can speak to a British, or any other audience. The play was well received and, most important of all, audiences seemed to relate to central issues such as the characters' isolation and inability to communicate, rather than their Italianness. Although the above production does not have the same political resonance as *The Odyssey*, it nevertheless subverts common British stage traditions that tend to focus on the cultural identity of foreign plays.

Returning to Fo and Rame, in December 2005 the world première of a new play, *Mother Courage, Cindy Sheehan's Real and Imaginary Diary*, translated by TomBehan, was staged at Pimlico School, in Central London, starring Frances de La Tour. It was directed by Michael Kustow and promoted by Stop the War Coalition at the time when Cindy Sheehan, mother of Casey, a 24-year-old US soldier who was killed in Iraq on April 4 2004, took her anti-war campaign to Britain. The performance was part of a peace conference that promoted global peace demonstrations to take place on 18 March, 2006. It is a monologue, based on newspaper articles and above all letters written by Sheehan to George W. Bush and to Barbara Bush. More precisely, as indicated in the press release by Stop the War Coalition:

> Her efforts to get an explanation from President Bush about the death of her and other mother's sons led her to pitch camp outside the presidential ranch throughout August this year. The persistence and growing anger of this woman who was nicknamed "Peace Mom" made her the focus of a nationwide movement against the war, which goes from strength to strength.

Mother Courage, a straightforward, colloquial monologue of a common, anonymous mother, is extremely powerful in voicing the anger and protest of thousands and thousands of US citizens who, like Cindy Sheehan, personally rebel against the war in Iraq and do not hesitate to condemn Bush and his government as criminals and killers. The immediacy of her words, combined with details of the events following her protest, have the effect of what the poet Buskaar calls "turning stones" in his ballad dedicated to Cindy Sheehan, as explained in the play:

> These stones are out in the Nevada desert, at the edge of the Great Prairies. They're round and almost hollow inside, apart from a small stone, which is round as well, but that acts like a shuttlecock. When the wind starts blowing the stones start turning, and inside them the smaller stone moves faster and increases the whole momentum. If you slightly push one of these stones you'll hear a strange sound come out, which makes a noise like somebody who's talking but who makes no sense. That'swhythese stones are also called the "talking stones" or the "singing stones." [...] Cindy's story is like the old Indian tale about the singing stone,

blown by the wind, it's forced to spin around out on the prairie. But its movement drags other stones along with it, and they all rub up against each other, creating sparks that set fire to the whole prairie.

As in the case of various plays by Fo and Rame, this monologue is the product of specific political events narrated and brought to life on stage to encourage everyday people in their struggle against injustice. This is confirmed by Sheehan's comments: "I hope the play can be used as an antiwar tool, to put a human face on this war, to show Casey had a life, was a person" (quoted in Higgins, 2005). To this end, after publishing a first draft on Jacopo Fo's website (www. alcatraz. it; accessed 10. 06), Fo and Rame's provided the final script, as requested by many, together with the English version (www. alcatraznews. com), accompanied by the following appeal to make the text known in the English-speaking world by sending it to US and British citizens: "*Lanciamo a tutti un appello affinché questo testo possa viaggiare nei paesi anglofoni e arrivi al maggior numero possibile di statunitensi e inglesi*" ("We launch an appeal to everybody in the hope that this text can be staged in English-speaking countries and reach as many US and British citizens as possible"). As indicated on the web, plans are afoot to contact Michael Moore for a version of the play to be produced in the United States.

There are numerous plays by Fo and Rame, which have never been translated into English and are unknown in Anglophone countries for various reasons, particularly because of their documentary or didactic structure, which makes them difficult to transpose to foreign countries. The world resonance of *Mother Courage*, the fact that, rather than being based on the Italian social or political context, refers to the war in Iraq, having therefore a significance for the whole international community, facilitates Behan's commitment to the translation and staging of unknown theatre texts by Fo and Rame. Moreover, the staging of this, together with other plays, particularly within politically-relevant contexts, as in the case of the peace conference promoted by Stop the War Coalition, makes it even more valuable since it can further contribute to reinforcing a *resistant* approach, which allows us to rediscover the political function of Fo and Rame's plays. Last but not least, given that *Mother Courage* is not set in Italy, nor has Italian characters, its cultural origins become irrelevant when it is put on stage, hence the monologue is safe from the above-mentioned British approach that focused on the cultural connotations of Fo and Rame's theatre.

The adoption of non-standard "langues," as shown by Tinniswood's adaptation, appropriate acting techniques, an innovative use of theatrical spaces, as in the case of *The Odyssey*, and, I would add, the translations of playwrights unknown to English-speaking countries are some of the ways through which it is possible to infuse new life into foreign theatre in the UK. My personal experience as a translator and, above all, current practices of translation and postmodern theatre, seem to confirm that British stagings of foreign plays are taking innovative and exciting directions. It is therefore vital that theatre scholars and professionals document and discuss the productions that adhere to such translation

strategies, in order to better understand if and how theatre translation practices affect our interaction with other cultures.

选文三　"Colonization," Resistance and the Uses of Postcolonial Translation Theory in Twenty-century China

Leo Tak-hung Chan

导　言

本文《"殖民"、抵抗和后殖民翻译理论在20世纪中国的应用》选自 *Changing the Terms: Translating in the Postcolonial Age*（2000）一书的第二章。作者陈德鸿（Leo Tak-hung Chan）是中国香港岭南大学（Lingnan College, Hong Kong）翻译系教授。新著《20世纪中国翻译理论：风气、问题与争辩》对中国的翻译理论进行了梳理，涵盖大陆、香港和台湾的有代表性的翻译论文42篇，给我们展示了一幅20世纪中国翻译理论研究的全貌。

20世纪80、90年代，最异常的学术现象就是当代西方批评理论的大量译介。西方一些主要理论家如杰姆逊、伊格尔顿、拉尔夫·科恩、杜威·佛克马、杰拉德·吉列斯比、马里奥·瓦尔德斯等被国内大学邀做讲座或参加学术会议作主题发言。很快，西方解构主义、女性主义、后殖民主义思潮进入中国。到了20世纪末，来自西方的后殖民理论已经很好地植入了中国知识界的沃土。文章认为，从上个世纪20年代起，中国知识界就开始对欧洲的语言殖民做出抵抗。西方理论引入之前，主要是通过抨击翻译，认为译者引入西方语言结构和表达方式污染了汉语。随着西方后殖民理论的引入，批评界认识到，语言和文化密不可分，要使文化不受损害，承载"文化货物"的语言绝对不能被污染。可以这样说，之前是一种无意识的抵抗，批评者自己就讨论的事件所采取的研究方法等都不甚明了；之后则是一种有意识的抵抗。但作者认为，这样的抵抗主要是由文化批评家促成的，而翻译后殖民理论的建构则仍未得到重视。

Discussions of postcolonial translations have come into vogue in recent years. Originally a term used extensively in literary theory, "postcoloniality" seems suddenly to have been given a prominent part to play in research on translation in Third World countries, particularly India. Undoubtedly, postcolonial theory should have some relevance to all countries that were colonized in one way or another. That being the case, much thought ought to be given to the relevance of postcolonial translation to China. To be sure, China has not been formally occupied by a foreign power in the past century, so she has not experienced a "colonial" period as did her Southeast Asian neighbors, India and most African countries.

Indeed, extraterritorial rights over certain parts of the country (like Shanghai and the Yangtze River) were claimed at certain times by foreign powers: Hong Kong was ceded to Britain (though she entered her postcolonial period with the 1997 Chinese takeover); and Taiwan was colonized by the Dutch and by the Japanese (from the end of the nineteenth century to the end of World War II). However, for mainland China, where the majority of translations are still carried out and published, the term "postcoloniality" may not mean much. What use do we have for postcolonial theories of translation in the Chinese context?

In hindsight, the influx of contemporary Western critical theory into China is among the most phenomenal intellectual events of the eighties and nineties. The chain of events connected with the introduction of deconstructionism, feminism and postcolonialism (not postcolonial translation theory, though) into China can be briefly recounted. Other than the proliferation of translated texts on "new theory," one can cite a sequece of academic events sponsored by China, but attended by major Western theorists. Fredric Jameson toured the major Chinese universities in 1985, and two conferences at which postcolonialism became a hot subject were held in Dalian (August 1995), scholars such as Terry Eagleton and Ralph Cohen were invited to give lectures; at the International Conference on Cultural Dialogue and Cultural Misreading (October 1995), which took place in Beijing, Douwe Fokkema, Gerald Gillespie and Mario Valdes were principal speakers. Another international conference that served as a forum for debating the applicability of Western critical theories, including postcolonial theories, was the Conference on Critical Theories: China and the West, sponsored by the Chinese Academy of Social Science and held in the summer of 1997 in Changsha, Hunan. Jameson was again one of the keynote speakers at the conference. Thus, before the century draws to a close, postcolonial theory from the West will have been well planted in Chinese intellectual soil; this is not dissimilar to the way in which sundry kinds of commodities have successfully found a place (at roughly the same time) on the Chinese market.

That postcolonial theory has become a reality in both the fields of literature and linguistics is evidenced by the spate of articles and books on the subject by Chinese scholars in the past decade. If this trend continues, translation studies in China will eventually have to face the postcolonial challenge. This article attempts to show how the new critical discourse on postcoloniality can become significant and meaningful in the Chinese context. I will consider the two "positions" that Chinese translation theorists, cultural theorists and translators have taken as a response to "colonization." Additionally, my discussion will be guided by the following insight: though the concepts of coloniality in translation throw new light on the Chinese situation, the uniqueness of the Chinese case forces us to revise the parameter within which postcolonial theorizing functions. To begin with, it must be noted that the terms "postcolonial" and "colonization" are used here in their broader sense, being restricted neither geographically nor temporally. This qualification is important in view of the fact that there has never been any form of territorial colonialism to speak of in the

Chinese context; rather, the Chinese have experienced, since the beginning of the century, a partly self-imposed kind of cultural and linguistic colonization. The difference between the Chinese situation and the Indian model, on which most recent postcolonial translation theorizing has been based, is probably as wide as can be imagined.

More specifically, to explicate the Chinese case I will use the elements that are the focus of analysis by postcolonial critics: the production of (Western) forms of discourse during periods of colonial expasion, the use of universalist discourses to subjugate colonized and marginalized peoples, and the resistance to the apparently well-meaning imperialist projects. Among these, the idea of native (or nativist) resistance will engage the greater part of my attention, especially as many texts, when examined from a postcolonial perspective, reveal the degree to which the "colonized" can react, and are not simply acted upon. The discussion below will centre around the different forms of resistance over a wide historical span, beginning with the 1920s and ending in the present. I will first detail the arguments, made prior to the nineties, against translators contaminating the Chinese language through the introduction of Europeanized structures and expressions. Then a reversal is shown to have occurred in the nineties, the counter-argument being that the language itself, carrying a unique "cultural cargo," simply cannot be contaminated. It can be said that the resistance prior to the nineties was very much an unconscious one, and by reading the statements of theorists with the benefit of postcolonial theory, we will see issues and approaches not obvious even to the writers of those statements. Subsequent to the work of those theorists, a conscious effort was made to combat "colonization" by European languages, but the still-ongoing resistance was forged in the main by cultural critics for whom translation theorizing was nevertheless of little interest.

Keeping the Language "Pure"

A clear contribution of postcolonial theory to our understanding of Chinese translation is the new light it sheds on existing translated texts. This comes about in an act of rereading: the theory is retroactively applied to a colonial, or even pre-colonial, period. The body of ideas associated with postcolonial translation theory, when shorn of its temporal-historical dimension, becomes applicable to earlier eras in which postcolonial translation practices, as we know them now, were only nascent. Thus, we can look at the first position, taken by translators and translation theorists in an earlier period, which we could designate as an act of resistance: the call for using a "pure" Chinese language when translating. A dominant trend since 1919 (the year the May Fourth Movement broke out in protest against the unjust treatment given China by the Western powers and Japan in the aftermath of World War I) was to adhere closely to the formal features of source texts and to import, on a huge scale, foreign terms and expression. For many, this was a means whereby the sterile Chinese language could be rejuvenated. There is no need at this point to pursue at length the continued (and still continuing) debate on the merits and drawbacks of using imported structures and expressions. Suffice it to say that the opponents of linguistic Europeanization were in fact fighting against a form of colonization; they were attacking a new language emerging primarily out of translations into Chinese, with the following features:

(1) the insertion of subjects where none was needed;

(2) the increased use of conjunctions and other linking devices;

(3) the proliferation of passive structures;

(4) the appearance of affix-like morphemes like *hua* ("-ze") and *fei* ("non-"); and

(5) the widespread use of length modifiers.

From our present-day perspective, it seems clear that the linguistic purists were fighting a losing battle. Lydia Liu has recently proven, with ample documentary evidence, that moder Chinese is a heteroglossic construction, incorporating elements from many languages—though predominantly, we must say, resulting from the aggressive cultural influence of Japanese, English and Russian. Nevertheless, the resistance efforts merit closer examination, and I will refer specifically to two of these, one in the thirties and another in the sixties.

In the "Language of the Masses Movement" (*dazhongyu yundong*) of the thirties, the target of attack was Europeanized Chinese; spoken Chinese as it was used in people's daily lives was considered superior because, crude as it was, it was at least more "alive." There are, however, deeper implications to the debate, for the question of the kind of language fit for use also engaged issues of ethnic and national identity. The leaders of the movement, such as Chen Wangdao (1890-1977) and Ye Shengtao (1894-1988), held that "language, being the supreme symbol of ethnic character," would be defiled if foreign elements were admitted into it (Fang, 1992: 343-48). Like these leaders, Zhao Shuli (1906-1970), a leading novelist of the era, advocated about avoiding Europeanizations; for him, every nation and every race has its own special linguistic habits, and it is precisely these habits that distinguish one language from another-and by analogy, one, one national or ethnic group from another. Zhao believed that Chinese is as fully capable of fulfilling its mission as other languages are of theirs. In fact, he was of the opinion that, of the two archrivals, Europeanized Chinese and classical Chinese (a language comparable to Latin of the Middle Ages, and a language which the vernacular has been trying to replace), the former is much more to be feared.

Translators and translation theorists resisted the Europeanizations as strongly as creative authors (such as Zhao and Ye) did, and as a group, they sought to launch an attack from another front. In a way, Frederick Tsai (1918-1996) and Yu Kwang-shung's (1928-) call to "purify" Chinese in the sixties must also be understood as a continuation of the flight against "linguistic colonization" by the West (and Japan). But this time, the alternative suggested was not the spoken language or the language of everybody; rather, it was the traditional vernacular used before the twentieth century. This vernacular was a written

language first developed near the end of the ninth century. Unlike classical Chinese, which remained the standard written language through the centuries, the traditional vernacular more nearly resembled the spoken language of the past and was used to serve "low-culture functions;" it was used in popular writings, such as plays and novels, of the late imperial era. Although the modern vernacular, having matured slowly since the beginning of the twentieth century, was developed in part from the traditional vernacular, they remain different in significant ways. Primarily, the modern vernacular has incorporated to a substantial degree European structures and expressions. For over a decade, Tsai and Yu issued repeated calls to free the Chinese language from the superimposed foreign influences; put simply, for them the modern vernacular needs to be replaced with the traditional vernacular. By so doing, they opened a new chapter in the history of resistance against Europeanizations.

Tsai and Yu followed nearly parallel careers: both lived in Hong Kong and Taiwan for extended periods of time; both achieved fame as creative writers (the former an essayist, the latter a poet) as well as translators; and both not only translated prodigiously, but also—as translation teachers—raised an entire generation of translators in Hong Kong and Taiwan. Most significantly, both sought to resurrect classic vernacular Chinese novels, such as *Dream of the Red Chamber* (the eighteenth century), as models of language used in traditional times that ought to be emulated by translators. Though their views did have a lasting impact, they were not without their detractors. For instance, Frederick Tsai's stand was criticized as impossible to maintain consistently by one of the most influential translation scholars from Taiwan (see Huang, 1974). Citing copious examples from Tsai, he shows why the existence of a plural form for "it" (*tamen*) is indispensable, and denounces as impracticable all of Tsai's suggested alternatives (like repeating the antecedent or not making a distinction between the singular and plural forms of pronouns). For him, all efforts to counter Europeanizations can be half-hearted as best. All in all, it did not seem as if the purists of the sixties were able to go very far in their attack on Europeanizations.

The Nineties: Foregrounding Chineseness

While efforts at defending the Chinese language against the onslaught of Europeanized translations have continued into present, since the eighties the signs of an alternative mode of resistance have become more and more conspicuous. This second "position" came into existence as a consequence of the recent introduction into Chinese critical and academic circles of new theories dubbed "post-isms:" postmodernism, postcolonialism, post-Enlightenment ideas, postcolonialism and so on. If Chinese culture in the May Fourth period (from 1919 to roughly the end of twenties) can be said to have been "colonized" for the first time, then Deng Xiaoping's era from the late seventies to 1997—divided by the 1989 Tiananmen Incident into the "New Era" (prior to 1989) and the "post-New Era" (after 1989 till his death)—has witnessed a "second colonization." Wang Jing has called this period China's "second colonization;" the similarities that it bears to the late 1910s and 1920s are unmistakable, for both of these eras saw a massive importation of Western ideas. In the late eighties and the early nineties, in particular, large-scale translation projects were carried out on key works of Western theory; what modernity meant for China was intensely discussed, and interest in comparative studies of Chinese and Western cultures flourished. The spirit of the age was such that culture, native as well as foreign, figured prominently in any discourse of contemporary relevance. It is in this context that linguistics and cultural theorists have directly and indirectly brought a postcolonial perspective to issues of translation.

What we have referred to as a second position in the reaction against Western linguistic imperialism was taken largely by linguistics and cultural theorists, but not translation scholars and practitioners. It is apparent that, the current situation in China being what it is, theorizing about the cultural role that translation is to play will originate with those who grapple with Western theory, rather than those who are primarily translators. In what follows, I will discuss the views of a linguist, a cultural critic and a translation theorist. All three provide perspectives on translation (indirectly, in the case of the first two) that can be appropriately termed "postcolonialist."

Shen Xiaolong (1952-), currently Professor of Chinese at Fudan University, Shanghai, is staunch exponent of a new approach to analyzing the Chinese Language that discards Western linguistic models (see Shen, 1992, 1995a). He set out to tackle the failure of Western linguistic theory to explain adequately the peculiarities of the Chinese language in his epoch-making study Interpreting Language (1992). For him, the time had come to revamp the entire Chinese linguistic tradition of the twentieth century, which began with the misguided attempt by Ma Jianzhong (1845-1900) in the late nineteenth century to borrow wholesale the Western model, and impose it on the Chinese language. The experience of the last ninety years—especially the insuperable difficulties in analyzing Chinese syntax—has shown that it is futile to try to account for features in the Chinese language simply by theorists that were developed in the West with reference to Indo-European languages.

The reception of Shen Xiaolong's ideas, however, has been extremely mixed. Considered currently as the leader of one of the three main schools of "cultural linguistics," a new field of study born of the mid-eighties, Shen is sharply differentiated from those cultural linguists whose focus is on the synchronic and diachronic study of how culture influences language and vice versa, and from those who seek to unravel the "cultural content" of a language (Chinese in this case) through an examination of how language adapts to social and communicative needs. Best known for the way in which he highlights language as a system understandable only by those using the language, Shen has been praised as the "hope of Chinese linguistics." Yet at the same time, others have openly derided him, saying that he is not worthy of serious attention. The debate on Shen's true significance (or lack thereof) reflects, in fact, an atmosphere where linguists are eager to revoke Western linguistic

methods that have been applied indiscriminately over the past century, and to establish cultural linguistics as the avenue for "rejuvenating" linguistic study in China. Whether they choose to argue or disagree with Shen, there is little doubt that Shen's system has arisen out of a unique historical—shall we say, postcolonial—situation.

Yet in stressing the need to sinicize the study of Chinese grammar, Shen is in fact furthering the cause of linguists of the thirties, like Fu Donghua (1893-1971) and Chen Wangdao, though he gives a new twist to the model being constructed (see Shen, 1992: 416-17). Freely adopting terms from traditional Chinese aesthetics, he notes the following peculiarities of the Chinese language:

(1) the preference for economy of expression (*jian*);

(2) the aspiration toward achieving phonological harmony;

(3) the close attention to balance between empty (*xu*) and concrete (*shi*) words; and

(4) the tendency to use the various parts of speech freely, so long as what is said makes sense.

He concludes in *Interpreting Language* that such peculiarities reveal the extent to which Chinese can be said to favour "associative thinking," allow the speaker's intentions to shape the language and generally privilege content (or "spirit") over form. This partly explains why the language does not fare well when Western linguistic models, with their strength in formal analysis, are applied. He argues (elsewhere) that the model of "subject-verb-object" ought to be abandoned in the analysis of Chinese sentences, since the clue to understanding Chinese syntax lies in explicating the use of "phrases" (*jududuan*), the fundamental unit of the Chinese sentence (see Shen, 1995b: 37-39). The essence of Shen's argument, which evinces a strong cultural and ethnic bias, adumbrated repeatedly in the dozens of articles and books that he has written, is that a language is inseparable from the culture in which it is nourished and that "when [Chinese] linguistics is severed from Chinese culture, the maternal sources of its being, it becomes stale and lifeless" (1990: 75). At one point in *Interpreting Language*, Shen talks about Europeanizations imported through translations, but curiously, he considers them to be present mainly in non-literary writings such as those of a technical or political nature; Chinese literature has not been much affected (1992: 451-52). While Shen seems to be only tangentially interested in translation, he puts forth a theory with serious implications for translation studies.

A similar statement could be made about Zhang Yiwu (1962-), presently Associate Professor of Chinese at Beijing University, and foremost among scholars who have applied a postcolonialist approach to literary studies in China. Zhang was one of the most powerful voices in early nineties against the Western presence in Chinese intellectual life, which, after all, has been pervasive since the May Fourth era. In contrast to the earlier opponents of Europeanizations in translations, he fights as much against cultural as against linguistic "colonization." In the first two chapters of his book *Exploring the Margins* (1993), he describes his resistance strategy: to fight back against Western ideological encroachment on its own terms. He points out that while Derrida advocates breaking down binary oppositions, the opposition between the First World and the Third World is one that has yet to be broken down and that China can be a test-case of how a new kind of cultural theory and discourse, pertinent to a Third World country, can be fruitfully developed (Zhang, 1993: 14).

In Chapter Three, in many ways the central chapter of the book, Zhang Yiwu elaborates on a key point that Shen Xiaolong had already made: a language must not be seen as a mere sign system, divorced from the culture in which it is embedded. Reiterated time and again by Zhang is the idea of the mother tongue (note the maternal metaphor, used also by Shen) and the ever-present, ever-powerful "collective memory" that it invokes for every Chinese. For the Chinese language carries a cultural residue, accumulated over a historical span of 5,000 years, that can never be erased in spite of overwhelming Western influence and violence done to the language through the importation of foreign words, structures and modes of expression. Like his predecessors who opposed Europeanizations in translation, Zhang sourly notes the irreparable damage done to the native tongue; for him, the impact is seen clearly in the realm of literature, for the language of literature is after all "the distilled essence of the mother-tongue, the agent for the spread of culture" (66). Thus Chinese literature becomes relegated to a subordinate and marginalized position, and pales besides Western literatures.

Unlike his anti-Europeanization predecessors, however, Zhang does not propose ways of further moulding the vernacular to serve as a medium of expression as effectively as Europeanized Chinese does. The attempt to enrich the Chinese language through the incorporation of elements from "real" spoken language is, for him, as ill-advised as the belief—first voiced by scholars like Hu Shi (1891-1962)—that this same language can be improved through the incorporation of translated foreign models. As method of resistance, Zhang advocates using a new kind of written Chinese, for which he coins the term "post-vernacular" (*haobaihua*). Drawing upon examples from works by major authors on the Mainland and in Taiwan since the eighties, he discusses the possibility of re-introducing elements of the classical language, denigrated since the May Fourth period, into contemporary written Chinese. It is his opinion that the classical language, the more refined, terse and compact language of the traditional literati that served high-culture functions for two millennia (from the second century BC to the end of the nineteenth century), should be given a greater role to play. Zhang sums up the postmodern view of language (with a Derridean touch) embodied by the postvernacular thus:

> [It] recognizes the fissure, the cleavage between the signifier and the signified, between language and reality. Language is no longer subordinate to the object of signification; it does not connect with reality; it is simply a moving and free-floating signifying system. (71)

Zhang takes pains to point out that his advocacy of the postvernacular does not amount to a rediscovery of (or a return to) the classical language, or the defeat of the vernacular language in the competition for ascendancy. What he stresses is the potency of the classical language as a carrier of cultural residue and its possible contribution to the emergence of a new mode of expression. Furthermore, Europeanizations are accepted, if only because it is no longer possible, in these *fin de siecle* time, to talk of completely purging them from the Chinese language. But Zhang is far from arguing for Europeanizations, as a wave of translation theorists in the twenties and thirties, such as Lu Xun (1881-1936) and Zhou Zuoren (1885-1968), did. The latter two did not think that the Chinese language was adequate for its purposes, whereas Zhang holds the opposite view and revalorizes the classical language, saying that it is more than adequate. Zhang's position is also different from those who suggested that Chinese language should be completely romanized or replaced with Esperanto, the "World-language." He restores dignity to the Chinese language while recognizing the difficulty of keeping it pure.

The postvernacular, then, is to be a hybrid language that admits elements of diverse sorts. It is reminiscent of the "in-between" language that Samia Mehrez describes in her study of Francophone North African texts in the postcolonial period—a "newly forged language" that is capable of "exploding and confounding different symbolic worlds and separate systems of signification in order to create a mutual interdependence and intersignification" (1992: 121-122). Seen from this perspective, a postcolonial critic (or a "nativist semiotician," as he has been called in China) such as Zhang Yiwu can be said to have moved to the other end of the spectrum on the issue of the proper language to be used for translations; as opposed to linguistic purity, he favours hybridity. In fact, the position that Zhang assumes is postcolonial in two senses: his recognition of hybridity and his refusal to accept the modern vernacular—very much a "colonial project"—as a replacement language for classical Chinese.

The view of Shen Xiaolong and Zhang Yiwu furnish a context for better understanding the recent work of Liu Miqing (1939-), our third perspective. A graduate of Beijing University and currently Associate Professor of Translation at the Chinese University of Hong Kong, Liu has written prodigiously on Chinese-English translation and to date has authored five books, which, taken together, present a systematic and coherent body of ideas on translation unmatched by any other theorist in this century. His earlier full-length studies deal variously with the translation of different genres, skills for translating from English to Chinese, and contrastive study of the two languages. However, *Present-day Translation Studies* (1993) is by common consent the most representative of Liu's works; it proffers a comprehensive re-examination of issues pertinent to translation theory and summarizes Liu's position on certain aspects of translation theory, such as the basic operating mechanisms in translating, translation as a mode of thinking, the stages in the translation process, translatability and untranslatability, and the translation of style. This work was followed in

1995 by the publication of *Aesthetic Studies of Translation*, in which the aesthetics of translation (already touched upon in one chapter of *Present-day Translation Studies*) are singled out for separate and detailed treatment.

As Liu Miqing himself has noted, his complete oeuvre forms a closely knit system that attempts to formulate a translation theory for modern China. As early as 1987, at the first Conference on Translation Theory in China, he expressed the need for "a Chinese translation theory," and this issue is brought up again in his *Present-Day Translation Studies*. Stating at the outset that there are no global translation theories and that all theorizing can only proceed from knowledge of a pair—or a very limited number—of languages, Liu advocates developing translation theory from the actual experience of translating from or into the Chinese language:

> Undoubtedly, the basic model for translation theory in China should begin and end with our *mother-tongue* ... We neglect at our own peril the distribution of lexical meanings and functions of the Chinese language. With this consideration in mind, we can summarily call this basic model a "descriptive semantic-functional model." (My emphasis) (1993: 30)

The maternal metaphor may or may not have been intended, but we already have here the basic ingredients of a counter-discourse. To be sure, Liu proceeds to expatiate on the specificity of the Chinese experience of translation by discussing the special features of the Chinese language in terms similar to those used by Shen Xiaolong.

Most notably, Liu stresses the idea that the Chinese language, unlike Indo-European languages, is composed of "sentence sections," which are the primary building blocks (*bankuai*) for clauses, sentences and even paragraphs. These sections are strung together rather loosely, as aggregates or conglomerates, and cohere around the "topic" or the thought to be expressed. It is in this sense that "spirit controls form" (to borrow Chinese terminology). By contrast, in Indo-European languages formal features play a significant role in sentence making, and instead of building blocks, a language like English is structured by means of "chain connections" (Liu, 1993: 33-35). While clearly an oversimplification, this mode of describing the difference of the "language of colonized" from the "colonizer's language" is gaining popularity in the discourse of societies emerging from the colonial yoke. Basil Hatim has noted how the Arabs—like the Chinese, perhaps—have been described as tending "to fit the thought to the word ... rather than the word to the thought"; for them, "the words become the substitutes of thought, and not their representative"(1997: 161). One may add that, besides this, the vagueness of thought that linguists have identified in Arabic is almost comparable to the so-called "expressive" nature of the Chinese language, which is prone to present ideas in a cinematographic manner. Elsewhere in the same book, Liu also opposes the form-oriented and analytical features typical of the English language against the thought-oriented and synthetic power of Chinese. Such overgeneralizations about

languages are, of course, quite dangerous, but one notice readily the "strategic" function they can serve in postcolonial discourse. Indeed, Liu's presentation of the Chinese language as different, but distinct, from other languages contrasts remarkably with the denigration of the language as inferior and inadequate by men of letters in the twenties, such as Lu Xun.

Seen in a broader context, Liu Minqng desire to theorize about translation on the basis of assumed "eqaulity" between Chinese and Western languages can be understood as the cumulative result of decades of thinking "positively" about their mother tongue on the part of translators. On the question of perniciousness (such as Zhang Yiwu) than to the harsh critics of Europeanized Chinese (such as Frederick Tsai) of earlier decades. In a brief section on translationese in *Present-day Translation Studies*, he calls the introduction of foreign terms and structures through translation an "alienation" process through which languages can reach even higher planes of perfection. This seems to point toward the more radical position that he takes in *Aesthetic Studies of Translation*. In this, his most recent book, Liu initiates a completely new view of translation as an activity, developing a discourse on translation that can be seen as almost counter-hegemonic. He blends traditional Chinese aesthetics with Western approaches to translation in order to rewrite translation theory from a Chinese perspective.

In striking contrast to his earlier works, which testify to his familiarity with Western translation theory, Aesthetic Studies of Translation is sprinkled everywhere with references to seminal texts by Chinese aestheticians, from Laozi and Liu Xie (c. 465-522), Zhong Rong (c. 465-518), Sikong Tu (837-809) to Wang Guowei (1877-1927). Among these figures, Laozi is raised to an eminent position. His dictum, from *Daode jing* [*The Classic of the Dao*], that "beautiful words are not truthful; truthful words are not beautiful" is cited time and again to clarify the debate between fidelity to the original and artistry in translating. Concepts corresponding to modern Western reception/semiotic theory are sought from Liu Xie and *The Book of Rites*—the latter, it is said, addressed two millennia ago the methods by which the translator "decodes the feelings" expressed in a literary text. In a lengthy section on the rendition of the source-text style, ten different styles of writing—reserved, bold, refined, natural, adorned, diluted, light-hearted, forceful, solid, humourous—are expounded with reference to at least one example of Chinese-English or English-Chinese translation in each case. In line with the sinicizing approach adopted throughout the book, the "Chinese" origins of each style are documented with quotations from traditional Chinese aesthetics texts.

If we understand postcolonial discourse broadly and see it as essentially a question of positionality—that is, where one places oneself in relation to existing modes of interpreting reality—then Liu can be seen as standing alongside Shen and Zhang in denying hegemonic narratives of what the Chinese language is like, and how translation should be understood.

The basic strategy of resistance developed by all three is to foreground Chineseness; by pointing out alternative (read "nativist") modes of understanding and contesting prevailing (read "Western") paradigms. They have effectively intervened into and altered perceptions of what the language of translation should be. Insofar as they have voiced similar oppositions to the epistemic violence done to the Chinese language, the earlier theorists can be regarded as postcolonialists, though they may have worked in the "colonial" period. One phenomenon worth pondering is that the resistance efforts were strongest at precisely those times when "colonization" proceeded most ferociously—first in the twenties, immediately after the May Movement, then in the eighties and nineties, when China was again opened to the outside world in the era of Deng Xiaoping's reforms. Though the occurrence of resistance is surely determined by many factors, the history of cultural resistance in China suggests that feelings for sinicization are most intense where Westernization poses the greatest threat (in the first case) and the impact of postcolonial thought is seen most powerfully not in the place of its origin, but in its place of destination, at which it arrives with allits colonial appendages (in the second case). Or there might even be a paradoxical love-haterelationship between the colonizers and the colonized, rendering it necessary to rethink the myth of the inevitable confrontation—or opposition—between the two.

Conclusion: A Third Position?

It may be worth our while, in our concluding remarks, to consider the possibility of a third position of resistance that we have not examined because it, paradoxically, is tantamount to a position of non-resistance. The proponents of Europeanized Chinese came close to endorsing this position, though none said so explicitly, and I will call this the "culturalist" argument for Europeanization/colonization. In her brilliant essay on postcoloniality in Hong Kong in the run-up to 1997, Rey Chow denounces the tendency on the part of some scholars to dilute the specificity of the term "postcolonialism" by allowing it to be construed as synonymous with "postmodernism." She stresses that postcolonialism as a body of ideas has its special value in cultural analysis, a value which is revealed through postcolonialism's application in individual cases (see Chow, 1992). If Hong Kong is one such case, then China must be another. The uniqueness of the Chinese situation needs to be taken into consideration if one is to talk about postcoloniality in the Chinese context.

In the first place, with the exception of Hong Kong, China has—strictly speaking—never been territorially occupied by a foreign power. As a consequence, though Western imperialism did indeed have an impact on Chinese life for the greater part of the twentieth century, colonization can only be conceived in cultural terms. Unlike India and most Southeast Asian countries (e. g., Vietnam, Cambodia, Thailand, Laos, Malaysia and the Philippines), mainland China has never come under French, British or American domination; thus, postcolonial theory may seem to furnish a less-than-perfect "tool" when extended to the Chinese case. Second, it must be admitted that China was (and still is) a cultural colonizer herself. Through the centuries Chinese culture has penetrated deeply into

Southeast Asian countries such as Vietnam, Thailand, Malaysia and Indonesia; this is borne out by the huge amount of translation of the Chinese classics as well as popular Chinese literature into Vietnamese, Thai, Malay, Makassarese and Madurese. How does one apply postcolonial theory to a colonized country that is at the same time a colonizer?

The actual situation seems to be that the majority of Chinese translators today use Europeanized structures and expressions almost unthinkingly; this goes against what the translation theorists and the cultural critics mentioned above have proposed as "proper." Of course it is true that in China as elsewhere, nations are losing their battle against the "linguistic colonization" by English (already on its way to becoming our *lingua franca*) and against the cultural dominance of the West. But the complicity of Chinese translators with Western colonizers can be looked at from a different angle. Among the Chinese there has always been an acute consciousness of China's positional superiority vis-a-vis the West. It is well known that, through the centuries of China's history, loanwords (from Mongolian, Pali, Sanskrit and Tibetan, to name just a few) have been ceaselessly absorbed into the Chinese language—just as non-Chinese ethnic groups were assimilated by the Chinese—and linguists have demonstrated that lexical items from diverse languages (such as Hindi) entered the Chinese lexicographical stock via translations. What is linguistic is also cultural. The culturalist view-point is precisely that Chinese culture is all-inclusive, and other cultures contribute to it like tributaries to the mainstream. (Similar arguments have been advanced by countries other than China. Of India it has been said that "the amazing capacity to assimilate alien cultural, linguistic, and literary elements is a unique and essential feature of Indian history" [Devy, 1997: 400].)

Following this line of thinking, Europeanizations need not be feared. The language, as much as the culture, is powerful enough to absorb alien influences. The recent arguments for the superiority of the Chinese language must be read against this background of linguistic confidence, asserted in the face the irreversible trend toward incorporating Europeanizations. The paramount concern for many linguistic researchers since the eighties has been to prove that the Chinese tonal system is better (than the non-tonal system of Western languages); monosyllabic characters lend themselves more readily to computerization; the flexibility in Chinese word-formation is an advantage; the absence of inflections is a positive features, as is the presence of words serving as more than one part of speech; and the use of ideograms is preferred to that of phonetic or alphabetic writing. Not unexpectedly, against such arguments, the "colonizers" have fought back: recently Wm. C. Hannas debunked the myth of the usefulness of the character-based Chinese writing system, along with much fallacious reasoning accrued around Chinese as a language. In spite of that, however, such rediscovered confidence has continued to grow in China, reflecting what for one critic is a "giant consciousness"—"a deeply seated superiority complex ... that dictated the sovereignty of China's cultural subjectivity even when it was conscious of its debt to the Western discourse" (Wang 1996, 169).

This is, then, the "colonizer's position," never explicitly presented as such, but perhaps always lurking somewhere in the Chinese subconscious as a viable position to be taken. The unspoken faith in the power of the Chinese language is reminiscent of what Goethe said in regard to German: "The force of a language is not to reject the foreign, but to devour it" (qtd. in Berman 1992: 1). This is also tantamount to a third position of resistance. Diametrically opposed to the first, it is similar in certain ways to the second. It is found on an unshaken belief in the superiority of Chinese culture, and in China's ability to emerge as the host of the cultural exchange process that we call translation.

Notes:

1. See Wang (1995) for a summary of these trends.
2. See, in particular, Niranjana (1992).
3. See Chan (1996) for a survey of the Europeanization debate.
4. For examples of Japanese, English, French, German and Russian terms that have entered the Chinese language in the past two centuries, see Lydia Liu (1995), 284-301, 343-78.
5. For a description in English of the differences between classical Chinese, the traditional vernacular and the modern vernacular, see Chen (1993).
6. Wang (1996), 48-52, depicts at some length the intellectual atmosphere of the eighties, calling it a "cultural fever." The impact of the West is clearly observable in this "second colonization."
7. This is an aspect of "culture fever" that Wang (1996) has not considered; her emphasis is on the literary scene. In the main, the reaction against Western linguistics takes the form of a refusal to continue using the analytical methods of the structuralists and an attempt to highlight the "humanistic" study of the Chinese language.
8. Shen makes abundant reference to Liu Xie's *Wenxin diaolong* [*The Literary Mind and the Carving of Dragons*], but other masters of Chinese aesthetics from traditional times are also called upon—among them the ancient philosopher Laozi and the Song dynasty poetry critic Yan Yu (fl. 1180-1235).
9. Shen ends this article by stressing the need "to develop a linguistic theory with Chinese characteristics," 41.
10. The promotion of Esperanto was most fervent during the early twentieth century; among the better known advocates were Ba Jin and Cai Yuanpei. For some time there was a craze for learning Esperanto among Chinese intellectuals in Shanghai. An abundance of literary works were translated from Esperanto by Zhou Zuoren and others, and an exchange of views concerning the use of this "World-language" that lasted for two years was documented in the 1917-1919 issues of the journal *Xin qingnian* [*New Youth*]. See Hou (1926) for a contemporary account.
11. The leading spokesman for the link between postcoloniality and hybridity is Homi Bhabha. See Bhabha (1994), 212-235.
12. These are *Wenti yu fanyi* [*Cenre and Translation*] (1985), *Ying Han fanyi jineng xunlian shouce* [*Training Handbook for English-Chinese Translation*] (1987) and *Han Ying duibi yanjiu yu fanyi* [*CE-EC Contrastive Studies and Translation*] (1991).
13. Liu Miqing (1989), 12-15, also stresses the importanceof building a Chinese translation theory. Another theorist making the same point is Luo Xinzhang; see Luo (1984), 1-19. For a recent discussion of Liu's research, see Lei (1993).
14. For an indispensable reference work on translations of Chinese works in East Asian and Southeast Asian

countries, see Salmon (1987).

15. For arguments in defence of Chinese superiority, see Xu (1992), 26-41. For the Western response, see Hannas (1997), 174-204.

【延伸阅读】

[1] Robinson, D. *Translation and Empire: Postcolonial Theories Explained*. Manchester: St. Jerome Pub., 1997.

[2] Anderman, G. (ed.). *Voices in Translation: Bridging Cultural Divides*. Clevedon · Bufflado · Toronto, NY: Multilingual Matters Ltd., 2007.

[3] Baker, M. *Translation and Conflict* [M]. London: Routledge, 2006.

[4] Tymoczko, M. & Gentzler, E. (eds). *Translation and Power*. Amherst, Mass.: University of Massachusetts Press, 2002.

[5] Carbonnel, O. The Exotic Space of Cultural Translation. In Román lvarez & M. Carmen frica Vidal (eds.), *Translation, Power, Snloversion*. Clevedon · Bufflado · Toronto, NY: Multilingual Matters Ltd., 1996.

[6] Álvarez, R. & Vidal, M. C. A. Translation: A Political Act. In Román Álvarez & M. Carmen África Vidal (eds.), *Translation, Power, Subversion*. Clevedon · Bufflado · Toronto, NY: Multilingual Matters Ltd., 1996.

[7] 蔡新乐. 后殖民状况下还有翻译吗? 中国比较文学,2002(4).

[8] 何绍斌. 后殖民语境与翻译研究. 天津外国语学院学报,2002(4).

[9] 蒋骁华. 巴西的翻译:"吃人"翻译理论与实践及其文化内涵. 外国语,2003(1).

[10] 孙致礼. 中国的文学翻译:从归化趋向异化. 中国翻译,2002(1).

[11] 王宁,薛晓源. 全球化与后殖民批评. 北京:中央编译出版社,1998.

[12] 许宝强,袁伟. 语言与翻译的政治. 北京:中央编译出版社,2001.

[13] 张京媛. 后殖民理论与文化批评. 北京:北京大学出版社,1999.

[14] 赵稀方. 翻译与新时期话语实践. 北京:中国社会科学出版社,2003.

[15] 朱立元. 当代西方文艺理论. 上海:华东师范大学出版社,1997.

【问题与思考】

1. 后殖民翻译和后殖民写作有何本质上的关联?
2. 如何理解后殖民翻译中的抵抗策略?
3. 说说劳伦斯·韦努蒂提出的"归化"和"异化"策略的文化批评背景。
4. 后殖民翻译研究关注哪些焦点问题?
5. 如何建构和完善独特的中国翻译理论话语体系?

主要参考文献

[1] Baker, M. *Routledge Encyclopedia of Translation Studies*. London & New York: Routledge, 1998/2001/2004.

[2] Bassnett-McGuire, S. Ways through the Labyrinth. Strategies and Methods for Translating Theatre Texts. In T. Hermans(ed.), *The Manipulation of Literature*. London & Sidney: Croom Helm, 1985: 87-102.

[3] Bassnett, S. & Lefevere, A. (eds.). *Translation, History & Culture*. London: Cassell, 1995.

[4] Bassnett, S. *Comparative Literature. A Critical Introduction*. Oxford: Blackwell, 1993.

[5] Bassnett, S. *Translation Studies* (Reprinted Revised Edition). London & New York: Routledge, 1996.

[6] Beddows, J. Translations and Adaptations in Francophone Canada. *CTR*, 2000 Spring.

[7] Berman, A. La traduction et la lettre, ou l'auberge du lointain. *In Les Tours de Babel: Essais sur la traduction*. Mauvezin: TransEurop-Repress, 1985.

[8] Berman, A. *The Experience of the Foreign: Culture and Tradition in Romantic Germany*. Trans. S. Heyvaert. Albany: State University of New York Press, 1992.

[9] Bhabha, H. K. How Newness Enters the World: Postmodern Space, Postcolonial Times and the Trials of Cultural Translation. In *The Location of Culture*. London & New York: Routledge, 1994.

[10] Billington, M. Family at War with Itself. *Guardian*, 29 June 1991.

[11] Blackburn, P. (ed. and trans.). *Proensa: An Anthology of Troubadour Poetry*. Berkeley & Los Angeles: University of California Press, 1978.

[12] Bourdieu, P. *Ce que parler veut dire*. Paris: Librairie Arthème Fayard, 1982.

[13] Bowman, M. Trainspotting in Montreal: From Scots to Joual. Unpublished paper presented at the University of East Anglia, 1998.

[14] Brisset, A. *Sociocritique de la traduction. Théatre et altérité au Québec* (1968-1988). Québec: Les éditions du Préambule, 1990.

[15] Brooke, N. *The Tragedy of Macbeth*. Oxford & New York: Oxford University Press, 1990.

[16] Buzelin, H. Opening the black box: Towards a study of translation as a production process. Paper presented at the Conference "Translating and Interpreting as a Social Practice," University of Graz, Austria, 2005.

[17] Casanova, P. *La République mondiale des Lettres*. Paris: Seuil, 1999.

[18] Chamberlain, L. Gender and the Metaphorics of Translation. In L. Venuti (ed.), *Rethinking Translation* (pp. 57-74). London & New York: Routledge, 1992.

[19] Chance, J. Gender Subversion and Linguistic Castration in Fifteenth Century English Translations of Christine de Pizan. In A. Roberts (ed.), *Violence Against Women in Medieval Texts* (pp. 161-193). Gainesville, FL: University Press of Florida, 1998.

[20] Cheng, V. J. *Joyce, Race and Empire*. Cambridge: Cambridge University Press, 1995.

[21] Chesterman, A. & Wagner, E. *Can Theory Help Translators*? Manchester: St. Jerome Publishing,

2002.

[22] Chow, R. Between Colonizers: Hong Kong's Postcolonial Self-Writing in the 1990s. *Diaspora: A Journal of Translation Studies* 2, no. 2,1992: 151-170.

[23] Courchene, M. "Mieux est de ris que de larmes écrire": entretien avec Antonine Maillet. *Revue Frontenac*: littérature acadienne 9,1992: 64-79.

[24] Culler, J. *Literary Theory. A Very Short Introduction.* Oxford & New York: Oxford University Press,1997.

[25] De Beauvoir, S. *The Second Sex* (H. M. Parshley, trans.). Harmondsworth: Penguin,1949.

[26] De Carolis, P. Judy Dench: Filumena diventa inglese. *Corriere della Sera*, 10 October 1998.

[27] De Filippo, E. *Filumena.* T. Wertenbaker (trans.). London: Methuen Drama,1998.

[28] De Geest, D. The Notion of "System:" Its Theoretical Importance and Its Methodological Implications for a Functionalist Translation Theory. In H. Kittel (ed.), *Geschichte, System, Literarische bersetzung* [*Histories, Systems, Literary Translations*](pp. 32-45). Berlin: Schmidt, 1992.

[29] Delabastita, D. & D'hulst,L. *European Shakespeares. Translating Shakespeare in the Romantic Age.* Amsterdam & Philadelphia: John Benjamins,1993.

[30] Delabastita, D. Translation Studies for the 21st Century: Trends and Perspective. *Génesis 3*,1993: 7-23.

[31] Delisle, J. (ed.). *Portraits de traductrices.* Ottawa: University of Ottawa Press,2002.

[32] Delisle, J. *Portraits de traducteurs.* Ottawa: Presses de l'Université d'Ottawa,1998.

[33] Devonshire, M. G. Intermediaries or Channels of Introduction. In *The English Novel in France*, 1830-1870(pp. 13-27). London: University of London Press,1929.

[34] Devy, G. N. Literary History and Translation: An Indian View. *Meta* 42, no. 2,1997: 395-406.

[35] Eco, U. *Interpretation and Overinterpretation.* Cambridge: Cambridge University Press,1992.

[36] Eco, U. *The Role of the Reader.* Bloomington: Indiana University Press,1979.

[37] Even-Zohar, I. *Papers in Historical Poetics.* Tel Aviv: Porter Institutue for Poetics and Semicotics, 1978.

[38] Even-Zohar, I. *Polysystem Studies. Poetics Today* 11,1990:1.

[39] Even-Zohar, I. The Making of Culture Repertoire and the Role of Transfer. *Target* 9,1997 (2): 355-363.

[40] Flotow, Luise von. *Translation and Gender.* Manchester: St. Jerome Publishing,1997.

[41] Flotow, Luise von. Genders and the Translated Text: Developments in Transformance. *Textus XII*, 1999: 275-288.

[42] Flotow, Luise von. *Women, bibles, ideologies. TTR: Traduction Terminologie, Redaction* 13, 2000 (1) :9-20.

[43] França, J. M. C. *Literatura e sociedade no Rio de Janeiro oitocentista.* Imprensa Nacional e Casa da Moeda,1999.

[44] Gadamer, H.-G. *Truth and Method.* Garrett Barden and John Cimming(trans.). London: Sheed & Ward Ltd., 1975.

[45] Gadamer, H.-G. *Philosophical Hermeneutics.* California: University of California Press,1977.

[46] Gentzler, E. *Contemporary Translation Theories.* London & New York: Routledge,1993.

[47] Gentzler, E. Translation, Poststructuralism and Power. In Maria Tymoczko & Edwin Gentzler (eds.), *Translation and Power*(pp. 195-218). Amherst & Boston, MA: University of Massachusetts Press, 2002.

[48] Graham, W. *English Literary Periodicals*. New York: Thomas Nelson & Sons, 1930.

[49] Gross, J. Old but still Smashing. *Sunday Telegraph*, 11 October 1998.

[50] Harvey, K. Translating Camp Talk: Gay Identities and Cultural Transfer. *The Translator* 4, 1998 (2): 295-320.

[51] Hatim, B. *Communication Across Culture: Translation Theory and Contrastive Text Linguistics*. London & New York: Routledge, 1997.

[52] Haugerud, J. *The Word for Us: Gospels of John and Mark, Epistles to the Romans and the Galatians*. Seattle: Coalition of Women in Religion, 1977.

[53] Hermans, T. Translational Norms and Correct Translations. In K. van Leuven-Zwart & T. Naaijkens (eds.), *Translation Studies: The State of the Art* (pp. 155-169). Amsterdam: Rodopi, 1991.

[54] Hermans, T. Revisiting the Classics: Toury's Empiricism Version One. *The Translator* 1, 1995 (2): 215-223.

[55] Hermans, T. *Translation in Systems. Descriptive and System-oriented Approaches Explained*. Manchester: St. Jerome Publishing, 1999.

[56] Higgins, C. Dario Fo's New Play: Anti-war Cry of a Peace Mom. *Guardian*, 12 December 2005.

[57] Holmes, J. S. The Name and Nature of Translation Studies. In Lawrence Venuti (ed.), *The Translation Studies Reader*. London & New York: Routledge, 1997/2000.

[58] Holmes, J. S. *Translated! Papers on Literary Translation and Translation Studies*. 2nd ed. Amsterdam: Rodopi, 1988/1994.

[59] *Inclusive Language Lectionary*. Philadelphia: Westminster Press, 1983.

[60] Jones, K. *La Revue Britannique, son Histoire et son Action Littéraire* (1825-1840). Paris: Librairie E. Droz, 1939.

[61] Keenaghan, E. Jack Spicer's Pricks and Cocksuckers: Translating Homosexuality into Visibility. *The Translator* 4, 1998 (2): 273-294.

[62] Kershaw, P. The Politics of Performance in a Post-modern Age. In P. Campbell (ed.), *Analysing Performance* (pp. 133-152). Manchester: Manchester University Press, 1996.

[63] Lefevere, A. *Translating Poetry: Seven Strategies and a Blueprint*. Assen & Amsterdam, 1975.

[64] Lefevere, A. Translation and Comparative Literature: The Search for the Centre. *TTR* 4, 1991(1): 129-144.

[65] Lefevere, A. *Translating Literature: Practice and Theory in a Comparative Literature Context*. New York: Modern Language Association, 1992.

[66] Lefevere, A. *Translation, Rewriting and the Manipulation of Literary Fame*. London & New York: Routledge, 1992a.

[67] Lefevere, A. *Transltion, History, Culture: A Scourcebook*. London & New York: Routledge, 1992b.

[68] Lévesque, S. Une nouvelle traduction. *Jeu* 67, 1993: 27-31.

[69] Levine, S. J. *The Subersive Scribe: Translating Latin American Fiction*. St. Paul, Minnesota: Graywolf Press, 1991.

[70] Limbeck, S. Plautus in der Knabenschule. In D. Linck (ed.), *Erinnern und Wiederentdecken: Tabuisierung und Enttabuisierung der miinnlichen und zveiblichen Homosexualitiit in Wissenschaft und Kritik* (pp. 15-68). Berlin: Verlag Rosa Winkel, 1999.

[71] Littau, K. Pandora's tongues. *TTR. Traduction Terminologie, Redaction* 13, 1999 (1): 21-35.

[72] Liu, J. J. Y. *The Art of Chinese Poetry*. Chicago & London: The University of Chicago Press, 1962.

[73] Liu, J. J. Y. *Chinese Theories of Literature*. Chicago & London: The University of Chicago Press,

1975.

[74] Maier, C. Issues in the Practice of Translating Women's Fiction. *Bulletin of Hispanic Studies* LXXV, 1998: 95-108.

[75] Maier, C. & Massardier-Kenney, F. Gender in/and Literary Translation. In M. Gaddis Rose (ed.), *Translation Horizons: Beyond the Boundaries of Translation Spectrum* (pp. 225-242). Binghamton: Centre for Research in Translation, 1996.

[76] Maillet, A. *William* S. Montréal: Leméac, 1991.

[77] Mehrez, S. Translation and the Postcolonial Experience: The Francophone North African Text. In Lawrence Venuti (ed.), *Rethinking Translation: Discourse, Subjectivity, Ideology* (pp. 120-138). London & New York: Routledge, 1992.

[78] Merkle, D. Antonine Maillet, femme de théâtre et traductrice de Shakespeare. In Maurice Basque, et al. (eds.), *L'Acadie au féminin: Un regard interdisciplinaire sur les Acadiennes et les Cadiennes* (pp. 267-293). Moncton: Chaire d'études acadiennes, 2000.

[79] Meylaerts, R. La traduction dans la culture multilingue: la recherche des sources, des cibles et des territoires. *Target* 16, 2004(2): 289-317.

[80] Mira, A. Pushing the Limits of Faithfulness: A Case for Gay Translation. In M. Holman and J. Boase-Beier (eds.), *The Practices of Literary Translation* (pp. 109-124). Manchester: St Jerome Publishing, 1999.

[81] Nida, E. A. *Toward a Science of Translating: With Special Reference to Principles and Procedures Involved in Bible Translating*. Leiden: E. J. Brill, 1964.

[82] Nietzsche, F. *The Gay Science*. Walter Kaufmann (trans.). New York: Random House, 1974.

[83] Pallares-Burke, M. L. G. *Nísia Floresta, O Carapuceiro e Outros Ensaios de Tradução Cultural*. São Paulo: Hucitec, 1996.

[84] Parker, M. *Literary Magazines and British Romanticism*. Cambridge: Cambridge University Press, 2000.

[85] Pavis, P. études théatrales. In Angenot, Marc (dir.), *Théorie littéraire, problèmes et perspectives* (pp. 95-107). Paris: Presses Universitaires de France, 1989.

[86] Pym, A. *Method in Translation History*. Manchester: St. Jerome Publishing, 1998.

[87] Pym, A. *Negociating the Frontier. Translators and Intercultures in Hispanic History*. Manchester: St. Jerome Publishing, 2000.

[88] Rechy, J. *City of Night*. New York: Grove, 1963.

[89] Robinson, D. *Translation and Empire: Postcolonial Theories Explained*. Manchester: St. Jerome Publishing, 1997.

[90] Robyns, C. Towards a Socio-semiotics of Translation. *Romanistische Zeitschrift für Literaturgeschichte* 1, 1992(2): 211-226.

[91] Scimone, S. *Nunzio*. S. Taviano and J. Varney (trans.). London: Arcadia Publishers and Agents, 1999.

[92] Sheffy, R. Repertoire Formation in the Canonization of Late 18th Century German Novel. University of Tel Aviv, unpublished dissertation, 1992.

[93] Shuttleworth, M. & Cowie, M. *The Dictionary of Translation Studies*. Manchester: St. Jerome Publishing, 1997.

[94] Simeoni, D. The Pivotal Status of the Translator's Habitus. *Target* 10, 1998(1): 1-39.

[95] Simon, S. Shakespeare en traduction. *Jeu* 48, 1988: 82-87.

[96] Simon, S. *Gender in Translation*. London & New York: Routledge, 1996.

[97] Snell-Hornby, M. The Bilingual Dictionary-Help or Hindrance. In R. K. Hartmann (ed.), *Lexeter '86 Procedings* (pp. 274-281). Tubingen: Niemeyer, 1984.

[98] Snell-Hornby, M. *Translation Studies: An Integrated Approach*. Amsterdam & Philadelphia: Benjamins, 1988/1995.

[99] Spencer, C. Binoche Bares Her Soul in a Play of Passion. *Daily Telegraph*, 19 February 1998.

[100] Spivak, G. C. The Politics of Translation. In G. C. Spivak (ed.), *Outside in the Teaching Machine*. London & New York: Routledge, 1993. Reprinted in L. Venuti (ed.), *The Translation Studies Reader* (pp. 369-388). London & New York: Routledge, 2000.

[101] Spivak, G. C. Diasporas Old and New: Women in the Transnational World. *Textual Practice* 10, 1996 (2): 245-269.

[102] Steiner, G. *After Babel: Aspects of Language and Translation*. London & New York: Oxford University Press, 1975/1998.

[103] Stokes, J. Priceless tears. *Arts*, 23 October 1998.

[104] Stratford, P. Translating Antonine Maillet's Fiction. *Québec Studies* 4, 1986: 326-332.

[105] Taviano, S. *Staging Dario Fo and Franca Ram: Anglo-American Approaches to Political Theatre*. Aldershot: Ashgate, 2005.

[106] Tieck, L. *Kritche Schriften*. Leipzig: Brockhous, 1848.

[107] Toury, G. *In Search of a Theory of Translation*. Tel Aviv: Porter Institutue for Poetics and Semicotics, 1980.

[108] Toury, G. *Descriptive Translation Studies and Beyond*. Amsterdam & Philadelphia: Benjamins, 1995.

[109] Venuti, L. Genealogies of Translation Theory: Schleiermacher. *TTR: Traduction, Terminologie, Redaction* 4, 1991(2): 125-150.

[110] Venuti, L. (ed.). *Rethinking Translation: Discourse, Subjectivity, Ideology*. London & New York: Routledge, 1992.

[111] Venuti, L. The Destruction of Troy: Translation and Royalist Cultural Politics during the Interregnum. *Journal of Medieval and Renaissance Studies* 23, 1993a(2): 197-219.

[112] Venuti, L. Translation as Cultural Politics: Regimes of Domestication in English. *Textual Practice* 7, 1993b(2): 208-223.

[113] Venuti, L. *The Translator's Invisibility. A History of Translation*. London & New York: Routledge, 1995.

[114] Venuti, L. *The Translation Studies Reader*. London & New York: Routledge, 2000.

[115] Verma, J. The Challenge of Binglish: Analyzing Multi-cultural Productions. In Campbell (ed.), *Analysing Performance* (pp. 193-202). Manchester: Manchester University Press, 1996.

[116] Weissbort, D. *Translating Poetry: The Double Labyrinth*. London: MacMillan, 1989.

[117] Wolf, M. (ed.). *Übersetzen—Translating—Traduire: Towards a Social Turn?* Münster, Hamburg, Berlin, Wien, London: LIT Verlag, 2006.

[118] Yip, W.-l. *Diffusion of Distances: Dialogues between Chinese and Western Poetics*. California: University of California Press, 1993.

[119] Yip, W.-l. *Chinese Poetry: An Anthology of Major Modes and Genres*. Durham & London: Duke University Press, 1997.

[120] Zuber, R. *Les "Belles infideles" et la forma-tion du gout classique: Perrot d'Ablancourt et Guez de*

Balzac. Paris: Colin,1968.

[121] 方珊. 形式主义文论. 济南:山东教育出版社,2002.

[122] 方锡德. 中国现代小说与文学传统. 北京:北京大学出版社,1992.

[123] 傅仲选. 实用翻译美学. 上海:上海外语教育出版社,1993.

[124] 郭延礼. 中西文化碰撞与近代文学. 济南:山东教育出版社,1999.

[125] 福斯特. 反美学:后现代文化论集. 上海:海湾出版社,1983.

[126] 黄宣范. 评析思果的《翻译研究》. 中外文学,1974(2):48-49.

[127] 刘宓庆. 当代翻译理论. 台北:书林出版社,1993.

[128] 刘宓庆. 翻译美学导论(修订本). 北京:中国对外翻译出版公司,2005.

[129] 罗新河. 鲁迅对尼采的接纳与疏离. 湖南工业大学学报:社会科学版,2006(4).

[130] 吕俊. 理论哲学向实践哲学的转向对翻译研究的指导意义. 外国语,2003(5).

[131] 吕俊,侯向群. 翻译学——一个建构主义的视角. 上海:上海外语教育出版社,2006.

[132] 陆扬. 西方美学通史. 上海:上海文艺出版社,1999.

[133] 罗新璋,陈应年. 翻译论集. 北京:商务印书馆,1984/2009.

[134] 毛荣贵. 翻译美学. 上海:上海交通大学出版社,2005.

[135] 萨莫瓦约. 互文性研究. 天津:天津人民出版社,2003.

[136] 申小龙. 当代中国语法学. 广州:广东教育出版社,1995a.

[137] 申小龙. 历史性的反拨:中国文化语言学. //邵敬敏,主编. 文化语言学中国潮:北京:语文出版社,1995b.

[138] 申小龙. 语文的阐释:中国语文传统的现代意义. 沈阳:辽宁教育出版社,1992.

[139] 申小龙. 中国文化语言学. 长春:吉林教育出版社,1990.

[140] 思果. 翻译研究. 台北:大地出版社,1972.

[141] 孙康宜. 文学经典的挑战. 南昌:百花洲文艺出版社,2002.

[142] 王秉钦. 20世纪中国翻译思想史. 天津:南开大学出版社,2004.

[143] 王宏印. 中外文学经典翻译教程. 北京:高等教育出版社,2007.

[144] 王宏印. 新诗话语. 天津:百花文艺出版社,2008.

[145] 汪立荣. 语法理论与英语研究. 长春:吉林人民出版社,2004.

[146] 韦勒克,沃伦. 文学原理. 刘象愚等,译. 北京:三联书店,1984.

[147] 谢天振. 译介学. 上海外语教育出版社,1999.

[148] 徐庆年,王达敏. 钱锺书与休谟哲学. 安徽大学学报:社科版,2005(5).

[149] 许钧,袁筱一. 当代法国翻译理论. 武汉:湖北教育出版社,2001.

[150] 许渊冲. 翻译的艺术. 北京:五洲传播出版社,2006.

[151] 许渊冲. Elegies of the South. 北京:五洲传播出版社,2012.

[152] 杨仕章. 篇章翻译概要. 哈尔滨:黑龙江人民出版社,2004.

[153] 叶威廉. 道家美学与西方文化. 北京:北京大学出版社,2002.

[154] 叶威廉. 中国诗学. 北京:人民文学出版社,2006.

[155] 张颐武. 在边缘处追索:第三世界文化与当代中国文学. 长春:时代文艺出版社,1993.

[156] 张智中. 许渊冲与翻译艺术. 武汉:湖北教育出版社,2006.

[157] 郑诗鼎. 评刘重德的《爱玛》重译版本. 中国翻译,1998(1).